American Epoch

A History of the United States since 1900

Volume II
Affluence and Anxiety, 1940–1992

American Epoch

A History of the United States since 1900

Volume II
Affluence and Anxiety,
1940–1992

SEVENTH EDITION

William A. Link
Professor of History
University of North Carolina at Greensboro

Arthur S. Link
George Henry Davis '86 Professor of
American History Emeritus
Editor and Director of The Papers of Woodrow Wilson
Princeton University

McGraw-Hill, Inc.
New York St. Louis San Francisco Auckland Bogotá
Caracas Lisbon London Madrid Mexico City Milan
Montreal New Delhi San Juan Singapore
Sydney Tokyo Toronto

This book was set in Palatino by ComCom, Inc.
The editors were Niels Aaboe and Larry Goldberg;
the production supervisor was Leroy A. Young.
The cover was designed by Keithley Associates.
R. R. Donnelley & Sons Company was printer and binder.

This book is printed on acid-free paper.

AMERICAN EPOCH
A History of the United States since 1900
Volume II: Affluence and Anxiety, 1940–1992

3 4 5 6 7 8 9 0 DOC DOC 9 0 9 8 7 6 5

ISBN 0-07-037952-1

Library of Congress Cataloging-in-Publication Data

Link, William A.
  American epoch.

  Rev. ed. of: American epoch / Arthur S. Link,
William A. Link, William B. Catton. 6th ed. c1987.
  Includes bibliographical references and index.
  Contents: v. 1. War, reform, and society —
v. 2. Affluence and anxiety, 1940–1992.
  1. United States—History—20th century.
I. Link, Arthur Stanley.   II. Title.
E741.L58   1993   973.9   92-16975
ISBN 0-07-037951-3 (v. 1)

About the Authors

WILLIAM A. LINK received his B.A. from Davidson College and his M.A. and Ph.D. from the University of Virginia. He has taught at the University of Virginia and at the University of North Carolina at Greensboro, where he is Professor of History. He is the author of *A Hard Country and a Lonely Place: Schooling, Society, and Reform in Rural Virginia, 1870–1920* (Chapel Hill: University of North Carolina Press, 1986), and *The Paradox of Southern Progressivism, 1880–1930* (Chapel Hill: University of North Carolina Press, 1993).

ARTHUR S. LINK, who received his B.A. and Ph.D. from the University of North Carolina, is the George Henry Davis '86 Professor of American History Emeritus at Princeton University and Director and Editor of *The Papers of Woodrow Wilson.* He has held Rockefeller, Guggenheim, and Rosenwald fellowships, in addition to memberships at the Institute for Advanced Study. He has been the Harmsworth Professor of American History at Oxford University and has lectured in South America, Japan, Western Europe, and Poland. Two of his many books have been awarded the Bancroft Prize, and he has received eight honorary degrees. He is a member of and has been an officer of many professional societies and is a past president of the Southern Historical Association, the Association for Documentary Editing, the Organization of American Historians, and the American Historical Association.

For William H. Harbaugh,
Teacher, Scholar, Friend

Contents

Part Four
WAR AND THE AMERICAN PEOPLE, 1940–1953

Part Five
QUIESCENCE AND CHANGE, 1953–1968

Part Six
TROUBLES AND TRANSFORMATIONS, 1968–1992

List of Graphs

List of Maps

Preface

Almost forty years ago, an energetic young historian at Northwestern University, Arthur S. Link, became frustrated, when teaching a popular course in twentieth-century American history, about the lack of a good textbook that both surveyed the period and provided an analytical framework in which students could understand it. The result was the publication of *American Epoch*, a history of the United States since the 1890s. Appearing in one volume, *American Epoch*, for its day, adopted a rather maverick approach: not only did it survey political and diplomatic history with thoroughness, it also sought to include—unlike most other historians of the immediate post-1945 era—material on labor, economic, and cultural history, as well as pioneering material on the history of minorities. Following the appearance of the first edition, *American Epoch* appeared in five subsequent editions. It is probably not completely immodest to describe it as a classic that educated new generations of students of twentieth-century American history.

This seventh edition of *American Epoch* seeks not only to continue this tradition of sturdy excellence but to blend in the mountain of scholarship on twentieth-century America that has appeared in print since 1955. The sheer amount of new studies is reflected in the length of the Suggested Additional Reading, which has grown steadily with each new edition. We have attempted to update our discussion in this edition, but we apologize for any inadvertent omissions. Since 1960, scholarship, which has remade the study of American history, has focused on nonelite groups in politics, society, and culture and has paid special attention to questions of class, gender, sexuality, and race.

Recent editions of *American Epoch* included much of this scholarship. This edition has included new material on these subjects appearing in print since the sixth edition in 1987, and, where appropriate, that material has been included in both volumes. The format of the two volumes has been somewhat altered, with the break occurring in 1940 rather than 1936. Users of Volume II will notice changes, including four new chapters, three of them on social changes since 1945, one of them including material on the second Reagan administration and the Bush administration.

The authors have incurred a number of debts in the writing of this book. This new edition was undertaken at the suggestion of David Follmer, then of McGraw-Hill, and has profited from the support and guidance of Niels Aaboe, also of McGraw-Hill. A number of anonymous readers made very useful suggestions about the revisions, and we have greatly profited from their advice, which we have attempted to include wherever possible. The advice and suggestions of two students who have used this book in their classes, Cheryl F. Junk and Judyth White, were of great help in preparing the revision. John D'Emilio of the History Department, University of North Carolina at Greensboro, was very generous in sharing his knowledge about post-1945 America, in suggesting materials to include, and even in lending works from his personal library. Finally, we owe a great debt to Margaret Douglas Link and Susannah J. Link, both of whom have patiently supported the revision, as well as to Percy, Maggie, and Josie for their customary good humor and inquisitiveness.

It is fitting that this seventh edition of *American Epoch* is dedicated to William H. Harbaugh, who has shared his own keen insights about twentieth-century America with several generations of students and in the process exposed them to high standards of thought and expression.

William A. Link
Arthur S. Link

American Epoch
A History of the United States since 1900
Volume II
Affluence and Anxiety, 1940–1992

PART FOUR

War and the American People, 1940–1953

CHAPTER 18

War and the Home Front

Not since the dark days of the Revolution had the American people confronted so dire a military menace or so staggering a task as during World War II. Within a few months after Japanese bombs fell on Pearl Harbor, the ensign of the Rising Sun floated triumphantly over all the outposts and bastions of the far Pacific region, while Hitler and his armies stood poised to strike at the Middle East and join forces with the Japanese in India.

It was perhaps fortunate that the American people in December 1941 little knew how long the war would last and what the costs would be. However, they had certain advantages that made victory possible: courageous allies, unity unprecedented in American history, enormous resources and industrial capacity, superb political and military leadership, and, most important, determination to win. These factors combined from 1941 to 1945 to achieve miracles of production that made earlier American war efforts look small by comparison.

The astonishing thing, however, was the fact that Americans could engage in total war without submitting to the discipline of total war at home. To be sure, the war intensified certain social tensions and created new problems of adjustment; but most Americans took the war in stride, without emotional excitement or hysteria.

1. MANPOWER FOR WAR

The adoption of the war resolutions found the United States in the midst of a sizable rearmament campaign, the momentum of which was daily increasing.

Congress quickly ordered the registration of all men between the ages of twenty (lowered to eighteen in 1942) and forty-four for war service and of men between forty-five and sixty-five for potential labor service. All told, draft boards registered some 31 million men, of whom 9.9 million were inducted into service. Including volunteers, a total of 15.2 million men and women served in the armed services before the end of the war—10.4 million in the army, 3.9 million in the navy, 599,693 in the marines, and 241,902 in the Coast Guard.

Because the first offensive blows could be delivered from the air, the army air forces were authorized at the outset to increase their strength to 2.3 million men and were given highest priority on manpower and materials. When the Japanese attacked Pearl Harbor the Army Air Force (AAF) had 292,000 men and 9,000 planes (1,100 of which were fit for combat). When the Japanese surrendered in August 1945, the AAF enlisted 2.3 million men and women and had 72,000 planes in service.

Thanks to the wealth, technology, and industrial and agricultural capacity of his country, the American soldier was the best-paid, best-clothed, and by 1943 the best-equipped fighting man in the world. In that year, for example, Americans achieved not only a quantitative but also a decided qualitative superiority in fighter planes and bombers. Even in areas of research in which the Germans had a head start, such as atomic fission, American scientists and engineers had won decisive advantages by 1945. On the battlefield the best American weapons were the light semiautomatic Garand rifle and the multiple-driven truck. They combined to give a superiority in firepower and mobility that the Germans were never able to overcome in spite of general equality in machine guns, mortars, rocket-launched missiles, and artillery.

In the meantime, the navy, marines, and Coast Guard had grown from relative weakness after Pearl Harbor to dimensions of gigantic strength at the time of the Japanese surrender. On December 7, 1941, the navy had a complement of 337,349 men, in addition to 66,048 in the Marine Corps and 25,336 in the Coast Guard. By the summer of 1945, the navy's manpower had increased to 3.4 million officers and men, the Marine Corps' to 484,631, and the Coast Guard's to 170,480. Before Japanese bombs disabled or sank part of the Pacific Fleet at Pearl Harbor, the navy had in operation some 4,500 ships, including 17 battleships, 7 fleet carriers, 18 heavy and 19 light cruisers, 200 destroyers and torpedo boats, and 114 submarines. By the end of 1945, the navy had grown to more than 91,000 ships of all sizes, including 24 battleships, 2 large cruisers, 29 fleet carriers, 73 escort carriers, 23 heavy and 45 light cruisers, 489 destroyers and torpedo boats, 500 escort vessels, and 274 submarines.

Finally, there was mobilization of women for war service. The Women's Auxiliary Corps, which grew in size to 100,000, sent 17,000 WACs overseas; the navy's counterpart, the WAVEs, numbered about 86,000 at the end of the war. There were also the Coast Guard's SPARs and the Marine Corps' Women's Reserve. Working as stenographers, clerks, technicians, cryptographers, and the

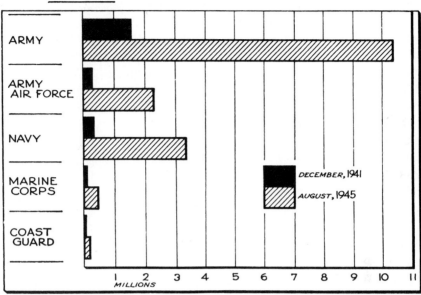

EXPANSION OF U.S. ARMED FORCES
1941-1945

like, female contingents not only performed indispensable functions but released over 200,000 men for service on the battle fronts.

Measured in human costs, the price of victory in World War II came high to the American people—253,573 dead, 651,042 wounded, 114,204 prisoners, and 65,834 men missing. For the men who died, however, Americans and their allies exacted a fearful retribution. Germany and Italy suffered 373,600 dead and lost 8.1 million prisoners to the Allies on the western front alone. The Japanese gave up 1.1 million battle dead in areas outside China.

For their comparatively low death lists, Americans in large measure could thank the medical corps of the several services. Although American soldiers lived and fought in deserts and jungles as well as in the temperate zones, the death rate from nonbattle causes was no higher than the rate for similar groups at home. And for the sick and wounded, there was extraordinary care, while use of sulfa drugs, penicillin, and whole blood brought such healing and relief from wounds and shock as would not have been possible a decade before. The result was to cut the rate of deaths from disease and battle wounds in half from the rate of World War I.

2.   SCIENCE AND THE WAR

In the last analysis the war was won as much in the laboratory and on the testing ground as on the battlefield. American scientists at the outset of the war lagged far behind the Germans in research in atomic fission, jet propulsion, and rockets, and they were behind the British in work on jet propulsion, radar, and other electronic devices. Alarmed by the prospect of his country entering the war scientifically unprepared, Dr. Vannevar Bush, president of the Carnegie Institution of Washington, persuaded the president in June 1940 to establish the National Defense Research Committee (NDRC), with representatives from the defense departments, universities, and private industry. Then Roosevelt reorganized the government's research program in June 1941 by creating the Office of Scientific Research and Development (OSRD). Bush was director of the OSRD, with power to approve or veto all projects and to initiate research.

Bush and his colleagues had accomplished a full mobilization of scientific personnel and facilities by the autumn of 1941. Some of the most significant results of this great effort include the development of radar and electronic devices, rockets for combat use, the proximity fuse, and, finally, the atomic bomb.

It was the British who first perfected radar and put it to large-scale use during the great German air assault of 1940–1941. Radar sets in patrol planes enabled the British and American navies to bring the German submarines under control. Perhaps even more effective in antisubmarine operations was so-called sonar, or underwater sound detection apparatus, developed by the NDRC in conjunction with the Harvard Underwater Sound Laboratory. Radar in fighters enabled the air forces to launch powerful night interceptors; in bombers, it provided a generally accurate bombsight. The American armed services alone had received $3 billion worth of radar equipment and $71 million worth of loran, a long-range navigational aid, by July 1945.

The outbreak of the war found research in the field of rocket warfare well advanced in Britain and Germany and practically nonexistent in the United States. But NDRC scientists had a sizable research program under way by the end of 1941. One of the first results was the "bazooka," a tube rocket-launcher perfected in 1942, which could be operated by two infantrymen and discharged a rocket powerful enough to destroy a tank. Subsequently, scientists developed a variety of rocket-launchers and rockets for use in land combat and antiaircraft operations, by airplanes, and in ship-to-shore bombardments. What this meant in terms of increased firepower can perhaps best be illustrated by the fact that a single fighter plane carrying rockets could discharge a salvo as heavy as a destroyer's.

Still another important wartime scientific achievement was the development, exclusively by the OSRD, of the proximity fuse. It was a miniature radio set in the head of the shell that detonated it by proximity to the target. Proximity fuses were first used by the navy against Japanese aircraft in 1943. Fearing that the Germans would recover an unexploded shell and put the fuse into production, the joint chiefs of staff did not allow ground forces in Europe to use the new weapon until December 1944. Put into use against the Germans in their Ardennes counteroffensive (see pp. 434–436), the proximity fuse compounded the effectiveness of American artillery and proved devastating against German ground troops.

The mobilization of American scientists paid numerous other dividends— among them the development of more powerful explosives and fire bombs, of DDT and other insecticides, of advanced techniques in the use of blood plasma and whole blood, of penicillin, and of new and deadly gases, which were never used. But the greatest triumph of American scientific and productive genius was the development of the atomic bomb. The perfection of this weapon marked a decisive turning point in history.

The Danish physicist Niels Bohr startled a group of American physicists assembled in Washington in January 1939 by announcing that two Germans at the Kaiser Wilhelm Institute in Berlin had recently accomplished atomic fission in uranium. Nuclear physicists had long understood the structure of the atom and known that atomic fission was theoretically possible. But the deed had now been done, and the road was open for the development of a bomb more powerful and deadly than the world had ever imagined. A real danger existed that the Nazis would produce atomic bombs and literally conquer the world. Therefore, Enrico Fermi of Columbia University, Albert Einstein of the Institute for Advanced Study, and others persuaded Roosevelt to begin a small research program. It was not until 1940, however, that work began in earnest. By the summer of 1941, research at Columbia, California, and other universities had confirmed the possibilities of atomic fission through a chain reaction. The chief problem now was to find a fissionable element in sufficient quantity. Earlier experiments had proved that the uranium isotope U-235 was fissionable; but, since U-235 was an infinitesimal part of uranium, the chances were remote of ever accumulating enough of the element to manufacture atomic bombs. This problem was solved by Dr. Ernest Lawrence of the University of California at Berkeley, who used a huge cyclotron, or "atom smasher," to convert the plentiful uranium element U-238 into a new element, plutonium, which was as fissionable as U-235 and much easier to obtain in quantity.

The next objective became a chain reaction in uranium, that is, the almost simultaneous fission of the uranium atoms through a chain bombardment by neutrons. A group of physicists under the direction of Dr. Arthur H. Compton built the first atomic pile, or apparatus, under the stadium at Stagg Field of the University of Chicago. They produced the first controlled chain reaction in December 1942. Production of an atomic bomb was now possible, provided a means of production could be devised. OSRD turned the problem over to the Manhattan District of the Army Engineer Corps, headed by General Leslie R. Groves, in May 1943. Drawing upon the combined resources of the OSRD, universities, and private industries, Groves pushed the project with incredible speed. Work on the bomb itself was begun in the spring of 1943 at a laboratory built on a lonely mesa at Los Alamos, outside Santa Fe, New Mexico. Here a group of American, British, and European scientists under the direction of Dr. J. Robert Oppenheimer worked night and day to perfect the bomb. They began the final assembly of the first atomic bomb on July 12, 1945, and tension mounted as the fateful day of testing drew near. Nearly $2 billion had been expended in an effort which yet might fail. The bomb was moved to the air base at Alamagordo and successfully detonated at 5:30 A.M. on July 16. A searing blast of light, many times brighter than the noonday sun, was followed by a deafening roar and a huge mushroom cloud. And relief mixed with a feeling of doom filled the minds of those who watched the beginning of a new era in human history.

3. MOBILIZATION AND AMERICAN INDUSTRY

The story of how changing agencies mobilized the American economy for the war effort is a tale full of confusion and chaos, incompetence and momentary failure, political intrigue and personal vendetta, but withal one of superb achievement on many home fronts. Government and industry accomplished one of the economic miracles of modern times before it was too late—the production of a stream of goods that provided a high standard of living at home and also supplied the American armed forces with all and the British, French, and Russians with a large part of the resources and matériel for victory.

The task during the first period of industrial mobilization, from August 1939 until about the end of 1941, was the comparatively easy one of utilizing idle plants and men to supply the inchoate American armed forces and the British. In August 1939, Roosevelt established the War Resources Board, headed by Edward R. Stettinius, Jr., of the United States Steel Corporation, to advise the administration on industrial mobilization. It soon fell victim to labor and New Deal critics, who charged that it was dominated by Morgan and Du Pont interests.

This was, of course, the time of the so-called phony war, when Allied victory seemed assured and the necessity for total economic mobilization seemed remote. Nevertheless, the War Resources Board, before its dissolution in October 1939, prepared an industrial mobilization plan that envisaged dictatorial economic authority for a single administrator in the event that the United States entered the war. Roosevelt rejected this plan and asked the former chairman of Wilson's War Industries Board, Bernard M. Baruch, to prepare another. Baruch presented a plan that met all Roosevelt's objections to the earlier proposal and provided for gradual transition to a total war economy.

Roosevelt, for reasons still unknown, suppressed the Baruch plan and permitted the partial mobilization effort of 1939–1940 to drift aimlessly. The fall of

France, however, galvanized him into action, inadequate though it was. Calling for vast new defense appropriations and the production of 50,000 planes a year, he reestablished the Advisory Commission to the old and nearly defunct Council of National Defense in May 1940. It was supposed to get defense production into high gear. In addition, Congress on June 25 authorized the RFC to finance the building of defense plants and, in the Revenue Act of October 1940, permitted businessmen to write off construction costs over a five-year period.

The Advisory Commission abdicated control over priorities to the Army-Navy Munitions Board and had lost all control of industrial mobilization by December 1940. Roosevelt still stubbornly refused to institute the kind of mobilization plan that Baruch had earlier suggested. Instead, in January 1941, he established the Office of Production Management (OPM), headed by William S. Knudsen of the Advisory Commission and Sidney Hillman of the CIO. It was directed to cooperate with the president and defense secretaries in stimulating and controlling war production. In addition, an Office of Price Administration and Civilian Supply, established in April, would work to protect consumers' interests.

The OPM went to work to improve the priorities system, to coordinate British and American orders, and especially to help automobile manufacturers prepare for conversion to production of tanks and planes. The result was a gradual shift during the spring and summer of 1941 to a wartime economy. Shortages of electric power, aluminum, steel, railroad stock, and other materials became acute. The priorities system nearly broke down, and internal bickering and public criticism mounted. Roosevelt attempted another superficial reorganization. He suspended the OPM in August 1941, but left an OPM Council. Then he created a Supplies Priorities and Allocation Board, headed by the Sears-Roebuck executive Donald M. Nelson, and added other agencies, many of which overlapped in a confusing way. The central force in the new apparatus, however, was the Supplies Priorities and Allocations Board. It had the power to determine and allocate requirements and supplies for the armed forces, the civilian economy, and the British and the Russians.

In January 1942, Roosevelt established a comprehensive economic mobilization by creating the War Production Board (WPB) under Donald Nelson. Nelson was an excellent technician, but he failed to meet the test of leadership. Because he continued to allow military departments to control priorities, he never established firm control over production. He permitted large corporations to dominate war production, and a near scandal ensued when the facts were disclosed by a special Senate committee headed by Harry S Truman of Missouri. Finally, Nelson allowed industrial expansion to get out of hand and occur in the wrong areas.

American industry was booming by the autumn of 1942, but chaos threatened. Alarmed by the prospect, Roosevelt brought Justice James F. Byrnes to the

White House as head of the new Office of Economic Stabilization in October and gave him complete control over economic mobilization. Byrnes forced adoption of a plan that established such total control over allocation of steel, aluminum, and copper that the priorities difficulty soon vanished. Then Roosevelt, in May 1943, created the Office of War Mobilization, a sort of high command with control over all aspects of the economy, with Byrnes as director or "assistant president." Representative Fred M. Vinson of Kentucky succeeded Byrnes as head of the Office of Economic Stabilization.

In spite of all its shortcomings, the American industrial mobilization did succeed far beyond any reasonable expectations. We can gain some understanding of the total achievement by considering the general performance of the American economy from 1939 through 1945. Measured by depression standards, 1939 was a relatively prosperous year. Gross national product stood at $91.3 billion—higher in real dollars than during the boom year of 1929. On the other hand, the gross national product had risen, in 1939 dollars, to $166.6 billion by 1945. Moreover, from 1939 to 1945 the index of manufacturing production increased 96 percent; agricultural production was up 22 percent; and transportation services increased 109 percent. Contrasted with the performance of the economy during World War I, when the total national output increased hardly at all, this was a remarkable achievement.

The main engine of these increases was, of course, war production. In 1941 it was a mere trickle—only $8.4 billion in value. A year later, it totaled $30.2 billion in value and equaled that of Germany, Italy, and Japan combined. American factories by 1944 were producing twice the volume of the Axis partners. A few examples illustrate these generalizations. The American airplane industry employed 46,638 persons and produced 5,865 planes in 1939. At the peak of production in 1944, the industry employed more than 2.1 million persons and turned out 96,369 aircraft. All told, American factories from Pearl Harbor to the end of the war produced 274,941 military aircraft. Production of merchant ships, an essential ingredient of Allied victory, which had totaled only 1 million tons in 1941, rose to a peak of over 19 million tons in 1943. As the need diminished, production declined to nearly 16.5 million tons in 1944 and nearly 8 million tons from January through July of 1945. All told, from July 1940 to August 1945, American shipyards produced a total of more than 55.2 million tons of merchant shipping—a tonnage equal to two-thirds of the merchant marines of all Allied nations combined.

Perhaps most remarkable was the creation, almost overnight, of a new synthetic rubber industry. Japanese conquest of Malaya and the Netherlands East Indies deprived the United States of 90 percent of its natural-rubber supply. Total imports could not exceed 175,000 tons during 1942, and the rubber shortage threatened to hobble the entire war effort. In August 1942, Roosevelt appointed a special committee headed by Bernard M. Baruch to investigate and recommend. It reported a month later and warned that the war effort and civilian economy might collapse if a severe rubber shortage occurred and urged immediate construction of a vast industry to produce rubber synthetically from petroleum. Roosevelt acted immediately and appointed William M. Jeffers, president of the Union Pacific Railroad, as rubber director in the WPB. Jeffers ruthlessly cut his way through the existing priorities system. By the end of 1943, he had brought into existence a synthetic rubber industry that produced 762,000 tons in 1944 and 820,000 tons in 1945.

4. THE SHAPING OF TAX POLICY

Federal expenditures aggregated in excess of $321.2 billion from 1941 to 1945. Some 41 percent of the money for the war effort came from tax receipts, which totaled nearly $131 billion during the fiscal years 1941–1945. The balance was raised by borrowing, which in turn increased the gross national debt from $49 billion in 1941 to $259 billion in mid-1945.

Meanwhile, the administration and Congress had revolutionized the tax structure. On the one hand, the president, Congress, and a vast majority of Americans, rich and poor alike, agreed that the few should not profit from the sacrifices of the many and that there should be no new millionaires as a result of the defense and war efforts. On the other hand, it became increasingly evident that it would be hopelessly inadequate to use the income tax as a tax principally on wealth, and that the costs of the war would have to be borne in part also by the lower and middle classes.

The administration's tax program evolved gradually in response to the need for revenues and the necessity for curbing inflation. Congress thus approved two revenue acts in 1940 that increased income and corporation taxes and imposed an excess profits tax graduated to a maximum of 50 percent. Congress again increased old taxes in 1941 and devised new means of finding revenue. Even so, the income tax still touched only the small minority with upper-middle- and upper-class incomes. A significant departure in federal tax policy occurred in January 1942, when Roosevelt, in his Budget Message to Congress, proposed a $7 billion increase in the tax burden. After months of agonizing delay, Congress responded with the Revenue Act of 1942, approved October 21.

Described by Roosevelt as "the greatest tax bill in American history," it was designed to raise more than $7 billion additional revenue annually, a sum exceeding total federal revenues in any peacetime year before 1941. The measure increased the combined corporate income tax to a maximum of 40 percent and raised the excess profits tax to a flat 90 percent. Moreover, it increased excise taxes and levied a host of new ones, and stiffly increased estate and gift taxes. The revolutionary feature of the Revenue Act of 1942, however, was its broadening of the income tax to tap low incomes as well as to increase the burden on large ones. Only 13 million persons had paid federal income taxes in 1941; in contrast, some 50 million persons were caught in the net cast in 1942. The difficulty of collecting income taxes from 50 million persons by the conventional method of individual returns led to the adoption, in 1943, of a measure requiring employers to collect the tax by payroll deductions.

Meanwhile, personal incomes, governmental expenditures, and inflationary pressures continued to mount. The president therefore came back in his Budget Message of 1943 to demand an increase of $16 billion in the federal tax load. Treasury officials later lowered the request to $10.5 billion. Even so, congressional leaders rebelled and adopted a Revenue Act in early February 1944 that yielded additional revenue of only $2.2 billion, chiefly by increasing the excess profits tax to 95 percent and by heavy increases in excise taxes. The president replied on February 22 with a veto so stinging that his spokesman in the Senate, Alben W. Barkley of Kentucky, resigned his post as majority leader. The Senate Democratic caucus promptly and unanimously reelected Barkley, and an angry House and Senate overrode the veto by enormous majorities. From this time forward administration and congressional leaders were concerned, not with increasing the tax burden, but with simplifying the withholding system and planning for the reconversion that would soon come with the end of the war.

In retrospect, perhaps the most significant aspect of the wartime tax program

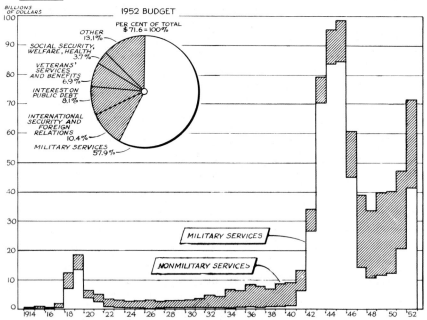

EXPENDITURES OF THE UNITED STATES GOVERNMENT, 1914–1952

was the way it reflected the nation's conviction that a war for survival should not become a war for the enrichment of the few. There could be no "swollen fortunes" when the federal income tax reached a maximum of 94 percent of total net income, to say nothing of state income and local property taxes. Indeed, the nation's top 5 percent of income receivers suffered their severest relative economic losses in the history of the country during this period. Their share of disposable income fell from 25.7 percent in 1940 to 15.9 percent in 1944. The relative status of the top 1 percent of income receivers declined even more. Their share of disposable income decreased from 11.5 percent in 1940 to 6.7 percent in 1944. And with an excess profits tax of 95 percent and corporation income taxes reaching a maximum of 50 percent, there were few cases of swollen profits. Net corporation income was $9.4 billion in 1941 and 1942, increased slightly in 1943 and 1944, and fell back to $8.5 billion in 1945.

5.   COMBATING INFLATION

Aside from the mobilization of fighting men and the maintenance of a steady flow of materials to the battle fronts, perhaps the most important problem at home was prevention of a runaway inflation that would compound the costs of the war and increase the burdens of many classes. To state the problem in its simplest terms, inflationary pressures existed after 1941 because the volume of

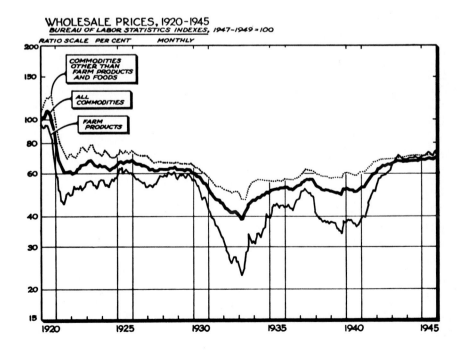

WHOLESALE PRICES, 1920-1945
BUREAU OF LABOR STATISTICS INDEXES, 1947-1949 = 100

disposable personal income greatly exceeded the supply of goods and services available for civilian consumption at the prevailing price level. Disposable personal incomes rose from $92 billion in 1941 to $151 billion in 1945, but the supply of civilian goods and services, measured in constant dollars, rose from $77.6 billion to only $95.4 billion during the same period. The danger of inflation stalked the home front because of this inflationary gap.

The most obvious weapon against inflation and the first to be tried was control of prices and rents. It will be recalled that Roosevelt, while reorganizing the defense mobilization machinery, had established an Office of Price Administration and Civilian Supply (OPA), headed by Leon Henderson, to work in conjunction with the Office of Production Management. Without any real power, Henderson was helpless to control prices during 1941. Consequently, retail prices were rising at the rate of 2 percent a month by February 1942. Roosevelt asked for new authority, and Congress responded with the Emergency Price Control Act of 1942. It empowered the price administrator to fix maximum prices and rents in special areas and to pay subsidies to producers, if that was necessary to prevent price increases. On the other hand, the powerful farm bloc denied the price administrator authority to control agricultural prices until they reached 110 percent of parity.

The OPA during the next three months launched a two-pronged campaign—to stabilize prices piecemeal and to establish a system of rationing for tires, automobiles, gasoline, and sugar and, somewhat later, for shoes, fuel oil, and coffee. In April 1942, the OPA issued its first General Maximum Price Regulation, which froze most prices and rents at the level of March 1942. Events soon revealed large loopholes in the stabilization program, the most obvious of which was the ban on a ceiling for food prices until they reached an extraordinary level. As food prices rose steadily—they increased a total of 11 percent during 1942—organized labor redoubled its demands for pay increases that in turn would mean higher prices for manufactured products. Somehow, somewhere, the inflationary spiral had to be stopped, Roosevelt exclaimed in a special message in September 1942. "I ask Congress to take . . . action by the first of October. . . . In the event that the Congress should fail to act, and act adequately, I shall accept the responsibility, and I will act."

Congress responded swiftly if grudgingly with the Anti-Inflation Act of October 2, 1942. It empowered the president to stabilize wages, prices, and salaries at their levels on September 15. Roosevelt established the Office of Economic Stabilization on the following day, October 3, and forbade any further increase in wages and salaries without the approval of the stabilization director, James F. Byrnes. In addition, Roosevelt froze agricultural prices at their level on September 15 and extended rent control to all areas of the country.

It was a good beginning, but even rougher storms lay ahead. The OPA administrator, Leon Henderson, had never been popular with Congress and the

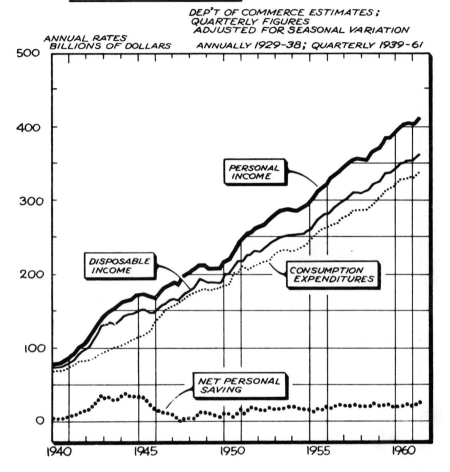

PERSONAL INCOME, CONSUMPTION, AND SAVING, 1940-1961

DEP'T OF COMMERCE ESTIMATES;
QUARTERLY FIGURES
ADJUSTED FOR SEASONAL VARIATION
ANNUALLY 1929-38; QUARTERLY 1939-61

ANNUAL RATES
BILLIONS OF DOLLARS

PERSONAL INCOME

DISPOSABLE INCOME

CONSUMPTION EXPENDITURES

NET PERSONAL SAVING

public. Roosevelt permitted him to resign in December 1942 and replaced him with Prentiss S. Brown, former senator from Michigan. Unfortunately, business, farm, and labor groups took Brown's appointment as a signal for an all-out campaign against stabilization. Congress tried to open a large hole in the dike in March 1943 by approving a bill to exclude subsidy and parity payments in determination of parity levels for agriculture. But Roosevelt vetoed the measure, pointing out that it would increase the cost of living by more than 5 percent. At the same time, labor spokesmen were growing restive under a formula by which workers had been allowed a 15 percent wage increase in 1942, and were threatening to break the no-strike pledge they had given after Pearl Harbor.

Roosevelt responded to this dangerous situation by ordering, in April 1943,

CONSUMER PRICES
1940 – 1960

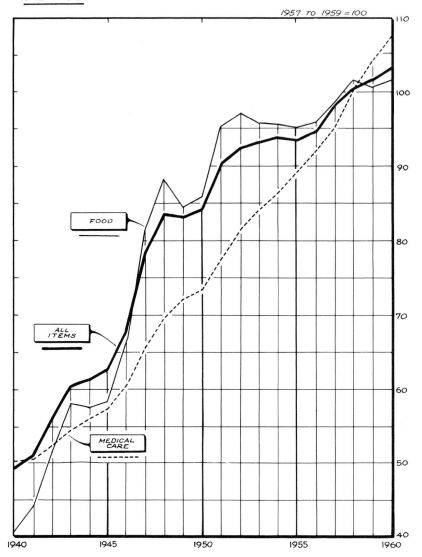

the stabilization agencies to "hold the line" against any further unwarranted price and wage increases. Nor was this all. When John L. Lewis called a general coal strike in May in defiance of the hold-the-line order, the president seized the coal mines and virtually ordered miners back into the pits. Moreover, the OPA began an aggressive campaign to roll back food prices. It culminated in a 10 percent reduction in the retail prices of meat, coffee, and butter in May. As a result of these efforts, the cost of living increased less than 1.5 percent between the spring of 1943 and the summer of 1945. The Consumer Price Index had increased by 28.3 percent during the entire period 1940–1945. This was a remarkable record in view of the power of organized pressure groups and inevitable public vexation at the inconveniences of direct controls.

6. WORKERS AND FARMERS

The nearly insatiable demands of the American and Allied war machines solved the unemployment problem almost overnight, as the number of civilian workers increased from about 46.5 million to over 53 million from 1940 to the middle of 1945. The chief factor in this expansion was the addition of about 7 million workers from the reservoir of the unemployed. To workers, the war boom brought unprecedented prosperity. Although the Consumer Price Index advanced 23.3 percent between 1941 and 1945, weekly earnings of those employed in manufacturing increased 70 percent.

It was not easy to mobilize this huge labor force, restrain labor's natural desire for higher wages, and bridle irresponsible labor leaders. Indeed, the administration never achieved comprehensive control over manpower resources. Roosevelt created the War Manpower Commission (WMC) in April 1942 and appointed former Governor Paul V. McNutt of Indiana to direct the flow of workers into war industries. The WMC gradually developed coercive measures that prohibited workers in defense industries from leaving their jobs without approval of the United States Employment Service. This system worked reasonably well, but it did not solve a more important problem—recruiting new workers and shifting workers from nondefense to war industries. One solution, of course, was national service legislation to draft men for war work. The CIO and AFL bitterly opposed such legislation, but the manpower shortage seemed so critical by the end of 1943 that Roosevelt supported a national service act in his annual message in January 1944. The House approved a labor draft bill in December 1944, but Germany collapsed before the Senate could act on the measure.

Much more important and difficult was the prevention of strikes and the reconciliation of labor's natural desires for economic advancement and union security with the general objective of winning the war without runaway inflation. This gigantic and at times nearly impossible task was entrusted to the War Labor Board (WLB), created by the president in January 1942. The WLB was established simply to settle labor disputes, but it soon discovered that mediation was impossible without a comprehensive labor policy. Inevitably, therefore, the WLB emerged as a powerful policy-making body in the war economy.

To the leaders of organized labor, the fundamental issue was protection of the right of collective bargaining. The WLB stood firm in defense of labor's rights under the Wagner Act, even the right to the closed shop when a majority of workers voted in favor of it. Moreover, it applied a compromise—the so-called maintenance of membership plan—that protected unions in rapidly expanding war plants. Union membership expanded under its aegis to nearly 15 million by the end of the war.

The thorniest problems of wartime labor administration were demands for higher wages and strikes to enforce such demands. Here the issue did not lie between labor and management—for management was usually eager to increase wages in order to hold and attract labor—but rather lay between the public interest and combined private interests. The WLB defended labor's right to enjoy a standard of living "compatible with health and decency." It also endorsed union demands for equal pay for blacks and women and the elimination of sectional differentials. On the other hand, the WLB also asserted that workers should be content to maintain and not improve their standard of living during wartime. In theory, most labor leaders concurred; the trouble was that they could never agree with the WLB on what that standard of living was. The rise in the cost of living during the early months of 1942 precipitated the first crisis. The WLB responded in July 1942 with the so-called Little Steel formula. It granted most workers a 15 percent wage increase to offset a similar increase in the cost of living since January 1941. But employers began to award pay increases that exceeded the Little Steel formula, and the president, under authority of the Stabilization Act of October 1942, empowered the WLB to forbid increases that imperiled the stabilization program.

Meanwhile, the WLB's determination to restrain wage increases had driven a minority of labor to irresponsible action. The AFL and CIO had given a no-strike pledge soon after Pearl Harbor and promised to "produce without interruption." Although responsible labor leaders kept this promise for the most part, restlessness among the rank and file of workers caused some labor strife. All told, there were 14,731 work stoppages involving 6.7 million workers and resulting in the loss of 36.3 million work days from December 8, 1941, through August 14, 1945. However, most work stoppages were short-lived, occurred in defiance of union leadership, and caused a loss of only one-ninth of 1 percent of total working time.

Even so, it was difficult for the mass of Americans to think in terms of averages when they saw workers in airplane factories and shipyards striking for higher pay or over union jurisdiction. Two major incidents—a coal strike and the near occurrence of a nationwide railroad strike in 1943—particularly alarmed the American people. John L. Lewis refused to appear before the WLB and called a general coal strike in May 1943. Roosevelt seized the mines, but the miners struck again in June because the WLB would not break the Little Steel formula and grant high wage increases. Miners returned to work when Roosevelt threatened to ask Congress to draft them, but Lewis forced the administration to surrender by threat of a third strike.

Lewis's cynical defiance of federal authority was more than Congress would tolerate. In June 1943, in hot resentment it approved and reenacted over Roosevelt's veto the Smith-Connally, or War Labor Disputes Act. It empowered the president to seize any struck war plant and required unions to wait thirty days before striking and to hold a secret vote of the workers before a strike was executed. More indicative of the rising antilabor sentiment was the enactment by many state legislatures of laws to prevent certain union practices and to subject unions to a measure of public regulation. In a number of states, these laws forbade the closed shop, mass picketing, secondary boycotts, and the like and required unions to file financial reports and obtain licenses for labor organizers.

For agriculture, the war boom brought new problems but also a stability and prosperity unknown since 1919. Net cash income from farming increased from $2.3 billion to $9.5 billion from 1940 to 1945, or by more than 300 percent. Two factors—increased production and higher prices, both of them stemming from vastly increased demands at home and abroad—restored agriculture to its long-sought position of parity in the American economy. Agricultural prices more than doubled between 1940 and 1945. During the same period, the index of all farm production rose from 108 to 123, while increases in food crops were even more spectacular. Incredible though it sounds, this expansion was accomplished in spite of a declining farm population and without any significant increase in acreage planted and harvested. It was, rather, the product of greater use of machinery, more productive hybrid crops, and fertilizers and insecticides.

7. WOMEN AND WORK DURING WARTIME

The advent of the war brought revolutionary changes for American women. Many of these changes had been apparent for at least a generation. During the late-nineteenth and early-twentieth centuries, for example, the participation of women in the work force grew significantly. Yet primarily because of the acute labor shortage that the departure of some 15 million men and women into the armed forces caused, women now experienced new opportunities.

Women had long been involved in the industrial work force, but for the most part they were confined to low-paying, low-status occupations. In the nineteenth century women were employed in nonunion, low-wage jobs in industries such as cotton textiles; in the twentieth century many women were employed in service sector jobs—also nonunion and low-wage—in department stores, offices, and clerical positions. Those professions that opened their doors to women, such as teaching and nursing, were also low-status and low-wage. Moreover, the great majority of working women were young and unmarried, and the prevailing pattern continued to be that married women (at least among white women, less so among black women) left the work force to be full-time homemakers. Meanwhile, the female work force had not increased since the early twentieth century;

the numbers of employed women remained the same between 1910 and 1940.

The prolonged labor shortage of World War II changed this configuration. As a direct result of the labor crisis, the numbers of women workers rose from 12 million in 1940 to 18 million five years later—an increase of 50 percent. Other important changes followed: the numbers of women belonging to unions quadrupled, while the proportion of married women who worked doubled. Although most women remained in underpaid occupations, they experienced wage increases. Women broke through barriers excluding them from white-collar occupations; during the 1940s, the number of women employed in these jobs grew 65 percent, as against a 27 percent increase for women workers overall. In banking, women were now employed in previously all-male jobs such as those of cashiers, tellers, and loan officers. Women were also employed in large numbers by the federal government. Nearly a million women worked for the federal government between 1940 and 1945, and by war's end, women constituted two-fifths of the federal work force.

Meanwhile, other women also realized new opportunities. The war-heated economy not only needed labor, it needed skilled labor—precisely those jobs in durable goods and heavy industries such as shipbuilding, steel, and automobiles that historically had excluded women. Although employers early on hesitated to employ women in these all-male occupations, the labor shortage convinced them otherwise, and government propaganda urged women to work as a patriotic duty. Millions of women, many of them previously employed in underpaid occupations, heeded the call. Because these sectors of the economy were not only skilled but heavily unionized, women could expect considerably higher wages in these occupations. In munitions and aircraft production plants, for example, women earned about 40 percent more than they could in traditional women's occupations. The war years saw the steady penetration of women into employment in durable-goods manufacturing. Overall, the numbers of women employed in heavy industry grew from 340,000 in 1941 to over 2 million in 1945. While in 1939 only 8 percent of all workers in durable-goods production were women, by 1944 that figure had increased to 25 percent. By late 1943, women constituted 10 percent of all shipbuilding workers, 40 percent of aircraft workers, and 34 percent of ammunition workers. While in 1939, only thirty-six women were employed in the shipbuilding industry, within three years over 160,000 women worked in occupations such as welding and riveting. Meanwhile, the numbers of women employed in the automobile industry grew from 29,000 to 200,000 and as electrical workers from 100,000 to 374,000.

The labor shortage created other work opportunities in addition to those of the war industries. Indeed, there were few traditionally male occupations that did not experience breakthroughs by women, many of whom were employed as post office employees, truck drivers, gas station workers, and civilian pilots, among many other occupations. Other women began to make inroads in previously all-male professions, working as engineers, scientists, physicians, lawyers, and journalists.

Although the war also brought new opportunities for African-American women, the disparities between men and women that prevailed generally in American society were greatest among black women. While they found new employment opportunities and higher wages during the war, they also found that many occupations continued to close the doors to their race. They were hit by a double whammy—they were women and black—and they were among the despised groups in American society. When the war ended, therefore, the expectation among many white Americans was that black women would return to a traditionally more subservient role. A white woman summed up the situation in 1944. "The first thing I'm going to do after the war is over," she declared, "is to get a vacuum cleaner. And a maid to run it."

Yet undeniably the war did open opportunities, even if limited, to African-American women. The most significant opportunities came in domestic work. Between 1940 and 1944, the percentage of the domestic workers who were black increased dramatically, from 13 percent to 60 percent. In other words, as white women domestics left these jobs in favor of better-paying war-related jobs, they created openings which black women, albeit reluctantly, filled. A similar pattern occurred in other occupations that ranked low in both pay and status, such as cafeteria work and laundry work. Domestic work was hard and low-paid, but it paid better than work on the farms from which many of the black women had migrated. Moreover, when they had the chance, black women frequently chose institutional work—as scrubwomen in factories, for example—over work in private homes.

African-American women worked under significant disabilities during the war. While approximately 30 percent of white women worked during the war years, the proportion for black women was 40 percent. Yet what is striking about the latter statistic is it represented no significant change over the pattern for the previous decade; for black women, the war did not unleash an avalanche of women participating in the American economy. The reasons for this lie less in the availability of the labor of black women than in discrimination. The sad fact is that African-American women almost always were last in line, following both white women and black men.

When the war ended, consequently, black women were among the first to be demobilized—that is to say, to lose their jobs. Through means such as layoffs, seniority lists that were separated by race and sex, and union opposition, black women lost their jobs, as did white working women, in the immediate postwar years. Thereafter, as opportunities for white women increased—even if in traditionally female occupations—those for black women did not. Two-fifths of working black women were employed as domestics in private households in 1950, and there they received low wages and few if any benefits, while nearly 20 percent of them toiled as scrubwomen, hotel help, and restaurant workers.

Perhaps the most revolutionary change of the war years had to do with the role and position of married women in the work force. Before 1941, a strong taboo discouraged married women from working. Although increasing numbers of married women sought jobs as a way to supplement family income during the depression, because of high unemployment opportunities were severely limited. The labor shortage provided incentives for this pattern to break down, and the war saw the entrance of scores of married women into the work force. Overall, the proportion of married women who worked grew from slightly more than 15 percent in 1940 to almost 25 percent by 1945.

A new trend with significant implications had begun. As wives entered the work force, long-standing attitudes began, out of necessity, to change. School boards, which had routinely excluded married women as teachers and had even fired teachers who married, now accepted them. Government positions in states and localities now became open to wives. Swift and Company abandoned its ninety-year ban against the employment of married women. Elsewhere, many other employers now also began to hire wives, and many of them also abandoned policies against employing older women. The new employment practices were reinforced by a widespread popular campaign to encourage women workers; "Rosie the Riveter" became a popular symbol of this kind of patriotism. By war's end, public opinion polls revealed a startling reversal in attitudes. In the 1930s, four-fifths of Americans believed that wives should remain in the home; by 1942, three-fifths supported work for married women.

The labor crisis and the war effort's campaign to attract women into the work force drew thousands of married women into employment. A majority of new women workers during wartime (about three-quarters) were married; most of these were older homemakers. Three-fifths of women workers had children. Increasingly, moreover, these new women entrants into the work force were older married women. Before 1941, the majority of working women were in their twenties. In contrast, three-fifths of the women workers employed during the war were over thirty-five.

By 1945, it is no exaggeration to say that, of the revolutionary changes that World War II wrought in the American home front, none was more revolutionary than the transformation of the role of women in the work force. Yet older patterns of unequal pay and job discrimination persisted, and positions that held large numbers of women tended to have diminished status and low wages. Although public opinion polls showed that most of the women joining the work force during the war were satisfied with the jobs and wanted to keep them, the end of the war saw a determined campaign to reduce the employment of women in historically all-male occupations. Although many women, especially married women, remained in the work force, a pattern of discrimination persisted.

8. PUBLIC OPINION AND CIVIL LIBERTIES

Never before had Americans gone to war with such determination and unity. Significant opposition to the war effort simply did not exist after the Pearl Harbor attack, mainly because Communists rallied to the defense and war efforts after the Germans attacked Russia. And because disloyalty was rare, there were no volunteer leagues of patriots, no committees of public safety, no war madness. This is not to say that the government abandoned control over news and expressions of opinion or that it was not ready to act ruthlessly to suppress dangerous dissent. For example, the Justice Department at Roosevelt's command convened a special grand jury in Washington in July 1941 and laid before it and two succeeding grand juries voluminous evidence on the far-flung network of Nazi and Fascist organizations in the United States. The upshot was the indictment under the Smith Act* of thirty leading seditionists for conspiring to establish a Nazi government in the United States and to incite disloyalty in the armed forces. The trial proceeded for more than seven months in 1944 until the judge died, apparently a victim of the badgering of defense attorneys. The seditionists were indicted a second time in 1945, and government attorneys rushed to Germany to obtain new evidence. However, the Circuit Court of Appeals of the District of Columbia ended the fiasco in November 1946 by dismissing the indictment on the ground that the government's proceedings were a travesty of justice.

The government was scarcely more successful when it tried to imprison individual champions of nazism and opponents of the war. The critical test arose when the Justice Department invoked the Espionage Act of 1917 against a man named Hartzel, who published a diatribe against American participation in the war in 1942 and mailed copies to army officers. The Supreme Court, in *Hartzel* v. *United States* (1944), made enforcement of the Espionage Act virtually impossible by declaring that the government had to prove specific intent to obstruct the war effort before it could obtain convictions under the law. Again, when the government obtained the conviction of twenty-four leaders of the German-American Bund for violating the Espionage Act, the court reversed the conviction on the ground of insufficient evidence of criminal intent.

Actually, the government knew that the assorted crackpots who made up the Bund and other pro-Nazi organizations were no menace, for the FBI had pene-

*Enacted in 1940, it forbade persons to advocate the violent overthrow of the government of the United States.

trated these groups and placed their leaders under surveillance. Espionage and sabotage, however, were different matters, and the Justice Department moved swiftly and sternly in dealing with them. The FBI broke a small Nazi espionage ring in 1938, destroyed the major Nazi network in 1941, and was prepared to move against potential spies and saboteurs on the eve of American entrance into the war. The FBI had taken more than 1,700 enemy aliens into custody within less than three days after the Pearl Harbor attack. By such effective countermeasures the Justice Department completely destroyed the elaborate German intelligence and sabotage systems, with the result that not a single known act of sabotage was committed in the United States after December 7, 1941.

Deprived of its underground in America, the German high command resorted to audacious plans. It trained two teams of saboteurs—composed of Germans who had lived in America and American citizens of German descent—and sent them by submarines in May 1942 to destroy the American aluminum industry and blow up bridges and railroad facilities. One team landed on Long Island, the other on the Florida coast. The eight invaders were captured almost immediately by the FBI, tried by a special military commission, sentenced to death, and executed on August 8. The father of one of the saboteurs, Hans Haupt of Chicago, was also convicted of treason for hiding his son and given life imprisonment. Another German-American, Anthony Cramer, was convicted of treason for assisting one of the saboteurs.

The one great blot on the administration's otherwise excellent civil liberties record during the war was the detention and forced removal of Japanese-Americans from the west coast to internment camps in the interior. It was the greatest single violation of civil rights in American history. The issue was not the arrest of Japanese subjects who were potential saboteurs, for they were rounded up immediately after the Pearl Harbor attack. It was the loyalty of some 41,000 Japanese ineligible to citizenship and 71,000 Nisei, or American citizens of Japanese ancestry. The general staff declared the west coast a theater of war in the panic following December 7, 1941, and newspapers and political leaders in California began a widespread campaign for removal of all Japanese-Americans, whether citizens or not. The demand was taken up in Washington by the congressional delegations from the Pacific coast states, and was seconded by the commanding general on the west coast, John L. De Witt. On February 19, 1942, Roosevelt authorized the army to take control. General De Witt soon afterward ordered removal of *all* Japanese-Americans from an area comprising the western third of Washington and Oregon, the western half of California, and the southern quarter of Arizona. Some 110,000 Japanese and Nisei were ruthlessly ejected from their homes and herded into temporary stockades surrounded by barbed wire. They were then transported to ten relocation centers established by the War Relocation Authority in western deserts and the swamplands of Arkansas. Eventually some 18,000 persons suspected of disloyalty were confined in a camp at Tule Lake, California, while the remainder were allowed to find new homes or go to colleges in the Midwest and East. Some 36,000 chose resettlement during the war.

The most disappointing aspect of the whole affair was the Supreme Court's refusal to vindicate the principle of civilian supremacy or defend elementary civil rights. A divided court, in *Korematsu* v. *United States* (1944), apologetically approved the evacuation on the ground that military leaders were justified in taking extreme measures against persons on account of race to protect national security, even though the situation was not serious enough to justify the imposition of martial law. The meaning of the decision was clear and foreboding: in future emergencies no American citizen would have any rights that the president and army were bound to respect when, *in their judgment*, the emergency justified drastic denial of civil rights.

9.   AFRICAN-AMERICANS AND THE HOME FRONT

World War II was a time of unrest and new striving on America's troubled frontier of black-white relations. There were race riots and national discriminations like the continued segregation of nearly a million blacks in the armed services and the separation of black and white blood in Red Cross blood banks. Racial tensions rose to the danger point in the South, as blacks acquired a measure of financial independence and social self-respect. Nonetheless, Negroes emerged from the war with a larger measure of self-esteem and economic and political power than they had ever enjoyed.

The most dangerous racial tensions developed in industrial areas outside the South, as a result of the sudden immigration of nearly 1 million southern blacks in search of jobs and new social opportunities. There were numerous minor clashes in many cities, and New York escaped a major race riot in early 1944 only because of the quick action of its mayor and police force. Tensions flared into large-scale rioting in Detroit, home of Gerald L. K. Smith and other Negro-baiters. A fight between a black and a white man in June 1943 led to other clashes. Soon mobs of whites were roaming the black section, killing and burning as they went. By the time that federal troops had restored order, twenty-five blacks and nine whites had been killed.

This was the dark side of an otherwise bright picture, for World War II was a time also of progress for American blacks. Blacks in the South enjoyed greater acceptance and security and larger political and economic opportunities than ever before. Lynching, long the extreme form of southern race control, became almost a historical phenomenon. The number of Negroes thus put to death declined from five in 1942 to one in 1945. A distinguished body of southern leaders, black and white, met in Atlanta in 1944 and organized the Southern Regional Council to combat prejudice and misunderstanding. Equally significant was the growth during the war of an advanced equalitarian movement outside the South. This campaign assumed the proportions almost of a crusade against Jim Crow and won many triumphs, the most important of which was a growing concern for civil rights by the major parties.

Blacks made greatest progress during the war, in both the North and the South, on the economic front. Of all groups they had suffered most during the depression and profited least from New Deal measures. Nor did the defense boom of 1940–1941 bring relief, as employers stubbornly refused to hire black workers. The administration moved slowly, until A. Philip Randolph, president of the Brotherhood of Sleeping Car Porters, called upon 50,000 blacks to march on Washington to protest. Randolph called off the threatened march; but he did so only after Roosevelt, in June 1941, issued Executive Order 8802. It directed that blacks be admitted to job training programs, forbade discrimination in work on defense contracts, and established a Fair Employment Practices Committee to investigate charges of discrimination on account of race.

The FEPC made progress slowly and performed its most effective service during 1942 and 1943 by conducting hearings on discrimination in most of the large cities of the country. It worked even more vigorously when Roosevelt, in May 1943, reorganized the agency, expanded its budget, and directed that antidiscrimination clauses in contracts be enforced. The FEPC established fifteen regional offices, heard some 8,000 complaints, and conducted thirty public hearings from 1943 to 1946. The results were unexpectedly successful. Nearly 2 million Negroes were at work in aircraft factories, shipyards, steel mills, and other war plants in the South and elsewhere by the end of 1944.

The millennium had not come for American blacks when the war ended. To men of good will, however, the steady enlargement of economic, social, and political opportunities for blacks during the war years was perhaps the most encouraging development on the American home front. Blacks in 1945 could look forward to a postwar era full not only of struggle but also of hope for a new era in which they might stand erect as free men and women and citizens of the great democracy.

CHAPTER 19

The United States and World War II

The American people were destined to play a leading and decisive role in the military operations that brought victory for the United Nations in 1945. In this chapter we will follow the Allies on the long and tortuous road from near defeat to victory. Since the war was won not only in the factory and on the battlefield but also around the conference table, we will also relate how Roosevelt and Churchill forged the bonds of Anglo-American unity, drew the Russian leaders into close association, and gave such an effective demonstration of allied cooperation in wartime as the world had rarely seen before.

1. THE GRAND ALLIANCE

American and British leaders gathered in Washington soon after the Pearl Harbor attack to lay plans for combined conduct of the war. Liaison with the Russians would come later, as soon as circumstances permitted. Prime Minister Winston Churchill arrived in Washington on December 22, 1941, for a week of conferences known by the code name of ARCADIA. These discussions continued on the military level until January 14, 1942. This was a time when Allied military fortunes were at their lowest ebb since the fall of France, but negotiations proceeded smoothly and yielded complete agreement on all important points. These were American production goals for 1942 and 1943, pooling of Anglo-American munitions and their disposal by a joint Munitions Assignment Board, and immediate establishment of a Combined Chiefs of Staff in Washington and a combined British, American, and Dutch command in the Pacific. ARCADIA's most

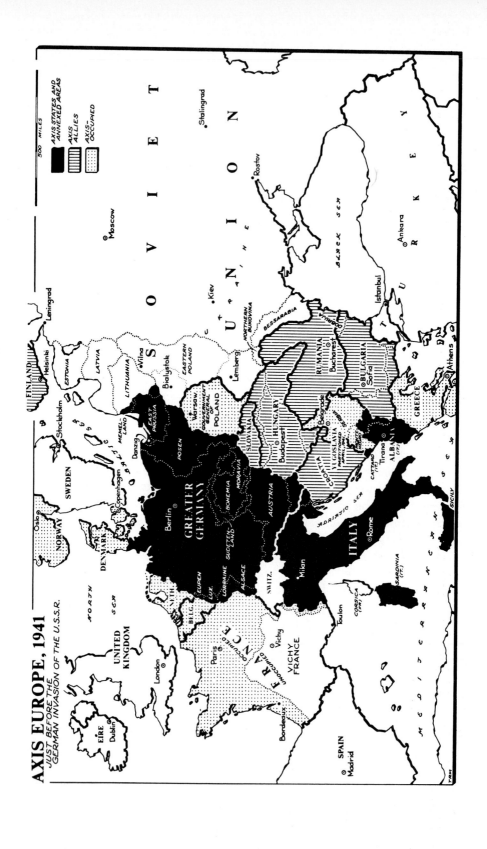

AXIS EUROPE, 1941

JUST BEFORE THE
GERMAN INVASION OF THE U.S.S.R.

500 MILES

AXIS STATES AND
ANNEXED AREAS

AXIS
ALLIES

AXIS-
OCCUPIED

important work was reaffirmation of the earlier staff decision to defeat Germany first since that nation was the stronger enemy and possessed industry and manpower superior to that of the Japanese. The Allies planned major offensives against the Continent first, with holding operations in the Pacific until Nazi power had been subdued.

On the diplomatic level, moreover, Roosevelt and Churchill worked in complete harmony for the formation of a grand coalition of the Allies. The fruit of their labor was the Declaration of the United Nations, signed at the White House on New Year's Day, 1942, by Roosevelt, Churchill, Maxim Litvinov for the USSR, and representatives of twenty-three other nations. The signatory powers reaffirmed the principles set forth in the Atlantic Charter, pledged their full resources to the defeat of the Axis nations, and promised one another not to make a separate peace.

The most uncertain link in the new Allied chain was Russia. By vigorous cooperation, the USSR could hasten victory and help lay the groundwork for postwar cooperation. By making a separate peace, on the other hand, Russia could postpone the hope of Allied victory perhaps indefinitely. The president's and the prime minister's most pressing diplomatic problem during early 1942 was Russian territorial ambitions in Europe and a Russian demand that Britain and the United States guarantee those ambitions in advance. The Kremlin presented the first installment of its demands during a visit of Foreign Secretary Anthony Eden to Moscow in December 1941. Josef Stalin, the Soviet dictator, then requested Great Britain's immediate approval of Russia's absorption of the Baltic states and parts of Finland, Poland, and Romania. He warned, moreover, that conclusion of a British-Soviet alliance would depend upon British endorsement of these territorial claims.

The issue came to a head when the Soviet foreign minister, Vyacheslav Molotov, arrived in London in May 1942 to press Russian territorial and military demands. Churchill and Eden had been strengthened by a warning from Washington that the United States might publicly denounce any Anglo-Russian agreement conceding Stalin's ambitions. They stood firm and persuaded Molotov to sign a general twenty-year Treaty of Alliance that included no reference to boundaries.

2. THE LOW POINT: 1942

Axis victories were so swift and far-reaching during the first six months of 1942 that it seemed that the United Nations might lose the war before they could begin fighting. The Japanese, following air attacks on British and American possessions on December 7, launched seaborne invasions of Hong Kong, Malaya, the Philippines, and lesser islands. They were free to roam and strike almost at will, for the once mighty Anglo-American Pacific naval power was nearly gone by the end of 1941. Guam fell on December 11, 1941; Wake Island, on December 23; Hong Kong, on Christmas Day. Meanwhile, Japanese forces pressed forward in conquest of Malaya, Burma, and the Philippines. Singapore, the great British naval base in the Far East, surrendered on February 15, 1942, to a Japanese force that came down from the north through Malaya. Most of Burma fell in March and April 1942, while Ceylon and India were threatened by a large Japanese naval force that momentarily controlled the Indian Ocean and the Bay of Bengal in April.

In the Philippines, General Douglas MacArthur, with a force of 19,000 American regulars, 12,000 Philippine Scouts, and 100,000 soldiers of the new Philippine Army, fought a desperate delaying action. When Japanese troops threatened Manila, MacArthur declared the capital an open city, moved to Corregidor, and withdrew his troops into Bataan Peninsula for a hopeless but gallant last stand. MacArthur was transferred to Australia in March 1942. His successor, General Jonathan Wainwright, continued the fight from Corregidor and other forts off the tip of the peninsula and held out there until disease, starvation, and superior enemy forces made further resistance impossible. He surrendered on May 6, 1942.

Meanwhile, large new Japanese forces were poised in Malaya and the Philippines by the end of December 1941 to strike at Borneo, the Celebes, New Guinea, and the Dutch East Indies. Only the small American Asiatic Fleet and a few Dutch and British cruisers stood athwart the path of Japanese conquest of the Indies. In the Battle of Macassar Strait, January 1942, American destroyers executed a daring night attack against a Japanese convoy and forced it to turn back. But in the subsequent engagements, known as the Java Sea campaign, the Allies lost their entire naval force, except for four American destroyers. By the end of March 1942, the Japanese were in possession of the East Indies, had pushed into New Britain and the Solomon Islands, and were in position to strike at Port Moresby, the Allied base in southern New Guinea, and at Australia itself. In little more than three months, the Japanese had gained control of a vast area which extended from the Gilbert Islands in the Central Pacific west and south through the Solomons and New Guinea to Burma. India and Australia lay virtually undefended.

Events almost as catastrophic for the Allies were transpiring in the Atlantic, on the eastern front in Russia, and in North Africa. German submarines came perilously close to winning the Battle of the Atlantic during 1942, when Allied and neutral shipping losses aggregated nearly 8 million tons. "The disaster of an indefinite prolongation of the war," to quote Churchill's phrase, threatened to upset Allied plans for military operations.

Meanwhile, the Germans had mounted a large offensive to drive through North Africa, cut the Suez Canal, and penetrate Arabia and the Middle East. General Erwin Rommel, the "Desert Fox," opened the campaign in Libya in May

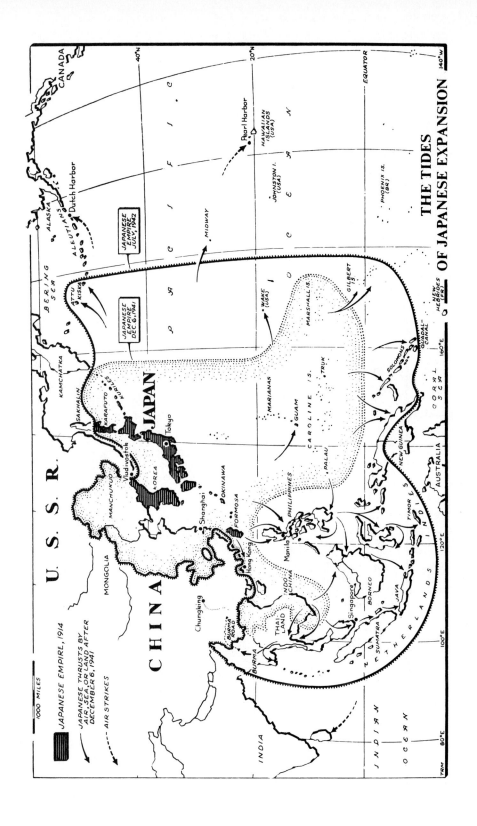

THE TIDES OF JAPANESE EXPANSION

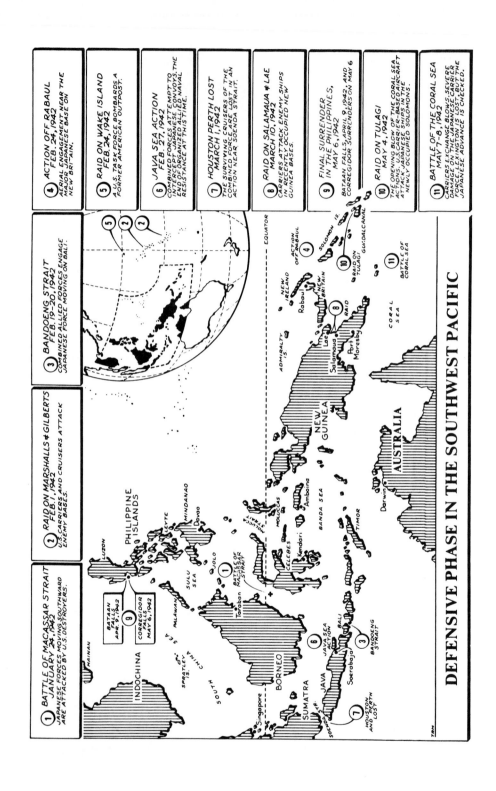

DEFENSIVE PHASE IN THE SOUTHWEST PACIFIC

① **BATTLE OF MACASSAR STRAIT**
JANUARY 24, 1942
JAPANESE FORCES MOVING SOUTHWARD ARE ATTACKED BY U.S. DESTROYERS.

② **RAID ON MARSHALLS & GILBERTS**
FEB. 1, 1942
U.S. CARRIERS AND CRUISERS ATTACK ENEMY BASES.

③ **BANDOENG STRAIT**
FEB. 19-20, 1942
COMBINED ALLIED FORCES ENGAGE JAPANESE FORCE MOVING ON BALI.

④ **ACTION OFF RABAUL**
FEB. 24, 1942
AERIAL ENGAGEMENT NEAR THE MAJOR JAPANESE BASE ON NEW BRITAIN.

⑤ **RAID ON WAKE ISLAND**
FEB. 24, 1942
A U.S. TASK FORCE BOMBARDS A FORMER AMERICAN OUTPOST.

⑥ **JAVA SEA ACTION**
FEB. 27, 1942
COMBINED FORCES ATTEMPT TO INTERCEPT JAPANESE CONVOYS. THE END OF ORGANIZED ALLIED NAVAL RESISTANCE AT THIS TIME.

⑦ **HOUSTON PERTH LOST**
MARCH 1, 1942
THE SURVIVING CRUISERS OF THE COMBINED FLEET ARE LOST IN AN ACTION NEAR SOENDA STRAIT.

⑧ **RAID ON SALAMAUA & LAE**
MARCH 10, 1942
CARRIERS ATTACK ENEMY SHIPS IN RECENTLY OCCUPIED NEW GUINEA BASES.

⑨ **FINAL SURRENDER IN THE PHILIPPINES,**
MAY 6, 1942
BATAAN FALLS, APRIL 9, 1942, AND CORREGIDOR SURRENDERS ON MAY 6

⑩ **RAID ON TULAGI**
MAY 4, 1942
THE OENUS. CARRIER-BASED AIRCRAFT ATTACK JAPANESE SHIPS IN THE NEWLY OCCUPIED SOLOMONS.

⑪ **BATTLE OF THE CORAL SEA**
MAY 7-8, 1942
CARRIERS EXCHANGE BLOWS. SEVERE DAMAGE ON THE JAPANESE CARRIER FORCE. LEXINGTON IS LOST, BUT THE JAPANESE ADVANCE IS CHECKED.

1942. The British, after several sharp defeats, retreated to El Alamein in Egypt, only seventy-five miles from Alexandria, to regroup and reinforce their shattered Eighth Army. The German lines were overextended by July 1, and Rommel's Afrika Korps was too exhausted to press the offensive.

These reversals during the spring and summer of 1942 had a nearly fatal impact on the Grand Alliance, when the hard-pressed Russians demanded assistance in the form of a second front in the west. The issue first arose prominently when Molotov arrived in Washington in late May 1942 for conferences mainly of a military nature with Roosevelt and his advisers. Stalin wanted, Molotov declared, an Anglo-American invasion of western Europe strong enough to draw forty German divisions from the eastern front. Without a second front in 1942, he continued, Germany might deal the USSR a crushing blow. Roosevelt turned to General Marshall for an answer. Marshall replied that there were enough men and supplies for the undertaking. The chief problem was to obtain adequate shipping for an expeditionary force without cutting off supplies to the Soviet Union.

Molotov returned to Moscow with a virtual promise that the United States would launch a cross-Channel invasion in 1942. The Germans drove deeper into southeastern Russia and penetrated the Caucasus, and the pressure from Moscow for relief in the west increased. At this point Roosevelt and his advisers

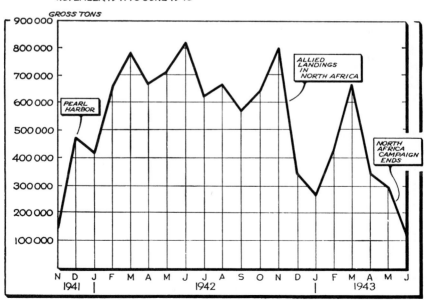

MERCHANT SHIPS SUNK
BY GERMAN SUBMARINES
NOVEMBER 1941 *TO JUNE* 1943

began to consider the feasibility of an Anglo-American thrust at the northern coast of France, known by the code name SLEDGEHAMMER, as a means of averting total disaster in eastern Europe. This was the issue that dominated the conferences among Roosevelt, Churchill, and their chiefs of staff that began in Washington during June 1942. Churchill stubbornly opposed any limited diversionary attempt. He admitted that the British would have six or eight divisions available for an invasion by September. They would participate if the Americans could guarantee the success of the undertaking. But were there not other ways, perhaps an invasion of North Africa, in which combined Anglo-American forces could attack more successfully? In the midst of these heated deliberations came news of Rommel's threatened drive into Egypt. It diverted the conferees' attention from the coast of France to the imperiled area, enabled Churchill to drive home his arguments for a North African invasion, and caused him to hurry home to face his critics in the House of Commons.

The president and his military staff moved swiftly to bolster British defenses in Egypt during the last week of June 1942. But this crisis soon passed, and Roosevelt decided to have the issue of the second front determined once and for all. He sent Harry Hopkins, General Marshall, and Admiral Ernest J. King, American naval commander, to London in mid-July. They joined General Dwight D. Eisenhower, now commander of the European theater of operations, and other Americans in London on July 18 for preliminary conferences. Marshall and Eisenhower were enthusiastic for an invasion of France, which they contemplated beginning on a limited scale until a large offensive could be mounted. But British staff officers refused to budge from their adamant opposition. And American naval officers agreed that a cross-Channel operation in September or October would be dangerous. Informed of the stalemate, Roosevelt replied that his spokesmen should now insist upon offensive operations somewhere, preferably in North Africa. When it seemed that the conferees would also postpone decision on GYMNAST, as the North African operation was then called, Roosevelt replied that plans must be made at once and that landings in North Africa should occur no later than October 30, 1942. Churchill agreed, and there now remained only the task of preparing for TORCH—the new code name of the North African operation—and the unpleasant job of telling Stalin why his western Allies could not open a second front in France in 1942. All apprehensions about a premature second front were confirmed in August. A commando raid by a force of 5,000 men, mainly Canadians, against Dieppe, on the French coast, was a disaster. The strongly entrenched Germans inflicted nearly 3,000 casualties.

3.   THE TIDE TURNS

Events of the autumn of 1942 began for the first time to bring some hope to the embattled United Nations. The American Navy and marines finally stemmed the onrushing tide of Japanese conquest and began their slow and painful progress on the road to Tokyo. The Anglo-American Allies began a campaign in North Africa that ended the Nazi threat to the Middle East and culminated in an invasion of Sicily and Italy in 1943. The Russians finally held firm on the banks of the Volga and then began a counteroffensive that would not cease until Soviet armies had captured Berlin.

The American Pacific Fleet, commanded by Admiral Chester W. Nimitz, had regrouped and given evidence of its valor and power even during the high tide of Japanese expansion. A spectacular blow came in April 1942, when United States Army medium bombers under Colonel James Doolittle took off from the carrier *Hornet* to raid Tokyo. But the most decisive engagement during this defensive phase was the Battle of the Coral Sea, in early May 1942, when planes from *Lexington* and *Yorktown* turned back a large Japanese force moving around the southeastern coast of New Guinea to attack Port Moresby.

The Japanese, shocked by the raid on Tokyo and unaware that the planes had come from a carrier, concluded that the Americans had launched the attack from one of the outlying islands in the Central Pacific. To avoid repetition of this air attack, they decided to extend their perimeter and sent a large armada and invasion force against Midway Island, an outpost guarding the Hawaiian Islands, in a bold bid to cut American communication lines in the Pacific and perhaps establish bases in the islands themselves. Warned of this attack by intercepted Japanese code messages, Nimitz had moved his carriers and cruisers into the Central Pacific, and one of the most decisive battles of the Pacific war raged with incredible fury from June 3 to June 6, 1942. Dive bombers and B-17s from Midway joined with dive bombers and torpedo planes from *Enterprise, Hornet,* and *Yorktown* to sink four Japanese carriers, a heavy cruiser, and three destroyers and to damage one heavy cruiser and two destroyers. In contrast, the Americans lost only *Yorktown* and a destroyer. The Battle of Midway not only removed the threat to the Hawaiian Islands but also restored the balance of naval power in the Pacific. It was, moreover, convincing proof of the importance of air power, for warships in this battle, as in the Battle of Coral Sea, did not exchange a single salvo during the engagement.

Now it was the Americans' turn to go on the offensive. The Japanese had recently moved into the southern Solomon Islands and were building an airfield on Guadalcanal, which imperiled the Allied position in the entire South Pacific and the line of communication to Australia. Assembling a large force of warships, transports, and marines in New Zealand, Admiral Robert L. Ghormley attacked Tulagi and Guadalcanal in the Solomons in August and soon won control of Tulagi and the airfield on Guadalcanal. At the same time, a Japanese cruiser and destroyer force surprised the Allies and sank four cruisers and damaged other ships in the Battle of Savo Island in one of the most humiliating defeats ever suffered by the United States Navy. The Japanese did not know what damage they had done, and they withdrew without attacking the Allied transports. But they soon returned with troops, and the battle raged on Guadalcanal and for control of the air and seas in the area of the Solomons during the next six months. The issue was long in doubt, as the Japanese enjoyed an advantage in land-based aircraft from their base in Rabaul on New Britain Island. However, the American Navy won control of the seas in a number of violent battles. Then American Army forces, relieving the battle-weary First Marine Division, gradually overcame the enemy on Guadalcanal. The Japanese withdrew in early February 1943.

In the meantime, Allied planners and diplomats had been at work preparing TORCH, the offensive in North Africa under General Eisenhower. The British Eighth Army opened an offensive against Rommel's forces at El Alamein in late October 1942, and three great Anglo-American convoys converged west of Gibraltar soon afterward. Two weeks later, they struck simultaneously at Oran and Algiers in Algeria and Casablanca on the Atlantic coast of French Morocco. They encountered heavy French resistance only around Casablanca. Marshal Henri-Philippe Pétain, head of the Vichy French government, severed diplomatic relations with the United States on November 9 and called upon his forces in North Africa to resist. But Pétain's deputy in North Africa, Admiral Jean Darlan, took control when the Germans invaded unoccupied France on November 11. He concluded an armistice agreement with the Allied supreme commander, General Eisenhower, that recognized Darlan's control and promised the cooperation of some 50,000 French colonial troops in North Africa.

During the two weeks following the conclusion of the Darlan agreement, American and British units from Algiers engaged in a race with the Germans for control of Tunisia, then occupied by small French forces. The Germans reached the province in large numbers first and poured additional men, tanks, and planes into North Africa, and the ensuing campaign became a crucial test of strength. Fighting began in earnest in February 1943. It mounted in intensity as General Sir Bernard Montgomery's British Eighth Army in the east and Eisenhower's combined armies in the west gradually closed the jaws of a gigantic vise on the Germans. The result was a complete Allied victory, signaled by German surrender on May 12, which cost the Axis fifteen divisions and 349,206 men killed and captured, 250 tanks, over 2,300 airplanes, and 232 ships. In contrast, the Allies suffered 70,000 casualties in a campaign that seasoned their troops and opened the Mediterranean once again to Allied shipping.

In the meantime, Roosevelt, Churchill, their political advisers, and the American and British chiefs of staff had met at Casablanca for a full-dress conference in January 1943. Two decisions—both arrived at reluctantly by the Americans—were reached: to invade Sicily in order to secure complete control of the Mediterranean and advanced air bases and to defer the invasion of France at least until 1944. General Marshall argued strenuously for a cross-Channel invasion in 1943, but without success.

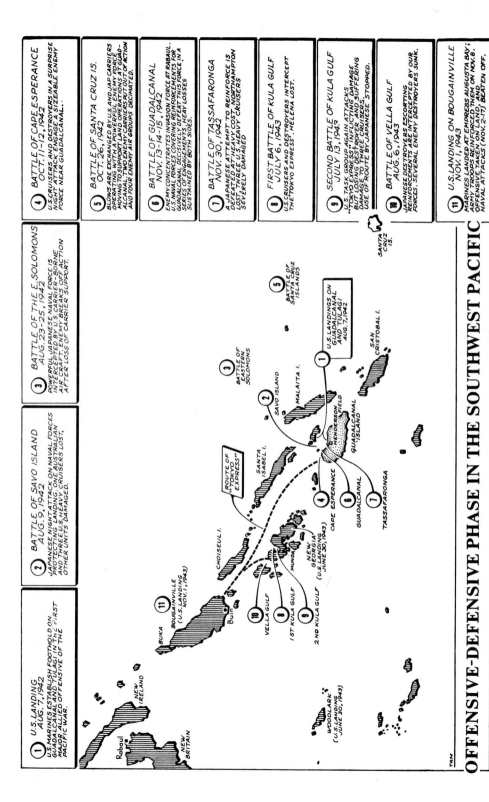

① BATTLE OF CAPE ESPERANCE
OCT. 11-12, 1942
U.S. CRUISERS AND DESTROYERS IN A SURPRISE NIGHT ACTION DEFEAT AN ENEMY FORCE NEAR GUADALCANAL.

⑤ BATTLE OF SANTA CRUZ IS.
OCT. 26, 1942
BLOWS ARE EXCHANGED BY U.S. AND JAP CARRIERS OPERATING WITH A POWERFUL ENEMY FORCE MOVING TO SUPPORT LAND OPERATIONS AT GUADALCANAL. TWO U.S. CARRIERS PUT OUT OF ACTION AND FOUR ENEMY AIR GROUPS DECIMATED.

⑥ BATTLE OF GUADALCANAL
NOV. 13-14-15, 1942
ENEMY CONCENTRATES INVASION FORCE AT RABAUL. U.S. NAVAL FORCES COVERING REINFORCEMENTS FOR GUADALCANAL DECISIVELY DEFEAT THIS FORCE IN A SERIES OF ENGAGEMENTS. HEAVY LOSSES SUSTAINED BY BOTH SIDES.

⑦ BATTLE OF TASSAFARONGA
NOV. 30, 1942
A JAPANESE ATTEMPT TO REINFORCE IS DEFEATED AT HEAVY COST. NORTHAMPTON LOST. THREE U.S. HEAVY CRUISERS SEVERELY DAMAGED.

⑧ FIRST BATTLE OF KULA GULF
JULY 6, 1943
U.S. CRUISERS AND DESTROYERS INTERCEPT THE "TOKYO EXPRESS". HELENA LOST.

⑨ SECOND BATTLE OF KULA GULF
JULY 13, 1943
U.S. TASK GROUP AGAIN ATTACKS "TOKYO EXPRESS", INFLICTING DAMAGE. BUT LOSING ONE CRUISER AND SUFFERING DAMAGE TO THREE CRUISERS. USE OF ROUTE BY JAPANESE STOPPED.

⑩ BATTLE OF VELLA GULF
AUG. 6, 1943
JAPANESE DESTROYERS ARE INTERCEPTED BY OUR FORCES. SEVERAL ENEMY DESTROYERS SUNK.

⑪ U.S. LANDING ON BOUGAINVILLE
NOV. 1, 1943
MARINES LANDED AT EMPRESS AUGUSTA BAY; ARMY TROOPS REINFORCED THEM ON NOV. 8. OFFENSIVE TAKEN ON LAND, AND NAVAL ATTACKS (NOV. 2-17) BEATEN OFF.

① U.S. LANDING
AUG. 7, 1942
U.S. MARINES ESTABLISH FOOTHOLD ON GUADALCANAL AND TULAGI IN THE FIRST MAJOR ALLIED OFFENSIVE OF THE PACIFIC WAR.

② BATTLE OF SAVO ISLAND
AUG. 9, 1942
JAPANESE NIGHT ATTACK ON NAVAL FORCES PROTECTING LANDING. ONE AUSTRALIAN AND THREE U.S. HEAVY CRUISERS LOST, OTHER UNITS DAMAGED.

③ BATTLE OF THE E. SOLOMONS
AUG. 23-25, 1942
POWERFUL JAPANESE NAVAL FORCE IS INTERCEPTED BY U.S. CARRIER-BORNE AIR CRAFT. ENEMY BREAKS OFF ACTION AFTER LOSS OF CARRIER SUPPORT.

OFFENSIVE-DEFENSIVE PHASE IN THE SOUTHWEST PACIFIC

The work of the conference completed, Roosevelt and Churchill held a joint press conference at Casablanca in which they reviewed their work and looked forward to victories ahead. But more important was Roosevelt's declaration, made after previous consultation with Churchill, that the Allies would insist upon the unconditional surrender of the Axis enemies. "It does not mean the destruction of the population of Germany, Italy, and Japan," Roosevelt explained, "but it does mean the destruction of the philosophies in those countries which are based on conquest and the subjugation of other people." It was, as one critic afterward said, one of the "great mistakes of the war." It hardened the German popular will to resist and shut the door to negotiations by an anti-Hitler faction. Worse still, it virtually precluded a negotiated settlement of the Pacific war, the one conflict that might have been terminated by negotiation.

4.   THE ALLIES ON THE OFFENSIVE

The decisive turning point of the European war in 1942–1943 occurred when the Russians held Stalingrad from September to November 1942 against furious German attacks. Then the Russians launched a counteroffensive that destroyed or captured a large German army in the blazing city in February 1943. From this point on, the Soviet armies pressed forward along the entire length of the eastern front. By October 1943, the Red armies had driven deep into the Ukraine and stood on the eastern bank of the Dnieper River, poised for a winter offensive that would drive through the Ukraine into Romania.

The year 1943 also witnessed the turning of the tide in the Battle of the Atlantic. The Germans had more than 100 U-boats constantly at sea by the spring of 1943. But the Anglo-American Allies had finally found the means of victory—aggressive offense through new methods of detection, air patrols both from land bases and escort carriers, and fast destroyers and destroyer escorts to protect the convoys. The turning point came from March through May 1943, when U-boat sinkings in the Atlantic declined from 514,744 tons in March to 199,409 tons in May, and the number of submarines destroyed rose from 12 to 40. Allied shipping losses had declined to 29,297 tons by May 1944, and not a single Allied ship was torpedoed in the summer of 1944. And for decreasing results the Germans paid such a high price—237 submarines sunk in 1943, 241 in 1944, and 153 during the first four months of 1945—as to make their underseas campaign a useless drain on resources and manpower.

Allied power increased so swiftly in the Pacific from March 1943 to March 1944 that the two major commanders in the area, Admiral Nimitz and General MacArthur, were able not only to overwhelm or neutralize the Japanese bastions in the Central and South Pacific but also to launch new offensives that pierced the outer perimeter of Japanese defenses.

The objective of the first great offensive was Rabaul on New Britain Island,

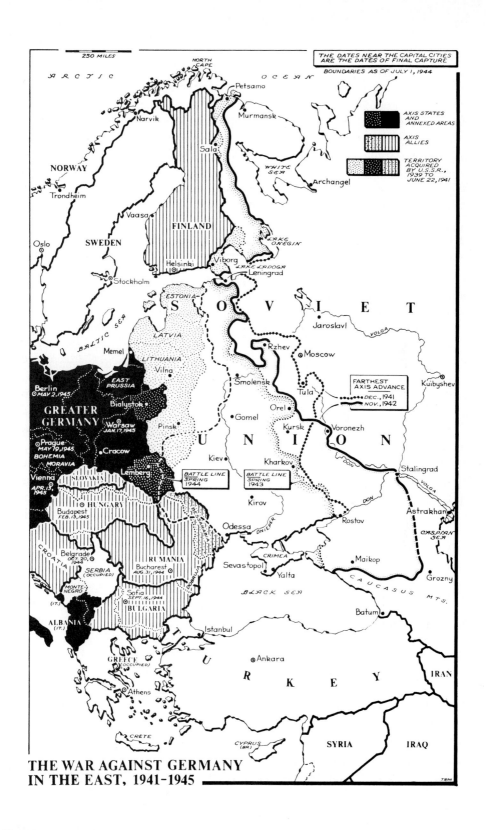

THE DATES NEAR THE CAPITAL CITIES
ARE THE DATES OF FINAL CAPTURE
BOUNDARIES AS OF JULY 1, 1944

AXIS STATES
AND
ANNEXED AREAS

AXIS
ALLIES

TERRITORY
ACQUIRED
BY U.S.S.R.,
1939 TO
JUNE 22, 1941

250 MILES

ARCTIC *OCEAN*

NORTH
CAPE

Petsamo

Narvik

Murmansk

Sala

*WHITE
SEA*

Archangel

NORWAY

Trondheim

Vaasa

FINLAND

*LAKE
ONEGIN*

Oslo

SWEDEN

Helsinki

Viborg

LAKE LADOGA

Leningrad

Stockholm

ESTONIA

S   O   V   I   E   T

Jaroslavl

VOLGA

LATVIA

Memel

Rzhev

Moscow

LITHUANIA

Vilna

Smolensk

Tula

FARTHEST
AXIS ADVANCE

Kuibyshev

Berlin
MAY 2, 1945

EAST
PRUSSIA

Bialystok

GREATER
GERMANY

Warsaw
JAN. 17, 1945

Pinск

Gomel

Orel

DEC., 1941
NOV., 1942

Prague
MAY 10, 1945

BOHEMIA

Cracow

U   N   I   O   N

Kursk

Voronezh

MORAVIA

Lemberg

Kiev

Kharkov

Stalingrad

Vienna
APR. 13,
1945

SLOVAKIA

BATTLE LINE
SPRING
1944

BATTLE LINE
SPRING
1943

DON

VOLGA

HUNGARY

Kirov

Astrakhan

Budapest
FEB. 13, 1945

DON

CROATIA

Belgrade
OCT. 20,
1944

RUMANIA

Odessa

DNIEPER

Rostov

*CASPIAN
SEA*

SERBIA
(OCCUPIED)

Bucharest
AUG. 31, 1944

Sevastopol

CRIMEA

Maikop

Grozny

MONTE-
NEGRO
(IT.)

Sofia
SEPT. 16, 1944

Yalta

C A U C A S U S   MTS.

ALBANIA
(IT.)

BULGARIA

Istanbul

BLACK   SEA

Batum

GREECE
(OCCUPIED)

Ankara

T   U   R   K   E   Y

IRAN

Athens

CRETE

CYPRUS
(BR.)

SYRIA

IRAQ

THE WAR AGAINST GERMANY
IN THE EAST, 1941-1945

the most important Japanese air and naval base in the Southwest Pacific area. The Allied attack was two-pronged. First came a tortuous drive up the New Guinea coast from Port Moresby to Hollandia by American and Australian ground forces, paratroops, and the American Fifth Air Force and Seventh Fleet—all under MacArthur's general command. The enemy had been cleared from the eastern part of New Guinea by February 1944. Meanwhile, American and New Zealand ground forces and strong air and naval forces under Admiral William F. Halsey began a drive in June 1943 through the central and northern Solomon Islands that had carried to New Georgia and Bougainville by November 1943 and to Green Island by February 1944. Finally, with the occupation of the Admiralty Islands north of New Guinea in late February 1944, Rabaul was cut off from communication with the Japanese base of Truk, and its encirclement was complete. Thereafter, Allied commanders were content to reduce Rabaul to impotence through aerial bombardment without attempting to capture it.

While Allied forces under MacArthur thus secured their hold on the South Pacific, the forces under Admiral Nimitz launched two major offensives in the Central Pacific that cracked the outer rim of Japanese defenses in that area. A new Central Pacific Force, including marine and army units, under the command of Admiral Raymond A. Spruance, attacked Tarawa and Makin islands in the Gilberts in late November 1943. Makin was lightly garrisoned and fell quickly to army troops; but the Second Marine Division, which invaded Tarawa after an inadequate bombardment, met fierce resistance from Japanese marines and had to fight for every inch of ground until the last defenders were wiped out on November 24. Striking next at the Marshall Islands, army and marine divisions rooted out Japanese defenders on Kwajalein, Roi, Namur, and Eniwetok between February 1 and 19, 1944. Next the American Navy steamed into the enemy's interior defenses in daring raids against Truk and Saipan in the Marianas, only 1,350 miles from Tokyo, in February 1944.

Meanwhile, the Allies began a major Mediterranean campaign when a huge Anglo-American armada disgorged 160,000 troops, 600 tanks, and 1,800 guns on the beaches of Sicily in July 1943. The British Eighth Army, under General Montgomery, and the American Seventh Army, under General George S. Patton, had routed the Italian and German defenders and overrun the island by mid-August. It was an important turning point, for a group of Italian conspirators persuaded King Victor Emmanuel to connive at the deposition and arrest of Mussolini on July 25 and formed a new government under Marshal Badoglio. He proceeded to open negotiations looking toward the surrender of Italy.

This sudden turn of events raised new perplexities for Roosevelt and Churchill—whether to negotiate with the Badoglio government, as Eisenhower and other Allied leaders requested, or to demand unconditional surrender in accordance with the Casablanca declaration. The situation was so uncertain that the president, the prime minister, and their respective entourages met in Quebec on August 17, 1943, for a conference known by the code name of QUADRANT.

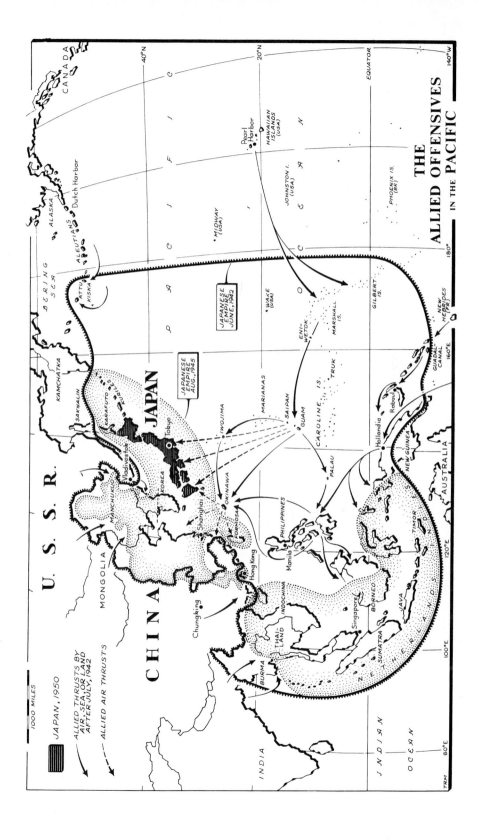

THE
ALLIED OFFENSIVES
IN THE PACIFIC

1000 MILES

JAPAN, 1950

ALLIED THRUSTS BY
AIR, SEA, OR LAND
AFTER JULY, 1942

ALLIED AIR THRUSTS

JAPANESE EMPIRE
JUNE, 1942

JAPANESE EMPIRE
AUG., 1945

The new Italian government made secret contact with the Allies. The Italians were eager to surrender but insisted that the Allies protect Rome, the king, and the government from the Germans, who had meanwhile taken control of most of Italy. Roosevelt and Churchill agreed to send an airborne division to capture the airfields around Rome, and the armistice was signed on September 3. By the time that preparations for an airborne assault on Rome were completed, however, the Germans had surrounded the city in force and seized the airfields. A German parachute force rescued Mussolini on September 12, 1943, and he then established a new Fascist government at Lake Como under German protection.

Meanwhile, the British Eighth Army crossed the Straits of Messina on September 3 and began the invasion of the Italian mainland in an operation called AVALANCHE. A week later a British airborne division seized the large Italian naval base at Taranto, while the United States Fifth Army, under the command of General Mark Clark, landed in the Gulf of Salerno south of Naples. The Fifth Army occupied Naples on October 7 in spite of furious German counterattacks and pushed northward to the Volturno River. Meanwhile, British forces had cleared the central and eastern sections of the Italian boot. Allied forces had pushed to a winter line south of Cassino by January 1, 1944.

A long and bloody campaign for Italy still impended, but the Italian surrender and successful invasion of Italy yielded large dividends to the Anglo-American Allies. It brought the surrender of the Italian Fleet and guaranteed complete Allied control of the Mediterranean. It gave the Allies advanced air bases from which to bomb the Balkans and Central Europe. It consumed some of Hitler's best divisions. Most important, it gave the British and Americans the incalculable advantage of being on the offensive.

5. THE SOVIETS AND THE GRAND ALLIANCE

The QUADRANT conferees at Quebec turned to other urgent problems after they approved final arrangements for the Italian surrender. They reaffirmed May 1, 1944, as the date for OVERLORD, the long delayed cross-Channel invasion. Hull and Eden discussed postwar plans for Germany and approved the draft of a Four Power Declaration—to be submitted to the coming conference of foreign ministers in Moscow—pledging America, Great Britain, Russia, and China to cooperate in the establishment of an effective postwar security organization. The conference was over on August 24, and Churchill accompanied Roosevelt back to Washington and stayed with him intermittently during the next three weeks. During this time the Badoglio government surrendered, and the Allies began their invasion of the Italian mainland.

Soon afterward, in October 1943, Secretary Hull made the arduous air journey to Moscow for the conference of foreign ministers that opened in the Russian capital. Before this time, no one in Washington or London knew what Russian

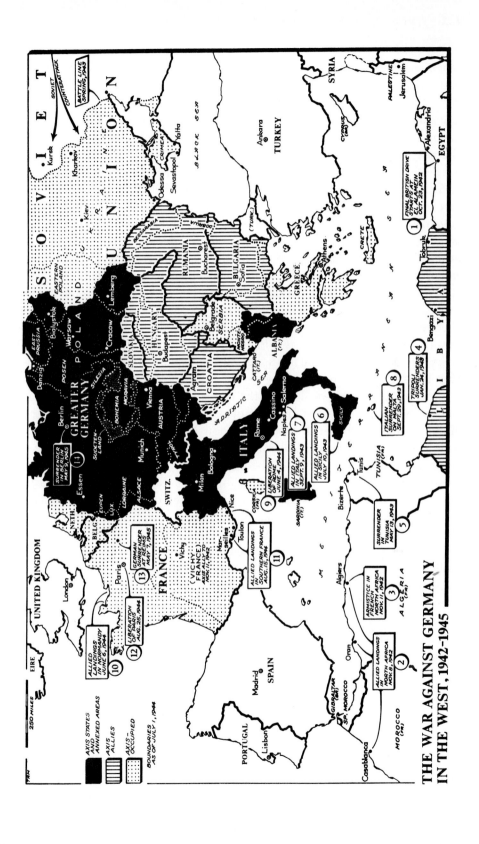

THE WAR AGAINST GERMANY
IN THE WEST, 1942-1945

postwar ambitions were, except for the territorial demands that Stalin had outlined to Eden in December 1941. In Moscow, Hull, Molotov, and Eden discussed immediate and postwar problems, with so little disagreement that future accord seemed assured. They completely endorsed an American plan for the postwar treatment of Germany. It called for the unconditional surrender of Germany by whatever government exercised power at the end of the war. An Inter-Allied Control Commission would supervise the surrender and occupation of Germany by Soviet, American, and British troops. It would undertake to destroy all vestiges of nazism and encourage establishment of a democratic government and the restoration of freedom of religion, speech, the press, and political activity. Moreover, Germany should be denied a standing army and general staff and prohibited from manufacturing any war materials or aircraft of any kind. Finally, Germany should be required to pay reparations in goods, equipment, and manpower, but not in money. The conferees agreed, moreover, that Austria should be reconstituted an independent nation and regarded as a liberated and not an enemy state, while Hull persuaded Stalin and Molotov to sign the Four Power Declaration. In addition, at a state dinner on October 30, Stalin told Hull the welcome news that Russia would join the war against Japan after the defeat of Germany.

Despite differences over Poland, the Moscow Conference was a resounding success. No one in the west knew absolutely whether Russia would cooperate in the postwar era, but such cooperation now seemed at least possible. As one milestone along the road to Allied unity, the conference prepared the way for the next—a personal meeting of the Big Three.

Roosevelt had long wanted to meet with the Russian leader, and he had invited Stalin before the Moscow Conference to join him and Churchill at Ankara, Baghdad, or Basra in Iraq. Stalin replied that he would go only to Teheran, since he could maintain personal control over his high command from the Iranian capital. The president agreed and left Hampton Roads on the new battleship *Iowa* in November 1943 for the long journey to Cairo. There he conferred with Churchill, Chiang Kai-shek, Lord Louis Mountbatten, Allied commander in Southeast Asia, and General Joseph W. Stilwell, American commander in the China area and adviser to Chiang. Most of these discussions revolved around an Allied drive in Burma to open supply lines to China, and a Chinese offensive in northern China.

Roosevelt and his party next flew from Cairo to Teheran. During the subsequent days, the Big Three thrashed over practically all outstanding military and political problems, including military operations in Italy and American plans for offensive operations in the Pacific. Stalin again promised that Russia would join the war against Japan after Germany's surrender.

The Russians were most concerned about OVERLORD and seemed desperately anxious to pin Roosevelt and Churchill to a definite time and place for the great invasion. Stalin pressed Roosevelt to name a supreme commander for OVERLORD, and, on his return from Teheran, the president chose Eisenhower for this position.

The Big Three also discussed the future of Germany and plans for postwar collaboration. They now seemed to favor partition. Stalin emphasized the danger of future German resurgence. Roosevelt outlined his plan for a future United Nations organization, which would assume responsibility for preventing wars and aggression. During all these conversations, Roosevelt became convinced that he had broken through the wall of suspicion and distrust surrounding Stalin, won Russian trust and friendship, and laid the basis for fruitful collaboration in the future. His feeling was well expressed in the concluding sentences of the Declaration of Teheran, issued on December 1: "We came here with hope and determination. We leave here, friends in fact, in spirit, and in purpose."

6. THE EUROPEAN AIR WAR, 1940–1945

After the failure of the German air blitz against England in 1940–1941, the British gained air superiority. The RAF Bomber Command conducted a limited number of night raids against selected industrial and transportation targets in Germany from 1940 to early 1942. Results were so unsatisfactory that the new chief of the Bomber Command, Sir Arthur Harris, executed a complete change in British bombing tactics—from the target system to mass bombing of industrial areas in order to disrupt the German economy and lessen the will of the German people to fight. The first 1,000-plane RAF raid, against Cologne on May 30, 1942, signaled the beginning of the new campaign. It was followed in 1942 by others against centers in the Ruhr, Bremen, Hamburg, and other German cities. This was only a small beginning, for less than 50,000 tons of bombs fell on Axis Europe in 1942, and German war production and civilian morale were not visibly impaired.

Meanwhile, the United States Eighth Air Force had established bases in England in early 1942 and joined in the air war in August 1942. The offensive power of the Eighth Air Force grew and was reinforced by the Ninth Air Force and the Fifteenth Air Force, and the Americans became a powerful factor in the air campaign during the summer of 1943. While the British continued their devastating night attacks, the Americans used their heavier armored Flying Fortresses and Liberators in daring daylight raids. However, extremely heavy losses in a raid on Schweinfurt for October 1943 convinced American commanders that further large daylight operations had to await production of long-range fighters to protect the bombers. All told, American and British bombers dropped 206,188 tons of bombs on European targets in 1943.

A new phase in the air campaign began in February 1944. The arrival in England of substantial numbers of long-range American fighters made resumption of daylight raids possible. The introduction of radar bombsights had already greatly increased the accuracy of night bombing. And there was a use of increasingly heavy bombs and a rapid buildup of the Eighth and Fifteenth Air Forces. The Americans first began a systematic campaign to destroy the German aircraft industry. Then the attack shifted in March to French and Belgian marshaling yards, railroads, and bridges. And, after the invasion of France, the American and the British air forces began a coordinated and relentless round-the-clock assault upon German synthetic oil and chemical plants. Some 8,000 to 9,000 Allied planes turned to the task of paralyzing the German transportation system in February 1945. Finally, the air forces joined the advancing Allied armies in April in reducing the German nation to utter impotence and ruin.

The overall dimensions of the Anglo-American air effort in Europe stagger the imagination: 1,442,280 bomber and 2,686,799 fighter sorties, which dropped 2,697,473 tons of bombs on Germany and Nazi-occupied Europe. This effort cost the Allies some 40,000 planes and 158,000 personnel. All told, Allied bombs dropped on Germany killed 305,000 people and wounded 780,000 others, destroyed or damaged 5.5 million homes, and deprived 20 million persons of essential utilities. By the beginning of 1944, according to a poll taken by the Strategic Bombing Survey immediately after the war, some 77 percent of the German people were convinced that the war was lost; and by May 1945 most Germans had lost all will to continue the uneven struggle.

7.   TOWARD VICTORY IN EUROPE

General Dwight D. Eisenhower, supreme commander of the Allied Expeditionary Forces, arrived in London in January 1944, with orders from Roosevelt and Churchill to "enter the continent of Europe and, in conjunction with the other Allied Nations, undertake operations aimed at the heart of Germany and the destruction of her armed forces." The Combined Chiefs of Staff and various technical staffs in Great Britain and the United States had been hard at work on OVERLORD since 1942. Planning for the actual invasion and subsequent operations continued in Eisenhower's London headquarters after January 1944.

The appointed time now approached rapidly. The great invasion armada was delayed by a sudden storm and put out to sea early in the morning of June 6. The Germans expected the invasion to come in the Pas de Calais area, where the English Channel is narrowest. Instead, the Allies struck at five beaches along a sixty-mile stretch of the Cotentin Peninsula in Normandy. First there were furious air and naval bombardments of the invasion area and beaches. Next came the landing of three airborne divisions behind the German lines a few minutes after midnight on June 6. Finally, the seaborne troops hit the beaches at 7:30 in the morning. German resistance was generally light; but American invaders met a fierce defense on Omaha Beach and suffered heavy casualties.

The German commanders, Field Marshals Rommel and Karl von Rundstedt, mistook the Normandy invasion as a screen for a larger invasion in the Pas de Calais. They were not able to bring up their reserve divisions in time to prevent the Allies from securing and capturing a bridgehead in Normandy. Within two weeks after D day, the Allies had landed more than 1 million troops with enormous quantities of supplies in a broad sector along the Normandy coast. They had also captured Cherbourg, Caen, and St. Lô, "eaten the guts out of the German defense," and were poised for a grand sweep through northern France.

The battle of the breakthrough began on July 25, with a lightninglike thrust by General Patton's Third Army into Brittany and a breakthrough to Avranches and Falaise by the American First Army and the British Second Army. Soon the battle for Normandy turned into the battle for France. The German Seventh Army in the area between Falaise and Argentan was under orders to stand firm. It was surrounded and partially destroyed or captured during a furious battle from August 19 to 23. The Allies completed the liberation of France in their own version of lightning warfare while the surviving German armies moved back to their Siegfried line. The American Seventh Army invaded southern France on August 15 and joined the race for the German frontier. Paris fell to French and American troops ten days later. By mid-September, American and British armies had captured Brussels and Antwerp, occupied Luxembourg, and crossed the German border at Aachen.

The Allies were on the move on other fronts as well. They had tried vainly to break the German lines in southern Italy. Then they tried to turn the German flank on January 22, 1944, by landings at Anzio and Nettuno on the Italian western coast, only thirty-six miles from Rome. This effort failed. But the British Eighth Army and the American Fifth Army pushed northward in the spring, joined the beleaguered divisions on the Anzio beachhead, and captured Rome on June 4, 1944. Under heavy Allied pressure and harassment, the Germans pulled back to their Gothic line, which ran across Italy some 150 miles north of Rome. There they managed to stabilize the fighting around September 1, 1944.

Meanwhile, the Russians, during the spring of 1944, began offensives along the entire eastern front fully as important in the Allied strategy as the Anglo-American sweep across France. One Russian drive on the northern sector forced Finland to sue for peace on August 25. The greatest Russian offensive, however, opened on June 23 to coincide with the Anglo-American drive in the west. Soviet armies captured the German stronghold of Vitebsk and then broke through to the Baltic on August 1. Five Russian armies in the central sector rolled into Poland, reached the Vistula River in late July, captured Warsaw on January 17, 1945, and reached the Oder River, only forty-five miles from Berlin, the following month. Farther to the south, two Red armies overran Romania in August 1944. Then they marched into Bulgaria, captured Belgrade on October 20, and entered Budapest in February 1945.

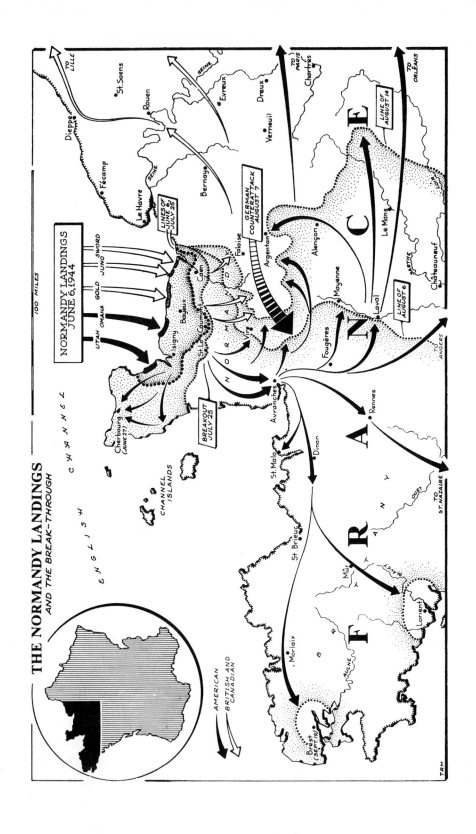

THE NORMANDY LANDINGS
AND THE BREAK-THROUGH

NORMANDY LANDINGS
JUNE 6, 1944

UTAH OMAHA GOLD JUNO SWORD

LINES OF
JUNE 6,
JULY 25

BREAKOUT
JULY 25

GERMAN
COUNTERATTACK
AUGUST 7

LINE OF
AUGUST 6

LINE OF
AUGUST 14

100 MILES

ENGLISH CHANNEL

CHANNEL
ISLANDS

AMERICAN

BRITISH AND
CANADIAN

FRANCE

NORMANDY

BRITTANY

TO LILLE

St. Saens

Dieppe

Fécamp

Le Havre

Rouen

SEINE

SEINE

Bernay

Evreux

Dreux

Vermeuil

TO PARIS

Chartres

TO ORLEANS

LOIRE

SARTHE

Le Mans

Châteauneuf

Alençon

Argentan

Falaise

Caen

Bayeux

Courseulles

Isigny

St. Lo

Cherbourg
(JUNE 27)

Mayenne

Fougères

Laval

TO ANGERS

Avranches

Rennes

St Malo

Dinan

St Brieuc

Morlaix

Brest
(SEPT.19)

Mûr

BLAVET

AULNE

OUST

Lorient

TO
ST. NAZAIRE

TRM

It was obvious to almost everyone by the autumn of 1944 that the German military situation was hopeless. Germany was now a beleaguered fortress awaiting final destruction because her fanatical master preferred complete destruction to unconditional surrender. Some high German officers, foreseeing inevitable ruin under Hitler's leadership, in cooperation with certain anti-Nazi groups, perfected plans to take control of the German government and assassinate Hitler. Their agent left a time bomb in Hitler's headquarters on July 20, 1944. Thinking Hitler dead, the conspirators proceeded to take first steps to seize control of the army and government. As it turned out, Hitler was only injured by the bomb's blast. With the support of loyal troops he rounded up the opposition, executed about 5,000 after drumhead trials, and sent another 10,000 enemies to concentration camps. In consequence, the war would proceed to its bitter end.

8.   THE CAMPAIGN AND ELECTION OF 1944

Meanwhile, partisan politics had persisted in the United States. The Republicans made a hard fight to win control of Congress in 1942. They failed, but they made such sweeping gains in the elections on November 3 that a GOP victory in 1944 seemed at least possible. The Democrats elected 222 and the Republicans 209 members to the House—a Republican gain of 47 seats. The Republicans, moreover, gained 9 seats in the Senate. Actually, what occurred in the federal and state elections in November 1942 was not merely a Republican revival but also a strong conservative upsurge. The significance of the upheaval became apparent after the organization of the Seventy-eighth Congress in January 1943, when many southern Democrats joined Republicans to form a majority coalition and seize control of legislative policy. This coalition gave the president aggressive support in all matters relating to war and postwar policies. In domestic matters, however, it proceeded as fast as it could to destroy certain parts of the New Deal.

Wendell L. Willkie was still titular head of the GOP, but he had no support among party leaders and had become so closely identified with the Roosevelt administration as to lose his status as leader of the opposition. He withdrew from the preconvention campaign after suffering an impressive defeat in the Wisconsin presidential primary in April 1944. Meanwhile, Willkie's chief rival, Governor Thomas E. Dewey of New York, was fast emerging as the new Republican leader. The presidential nomination went to him on the first ballot when the Republican National Convention met in Chicago on June 26, with the vice-presidential nomination going to Governor John W. Bricker of Ohio. The convention adopted a platform that was aggressively internationalistic and essentially progressive in tone. It roundly condemned the Roosevelt administration's alleged inefficiency, waste, excessive centralization, and destruction of private enterprise. However, it made it clear that Republicans had no fundamental quarrel with Democrats on domestic issues. On the contrary, it promised to strengthen the New Deal's labor, social security, and agricultural programs. All in all, it was the most significant endorsement of the Roosevelt policies yet written.

There never was much doubt that the Democrats would nominate Roosevelt for a fourth term, and he was willing to accept even though he had recently suffered from cardiac failure, hypertension, and hypertensive heart disease. On July 11, the president announced that he would accept renomination, and his announcement settled the matter when the Democratic National Convention opened in Chicago on July 19.

In view of Roosevelt's precarious health and poor chances of serving out a fourth term, the crucial struggle revolved around the nomination of a vice-presidential candidate. This battle was bitter and created divisions in the party that persisted for years afterward. Vice-President Henry A. Wallace enjoyed the support of the advanced progressive wing and large elements in the CIO. But he was almost unanimously opposed by party bosses, Southerners, and many moderates who suspected that he was temperamentally unfit for the presidency and hopelessly inept at political leadership. Roosevelt endorsed Wallace publicly but refused to insist upon his nomination. In fact, the president had apparently promised the succession to Byrnes and actually tried to obtain the nomination for the South Carolinian.

The president's plans, however, were upset on the eve of the convention by a newcomer in high Democratic councils, Sidney Hillman, a vice-president of the CIO and former codirector of the defense effort. Alarmed by the rising tide of antilabor sentiment and the failure of workers to go to the polls in 1942, Hillman organized the Political Action Committee (PAC) of the CIO in 1943. His purpose was not only to rally workers and progressives but also to win new bargaining power for labor within the Democratic party.

Hillman used his power in a spectacular way at the Democratic National Convention. He virtually vetoed Byrnes's nomination by warning the president that the South Carolinian was unacceptable to labor and northern blacks. The president concluded that his assistant must give way to a compromise candidate. He therefore declared that either Senator Harry S Truman or Justice William O. Douglas would be an agreeable running mate. And he agreed with Hillman that the PAC should shift its support from Wallace to Truman when it became obvious that Wallace could not be nominated. In any event, Roosevelt declared in his final instructions to National Chairman Robert E. Hannegan that the party managers had to "clear it with Sidney," that is, had to win Hillman's approval for any vice-presidential candidate.

The issue was actually settled during the three days before the convention opened in Chicago on July 19, 1944. Hillman declared that he would fight Byrnes's nomination to the bitter end, and the president on July 17 asked the

South Carolinian to withdraw. Byrnes's withdrawal narrowed the field to Wallace, who still enjoyed the PAC's seeming support, and Truman, upon whom administration and party leaders had finally agreed. During the balloting for the vice-presidential nomination on July 19 and 20, Wallace led on the first ballot and Truman won on the third, as the leaders had planned. The convention had nominated the president on the first ballot a short time before. The Democratic platform promised continuation of progressive policies at home and vigorous American leadership abroad in the postwar era.

Dewey campaigned hard under tremendous handicaps during the ensuing summer and autumn. He was beaten before he started—by smashing Allied victories in Europe and the Pacific, a general reluctance to change governments in the midst of the world crisis, and above all by his own general agreement with basic administration policies. This latter handicap forced him to make criticisms that could only sound captious. Dewey's chief advantage was Roosevelt's failing health and a growing suspicion that perhaps the president was incapable of managing affairs of state. This suspicion increased after Roosevelt's address at Bremerton, Washington, on August 12, during which he was halting and ineffective because he was suffering at this very time from an attack of angina pectoris. However, Roosevelt, his health substantially recovered, came back in a speech before the Teamsters' Union in Washington on September 23 that convinced millions of voters that he was still the champion campaigner. He followed this masterpiece with strenuous tours and speeches in Chicago, New York, Wilmington, Delaware, and New England.

This aggressive campaign gave Roosevelt the initiative that he had seemingly lost. He also recovered lost ground by committing himself squarely to a full resumption of progressive policies in the postwar era. Almost as decisive was the PAC's success in getting workers to the polls. In the election on November 7, Roosevelt received 25,602,505 popular and 432 electoral votes; Dewey, 22,006,278 popular and 99 electoral votes. The Democrats lost one seat in the Senate, but they gained twenty seats in the House, all but four of them in the large cities, and captured governorships in Ohio, Massachusetts, Missouri, Idaho, and Washington. The most important outcome of the election was not the continuation of Democratic control but rather the fact that Americans of both parties were now irrevocably committed to assume the leadership in world affairs that they had so often rejected before 1941. For better or for worse, there could be no turning back on the high road to international responsibility.

9.   THE YALTA CONFERENCE

The rapid progress of Allied and Russian armies raised the possibility that the war in Europe might end before the three great powers had come to definitive agreement on plans for future collaboration. Indeed, there was little evidence

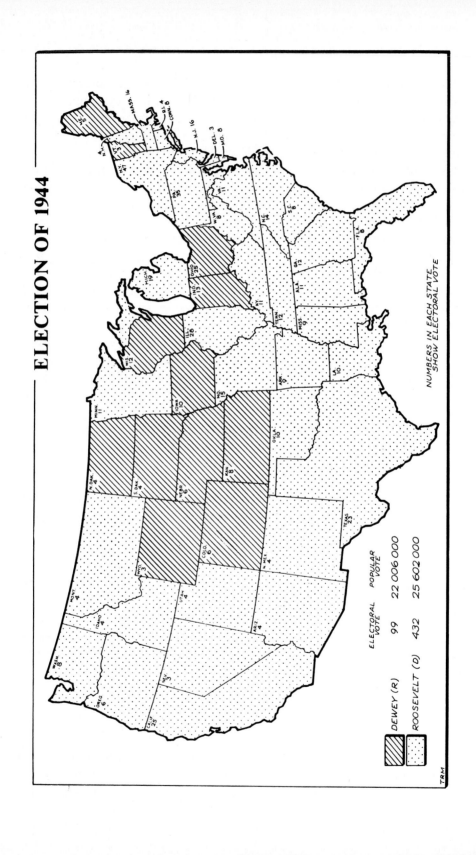

ELECTION OF 1944

NUMBERS IN EACH STATE
SHOW ELECTORAL VOTE

	ELECTORAL VOTE	POPULAR VOTE
DEWEY (R)	99	22 006 000
ROOSEVELT (D)	432	25 602 000

T.R.M.

that the American leaders yet knew even their own minds on the most important aspect of postwar planning—a policy for the control of Germany. More disturbing, however, were signs of growing Allied dissension that threatened to split the Grand Alliance and prevent organization of a postwar United Nations. British, American, and Russian delegates met at Dumbarton Oaks in Washington in September 1944. They agreed on a basic structure for a United Nations but could not agree upon certain fundamental aspects of voting procedure. Following this, the State Department and the British Foreign Office engaged in heated controversies over the organization of a new Italian government and the methods and objectives of British intervention in Greece. The most dangerous potential source of trouble was Russian policy in eastern Europe, especially in Poland.

Roosevelt's thoughts inevitably turned toward another meeting of the Big Three to discuss matters that could be settled only on the highest level. Churchill and Stalin were agreeable, although Stalin insisted that he could not leave Russia because he was personally directing the Russian armies. The three leaders soon agreed upon Yalta in the Crimea as the place and early February 1945 as the time of the conference.

The Yalta meeting would obviously be the last Big Three conference before the surrender of Germany, and the president and the new secretary of state, Edward R. Stettinius, Jr., went to unusual effort, first, to formulate an American program and, second, to come to firm agreement with the British before the Big Three met. Stettinius took his staff to Marrakech in French Morocco for a briefing session in January 1945, and they then went to Malta for conferences with Churchill and Eden.

The Anglo-American-Russian conferees assembled at Yalta on February 3 and 4, 1945, for the opening of the conference called ARGONAUT on the latter day. The Big Three discussed almost every conceivable problem related to the future of Europe, Asia, and the United Nations from February 4 through 11. In addition, the foreign ministers and military and naval leaders of the three powers worked behind the scenes to smooth out minor differences and lay the groundwork for major understandings. Without following the conferees in their long deliberations, let us now summarize their major agreements and decisions.

Germany   The discussions relating to Germany revolved around the questions of dismemberment, reparations, future Allied control, and French participation in the Inter-Allied Control Commission. The conferees approved dismemberment in principle and agreed to consider details in future negotiations. However, they agreed that northern East Prussia, including Königsberg, should go to Russia; that Poland should annex the southern half of East Prussia; that Russia should annex certain former eastern Polish provinces; and that Poland should receive territory in eastern Germany as compensation. As for reparations, the Russians proposed exacting a total of $20 billion, half of which should be paid to the USSR. Roosevelt and Churchill would not approve any fixed sum.

But they agreed to accept the Russian proposal as the basis for future negotiations and to establish a reparations commission with headquarters in Moscow. The Russians withdrew their objection to French participation in the occupation of Germany, and Stalin agreed also that France should have a seat on the Control Commission. As the several occupation zones had already been drawn by the European Advisory Commission in London, there was no discussion of this matter at Yalta.

The Governments of Poland and Eastern Europe   The crucial question was Poland's political future. Stalin and Molotov said quite frankly that they would not tolerate a Polish regime unfriendly to the USSR. As they pointed out, the Germans had twice within twenty-five years used Poland as the corridor for attacks against Russia. They insisted that Great Britain and the United States recognize a provisional Polish government in Lublin that Russia had sponsored and recognized. Roosevelt and Churchill adamantly refused. Then Stalin suggested that the Lublin government be enlarged to include some of the leaders of the Polish government-in-exile that the western powers supported and which was now in London. Roosevelt and Churchill again refused. Stalin finally agreed that the Lublin government should be reorganized to include Polish democratic leaders at home and abroad, and that free elections should be held at an early date to determine the future government of the country. Roosevelt made it clear that the British and American ambassadors in Warsaw would judge whether this pledge had been honestly kept.

The three powers pledged themselves to assist the peoples of other so-called liberated countries of eastern Europe to establish, through free elections, democratic governments responsive to popular will.

Churchill and Eden had had conferences with Stalin in Moscow over the future of the Balkans in October 1944 in which they agreed that Russia should have predominance in Romania and Bulgaria, that Britain should have predominance in Greece, and that the two countries would share responsibility in Yugoslavia and Hungary.

The Yalta agreements were to supersede the Churchill-Stalin agreement.

The Organization of the United Nations   The Russians conceded almost everything for which Americans had contended at the Dumbarton Oaks Conference in discussions at Yalta over organization of the United Nations. First, they accepted the American formula for voting in the Security Council. Second, the Soviets withdrew their demand for sixteen votes in the General Assembly and received in return additional representatives and votes for the Ukraine and White Russia. Third, Stalin agreed to Roosevelt's proposal that all nations at war with Germany by March 1, 1945, might become members of the United Nations.

The Far East   By secret agreement between the Americans and Russians, which Churchill approved but did not help make and which was not published until February 1946, Stalin agreed to bring Russia into the war against Japan within two or three months after the surrender of Germany. In return, Roosevelt approved the transfer of the Kurile Islands from Japan to Russia, recognized Russian control of Outer Mongolia, and agreed that Russia should recover all rights and territory lost at the end of the Russo-Japanese War. Finally, Stalin agreed to recognize Chinese sovereignty over Manchuria and to conclude a treaty of friendship and alliance with the Nationalist government of China.

Millions of words have since been spoken and written about the Yalta agreements. Critics have called them base appeasement of Russia, betrayal of Poland and eastern Europe to Soviet imperialism, and useless surrender to communism in the Far East—all by a mentally incompetent president who was hoodwinked by the wily Stalin. Defenders have replied that the agreements were necessary and realistic.

The charge that Roosevelt was mentally incompetent is most easily disposed of. Roosevelt was obviously tired at Yalta and exhausted afterward by the strain of the grueling sessions and of his long journeys. But there is no evidence that he was not in full possession of his mental faculties during the conference itself. The consensus of historical judgment rather emphatically supports the conclusion that Roosevelt and Churchill achieved nearly everything that circumstances permitted. They undoubtedly knew the risks they were running in the agreements on Poland and eastern Europe. They knew also that they had no alternative but to accept a compromise and to hope that the Russians would honor it. The Russians were already in eastern Europe. The United States and Britain might conceivably have driven them out, but neither the Anglo-American peoples nor soldiers would have tolerated even the suggestion of a long and bloody war to save Poland or Romania from Communist domination. These were the two prime historical realities with which Roosevelt and Churchill had to reckon, and from which Stalin could benefit, at Yalta. The Anglo-American leaders obtained important concessions from Stalin in spite of their weak bargaining positions. Future conflicts with the Soviet Union developed, not because the Russians honored the Yalta agreements, but precisely because they violated them.

We now know that Roosevelt concluded the secret Far Eastern agreement with Stalin because he and his military advisers believed that the Japanese would not surrender unconditionally without invasion and occupation. Moreover, no one yet knew whether the atomic bomb would explode or what damage it would do. Acting on the advice of his military advisers, Roosevelt made the agreement with Stalin, he thought, in order to prevent the death of perhaps 1 million American men in bloody campaigns in Japan and on the Asiatic mainland. To avert this catastrophe, the president virtually let Stalin name his own price for Soviet participation. Actually, Soviet Far Eastern policy was neither determined nor defined at Yalta. It is a fair assumption that the Russians would have entered the war against Japan and reestablished themselves as a major Far Eastern power whether the Americans liked it or not.

Critics of the Yalta agreements tend to forget that the Russians also made substantial concessions. They agreed to participate in a United Nations that would certainly be controlled by the Anglo-American bloc, to give France a share in the control of Germany, and to respect the integrity of the peoples of eastern Europe. They seemed determined to act reasonably and to meet Churchill and Roosevelt halfway on all important issues. Roosevelt and Churchill, therefore, acted in the only manner that was historically possible.

10. VICTORY IN EUROPE

The British and American armies approached the Siegfried line in September 1944. Eisenhower made an effort to turn the northern flank of the German defenses by landing three airborne divisions to capture bridges across the Meuse, Waal, and Rhine rivers. This effort failed when the British First Airborne Division was unable to hold a bridge across the Rhine at Arnhem, and the Allies were denied the opportunity to make a rapid drive across the north German plain. Instead, they brought up reinforcements for a winter campaign through the heavy German defenses manned by armies now regrouped and strengthened.

While American and British armies were probing along the length of the Siegfried line, Hitler laid plans for one final gamble—a counteroffensive through the weak center of the Allied lines in the Ardennes Forest. This, he hoped, would split the enemy's forces and carry to Liège and perhaps Antwerp. Bad weather in late November and early December enabled Von Rundstedt, the German commander, to bring up his forces in secret. They struck furiously in the Ardennes on December 16 and scored heavily until Allied counterattacks forced them to withdraw. The Battle of the Bulge, as the German offensive is commonly known, was over by January 1945. Hitler's gamble had cost him his last reserves of aircraft and some of his best divisions.

In fact, the German army in the west was so weakened by ruinous losses in the Ardennes counteroffensive that it could no longer prevent the Allied armies from advancing to the Rhine. Forces under Field Marshal Montgomery captured Cleves, in the north, on February 12. Cologne fell to the American First Army on March 6. Troops of the French First and the American Third and Seventh armies had cleared the Saar and Palatinate areas in the south by March 25. Meanwhile, American troops, by an unbelievable stroke of good luck, captured the Ludendorff Bridge across the Rhine at Remagen on March 7 before it could be demolished. They quickly established a bridgehead on the other side of the river.

Anglo-American armies were now poised along the Rhine for a final drive into the heart of Germany, and Russian armies were massed on the Oder River for an assault upon Berlin. But new tensions between the western democracies and Russia gave warning of troubled times ahead. For one thing, the Russians,

ALLIED OFFENSIVES TO THE RHINE
1944-1945

in February 1945, had imposed a Communist government on Romania. For another thing, Anglo-American negotiations with a German general for surrender of German forces in Italy had caused Stalin to address a letter to Roosevelt virtually accusing him and Churchill of treacherously negotiating for surrender of all German forces in the west so that British and American armies could occupy Berlin before the Russians.

Even more ominous were Russian actions in Poland. The Russians had not only refused to honor the Yalta agreement to reorganize the puppet Lublin government, but they had also refused to allow American and British observers to enter Poland and had proceeded to liquidate the leaders of the democratic parties in that unhappy country. It was plain that Stalin would tolerate no Polish government that he could not completely control; indeed, he admitted as much in correspondence with Churchill. The Polish dispute was nearing the point of open rupture by mid-March, but Roosevelt was now so weak that he had lost his grasp and could not take leadership in opposing Soviet violations of the Yalta agreements. Actually, Poland was irretrievably lost to Soviet domination, as Stalin's blunt replies to Churchill's vigorous protests revealed.

Poland was lost, but not yet Prague and Berlin, if the Allies resolved to act quickly and send their armies hurtling across Germany. Churchill perceived clearly enough that "Soviet Russia had become a mortal danger to the free world." He pleaded all through April and early May with his American colleagues to push as rapidly as possible toward the two central European capitals. Even more important, he proposed that the Allies stay in force on this forward eastern line until the Russians had honored earlier promises.

The reasons for the failure to attempt to seize strong outposts in central Europe can best be seen in an account of military and political events. The combined Anglo-American armies began their crossing of the Rhine on March 24. Montgomery's forces in the north and Omar N. Bradley's in the center had converged by April 1 to encircle the Ruhr and trap more than 250,000 German troops. General Montgomery was all for driving straight to Berlin. But Eisenhower, for what seemed to be sound military reasons, decided to drive from the Kassel-Frankfurt area to the Elbe in order to split the German forces and prevent them from retreating to the Bavarian mountains. Eisenhower would then turn his armies directly to the north and southwest of the Elbe. In late March, Eisenhower relayed this decision to Stalin, who approved it. At this point, Churchill appealed personally to Roosevelt to join him in ordering Eisenhower to use his main forces in a drive to capture Berlin.

When the vanguard of the American army reached the Elbe, only fifty-three miles from Berlin, the Russians stood on the banks of the Oder, thirty to forty miles from the German capital. Churchill now redoubled his pleading, but his voice was no longer heard in Washington. Roosevelt was tired and unable to stand any longer at the helm. He wanted rest and recovery, not a new quarrel with the Russians. He went to Warm Springs, Georgia, early in April to renew his strength before opening the San Francisco Conference of the United Nations on April 25. On April 12 he complained of a terrific headache, lost consciousness, and died at 4:35 P.M. of a massive cerebral hemorrhage.

Roosevelt's growing weakness and death came at a fateful time in the history of the world. The new president, Harry S Truman, had been utterly unprepared by his predecessor. Eisenhower had submitted a plan for further action to the Combined Chiefs of Staff on April 7. He proposed pushing through to the Elbe near Leipzig and then turning northward to the Baltic coast in order to prevent the Russians from occupying any part of the Danish peninsula. He added that he saw no point in making Berlin a military objective but that he would cheerfully accept the decision of the Combined Chiefs of Staff on this matter. The military leaders did not discuss the question of Berlin. President Truman supported Eisenhower's proposal. Even Churchill agreed on April 19 that the Anglo-American forces were "not immediately in a position to force their way into Berlin." Eisenhower informed Stalin of this plan on April 21, adding that he intended to send forces not only northward but also southward into the Danube Valley. He sent General Patton into Bavaria on the following day.

Even at this date Eisenhower could have captured Prague with ease, and Churchill pleaded for action that "might make the whole difference to the postwar situation in Czechoslovakia." Eisenhower in response decided to send Patton into Prague and so informed the Soviet high command. But he called Patton back after receiving a vehement protest from Stalin. Thus, while the Americans waited, the Russians occupied Prague on May 9.

Meanwhile, Hitler remained in Berlin, confident that a miracle would yet save the Third Reich. He was heartened by Roosevelt's death and certain that the western Allies and Russia would soon turn against each other. But *Götterdämmerung* was near. Marshal Georgii K. Zhukov began a massive offensive across the Oder on April 15 that reached the suburbs of Berlin a week later. American and Russian troops met on the Elbe near Torgau on April 27. Italian partisans captured and shot Mussolini on the following day. Hitler married his mistress, Eva Braun, in his bunker in Berlin and appointed Admiral Karl Doenitz his successor on April 29. He committed suicide on the next day, and his body was burned in the garden of the Reich chancellery.

Nothing remained but to end the war as quickly as possible. Nearly 1 million German troops in northern Italy and Austria surrendered on May 2. Two days later, German troops in northwest Germany, Holland, Schleswig–Holstein, and Denmark laid down their arms. Then Colonel General Alfred Jodl surrendered unconditionally the remnants of the German Army, Air Force, and Navy at Eisenhower's headquarters at Reims at 2:41 A.M. on May 7. All hostilities ceased at midnight May 8, 1945.

11.   VICTORY IN THE PACIFIC

American ground, naval, and air power in the Pacific was overwhelmingly preponderant by the early summer of 1944. The American Navy was now five times stronger than the imperial fleet. The time had come to close in on the stronghold of the enemy's inner ring. Admiral Raymond A. Spruance with a huge force of ships, aircraft, and troops moved against the strongly held Marianas, about 1,350 miles south of Tokyo. After a bitter struggle, in which the Japanese fought fanatically, the three principal islands in the group—Saipan, Tinian, and Guam—fell before the overpowering assault. While Americans were invading Saipan, a large Japanese force of nine aircraft carriers, five battleships, and other ships sailed from the Philippines to intercept the invaders. In June 1944, over 500 Japanese airplanes attacked and slightly damaged a battleship and two carriers. But the Japanese lost 402 airplanes and pilots, the core of their naval aviation, and pursuing American submarines and aircraft caught up with the Japanese Fleet. They sank three Japanese carriers and two destroyers and severely damaged one battleship, four carriers, and other craft in the first Battle of the Philippine Sea. American naval and ground forces then attacked the western Caroline Islands in September. They overpowered fierce resistance on Peleliu, Angaur, and Ngesebus islands and neutralized the main Japanese garrisons on the islands of Babelthuap and Yap.

While Admiral Nimitz's forces were clearing the Central Pacific route to the Philippines, farther in the Southwest Pacific General MacArthur was making final preparations for an invasion of those islands. First came an Allied drive in April and May 1944 that cleared the northern coast of New Guinea; next, amphibious offensives against Wakde, Biak, Noemfoor, and other islands off the northwestern coast of New Guinea that cleared the lower approaches to the Philippines. Finally, the capture of Morotai Island in September put the Southwest Pacific forces within striking distance. As prelude to an invasion, land-based bombers and planes from carriers of the Third Fleet scourged Japanese airfields and installations in Mindanao, Luzon, and Formosa during September and October. These operations practically destroyed Japanese air power in the area and disrupted Japanese sea communications. Then Americans returned in October to redeem their pledge to liberate the Philippines—with an invasion of Leyte Island by the Sixth Army, the Seventh Fleet under Admiral Thomas C. Kinkaid, and the Third Fleet under Admiral Halsey.

The Japanese admirals well knew that American conquest of the Philippines would spell the doom of the empire, because it would cut communication between Japan and Indochina, Malaya, and the East Indies. They made one last desperate effort to destroy the American invaders in Leyte Gulf. The three naval engagements that ensued between October 24 and 25—the battle of Surigao Strait, the battle off Samar, and the battle off Cape Engaño, collectively known as the Battle for Leyte Gulf—ended disastrously for the Japanese. In this greatest naval battle in history, the Japanese lost practically their entire fleet—three battleships, four carriers, nine cruisers, and eight destroyers.

The threat of Japanese naval intervention was forever ended, and MacArthur could now press forward with his overwhelming campaign in the Philippines. While the invasion of Leyte was at its height, MacArthur launched an attack against Mindoro in December and then attacked Luzon from Lingayen Gulf in early January 1945. Not until July, however, were the Japanese rooted out of the mountains of northern Luzon and out of Mindanao and dozens of smaller islands. All told, Japan lost over 400,000 men and 9,000 planes in the entire Philippines campaign.

The American conquest of the Marianas, western Carolines, and Philippines blasted the inner rim of Japanese defenses, cut communications between the home islands and Indochina, Malaya, and the East Indies, and reduced the Japanese Navy to the size of a single task force. Equally important, it afforded advanced bases from which to bomb the empire. Indeed, the air war against Japan had already begun in June 1944, when a force of large new B-29 Superfortresses of the Twentieth Air Force, operating from bases in China, attacked steel works in Kyushu. The Twentieth Air Force made subsequent raids on Japan and Manchuria, but its operations were limited because all its supplies and bombs had to be flown over the Himalayan Hump from India. A massive B-29 attack became possible only with the capture of Saipan in the Marianas. The capture of Iwo Jima later yielded bases for American fighter planes and fighter bombers that joined in the increasing aerial assault. All told, American planes dropped about 160,000 tons of bombs on the Japanese home islands from November 1944, when the bombardment from the Marianas began, to September 1945, when the war ended.

Although the tonnage of bombs dropped on Japan was about one-ninth of that dropped on Germany, the physical destruction in Japan almost equaled that in Germany. American bombs killed 330,000 Japanese civilians and injured nearly 500,000; moreover, they destroyed 2,510,000 buildings and 40 percent of the built-up areas of sixty-six cities. The effects on the Japanese war economy were equally devastating. Air attacks by July 1945 had reduced the productive capacity of Japanese oil refineries by 83 percent, aircraft engine plants by 75 percent, electronics and communication equipment plants by 70 percent, and munitions factories by some 30 percent. For a nation with an industrial capacity only 10 percent that of its chief enemy, these losses were fatal.

Let us now turn back to the last phase of the relentless American drive by land and sea toward Japan. While MacArthur was bringing the Philippines campaign to its climax, marine divisions invaded Iwo Jima, 750 miles south of Japan, on February 19, 1945. The Japanese defenders had made the island virtually one vast pillbox. They fought so courageously that the Iwo Jima operation was the

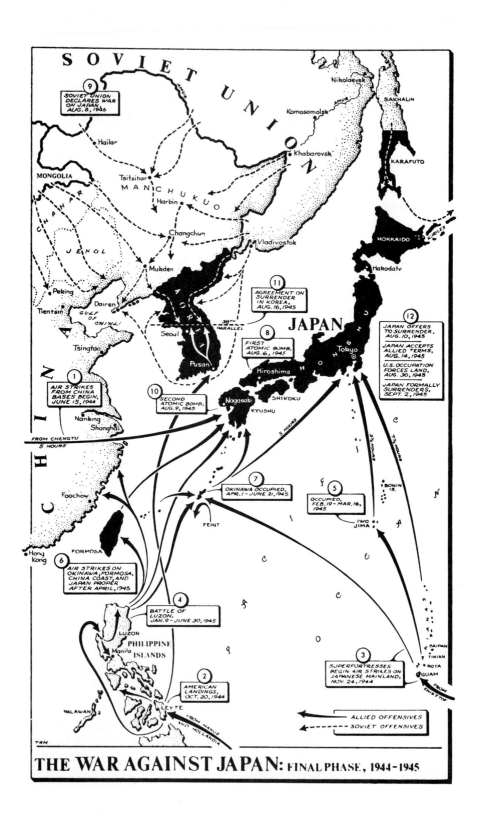

THE WAR AGAINST JAPAN: FINAL PHASE, 1944–1945

bloodiest in the history of the United States Marine Corps. However, the entire island, with its two airfields, was in American hands by March 16. Next came a larger attack, beginning April 1, by marine and army forces against Okinawa, a large island in the Ryukyus only 350 miles southwest of Japan. The Japanese and American leaders both knew that the fall of Okinawa would spell the early doom of the empire. The defenders, therefore, fought fanatically during the battle that raged from April 1 to June 21 and lost nearly 111,000 dead and 9,000 prisoners. The most spectacular aspect of the defense was the unrelenting and often effective Kamikaze, or suicide, attacks by Japanese aircraft against American warships and transports. All told, the Japanese lost some 4,000 aircraft, 3,500 of them in Kamikaze attacks, during the Battle of Okinawa.

By this time the main question was whether Japan would collapse internally before the Americans had launched their final invasion of the island empire. We have noted the terrible devastation wrought by the Superfortresses from Saipan. They were joined in February 1945 by thousands of planes of the Third Fleet and in April by fighter bombers from Iwo Jima and Okinawa. American battleships and heavy cruisers joined in the attack in mid-July by shelling steel works, synthetic oil plants, and other industrial targets on the mainland and by heavy attacks upon Japanese shipping. But Japan was suffering most from a combined sea, air, and mine blockade that had reduced her once large merchant fleet to ineffectiveness and deprived her people of food and her industries of vital raw materials.

Indeed, it had been evident to certain Japanese leaders since the autumn of 1943 that they were fighting a losing battle and that the imperial government should seek peace, even at the cost of giving up China, Korea, and Formosa. In July 1944, soon after the American invasion of the Marianas, a moderate group led principally by the naval chieftains forced Tojo to resign and establish a new cabinet under General Kuniaki Koiso. An important element in the new government, led by Navy Minister Mitsumasa Yonai and allied with officials in the imperial court, was determined to end the war as quickly as possible. The emperor threw his full support to the peace party in February 1945. After the invasion of Okinawa on April 8, he appointed Baron Kantaro Suzuki as premier and ordered him to end the war. Suzuki, however, did not control the army, which was determined to fight to the bitter end and threatened to revolt if the cabinet moved for peace. Thus the cabinet began secret discussions in May with the Russian ambassador, Jacob Malik, looking toward Russian mediation. In addition, the emperor appealed directly to the Soviet government in June and July to help to arrange peace talks with the United States.

This was the situation when Truman, Churchill, Clement Attlee, soon to be Churchill's successor, and Stalin met at Potsdam on July 17, 1945, for the last conference of the Big Three. Truman almost certainly knew about the Japanese peace overtures even before the Potsdam Conference met; in any event, Stalin soon gave full information about them. Truman was not inclined to take the overtures seriously. He did not trust the Japanese, and his military advisers believed that Japan would not surrender until Allied forces had invaded and occupied the islands. He therefore approved a discouraging Soviet reply to Tokyo.

Meanwhile, word had come to the American leaders at Postdam on July 16 that an atomic bomb had been exploded in New Mexico. Knowing that the bomb was a reality (there were materials on hand to assemble two additional bombs at once) and that its use might avert the necessity of a long and bloody campaign, Truman now concentrated on a public warning to Japan. It was the Potsdam Declaration, issued on July 26 under Truman's, Churchill's, and Chiang Kai-shek's signatures. It promised stern justice to Japanese war criminals and enforcement of the Cairo Declaration stripping Japan of all conquests. But it also held out the hope of generous treatment of a Japan purged and reformed. "The alternative for Japan," it concluded, "is prompt and utter destruction."

The leaders of the Suzuki government in Tokyo agreed to accept the Potsdam Declaration but could not persuade the army leaders to surrender. When Suzuki declared on July 28, only for home consumption, that the Potsdam Declaration was "unworthy of public notice," President Truman and his advisers took this as a refusal and decided to use the atomic bomb. The decision was made largely on military grounds. The Japanese were doomed, to be sure, but they still had large supplies of weapons and an army of 2 million in the home islands. An invasion would surely have succeeded only at great human costs on both sides.

Thus a lone B-29 flew over Hiroshima on August 6 and dropped the first atomic bomb used in warfare. It leveled 4.4 square miles of the city and killed between 70,000 and 80,000 persons. On the same day, President Truman announced the news to the world and warned the Japanese that if they did not surrender they could expect "a rain of ruin from the air, the likes of which has never been seen on this earth." Still the Japanese Army refused to surrender. Then, on August 9, news came to Tokyo that Russia had entered the war and that the Americans had dropped a second atomic bomb on Nagasaki. When hurried conferences failed to yield agreement to accept the Potsdam ultimatum, the emperor made the decision for peace. The cabinet informed Washington on the following day that it accepted the Potsdam terms, provided that the status of the emperor would not be changed. The military and naval chieftains balked when Washington replied on August 11 that the emperor must be subject to the supreme commander of the Allied powers. But the emperor insisted, and the Suzuki government formally accepted the Allied demands on August 14. The emperor at once prepared records of an imperial rescript ordering his armed forces to surrender; and the cabinet, after suppressing an insurrection of army fanatics, sent emissaries to General MacArthur to arrange the details of surrender. A great Allied fleet entered Tokyo Bay on September 2. Soon afterward Foreign Minister Mamoru Shigemitsu and a representative of the imperial general staff signed articles of surrender on board the battleship *Missouri.* General MacArthur and representatives of the Allied powers accepted on behalf of their respective governments.

CHAPTER 20

The Politics of Postwar America

The end of World War II brought a new period of change and turbulence to American politics. The death of Franklin Roosevelt left a leadership vacuum in his party; later New Deal and wartime policies had created significant internal strains in the Democratic coalition. Torn by struggles over civil rights and labor policy, Democrats were further weakened by a growing conviction that the Truman administration was riddled with corruption and tainted with communism. The Republicans, long out of office and out of power, were beset with equally difficult problems. Torn by divisions between internationalists and neoisolationists on foreign policy and between moderates and conservatives on domestic policy, Republicans were weakened by a long absence from power and plagued by irresponsibility.

1. HARRY S TRUMAN AND AMERICAN LIBERALISM

A distraught man stood in the White House at 7:09 P.M. on April 12, 1945, and took the oath as president of the United States. Franklin D. Roosevelt had died a few hours before, and leadership was now entrusted to his vice-president, Harry S Truman. For Roosevelt, as for Lincoln, death was a merciful deliverer, sparing him a host of troubles at the moment of his greatest triumph. For Truman, Roosevelt's passing meant not only a new life of trials and challenges but also rare opportunities.

"Who the hell is Harry Truman?" Admiral William D. Leahy had asked when

444

Roosevelt told his chief of staff of the vice-presidential nominee in the summer of 1944. That question was often repeated during the days of mourning that followed Roosevelt's death. Harry S Truman was born at Lamar, Missouri, on May 8, 1884, the grandson of pioneers from Kentucky, and grew up in the Kansas City area. After graduation from high school in 1901, he worked as a bank clerk and farmer, then went to France with his National Guard artillery regiment and rose to the rank of major. He married his childhood sweetheart and entered the clothing business in Kansas City in 1919. Ruined by the postwar recession in 1922, Truman accepted nomination as county judge, or commissioner, of eastern Jackson County from the Pendergast Democratic machine of Kansas City. He was defeated for reelection in 1924, in part because of his opposition to the Ku Klux Klan, but he returned to the courthouse in Independence as presiding judge in 1927. During the next seven years he rebuilt the county's roads and courthouse, helped to plan a system of parkways for Kansas City, and earned a reputation as an able and incorruptible administrator.

Truman was nominated for the United States Senate in 1934 with the help of the Pendergast machine and won easily in the Democratic landslide that fall. In Washington he was known as the "Gentleman from Pendergast," and his political career seemed at an end when his patron, Tom Pendergast, was sentenced to prison in 1939 for income tax evasion. Truman surprised friends as well as enemies when he won reelection to the Senate on his own in 1940 by attracting the votes of workers, farmers, and blacks in a campaign prophetic of his more famous battle eight years later.

His political stature, enhanced by this victory, increased still further with the coming of war. Appalled by waste in defense spending and by the army's neglect of small business in awarding contracts, he obtained appointment in 1941 as chairman of a special Senate committee to investigate the defense effort. His committee worked assiduously to prevent waste and favoritism, and his fairness and insistence upon constructive criticism won him the admiration of President Roosevelt and the vice-presidential nomination in 1944. The country knew little about Truman when he became president. Because he was modest in demeanor, unpretentious in appearance, and obviously lacking in Roosevelt's histrionic abilities and patrician touch, many Americans assumed that Truman epitomized the average man.

Yet in most aspects the new president was extraordinary indeed. He had personal warmth and charm, a breadth of learning that often astonished scholars, and an ability to understand difficult situations. He was also extraordinary in his personal honesty and integrity. Although supported by a corrupt political organization, he never allowed the machine to use him; nor had he misappropriated a single dollar of county funds. He was extraordinary in his devotion to duty and the general interest and in his capacity for hard work. He was extraordinary in his feeling for the underdog, hatred of pretense, and broad sympathy that tolerated no racial or religious distinctions. Above all, he was extraordinary in his courage—whether in defying the Ku Klux Klan in Jackson County, fighting a seemingly lost battle on the hustings, dismissing a renowned general, or leading his country in bold pursuit of peace and security.

Some traits limited Truman's effectiveness as a leader. A number of these weaknesses stemmed in the beginning from an undue modesty and feelings of inadequacy. "I don't know whether you fellows ever had a load of hay or a bull fall on you," he told reporters on April 13, 1945. "But last night the moon, the stars and all the planets fell on me." Inheriting a cabinet and administration of strangers, he turned to friends in the Senate and gathered around him a group of intimates known as the Missouri gang. Absolutely honest himself, Truman was a professional politician who accepted the game as he found it. Consequently, he sometimes seemed blind to dishonesty, trusted too much, and refused to move quickly against corruption. President during a period of intense partisanship, he did little with his own campaign oratory to elevate the tone of public discourse. Usually cautious in matters of state, he was often rash and impulsive in personal controversy and sometimes resorted to name-calling in public. Yet historians have been kind to Truman. His personal defects, they have realized, were far outweighed by his positive qualities: strength, courage, and an ability in large matters to put the national interest above personal and party advantage. Historians have also remembered his many contributions, the difficulties of his tasks, and his great growth in leadership.

2.   DEMOBILIZATION, RECONVERSION, AND NEW FEDERAL STRUCTURES

The immediate postwar years were characterized by inflation and labor unrest—but also by tremendous economic growth and prosperity. They were characterized also by growing international tension, which caused foreign-policy considerations to intrude into other concerns. An early decision Truman faced was how—and at what speed—to demobilize the armed forces and convert the economy from a war to a peace footing. It was apparent to the new president and his advisers, even before Japan surrendered, that the world was entering an uncertain period of potential conflict and realignment of power and that national security demanded large, permanent armed forces. But the dimensions of these future military needs were unclear in the autumn of 1945, while the popular demand for speedy and drastic demobilization was so overwhelming that probably no administration could have resisted it.

Beginning with a limited demobilization in May 1945, the armed services dischared personnel as rapidly as possible once Japan had surrendered. When the army slowed its pace in January 1946, there were riots among enlisted men abroad and frenzied protests at home, and demobilization proceeded in response to public demand. As Truman later wrote, this "was no longer demobilization—it was disintegration of our armed forces." By its completion in midsummer of 1946, the great wartime army and navy had been reduced to 1.5 million and 700,000 men, respectively.

Truman and his military advisers repeatedly claimed that American armed strength was insufficient to meet postwar needs. Congress grudgingly extended a weak Selective Service in 1946 and reinstituted the draft on a broader basis a year later. At the same time, Congress refused to approve universal military training and insisted on further military cuts after 1946. The Communist coup in Czechoslovakia and the Berlin blockade brought both greater Soviet-American tension and temporarily larger defense appropriations in 1948, but new reductions brought American armed strength to a postwar low. By early 1950, the administration and Congress had imposed a $13 billion ceiling on defense expenditures and reduced the army to 600,000 men and ten active divisions.

Another major readjustment of the immediate postwar years was the reconversion of human and material resources. The bipartisan consensus was that veterans should have generous help in finding jobs, adjusting to civilian life, and recovering lost educational opportunities. Congress in June 1944 had enacted the Servicemen's Readjustment Act, known as the G.I. Bill of Rights. Expenditures of the Veterans Administration rose from $723 million in 1944 to a peak of $9.3 billion in 1950, declining to about $6 billion in 1951 and 1952, and averaging $5 billion annually for the balance of the decade. During the peak period 1945–1952, the government spent $17.5 billion on education, training, unemployment benefits, and self-employment help. The Veterans Administration guaranteed or insured nearly $16.5 billion in veterans' loans for homes, farms, and businesses and operated a chain of some 150 hospitals that served over 100,000 patients a day in 1950.

There was also general agreement about the desirability of tax reductions and assistance to industry in its conversion to civilian production. Congress responded to public pressure by reducing taxes nearly $6 billion in November 1945, while the administration in 1945–1946 disposed of government-owned war plants representing a total investment of $15 billion—some 20 percent of the nation's industrial capacity.

Overshadowing the end of World War II was the fear of a catastrophic postwar depression that might bring national bankruptcy and world chaos. Success in organizing industry and labor during the war stimulated bold ideas. Henry A. Wallace and spokesmen of the CIO, countering the assumption that the nation must inevitably experience alternating periods of "boom and bust," proposed that the government assume responsibility for full employment through indirect stimulation of purchasing power and, if necessary, sufficient compensatory spending to prevent recession. The promise of "full employment" after the war, a major Democratic pledge during the campaign of 1944, was reaffirmed by Truman in September 1945. A full-fledged debate on postwar domestic policy ensued.

Embodied in a full employment bill submitted by Democratic Senator James E. Murray of Montana, the administration plan stipulated that the president and his staff should prepare an annual budget estimate of the investment and production necessary to maintain full employment, and that a congressional committee should assume responsibility for such "federal investment and expenditure as will be sufficient to bring the aggregate volume . . . up to the level required to assure a full employment volume of production." To conservatives, however, the Murray bill threatened to inaugurate a permanent program of deficit spending, and they proposed instead a nonpartisan commission to advise the president and Congress on the state of the economy and measures necessary "to foster private enterprise . . . and promote a high and stable level of employment."

Although they disagreed about means, the significant result of the debate over the Murray bill was that both sides agreed that chief responsibility for economic stabilization lay with the federal government. The outcome was the Employment Act of February 1946, a compromise that affirmed national responsibility for prosperity without prescribing an inflexible method to achieve it. The act created a three-member Council of Economic Advisers, each of them presumably expert and nonpartisan, to study economic trends and suggest ways to promote national economic welfare. The act also established a new congressional joint committee to study and propose stabilization measures. The Employment Act was a milestone in American history. It established machinery for mobilizing all public and private resources in order to sustain a high level of national production, employment, and income.

Devising a postwar policy for development of nuclear energy was, as events turned out, considerably more urgent. Most Republicans and Democrats agreed that national security demanded retention of a governmental monopoly over research and production of fissionable materials. On the issue of civilian or military control of the program, however, a heated controversy ensued when a special Senate committee, headed by Brien MacMahon of Connecticut, set to work on a nuclear energy bill in late 1945. At Truman's urging, MacMahon drafted a measure that established exclusive civilian control through an Atomic Energy Commission (AEC). This bill won the support of most reformers, scientists, and religious and educational leaders. On the other hand, Senator Arthur H. Vandenberg of Michigan won committee support for a proposal to give military and naval leaders a full voice with—even a veto over—civilian authorities in the determination of nuclear energy policies.

After the Senate committee adopted Vandenberg's amendment to the MacMahon bill in early 1946, Truman and public opinion reacted strongly against the proposed law. Vandenberg then agreed to a compromise amendment which established a Military Liaison Committee to work with the AEC but placed

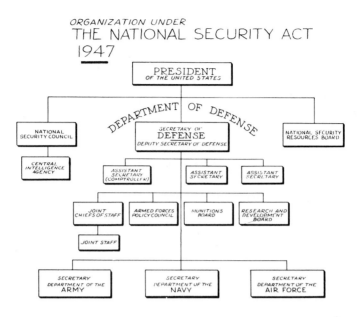

ORGANIZATION UNDER
THE NATIONAL SECURITY ACT
1947

exclusive control in civilian hands. The Atomic Energy Act, approved in August 1946, preserved governmental monopoly on fissionable materials, vested control of research and production in the hands of a five-member AEC, and gave to the president alone the power to order the use of the atomic bomb in warfare. It also barred divulgence of classified information to foreign governments, even friendly ones—which drew a sharp protest from the British.

Meanwhile, another problem—unification of the armed services—was the subject of bitter controversy. Almost everyone, including military and naval spokesmen, agreed that the Pearl Harbor disaster and wasteful interservice competition during the war had proved the need for common control and direction of the defense establishment. Beyond this, however, there was disagreement on virtually every important issue. The army's friends in Congress favored unification, but the navy's champions feared that army domination of a unified defense structure would mean the end of the Marine Corps and favor land-based air forces at the expense of sea power. Advocates for the two services maneuvered and skirmished from late 1945 to mid-1947.

The result of this give and take was the National Security Act of July 1947. It created a single Defense Department, headed by a secretary with cabinet rank who was to supervise secretaries of the army, navy, and air force. It charged the Joint Chiefs of Staff, representing the three services, with the preparation of defense plans and with consideration of matters of strategy. Finally, it created the Central Intelligence Agency, supreme in that sphere, and two advisory bodies, the National Security Council and the National Security Resources

Board. Although it was easier to erect the façade of a new defense structure than to compel genuine unification, the National Security Act was a major accomplishment.

Largely at Truman's insistence, Congress approved another major governmental change, the Presidential Succession Act of 1947, which placed the speaker of the House and the president pro tem of the Senate ahead of cabinet members in line of presidential succession after the vice-president. Another constitutional alteration was the Twenty-second Amendment, passed in 1947 and ratified by the thirty-sixth state in 1951. It forbade election to the presidency for more than two full terms or the reelection of a president for more than one term if he had served more than two years of an unfinished term. The amendment, which specifically exempted Truman from its interdiction, reflected a widespread conviction that the powers of the presidency were too great to justify the risk of unlimited reelections.

3. TRUMAN AND CONGRESS, 1945–1948

Republicans in Congress, often in alliance with conservative Democrats, bitterly opposed several aspects of Truman's domestic policies. During the first months of his presidency, Truman had led conservatives to believe that he planned to preside over a period of consolidation rather than of reform. This brief "honeymoon" came to an end in September 1945, when Truman sent his first important domestic message to the Capitol. He called for a full revival and extension of New Deal policies—expansion of Social Security, increase in the minimum wage, national health insurance, a greater federal role in public housing, regional developments along the lines of the Tennessee Valley Authority, a full employment bill, executive reorganization, and continuation of wartime economic controls.

This manifesto clearly demonstrated Truman's determination. More difficult, however, was finding majority support in Congress. Despite Truman's success on nonpartisan issues and some acceptable compromise solutions, he often found a conservative coalition of Republicans and southern Democrats in control of both houses: this combination blocked Truman's welfare and civil rights measures and defeated him in hard battles over economic controls and revision of federal labor policies.

Soon after the Japanese surrender, Truman and the Office of Price Administration announced that they would undertake "continued stabilization of the national economy" by gradually relaxing wartime controls over prices, wages, and scarce commodities. During late 1945 and early 1946, the OPA ended most rationing, retained priorities on scarce industrial materials, and held wholesale prices and the general cost of living to increases of only 7 and 3 percent, respectively. Yet strong pressure was building among consumers, organized labor, manufacturers, and farmers to end all controls. A battle in Congress ensued during the spring of 1946 over extension of the OPA, and Truman was presented with a price control bill in June that extended the agency for one year but severely weakened its power and commanded it to decontrol prices "as rapidly as possible." In response, Truman vetoed the bill and allowed price controls to end altogether on July 1. After prices rose wildly in the severest inflation since 1942, Congress approved a second bill extending price and rent controls for one year in late July 1946. But the new measure was even weaker and more confusing than the one Truman had vetoed. Giving up the fight after the Republican victory in the congressional elections that autumn, Truman ended all wage and price controls except for those on rents, sugar, and rice, and the OPA began to wind up its affairs in December 1946.

All during the congressional campaign of 1946, Republican speakers and advertisements capitalized on the confusion and failure of the price control program. In one particularly damaging incident, farmers withheld beef from the market after the OPA reimposed price ceilings in August 1946. While housewives waited in line in vain for hamburger at any price, Republicans pressed their telling question, "Had enough?" Truman meanwhile had alienated almost every major constituency. Labor was embittered by his bridling of John L. Lewis and his stern action in breaking the railroad strike that spring. Conservatives were already disenchanted by his advocacy of welfare and civil rights legislation. New Dealers, on the other hand, were disgruntled by the dramatic resignation of Harold L. Ickes as secretary of the interior following a dispute with Truman over a recent appointment. They were also dismayed by Truman's dismissal of Secretary of Commerce Henry A. Wallace after the former vice-president publicly opposed the administration's increasingly hard line toward the Soviet Union. But the Democratic party's chief liability that fall was Truman himself, who had given millions of Americans an impression of total inability either to lead or to govern.

Few observers were surprised, therefore, when the GOP won control of the House and Senate for the first time since 1928 and captured governorships in twenty-five of the thirty-two nonsouthern states in November 1946. What was surprising were the dimensions of the landslide and the sharp decrease in the urban Democratic vote. Party machines in many cities had been weakened by prosperity and the suburban migration, and the hitherto solidly Democratic labor bloc had crumbled in a number of places.

The significance of the Republican triumph became evident soon after the Eightieth Congress convened in January 1947. There were many new faces and new conservative leaders in both houses, but above them all stood Robert A. Taft of Ohio, chairman of the Republican Policy Committee in the Senate, champion of business interests, and trenchant conservative. This son of a former president would lead such a vigorous opposition during the next five years as to earn the title "Mr. Republican" and come within a few votes of winning his party's presidential nomination in 1952.

All during 1947 and 1948, Republican leaders in Congress fought with Truman and his supporters. Although the president and Congress cooperated on foreign policy, sharp differences existed over domestic policies. Truman, for example, vigorously opposed the Taft-Hartley bill, and its adoption over his veto in June 1947 was the most important conservative triumph of the immediate postwar era. Truman and the Republican Congress also differed over a proper anti-inflation policy. While Truman opposed further tax reduction, which he believed would aggravate inflation, the Republicans—their eyes on 1948—enacted a tax bill over a presidential veto in July 1947 that gave greatest relief to those with low and middle incomes. When prices continued to rise during the summer and autumn, Truman called Congress into special session in November to consider an anti-inflation program. Republican leaders responded with a bill that carefully avoided giving the president effective power. Congress extended rent controls for another year in March 1948, but added to inflationary pressures by adopting, again over Truman's veto, another measure for tax reduction.

Precampaign battles were also fought over housing and agricultural policies. Truman and moderate Republicans, led on this occasion by Senator Taft, supported a bill that would have inaugurated a broad program of public housing designed to benefit lower-income groups. All that the Republican majority would permit, however, was a measure providing governmental credit for veterans' homes and cooperative housing projects. As for agriculture, Congress approved a measure in June 1948 that continued support of farm prices at 90 percent of parity through 1949, to be followed by a program of flexible supports ranging from 60 to 90 percent of parity.

4. THE ELECTION OF 1948

Not for two decades had the GOP been so confident as it was in early 1948. Among Republican hopefuls the most eager candidate for the presidential nomination was former Governor Harold E. Stassen of Minnesota, who won much popular backing by his frank support of reform policies at home and internationalism abroad. After victories in the Wisconsin and Nebraska presidential primaries in April, Stassen seemed on his way, but party leaders looked elsewhere. They preferred Taft, whose conservatism had won enthusiastic support from the business community, particularly in the Middle West. Taft's chances, however, were weakened by his isolationist background, lukewarm support of postwar internationalism, and a popular feeling that he was a cold man and a poor campaigner. Republican leaders were too eager for victory to run the risk of nominating Taft. They approached General Eisenhower, who declined. Then they turned to their titular leader, Governor Thomas E. Dewey of New York, who had gained a reputation as a moderate and an internationalist. Meeting in Philadelphia in June 1948, the Republican National Convention nominated Dewey on the third ballot and named Governor Earl Warren of California as his running mate. A brief platform approved the New Deal reform structure and postwar bipartisan foreign policy and promised further tax reductions, greater efficiency, and more legislation favoring civil rights, welfare, and housing.

Meanwhile, the Democratic party was suffering from serious internal conflict. Henry Wallace proposed a domestic program of collectivism and a foreign-policy program of conciliation with the Soviet Union. His appeal was strongest among idealistic college students. When he announced in December 1947 that he would run for president on a third-party ticket, observers predicted that he would poll between 5 and 8 million votes and thereby blast Democratic chances. Southern Democrats were up in arms against Truman's civil rights program and threatening to bolt if the convention adopted a strong civil rights plank. Other liberal Democrats, organized in Americans for Democratic Action (ADA), wanted to avoid having to choose between Truman and Wallace. They tried to force Truman to retire and sought a winning candidate in Justice William O. Douglas or General Eisenhower. Powerful urban Democrats like Edward Flynn of New York and Jacob Arvey of Chicago also joined the movement to oust Truman and draft Eisenhower.

It was, therefore, a gloomy and contentious Democratic convention that assembled in Philadelphia in July 1948. ADA liberals, led by Mayor Hubert Humphrey of Minneapolis and supported by city leaders, were determined to draft a program for the future even while they expected defeat in 1948. They put through a platform that strongly reaffirmed the reform tradition. Then, after a bitter floor fight, the convention endorsed a civil rights plank demanding a fair employment practices commission and federal laws against lynching and the poll tax. Because the harassed convention had no other choice, it nominated Truman for president and Alben W. Barkley, president pro tem of the Senate, as his running mate.

What Democratic leaders most feared—a party rupture—occurred a few days later. The rebel left wing met in Philadelphia in late July, organized the Progressive party, and nominated Wallace for president and Senator Glen Taylor of Idaho for vice-president. Their platform demanded gradual nationalization of basic industries, an end to segregation, and reorientation of foreign policy toward friendship with Russia. This was, actually, the high point of Wallace's strength, for the convention revealed what many already suspected: the Progressive organization was controlled by Communists and fellow travelers, and Wallace had allowed himself to be used by the Communists. Wallace's support dwindled steadily thereafter.

Meanwhile, the smoldering southern rebellion had also erupted. So-called

Dixiecrats met in Birmingham on July 17, 1948, waved Confederate flags, formed the States' Rights Democratic party, and nominated Governor J. Strom Thurmond of South Carolina and Governor Fielding L. Wright of Mississippi. Their opposition to the president's civil rights program had a powerful appeal to southern white sentiment and enabled them to control the Democratic party in four southern states. But they failed to achieve their main objective—an all-southern rebellion that would throw the election into the House of Representatives.

Republican confidence mounted as both wings of the Democracy pummeled Truman. Governor Dewey conducted a mild and dignified campaign. He repeated old strictures against alleged Democratic incompetence but made it clear that he approved the essentials of Democratic domestic and foreign policies. Dewey was so encouraged by the Gallup poll, which showed him far in the lead, that he bestirred himself only to make plans for his inauguration. Most newspapers and magazines shared his confidence.

Indeed, Truman was one of the few people in the country who thought that he had a chance to win. He startled everyone by announcing that he would call Congress into special session and give the Republicans an opportunity to enact their platform into law. Congress met from July 26 to August 7 without, as he expected, adopting any important legislation. Then Truman went to the country in perhaps the most strenuous personal campaign in American history. Traveling more than thirty thousand miles, he made 351 speeches, many of them "whistle-stop" talks in railroad yards from the rear platform of his car, to an estimated 12 million people. "The technique I used," he later wrote, "was simple and straightforward. . . . I had simply told the people in my own language that they had better wake up to the fact that it was their fight." Castigating the "do-nothing" Eightieth Congress, he urged an extension of New Deal policies. Moreover, he went into Harlem to become the first presidential candidate ever to speak seeking black votes.

Americans admired the president's pluck and assumed that Dewey was bound to win. As one writer observed, they seemed willing to give Truman anything but the presidency. But he knew better than the pollsters and commentators, and he went to bed on election night, November 2, 1948, confident and serene. In the most surprising political upset in American history, Truman won 24.1 million popular and 303 electoral votes, Dewey 22 million popular and 189 electoral votes. Thurmond, with 1.2 million popular and 39 electoral votes, and Wallace, with 1.2 million popular votes, trailed far behind. The Democrats won control of the next Congress by majorities of ninety-three in the House and twelve in the Senate.

Republican critics like the *Chicago Tribune* charged that Dewey had no one but himself to blame for his debacle because he had offered no alternative to Democratic policies. But a careful survey later indicated that Dewey received

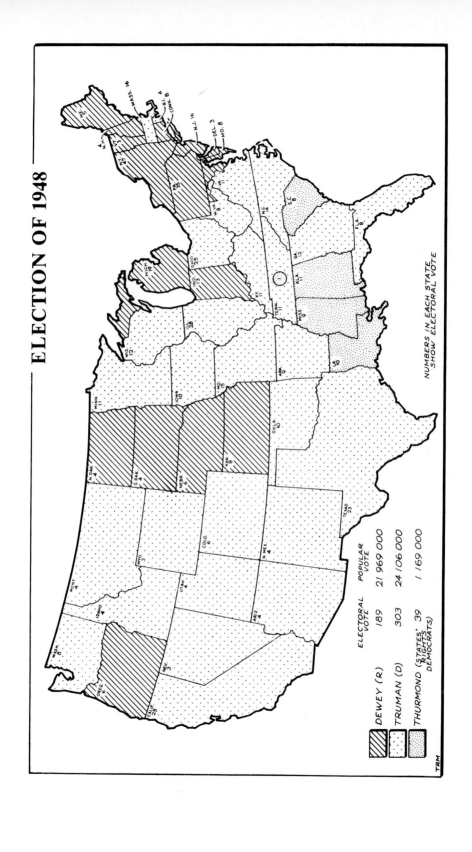

ELECTION OF 1948

NUMBERS IN EACH STATE
SHOW ELECTORAL VOTE

	ELECTORAL VOTE	POPULAR VOTE
DEWEY (R)	189	21 969 000
TRUMAN (D)	303	24 106 000
THURMOND (STATES' RIGHTS DEMOCRATS)	39	1 169 000

TRM

about the maximum normal Republican vote and that Truman would have been the gainer by a larger turnout on election day. Truman and the Democrats retained control of the federal government for a number of reasons. The country was at peace, prosperous, and relatively united on foreign policy. The party recaptured labor support by its advocacy of the repeal of the Taft-Hartley Act and gained an almost solid black allegiance by its firm support of new civil rights legislation. The Wallace and Dixiecrat rebellions on balance probably helped the Democrats more than they hurt them. They removed the Communist issue from the campaign and made it clear to blacks and other minority groups that the southern wing did not dominate the party. Another critical factor was the unexpected behavior of farmers in the Middle West and border states, all of which except Indiana went for Truman. Farmers had feared a depression since the war, and farm prices began a precipitate decline in 1948. Yet Republicans advocated "flexible" price supports that could mean disaster in the rural areas, while Truman promised to continue a program that had brought prosperity. Finally, the party ticket was strengthened in crucial areas by strong local candidates like Humphrey in Minnesota and Adlai E. Stevenson in Illinois, who ran far ahead of Truman and probably helped him to carry their states by small majorities.

5. THE FAIR DEAL

Truman was a new political creature after the election of 1948—a president in his own right—and the liberal wing of the Democratic party was happier than at any time since 1936. With new and vigorous leaders in Congress, they possessed a champion in the White House. Chastened Republican leaders, surveying the wreckage of their efforts, agreed with Dewey that the GOP's only hope lay in a less conservative posture. Reform seemed once again ascendant. When Truman formally launched what he called the Fair Deal in his annual message in January 1949, he began to consolidate past proposals into a comprehensive program. To state the matter briefly, Truman won less than he asked for and a good deal more than cynics thought that he could get from the Eighty-first Congress. For labor, he obtained an amendment to the Fair Labor Standards Act which increased the minimum wage from forty cents to seventy-five cents an hour, plus amendments to the Social Security Act that brought 10 million new beneficiaries into the system and increased benefits for retired workers by an average of 77.5 percent. For the millions who lived in rented homes and apartments, he won extension of rent control to March 1951.

Another triumph, climaxing a bitter four-year struggle, was the Housing Act of 1949, which provided for slum clearance and authorized construction of 810,000 units for low-income families. Truman failed to win approval for the St. Lawrence Seaway, a Missouri Valley Authority, and other regional projects. But he obtained large increases for the Reclamation Bureau's ambitious hydroelectric, water control, and irrigation program in the West. He won higher appropriations for the TVA, the Rural Electrification Administration, and the Farmers' Home Administration, which since the war had continued the work of the Farm Security Administration in extending loans to farmers for rehabilitation and farm ownership. Finally, he gained approval in June 1950 of a new displaced persons bill to admit some 400,000 European refugees.

On other domestic fronts, Truman was less successful. In striving to achieve labor's most important goal—repeal of the Taft-Hartley Act—Truman and his supporters in organized labor overreached themselves. The Senate, with Taft's approval, adopted a series of amendments that revised the measure substantially in labor's favor, but Truman and his labor allies, gambling on the future, ruined the opportunity by rejecting the compromise and demanding nothing less than complete repeal. Truman and his supporters also pushed too hard too fast on other important Fair Deal objectives. The administration's program for agriculture, the Brannan Plan, proposed by Secretary of Agriculture Charles Brannan in April 1949, guaranteed a "farm income standard," or a dollar income as high as the average of the preceding ten years, through price supports, loans, and storage of nonperishable commodities. The Brannan Plan aroused charges of regimentation and socialism and provoked the strong opposition of large farmers. Although the plan failed, the administration could claim that the Agricultural Act approved by Congress in October 1949—which continued rigid price supports at 90 percent of parity through 1950 and provided for flexible supports ranging from 75 to 90 percent afterward—redeemed Democratic pledges and reaffirmed New Deal farm policy.

In other, more controversial projects, Truman encountered bitter opposition and defeat. His proposal for national health insurance was beaten by the American Medical Association's gigantic advertising and lobbying campaign. His plan for federal aid to education had substantial bipartisan support, but it met resistance from the Roman Catholic Church because it did not include subsidies to parochial schools. Truman's most discouraging defeat was on civil rights. In 1946, he had appointed a Committee on Civil Rights, composed of distinguished Southerners, blacks, educators, and churchmen, to investigate and recommend "more adequate and effective means and procedures for the protection of the civil rights of the people of the United States." The committee report, *To Secure These Rights,* issued in 1947, exposed the operation and consequences of the caste system and called for systematic federal-state programs to root out racial injustice.

Although Truman appealed to Congress to implement these recommendations, he could not overcome the threat of a southern filibuster in the Senate. But he struck hard at the caste system in other ways. He strengthened the civil rights section of the Justice Department and began a practice of having the department assist private parties in civil rights cases. He invited blacks to the inaugural reception and ball in 1949. He appointed the first black governor of the Virgin Islands and the first black federal judge. Most important, he began abolition of segregation in governmental departments and the armed services in 1948.

6. THE CAMPAIGN OF 1952

Truman's frustrations over domestic policy were accompanied by abundant signs after 1950 of mounting popular discontent with administration policies at home and abroad. Indeed, probably a majority of Americans for one reason or another desired a change of government by early 1952. Practically the entire white South stood on the verge of revolt against the president's civil rights program and was gripped by an intense fear that the Supreme Court would outlaw public school segregation. Democratic leaders and private interests in Texas, Oklahoma, Louisiana, and Florida were near rebellion because of presidential and northern Democratic opposition to their demands for state ownership of offshore oil lands and exclusive state regulation of the natural gas industry.

After 1950, Senator Joseph R. McCarthy led a partisan attack on alleged Communist infiltration in government (see pp. 501–505). Other Republican leaders were less abusive, but they joined his attack by charging that Roosevelt had "sold out" to Stalin at Yalta and by asserting that sympathizers in the State Department had facilitated Communist victory in China. These persistent attacks succeeded in planting in millions of minds the suspicion that the Democratic party was tainted with treason and communism.

Opposition to Democratic rule was also fueled by revelations of widespread corruption in Washington. A Senate investigation of the Reconstruction Finance Corporation in 1951 revealed corruption in the granting of loans. Soon afterward, in a nationally televised investigation, a Senate committee headed by Estes Kefauver of Tennessee exposed embarrassing connections between Democratic city machines and crime syndicates. Americans also learned that the Bureau of Internal Revenue was riddled with corruption and that the assistant attorney general in charge of tax evasion cases had accepted expensive gifts, including two mink coats for his wife, from "fixers" and persons accused of income tax fraud.

Even more damaging was Truman's failure to uproot corruption vigorously. Although he reorganized the RFC and Bureau of Internal Revenue, he acted slowly and, it seemed, reluctantly. And when he finally launched a housecleaning early in 1952, the affair turned into a farce. Attorney General J. Howard McGrath would not permit the special investigator to question Justice Department employees about their incomes. Truman upheld McGrath, causing the investigator to resign, then dismissed his attorney general in April and appointed James P. McGranery—who quietly abandoned the project of a special investigation.

Economic developments also contributed to popular dissatisfaction with the Democrats. Wholesale prices rose 13 percent from June 1950 to January 1952, spurring new rounds of wage demands and a sharp increase in the number of work stoppages. Although income kept pace with higher taxes and prices, persons on fixed incomes and farmers suffered much hardship.

Moreover, the dragging on of the Korean War (see pp. 487–489) generated popular discontent. Although Truman at first enjoyed popular support for intervention, disillusionment and a kind of despair swept through large elements of the country following China's entry and the administration's refusal to make an all-out bid for victory. Few Americans actually wanted to risk a third world conflict, but millions of them could not comprehend the concept of limited war and longed for some quick and easy way out of the stalemate.

Republican leaders thus exuded confidence about the impending presidential election. But basic disagreement between the two important wings of the GOP quickly erupted into a battle for party control. Since his smashing reelection in 1950, Senator Taft was more than ever the unchallenged Republican leader in Congress, spokesman for the nation's conservatives and neoisolationists, and preeminent foe of Democratic foreign and domestic policies. With the support of business interests, conservative-isolationist newspapers like the *Chicago Tribune,* and party organizations in the South and Middle West, he seemed irresistible as he opened an all-out campaign to win the presidential nomination and wrest control from the eastern internationalist leaders who had guided the party since 1940.

The eastern wing moved to counter this challenge. Led by Governor Dewey of New York and party heads in New England, Pennsylvania, New Jersey, and Maryland, the Easterners enjoyed a working alliance with west coast GOP leaders. They were moderate in domestic affairs and favored preserving the New Deal reform structure. In foreign policy, they were firmly committed to support of the United Nations and the non-Communist world. Their task was to find a candidate who could defeat Taft and then go on to victory in November. Former Governor Harold E. Stassen was eager but unacceptable because of his strong support of the New Deal, while the GOP's most prominent spokesman, Governor Dewey, was already a twice-beaten candidate. They turned, therefore, to General Eisenhower, supreme commander of NATO forces. He agreed reluctantly, as he told intimate friends, in order to prevent Taft's nomination and the triumph of isolationism in the Republican party.

Eisenhower's manager, Senator Henry Cabot Lodge, Jr., of Massachusetts, entered the general's name in the New Hampshire primary in January 1952, while Taft's forces began a drive in the South and Middle West. Eisenhower won easily in New Hampshire, Pennsylvania, and New Jersey, but Taft won such impressive victories in Wisconsin, Nebraska, and elsewhere in the Midwest that Eisenhower resigned his NATO command, returned to the United States, and entered the campaign in person in early June. Not since the William H. Taft–Theodore Roosevelt contest in 1912 had Republicans waged such a close and bitter prenomination battle. Taft and Eisenhower each controlled about five hundred delegates. The nomination would go to whoever won Minnesota and California—initially committed to favorite sons—and the contested delegations with sixty-eight votes from Texas, Georgia, and Louisiana.

The Taft forces controlled the Republican National Committee when the convention opened in Chicago in July 1952. But they were outmaneuvered by Dewey and Lodge in a struggle for the crucial contested delegates. The Easterners won a savage floor fight and were thereby able to nominate Eisenhower on the first ballot. It was an impressive victory but a potentially fatal one, for Taft and his embittered supporters were threatening to bolt or stay at home, and GOP chances rested upon Eisenhower's ability to close this breach. Meanwhile, the convention nominated Senator Richard M. Nixon of California for vice-president and adopted a platform broad enough to accommodate both factions.

The Democrats also waged a long, hard campaign to determine party control and a presidential ticket. There were a host of contenders—Vice-President Alben W. Barkley of Kentucky, Governor Averell Harriman of New York, and Senators Robert S. Kerr of Oklahoma, Richard B. Russell of Georgia, and Estes Kefauver of Tennessee. Kefauver made the most vigorous bid and scored the earliest successes by his open opposition to the Truman administration. Yet power remained with leaders of the northern and midwestern organizations and in large measure with the president himself. Truman played a cautious game at first. Then he announced on March 30 that he would not run again and soon afterward began a campaign to draft Governor Adlai E. Stevenson of Illinois. Stevenson insisted that he was not a candidate and continued his protestation until just before the convention. Truman and his allies therefore promised to support Barkley. But on the eve of the convention a group of labor leaders, including Walter Reuther of the CIO and George M. Harrison of the AFL, told Barkley that he was too old to run and asked him to withdraw. They spoke without authority, but they gained their objective.

When the Democratic convention assembled in July 1952, Truman and his friends, securely in control, turned again to Stevenson, who this time consented and won the nomination on the third ballot. The convention named Senator John J. Sparkman of Alabama as his running mate and adopted a platform demanding repeal of the Taft-Hartley Act, enactment of a full civil rights program, including a compulsory Fair Employment Practices Committee, and maintenance of high price supports for farmers. The platform also promised continuation of administration policies in Asia and Europe.

Stevenson, once he accepted the nomination, acted like a man who wanted to win. In a series of addresses unparalleled for literary excellence since Wilson's day, he told the American people that there was no easy road to peace and security. On domestic issues he began as a moderate but was drawn inevitably into full espousal of Fair Deal reform. He won AFL and CIO endorsement by demanding repeal of Taft-Hartley. He won wide support among blacks by championing advanced civil rights legislation. He drew most intellectuals to his side by his high seriousness and rhetorical abilities. On the other hand, he was less successful in his bid for general support. Many farmers and suburbanites, tired of both the Korean War and the administration, simply refused to listen to a Democratic candidate.

Stevenson's eloquence was not enough to withstand the Republican assault. Launching a "great crusade" for honest and efficient government at home and for "freedom in the world," Eisenhower supported liberation of captive peoples. This theme was first developed by John Foster Dulles and was included in the party platform. Eisenhower condemned the administration's "appalling and disastrous mismanagement" of foreign affairs, although he never precisely explained his alternative. On domestic issues, he spoke in generalities broad enough to please almost all classes and interests.

In the early part of the campaign, Eisenhower remained above partisan political strife. Soon, however, he shifted strategy toward working for a sweeping Republican triumph. Inviting Taft to New York to conciliate the party's right wing, Eisenhower won the Ohioan's promise of cooperation and soon afterward opened a strongly partisan attack upon the Truman administration. He also clearly endorsed Taft's view that one objective of his administration would be to destroy such products of "creeping socialism" as the TVA and federal hydroelectric projects in the Northwest. Finally, he tried to cement party unity by supporting all Republican candidates, including the rabid anti-Communists, Senator McCarthy and Senator William Jenner of Indiana.

Most important, Eisenhower capitalized upon the overriding popular desire for peace in Korea. Refusing to say that intervention had been unwise, Eisenhower charged that Truman's blundering had helped to cause the conflict and that the United States had walked into a Soviet trap by agreeing to a cease-fire in 1951. He struck the high note of his campaign at Detroit in October by promising "an early and honorable end" to the war. "That job," he said, "requires a personal trip to Korea. I shall make that trip. Only in that way could I learn how best to serve the American people in the cause of peace. I shall go to Korea."

Meanwhile, a united Republican party waged one of the most powerful and best-financed campaigns ever seen. Effectively using television and radio advertising, the GOP mounted a devastating attack. Practically all Republican campaigners exploited the Communist issue. A few, like McCarthy, went so far as to charge that Stevenson was tainted with Communist associations. Even more effective was the attack on American participation in Korea. The Republican

ELECTION OF 1952

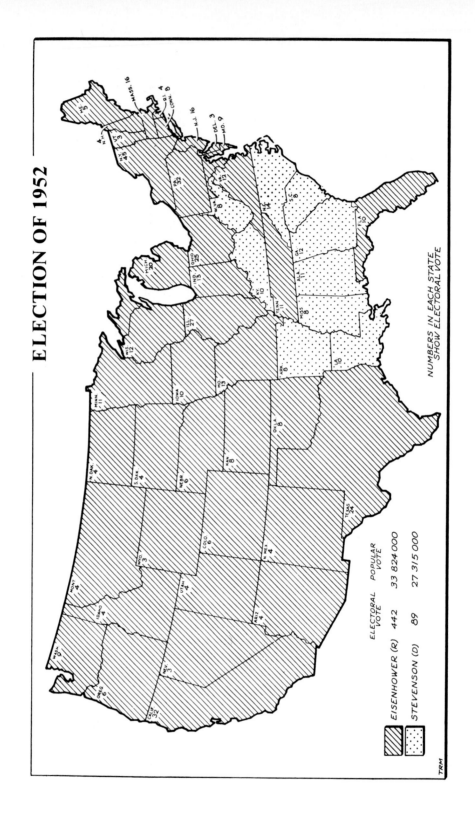

NUMBERS IN EACH STATE
SHOW ELECTORAL VOTE

	ELECTORAL VOTE	POPULAR VOTE
EISENHOWER (R)	442	33 824 000
STEVENSON (D)	89	27 315 000

TRM

momentum was halted only once, when the Democrats published proof that Nixon had enjoyed access to a modest fund provided by friends in California. Eisenhower was so furious that he commissioned Dewey to ask Nixon to withdraw. But Nixon fought back in an emotional television broadcast—his famous "Checkers" speech—that renewed support for his ticket. Eisenhower was convinced and rushed to a dramatic public reconciliation.

Although all signs pointed to a Republican victory on November 5, GOP campaigners fought hard to avert a last-minute swing to Stevenson. It did not occur. Stevenson, with 27.3 million popular votes, carried only West Virginia, Kentucky, the Carolinas, Georgia, Alabama, Mississippi, Louisiana, and Arkansas. Eisenhower won 33.8 million popular votes and carried thirty-nine states with a landslide electoral total of 442 to Stevenson's 89.

This victory was, in part, a personal triumph of a much-loved and widely respected national hero. In addition, the Republicans won because widespread discontent disrupted normal voting habits and broke the Democratic coalition of farmers, workers, ethnic minorities, and Southerners. Many southern Democrats voted as much against Truman's civil rights program and for their states' ownership of the tidelands as for Eisenhower. Many Democratic workers defected because, as Catholics or persons of eastern European ancestry, they were particularly susceptible to Republican denunciations of Communists and Yalta. Midwestern farmers voted Republican, in part, because Eisenhower simply outbid Stevenson for their support. People on fixed incomes were obsessed by fear of inflation. All observers agreed, moreover, that the issue with the greatest impact was the Korean War.

The presidential election of 1952 was, in several respects, an important turning point in postwar politics. It ended twenty years of Democratic dominance in national politics and inaugurated a new era of Republican strength and the partial erosion of the New Deal coalition. Eisenhower's coalition in 1952— white Southerners, farmers, Westerners, and ordinary middle-class Americans— would continue to vote Republican in presidential elections during the next thirty years. Yet Eisenhower's election crystallized another new phenomenon in American politics—the increasing practice of ticket splitting and the bifurcation characteristic of elections in which Republicans won the presidency but Democrats tended to win congressional contests. Indeed, one astonishing result of the election of 1952 was the continued strength of congressional Democrats. In spite of Eisenhower's personal popularity, the widespread discontent, and an effective campaign against an increasingly unpopular administration, the Republicans managed only to elect a majority of eight in the House and, because of the defection of Wayne Morse of Oregon from the GOP, to break even in the Senate. Since Eisenhower ran far ahead of most other Republican candidates, it was clear that he carried this slight congressional majority along with him into office.

CHAPTER 21

The Origins of the Cold War, 1945–1949

Probably most Americans in the summer of 1945 believed that the end of the war would bring a new world order. Events soon made a mockery of these hopes. The Allied victory confirmed American power, but it also propelled Soviet expansionism. The total defeat of Germany and Japan removed counterbalances to Soviet power, and Americans now faced two unwelcome alternatives. They could either allow Russia to fill the European and Far Eastern power vacuums, or they could build and support a new power structure to prevent it.

The years immediately after the war were crucial in the formation of a new Soviet-American relationship. In some respects, the development of superpower competition—and of what came to be known as the "cold war"—followed its own logic. It was at least partly the product of two inexperienced powers, both isolationist and xenophobic, testing the limits of their new world responsibilities. The Soviets, run by an oppressive political system, saw no inconsistency in imposing it upon a cordon of buffer states in Eastern Europe. Alarmed by the threat of Soviet imperialism, the United States, on the other hand, came to internationalize the danger from world communism.

1. BUILDING THE POSTWAR ORDER

One of Roosevelt's primary postwar objectives was the creation of a permanent international organization. He and his policy makers found an almost unanimous response in the United States; abroad they found disagreement only upon details. Leaders of the three great powers resolved their differences at the

Dumbarton Oaks and Yalta conferences in 1944 and early 1945. They also approved the structure of a United Nations and convoked an international conference to meet in San Francisco in April to draft a charter for the new organization.

Although disagreement over Poland threatened to disrupt the conference, Truman bluntly told Soviet Foreign Minister Molotov in April 1945 that the United States would help form an international organization—with or without Soviet cooperation—and the Russians abruptly changed their attitude. The San Francisco Conference was an inauspicious beginning for the reign of universal brotherhood. American and Russian delegates wrangled incessantly over questions large and small, and Truman saved the conference from disruption on one occasion only by appealing personally to Stalin. In the end, the Charter of the United Nations—signed in June, approved by the United States Senate in July, and promulgated in October 1945—conceded some points to the Soviets. Even so, it was an American document in all its strengths and weaknesses.

Under the terms of its Charter, the UN was governed by a bicameral legislature—an "upper house" Security Council and a "lower house" General Assembly. The Charter also established an executive agency, the Secretariat, headed by a secretary-general, and dozens of subsidiary and allied agencies. It was an imposing structure, calculated to fit every need and to please all but the most extreme nationalists. But it was a structure for world confederation and cooperation, not for effective world government. On paper, members agreed to follow the path of arbitration rather than resort to war. Yet the United Nations lacked power sufficient to its task. It was an association of sovereign states, with no authority except such as its leading members condescended to let it use. Established primarily to prevent war, it could be blocked in performing this elementary function by the veto of any permanent member of the Security Council. Powerless to prevent aggression by its leading members, the UN in this respect was a weaker peacekeeping instrument than the League of Nations. Nor was there much hope of reform, for permanent members of the Security Council had the right to veto proposed amendments to the Charter.

American leaders were largely responsible for these constitutional defects. Fearing isolationist sentiment at home and willing to make concessions to obtain Russian membership, they insisted upon an agency that would not impair national sovereignty and could function effectively only so long as all great powers cooperated. Thus the veto was more an American than a Russian invention. The provision for "regional" defensive associations, creation of which later emphasized the UN's failure as a peace agency, was also included at American insistence.

These weaknesses were only dimly perceptible in 1945. To the most urgent task—relief for war-ravaged areas—Americans responded generously. The United States contributed some $2.7 billion through the United Nations Relief and Rehabilitation Administration (UNRRA) in food and supplies to the peoples of China and central and eastern Europe. The army assumed the burden of relief in Japan and the American zone of Germany, while the Red Cross, church groups, and private organizations added several hundred million dollars' worth of clothing and food. Through the sale on credit of surplus property and extension of credits by the Export-Import Bank, Washington made some additional $4.7 billion available, chiefly to western Europe.

The American government also worked to restore international trade. Accumulated foreign deficits—over $19 billion in 1946–1947—were so staggering that world trade would have collapsed without decisive American support. Washington solved the problem before 1948 by stopgap expedients such as UNRRA and other aid, loans by the Export-Import Bank, and a credit of $3.75 billion to Great Britain in 1946.

An even more difficult task was the reconstruction and reform of Germany and Japan. Americans were unprepared for this undertaking, and in retrospect many of the occupation policies seem unwise, unnecessarily harsh, and utopian. American policy in Germany was shaped by a desire to visit condign punishment on criminals and then remake German society in the American image. All four occupying powers were pledged to destroy nazism and help build new democratic institutions, but American authorities outdid all others in zeal. The United States cooperated with other powers in limiting German steel production, destroying armament plants and industries with war potential, and dismantling other plants and sending them to Russia, Poland, and elsewhere as reparations. The result was to limit the German contribution to European recovery and aggravate the huge burden of relief for refugees, displaced persons, the homeless, and the unemployed.

By 1949, when "denazification" was supposedly complete, military authorities and German courts had punished 1,635 major and some 600,000 minor Nazi offenders. Allied vengeance culminated in the trial of twenty-two high Nazi officials by an International Military Tribunal at Nuremberg from November 1945 to October 1946. Three of the defendants were acquitted and nineteen were convicted—of whom twelve were sentenced to death. Although the tribunal tried to avoid the appearance of a kangaroo court and observed some forms of justice, the trial violated nearly every tradition of Anglo-American jurisprudence. Conviction of political officials for planning and waging aggressive war, for example, violated the ancient prohibition against ex post facto laws. Execution of military commanders established the new and dubious doctrine that soldiers might be punished for obeying orders. Above all, the trial of defendants for war crimes and atrocities established the principle that, as Churchill put it, "the leaders of a nation defeated in war shall be put to death by the victors."

The United States exercised complete control over occupation and reconstruction policies in Japan, vesting all authority in General Douglas MacArthur as supreme commander for the Allied powers. Thousands of alleged militarists and supporters of aggression were purged, and hundreds of military leaders were tried and executed for war crimes. An International Military Tribunal for the Far East prosecuted twenty-eight high officials for waging aggressive war in violation of international law. But MacArthur and his subordinates came to reform as well as to punish. They sought not only to preserve or modify institutions and customs that had served the Japanese people for hundreds of years, but also to create a new political, economic, and social order inspired by American utopian traditions. This new order included renunciation even of defensive war, demilitarization, land distribution, an antitrust campaign, and social democracy. Most Americans hailed the building of this new Asian society, as, indeed, did the great majority of the Japanese people.

2. SOVIET-AMERICAN TENSIONS, 1945–1947

Until his death, Roosevelt believed that he could remove Soviet suspicions and create an atmosphere of mutual trust in which genuine collaboration could develop. Truman took command of foreign policy in April 1945 in an atmosphere of suspicion about Soviet bad faith and expansionist ambitions. In imposing Communist governments on Romania and Poland and in accusing Roosevelt and Churchill of conspiring to conclude a separate peace at the end of the war, Stalin had raised grave doubts about the permanence of the Grand Alliance. Tensions increased further at the San Francisco Conference, and Truman sent Harry Hopkins to Moscow in May 1945 for talks with Stalin. The Soviet dictator, in an angry mood, repeated the Russian indictment of American policy. He accused the American government of insulting the USSR at San Francisco and ending lend-lease aid abruptly after the German surrender in order to apply pressure on Russia—charges which were well founded. But Stalin mellowed in conversation and agreed to admit non-Communist Poles to the Polish government and to meet President Truman and Prime Minister Churchill for a full discussion of outstanding problems.

Soviet-American tensions dominated the meeting of Truman, Stalin, and Clement R. Attlee, the new British prime minister, at Potsdam in July 1945. Almost interminable disagreement over the sensitive issues of reparations and implementing the Yalta Declaration on Liberated Countries dominated the conference's proceedings. Under strong pressure from Truman and Churchill, the Russians finally agreed to permit Anglo-American observers in Romania, Hungary, Bulgaria, and Finland to move about freely. In return, the American and British leaders approved Polish occupation and administration of German territory east of the Neisse River until a peace conference could settle German boundaries. As for reparations, Stalin accepted Secretary of State James F. Byrnes's proposal that each power obtain reparations from its own zone and that the western Allies transfer 25 percent of the capital equipment available for reparations in their zones. Other issues were deferred for future discussion.

Soviet-American relations were not helped by Washington's failure in the immediate postwar period even to acknowledge a Soviet request for a large loan from the United States. Nonetheless, Byrnes worked hard, despite serious obstacles, to reach an accommodation with the Soviets on outstanding problems—a united policy for Germany, peace treaties for Italy and the central European and Balkan countries, and international agreement for disarmament and control of atomic energy. Byrnes, who shared Roosevelt's conviction that American cooperation with Russia was the indispensable cornerstone of postwar peace, sought to overcome Soviet suspicion by concession and compromise.

Yet the failure of this policy during the next seventeen months and the further deterioration of Soviet-American relations confirmed to Truman and Western European leaders the apparent need for a firmer anti-Soviet posture. The status of postwar Germany was another troublesome question. In order to destroy the German threat to European security and world peace, Roosevelt had envisioned, and apparently won Stalin's support for, the future demilitarization and neutralization of Germany. When Truman, Stalin, and the British and French foreign ministers approved a twenty-five-year alliance against the resurgence of German militarism, Byrnes prepared a treaty, but it encountered strong Soviet opposition in early 1946. Byrnes's successor, George C. Marshall, raised the proposal again in April 1947 and met the same response. It was clear that the Grand Alliance was permanently disrupted and that the Soviets were committed to keeping Germany divided as a way to prevent any future European invasions.

Byrnes meanwhile negotiated peace treaties with Hitler's allies. The Russians refused to approve an Austrian treaty because it would have ended their control of a vital outpost in central Europe. On the other hand, Byrnes finally obtained treaties for Italy, Hungary, Romania, and Bulgaria at Paris in February 1947. They confirmed Western supremacy in Italy and North Africa and Soviet predominance in Hungary and the Balkans. This was perhaps the only settlement possible, but it marked American recognition of Russian control of southeastern Europe, which, in the circumstances and in view of Russian security needs, was inevitable in any event. However, it was obvious, as former Prime Minister Winston Churchill said in a speech at Fulton, Missouri, on March 5, 1946, that the Russians had lowered an "iron curtain" around Eastern Europe.

Another issue, of ever greater importance, was international control over nuclear weapons and nuclear energy. Between 1945 and mid-1949, when the Soviets detonated their first nuclear device, the United States possessed a monopoly over nuclear weapons, and these became still another source of international tension. One solution was proposed to the United Nations Atomic Energy Commission by Bernard M. Baruch in June 1946. The Baruch Plan provided for an international Atomic Development Authority to own, control, and operate all

CENTRAL
AND EASTERN
EUROPE

TERRITORIAL CHANGES
1939-1947

uranium and thorium mines and production facilities and alone conduct research in atomic explosives. The authority might permit use of atomic energy for peaceful purposes, but it would have full power, unrestrained by any veto, of inspection and punishment of those who violated the atomic energy statute.

This ambitious proposal to internationalize nuclear weaponry would have transcended the short-term interests of both the United States and the Soviet Union. In the tense atmosphere of 1946, it perhaps seemed a plan which perpetuated the American atomic monopoly, and it was more than the Soviets could safely approve. They instead countered with a proposal simply to outlaw the manufacture and use of nuclear weapons and to vest enforcement in the Security Council, where they might veto action against violators. The Russians subsequently made important concessions by accepting unlimited international inspection, but they would never yield the power to veto punishment of violators. The American government, unwilling to accept any compromise that impaired the principle of effective international control, rejected the Soviet overtures and effectively ended all hopes for nuclear disarmament for the next generation.

Failure here merely underscored the larger failure of the United States and the Soviet Union to find a basis for common action on Germany, disarmament, and the creation of armed forces for the UN. Perhaps Russia would have been more cooperative had the United States extended material aid for civilian reconstruction after the termination of lend-lease, shared the secrets of the atomic bomb (which Roosevelt had also refused to do), and more readily conceded what in retrospect seem to have been Russia's legitimate security needs in eastern and central Europe. Perhaps American leaders, by moving too boldly and quickly on disarmament, confirmed Russian suspicions that the United States sought world domination. On the other hand, it does seem fair to say that Russian leaders, out of ignorance, isolation, a distorted view of international politics, or a desire to extend their own power, were primarily responsible for wrecking the world's hopes for a stable peace.

3.   THE UNITED STATES AND CHINA

The Chinese Revolution and the victory of the Communists in 1949, coming on the heels of the frustrating postwar experience with the Soviets, was a telling blow to American hopes in the Far East. For the United States, the impact of the Chinese Revolution was supremely ironic. The American government had sought for half a century to maintain Chinese independence and give to China what it regarded as the benefits of Western civilization, democracy, and Christianity. The United States, among all of the major Far Eastern powers, had been the least imperialistic and had defended Chinese integrity even to the point of fighting a bloody war with Japan. Yet, only five years after the Japanese surrender, the American people found themselves at war with a Chinese government that reviled them as China's most dangerous enemies.

The stage was set for a Communist triumph during the war years. By the end of 1941, Chiang Kai-shek's Nationalist government at Chungking (Chongqing) was exhausted and nearly fatally weakened after four years of seemingly hopeless resistance to Japan. It managed to survive after 1941 only because the Japanese concluded that its final destruction was not worth the effort. The American government did its best to keep China in the war—by extending a $500 million credit in 1942, airlifting supplies over the treacherous Himalayan Hump, and dispatching military advisers to Chungking. But these efforts were totally inadequate to the main task of strengthening and supplying Chinese armies. Allied forces in Burma finally broke the siege of China and opened a supply route from India to Kunming in early 1945. But the war was nearly over, and the Nationalist government was weaker than ever.

Roosevelt meanwhile began measures to build China into a postwar power. The Cairo Declaration of December 1943, approved by the Big Three, promised the return of Japanese-held Manchuria and Taiwan to China. At Yalta, with American support, China won a permanent seat on the Security Council and Stalin's pledge of support for the Nationalist government. Yet Chiang's most important challenges were domestic rather than international: how to defeat the Communists and establish Nationalist control of the Chinese countryside. The Chinese Communists, driven out of southern China in 1934–1935, had fought their way to Yenan (Yan'an), in the Shensi (Shoanxi) Province in northwestern China, where they established a precarious government, harassed but never conquered by Nationalist forces. Growing stronger after the Japanese invasion in 1937, the Communists rejected Chiang's appeals to submit to the central government and join in common defense of the homeland. They were so strong by early 1944 that Chiang had diverted 400,000 of his best troops in order to contain them.

At this point the Allied need for manpower in Burma and the beginning of a new Japanese offensive in China led Washington to try to unify the Chinese forces. Stalin and Molotov reassured Roosevelt that Russia had no interest in controlling China and that, in any event, Chinese Communists were not good Communists. Vice-President Wallace went to Chungking in June 1944 and urged Chiang to come to terms with Yenan so that all Chinese troops could combine against the common enemy. A short time later Roosevelt sent General Patrick J. Hurley as his personal representative to Chiang. Hurley went by way of Moscow and learned that the Kremlin was not interested in or responsible for the Chinese comrades and would take no part in the civil war.

But the more American leaders urged Chiang to come to agreement, the more stubbornly did Chiang insist that Chinese Communists were revolutionaries bent upon domination of China. And the more Chiang refused to approve unification upon any basis except Yenan's military submission, the stronger the American conviction grew that Chiang and his government were unreasonable, corrupt, incompetent, and unrepresentative. Chiang did allow American newspaper reporters and official observers to go to Yenan in the spring of 1944. These reporters sent back glowing accounts, while foreign service officers confirmed newspaper reports that the Communists were primarily agrarian reformers, extraordinarily efficient, and devoted to the cause of democracy.

As the showdown between Communists and Nationalists approached in 1945, a rational American policy would have been difficult at best. The two chief American officials in China—General Hurley, who became ambassador in December 1944, and General Albert C. Wedemeyer, who succeeded General Joseph W. Stilwell as Chiang's chief of staff and commander of American forces in China in October 1944—favored Chiang's government. Foreign service experts, on the other hand, argued that the Nationalist government was hopelessly corrupt and tyrannical and that the Communists would prevail because they were genuinely representative of the people. They appealed over Hurley's head to Washington, urging that the United States should either compel Chiang to come to terms with the Communists; if Chiang refused, the experts advocated support for the Yenan regime.

When Roosevelt backed Hurley at a showdown meeting in Washington in March 1945, American policy seemed reasonably clear. The United States would continue to support Chiang but would also seek to end the civil war by bringing the Nationalists and Communists together in a coalition government. Hurley, cordially supporting this decision, began intense mediation efforts upon his return to Chungking in May 1945. In Moscow, Harry Hopkins received Stalin's unequivocal pledge of support for the Nationalist government.

Then the war in the Pacific suddenly ended, and the United States had to redefine its policy. It quickly assisted Chiang in accepting the surrender of Japanese forces and occupying key Chinese ports and cities before the Communists could do so. Americans airlifted three Nationalist armies from the interior to eastern and northern provinces during September and October 1945, while the American Navy later transported 400,000 Nationalist troops to Manchurian ports. American marines occupied strategic cities like Tsingtao (Qingdao), Tientsin (Tianjin), and Peking (Beijing) until Nationalist forces could take over. By the end of 1945, American and Chinese troops had accepted the surrender of Japanese forces everywhere in China but Manchuria, and Chiang controlled the important cities in Manchuria and the southern and eastern provinces. Yet the Nationalists were in a precarious position. The Chinese Communists were powerfully entrenched in the north and in Manchuria, where Russian occupation forces were supplying them with Japanese arms. Nationalist armies were badly overextended, while Chiang's political agents were often inexperienced, inefficient, and corrupt. Before the Russians withdrew from Manchuria in February

1946, they stripped that province of some $2 billion worth of industrial and railroad equipment, thus leaving the area useless to assist in national reconstruction. It was obvious that China stood on the brink of full-scale war.

American policy makers faced several uncomfortable alternatives. Should they occupy China and Manchuria, at least with token forces, and give material assistance to the Nationalists? Should they seek to halt the civil war through mediation and threaten to withdraw support if Chiang refused to cooperate? Or should they leave China altogether and let the two opposing forces fight it out? There was no lack of reliable information as the Americans weighed their distasteful choices. General Wedemeyer warned in a series of messages that the task of unifying and pacifying China was too great for Chiang and his incompetent government to accomplish. Other military observers confirmed this analysis and agreed that abandoning Chiang meant abandoning China to the Communists. And yet there was no disposition in Washington or the country at large to give wholehearted support to Chiang's discredited regime in a war against what many thought was an honest, efficient, and democratic opposition. In fact, the administration's desire to stay out of the civil war enjoyed almost universal support in the United States.

With this domestic support, Truman made his decision in late 1945. He sent General Marshall to China to press for a truce and to conduct mediation looking toward a coalition government in which both the Kuomintang, or Nationalist, and Communist parties would compete peacefully for power. Marshall arrived in Chungking at the end of December and immediately set to work. It seemed for several months that his efforts to achieve peace and unity might succeed, for the opposing groups approved a cease-fire and a plan for governmental reorganization. Actually, Marshall merely delayed the inevitable war—inevitable because neither side would trust the other or yield on essential points. Marshall abandoned his mission in January 1947 with a blast at Nationalist reactionaries and Communists alike, declaring that the hope of Chinese salvation lay with a liberal group who were without power and prestige in the Kuomintang.

Marshall returned to Washington to become secretary of state, and the war in China began in earnest. The Nationalists were well equipped and greatly superior in numbers at the outset. But the Communists had the edge in training, discipline, and leadership, plus the advantage of interior lines. At the same time, Nationalist commanders were content to occupy isolated cities and seemed unable to wage aggressive campaigns. The tide was beginning to turn by mid-1947. Defeatism swept through the Nationalist armies, and Chiang's government at Nanking (Nanjing) lost further popular support through its failure to curb inflation, suppress warlords and bandits, and govern competently.

Resumption of the Chinese civil war forced Washington to face a new situation. Convinced that the Nationalist armies were adequately equipped, American leaders felt that they could do nothing more without running heavy risks of full-scale participation. Hence they withdrew all military forces, except for a small contingent of marines at Tsingtao, and refused to extend any large new assistance to Chiang in 1947. President Truman did send General Wedemeyer back to China in July to investigate and then recommend appropriate policy. The general reported on the dangers of the Chinese situation in September 1947. While admitting that "reactionary leadership, repression and corruption" had caused the people to lose faith in Chiang's government, he held out hope for genuine reform, provided that the United States gave effective moral and material support. Communist control of China, Wedemeyer warned, would imperil American interests and peace in the Far East. Yet the situation was far from hopeless, Wedemeyer said. The United States should insist that the UN take control of Manchuria to prevent that province from falling into the Soviet orbit. It should also inaugurate a large program of "moral, advisory, and material" assistance to China "to protect United States strategic interests against militant forces which now threaten them."

Even such action would probably not have sufficed, given the incompetence of Chiang's regime and the Chinese Communists' determination to win and reconstruct their country. Knowing that the American people would not tolerate full-scale participation in the Chinese civil war, the administration not only refused to sanction Wedemeyer's report but kept it secret until Chiang had been driven from the mainland. As Secretary Marshall declared, there was nothing the United States could do to "make the present Chinese Government capable of reestablishing and then maintaining its control throughout all of China."

The Communists captured Mukden (Shenyang) in October 1948 and then, assisted by the rapid disintegration of the Nationalist government and armies, swept on to victory with incredible speed. They crossed the Yangtze in April 1949 and quickly captured Hankow (Wuhan), Shanghai, Canton (Guangzhou), and other southern ports and cities. Chiang retired to Chungking in October and fled by air with remnants of his government to Taiwan in December. Meanwhile, the Chinese Communist leaders, Mao Tse-tung and Chou En-lai, had established the People's Republic of China at Peking, declared their friendship for the USSR, and begun an intensive campaign to expel American officials, missionaries, and other citizens.

4.   THE DECLINE OF THE GOOD NEIGHBOR POLICY

Evidence of the success of the Good Neighbor policy came within a few days after Pearl Harbor, when twelve Latin American governments either declared war upon the Axis or broke diplomatic relations. All the rest, except Argentina and Chile, followed suit after approving a United States resolution to that effect at a conference in Rio de Janeiro in January 1942. The American republics then began a genuine collaboration. Brazil participated in the campaign against German U-boats, provided airfields for an "air ferry" to Africa, and sent a division to the Italian front. Most other Latin American countries cooperated by sending vital raw materials, offering air bases, and joining with American agents to root out Axis influences.

The one important and dangerous exception was Argentina. Its leaders not only refused to break with the Axis but also maintained intimate relations with Nazi agents and sympathized with the German cause. A group of army officers, led by Colonel Juan Perón, seized control of the Buenos Aires government in June 1943 and launched a campaign to destroy the democratic opposition. Although a new president, General Edelmiro Farrell, consequently came to power in February 1944, Perón remained dominant, and Washington undertook to persuade the other American republics to withhold recognition and several months later froze Argentina's gold assets in the United States.

The State Department, to quiet Latin American fears that even stronger unilateral measures impended, called a special Pan-American conference, which met in Mexico City in February 1945. After first inviting Argentina to return to the inter-American fold, the delegates then approved the Act of Chapultepec on March 3. It completed the mutualization of the Monroe Doctrine by declaring that any attack upon the territory or sovereignty of one American state would be met by the combined forces of all of them. The Argentine government soon afterward declared war on Germany and Japan and ratified the Act of Chapultepec, and the United States accorded the Argentine government diplomatic recognition.

For a brief time the breach appeared healed, especially when the American delegation at San Francisco joined Latin Americans in winning UN membership for Argentina. Actually, however, the United States was already hard at work on new strategies against the Farrell government, which had suppressed free speech, opposition parties, and the press. Spruille Braden, American ambassador to Argentina, worked secretly with opposition leaders and publicly urged Argentines to change their government. Further, in February 1946, the State Department, issuing the so-called Argentine Blue Book, accused the Argentine regime of "aid to the enemy, deliberate misrepresentation and deception in promises of hemispheric cooperation, subversive activity against neighboring republics, and [forming] a vicious partnership of Nazi and native totalitarian forces." American friendship could be restored, the document warned, only when the Argentine people were represented by a government that commanded "full faith and confidence at home and abroad."

This intervention in the political affairs of a sovereign, suspicious, and proud people was stern but ill-considered diplomacy. In what was probably a fair election, Argentinos gave a large majority to the Argentine nationalist, Colonel Juan Perón—and sent a clear answer to their northern neighbor. Although

Washington accepted this popular verdict, relations between the United States and Argentina remained tense during 1946, and the former refused to participate in any regional defense association that included Argentina. Facing mounting Latin American criticism, Truman and Marshall agreed to begin discussions about a hemispheric defense pact.

Meeting in Rio de Janeiro in August 1947, delegates from all twenty-one American republics approved an Inter-American Treaty of Reciprocal Assistance. It obligated all signatories, when two-thirds of them so voted, to sever diplomatic and economic relations with any internal or external violator of the Act of Chapultepec, but no signatory would be required to use its armed forces without its own consent. A ninth Inter-American Conference, assembling at Bogotá in early 1948, established a charter for an Organization of American States and gave full constitutional status to the hemispheric system.

Although the structures erected at Mexico City, Rio, and Bogotá indicated that the Good Neighbor policy had been thoroughly mutualized, they provided more form than substance, and hemispheric cooperation actually declined after 1945. The postwar era was a time of great political unrest and turmoil, as leaders of downtrodden urban workers and a landless peasantry and representatives of the privileged classes, usually military regimes, contended for power. Most important, Latin America ceased to be of prime importance to the United States. New global responsibilities shifted the direction of American foreign policy toward Europe and Asia. The result was a policy of neglect during a crucial period of Latin American economic and political problems.

5. THE TRUMAN DOCTRINE AND CONTAINMENT

In the spring of 1947, Truman inaugurated a departure in American foreign policy as important as the Monroe Doctrine and the decisions to enter the world wars. With Byrnes as secretary of state, Truman had attempted to strike an accommodation with Soviet desires for secure borders and worldwide influence. Yet Truman, never entirely happy with this approach, began a new foreign-policy approach designed to halt, or contain, Soviet expansion aggressively in the Middle East and Europe. "Containment," as this approach came to be known, did not stem merely from irritation and disappointment over Russian behavior. It was a radical new departure grounded upon certain harsh assumptions and devised to meet a perceived threat of Soviet control of the eastern Mediterranean.

Well before containment, many American and British leaders had already abandoned faith in accommodation with the Soviets. Truman himself never fully shared Roosevelt's belief in the chances of successful cooperation, and he saw a threat of Soviet expansion in the Middle East and Greece as early as January 1946.

But it was George F. Kennan, counselor of the American Embassy in Moscow, who first fully elaborated the assumptions behind the policy of containment. In February 1946, Kennan drafted an eight-thousand-word dispatch to clarify the character, tactics, motivation, and ambitions of the Soviets. After exploring the historical background of Russian distrust of the West, Kennan pointed up the danger: "We have here a political force committed fanatically to the belief that with the U.S. there can be no permanent *modus vivendi*, that it is desirable and necessary that the internal harmony of our society be disrupted, our traditional way of life be destroyed, the international authority of our state be broken, if Soviet power is to be secure."

To Kennan, the realities of the Soviet system—which was fundamentally both inward-looking and suspicious of outsiders but also aggressively expansionist—necessitated a policy of containment. The nation could live at peace with the Soviet Union only by building its own strength and by erecting effective counterweights in order to contain Communist power at least in Europe, Kennan wrote in *Foreign Affairs* in July 1947. "It is clear that the main element of any United States policy toward the Soviet Union must be that of a long-term, patient but firm and vigilant containment of Russian expansive tendencies."

Events in the Middle East provided an opportunity for Truman and his new secretary of state, George C. Marshall, to articulate this new policy. During the war, the Soviets created a puppet regime in the northern Iranian province of Azerbaijan. They withdrew their troops in early 1946 only after sharp State Department protests and "a blunt message" from Truman to Stalin. Even more threatening was the extraordinary Russian pressure on Turkey between 1945 and 1947 for cession of territory and the right to build naval bases in the Bosporus. In brief, Soviet leaders seemed determined to achieve a historic Russian objective—control of the Bosporus Strait and the eastern Mediterranean.

Soviet expansionism appeared to be connected with a civil war in Greece, where a popular but Communist-controlled guerrilla movement had the upper hand in early 1947. The British had supported a rightist Greek government since late 1944 in a protracted and bloody effort to suppress a Communist-led partisan group known as the EAM. The British ambassador informed Washington in February 1947 that Great Britain would soon have to withdraw entirely from Greece. Truman's response to the end of British power in the eastern Mediterranean marked a fateful turning point in American foreign policy. The implications seemed clear enough: "If Greece was lost, Turkey would become an untenable outpost in a sea of Communism. Similarly, if Turkey yielded to Soviet demands, the position of Greece would be extremely endangered." After discussions with congressional leaders, Truman went to Capitol Hill on March 12 to seek $400 million for military assistance to Greece and Turkey. Even more important was his enunciation of the so-called Truman Doctrine. It went far beyond Kennan's concept. American foreign policy, Truman said, should support "free peoples who are resisting attempted subjugation by armed minorities or by outside pressures." "If we falter in our leadership," he declared, "we may endanger the peace of the world—and we shall surely endanger the welfare of our own Nation."

The declaration of the Truman Doctrine marked the beginning of a new era in Soviet-American relations. Although mutual suspicion and bad feeling had existed since 1945, the two powers had tacitly agreed to respect each other's spheres of influence. Whether the president overreacted in seeking aid to Greece and Turkey and enunciating the Truman Doctrine, it is impossible to say, since the documents essential to a full understanding of Soviet plans and purposes are not open to scholars. What is clear is that the United States was now committed to oppose any further expansion of Soviet power and, in the Truman Doctrine, had identified the Greek civil war with these ambitions. With this important precedent for the internationalization of Soviet-American competition established, the cold war had begun.

Truman's pronouncement shocked the American people, then inadequately prepared to assume such enormous new responsibilities. With the crucial help of Arthur Vandenberg of Michigan, chairman of the Senate Foreign Relations Committee, Truman won congressional support for his Greek-Turkish aid bill in May 1947. All told, Washington spent some $659 million under the Greek-Turkish aid program from 1947 to 1950. The task in Turkey was quickly and inexpensively accomplished, for the Turkish government was undisturbed by civil war and relatively honest. American aid helped the Turks to achieve economic stability and modernize their sizable army without much friction on either side.

The Greek problem, on the other hand, proved immensely difficult. The United States found itself in the embarrassing position of defending democracy in Greece by supporting a reactionary government that refused to do anything effective about the basic economic and social evils which had stirred the masses to revolt. In any event, American supplies and a military mission enabled a reorganized Greek Army to undertake a determined campaign to end the civil war. Government forces cleared the Peloponnesus of guerrillas and then turned northward toward the EAM stronghold. Success was assured when Yugoslavia broke with the Soviet bloc in 1948 and abandoned its support for the Greek Communists in mid-1949. The long civil war was over by October, and the Greek people could turn to urgent problems of domestic reconstruction.

6.   THE MARSHALL PLAN

As winter turned into spring in 1947, it seemed that the Greco-Turkish situation was merely a symptom of a more momentous crisis that threatened all of non-Communist Europe. To a varying extent, Great Britain, France, Italy, and the other nations of Western Europe were staggering under nearly impossible burdens of reconstruction. Careening from one economic crisis to another, they faced the grim prospect of violent social upheaval if they failed to accomplish virtual miracles of recovery.

In a little-noticed speech at Cleveland, Mississippi, in May 1947, Undersecretary of State Dean Acheson pointed up the necessity of strengthening governments that were "seeking to preserve their independence and democratic institutions and human freedoms against totalitarian pressures, either internal or external." Then, in an address at Harvard University in June, Secretary Marshall embraced suggestions made by Kennan and the Policy Planning Staff of the State Department. The European governments, he declared, should work out a comprehensive reconstruction program and tell the United States how it might best help them to achieve lasting recovery. "Any government willing to assist in the task of reconstruction," he promised, "will find full cooperation on the part of the United States."

What the secretary envisaged was nothing less than the rebuilding of the Western European economy and social order. Although Marshall did not exclude the Soviet bloc from the offer of American aid, he knew that Russian rejection was very likely. When the British, French, and Russian foreign ministers met in Paris in late June to consider a reply, the British and French ministers voiced the overwhelming enthusiasm and gratitude of Western Europe, while Molotov expressed the opposition of the Communist bloc and left the meeting when he could not disrupt it. Representatives from Great Britain, France, Italy, Turkey, and other non-Communist nations met in Paris in July and appointed a Committee of European Economic Cooperation (CEEC). It submitted a master recovery plan two months later, calling for $22.4 billion in American assistance and loans. In late 1947, therefore, a struggle also ensued to exclude Communists from political power in Western Europe. That struggle was already acute in France and Italy, where Communists, expelled from coalition cabinets early in the spring, were now working to destroy moderate governments.

Meanwhile, lines were also being drawn in the United States between champions of the European Recovery Program (ERP), as the Marshall Plan was called, and their opponents. Debate began in earnest when Truman submitted an economic cooperation bill in December 1947 calling for $17 billion in aid during the next four years. Opponents of the measure, handicapped by the fact that Communists also opposed it, were soon overwhelmed by a coalition that included farm organizations, the AFL and CIO, the National Association of Manufacturers, and other pressure groups. Any doubts that Congress would approve the bill were ended when a Soviet-backed coup put Communists in power in Czechoslovakia in February 1948. Truman signed the Marshall Plan into law in April 1948.

The Marshall Plan, soon one of the most successful foreign-policy programs in American history, forged a permanent link between the United States and Western Europe. But, more important, it brought a new period of economic prosperity and political stability to American allies there and thus fulfilled its chief objective—preventing Communist electoral successes and the further expansion of Soviet influence. By 1950, it was clear that the Marshall Plan was providing a strong stimulus to economic growth. From 1947 through 1950, the GNP in Marshall Plan countries as a whole increased 25 percent; industrial production, 64 percent; and agricultural output, 24 percent. In most categories recovery not only attained but exceeded prewar levels.

7.   THE BERLIN CRISIS AND THE NORTH ATLANTIC TREATY

So far, we have viewed the European Recovery Program in part outside the context of other events that were impelling Western nations toward closer unity and driving the Soviet Union to a desperate campaign to consolidate its control over Eastern Europe. Most important in this context was the fate of war-ravaged Germany. American, British, and French leaders continued to press for German unification and neutrality until the end of 1947. But the Soviets made it clear at the Moscow and London meetings of the Council of Foreign Ministers in 1947 that they would approve no agreement on Germany that did not give them a large voice in the control of the Ruhr Valley, the industrial heart of Europe.

Western leaders, concluding that agreement with the USSR on its own terms was impossible, began to devise their own plan for Germany. German recovery was the key to European recovery, and the defense of western Germany was the key to the defense of Western Europe. British and American leaders moved fast. After consolidating their zones in February 1948 and creating a provisional German government at Frankfurt, they won French approval for a West German Federal Republic with limited sovereignty. They also won French consent to currency reform in the three western zones and measures to include West Germany as a full partner in the ERP. The Germans organized state governments in October 1948, adopted a federal constitution in May 1949, and elected a federal congress that met at Bonn in September and established a full-fledged constitutional government.

Russian reaction to the Marshall Plan and to Western policy in Germany was immediate. Soviet leaders created the Cominform in October 1947 to unite Eastern Europe in a campaign of complete "sovietization," that is, a final destruction of all anti-Communist elements. They launched a campaign of strikes and violence through Communist parties and Communist-controlled trade unions that impeded but did not prevent Italian and French recovery. They engineered the coup that overthrew a coalition government in Prague in February 1948, after which they established a Communist regime in Czechoslovakia.

The climax to this dangerous new period of international tension was the Berlin blockade. In April, Soviet authorities began to restrict the movement of people and freight from the western zones of Germany into Berlin, then under four-power control but isolated in the Russian-held eastern zone of Germany. This action provoked violent controversies in the Allied Kommandatura, the four-power control council for the German capital, and eventuated in Soviet withdrawal from that body in July. Meanwhile, in retaliation against Allied introduction of the new West German currency, Russia halted all surface traffic to Berlin from the western zones in late June. The Soviets made no effort to conceal the objectives of the Berlin blockade—either to force the Allies from their advanced position in eastern Germany or else to compel them to abandon their plans to create an independent West Germany. Yet withdrawal would signify surrender in the face of superior force, the end of Allied influence in Germany, and a Soviet diplomatic victory of major proportions. This, clearly, was the first open test of strength between the West and the Soviet Union.

Rejecting the suggestion that the army send armed convoys and fight its way into Berlin, Truman approved a more ingenious and less risky plan—to supply West Berlin by air and thereby force the Russians to make the decision for peace or war. Soon afterward, Truman sent two groups of B-29 bombers to English bases. While the siege of Berlin lasted, from June 1948 to May 1949, the British RAF and the United States Air Force accomplished a miracle. The airlift was soon carrying a daily average of 4,000 tons of supplies, including quantities of coal, to the western sectors of Berlin. All told, British and American planes made over 277,000 flights and carried nearly 2.5 million tons of supplies, enough to sustain the outpost.

The airlift succeeded, but it was no permanent solution. That would have to come through diplomacy. The Americans, British, and French began negotiations in July 1948, but efforts at compromise were impeded by Russian insistence that there be no West German unification without Soviet participation and by Allied refusal to discuss this larger issue so long as the blockade was in effect.

Russia finally yielded and lifted the blockade in May 1949, in return for Allied agreement to hold a prompt meeting of the Council of Foreign Ministers in Paris. Although the Paris conference brought no important agreement on Germany, it did reveal Soviet indecision and obvious unity among the Allied powers. Indeed, by 1949, the Berlin crisis and Western unity led directly toward another important step in the cold war: the formation of Soviet and American alliance systems. In January 1948, British Foreign Secretary Ernest Bevin, in a speech in the House of Commons, announced his country's readiness to join a Western European union. Great Britain, France, the Netherlands, Belgium, and Luxembourg signed a fifty-year treaty of economic cooperation and military alliance at Brussels in March and quickly established machinery to speed such collaboration. A Council of Europe, created in January 1949, included not only the Brussels powers but

DIVIDED GERMANY AND AUSTRIA

FEDERAL REPUBLIC OF GERMANY — FULLY SOVEREIGN ON MAY 5, 1955

GERMAN DEMOCRATIC REPUBLIC

FORMERLY GERMAN TERRITORY UNDER U.S.S.R. AND POLISH ADMIN.

SOVIET UNION

DENMARK

Danzig

EAST PRUSSIA

Hamburg (U.S.)

Bremen (U.S.)

Stettin

Berlin (JOINT OCCUP.)

SOVIET ZONE

Warsaw

NETHERLANDS

BRITISH ZONE

P O L A N D

Cologne

Bonn

BELGIUM

LUX.

SAAR

FRENCH ZONE

EAST GERMANY

WEST

Leipzig

Dresden

Prague

CZECHOSLOVAKIA

Frankfurt

Nuremberg

UNITED STATES ZONE

FRANCE

Stuttgart

Freibourg

Munich

REPUBLIC OF AUSTRIA — REGAINED FULL SOVEREIGNTY JULY 27, 1955

(U.S.S.R.)

Vienna (JOINT OCCUP.)

(U.S.)

(FR.) A U S T R (BR.)

Graz

HUNG.

SWITZERLAND

ITALY

YUGOSL.

100 MILES

BERLIN'S CHANNELS TO THE WEST

AIR CORRIDORS
RAILROADS
HIGHWAYS
WATERWAYS

50 MILES

BALTIC SEA

WEST

Hamburg

EAST

Stettin

POLAND

Hannover

BERLIN (JOINT OCCUP.)

GERMANY

Helmstedt

Potsdam

GERMANY

Leipzig

Frankfurt

CZECHOSL.

DIVIDED GREATER BERLIN

FRENCH SECTOR

TEGEL AIRFIELD

BRITISH SECTOR

SOVIET SECTOR

GATOW AIRFIELD

TEMPELHOF AIRFIELD

SCHOENFIELD AIRFIELD

UNITED STATES SECTOR

5 MILES

T.R.M.

Italy, Ireland, Denmark, Norway, Sweden, the Saar, and the German Federal Republic as well.

Western European leaders now turned to Washington. The Vandenberg Resolution, adopted by the Senate in June 1948, had implicitly promised American cooperation. Negotiations looking toward an Atlantic alliance began in the American capital in July. A draft treaty was completed in December and signed in April 1949 by representatives of the United States, Britain, France, Italy, the Netherlands, Belgium, Canada, Iceland, Luxembourg, Denmark, Norway, and Portugal. This North Atlantic Treaty declared that an armed attack against any member in Europe, North America, or French Algeria would be considered an attack against all signatories. It also looked forward to the creation of joint military forces under the aegis of a North Atlantic Treaty Organization (NATO). Congress in September 1949 approved the Mutual Defense Assistance Act appropriating $1 billion for arms and equipment for the signatories and an additional $211 million for Greece and Turkey.

One meaning in these momentous events stood out above all others. In signing the North Atlantic Treaty, the United States revealed a determination to abandon its historic traditions against alliances and do what was necessary to protect Western Europe. President Truman and Secretary Acheson had wisely drawn Republican as well as Democratic senators into the negotiations. Consequently, a solid bipartisan phalanx overwhelmed the opposition when debate opened in the Senate on the Atlantic alliance in July 1949. It approved the pact without reservation on July 21 by a vote of 82 to 13.

CHAPTER 22

The Triumph
of Anticommunism

The years following the signing of the North Atlantic Treaty were a period of rising tensions at home and abroad, which were in turn a direct result of the onset of the cold war. The North Korean invasion of South Korea and the American and Chinese interventions in the ensuing war raised the stakes by extending the doctrine of containment from Europe to Asia. Soviet-American relations further deteriorated after the inauguration of Dwight D. Eisenhower: efforts to restrain escalating military competition between the two superpowers were generally unsuccessful. The cold war also had extensive political implications inside the United States, where the emergence of a domestic anti-Communist consensus bolstered Republican strength and inaugurated a period in which dissent and radicalism became equated with communism.

1. ORIGINS OF THE KOREAN WAR

Despite the conviction that the United States could not keep spending billions on foreign aid, the Truman administration continued to enjoy large bipartisan support for its policy of assistance to Western Europe. Truman also won considerable Republican support in 1950 in obtaining $35 million to launch a program, called Point Four, to check communism by rendering technical assistance to underdeveloped areas.

Yet, by 1950, communism had become a major domestic political issue. Nothing disrupted the political peace more than the impact of developments in Asia on American public opinion. The Truman administration probably would have followed Great Britain, India, and other powers in recognizing the People's Republic of China had Beijing not launched a violent campaign in late 1949 to expel American diplomats, missionaries, and private interests. Bitter anti-Beijing sentiment in the United States was exacerbated by a so-called China lobby and by a Republican campaign to discredit the administration and force it to extend military assistance to the Chinese Nationalists on Taiwan.

The State Department, in 1949, washed its hands of responsibility for the Chinese debacle by releasing a white paper that blamed the Nationalists for their own defeat. The president, in January 1950, reaffirmed his determination not to be drawn into Chinese affairs, even if that resulted in Communist capture of Taiwan. And, a week later, Secretary of State Dean Acheson, who had succeeded Marshall in January 1949, announced what was in effect a new American policy in the Far East. The United States, he declared, would protect a "defensive perimeter" that ran from the Aleutians to Japan, the Ryukyus, and the Philippines. Japan, as American strategists saw it, would become the pivotal center of a new American presence in the western Pacific. But aggression against areas outside the perimeter—Korea, Taiwan, and southeast Asia—would have to be met by the peoples involved and by the United Nations.

This speech gave new impetus to the Republican attack. It took an extreme turn as Senators McCarthy, Taft, Kenneth S. Wherry of Nebraska, and other GOP spokesmen opened a campaign to drive Acheson from office and prove that the State Department was riddled with Communists and fellow travelers who, as Taft put it, had "surrendered to every demand of Russia . . . and promoted at every opportunity the Communist cause in China." This violent assault wrecked the previous bipartisan policy, made the formulation of a rational Far Eastern program impossible just when it was most needed, and raised grave doubts abroad about the quality of American leadership.

Other developments contributed to even greater soul searching. Truman's revelation in September 1949 that Russia had detonated a nuclear device upset the assumptions of American defensive strategy. It also renewed a fierce debate in administration circles, particularly between physicists J. Robert Oppenheimer and Edward Teller, over the development of a hydrogen bomb, potentially a thousand times more powerful than the atomic bombs that had destroyed Hiroshima and Nagasaki. When Truman announced in January 1950 that he had ordered the AEC to proceed with work on the hydrogen bomb, thoughtful Americans were stunned by the gloomy prospects, even while agreeing that their government had no recourse. The American people were entering, as Acheson put it, a new era of "total diplomacy," in which their fortitude and wisdom would be put to severe and numerous tests.

Not many months after Acheson spoke, an invasion of South Korea threatened world peace and sorely taxed American capacities. Although Roosevelt had decided that a postwar Korea should become independent from Japan, he had formed no concrete policy, even though Japan and Russia had fought a war for control of this strategic peninsula in 1904–1905 and Russian dominance there would gravely threaten Japanese security. Russian troops had entered northern Korea in August 1945; American forces had occupied southern Korea in September. The two powers agreed to divide their occupation zones at the thirty-eighth parallel, which runs north of the capital city of Seoul.

American leaders assumed that the Korean people would soon organize a government and that all occupation forces would thereupon be withdrawn. The Soviets in fact approved a plan in December 1945 to create a Korean government guided by a joint American-Soviet commission. But Russian representatives on the commission blocked all efforts at unification, established a Communist "people's government" in North Korea, and trained and equipped an army of 150,000 men. The United States then appealed to the UN General Assembly, which established a Temporary Commission on Korea in November 1947. It visited Seoul in January 1948 and, after being denied entry into the Soviet zone, held elections in South Korea. A constituent assembly met in July 1948, adopted a constitution, and elected Syngman Rhee as president. The UN, the United States, and other non-Communist powers recognized Rhee's regime as the only lawful government of Korea. Washington, following the advice of the Joint Chiefs of Staff and of General MacArthur in Japan, withdrew its last troops from South Korea in June 1949. It also gave substantial assistance to Rhee's government.

This, in general, was the situation when North Korean forces crossed the thirty-eighth parallel in an all-out invasion of South Korea at 4 A.M., Korean time, on June 25, 1950. The Soviet government's precise role and objectives remain unclear. In all likelihood, the withdrawal of American troops and Acheson's statement that Korea lay outside the Far Eastern defense perimeter of the United States encouraged a belief on the part of the North Koreans, and perhaps the Soviets, that the United States would not fight to repel an invasion.

News of the war reached Washington at 9:26 P.M., June 24, Washington time. Acheson held hurried conferences and called the president (who was then in Independence, Missouri) at about midnight. Truman agreed that the secretary should bring the matter before the UN Security Council at once. By the following afternoon, when the Council met in emergency session, it was evident that North Korea had launched not a border raid but a full-scale war. With the Russian representative absent, the Council, by a vote of nine to zero, adopted a resolution which condemned the invasion as aggression and demanded withdrawal of Communist troops from South Korea.

Truman hastened to Washington on June 25 and conferred immediately with civilian and military advisers. He ordered the Seventh Fleet to protect Taiwan and directed General MacArthur to furnish arms and limited air support to South Korea. After hearing the views of his advisers, Truman subsequently announced that American naval and air forces in the Far East would render full assistance to the South Koreans. Events now moved swiftly to a climax. Truman summoned congressional leaders to the White House on June 27 and told them of his decision to resist the invasion and his determination to secure United Nations support for a collective effort. The Security Council that same day adopted an American-sponsored resolution calling upon member nations to render all necessary assistance to the Republic of Korea. On June 29 and 30, it became evident that the North Koreans would quickly overrun the peninsula unless American forces stopped them. Making a difficult decision, Truman sent two divisions of ground troops from Japan to South Korea and authorized a naval blockade of North Korea. This action was approved by the Joint Chiefs of Staff, the State Department, General MacArthur, and other advisers, all of whom assumed that American intervention would turn the tide and would not provoke Soviet or Chinese participation.

2. THE KOREAN WAR

Truman's decision to intervene earned him, at least for the time being, widespread popular support. Republican leaders like Governor Dewey and John Foster Dulles were effusive in praise. Members of the House of Representatives stood and cheered when they learned that the president had ordered air and naval forces to defend South Korea. Even Senator Taft declared that he would vote for a resolution authorizing use of American forces in Korea, although he opposed Truman's acting without formal congressional approval. Meanwhile, the Security Council established a UN command and requested the American government to name a commander in chief. Some nineteen nations soon made a military contribution, and by the end of 1950, British, Turkish, Australian, and Philippine troops were fighting alongside Americans and South Koreans, with General MacArthur in command.

Meanwhile, North Korean troops almost overran the entire peninsula before American power could be brought to bear. They had pressed the defenders into Korea's southeastern corner by September 12 and were threatening to drive them from Pusan, their remaining supply port. But UN defenses stiffened and held firm, and MacArthur counterattacked with large reinforcements on September 15, making a daring landing on the North Korean flank at Inchon. He soon recaptured Seoul, reoccupied southern Korea, and destroyed or captured more than half the invaders. UN forces had reached the thirty-eighth parallel by October 1 and were preparing to launch an invasion of North Korea.

Having cleared South Korea, victorious allied forces halted at the thirty-eighth parallel until the General Assembly of the United Nations, on October 7, 1950, called upon MacArthur to take all necessary steps to establish UN control throughout Korea. Although the Chinese foreign minister informed the Indian

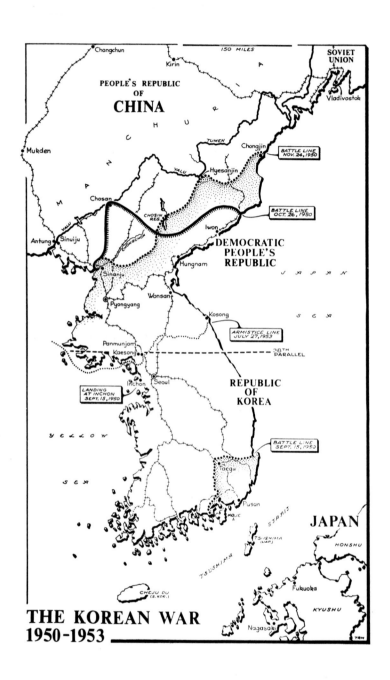

THE KOREAN WAR
1950-1953

ambassador in Peking that "if the U.S. or U.N. forces crossed the Thirty-eighth Parallel, China would send troops to the Korean frontier to defend North Korea," few took the threat seriously. MacArthur assured Truman that there was little danger of Chinese intervention and promised a great slaughter if China's armies entered the fight.

MacArthur's forces drove triumphantly northward toward the Yalu River separating Korea from Manchuria. Just as it seemed that North Korean resistance had entirely collapsed, advanced American troops encountered large Chinese units fifty miles south of the Yalu in late October. Later reconnaissance revealed that China had massed armies of some 850,000 men in Manchuria and moved advanced units into northern Korea. While Chinese soldiers skirmished defensively, the Security Council heard Peking's representatives demand prompt American withdrawal from Korea.

MacArthur, on November 24, launched an offensive to drive the Chinese beyond the Yalu and end the war before Christmas. In this action he violated the spirit, if not the letter of his instructions. It was the Washington government's policy to send only South Korean troops into this area in order to avoid provoking the Chinese. MacArthur's decision was also a nearly fatal strategic blunder, for he drove his men into a huge trap. The Chinese counterattacked on November 26 and split the center of the UN line, held by South Korean troops. The United States Eighth Army on the western flank withdrew in an orderly retreat toward the thirty-eighth parallel, but X Corps on the northeastern flank was isolated and cut off. It took the unit two weeks of desperate fighting to reach the port of Hungnam. From there, X Corps was evacuated and transferred to the main defensive line north of the thirty-eighth parallel, in one of modern warfare's most spectacular operations.

3. DOMESTIC DEBATE AND THE KOREAN ARMISTICE

In clear response to the heightened level of Soviet-American tension and to the perception of the need to contain Soviet expansionism, the Truman administration made a crucial decision to remobilize the United States. This historic change was clearly enunciated in an influential document, NSC-68, written by Paul Nitze of the State Department's Policy Planning Staff during the spring of 1950. Nitze, drawing on Kennan's conception of the roots of Soviet expansionism, argued that the United States had to be prepared to respond to communism around the world. The Soviets, and world communism, were motivated by a "fanatic faith, antithetical to our own," which sought to "impose its absolute authority over the rest of the world." A proper American response, according to Nitze, was preparation for long-term military and diplomatic competition with the Soviets. He proposed a wholesale militarization of peacetime society that would increase defense appropriations from an average of $15 billion to $30 to $40 billion a year.

The outbreak of the Korean War inspired broad political support for a program of remilitarization. In August 1950, Congress approved the Defense Production Act. This measure, which announced a determination to "oppose acts of aggression and . . . to develop and maintain whatever military and economic strength is found to be necessary," empowered the president to determine allocations and priorities, authorize tax incentives to encourage defense production, including the construction of industrial plants, and impose limited price and sweeping credit controls. Congress also approved plans to double the armed forces from 1.5 million to 3 million men by mid-1951. It adopted a revenue bill designed to raise nearly $4.5 billion in additional income and corporate taxes, and it appropriated another $12.6 billion for defense and over $5 billion for military assistance.

This increase in defense expenditures established a new level which remained high even after the Korean armistice in 1953. The militarization of American society and the rise of a national security state that accompanied it brought several clear consequences. It stimulated the growth of what Eisenhower later called the "military-industrial complex" and committed the United States, historically a nation without large peacetime forces, to support a buildup of both nuclear and conventional forces. It also spawned an array of new executive agencies, the most important of which was the National Security Agency. Their primary duty was to wage the cold war through diplomatic, military, and sometimes covert means. All of these presidentially controlled agencies, moreover, caused further erosion of congressional control over foreign policy.

It would be perhaps easy for the historian to conclude that Americans made this transition from isolation to global involvement calmly and wisely. The truth is, however, that the people nearly lost their heads, the Truman administration nearly lost control of foreign policy, and the United States almost lost its allies as a result of a domestic debate and of the events that followed the Chinese intervention in Korea.

The debate began in November 1950, when Senator Taft, reacting to Truman's announcement that he would send additional divisions to Europe, proposed a reexamination of foreign and military policies. Fundamentally, Taft questioned whether the defense of Western Europe was essential to American security. Former President Hoover subsequently declared that the United States should defend the Atlantic all the way to Great Britain and the Pacific all the way to Japan, but should withdraw troops and withhold further support until Western Europe had organized and equipped sufficient forces to withstand a Russian assault. These were only two indications of the surging growth of Republican neoisolationism, based partly upon fear of excessive governmental spending and the expansion of presidential power.

The debate exploded with exceptional bitterness in January 1951, when Senator Kenneth S. Wherry of Nebraska offered a resolution declaring that "no ground forces of the United States should be assigned to duty in the European area for the purposes of the North Atlantic Treaty pending the adoption of a policy with respect thereto by Congress." Administration and military spokesmen replied that defense of Western Europe was essential to defense of the United States. General Eisenhower returned from his command in Paris to report to Congress that Western European nations could build a strong anti-Soviet barrier if America did not desert them. Even so, debate raged on, and the issue was long in doubt, especially after a majority of House Republicans signed a manifesto in February endorsing Hoover's proposals. Although the Senate in April reaffirmed American commitments under the North Atlantic Treaty by approving the dispatch of four more divisions to Europe, it warned Truman not to send additional troops without further congressional approval.

This furor was nothing as compared with that of the so-called MacArthur affair. The conflict between Truman and MacArthur first centered around relations between the United States and Nationalist China. MacArthur made a widely publicized visit to Taiwan in July 1950. He then sent a message to the annual convention of the Veterans of Foreign Wars in August which called for the incorporation of Taiwan into the American security system and talked about "offensive strategy" in the Far East. Truman was shocked and considered relieving the general of his command. Instead, he met MacArthur on Wake Island in October, again explained that he had no intention of becoming involved in the Chinese civil war, and warned the general to make no more provocative statements.

Although temporarily silenced, after the Chinese intervention MacArthur began a campaign to force the administration to permit him to bomb Chinese bases in Manchuria. Truman replied by forbidding the release of any statement on foreign policy by civilian or military officials without prior approval by the State Department. During the following weeks, when the Chinese and North Koreans seemed about to drive UN forces from Korea, MacArthur suggested that the United States blockade the Chinese coast, bombard China by air and sea, and support a Nationalist invasion from Taiwan.

The issue was decided when the American Eighth Army halted the enemy drive in Korea and began a limited offensive in January 1951. With the UN presence in Korea secure, Truman and the Joint Chiefs quickly agreed upon a policy of conducting a limited war designed to maintain the integrity of South Korea, but one which would avert the danger of a general war with China—"the wrong war, at the wrong place, at the wrong time, and with the wrong enemy," as General Omar N. Bradley, chairman of the Joint Chiefs of Staff, later called it. Full-scale war with China might absorb all available manpower and resources and thus invite a Russian attack on Western Europe; limited war might inflict such punishment on Chinese and North Korean forces that they would have to abandon their aggression and thereby acknowledge a defeat that would vindicate the principle of collective security. NATO leaders fully shared these convictions.

MacArthur, however, was temperamentally incapable of accepting the concept of a limited war. Believing that America's destiny lay in Asia, he was prepared to abandon Europe to its inevitable doom. Blundering, if not treasonable, political leadership, MacArthur maintained, was depriving America of an opportunity to settle the Far Eastern question for generations to come. He therefore resorted to extreme measures. Informed on March 20, 1951, that the president was about to attempt to settle the Korean conflict by diplomacy, MacArthur issued a public statement calculated to prevent a peaceful settlement. Then, in reply to a letter from the House minority leader, Joseph W. Martin, Jr., of Massachusetts, the general called for a war to defeat communism in the Far East. "We must win," he concluded. "There is no substitute for victory."

Martin read this letter to the House of Representatives on April 5. The country was now convulsed by a frenetic Republican campaign to force the administration to adopt MacArthur's proposals for a victory offensive in Korea and possible war against China. Publication of MacArthur's letter was an open challenge to Truman's foreign policy by a military commander who had joined hands with the opposition. On April 10, Truman relieved MacArthur of his commands in Japan and Korea.

The recall of a general who, in the eyes of millions, was the greatest living American required courage. And all the furies of hell seemed abroad in the country in consequence. Republicans, the China lobby, and many commentators poured out streams of invective and abuse. MacArthur, with a large entourage, returned to his native land for the first time in more than a decade. He made triumphal tours in San Francisco, Chicago, New York, and Washington and basked in the warmth of popular applause. The peak of his triumphal return was an address to a joint session of Congress. Congressional leaders agreed that the Senate Armed Services Committee should investigate MacArthur's recall and review American policy. The committee heard more than 2 million words of testimony from MacArthur, Bradley, Acheson, and dozens of others during May and June 1951. Headed by Richard B. Russell of Georgia, the committee tolerated no nonsense, and the inquiry ended in a vindication of the administration.

In retrospect, we can see that the MacArthur affair cleared the air of popular confusion over Far Eastern policy. The United States neither adopted MacArthur's program nor abandoned Korea. In a limited war, it sought to inflict high casualties upon, and break the morale and discipline of, the Chinese and North Korean armies. Unification of Korea remained a political and diplomatic objective. But, as it had never been a military objective, the UN could accept a compromise that provided for Communist withdrawal above the thirty-eighth parallel. In short, the United States would fight a limited war for limited objectives to avert the risk of world conflict.

Meanwhile, on several fronts, the Americans had moved to convince the North Koreans and Chinese that a settlement would be to their advantage. Secretary Acheson won United Nations approval in May 1951 of an embargo against the shipment of arms, munitions, and critical raw materials to China. He made it clear that the United States would strenuously oppose Beijing's effort to join the UN and would prevent China's seizure of Taiwan. In Korea, UN forces repulsed two major offensives in April and May 1951 with staggering losses to the attackers. By midyear, it appeared that American policy was succeeding. The Communists had suffered over a million casualties; the best Chinese armies had been decimated; and China was isolated diplomatically and economically from the non-Communist world and and had no hope of forcing a military decision.

Moreover, Chinese hostility confirmed American determination to conclude a peace treaty with Japan that would both restore its sovereignty and make it the cornerstone of a new security system in the far Pacific. Negotiations directed by John Foster Dulles, Republican adviser to the State Department, proceeded smoothly during 1950 and 1951. The Soviets objected, but their opposition only strengthened Western unity and facilitated the signing of a "peace of reconciliation" in San Francisco in September 1951. The treaty stripped Japan of its overseas empire but was extraordinarily generous in all other respects. It imposed no restrictions upon Japanese economic development, levied no reparations, and recognized Japan's right to rearm. By this time a new security system in the Pacific had taken shape. The United States concluded a mutual defense treaty with the Philippines in August and a tripartite security treaty with Australia and New Zealand in September. A security treaty with Japan that same month permitted the United States to maintain land, sea, and air bases in Japanese territory.

When it became clear to both sides that a military victory was not possible, truce negotiations began in July 1951. The Chinese and Koreans in November 1951 dropped their demand for UN withdrawal southward to the thirty-eighth parallel and accepted the American demand for demarcation along the military line at the time an armistice was signed. But, in October 1952, these negotiations were broken off after the Communists demanded the forcible delivery of some 46,000 Chinese and North Koreans who did not wish to go home. Only after the inauguration of the new Eisenhower administration was the impasse ended. Eisenhower and Dulles were determined to use nuclear weapons to resolve the stalemate, and the Chinese knew this fact. Rather than face nuclear weapons, the Chinese and South Koreans yielded, and an armistice was signed at Panmunjom on July 27, 1953. It ended the Korean War, a military conflict that had cost the United States 54,246 dead, 103,284 wounded, and billions of dollars.

4.   THE "NEW LOOK"

By 1952, many Americans believed that Roosevelt and Truman had made a series of disastrous blunders: conceding too much at Yalta, allowing the Soviets to solidify their control over Eastern Europe and develop nuclear weapons, permitting a Communist triumph in China, and bogging down in an indecisive war in Korea. To these Americans, the Democratic policy of containment now seemed a defensive policy, and they were receptive to the Republican call in 1952 for a "new look" in foreign policy.

The chief spokesman for the new look was John Foster Dulles, who served as secretary of state from 1953 until a fatal illness forced his retirement in 1959. An experienced diplomat and international lawyer, grandson of one secretary of state and the nephew of another, Dulles was eminently qualified for his important post. In office, Dulles possessed abundant energy, profound self-assurance, and a domineering personality. He was seldom plagued by doubt, and it was often difficult to distinguish between his moral certitude and self-righteousness. Most important, he enjoyed the complete confidence of President Eisenhower.

Yet Dulles was also a controversial secretary of state, often because of his rhetorical excesses. In the foreign-policy sections of the GOP platform of 1952, which he drafted, Dulles condemned Yalta by promising to repudiate all "secret understandings," indicted the Democrats for "neglect of the Far East," and promised that Republicans would find a "dynamic" substitute for the "negative, futile, and immoral" policy of containment. Later he confidently predicted a "rollback" of Soviet power in Eastern Europe and "liberation" of countries under Soviet domination. He also helped to popularize the notion that Chiang Kai-shek and his Nationalist forces on Taiwan should be "unleashed" to recover China.

It was bold rhetoric, but the Eisenhower administration did not have a workable alternative to containment. In fact, the basic principles of Truman-Acheson diplomacy—regional alliances, collective security, foreign aid, and support of the UN—not only were maintained but also were extended after 1953. It could hardly have been otherwise. Both Eisenhower and Dulles had helped to formulate American policy during and after World War II. Both were firmly committed to the postwar system of alliances and mutual obligations. The extreme revisions advocated by neoisolationists were totally unacceptable to the new president and secretary of state. Any changes which they undertook would be made within the framework of internationalism and collective security.

Eisenhower and Dulles shaped a defense policy aimed at achieving the power to deter most attacks. The United States, as Dulles put it, would "retaliate, instantly, by means and at places of our choosing." A massive nuclear arsenal, combined with leaner conventional forces, gave defense policy a new degree of flexibility. It permitted economy—a prime goal of the new administration—by obviating the need to deploy extensive ground forces against potential attacks.

As a result of advancing technology and the increasing importance of air power, the Eisenhower administration effected substantial reductions in defense spending between 1953 and 1956. The army dwindled from a postwar peak of 1.5 million men in 1953 to less than 900,000 by 1960; navy personnel (including marines), from over 1 million to less than 800,000. Army expenditures dropped from $17 billion in 1953 to an annual average of under $10 billion in 1955–1960. Naval expenditures were reduced from almost $12 billion in 1953 to $9.7 billion in 1955 and 1956, and then began to rise. Air force expenditures, in contrast, mounted steadily from $15 billion in 1953 to over $19 billion in 1959.

Air power, of course, figured most prominently in Eisenhower's defense system. Concentration on the air arm was doubly attractive to policy makers. It offered savings through reduced manpower and equipment for ground and naval forces, and it seemed to provide a way to meet aggression without the heavy commitment of troops and attendant casualties. But technological change was nowhere more dynamic than in the field of aviation, and maintaining an up-to-date air force belied hopes for economy. Greater range, maneuverability, and firepower likewise added to rapid turnover and mounting costs of combat planes—as did other advances like aerial refueling, all-weather navigational and bombing systems, and air-to-air and air-to-surface rockets. All these improvements were eclipsed in the late 1950s by progress in missile development. Intercontinental (ICBM) and intermediate-range (IRBM) ballistic missiles promised to supplement, and perhaps eventually replace, the manned bombers of the Strategic Air Command as America's ultimate offensive weapon.

By the late 1950s, the new look in defense policy had lost much of its luster. Despite efforts at economy, expensive new weapons and research programs more than offset savings in manpower and conventional equipment. The administration slashed its military program drastically in 1958 by, among other things, retiring nearly one hundred warships and eliminating five tactical wings from the air force. Four army divisions, two proposed missile commands, and several antiaircraft battalions were also pared from the rolls.

At the same time, Eisenhower's emphasis on economy coincided with growing public alarm about Soviet nuclear superiority. When the Russians test-fired their first ICBM—a year before the United States had done so—and then launched the *Sputnik* space satellite in 1957, angry critics accused the administration of complete failure. It had first weakened conventional forces and limited-war capability in the interest of economy and nuclear air power, they claimed, and then fallen so far behind Russia that a dangerous "missile gap" now existed. Defense expenditures rose in response; they reached record peacetime highs of over $45 billion annually from 1959 through 1961. But public confidence, despite official reassurances, was badly shaken.

Actually, the state of American defenses was sounder than critics claimed. Progress in some aspects of missile development lagged behind Russia's, but

American strength was clearly sufficient, at any time during the Eisenhower era, to deter an all-out Soviet attack and, failing that, to retaliate with crushing effectiveness. It is probably true that less concern for economy would have advanced the missile and space programs and reassured the nation's allies about its ability to fight limited wars by nonnuclear means. But the overshadowing fact of the decade was that both the Soviet Union and the United States were acquiring and enlarging nuclear arsenals capable of destroying each other and possibly the rest of the world as well.

5. SOVIET-AMERICAN RELATIONS, 1953–1960

The inauguration of President Eisenhower virtually coincided with the death, on March 5, 1953, of Josef Stalin. The vacuum thus created at the top of the Soviet hierarchy, after twenty-five years of dictatorial rule, led to a long struggle for control in which power was shared and a number of pretenders attempted to consolidate power. By 1957, however, it was clear that the one who was increasingly solidifying his power with each shake-up was Nikita S. Khrushchev, first secretary of the Communist party's Central Committee. Khrushchev became premier in 1958.

Primarily because of the uncertainties of the post-Stalin succession, the Soviet leaders undertook a less aggressive foreign policy. They talked of relaxing tensions, evinced a seeming readiness to negotiate deadlocked questions, and hinted at concessions. They also began to speak of the "peaceful coexistence" of socialist and capitalist nations. Prime Minister Churchill had long urged a four-power summit conference to ease tensions, but the Soviets and Americans had responded slowly and cautiously. When Russia agreed in May 1955 to conclude a treaty restoring Austria's independence and ending the four-power occupation, it did much to persuade the West that the new Soviet leaders genuinely desired better relations. Plans for a summit meeting were quickly drawn, and President Eisenhower, Soviet Premier Nikolai A. Bulganin, Prime Minister Anthony Eden of Great Britain, and Premier Edgar Faure of France met at Geneva in July 1955 to define and review the issues dividing East and West. It was the first time that an American and a Soviet chief of state had talked directly since Truman's meeting with Stalin at Potsdam ten years before.

The Geneva meeting raised high hopes. Its relaxed atmosphere, encouraged by an abundance of vodka, martinis, and mutual cordiality, seemed to suggest that a major turn for the better in world affairs was taking place at last. The Soviet leaders, smiling and seemingly well disposed, made a favorable impression. They were obviously impressed in their turn by Eisenhower's manifest good will and desire for peace. These feelings of harmony, often invoked as the "spirit of Geneva," remained in evidence for over a year and kept hopes alive for an East-West détente.

Actually, the summit conference amounted to little more than an earnest gesture. It had been decided in advance that the heads of government would try to identify rather than solve the pressing issues, and agree, if possible, only upon methods to be followed. The four leaders defined the paramount problems as German reunification, European security, disarmament, and greater East-West contact. They recommended free elections in Germany, a general treaty renouncing force or aid to aggressors, pursuit of disarmament through the UN, and elimination of barriers to the flow of people and ideas between East and West. A follow-up conference of foreign ministers in Geneva in late 1955 was no more successful in finding agreement on these issues.

In 1957, the Soviets, inaugurating another peace offensive, pushed for a second summit meeting. Following a preliminary meeting of foreign ministers in 1958, Khrushchev visited the United States in September 1959. His American tour ended in such a friendly mood, induced especially by private talks between the premier and president at the latter's mountain retreat west of Washington, Camp David, that observers soon began speaking hopefully of the "spirit of Camp David." But this spirit proved even more illusory and short-lived than that of Geneva. Well in advance of the summit meeting, scheduled to open in Paris in May 1960, it became evident that little would be achieved there. The powers had made slight progress toward agreement on a nuclear test ban but none whatever on German reunification, Berlin, or arms control. Khrushchev's general posture for some weeks before the conference did not augur well for its success.

Two weeks before it opened, a high-altitude American U-2 reconnaissance plane was shot down over the interior of the Soviet Union. Washington at first claimed that a routine weather flight from an overseas base near the Soviet border had gone astray. Then Khrushchev revealed that the pilot had been captured and had freely confessed that aerial espionage was the real purpose of the flight. The American government not only admitted this but added, in a display of frankness that amazed foreign diplomats, that such photoreconnaissance flights had been taking place over Soviet territory since 1956.

Khrushchev came to Paris in a dangerous temper. He voiced all manner of threats, not only against the United States but against nations that permitted "spy flights" to take off or land on their soil. (The U-2 aircraft in question had been flying across Russia from Pakistan to Norway.) He demanded that Eisenhower apologize for these violations of Soviet air space and promise their immediate discontinuance. He added that, whatever the United States did about the U-2 flights, it would be necessary to cancel Eisenhower's scheduled visit to the Soviet Union in June because the Soviet people were too upset by the recent episode to greet the American president with proper "cordiality."

Eisenhower ordered suspension of the flights but refused to apologize. His own temper mounted wrathfully as Khrushchev's diatribes continued, and the efforts of Prime Minister Harold Macmillan of Great Britain and President

Charles de Gaulle of France to restore harmony and save the meeting were futile. It broke up in mutual frustration and anger before it actually convened.

Many observers felt that Khrushchev had used the U-2 incident as a pretext for disrupting a conference that he no longer saw an advantage in attending. Certainly the propaganda value of the affair was of greater benefit to him than the inevitable deadlock would have been. Despite his anger, the Soviet premier spoke in favor of a summit conference at some future date—adding, however, that it could not take place while Eisenhower was president. Eisenhower left office, therefore, with Soviet-American relations at a low point and the record of summit diplomacy a distinct failure.

A similar degree of frustration also characterized attempts to reduce or control nuclear weapons. In 1953, Eisenhower and Dulles renewed attempts to negotiate an arms control agreement. Various UN commissions had tried since 1946 to produce such agreements, but progress had been stymied by unyielding attitudes on both sides. Although both the NATO powers and the Soviet Union said that they favored disarmament, a fundamental difference separated their views. The Western allies, not trusting the Soviet Union, had insisted that disarmament could neither begin nor proceed except under an effective system of international inspection and control. The Soviets had flatly rejected this approach and hammered away on a sweeping formula of their own: immediate abolition of atomic weapons, a one-third across-the-board reduction in conventional forces by all countries, and abandonment by every nation of all military bases on foreign territory. Since this would, in effect, abolish the Strategic Air Command and debilitate NATO while the Red Army retained its decisive numerical superiority, the West found it unacceptable.

Although shifts, new proposals, and partial concessions on both sides marked negotiations from 1953 to 1960, this basic pattern of negotiation did not change. None of the various Western proposals for "phased" and controlled disarmament or international inspection was acceptable to the Soviets, whose deep-seated dislike of opening their country to foreign observation stemmed in part from fear of espionage. For this reason the Soviets also opposed Western suggestions for preventing surprise attacks, including Eisenhower's "open skies" plan put forth at Geneva in 1955. This plan proposed a complete exchange of information about military installations, equipment, and organization, and monitored but unrestricted aerial reconnaissance.

The superpowers came closest to accord on the issue of a nuclear test ban. World opinion justly regarded this as the least difficult and most imperative aspect of the disarmament controversy, especially since repeated tests by the United States, the Soviet Union, and Great Britain (which developed the hydrogen bomb in 1957) demonstrated the weapon's terrifying potential.

The Soviets soon made a test ban a principal item in their disarmament proposals, and gradually the two sides moved toward an agreement. The Soviet demand for a test ban culminated in a dramatic announcement in March 1958 that the USSR would suspend nuclear tests, although it reserved the right to resume them if other powers did not join the moratorium. After the United States countered by citing the need for verification, a panel of scientific experts from four Soviet-bloc states and four Western nations held closed meetings in Geneva in mid-1958. The scientists conducted their deliberations in a cooperative spirit and with remarkable objectivity and concluded that it was possible to establish a workable control system which would detect violations. The system required land-based control posts on every continent, including both Soviet and American territory, plus naval and air patrols and mobile inspection groups—all to be operated by an international agency.

The American and British governments now seized the initiative by announcing their willingness to negotiate a three-power treaty that would establish an international system of control and provide for permanent cessation of nuclear tests. The Soviets accepted the invitation in August 1958, and a three-power Conference on the Discontinuance of Nuclear Weapons Tests assembled in Geneva in October. Prospects for success seemed bright for a time, then dimmed in 1960. As in almost all previous negotiations, the issue of controls was the major obstacle. Despite agreement on general principles, the United States consistently held out for a more extensive system and a larger number of on-site inspections than the Soviet Union was willing to grant. The conferees continued their sessions in good spirit until the end of 1960. They gradually narrowed their differences and then recessed to await the inauguration of President Kennedy.

6. ORIGINS OF POSTWAR ANTICOMMUNISM

Soviet-American global competition, especially the onset of the Korean War, seemed to confirm growing suspicions about a worldwide Communist conspiracy. By that fateful day in June 1950 when North Korean Communists invaded South Korea, the American people had become consumed by fear of foreign infiltration of their government and institutions. This xenophobic obsession with a Communist conspiracy, what some historians have called the Second Red Scare, grew stronger before it weakened and left a residue of personal and partisan bitterness unparalleled since Reconstruction. In a time when Americans needed unity of will and purpose, its effects were tragically disruptive.

Fear of Communist infiltration after 1945 was in some measure justified. The rise and decline of American communism during the 1930s resulted in the success of underground party members in infiltrating key positions in the federal government (see Vol. I, pp. 329–330), and this infiltration continued unabated after 1941. Several events during 1945 and 1946 seemed to demonstrate extensive subversion. The Office of Strategic Services (OSS) discovered early in 1945 that certain of its most secret documents had fallen into the hands of Philip J.

Jaffe, editor of *Amerasia,* a Communist-sponsored magazine established for the purpose of influencing American policy in the Far East. OSS agents raided the *Amerasia* offices in March 1945 and found piles of diplomatic and military documents. The FBI then took jurisdiction and established an intimate connection between Jaffe and his associates and Soviet and Chinese Communist officials. Jaffe and an accomplice subsequently received light fines for conspiring to receive government property illegally. Even more jarring was the report issued in 1946 by a Canadian royal commission appointed to investigate charges of Communist espionage. The commission demonstrated that the Communist party in Canada was an arm of the Soviet government and exposed the operations of several Soviet spy rings. More important, it revealed that at least twenty-three Canadians in "positions of trust," one of them a member of Parliament, another a leading atomic scientist, were agents of the Communist ring and had sent atomic secrets and samples of uranium to Moscow.

These revelations spurred the FBI and security officers of Washington departments into action. In March 1947, President Truman issued an executive order which inaugurated a comprehensive investigation of all federal employees. Some features of the program evoked strong opposition from liberals. They charged that the government had introduced the principle of "guilt by association" and failed to provide adequate safeguards against dismissal on account of rumors and unknown accusers. On the whole, however, the administration showed considerable regard for justice and civil rights during its loyalty probe. The gigantic task was completed by early 1951. The Civil Service Commission cleared more than 3 million federal employees, while the FBI conducted some fourteen thousand full-scale investigations of doubtful cases. Over two thousand employees had resigned, and 212 persons had been dismissed on the ground that their loyalty was in reasonable doubt. In addition, Truman approved a bill in August 1950 authorizing the heads of ten so-called sensitive departments and agencies to dismiss persons who, though not necessarily disloyal, were deemed to be security risks. Those discharged might demand a hearing by the security board of their own agency but were denied the right of appeal to a review board.

In spite of the thoroughness and severity of the administration's loyalty probe, it was not enough to quiet popular alarm or prevent Republicans from exploiting the issue. This was pure demagoguery, but sensational exposures revealed the former extent of Communist infiltration and the devastating effectiveness of Soviet espionage in acquiring secrets vital to American security. The situation was especially poignant because Truman and several public leaders were drawn into a compromising position in one of the most celebrated cases in American history—the trial of Alger Hiss, ostensibly for perjury but actually for espionage.

Hiss, a member of an important Communist cell in Washington during the New Deal era, had risen rapidly through various departments to a position of considerable trust in the State Department. He had in a sense become the model of the able young civil servant. Among a host of friends, he could count a justice of the Supreme Court and a future secretary of state. Hiss resigned from the State Department in 1947 to accept the presidency of the Carnegie Endowment for International Peace.

Whittaker Chambers, a former Soviet agent, had denounced Hiss and other Communists to the State Department in 1939 but had failed to offer proof or even to describe the espionage network to which Hiss belonged. Events subsequently convinced Chambers that democracy and communism were engaged in a life-and-death struggle, and he told his story to the public and the House Un-American Activities Committee in 1948. Hiss sued for libel, and Chambers produced microfilms of sixty-five State Department documents that he said Hiss had passed to him in early 1938. Called before a federal grand jury in New York, Hiss denied that he had ever delivered such documents to Chambers. Hiss was then indicted for perjury and convicted in January 1950, after the first trial had ended in a hung jury. Added to the tragedy of Hiss was his betrayal of the president—who had earlier denounced the House committee's investigation as a "red herring"—and of a large body of distinguished public leaders who testified to his integrity. The Hiss trials, more than any other event, contributed to a growing public conviction that the Roosevelt and Truman administrations had been oblivious to the danger of Communist subversion.

Other shocks followed. While the rehabilitated House Un-American Activities Committee launched new investigations, a young employee in the Justice Department was arrested, tried, and convicted in 1948 for passing vital information on the FBI's counterespionage system to a Soviet agent. Further public outrage followed the revelation in 1950 that a group of Anglo-American agents had succeeded in delivering full information on the atomic bomb to the Soviet government from 1943 to 1947. One result was the trial of Julius and Ethel Rosenberg for espionage and their execution in 1953.

These disclosures and their implications set the stage for the spectacular rise of Joseph R. McCarthy of Wisconsin. Elected to the Senate in 1946, McCarthy had already acquired a reputation for moral callousness, doubtful integrity, and utter ruthlessness. He decided early in 1950 to use the issue of Communist infiltration to improve his ebbing political fortunes. By his indiscriminate and reckless attacks during the next four years, he won clear title as the most unprincipled man in public life since Aaron Burr and the most successful demagogue since Huey Long.

McCarthy opened his campaign on February 9, 1950, by announcing that he held in his hand the names of Communists in the State Department. Unable to identify a single one of these, McCarthy countered by naming Owen Lattimore of the Johns Hopkins University, an expert on the Far East, as leader of "the espionage ring in the State Department." When J. Edgar Hoover, head of the FBI, affirmed that there was no evidence to substantiate this charge, a special Senate committee headed by Millard Tydings of Maryland gave Lattimore a clean bill of health. Such failure only stirred McCarthy to more brutal attacks. He turned next against Philip C. Jessup, American representative in the General Assembly of the United Nations, charging savagely that this distinguished public servant had Communist connections. Then he assaulted Senator Tydings. Finally, McCarthy attacked Generals George C. Marshall and Dwight D. Eisenhower, both of whom he accused in June 1951 of assisting the Russians in their drive for world domination. Although McCarthy's anticommunism filled many with loathing, many Americans, frightened by revelations of Communist espionage and infiltration, were receptive to his message.

Moreover, Republican leaders encouraged the Wisconsin demagogue and used him with telling effect. "McCarthyism"—temporarily, at least—won the approval, if not the open endorsement, of the GOP, and the summer and autumn of 1950 witnessed one of the bitterest congressional campaigns in American history. Republicans did not openly repudiate the Korean intervention, but they charged that Truman and Acheson had blundered so badly as to make that war inevitable. They also warned of further inflation, socialization, and federal aggrandizement if the Truman policies were not abandoned. But the main Republican issue was communism—the alleged Democratic failure to recognize and cope with Communist infiltration and influence in government. Not all Republican leaders followed McCarthy's example, but he clearly dominated the campaign. McCarthyites capitalized on discontent with Truman's policies and on obsessive anticommunism to defeat the veteran Democratic senator from Maryland, Millard Tydings. Similarly, Representative Richard M. Nixon exploited this fear in his successful campaign for a California Senate seat. Republican campaigners capitalized on the issue almost everywhere with considerable success.

The Democrats narrowly retained control of both houses in the election of 1950, but the overall result was a smashing reversal for the administration. Two Fair Deal stalwarts, Senators Frank P. Graham of North Carolina and Claude W. Pepper of Florida, had been defeated by anti-Truman conservatives in the primaries, while other Truman allies followed them into retirement after losing in the general election. An all-out Democratic effort to unseat Senator Taft in Ohio failed so dramatically as to make Taft a leading contender for the Republican nomination for the presidency in 1952. Even more important were three underlying developments—the return of the agrarian Middle West to the Republican fold, the obvious success of the Communist issue as a vote getter, and the fact that Republicans polled a larger total vote than Democrats in contests for House seats nationwide.

7.   EISENHOWER AND McCARTHYISM

National alarm over alleged Communists in government remained a major issue well into Eisenhower's first term (see p. 504). Anti-Communists were a bizarre cast of characters, but the central figure, the man who did most to shape the campaign and stamp it with his own personality and character, was still Senator McCarthy.

It was widely assumed that the inauguration of the Eisenhower administration would bring McCarthy's days of power and influence to an end. His reputation was based on savage and reckless attacks on the party in power. But, now that the Democrats were gone, how would the Wisconsin senator react? Confidence among Republican leaders that they could control McCarthy persisted for a few weeks after the election. Senator Taft, who disapproved of McCarthy while condoning his scurrilous attacks, believed that GOP strategists could now contain the Wisconsin demagogue. Taft planned to neutralize McCarthy by assigning the chairmanship of the Internal Security Committee, which would handle loyalty investigations, to the devoutly anti-Communist but colorless William Jenner of Indiana. Meanwhile, McCarthy could be relegated to obscurity as chairman of the innocuous Committee on Government Operations. "We've got McCarthy where he can't do any harm," Taft concluded.

This was as mistaken a judgment as the astute Ohioan ever made. McCarthy's new committee had a permanent subcommittee on investigations. Making himself chairman of the subcommittee, he quickly resumed his flamboyant crusade against Communists in government. For the next year and a half, McCarthy was rarely out of the headlines, and few men in public life were willing to challenge him when opinion polls reported in early 1954 that 50 percent of the people approved of McCarthy and another 21 percent "did not know." The Senate was reluctant to oppose him. More important, his own party, which had earlier encouraged his subversion-in-government charges, did not restrain him even now that it was a Republican bull he was goring. Even Eisenhower remained aloof. Desiring party harmony and disliking personal controversy—especially of the sort that McCarthy relished—Eisenhower also apparently hoped that forbearance and time would solve the problem with the least friction and damage.

The president's forbearance was sorely tested during his first eighteen months in office. McCarthy conducted a vituperative campaign against the appointment of Charles E. Bohlen as ambassador to Russia in 1953. Although Taft intervened to secure Bohlen's confirmation, the price of Bohlen's confirmation was the administration's promise to make no more diplomatic appointments without McCarthy's approval. The State Department appointed a McCarthy man as its security officer, thereby giving the senator from Wisconsin a hand in departmental personnel policy. McCarthy announced in March 1953 that he had "negotiated" an agreement with Greek shipowners to stop trading at Soviet and other Communist ports. When Harold Stassen, director of mutual security, indignantly charged that McCarthy was usurping executive functions and undermining American foreign policy, the administration made peace by issuing a mild rebuke to McCarthy and forcing Stassen to tone down his statement. Meanwhile,

McCarthy's subcommittee hunted alleged Communists in the Voice of America program, finding none but managing to devastate that agency's efficiency and morale. He performed a similar operation in 1953 upon the State Department's overseas information program, forcing it to remove books from its overseas libraries by authors the McCarthy subcommittee regarded as subversive.

Meanwhile, the Justice Department and other federal agencies conducted loyalty probes of their own. Fears of subversion, along with exaggerated new security regulations, were beginning to affect the functioning of government adversely, especially in the vital fields of scientific research, national defense, and foreign policy. Attacks on the State Department shattered morale among loyal public servants and caused a sharp decline in the numbers entering the foreign service. Equally damaging was a sustained attack upon J. Robert Oppenheimer, former director of the Los Alamos laboratory and a scientist of international renown. The Atomic Energy Commission, on the initiative of its new chairman, Lewis L. Strauss, barred Oppenheimer from access to classified materials in July 1953 on the ground that he was a security risk. A special board affirmed Oppenheimer's loyalty in May 1954 but, based upon security regulations, denied him access to classified data—including work he had done himself.

In early 1954, McCarthy overreached himself, initiating a series of events that culminated in his public disgrace. When he discovered that a reserve corps dentist at Fort Monmouth in New Jersey had been promoted and honorably discharged despite his refusal to sign a loyalty oath, McCarthy claimed there was a wide extent of subversion in the armed forces and began a new round of hearings. After McCarthy bullied and humiliated Brigadier General Ralph Zwicker, the dentist's commanding officer, Secretary of the Army Robert Stevens indignantly defended the general. Stevens denounced the subcommittee, ordered Zwicker and other officers not to testify before it, and prepared a strong statement which he planned to read before it himself. McCarthy, calling Stevens an "awful dupe," conferred with the secretary and obtained his signature to articles of surrender requiring Zwicker to testify after all. The army responded with the charge that McCarthy had attempted by various improper means to obtain preferential treatment for Private G. David Schine, former "consultant" to the subcommittee.

During the spring of 1954, televised hearings ensued that captivated millions. McCarthy dominated these proceedings as he had dominated all such affairs— interrupting, raising "points of order," evading questions, bullying witnesses, glowering, sneering, and obstructing. Many Americans saw McCarthy in action for the first time. They saw uncouth arrogance, rank brutality, and a callous disregard for established rules, law, the rights of others, and human decency in general. Equally important, McCarthy's performance goaded both the Senate and Eisenhower into open defiance. Democratic members of the subcommittee could hardly acquiesce or look away while under the scrutiny of a national television audience: they bluntly opposed their chairman for the first time.

President Eisenhower delivered a sharp rebuke. During the hearings, McCarthy had produced a letter containing secret material from the FBI files and announced that federal employees were "duty bound" to give him information "even though some bureaucrat may have stamped it secret." This was open aggression, and the White House responded with the flat statement that executive responsibility could not "be usurped by any individual who may seek to set himself above the laws of our land or to override orders of the President of the United States."

McCarthy's star was on the wane when the hearings closed in June 1954. They ended in victory for neither side, but McCarthy was the real loser. His investigation of Fort Monmouth had collapsed; he had lost his dictatorial control over the subcommittee; and both the Senate and the president were now in open opposition. In August, following debate over a censure resolution introduced by Ralph Flanders of Vermont, the Senate voted to appoint a committee to investigate McCarthy's conduct. After prolonged hearings, in which McCarthy for once appeared as defendant rather than prosecutor, the committee recommended censure on two counts. By a vote of sixty-seven to twenty-two, the Senate adopted a resolution in December 1954 "condemning" certain of McCarthy's actions.

There followed a downhill trail to obscurity and death. The Democratic victory in the election of 1954 cost McCarthy his committee chairmanships. The Senate thereafter ignored him. Physical ailments drained his vitality. His will to resume the struggle seemed to have been sapped, and he never again captured the headlines or strode into the limelight. A hard core of devoted followers remained loyal to the end—and afterward—but most Americans simply forgot about him. When McCarthy died on May 2, 1957, of complications induced by hepatitis, the era to which he had given his name was itself already dead.

McCarthy's decline was as much a symptom as a cause of the subsidence of the Second Red Scare. Except for a determined minority on the far right, the search for Communists in government abated. McCarthy's humiliation in early 1955 was followed by the discrediting of the loyalty probes. Harvey Matusow, a voluble ex-Communist and prize witness in the government's case, suddenly went back on his testimony and confessed to perjury. Other ex-Communists, some of whom had been retained by the Justice Department as consultants in preparing cases against alleged subversives, also repudiated earlier testimony. As a result, the whole process of anti-Communist investigation was thrown into confusion and disrepute, and it never fully recovered.

8. ANTICOMMUNISM AND THE AMERICAN PEOPLE

McCarthyism was only the most extreme manifestation of anticommunism. In varying degrees, it affected popular culture, the press, schools, churches, courts, the executive branch, and Congress. It created an atmosphere of fear and stimulated a belief that it was safer to conform than to disagree with the majority. While some pleaded for sanity and preservation of civil liberties, the government carried through, and the courts approved, an anti-Communist program that greatly diminished such liberties.

The apparently sudden spread of anticommunism actually had its roots deep in American society and politics. Domestic opponents of the New Deal, such as followers of the Liberty League, had long tried to establish a connection between domestic reform and subversion by foreign influences. After 1938, the notorious House Special Committee on Un-American Activities, led by Martin Dies of Texas, investigated New Deal agencies and attempted to find evidence of Communist subversion. Although the Dies committee attracted attention, it did not acquire extensive powers of investigation until 1945, when, in a resolution by John Rankin of Mississippi, it was reorganized as the House Committee on Un-American Activities (HUAC) and was granted a broad mandate to investigate all so-called subversive groups.

The success of HUAC in the Hiss case emboldened it to widen its investigation into the far reaches of American society. In March 1947, HUAC began an inquiry into the motion-picture industry, long regarded by anti-Communists as a haven for organized labor and pro-Soviet unions. In September, the committee subpoenaed forty-one witnesses, ten of whom, as "unfriendly" witnesses—later known as the Hollywood Ten—were pilloried. When the Hollywood Ten—all of whom were screen writers—refused to testify about whether they were members of the Communist party, the full House in November 1947 cited them for contempt of Congress. As it turned out, at least some of the ten had been active Communists, and, after the Supreme Court refused to hear an appeal in April 1950, all of them served prison terms. Severely shaken by the HUAC investigation, the film industry began a policy which went beyond uprooting Communist actors and writers. In 1947, the industry began a policy of "blacklisting," or denying employment to, anyone with even vague Communist associations.

The turn to anti-Communist repression in the late 1940s gained added momentum partly because of vigorous support from the Truman administration. In 1949, it obtained the indictment of eleven Communist leaders for conspiring, in violation of the Smith Act of 1940, to *teach* the violent overthrow of the United States government. The government had prepared its case thoroughly and could support its charges by the testimony of FBI agents and former Communists. The long trial culminated in the conviction of all eleven defendants in 1949. After the court of appeals upheld the decision, the case—*Dennis et al.* v. *United States*—came before the Supreme Court for final review.

The Court upheld the Smith Act and confirmed the convictions by a vote of six to two in June 1951. The charge was not conspiracy to overthrow the government by force, but conspiracy to teach or advocate revolution. Chief Justice Fred M. Vinson, speaking for the majority, reconciled the conviction with the right of free speech by affirming that the government could justify conviction under the doctrine of the "clear and present danger" of Communist subversion.

Government prosecutions of Communists under the Smith Act continued through the mid-1950s. The Justice Department obtained indictments and convictions of Communist leaders in California, Baltimore, Seattle, Detroit, Philadelphia, and Cleveland. Even more ambitious was use of the Smith Act against *members* of the Communist party. In well-publicized cases, Claude Lightfoot, a black Communist, and Junius Scales, a Communist from Greensboro, North Carolina, were sent to jail under the Smith Act.

Congress, too, overreacted in 1950 by approving, over Truman's veto, the McCarran internal security bill—easily the severest measure since the Sedition Act of 1918 and one of the most confused. It required Communist organizations to register with the attorney general and furnish membership lists and financial statements. But it specifically declared that membership or officeholding in a Communist organization was not, per se, a crime. In a second breath, the bill made it illegal knowingly to conspire to perform "any act" that would "substantially" contribute to the establishment of a totalitarian dictatorship in the United States. It also forbade granting passports to Communists or employing them in defense plants; authorized their internment in time of war; and established a bipartisan Subversive Activities Control Board to assist in exposing subversive organizations.

If, as Truman charged in his veto message, the McCarran Act's internal provisions were mainly blundering and ineffective, those relating to immigration, deportation, and naturalization actually damaged American security. By forbidding the entry into the United States of any person who had once been a member of a totalitarian organization, for example, the measure deprived the American government of its most effective means of inducing Soviet and other Communist leaders to defect to the United States.

CHAPTER 23

American Society
in the Postwar Era

With the end of World War II, the United States underwent a long era of tumultuous social, economic, and cultural change. Over the next three decades, Americans achieved the greatest period of prosperity in their history, as gains in productivity, the availability of cheap fossil fuel, and, above all, the introduction of new technologies resulted in an increase in the standard of living for the majority of the people. Even more radical social and cultural changes accompanied the economic transformation. Affluence reshaped the family and the position of women and children within it. The size of the postwar American family grew rapidly, setting off what became known as the "baby boom." Although this appeared to affirm a new traditionalism in American life, the emergence of the baby boom family in fact marked a distinctly new period in the history of American families. As American wives took up domesticity with new vigor, they also expressed new restiveness with it. Meanwhile, baby boom children, with similar ambivalence, endorsed the new domesticity yet also developed new ways to defy it.

As a whole, the post-1945 era witnessed a remade social and economic landscape. In the South, before the war the poorest region in the country, agriculture, industry, and folkways underwent permanent change. No greater change came to that region than the collapse of the Jim Crow system, the de jure system of legally required segregation that had existed since the end of the nineteenth century. For African-Americans, the Age of Affluence provided new opportunities in migration to new northern homes and, eventually, in the civil rights revolution.

In the decade after World War II, these dizzying changes were, of course, not as apparent as they are in hindsight. Thoughtful Americans in 1945 were deeply troubled about more immediate problems—a high rate of inflation, labor conflict, and ability of the war-heated American economy to make the transition to a peacetime footing. Yet they were aware that the war itself had unleashed social forces and had inaugurated changes whose full implications they did not entirely comprehend.

1. THE POSTWAR ECONOMIC BOOM

Unknown to most Americans of the 1940s was a force that would soon reshape most of their lives: the unfolding of a period of economic growth that was unprecedented in their history. Actually, World War II inaugurated a long era of steady and unprecedented expansion, as Americans not only recovered from the depression but enjoyed a real improvement in living standards and income. This period of growth had peaks and valleys; it was interspersed with both boom and recession. But, beginning with the wartime boom and ending in the early 1970s, it resulted in a transformation of American living standards.

Steady increases in wealth and income resulted. Measured in constant dollars, gross national product (GNP) more than trebled between 1940 and 1969, while per capita disposable income roughly doubled. Growth affected every part of the economy, from manufacturing to agriculture to the service sector. Although growth affected these sectors differently, over the long term the entire American economy benefited. Farmers, for example, experienced great prosperity during the war, as net income per farm more than doubled between 1940 and 1946, but then experienced a sharp drop in net income, which declined by a third in the next nine years. Between the late 1950s and 1970, farmers enjoyed renewed gains in income; by the latter years, farm income stood at 25 percent greater than its level in the peak year of 1946. Workers in industry, mining, transport, construction, and other fields experienced a steadier rate of growth. During the period 1940–1970, the real income of the average worker increased by 80 percent, and this constituted a sort of golden age for the American worker. Unemployment, which had sharply declined during World War II, never reached troublesome levels, at least before 1970. It hovered between 3 and 5 percent from 1940 to 1970 and rose above 5.5 percent only during recessions in 1948–1949, 1954–1955, and 1958–1960.

Increases in the GNP and individual income were, at least partly, the direct product of an expanding technological revolution which increased productivity in mines and factories and on farms, emancipated the housewife from numerous drudgeries, and freed unskilled labor from its ancient bondage to the pick and shovel. Mass-production work organization and technologies were applied more extensively than ever before. Further use of the assembly line and interchangeable parts, which had slowed during the 1930s, rapidly increased during and after the war. New electronic measuring devices enabled machine tools to produce engines of almost perfect quality and virtually eliminated the need for hand tooling.

A crucial precondition of these technological changes was the use of more and different forms of energy. The use of electricity became a commonplace; a mainstay, both to generate electricity and to provide other forms of energy, was the use of the fossil fuels natural gas and petroleum. Coal, which had powered the industrial revolution, experienced a relative decline. Another important factor in the heightened importance of technology was research and development (R&D), which increasingly was supported and financed by government. Growing modestly during and after World War I, industrial research became a vitally important exercise. Greater use of energy and expanded technological innovation resulted in the greatest productivity increases in American history. Between 1940 and 1969, industrial production tripled and output per work-hour in manufacturing doubled. Output per work-hour in agriculture meanwhile rose by a staggering 430 percent.

2.   SUBURBANIZATION

One of the most significant physical changes of the postwar period was the transformation of American residential patterns. During the first two decades of the twentieth century, the center of population shifted from farm to city, yet the majority of Americans who lived in urban areas lived in inner-city locations. In the decades after 1945, that pattern changed. With the further development of the automobile culture, a boom in highway and road construction, and the spread of affluence, middle-class Americans fled cities in favor of suburbs.

The end of World War II saw an acute housing shortage for returning veterans and for many other Americans who had long deferred, because of either the depression or the war, the purchase of a home. For much of the 1930s and the war years, single men and women and often young couples shared lodgings with an extended family. In 1947, a total of 6 million families fell into this category, while a half a million inhabited temporary housing. The return of 16 million veterans only aggravated the shortage. In response, Congress appropriated additional funds for the Federal Housing Authority (FHA) and, in 1944, enacted the Servicemen's Readjustment Act. This act created what became popularly known as the Veterans Administration (VA) loan program, which provided federally subsidized, low-interest home mortgages for veterans.

Federal intervention was crucial in setting off a postwar housing boom, as housing starts for single families grew rapidly. In 1944, there were 114,000 housing starts. Two years later that figure had risen to 937,000; by 1950, it had reached almost 1.7 million. The industry meanwhile became increasingly dominated by builders who employed new mass-production technologies and work organization. The typical pre-1945 home builder was highly skilled but small. In contrast, the postwar period saw the emergence of larger operators. The median single-family builder in 1945 constructed fewer than five houses, while by the end of the next decade the median builder accounted for twenty-two homes.

The triumph of mass production in home building was personified in Abraham Levitt. Operating with his sons, William and Alfred, Levitt mastered new opportunities in the postwar housing industry. Soon after the war, the Levitts purchased a 4,000-acre tract in Long Island that they turned into the nation's largest planned suburban development. Employing new economies of scale, the Levitts were able to achieve significant reductions in cost. Homes were constructed on concrete slabs rather than basements, bulldozers accelerated production, and plywood and composition board were used.

Tailored to the market of G.I.s in the metropolitan New York area who needed inexpensive housing, the massive new development—known originally as Island Trees but later as Levittown—eventually included 17,400 residences and 82,000 people. Levittown offered cheap, affordable housing for the masses. Buyers could choose between Cape Cods, which cost $7,990 and had two bedrooms and one bath, or ranches, which cost $9,500 and were slightly larger. The Levitts offered buyers not only low costs but also cheap credit through the extension of FHA and VA subsidized loans; the sales pitch included an offer of no down payment and no closing costs.

The example of Levittown was duplicated across the nation. The Levitts themselves constructed two other large suburban developments, one outside Philadelphia, in Bucks County, Pennsylvania, in the 1950s, and the other east of Philadelphia in Willingboro, New Jersey, in the 1960s. In both communities, they employed a similar formula: suburban tract homes that were produced by using cheap materials, modern labor management, and power tools, with a price and a look that appealed to a large middle-class market. Elsewhere other developers took advantage of many of the Levitts' innovations. By the early 1950s, suburban construction was dominating the home-building industry; according to one estimate, about 9 million people moved to suburbs in the decade after 1945.

Although dispersed throughout the nation, suburban America shared important characteristics. While suburbs were located outside the inner city, they extended the boundaries of urban America into what had been, often literally, cow fields and corn rows. Suburbs offered Americans an attractive refuge from city congestion. Spread apart and detached, suburban homes were situated in pastoral landscapes of green lawns, trees, and winding lanes and appealed to an exclusively urban constituency. Yet to an unprecedented degree the new suburbs were standardized; many critics bemoaned the monotony and dreariness of suburban tracts. But, because builders were able to offer homes at a low, mass-produced cost, suburbs made home ownership available to a larger segment of Americans and contributed to the move of many upwardly mobile persons out of the working class.

By the mid-1950s, suburbanization had become a major part of the social changes of the postwar period. The end of the war witnessed a era of sustained economic growth that benefited a large segment of the population and lifted millions of Americans into the middle class. The new affluence made possible larger families; the baby boom reflected confidence in the economic future. Raised in a culture of affluence, the baby boom suburban families lived in a new spatial environment, where they pioneered a starkly new pattern of life. Dependent on automobiles for transportation, they traveled on new roads and highways constructed for that purpose. In many instances they created local governments where none had existed before. For their children, they constructed new schools, parks, and playgrounds. Suburban Americans enjoyed totally new forms of recreation, as television became a common feature of life, as did the new shopping centers and, eventually, shopping malls that catered to suburban markets.

The rise of suburbs largely depended on a degree of spatial mobility unheard of in pre-1945 America. That, in turn, was made possible by growing ownership of automobiles and construction of highways. In 1950, two-fifths of all Americans did not own a car; by 1984, in contrast, there were more cars than either householders or workers. Americans owned cars, in part, for cultural reasons: the automobile became an important part of status. Yet they also owned them because, in the suburbs that so many Americans inhabited, transportation and subsistence were impossible without them.

With the spread of automobile-dependent suburbanites, federal, state, and local governments poured resources into a virtually complete rebuilding of the nation's highway system. In the 1940s and 1950s, localities improved existing roads and thoroughfares, while building state and federal highways continued. But the most important development of the 1950s was the creation of the Interstate Highway System in 1956. Powerful lobbying by automobile manufacturers, highway administrators, the trucking industry, the construction industry, and an assortment of other interest groups resulted in the appointment, in 1954, of a national committee to examine the nation's highway needs. The committee, headed by a former general, Lucius D. Clay, recommended a massive infusion of federal funds into a national highway system. Two years later, Congress enacted the Interstate Highway Act. It provided for the creation of a 41,000-mile system, with the great proportion of the costs to be borne by the federal government. The succeeding decades witnessed the final triumph of interstate highways and automobiles in American life. Interstate highways helped to create a more mobile society and spurred on suburbanization. They also spawned highway-related industries. The first Holiday Inn, a pioneer in the burgeoning chain motel industry, was established in Memphis, Tennessee, in 1952, and the chain subsequently grew to dominate the industry. By 1960, there were 60,000 motels nationally, a figure that was to double by 1972. Along with motels came other enterprises that sought to appeal to a mobile suburban market. Fast-food enterprises were becoming a growing sector of the service industry by the late 1950s; McDonald's began in a Chicago suburb, Des Plaines, in 1954. By 1960, the entrepreneurial genius behind McDonald's, Ray Kroc, had established 228 franchises nationwide.

Together, the automobile and suburbs combined to create an entirely new social environment for many Americans in the postwar era. Instead of living in small towns or cities—the two most familiar locales in pre-1945 America— middle-class children grew up entertained by television and transported by automobile. They and their parents lived in houses with garages. For entertainment, they turned to drive-in movie houses rather than downtown movie palaces. Drive-ins reached their peak of popularity during the 1950s (they thereafter declined), and by 1958, more than 4,000 drive-ins existed nationally. For most of their necessities, moreover, suburban Americans drove to shopping centers or suburban-located shopping strips, which first appeared during the 1950s.

To be sure, suburbanization had negative effects. The diversion of a massive amount of public resources toward highways meant that the United States had a superior highway system, as opposed to deteriorating and underfunded mass transit and public transportation systems. The growth of suburbs accentuated the further segregation of life according to race and class. Virtually all the post-1945 emigrants to suburbs were white; most of them either occupied a place in or aspired to the middle class. Developers advertised suburbs as a refuge from the inner city, and the thinly veiled message was that this also meant a refuge from black migrants in inner cities. Often the message was not so subtle, as developers openly refused to sell to black families. Local governments employed zoning as a tool to discourage any threats from minority or low-income people from the city; public housing, which was confined to the inner city, further segregated the poor from the rest of society. By the 1950s, then, suburbs had become stratified to the extreme, and they played a major role in shielding the new affluence from the persisting poverty of portions of society.

3. ROOTS OF THE SEXUAL REVOLUTION

The transformation of the American economy and the impact of unprecedented prosperity were matched by an equally startling transformation in family and sexual patterns. The sexual lifestyles of Americans depended, in turn, upon a revolution in the technology and availability of contraceptives. By the middle of the twentieth century, contraception—especially the diaphragm, a device that provided greater choice and control for women—had become routine within the institution of marriage. One study found, for example, that the use of the diaphragm among married white college-educated women born in the second decade of the twentieth century doubled (to slightly more than three-fifths) over that of their parents' generation. Although significant class and racial differences remained—poorer white and black families were less prone to use birth control—these differences had narrowed by the middle twentieth century.

Before 1960, the most significant effects of the birth control revolution occurred within the family. Although families increased in size during the post-war era, this rising fertility did not take place in unrestricted fashion. Rather, postwar families, especially middle-class white families, grew to three, four, or more children through conscious choice and careful planning. Survey data from the 1950s confirmed these tendencies. Among women of childbearing age during that decade, more than nine-tenths either used or expected to use contraception. These same data also show that the use of birth control was most extensive among middle-class whites and least extensive among blacks, poorer whites, and Roman Catholics. Family planning in the delay of the birth of the first child and the spacing of subsequent children became a fundamental feature of postwar family life.

The transformed sexual practices that contraception at least partly evoked became fully evident in 1948 and 1953, when Alfred Kinsey published two landmark works, *Human Sexuality in the American Male* and *Human Sexuality in the American Female.* Achieving rapid commercial success, both volumes revealed a startling profile of the sexual habits of mid-twentieth-century Americans. Kinsey's studies, based on extensive interviews of 18,000 subjects conducted over a decade, offered a valuable sociological and historical view of American sexual habits and preferences.

Kinsey's publications suggested a disparity between mainstream, straitlaced morality and the actual sexual practices of ordinary Americans. Among other findings, he reported that, among males, nine of out of ten Americans participated in premarital intercourse, while about 50 percent had at some point been involved in extramarital sex. Among women, the results were equally startling. The vast majority of women had engaged in masturbation and "petting"—a form of foreplay that may or may not have led to actual intercourse—while a significant portion had been involved in premarital sex (about half) and extramarital relations (about a quarter).

The Kinsey reports had a wide-ranging impact. On the one hand, they revealed to public opinion the divergence between public and private sexuality. American culture during the 1920s and 1930s had been increasingly sexual in its message and symbols; Kinsey's studies offered nothing new in this respect. From the flappers of the 1920s to the cultural iconography of movies, to the new popular music emerging, and to the widespread format and message of advertising, American culture was becoming increasingly sexual. Yet there remained strong taboos against the public display or open discussion of sexuality. Nothing better displayed this factor than the self-regulation of the film industry. Beginning in 1934, Hollywood movie producers established a code that banned the portrayal of all scenes involving adultery, suggestive embraces, and nudity. During the next two decades, the industry effectively eliminated any evidence of sexuality on the silver screen, and the new television industry of the 1940s and 1950s quickly adopted similar standards.

Into the 1950s, then, a clear tension existed between the changing sexual practices of Americans, as described by Kinsey, and the wide-ranging system of restrictions over the public display of sexuality, some of which dated to the Comstock laws (named for the antivice reformer Anthony Comstock) of the nineteenth century. This tension became, at times, part of the central tensions of cold war society. Beginning especially with World War II and the congregation of single-sex associations that it fostered, homosexuality became, for the first time in American history, openly expressed. In his studies, Kinsey found an extensive prevalence of homosexuality: among males, he reported that half admitted same-sex sexual attraction, while one-eighth of his respondents were primarily homosexual over a three-year period. Out of the war, which for many men and women marked a "coming out," American homosexuals began to develop an independent and largely self-sufficient economy and culture of their own. Gay culture first appeared in large cities such as New York, Los Angeles, and San Francisco, and in the aftermath of the war, gay businesses and meeting places, such as bars, sprang up in these cities.

Nothing threatened the sexual status quo or its notion of sexual order more than the phenomenon of homosexuality. Domesticity and traditional heterosexual marriage were the bedrocks of cold war society; to challenge them, many Americans believed, was to undermine the foundations of American security. As a minority that was largely dispersed and disorganized, moreover, homosexuals made an easy target. Running congruently with the anticommunism of Joseph McCarthy and others, then, was an attempt to locate and persecute homosexuals. In February 1950, Republican anti-Communists charged in the Senate that the State Department was filled not only with Communists but also with homosexuals. According to the chairman of the Republican National Committee, "sexual perverts" had infiltrated the government; they were "as dangerous as the actual Communists." The result was a formal inquiry by the United States Senate investigating the presence of "homosexuals and other moral perverts" in June 1950 and the writing of a report at the end of that year. That report, released in December, warned that homosexuals were present in American government and, like Communists, could have a "corrosive influence" that could "pollute a Government office."

The Senate homosexual report of 1950 provided the basis for a witch-hunt paralleling the anti-Communist purges of the same era. In April 1953, President

Eisenhower, soon after his inauguration, prohibited the employment of gay men and women by federal agencies. Over the decade of the 1950s, the FBI introduced a system of screening and surveillance to search out homosexuals. Meanwhile, state and local governments followed suit by also banning the employment of gays, while the numerous corporations that received federal funds were expected to follow this same antigay standard. Local police forces were also encouraged to harass gays, and they periodically engaged in mass arrests and sweeps.

Despite cold war vigilance against alleged moral perversion, it was clear that American public attitudes about sexuality—along with actual practices—were undergoing fundamental change. The Victorian emphasis on private passion had given way increasingly to a public emphasis on all things sexual. Meanwhile, the growing availability of contraception made it possible for intercourse to occur without fear of pregnancy. In spite of cold war proscriptions, a new form of sexual free choice was becoming increasingly popular by the 1950s. For most of the immediate postwar period, that sexual free choice was contained within the institution of marriage: premarital sexuality was, more often than not, in anticipation of marriage, while nonmarital or extramarital promiscuity was the exception.

4.   THE BABY BOOM AND
THE NEW DOMESTICITY

The American family underwent a rapid and extensive transformation during and after World War II. With the end of hard times and the onset of prosperity, Americans became more willing to marry earlier. During the depression years, the marriage rate had declined to a historic low as potential marriage partners deferred matrimony for economic reasons. Though this development increased the instances in which single women were, in effect, forced to become autonomous, it placed a serious strain both on prospective families and on existing ones as the divorce rate increased significantly. Not surprisingly, the birthrate also dropped to a new low during the 1930s.

The war fundamentally altered these conditions. Women streamed into the work force and participated in jobs that had previously been all-male. The entrance of working women, particularly married women, disrupted male-dominated families, to be sure. Yet, by providing greater wealth, the war also made possible the resurgence of the traditional male-headed family. With the war, the marriage rate experienced a steady increase. Between 1940 and 1943, a million more marriages were formed than might have been expected according to the marriage rate of the 1930s. Even more startling, the birthrate took off during the war years. From 19.4 per thousand in 1940, it increased to 23.0 per thousand in 1950.

A sharp upsurge in births, soon known as the baby boom, became a clear social trend by the late 1940s and 1950s. In the five years between 1948 and 1953—the peak years of the baby boom—more babies were born than during the previous three decades combined. Beginning during the war, as couples married at younger ages, they had babies earlier and extended their childbearing years. During the 1930s, women of childbearing age had, on the average, 2.4 children; the rate for the 1950s, in contrast, was 3.2 children. In more concrete terms, what this meant was that the standard American family, which had included two or perhaps three children in the 1930s, now more commonly included four or more children. In the postwar era, some 70 percent of couples had two to four children. Meanwhile, between 1940 and 1960, the birthrate for third children doubled and that of fourth children tripled.

Clearly, these demographic changes occurred just as a new sexual ethos was acquiring clearer definition. Kinsey had been able to document that the patterns that had begun in the late nineteenth century and become more clearly focused in the 1920s achieved full fruition in the postwar era. Most married couples shared the experience of having had premarital sex; Kinsey discovered, for example, that about half of all postwar American women and almost 70 percent of American men had experienced premarital intercourse. Yet these patterns were intertwined with a new code of domesticity. Although there was widespread premarital intercourse, it was often followed by marriage; sex before marriage became a part of the last stages of the courtship ritual. Kinsey and other students of postwar sexuality demonstrated that the vast majority of dating couples engaged in some kind of petting; yet this meant that women felt increasing pressure to engage in sex. Most of these women felt constrained by taboos against premarital sex, but they also felt the pressures of social standards of their peers that sanctioned relationships that appeared to lead to marriage.

These new norms of sexuality were very much a part of American life, but they suggested that sexual awareness and consciousness prevailed among the new parents of the baby boom. Increased awareness of sexuality was accompanied by greater attention to family planning; the prevalent families of four were usually not accidents of passion but reflected planning and deliberate consideration. The use of contraception for purposes of family planning was almost universal. Kinsey found, for example, that 94 percent of white women in the postwar era used contraception; of these, 57 percent used diaphragms, while 37 percent of the males used condoms. Among white married women, a pattern of contraceptive use was common: 81 percent of them used birth control. For many women of the postwar era, the use of contraceptives helped to defer the birth of the first child—which most middle-class white wives postponed until after the first year of marriage—and made the spacing of further children possible.

The baby boom affected diverse strata of American society. By the early 1950s, the pattern of larger families with mothers not employed outside the home became, to be sure, a middle-class ideal. In Hollywood, the war years brought a new celebration of domestic life; in contrast, in the 1930s, the studios had exalted single, unattached women who exuded sexuality. In popular magazines and in the advertising industry a new pitch was made to the stability of home life, the happiness of women in the home, and the higher calling of motherhood and matrimony.

The white middle-class participants in the new domesticity were often highly educated, and although they partly or completely relinquished the option of careers, they pursued the activities of the home with unprecedented energy and zest. They organized themselves into clubs and organizations, they operated car pools to transport their large families, and they participated in school PTAs with great energy. In a certain sense, then, the role of homemaker became a professionalized, demanding occupation whose requirements were often stressful.

The baby boom had a profound impact on postwar American life. The new families sought homes that exemplified their new domesticity; suburban communities became the ideal to which many Americans aspired. These communities developed a distinctive flavor, but they came to typify the kind of environment that prevailed among middle-class whites. By comparison, these communities were affluent; suburban families had new spending power and a new ability to exercise their cultural, political, and economic influence. Not the least important, the baby boom resulted in a huge new demand for public services in roads, hospitals, and, above all, schools to attend to these new and growing families.

But the baby boom was also a complex historical phenomenon. It seemed to suggest that Americans were returning to a pristine past and were reasserting a new kind of familial traditionalism in which men dominated the workplace and women were segregated to the sphere of unpaid domestic work. Yet there was clearly a fundamental ambivalence about this development. The war years, which had brought to fruition most of the changes discussed above, also brought thousands of women into the work force; unlike previous generations of working women, moreover, many of these workers were married. The mothers of the baby boom, far from subservient, were participating in a new assertiveness both within the family and, as we shall see, in the public sphere.

5.   WOMEN IN THE WORKPLACE

The postwar era was characterized by increased numbers of marriages and larger families, but it was also marked by another trend: the continuing participation of women in affairs of work and life outside the home. The years immediately after the war brought a shrinking in the participation of women in the work force. The "Rosie the Riveters," who during wartime had entered previously all-male occupations, were now expected to relinquish their jobs. As a result, some 2 million women left their jobs when the war ended, with most of the layoffs coming in previously all-male occupations for which women had been temporarily hired. The impact of shrinking job participation by women was most profound among younger women—those whose chances of job advancement, it was assumed by employers, were the brightest. Nonetheless, over the long term women, and especially married women, entered the work force in greater numbers. In 1960, about twice as many women were at work as in 1940; two-fifths of all women older than sixteen worked. Among married women during the same years, the proportion who worked grew from 15 to 30 percent, while the number of working mothers increased from 1.5 million to 6.6 million. Clearly, despite the reassertion of traditional familialism, other pressures were motivating women to seek work outside the home.

Other evidence bears out the contradictory tendencies of family and work in the 1950s. Before World War II, women had worked only as a temporary expedient; jobs usually preceded marriage and continued thereafter only to supplement the male breadwinner's earnings. Yet, in the postwar era, many women maintained their jobs after marriage. When the first child arrived, they may have quit their jobs, but they returned to them once the last child entered school. Most of the increasing numbers of new working women were women older than forty-five, at about the age that many of them saw their last child leave for school. Yet even in this social environment the number of younger mothers who worked increased; during the 1950s the number of working women with children under age of six grew by a third. The number of working women among working-class and minority families had long been relatively high. What was different about the postwar era was the growing proportion of middle-class white women who worked outside the home. Many of these more affluent women were well educated. By 1962, over half of the women who held college degrees worked outside the home; for women with postgraduate education, the figure was 70 percent.

In the breakdown of stubborn taboos that prevented women from working, American society was experiencing revolutionary change. The war played a major role in breaking this pattern, yet over the next decades that pattern of working women became more fully elaborated. A diverse number of reasons explains why this revolutionary change occurred. Once the wartime experience had shattered the taboo against married women in the work force, like most taboos it never reacquired its force or impact. For many women, working became a means of greater fulfillment; working women enjoyed their jobs and the chance to get out of the house. Much of this transformation was also undoubtedly economic; new expectations of consumer goods, education, and home appliances, among other things, accompanied the revived domesticity. Married women entered the work force to supplement family income and to sustain the family's standard of living. Families with both spouses working could spend more on luxuries, could afford to send their children to better colleges, and could buy the new appliances and automobiles that American factories were producing in the 1950s.

In large part, consumerism explains the apparent contradiction between domesticity on the one hand and working wives on the other. In the 1940s and 1950s, there were significant increases in family income; most families chose to spend rather than to save. Between 1945 and 1950, consumer spending jumped 60 percent; for goods such as household furnishings and appliances the figure was 240 percent, while for food and clothing it was 33 percent and 20 percent, respectively. Rather than bare necessities, Americans were spending their increased incomes on appliances, television sets, and new homes. In the four years just after the end of the war, they bought 1 million new homes, 21.4 million cars, 20 million refrigerators, 5.5 million stoves, and 11.6 television sets. In many instances, women sought work not to challenge the traditional family but to bolster it.

Although significantly larger numbers of women worked, they remained underpaid. Most of the jobs available to older wives who took them were nonprofessional; the proportion of women in the professions by 1960, for example, was actually lower than the proportion three decades earlier. Public opinion polls of the era revealed that, rather than seeking professional fulfillment, most working women cited additional income as the main reason for their entrance into the work force. Yet the result was that disparities between the earnings of women and men persisted despite the rise in the number of women workers. Much of the expansion in the clerical labor force, which had long been both underpaid and overwhelmingly female, was fueled by women entrants to the job force. By the end of the 1950s, fully a third of all working women held clerical positions. With the mechanization of household work, the numbers of domestic workers, another underpaid women's occupation, declined, as did the numbers employed in that occupation. Instead, women moved into other service jobs, such as waitressing, health care, and hairdressing. Almost four-fifths of all women in the work force by the end of the 1950s were employed in jobs that were stereotypically female.

Overall, as women entered the work force, the historical disparity in pay between men and women continued. In fact, wage rates during the 1950s in many if not most occupations actually fell, especially in traditional female occupations. By 1960, women workers were earning only three-fifths what men were, a disparity that reflected the high degree of gender segregation and the low pay in female occupations.

6.   AFRICAN-AMERICAN WOMEN IN THE POSTWAR ERA

The foregoing generalizations about working women, it should be reiterated, refer primarily to white middle-class working women. The case of African-

American working women during and after World War II offers a different perspective. On the one hand, the same demographic, economic, and social forces affected black as well as white women. Black families, like white families, experienced an increase in fertility and the baby boom. They also directly benefited from wartime and postwar prosperity. And they aspired to similar ideals of domesticity and a nuclear child-centered family that had become so common among white families by the late 1950s.

At the same time, the experience of African-American women was distinctive. With the migration of millions of blacks to cities in the Northeast, Middle West, and West Coast, the daily experiences of an increasing share of African-Americans became urban. Black women in the postwar era had even larger families than white baby boom families. By 1950, indeed, black fertility rates were a third higher than those of whites. Yet the baby boom for black women, especially those migrants or children of migrants in cities, occurred in a context of at least partial family disintegration; the chances that children would be born to single-parent black families rose sharply during this era. By 1950 a quarter of all black women who had married were now either divorced, separated, or widowed, while the separation rate for black women was four times that of white women. Meanwhile, the disparities between men and women that prevailed generally in American society were greatest among black women. Although they had found new employment opportunities and higher wages during the war, they also found that many occupations continued to close their doors to their race, as black women remained among the most despised of all American social groups. When the war ended, therefore, the expectation among many white Americans was that black women would return to a traditionally more subservient role.

The war created new opportunities for African-American women, the most significant of which came in domestic work. White women domestics left these jobs in favor of better-paying war-related jobs, creating openings which black women reluctantly occupied. Black women also filled other occupations that ranked low in both pay and status—occupations which white women had deserted during the war, such as cafeteria and laundry work. These jobs required hard work and received low pay, but they paid better than work on the farms from which many of the black women had migrated. Moreover, when they had the chance, black women frequently chose institutional work—as scrubwomen in factories, for example—over work in private homes. While approximately 30 percent of white women worked during the war years, the proportion for black women was 40 percent. Yet what is striking about the latter statistic is that it represented no significant change over the pattern for the previous decade; for black women, the war did not unleash an avalanche of new opportunities in jobs and upward social mobility through participation in the American economy. The reason for this lies less in the availability of the labor of black women than in discrimination. In the South, working African-American women continued to face open hostility and exclusion; in the North, they confronted subtler forms of racism. North or South, the fact is that African-American women almost always were last in line, following both white women and black men.

When the war ended, consequently, black women were among the first to be demobilized, that is to say, to lose their jobs. Through layoffs, seniority lists that were separated by race and sex, and union opposition, black women lost their jobs, as did many white working women, in the immediate postwar years. Thereafter, as opportunities for white women increased—even if in traditionally female occupations—those for black women did not. Two-fifths of black working women were employed as domestics in private households in 1950, and there they received low wages and few if any benefits, while nearly 20 percent of them toiled as scrubwomen, hotel help, and restaurant workers.

7. THE TRANSFORMATION OF THE RURAL SOUTH

In the postwar era, perhaps no other region of the country experienced greater and more wrenching social change than the rural South. Long the poorest region of the nation, it had historically resisted the penetration of socioeconomic forces that had, for the previous century, been remaking much of the rest of the country. Up until World War II, for example, migration out of the rural South had been minimal. This meant not only that the South remain overwhelming rural into the middle of the twentieth century but also that the rural areas were overpopulated, given scarce available resources and wealth. The result was widespread and grinding poverty in the rural South that contrasted with relative prosperity in southern towns and cities and outside the region.

Change came to the region, however, during and after the New Deal. Until then, cotton, tobacco, and rice planters remained rooted in a system of agriculture that differed little from that of their great-grandparents. The system relied on a single cash crop. Lacking much investment capital, the system was starved for credit; its scarcity affected every aspect of the plantation system. The system was highly exploitative of the land and tended to accelerate soil exhaustion. It was labor-intensive and depended upon the availability of a large pool of relatively stable and cheap laborers, many of them descendants of the former slaves of region. By the early twentieth century, changes in this system were on the horizon, even if dimly so. Beginning in 1894, crossing from Mexico to Texas, a new insect, the boll weevil, invaded the cotton South. Farmers soon discovered that weevils, which nested in the young buds of the cotton plant and killed them, devastated the cotton crop. Over the next decades, the boll weevil spread northward and eastward. By 1908, it had traveled into Arkansas and, thereafter, into the Gulf Coast South. By the third decade of the twentieth century, the boll weevil was reshaping the pattern of southern agricultural life.

The advent of the boll weevil dramatized the overdependence of southern agriculture on single crops and accelerated efforts to diversify. The United States Department of Agriculture, in what eventually evolved into the county extension program, intervened in the 1890s and attempted a variety of measures, most of them unsuccessful, to turn back the tide of weevils. Eventually, the USDA embraced through its county agents a different approach: that the whole system of southern agriculture needed fundamental revision. The basic elements of this revision reached fruition during the New Deal and World War II. In response to the depression collapse in agricultural prices, New Deal agricultural policies brought on federal relief, subsidies, and other intervention. In the cotton South, for example, the AAA played a decisive role in transforming agriculture. That agency's subsidies, designed to prevent "overproduction," provided capital to planters and landlords; subsidies, along with the incentive to reduce production, encouraged the displacement of landless tenants and sharecroppers. Meanwhile, federal relief provided cover for massive displacement. By the late 1930s, federal policies were helping to push the plantation work force, black and white, off the land. This amounted to an enclosure movement, in which a labor-intensive society was transformed into one that was more capital-intensive.

The transformation of southern agriculture was fueled by another factor: increasing mechanization. Since the 1920s, the tractor had become more prominent on southern farms. Yet relative to the rest of the nation, southern farmers before 1930 invested in tractors slowly. In that year, only about 4 percent of southern farmers possessed tractors, as compared with almost 14 percent nationally. Over the next decades, the tractor entered southern life and became a commonplace. With a guaranteed "parity" price determined by the federal agricultural bureaucracy, landowners enjoyed a regular and predictable infusion of cash. By the 1930s they were investing that cash in new tractors. The triumph of the tractor had a sweeping impact. Not only did it account for the disappearance of the ever-present mule in southern rural life, it also contributed mightily to forces pushing southern masses off the land. According to one estimate, the introduction of tractors in cotton-growing states during the 1930s alone contributed to the displacement of as many as 2 million Southerners. During and after World War II, a mechanical cotton picker became widely available for the first time, and it transformed cotton culture across the South. The Rust cotton picker, the most popular by the mid-1940s, extended mechanization into a previously labor-intensive form of agriculture, while it also displaced thousands of mostly black agricultural laborers.

Federal industrial policy also had a decisive impact. In 1937, FDR had identified the South as the "nation's number 1 problem" and endorsed wide-ranging policies to transform it. Among the most important of these were policies designed to make the labor practices and wages of southern industry consistent with those of the rest of the nation. Policies advanced by the National Recovery

Administration sought to increase the presence of unions and to raise wages, but it was not until the enactment of the Fair Labor Standards Act of 1938 that truly effective federal intervention in southern industry occurred, including the final elimination of child labor, the institution of national standards of overtime, and, most important, the institution of a national minimum-wage policy.

The minimum wage was to southern industry what the AAA had been to southern agriculture: it provided a powerful incentive for sweeping structural changes. Cheap labor and a labor-intensive society had long been a chief feature of southern industry. With the minimum-wage requirement, employers reduced cheap unskilled labor and turned to the introduction of more efficient machinery. The result, once again, was dislocation in higher unemployment and the displacement of a marginal industrial labor force.

Federal policies, by the postwar era, had brought major changes to the South. The wartime boom saw the building of roads, airports, and a host of facilities to house and train American military forces. It spawned the profusion of defense industries across the regions that accounted for new jobs for Southerners. Into the 1950s, the South was experiencing the most significant social changes since the colonial era. The southern plantation had by then disintegrated, replaced by an agribusiness system of farming that, like agriculture elsewhere, was capital-intensive and employed far fewer laborers than it had a generation before. With the shift in the structure of southern agriculture, millions of black and white Southerners moved, many of them settling in southern cities, which grew rapidly in the post-1945 era. Many others migrated to northern cities. Together the displacement of the large portion of the southern population constituted one of the most significant population shifts in American history. Before the 1960s, all of the southern states, with the exception of Florida (which experienced a development boom in the 1920s), had been majority-rural. By 1960, six southern states now possessed majority-urban populations, while in the remaining states significant increases in the urban proportion had occurred. In eight southern states, almost 3 million Southerners left rural areas for cities.

8. AMERICAN CULTURE IN THE POSTWAR ERA

The most important postwar cultural phenomenon was the further spread of commercialized, nationally standardized forms of mass entertainment. Although postwar popular culture followed well-established patterns, it underwent significant changes. Like early-twentieth-century popular cultural forms, mass culture after World War II was dominated by highly integrated corporate enterprise whose chief objective was profit. At the same time, however, the influence of popular culture became greatly extended through a new medium, television, which possessed almost limitless potential for commercial entertainment.

Indeed, television broadcasting became the single most important form of postwar mass culture. Although the technology for televised broadcasting had existed since the 1930s, it was not until the end of World War II that television sets became widely available—nor until then that the major radio broadcasting networks energetically moved into television programming. The year 1946 inaugurated the television age. In June of that year, NBC aired a telecast of the Joe Louis–Billy Conn heavyweight championship bout. In January 1947, the opening of Congress was televised for the first time. Then, in May of that year, the first television dramatic series, the *Kraft Theater*, began on NBC.

Thereafter, despite a freeze in the number of licenses for new television stations lasting from 1948 to 1952, television quickly became the dominant form of popular amusement. By 1953, it contributed to a noticeable decline in audiences for radio and motion pictures, while a shift in the resources of commercial entertainment occurred in these industries. The immediate effects of television during its first decade were nothing less than disastrous for the radio industry, as gross receipts declined throughout the 1950s. Radio broadcasting recovered only after a thorough, industrywide reorganization. Abandoning the national programming of the interwar period, radio grew as a decentralized industry which adapted to specialized and regional differences in taste. The loosening of federal controls over FM bands made possible a profusion of stations which could broadcast with a higher-fidelity sound. By the mid-1950s, most of the radio dramas had either moved into television or passed out of existence. They were replaced, increasingly, by a close relationship between radio and the popular music industry.

By this time, moreover, the tone and emphasis of television had taken shape. Like radio, it was dominated by advertising, and its programming was dictated by commercial sponsors. Moreover, the same large national networks which controlled radio entertainment—CBS, NBC, and ABC—quickly moved their organizational and capital resources into television. Radio personalities such as Bob Hope and Jack Benny made a smooth transition to television. Early television also openly borrowed content and format from radio. Mysteries and situation comedies, both popular on radio, quickly appeared on television. The most successful dramatic transplants from radio followed familiar plots—and even scenes—which were often dictated by commercial sponsors. Although most of television's dramatic fare during the 1950s was performed live, television increasingly borrowed from Hollywood and employed the technology of film-making.

Innovation and development made television a rapidly changing and dynamic cultural industry. The first decade of television witnessed not only the application of radio's formulas to television but also experiments in the broadcasting of original plays, which attracted top-flight playwrights and actors and actresses to television. News programming was another area of development innovation. Television news had arrived by 1955.

Television's primacy in mass entertainment was well established by the late 1950s, and, in both earnings and audience, it had superseded radio and motion pictures as the primary form of American entertainment. With a new period of stability, moreover, came a greater degree of uniform program and technological prowess. The earlier experiments in high-quality television drama were abandoned, and the early live episodic dramas were replaced by filmed versions.

Television had a profound impact on two early-twentieth-century manifestations of popular culture—spectator sports and radio. The national spectator sport, baseball, had developed as a professional, profit-oriented industry because of its direct access to urban fans in midwestern and northeastern urban-industrial centers. After 1920, the spread of radio broadcasting, along with the profusion of minor-league teams, extended baseball to a wide audience. The popularity of the national pastime peaked about the time of World War II.

The advent of televised sports broadcasting transformed baseball. It coincided with and probably caused a long decline in attendance, particularly in minor-league attendance, which dropped from 42 million fans annually to 10 million in 1969. Baseball was less suited to the visual impact of television than sports like boxing, football, and basketball, which became growth sports after 1960. One response of baseball owners facing declining attendance was to seek out lucrative new markets elsewhere by moving their teams. For example, the Boston Braves, which had won the National League pennant in 1948, attracting 1.5 million fans, sold the rights to televise their games and then experienced a decline in attendance of 81 percent by 1952. Faced with catastrophe, the Braves moved in 1953 to Milwaukee, where they recorded the highest league attendance for six straight years. Other relocations, such as the move of the Brooklyn Dodgers to Los Angeles and the New York Giants to San Francisco, had followed by the late 1950s.

American literature also reflected many of the larger social and cultural trends affecting life in the postwar era. In contrast to the apparent security of the time, both in the reassertion of domesticity at home and in the expression of American supremacy abroad, in literature the trends of alienation and modernism that had first become prominent in the 1920s continued to dominate the writing of fiction during the 1940s and 1950s.

World War II marked the close of a literary era. Postwar authors possessed less clarity of purpose than did their predecessors, while prewar literary giants, with a few exceptions, spoke with declining power. One such exception was William Faulkner, whose reputation as America's foremost living novelist was firmly established by 1945 and endured until his death in 1962. In all of his major novels, Faulkner probed fundamental human questions through a many-sided portrayal of southern society, with its tensions between a meaningful but archaic past and a rapidly changing present, between the established but often degenerate code of older families and the rapacious, materialistic instincts of those on the rise. In later works—*The Hamlet* (1940), *Go Down, Moses* (1942), *Intruder in the Dust* (1948), *Requiem for a Nun* (1951), *A Fable* (1954), *The Town* (1957), and *The Mansion* (1960)—Faulkner strongly reaffirmed the value and dignity of the human spirit.

Although Ernest Hemingway's position as the other undisputed master of American fiction survived, he did little to sustain it after 1940. Between his triumph with *For Whom the Bell Tolls* in that year and his suicide in 1961, Hemingway produced only one major work, *The Old Man and the Sea*. Hemingway's literary power was more, and finally, evident in this tale of an aging fisherman adrift in the Gulf Stream, battling for his own survival in the protracted effort to land a great fish.

Taken together, the best writing of the postwar generation did not constitute a literary revival. A talented group of southern writers maintained the high literary standards earlier established by Ellen Glasgow, Willa Cather, and Katherine Anne Porter. Among the best postwar writers in this tradition were Caroline Gordon, Joan Williams, Carson McCullers, Harper Lee, Eudora Welty, and Reynolds Price. There was also a flood of war fiction. Among the best of this genre were three probing portrayals of military life in which the war formed a backdrop for a study of relationships among men in uniform: James Gould Cozzens's *Guard of Honor* (1948), James Jones's *From Here to Eternity* (1951), and William Styron's *The Long March* (1953). There were also the neo-Hemingways, to borrow a name—Alfred Hayes, John Horne Burns, Norman Mailer, and Irwin Shaw—who wrote powerfully of war's horrors and brutality. Other young writers, like John Hersey, Herman Wouk, and James Michener, found courage and nobility in the great tragedy.

Although vigorous and forceful, postwar writers suffered from an exaggerated indecision and an inability to find intellectual and moral bearings. Like other twentieth-century intellectuals, they were chiefly concerned with the search for meaning in an increasingly impersonal and complex society. Perhaps the outstanding difference between most younger novelists and their illustrious predecessors lay in the assumption with which they confronted modernism. More than any other previous literary generation, the writers of the Lost Generation had dealt with the moral confusion of modern life, and they shed all their illusions save one: hope that humankind had retained enough heroic potential not merely to endure, as Faulkner put it, but to prevail.

It was precisely this hope that many postwar novelists seemed to have lost. Some moved in the direction of subjectivism and a new way of expressing or identifying the self. This, at least in part, characterized the efforts of such otherwise dissimilar novelists as John Updike and Norman Mailer. Both were talented writers, yet Updike's brilliant style and sharp wit could not remove the taint of dullness and joylessness that marked the lives of most of his fictional characters. Mailer sought experience so avidly through playing the roles of tormented genius, brash social critic, and male sex symbol that his potential seemed unlikely to be fully realized.

The postwar era was also marked by the further development of talented African-American novelists, dramatists, and poets. Most of them, like their white counterparts, wrote about the problems of modernism and alienation while exploring the themes of racism and the impact of discrimination upon blacks in a white-dominated society. The novelist Ralph Ellison treated alienation in his *Invisible Man* (1952). Richard Wright, in *The Outsider* (1953), attempted to combine French existentialism with the black experience in postwar America. A clearer expression of frustration and rage came from James Baldwin. Born in Harlem, Baldwin in 1948 began a long exile in France and Switzerland, where he wrote his first and best novel, *Go Tell It on the Mountain* (1953). Subsequently, Baldwin continued to fuse themes of alienation and moral rootlessness with a message of racial conflict and confusion.

American postwar drama was also dominated by the themes of confusion about the modern world. To be sure, the brooding genius of Eugene O'Neill survived, and, although illness slowed his productivity, he completed four plays after 1940—*The Iceman Cometh* (1946), *A Moon for the Misbegotten* (1947), *A Long Day's Journey into Night* (1956), and *A Touch of the Poet* (1957). There were many outstanding musicals and light comedies in the 1940s and 1950s, but only three significant new playwrights: William Inge, Arthur Miller, and Tennessee Williams. Among this group, Tennessee Williams was unquestionably the most gifted and influential. He both captivated and shocked his audiences by liberally infusing his plots with sex and violence and by exploring the darker side of human nature. His plays included many theatrical landmarks: *The Glass Menagerie* (1944), *A Streetcar Named Desire* (1947), *Summer and Smoke* (1948), *The Rose Tattoo* (1950), *Camino Real* (1953), *Cat on a Hot Tin Roof* (1955), and *The Night of the Iguana* (1962).

American poetry also displayed excitement and virtuosity. The best poetry revealed great vitality and a sustained interest in experimental forms. Robert Penn Warren, John Malcolm Brinnin, and Robert Lowell reflected a thoughtful quest for identity with the past. Readers learned to appreciate the wide-ranging themes and varied styles of poets such as Lowell, Karl Shapiro, Randall Jarrell—who began to publish during World War II—and Theodore Roethke. Robert Frost, the dean of American verse, continued to captivate readers with his unique New England magic, controlled but exuberant energy, dry humor, and sympathetic wisdom until his death in 1963.

Many regarded another venerable writer, Wallace Stevens, as one of the greatest of modern poets. Stevens, like Frost, began writing verse before World War I; unlike Frost, Stevens did not win wide recognition until late in life. Intuitive rather than rational, Stevens wrote with eloquent simplicity about nature and the seasons and "gusty emotions on wet roads on autumn nights

. . . the bough of summer and the winter branch." A constant experimentalist in the Eliot-Pound tradition, he employed both bizarre words and obscure allusions. Yet persevering readers discovered that his poems contained much beauty, force, and meaning. Three well-established poets of the preceding generation, also in the Eliot tradition—Marianne Moore, William Carlos Williams, and e. e. cummings—continued to display their diverse talents in the postwar years.

By 1960, American poetry had begun a period of transition. Several major figures abruptly passed from the scene: Stevens died in 1955, e. e. cummings in 1962, Roethke, Williams, and Frost in 1963, and Jarrell in 1965. Yet American verse lost little of its force, momentum, or vitality, primarily because no form of creative writing was better suited for this disjunctive, unconventional, individualistic, desperately questioning era. Poets had been experimenting in these directions for half a century and were far less dependent than novelists or dramatists upon traditional forms and structures. Reflecting the mood of the times, contemporary verse became increasingly personal in subject matter, increasingly informal in style.

9. SCHOOL AND CHURCH

The postwar era brought new challenges for two mainstays of American society, schools and churches. Culminating decades of growth, education acquired a new position of preeminence in American society. As the school population grew as a result of the baby boom, a virtual reconstruction of the elementary school physical plant occurred beginning in the 1950s. For churches, the apparent solidification of the domestic family unit was accompanied by a resurgent interest in organized religion, yet dark clouds lay on the horizon for the stability or security of that interest.

The end of the war inaugurated a long period of expansion in education. The war had severely taxed schools. Not only was there severe overcrowding, but there were also acute shortages of teachers as well as of material and equipment. Many schools closed, as a result; others went on double sessions or used abandoned buildings. This situation became worse once the war ended, as about 350,000 teachers—nearly 40 percent of 1941 work force—left the profession for better-paying jobs in business and government. Desperate authorities issued emergency certificates to over 100,000 teachers, but the shortage persisted and, if anything, worsened during the immediate postwar years. Not surprisingly, teacher pay also grew, from an average of $1,440 in 1940 to $3,000 in 1950, to almost $5,000 in 1960.

Postwar growth stimulated a rethinking of teaching methods and curriculum and of progressive education, the dominant educational philosophy of the early twentieth century. Progressive education, said its critics, sacrificed scholarship, ignored basic skills, and sapped intellectual vitality, rigor, and discipline—all to further such amorphous objectives as "life adjustment." Critics, such as Albert Lynd, Robert M. Hutchins, and Arthur E. Bestor, Jr., called for a shift in emphasis from "child-centered" to "subject-centered" education and more rigorous training in basic academic disciplines like English, history, mathematics, science, and languages. The drive for improved standards moved into high gear in the decade after 1955.

Similar trends also affected higher education in the postwar era. Like elementary and secondary schools, colleges and universities experienced phenomenal growth after 1950, and enrollments and expenditures began to increase by the 1950s. Higher education in the United States experienced a renaissance during the decades after 1945. First came a sweeping victory for the proponents of an integrated curriculum designed to provide a general education for American undergraduates. A revolt against the intellectual chaos of the elective system, led in the 1930s by President Robert M. Hutchins of the University of Chicago, culminated in the publication of *General Education in a Free Society* in 1945. A milestone in the development of educational philosophy in the United States, this Harvard report strongly advocated a general education that would acquaint students with the whole of human experience rather than with isolated fragments. Curricular changes embodying the substance of this concept were adopted in many colleges and universities in the years that followed.

This reexamination, once set in motion, led to other changes and experiments. Recognition of the importance of Judaism and Christianity in the development of Western civilization led to the establishment of religion departments in many institutions that had once gladly abandoned such studies. Awareness of America's new world responsibilities stimulated academic interest in international affairs and foreign areas and especially in institutes to promote study about Russia, the Far East, and the Middle East. New or enlarged programs in American civilization and expanded offerings in cultural anthropology, sociology, and psychology reflected new concerns.

Organized religion also experienced change and new challenges in the postwar era. In an age of further secularization of American culture, churches not only maintained their spiritual and moral authority but underwent growth in size and material resources. During the 1950s, religion became a fundamental of the new domesticity of the era; Americans surged into churches and synagogues. In 1940, 37 percent of American adults had attended church or synagogue during an average week; by 1958, this figure had reached a postwar high of 49 percent. Nearly every religious group recorded substantial gains. Membership in the three Jewish confessional groups grew from an estimated 3 million in 1940 to over 5.7 million in 1982. All Protestant denominations grew faster than the general population, with Southern Baptists registering the biggest gains. The various bodies on the socially acceptable margins of Protestantism—the Church of the Nazarene, the several Churches of God, the Pentecostal Assemblies, the

Foursquare Gospel movement—also grew rapidly and evolved from fringe sects into established denominations. Although the United States remained a predominantly Protestant country, a striking feature of the postwar era was the growth in size and influence of the Roman Catholic Church.

Another important change in organized religion that became apparent in the postwar era was the growth of interfaith toleration and cooperation. Gaining headway after World War I, ecumenism gathered speed after 1940. The Federal Council of Churches in America combined with eight interdenominational agencies in 1941; the entire structure was reorganized in 1950 and reintegrated into the National Council of Churches of Christ. In addition to the Orthodox churches in America, the council included every important Protestant denomination except the Southern Baptists and the Missouri Synod Lutherans. A further outgrowth of the ecumenical spirit was the World Council of Churches, organized in Amsterdam in 1948 after years of preparation. It combined practically all the non-Roman Catholic churches of the world, including the Russian Orthodox Church, by 1961.

Another important ecumenical development was the steady improvement of relations between Protestants and Roman Catholics. The Roman Church contributed significantly to this new spirit. The Second Vatican Council (1962–1965) and the brief but epochal tenure (1958–1963) of the most influential pontiff in recent church history, John XXIII, featured a thorough reexamination and liberalization of Roman Catholic beliefs and doctrine. As the Roman Church began to recognize the legitimacy of Protestant churches and theology, the distinctions that had long set it apart from other Christian churches blurred and softened. Not since the Reformation had Roman Catholicism been so affected by internal criticism, questioning, and intellectual independence at all levels of its complex hierarchy. Catholic bishops increasingly took part in meetings of the World Council of Churches and other interfaith bodies.

PART FIVE

Quiescence and Change, 1953–1968

CHAPTER 24

The 1950s and American Politics

The presidency of Dwight David Eisenhower offers vivid evidence of how the evaluations of historians change with the passage of time and the increasing availability of historical evidence. The majority of presidential scholars in the 1950s and 1960s regarded Eisenhower as a mediocre and weak president. Historians and political scientists alike judged him harshly for his alleged failure to provide aggressive leadership in resolving foreign-policy and a host of pressing domestic issues. The pressures and crises of the cold war continued undiminished. Inflation and recession posed threats to prosperity. Racial, religious, and ideological tensions added their disruptions to the normal problems of a mobile society. The emphasis had shifted somewhat, but doubt and uncertainty were as rife, so it was said, at the end of the Eisenhower era as they had been at the beginning.

We now know that this portrait of the Eisenhower years was much overdrawn. In an age of instability in the institution of the presidency, he enjoyed widespread popular support; indeed, he recorded among the highest public opinion poll approval rates since they were first recorded. Recent biographers have convincingly shown, moreover, that Eisenhower's style of affability and avuncular leadership disguised a strong command over the process of presidential decision making. Perhaps most important, the eight years of the Eisenhower presidency were good years for the American people—years, for the most part, of uninterrupted peace, prosperity, and national unity. Before the end of Eisenhower's first term, the nation had largely recovered from the excesses of its Second Red Scare. There was progress in the field of civil rights. The new administration prevented runaway inflation and presided over the most prosperous decade Americans had ever known. And the GOP's return to power—after twenty years in the political wilderness—resulted in a cautious expansion of the New Deal reform structure rather than its dismantling. The anticipated break with the Democratic era did not occur.

1. THE EISENHOWER PRESIDENCY

Eisenhower brought and retained a degree of popularity to the presidency accorded to few if any of his predecessors. Not since Hoover had a new presidential candidate been as widely known and respected at the time of his nomination. Not since Grant had the American people turned so hopefully to a military hero.

Eisenhower was born in Denison, Texas, on October 14, 1890, and grew up in Abilene, Kansas. After graduation from West Point in 1915, he began twenty-seven years of routine duty at regular army posts, attendance at various service schools, and a tour of duty as aide to General MacArthur in the Philippines from 1935 to 1940. Eisenhower was a lieutenant colonel with the temporary rank of brigadier general when the Japanese attacked Pearl Harbor. During the next three years, after brief service in the War Department, he commanded United States forces in the European theater, directed the North African campaign, led the Allied Expeditionary Force that landed on the beaches of Normandy in June 1944, and achieved the five stars of a general of the army. He commanded American occupation forces in Germany following the German surrender, succeeded George C. Marshall as chief of staff in late 1945, and resigned from active service in 1948 to become president of Columbia University. In 1950 he took leave of absence from Columbia to become supreme commander of the newly formed NATO forces.

Eisenhower entered the campaign of 1952 with no political experience and almost no working knowledge of the political process. Indeed, his political views were so ill defined after the war that no one, including the general himself, was quite sure of his party preference, with the result that both parties sought his candidacy in 1948. Although he was free of intense partisanship, this meant that his style of political leadership was largely a product of his army career.

In his military experience, Eisenhower had proved to be an administrative genius who was able to direct gigantic operations, work harmoniously with others and reconcile divergent viewpoints, and shoulder the burdens of large responsibility. A gifted coordinator, Eisenhower detested controversy and constantly sought to reconcile opposing viewpoints. He employed approaches that were second nature to him: persuasion, discussion, tact, charm, patience, and good will. Teamwork was the key to accomplishment. The leader's role was to harmonize the functioning of the team and ratify decisions and policies carefully prepared by subordinates. At a time when questions of national defense were crucial, he brought to the presidency a high level of competence in that field. His overseas experience had instilled in him a mature internationalist outlook, an invaluable familiarity with European leaders and problems, and a determination to maintain and strengthen the Western alliance system and the non-Communist world generally. All this gave a strength and a focus to his presidency that no specific errors or failures could undermine.

The new president was not an intellectual, nor was he given to serious reading in history, politics, or current affairs. "Eisenhower's mind is, like his personality, standard-American," one observer noted. "It is unschematic, distrustful of fine distinctions into the realm of matter and things, concerned with the effect of ideas rather than with their validity." He sometimes expressed commonplace ideas in a rambling and labored syntax. Yet he spoke in terms and voiced sentiments that millions of Americans understood and shared.

Indeed, Eisenhower was "standard-American" almost to the point of caricature. He liked westerns, bourbon, bridge and poker, golf, fishing, gardening, and hunting. He admired the successful businessman. In a generation that had experienced bewildering changes and looked nostalgically toward a vanished past, Eisenhower seemed to embody traditional American virtues: decency, self-reliance, thrift, and individualism. The political views that began to emerge with his candidacy in 1952 expressed traditional Republican devotion to free enterprise and a balanced budget, a preference for liberty over security, respect for state rights, and distrust of "creeping socialism." Yet he agreed that the essentials of New Deal reform should be maintained. This seemingly inconsistent attitude exemplified the middle-road position that Eisenhower consciously sought to occupy, and it was an excellent approximation of majority sentiment in the 1950s.

Yet there was an undeniable gap between promise and performance. The military staff system, with its chains of command and sweeping delegations of pyramided authority, lent itself only moderately well to the operations of the federal executive. It also resulted in an unprecedented bureaucratization of the presidency through the growth of the White House staff. Moreover, teamwork and coordination, which had made Allied landings on D day so huge a success, were poorly designed to absorb the frictions and pressures of the political process. Conciliation and compromise had a way of deferring or diluting decision, and moderation began to look like drift. Eisenhower avoided, when possible, systematic exposure to the details, close political contacts, and daily burdens of his office. Although beneath his open and uncomplicated manner lay an impressive fund of political ability and shrewdness, he failed to grasp the immense possibilities that his skills, prestige, and the powers of office had placed at his disposal.

And yet Eisenhower's outlook, temperament, and style fitted the public mood like a tailored uniform. Americans wanted just such a president—a respected figure above the political battle, a cautious moderate, an embodiment of the "American way." Twenty years of one-party dominance had weakened the vitality and responsibility of Republicans and Democrats alike. New Deal reform needed the kind of bipartisan ratification that only a well-disposed Republican administration could provide. Republicans needed to learn, as only the burdens of leadership could teach them, that neither the New Deal nor the postwar world could be wished into oblivion.

2. POLITICAL PATTERNS, 1953–1960

Although Eisenhower was instrumental in restoring unity and confidence, the most striking features of American politics during the 1950s was its confusion and instability. Eisenhower's huge majority in 1952 signaled the breakup of the Roosevelt coalition of laborers, farmers, urban minorities, and Southerners. Yet no new majority coalition took its place. As we have said before, Eisenhower's election seemed to signify "decomposition"—the decline in traditional party allegiances among almost every group, class, and section, and the growth of political independents and undecideds. Millions of Americans began to vote a split ticket, supporting a candidate or an issue rather than a party, and shifting sides in response to circumstances. Ticket splitting encouraged another tendency—a two-leveled political system in which Republicans dominated presidential politics while Democrats controlled Congress and state legislatures.

The partial erosion of New Deal political patterns and the partial emergence of a new political pattern were the product of several factors. Short-term issues, such as anticommunism and resentment over the Korean War, swung many traditionally Democratic votes into the Republican column in 1952. Over the long term, prosperity eroded older voting habits. Among farmers, for example, the dire economic plight that had produced Democratic majorities in most rural areas in the 1930s was largely gone. Farmers, while relying upon governmental price supports and other New Deal benefits, now disapproved of governmental spending—except, of course, for agricultural price supports—and regarded Democratic fiscal and welfare policies as inflationary.

Comparable pressures were at work in cities, where traditionally Democratic urban voters were entering the middle class. As millions of families moved from city tenements to suburban homes after 1945, a new property-owning, taxpaying outlook often outweighed older class prejudices and party loyalties. A Republican majority in the suburbs began to offset the Democratic big-city vote. Among urban groups, only blacks retained the staunch Democratic loyalty fostered during New Deal days. Meanwhile, two other bulwarks of the New Deal coalition—the South and organized labor—could no longer be depended upon to deliver large Democratic majorities.

Notwithstanding all these changes, Republicans were unable to construct a stable national majority of their own. The Roosevelt coalition had been broken because conditions that gave it birth were largely gone, but, for the next thirty years, the Democrats still retained a majority of several million registered voters. It was no longer a reliable majority, but the country remained "normally" Democratic in congressional and state elections, and neither prosperity, Eisenhower's popularity, nor the frustrations and resentments of the cold war could make permanent Republicans out of the millions of Democrats who backed Eisenhower in 1952.

As a reflection of this political ferment, the GOP could do no better in 1952 than break even in the Senate and win a majority of eight in the House. The balance of the decade, with one major exception, witnessed a resurgence of Democratic strength in Congress. In 1954, recession, a rise in unemployment, and rural discontent over administration farm policy contributed to a Republican reversal in the midterm elections. The Democrats won a precarious majority in the Senate and regained control of the House by a margin of 232 to 203—a gain which was, however, below average for a midterm election.

More indicative of general political patterns were the results of the presidential election of 1956. The only serious question for Republicans was Eisenhower's health. He had suffered a major heart attack in the autumn of 1955 and had undergone an operation for ileitis in the spring of 1956. His recovery in both cases had been so remarkable as to remove most doubts about his ability to serve a second term. GOP leaders were also determined to renominate the more controversial Nixon for vice-president, who, although offensive to liberal Republicans because of his strident anticommunism, was regarded by GOP strategists as an indispensable link between the moderate and conservative wings. After the appearance of no real opposition, the Republicans met in San Francisco in August 1956 and quickly renominated Eisenhower and Nixon. The platform promised flexible farm price supports, federal aid to schools, stiffening of the Taft-Hartley Act, and possible tax reductions. It approved the Supreme Court's desegregation decision of 1954 (see p. 550) but opposed the use of force to implement it.

Meanwhile, the Democrats, meeting in Chicago, renominated Adlai Stevenson. But he did not win this second nomination without strong opposition from Senator Estes Kefauver of Tennessee, a southern liberal whose national reputation was based largely upon his investigations of organized crime. He announced in early 1956 that he would enter certain primaries and seek the nomination, but after a long, exhausting, and uninspiring primary battle, Kefauver withdrew. Stevenson announced after his nomination that he would leave the convention free to choose a vice-presidential candidate, and, following a feverish battle, Kefauver was nominated. The Democratic platform endorsed the further extension of New Deal policies—more generous agricultural subsidies, a higher minimum wage, repeal of the Taft-Hartley Act, better conservation of natural resources, and tax reduction for lower-income groups. Another plank, cautiously endorsing the Supreme Court's recent desegration decision, called for continued efforts to wipe out discrimination, but it contained no pledge to implement desegregation and was weaker than its Republican counterpart.

The Democrats, to be sure, labored under huge disadvantages. Eisenhower, at the peak of his popularity, was almost invulnerable to criticism, while Stevenson groped vainly for an issue. Nothing in the Democratic arsenal could possibly match the Republican appeal of "peace and prosperity." Neither farm discontent nor unemployment was acute enough to cause a major upheaval, and the civil rights question was more a liability than an asset to the Democrats. When Stevenson tried to discuss the perils of radioactive fallout and the need to stop nuclear testing, the country seemed satisfied that Eisenhower knew best about such matters.

In retrospect, it is doubtful that anything Stevenson might have said or done would have significantly affected the outcome, and the result was an Eisenhower landslide of almost staggering proportions. The Republican candidate received a record number of 35.6 million popular votes and carried forty-one states with 457 electoral votes. Stevenson, with 26 million popular votes, won only the 73 electoral votes of Missouri, Arkansas, Alabama, Mississippi, Georgia, and the Carolinas. Only in Missouri, California, and a few farm states did Eisenhower fail to run more strongly than in 1952. While the GOP decisively retained control of the presidency, the Democrats carried both houses of Congress, retaining their narrow majority in the Senate and slightly enlarging their House margin. Never before had a party won both branches of Congress while losing the presidency.

Two years later, Democratic control of Congress was further extended, as Republicans suffered a severe midterm defeat. A recession beginning in late 1957 brought a sharp rise in unemployment, while the launching of the Russian *Sputnik* satellites created public alarm about the state of American education, science, and defense. Beset by these liabilities, the Republicans received a stunning rebuke at the polls in 1958. The Democrats enlarged their congressional majorities to veritable New Deal proportions: 62 to 34 in the Senate and 283 to 153 in the House. There was a resurgence of Democratic strength among white-collar workers, young voters, and suburbanites.

This huge Democratic congressional majority created a deadlock in national politics during the last half of Eisenhower's second term. Warning against inflation, Eisenhower freely vetoed Democratic domestic-policy initiatives, and, on most matters, the Democratic majority was less impressive than it looked. While a coalition of southern Democrats and conservative Republicans often modified or blocked liberal measures, the skillful Texas politicians who led the Democrats in Congress—Senate Majority Leader Lyndon B. Johnson and veteran Speaker Sam Rayburn—followed a deliberate strategy of compromise and cooperation in their dealings with the White House.

ELECTION OF 1956

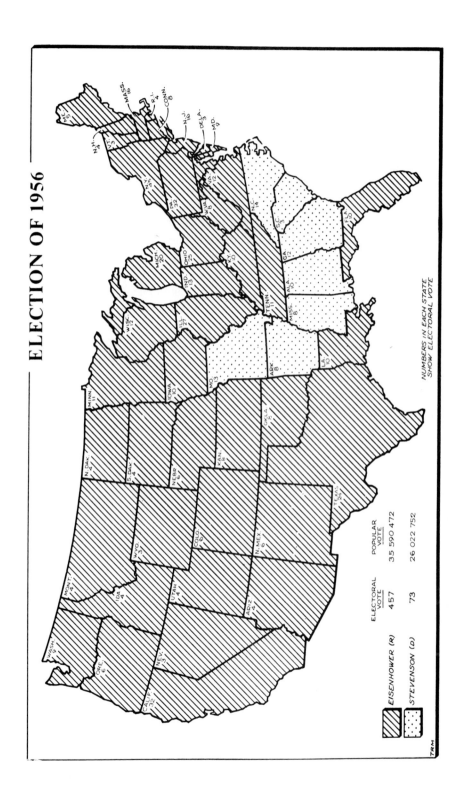

NUMBERS IN EACH STATE
SHOW ELECTORAL VOTE

	ELECTORAL VOTE	POPULAR VOTE
EISENHOWER (R)	457	35 590 472
STEVENSON (D)	73	26 022 752

TRM

3.   DYNAMIC CONSERVATISM

Although many observers predicted a rightward swing in domestic policy as the Eisenhower administration took office in 1953, it proved far less conservative than many liberal Democrats feared and many conservative Republicans hoped. As Eisenhower put it, the main emphasis in domestic policy would be "dynamic conservatism"—caution in financial and economic matters combined with careful attention to problems of human welfare.

The new cabinet seemed, however, to suggest an approach much more conservative than dynamic. For secretary of state, the president chose John Foster Dulles, an experienced diplomat and wealthy corporation lawyer. Two prominent business executives, George Humphrey of the M. A. Hanna Steel Company and Charles E. Wilson of General Motors, headed the Treasury and Defense departments. The new attorney general was Herbert Brownell, Jr., of New York, legal aide and political ally of Thomas E. Dewey. Ezra Taft Benson of Utah, conservative farm marketing specialist, became secretary of agriculture, while the Commerce Department went to Sinclair Weeks, a New England industrialist.

Eisenhower's cabinet, by the looks of it, was a big businessman's dream. All the same, its members were hardheaded pragmatists who accepted the New Deal–Fair Deal framework. Even so, the new administration attempted to roll back governmental intervention in the economy. It promptly eliminated wartime price, wage, rent, and other controls, sold twenty-eight federally owned synthetic rubber plants to private companies, and allowed the Reconstruction Finance Corporation to go out of business in 1953. Even more indicative was a new policy of tax cutting. Reductions for individual and corporate income taxes went into effect in January 1954, and a vigorous attempt was made to balance the budget. The attempt failed, but the Republicans did succeed in slashing federal expenditures in 1954 by fully $6.5 billion, or almost 10 percent.

Still another example of dynamic conservatism concerned the role of government in electrical and natural resource management. Eisenhower believed that, in both of these areas, waste and "creeping socialism" were the result of excessive governmental intervention and too little participation by private enterprise. While public ownership of natural resources often infringed upon state rights, public power should be replaced by a partnership between government and industry. Three controversies brought attention to the proper role of government in hydroelectric power and natural resources management: the tidelands oil deposits, the Hell's Canyon Dam project, and the Dixon-Yates contract with the Atomic Energy Commission.

The tidelands oil controversy began during the 1930s, when discovery of huge oil deposits off the California and Gulf coasts provoked a dispute between state and federal governments over ownership of the submerged lands. President

Truman vetoed bills in 1946 and 1952 granting title to the states, and Supreme Court decisions in 1947 and 1950 affirmed the federal government's "paramount rights" to the offshore lands. Opposing "federal encroachment upon the rights and affairs of the states," Eisenhower signed a Submerged Lands Act in May 1953 after it had passed both houses by large majorities. The act gave title to submerged coastal lands within their "historic boundaries" to the states but recognized federal jurisdiction over the continental shelf extending beyond these boundaries.

Meanwhile, the historic power controversy flared anew during the 1950s. Public power advocates wanted the government to build and operate a huge dam and hydroelectric plant in Hell's Canyon on the Snake River in Idaho. Eisenhower opposed further expansion of federal involvement and threw his support behind the proposal of a private firm, the Idaho Power Company, to develop power in the region by building three smaller dams. After a bitter two-year battle, the Idaho company obtained a license from the Federal Power Commission for its project in 1955. Democratic attempts to pass a Hell's Canyon bill in the next two sessions of Congress ended in failure.

The Dixon-Yates controversy began in 1953 over the means of providing increased electrical power to the AEC's atomic energy plant at Paducah, Kentucky. Congress rejected a $100 million request by the Tennessee Valley Authority to erect a new steam plant for this purpose, and Eisenhower supported a proposal already under consideration by the AEC to obtain its power from private sources. A newly formed group headed by utilities executives Edgar H. Dixon and Eugene A. Yates had offered to construct a generating plant at West Memphis, Arkansas, and to sell power to the TVA, which could then divert more of its own electricity to the AEC. This proposal immediately became the focus of a slashing battle between friends and opponents of public power. While the AEC voted approval of the Dixon-Yates contract in November 1954, the Joint Congressional Committee on Atomic Energy, whose approval was also necessary, found that there had been no competitive bidding and that the TVA, which bitterly opposed the plan, had not been adequately consulted. Although the joint committee also endorsed the contract by a strict party vote after obtaining a few revisions, new disclosures and heightened Democratic opposition finally brought the project to defeat. Eisenhower was quick to seize an alternative, and, when the city of Memphis announced that it was ready to build a municipal power plant with ample capacity to supply the needed electricity, he canceled the Dixon-Yates contract in July 1955. Later that year, the AEC formally ruled the contract invalid because of a possible conflict of interest in its negotiation.

Another phase of the power controversy centered around Eisenhower's program for nuclear power. In an atoms for peace address before the United Nations in December 1953, he proposed the international pooling of nuclear technology and materials and the use of this common fund in peaceful pursuits. The plan was favorably received at home and abroad, and Congress embodied it in the Atomic Energy Act of 1954, but the domestic side of this program rekindled the power controversy. Eisenhower's plan contained another important element: a stipulation that the nuclear power industry be under private rather than public auspices. Battle lines formed immediately in Congress. Private power clauses in the Atomic Energy Act passed only after a long struggle that included a thirteen-day filibuster by Democratic opponents of the bill. As finally adopted, the act made material and production facilities available to private companies under AEC safeguards. It also authorized the AEC to license private construction of nuclear reactors and pay a fair price for their output. All in all, the act was a victory for Eisenhower's nuclear power policy.

4.   THE MIDDLE ROAD

Although Eisenhower favored a moderate expansion of New Deal economic and social policies, he was constantly hampered by conservatives who wanted no expansion at all and by liberals who wanted more than he was willing to approve. His desire for an adequate welfare program was also circumscribed by his own dislike of spending and big government. Yet, despite setbacks in some areas and small results in others, Eisenhower succeeded in preserving and enlarging the complex body of welfare legislation initiated by Roosevelt and Truman.

It was not easy going during Eisenhower's first two years in office. Conservative Republicans refused to permit revision of the Taft-Hartley Act, notwithstanding the platform pledge in 1952. They rejected Eisenhower's proposals for federally supported health insurance, larger highway appropriations, and aid to education. And they nearly approved a constitutional amendment offered by Senator John W. Bricker of Ohio to limit the president's treaty-making power. The death of Senator Taft due to cancer in 1953 only exacerbated a rift between moderate and reactionary elements within the Republican party, for Taft had supported the administration in its first months and used his great prestige and influence to win a measure of cooperation from the right wing. On the whole, in fact, Eisenhower's programs fared better in the narrowly Democratic Eighty-fourth, Eighty-fifth, and Eighty-sixth Congresses (1955–1960) than in the Republican Eighty-third (1953–1954).

The most difficult New Deal policy to maintain rationally was that of agricultural price supports and crop controls. Farmers, while more efficient and productive than ever before, were squeezed by rising costs for equipment, labor, and distribution. As a result, net income per farm declined by 29 percent from 1947 to 1957. Overproduction was the major problem, as increasing use of machinery, fertilizer, and better scientific methods swelled the yield per acre. A gigantic surplus overburdened granaries and warehouses every year. The Eisenhower administration remained committed to the principle of farm price supports, but considerable disagreement ensued over the formula for determining reduced production and fair prices.

Most farm spokesmen, favoring the highest supports obtainable, opposed any changes in the Agricultural Act of 1949. The Eisenhower administration, following the lead of Secretary Benson, advocated lower supports on a flexible, sliding scale. According to Benson, high and rigid price supports stimulated overproduction and thereby insured falling prices for the farmer and a costlier and less manageable surplus for the government. Congress, mindful of the farm vote, was cool to the Benson program, but the administration succeeded in making it the basis for the Agricultural Act of 1954. The act established a flexible scale of supports on basic commodities, ranging from 82.5 to 90 percent of parity for the 1955 crop and from 70 to 90 percent in succeeding years. The administration subsequently worked for lower and flexible price supports. The principle was retained in the Agricultural Act of 1956, which Eisenhower signed after vetoing a Democratic bill to reestablish 90 percent supports. The new act encouraged farmers to set aside several million acres each year under a "soil bank" program, but higher yields per acre produced a succession of record-breaking bumper crops from 1956 through 1960, and the formidable surpluses remained as large as ever.

The last major farm legislation during the Eisenhower era was the Agricultural Act of 1958, signed in August after another hard battle between advocates of rigid and flexible price supports. The act was a compromise, achieved with the aid of Democratic votes after Eisenhower, in March, had vetoed a bill which froze price supports at their existing level. Under the new law, supports were to be lowered gradually to a minimum of 65 percent on most basic crops in 1961–1962. Critics claimed that a progressive lowering of price supports was self-defeating because it merely encouraged farmers to produce more and thus create larger surpluses. Defenders responded that high supports had the same effect but at greater cost to the taxpayer.

The farm problem, surely one of the most intricate ones confronting the American people, had clearly not been solved by 1960. The basic principle of federal support had, however, become permanently established, and the role of government in agriculture grew markedly during the 1950s. Agricultural research programs continued their valuable work. The Rural Electrification Administration celebrated its twenty-fifth birthday in 1960 with the announcement that 97 percent of all American farms now had electricity, as compared with 11 percent in 1935. The Farmers Home Administration made and insured farm loans at a rate of over $300 million a year during the late 1950s. And a Rural Development Program, designed to provide opportunities for farmers and rural dwellers in low-income areas, was operating in 262 counties in thirty-one states by 1960, with more than two thousand local improvement projects under way. Meanwhile, as a partial solution to the problem of farm surpluses, the Agricultural Trade Development and Assistance Act of 1954 authorized the sale and export of surplus farm products to other nations in exchange for foreign currencies. It also made available outright gifts of surplus food to needy nations, milk for American schoolchildren, and, by an amendment in 1959, up to $1 billion in surplus food to needy families by issuing free stamps redeemable at grocery stores.

In order to promote American commerce, the Eisenhower administration increased governmental activity in two areas—by expanding liberal trade policies begun during the New Deal and by creating the St. Lawrence Seaway Development Corporation. Improving navigation on the St. Lawrence River, through a system of locks and dredging, would open the Great Lakes and Middle West to large ocean-going vessels. Advocated without success by Presidents Hoover, Roosevelt, and Truman, American participation in the seaway was approved by Congress in 1954, after strong support from Eisenhower. In a jointly constructed project involving the Canadian and United States governments, the St. Lawrence Seaway was opened in 1959. Tonnage passing between Montreal and Lake Ontario during the first season was 75 percent greater than in 1958, and several foreign shipping lines took steps to inaugurate or enlarge direct trade between European and Great Lakes ports. Eisenhower rightly regarded the seaway as one of the most valuable achievements of his administration.

Support of the seaway was one of several indications that Eisenhower was more sympathetic to public works projects than many persons assumed. He disapproved of pork-barrel legislation, opposed federal spending as an antidote to recession, and continued to favor federal partnership with state, local, and private enterprise whenever possible. He insisted that public works programs meet tests of legitimate need and fiscal responsibility. And, as we have seen, he wanted to restrict governmental activity in the realm of power development. Yet, within these limits, Eisenhower supported a variety of public works measures, including increased funds for flood control and other projects in the Columbia River Valley in 1953; a $1 billion appropriation for river, harbor, and flood control projects in 1954; a gigantic Colorado River Storage Project; and an agreement to participate with Mexico in building a huge dam and power plant on the Rio Grande in 1960.

But most ambitious of all was Eisenhower's highway construction plan, which failed to pass in 1955 but was enacted, after some compromise, in 1956. The Federal Aid Highway Act projected a 42,500-mile network of superhighways linking all major urban areas, with the federal government paying 90 percent and the states 10 percent of the estimated cost of $27.5 billion.

Eisenhower also supported the expansion of New Deal welfare legislation. Amendments to the Social Security Act in 1954 and 1956 extended coverage and benefits to millions not previously covered—salaried and self-employed

FOREIGN TRADE
1940 – 1970

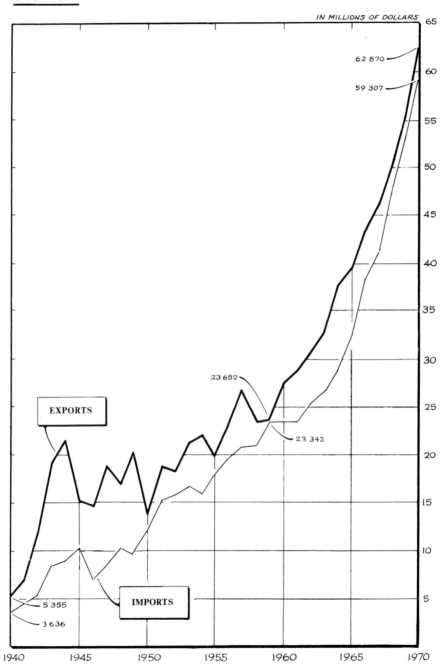

IN MILLIONS OF DOLLARS

EXPORTS

IMPORTS

62 870

59 307

23 652

23 342

5 355

3 636

professionals; religious, domestic, and clerical workers; farm operators and workers; and members of the armed forces. A 7 percent increase in Social Security benefits, although opposed by the administration, received bipartisan support in Congress and became law in January 1959. Social Security legislation covered some 58 million people by 1960. Similarly, Congress increased the minimum wage from seventy-five cents to $1 an hour. Congress twice refused to act on Eisenhower's request for federal participation in a national health insurance program, but federal spending on public health, medical research, and hospital construction increased steadily during the Eisenhower years—from $290 million in 1954 to almost $1 billion in 1961.

5.   EISENHOWER, EDUCATION, AND CIVIL RIGHTS

In two other areas—education and civil rights—the Eisenhower administration inaugurated a new era of federal involvement. Advocates of massive intervention could claim no clear victory by 1960. A combination of Eisenhower's reluctance about increasing the federal role and outright opposition from conservative Republicans meant that activism on these fronts would come from neither the president nor Congress.

After the mid-1950s, a national debate raged over the proper extent of federal involvement in public education, which had been historically the preserve of state and local governments. The high postwar birthrate and a growing shortage of classrooms and qualified teachers was an inescapable fact of the postwar era (see pp. 529–530). Because state and local budgets were strained, there was a growing call for massive federal aid. Others opposed federal aid for a variety of reasons. Private and parochial educators feared its effect. Southerners meanwhile opposed federal aid because it offered a means to enforce desegregation.

When Eisenhower introduced an education bill in 1956, basing aid on per capita income and relative state expenditures on schools, Democrats substituted a bill making population the basis for apportionment of aid. In a maneuver that was to be repeated, House Democrats adopted an amendment which made public school desegregation a condition of federal aid. In response, a bipartisan conservative majority defeated the measure altogether. A similar fate befell the administration's school aid bill in 1957.

Eisenhower's lone accomplishment in education came a year later. In the shocked aftermath of *Sputnik*, Congress enacted the National Defense Education Act of September 1958. It provided funds for long-term, low-interest loans to college students, with half the debt to be canceled if the student taught in elementary or secondary schools for at least five years after graduation. It offered matching grants to public schools for laboratories, textbooks, and other facilities in the sciences, mathematics, and foreign languages, as well as funds for 5,500 fellowships for graduate students interested in college or university teaching.

Finally, it provided grants to state agencies for counseling, vocational education, and other purposes.

At the same time, the act sidestepped the crucial issue of federal aid for new classrooms and teachers' salaries. Bills containing such provisions were debated by Congress in 1959 and 1960. A compromise measure providing funds for classrooms but not salaries seemed within reach in the latter year. However, the House Rules Committee, controlled by its four Republican and three southern Democratic members, stubbornly refused to authorize the official House-Senate conference that was prepared to adjust differences and devise an acceptable bill.

The administration's record was equally inconclusive in the crucial area of civil rights. After months of bickering and southern obstruction, Congress adopted a Civil Rights Act in September 1957. It was a landmark, but mainly for the symbolic reason that it was the first federal civil rights law in eighty-two years. The bill overcame a southern filibuster only after it was clear that it posed no danger to Jim Crow.

The Civil Rights Act established a bipartisan commission with power to subpoena witnesses and investigate denial of voting rights and equal protection of the laws on account of color, race, religion, or national origin. It also provided for a new assistant attorney general who might initiate injunctive proceedings in federal district courts when voting rights were interfered with. Congress extended the commission for two more years in 1959. But more legislation was clearly needed, and Congress finally responded, after long debate, with another Civil Rights Act in 1960, which empowered federal courts to appoint referees to consider state voting qualification laws whenever a petitioner had been deprived of the right to register or vote because of race or color. It also imposed heavy penalties against illegal acts by private citizens. With what seemed to civil rights advocates like agonizing slowness, the power of the federal government was thus extended in behalf of fair and equal treatment for all Americans.

6. THE WARREN COURT AND A JUDICIAL REVOLUTION

Perhaps far more important in shaping the course of American history after 1950 than Eisenhower, Congress, or political parties was the Supreme Court and its chief justice, Earl Warren, who was appointed by Eisenhower less than nine months after he took office. Civil rights and civil liberties had been the Supreme Court's major concern since the late 1930s. In the 1940s and early 1950s, the Court took important steps toward breaking down legally enforced segregation. In *Smith* v. *Allwright* (1944), it reversed a previous decision and declared that Negroes could not be denied the right to participate in party primaries. When South Carolina responded by removing all regulations for party primaries from its statute books, District Judge J. Waites Waring of Charleston ordered Democratic registrars to enroll qualified black voters in 1948, and the Supreme Court upheld Waring by refusing to review the case. And in *Terry* v. *Adams* (1953), the Court outlawed a Texas organization, the Jaybird Association, which limited its membership to whites and chose nominees for the local Democratic primary. The Court noted that Jaybird candidates almost invariably won both the primary and general election and identified this as another illegal method to circumvent the Allwright decision and to exclude blacks from voting. Such decisions brought southern blacks measurably closer to full political citizenship.

The Court found cause to strike down the historic "separate but equal" concept, the legalism upon which southern states had built their elaborate system of Jim Crow legislation, on the question of school segregation. Chief Justice Hughes opened the assault in the *Gaines* decision in 1938 (see Vol. I, pp. 323–324). In *Sweatt* v. *Painter* (1950), the Court decreed that separate law school facilities could never be really equal and ordered the University of Texas to admit a black student who had refused to attend the state law school for Negroes in Houston. One effect was to compel many southern state universities to admit blacks to law, medical, and graduate schools. More important was the clear implication of the Sweatt case: segregated public education on any level was unequal education. Thus encouraged, the National Association for the Advancement of Colored People's Legal Defense Fund stepped up its campaign to end segregation in public schools.

The stage was set for a momentous decision in 1954. A number of cases challenging public school segregation had come before the Vinson Court in 1952. Unable to reach a decision, the justices ordered reargument of these cases in 1953 and requested counsel to answer certain key questions regarding the intent and meaning of the Fourteenth Amendment. With Warren on the bench during the reargument, the justices handed down their decision on a representative case—*Brown* v. *Board of Education of Topeka*—on May 17, 1954. A unanimous Court, declaring that public school segregation was unconstitutional under the Fourteenth Amendment, completely reversed the separate but equal doctrine enunciated in *Plessy* v. *Ferguson* in 1896. Impressed by the trenchant logic of Thurgood Marshall, counsel for the Legal Defense Fund, the justices emphasized sociological and psychological factors in their decision. "In the field of public education," Warren declared, "the doctrine of 'separate but equal' has no place. Separate educational facilities are inherently unequal."

The Court outlined implementation procedures a year later. It instructed federal district courts to order school desegregation in their respective areas and to require "good faith," "a prompt and reasonable start," and "all deliberate speed" from local authorities. Though demanding compliance with the principle, these instructions recognized that the timing and mode of desegregation would vary according to conditions, and they permitted district judges to use discretion in setting specific deadlines and other details. Nevertheless, the broad import of the Brown decision was momentous and unmistakable. Affecting the school systems of twenty-one states and the District of Columbia, it promised to alter the pattern of education for over 8 million white and 2.5 million black children, representing nearly 40 percent of American public school enrollment. The Warren Court had erected a historic landmark in American constitutional law.

The Court, having destroyed the separate but equal doctrine in public school education, quickly rendered it inapplicable elsewhere. It steadily ruled in favor of blacks who sought admission to southern colleges, universities, and graduate schools. Out of 195 formerly all-white public institutions of higher learning in fourteen southern states, fully 124 had admitted Negro students by 1960. In a series of other rulings, federal courts also invalidated segregation of parks, public housing, municipal golf courses, public beaches and bathhouses, intrastate buses, and bus, railway, and air terminals serving interstate passengers. On the basis of the Brown decision, the ICC in 1955 ordered railroads to end all rules and practices maintaining segregation. Like emancipation a century earlier, the long-overdue extension of equal justice under law to black Americans was a beginning, not an end. It was, nevertheless, a forward step of lasting importance.

On the related issue of civil liberties, which involved the reconciliation of individual freedoms with demands of national security, the justices proceeded understandably more cautiously. Civil rights essentially pitted elementary justice against entrenched prejudice; civil liberties involved legitimate needs and rights on both sides. Rather than attempt to enunciate a fundamental principle that would guide and control future action, as in the Brown case, the Court dealt with civil liberties on a case-by-case basis. It questioned procedure and wording, sought to curb excesses, and invited state and federal bodies to tighten and improve their loyalty programs. The justices, often divided on details, groped for a middle ground that would preserve the substance of individual liberties without crippling the government's right to protect itself from disloyalty and subversion.

We have noted the general timidity of the Vinson Court, which sat during the worst years of the McCarthy era. As McCarthyism declined after 1954 and the influence of the new chief justice began to be felt, the federal judiciary took a bolder stand. Two lower-court decisions in 1956, for example, narrowed the investigative authority of the Senate Committee on Government Operations by applying the standard of pertinency. The Supreme Court in 1955 strongly upheld the controversial right of witnesses to avoid incrimination by invoking the Fifth Amendment before congressional committees. Congress attempted to circumvent the Fifth Amendment by passing the Immunity Act of 1954, under which witnesses could be granted immunity from criminal prosecution and then be *compelled* to testify in national security cases. Not unmindful of the government's need, the Court upheld the Immunity Act in *Ullman* v. *United States* (1956), but it warned that Fifth Amendment protections must not be downgraded or diminished.

An early high-water mark in the Court's defense of civil liberties came with a spate of decisions in 1957. In *Jencks* v. *United States*, the Court held that, in certain circumstances, a defendant was entitled to inspect FBI reports used in his trial and ordered the government to dismiss criminal action if it chose to withhold such reports. In *Yates* v. *United States*, the justices narrowed the meaning of the Smith Act by ruling that an individual might advocate the "abstract principle" of overthrowing the government so long as he did not advocate specific action to that end. And in *Watkins* v. *United States*, the Court invalidated a contempt citation by the House Un-American Activities Committee because HUAC's legislative mandate was "loosely worded" and "excessively broad" and because the committee had failed to show the pertinency of its questions to the inquiry at hand.

The justices also reviewed and set aside certain state actions against subversives. The most important of these rulings was *Pennsylvania* v. *Nelson* (1956), in which the Court invalidated a conviction under a state sedition law on the ground that Congress had in effect reserved to itself the field of sedition, which was a national question, and had thus "superseded" state laws on this subject. The effect was to set aside, at least temporarily, anti-Communist laws in forty-two states.

The expansion of the Court's authority—and the beginning of what became a period of judicial activism—provoked attempts to restrict its power. Southern congressmen repeatedly introduced bills to nullify the desegregation decision of 1954. Among the more extreme and farfetched proposals were constitutional amendments aimed at destroying the power of judicial review, limiting the Supreme Court's appellate jurisdiction, and choosing justices by popular election or by vote of state supreme court judges. Such schemes got nowhere; nor did proposals to strengthen the government's security program. Bills which protected state antisubversion laws and broadened the "violent overthrow" provision of the Smith Act passed the House in 1959 but died in the Senate. The one enactment that emerged from the debate was a law adopted in 1957 that protected the security of FBI files against undue exposure, but it did not overturn the basic principle affirmed in the Jencks decision.

7. AFRICAN-AMERICANS AFTER THE BROWN DECISION

The postwar era was a period of unparalleled striving, ferment, and progress for American blacks. In the years after World War II, the federal government had begun, for the first time since Reconstruction, to intervene in order to protect the civil rights of African-Americans. Perhaps the most revolutionary development in federal civil rights policy in a century was Harry Truman's decision to integrate, by executive order, the armed forces in July 1948. Yet the postwar era was also a time of heightened tension. New onslaughts against racial discrimination challenged traditional attitudes, altered the status quo, and met the resistance born of prejudice, ignorance, and fear. The most significant feature in this changing pattern of race relations was neither black progress nor the tension that accompanied it, but rather the fact that various developments at home and abroad had finally forced the nation, after generations of evasion and indifference, to begin to face its biggest social problem.

Such a confrontation could no longer be deferred. To a few Americans, it had long been apparent that the status of blacks represented American democracy's most glaring failure. The fight against German racism abroad dramatized the injustice of systematic racial discrimination at home. Subsequently, the cold war and the ideological struggle against Soviet totalitarianism pointed up the inconsistency of a foreign policy designed to promote democracy and a domestic policy that denied basic civil and political rights.

Even more important, black Americans had reached a point where they were both able and determined to mount an aggressive challenge to segregation. They had shared largely, if somewhat belatedly, in wartime job opportunities and high wages, and they further expanded their economic strength in the prosperous postwar years. Their growing concentration in northern urban centers conferred a political power which both parties had to recognize. The efforts of President Truman and other national leaders in behalf of civil rights raised black expectations.

At the same time, a significant number of white or white-dominated groups began to favor an end to Jim Crow. The federal government, as we have seen, instituted desegregation in both the civil service and the armed forces, promoted equal job opportunities, and eventually legislated to protect black voting rights. Most northern states passed or strengthened antidiscrimination laws aimed at removing inequities in employment, housing, and public accommodation. National labor organizations strove to end segregation and other discriminatory practices in union membership, although many local unions remained strongholds of prejudice. Youth organizations and urban welfare agencies were active in promoting racial harmony. Religious bodies, including most Protestant denominations, took a far more liberal and enlightened stand on the race question than in previous times.

Interracial organizations occupied the vanguard in the civil rights campaign. The Southern Regional Council, with headquarters in Atlanta, worked quietly but effectively to promote equal opportunity and friendly contact between the races. The National Urban League, founded early in the twentieth century, was operating in forty-one states by 1960. Moderate in approach, dependent largely upon local resources and contributions, the Urban League maintained a variety of services but concentrated primarily upon advancing black employment opportunities. A more recent organization, the Congress of Racial Equality (CORE), supported a wide range of antidiscrimination campaigns, with an emphasis upon direct nonviolent action.

The most influential of these groups was undoubtedly the National Association for the Advancement of Colored People. Supported by 350,000 members, white and black, the NAACP, through its Legal Defense Fund, conducted an intensive and highly successful legal campaign to destroy segregation. Victorious in all but four of forty-six appeals to the Supreme Court, the NAACP was instrumental in the epochal decisions that advanced voting rights, invalidated restrictive housing covenants, and upset the separate but equal doctrine in transportation, public facilities, and education.

Yet, especially after the Brown decision in 1954, white attitudes toward segregation hardened. Although an initial reaction was to comply with Brown, within weeks the decision had sent shock waves across the white South. Only a year after the ruling, southern extremism was ascendant over southern moderation. While moderates spoke in muted tones or not at all, more rabid southern politicians assumed postures of defiance and mobilized to meet the challenge. Most important among their numerous local organizations were the White Citizens Councils, modeled after a prototype that sprang up in Indianola, Mississippi, in 1954. The idea spread rapidly, especially in the black-belt regions of the lower South, until a network of Citizens Councils had appeared in several southern states. The Citizens Councils officially renounced violence, terrorism, and hooded night raids. Instead, they employed the weapons of propaganda, pressure, persuasion, and agitation to solidify white opinion. Relying heavily upon state rights arguments, they denounced the Brown decision as unconstitutional and promoted their ideas in a flood of pamphlets, books, speeches, letters, radio programs, and lectures. So effective a pressure group did the Councils become in most southern states that opposition was silenced. Even rational discussion of the problem soon became impossible. Southern legislatures passed a barrage of resolutions, laws, and constitutional amendments designed to circumvent the Brown ruling, including measures that would permit or require state officials to close public schools rather than allow integration.

The white South, of course, was not monolithic on this or any other question, and the speed and degree of compliance with the Brown decision varied greatly. On the whole, school integration was accomplished rapidly and without undue difficulty in the District of Columbia and the border states. "Token integration" was achieved in North Carolina, Tennessee, Arkansas, and Texas by 1957. Despite resistance from state authorities and the pressure of local opinion, most federal district judges implemented the Brown decision. Appellate courts were quick to sustain their integration orders or reverse their rulings and demand more vigorous action when they encountered evasion or undue delay.

The first major clash between federal and state authorities occurred in Arkansas, when Governor Orval E. Faubus posted state national guardsmen outside Central High School in Little Rock to bar the entry of nine black students in the fall of 1957. President Eisenhower immediately federalized the National Guard and sent federal troops to Little Rock to preserve order and enforce integration.

Openly encouraged by their state's policy, aroused white citizens prepared to bar the reentry of the black students in 1958. So threatening had the situation become that a federal district judge granted the local school board a two-and-a-half-year delay in integration in order to avoid violence. This order was quickly appealed, and the Supreme Court, in *Cooper* v. *Aaron* (1958), unanimously set it aside. The state of Arkansas thereupon closed the four Little Rock high schools but reopened them again in 1960 with limited integration.

Schools facing integration were also closed in 1958–1959 in Virginia, where Senator Harry F. Byrd had announced a "massive resistance" to desegregation. But both state and federal courts in 1959 held Virginia's school-closing law unconstitutional, and local opinion soon concluded that a little integration was better than no schools at all. State authorities yielded, and token integration was peacefully accomplished in several Virginia schools in 1959 and 1960. Even in the Deep South the wall was finally breached: a few blacks began attending formerly all-white schools in Florida in 1959 and, despite an angry boycott by white parents, in Louisiana in 1960. When Georgia yielded to the extent of permitting local school boards to comply with federal court orders if they chose, Atlanta drew up an integration plan, and nine black students entered a white school there in 1961. By the latter date, only South Carolina, Alabama, and Mississippi had failed to make at least a token compliance with the Brown decision.

And yet the "tokens" were small. White citizens soon realized that they could better preserve the substance of segregation in practice by accepting a small measure of integration in principle. Devices to limit integration by "pupil placement" laws, permitting assignment on some basis other than race—psychological factors, mental aptitude, availability of classrooms and teachers, and so on—appeared less apt to be struck down if carefully drawn. The Supreme Court held in 1958, for example, that an Alabama school placement law was not unconstitutional on its face. As of 1960, six years after the Brown decision, only about 181,000, or 6 percent, of some 3 million black students in the South were attending public schools with white students, and all but a fraction of these were in the border states and the District of Columbia.

CHAPTER 25

Global Diplomacy, 1953–1960

Although Americans were well acquainted with international tension when Eisenhower became president, they were not prepared for the degree and extent of change in world politics after 1953. In former colonies in Asia, Africa, and Latin America, nationalism became a potent force for both the Soviet Union and the United States to reckon with. The United States and its allies worked earnestly, if not always harmoniously, to preserve their security and contain the spread of communism. East-West rivalry and the cold war came to seem limitless in scope—featuring a costly arms race that increased the dangers and destructive potential of nuclear war at every step and impelled both sides toward involvement in border quarrels, political upheavals, and social revolutions in every corner of the globe.

1. EUROPE AND THE UNITED STATES IN THE 1950s

Europe remained the central battleground in the cold war. The strength and solidarity of the North Atlantic alliance continued to be America's primary concern; the weakening or disruption of that alliance retained a high priority among Soviet goals. There was no doubt in either Washington or Moscow that the renascent countries of Western Europe, with their booming economies, vast industrial and human resources, and quickening sense of unity, were the pivot in the world balance of power. Conversely, retaining control of its satellite empire in Eastern Europe was of crucial importance to the Kremlin.

The European NATO allies had concluded by midcentury that they could not rely solely upon American strategic air power to deter a Soviet attack on Western Europe. Conventional ground forces would also be necessary, although numerical parity with Russia was never contemplated. It was hoped, rather, to raise and equip a sufficient number of divisions—a so-called defensive shield—to prevent Europe from being overrun before American retaliatory bombing could take effect. The alliance promptly took steps to formulate a defensive strategy, integrate its command system, and rearm, backed by a flood of American supplies. By 1953, NATO could deploy five thousand tactical aircraft and had large stockpiles of weapons and equipment. Troop strength was another matter. Main reliance was on a handful of well-equipped divisions, mainly American, British, and French, backed by a larger number of undermanned reserve units. The entire NATO army was less than half the size of the forces immediately available to the Soviet bloc.

The British, French, and Americans had united their respective zones in the West German Federal Republic in 1948–1949. Then, in 1950, the United States proposed the delicate question of German rearmament, an issue which threatened NATO unity for years. Most Europeans, especially the French, viewed the idea with unease. Yet European leaders agreed reluctantly with the American view that German manpower was indispensable, and the first major design for rearming West Germany came from French Premier René Pleven in 1950. He called for an integrated European Defense Community, linked to NATO, with German units subordinated to a supranational army under joint control of the member nations. A treaty creating the EDC was signed in Paris in May 1952 by France, Belgium, the Netherlands, Luxembourg, Italy, and West Germany. But the French National Assembly rejected it in August 1954, after over two years of debate. Prime Minister Anthony Eden of Great Britain came forward with an alternative. In brief, an agreement, signed in Paris in October 1954, ended the joint occupation, restored full sovereignty to the West German government, and admitted West Germany to NATO. It also provided for a maximum of twelve German divisions and expanded NATO's authority over the armed forces of all member nations.

But admission of West Germany alleviated none of NATO's difficulties. Its military posture, which German adherence was designed to improve, had begun to decline well before the agreement of 1954 made possible the raising of German contingents. An ambitious three-year program to increase the size and strength of defensive-shield forces had been adopted in February 1952, only to prove unworkable within a few months and slide steadily further out of reach. Both Western Europe and the United States were prospering, and the peoples involved had little taste for high taxes, austerity, and sacrifice in peacetime. The Eisenhower administration's economy drive in military spending had its counterpart in every NATO capital. As late as 1959 only seven of the projected twelve

German divisions were ready, and NATO never achieved the thirty-division strength described by its commanders in 1958 as a necessary minimum.

While prosperity brought a greater degree of stability to continental politics, it also instilled new confidence and independence among European leaders. It also tended to make them susceptible to a long-standing Soviet objective—"decoupling" the United States from the Western alliance. A degree of European-American tension was thus evident during the 1950s. Europeans complained that Americans were rigidly anti-Soviet, unreasonable in their refusal to recognize Peking, obsessed with internal security and military preparedness, and intolerant of the needs and problems of Western Europe. Americans in turn sometimes felt that Europeans were "soft" on communism, prone to appease the Soviets, and unwilling to assume a fairer share of the Western defense effort.

The Soviet government naturally tried to exploit these frictions. When its attempt to prevent German rearmament failed, it created a regional grouping of its own—the Warsaw Pact of May 1955. It bound Albania, Bulgaria, Czechoslovakia, East Germany, Hungary, Poland, and Romania to the USSR in close military alliance. Still hopeful of driving a wedge between America and Western Europe, the Soviets later renewed their proposal to form a continental security system by excluding the United States from a merger of the defense mechanisms of the NATO and Warsaw Pact countries.

The Soviets also sought to woo the Federal Republic. Reunification was the Soviet trump card, and all Western efforts to reach agreement with Moscow on this important issue ended in failure. From the very beginning, the Eisenhower administration had sought to rearm the Federal Republic within NATO and unify the two Germanys through free elections. These were not easily reconcilable goals, and achievement of the former made the latter more remote than ever. The Western allies had urged reunification upon Russia at the Berlin conference in 1954 without success. They tried again at Geneva in 1955 and did obtain Bulganin's agreement that free elections should be the basis for future settlement. But Soviet intransigence had not abated. Russia first insisted that the two Germanys negotiate directly, in order to guarantee East Germany a voice in any united government thus formed. Next came a plan suggested by Polish Foreign Minister Adam Rapacki in October 1957. It called for the military disengagement of central Europe by banning nuclear weapons in both Germanys, Poland, and Czechoslovakia. Another Soviet proposal, in 1959, demanded that all foreign troops leave German soil, that German armaments be restricted, and that a reunited Germany be prohibited from joining any alliance that did not include the Western Big Three and the USSR.

Another serious challenge to Western unity was colonialism and the challenge posed to it by growing nationalism in Asia and Africa. Whether by war and revolution or by patient negotiation—or both—most of the colonies and protectorates in the once extensive empires of Great Britain, France, Belgium, and the Netherlands either won independence or advanced to its threshold between 1945 and 1962. By the latter date only Portugal, oldest of the imperial powers, still clung tenaciously to most of its overseas possessions. All in all, some thirty-five new countries, with a total population of over 600 million, emerged from colonial status during the postwar years.

Decolonization was a difficult process, both for the former colonies and for the former imperialists. Most of the former colonies gained independence with only weakly formed political institutions. Most of them also possessed all the structural problems endemic to colonial economies: poverty and maldistribution of income, excessive dependence on one crop or extractive industry, and under-developed human, industrial, and financial resources. For European powers, the economic and psychological readjustments were also enormous. NATO suffered both because it included all the major imperial powers and because Americans were highly critical of colonialism. The United States, seeking to combat the rising anti-Western sentiment that European imperialism had fostered, was not always patient in urging decolonization upon its allies, who often felt that Washington failed to appreciate the complexity of their problems and was oversensitive to the frequently unreasonable demands of the former colonies. This tension underlay a rupture that almost destroyed NATO in late 1956.

Meanwhile, the solidarity of the Eastern European bloc was also crumbling. The first break had occurred in 1948, when the Yugoslav leader, Marshal Tito, defied Stalin and embarked upon independent foreign and domestic policies. The satellite nations, emboldened by an apparent loosening of Soviet control and encouraged by Tito's example, stirred restlessly. Their peoples dreamed variously of greater independence, improved economic conditions, and possibly even freedom from communism. Pent-up economic and political discontent burst forth during the summer and autumn of 1956. Unorganized riots by workers demanding "bread and freedom" broke out in the Polish industrial city of Poznań in late June, and demands for an end to Soviet control over Polish affairs reached revolutionary proportions in October. With strong public support, a major element within the Polish Communist party moved to end Soviet domination by elevating Wladyslaw Gomulka, who had once been jailed in a Stalinist purge, to the important post of first secretary. Soviet leaders, backed by Soviet troops moving into Poland from Russia and East Germany, hastened to Warsaw to face down this challenge. Minor clashes between Polish and Russian military units seemed to presage full-scale war. But tense discussions resulted in a victory for Polish nationalism. The Soviets backed down in late October. They withdrew their troops and acquiesced in Gomulka's installation as first secretary and head of state. Gomulka won enough concessions from Moscow to launch Poland on a "national Communist" policy along Titoist lines.

Nationalist dissent immediately erupted in Hungary, beginning with a revolt in Budapest on October 23–24. The uprising led to bloodshed and intervention

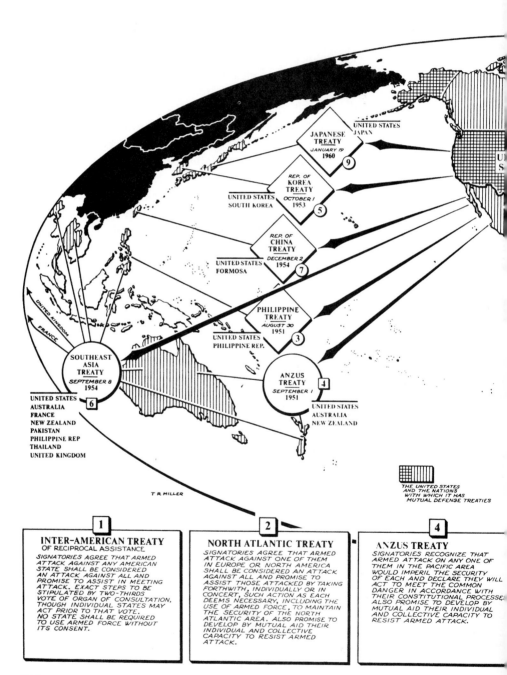

UNITED STATES
JAPAN

JAPANESE TREATY
JANUARY 19
1960
9

REP. OF KOREA TREATY
UNITED STATES
SOUTH KOREA
OCTOBER 1
1953
5

REP. OF CHINA TREATY
UNITED STATES
FORMOSA
DECEMBER 2
1954
7

PHILIPPINE TREATY
AUGUST 30
1951
UNITED STATES
PHILIPPINE REP.
3

UNITED KINGDOM

FRANCE

SOUTHEAST ASIA TREATY
SEPTEMBER 8
1954

UNITED STATES
AUSTRALIA
FRANCE
NEW ZEALAND
PAKISTAN
PHILIPPINE REP
THAILAND
UNITED KINGDOM
6

ANZUS TREATY
SEPTEMBER 1
1951
4
UNITED STATES
AUSTRALIA
NEW ZEALAND

U
S

THE UNITED STATES
AND THE NATIONS
WITH WHICH IT HAS
MUTUAL DEFENSE TREATIES

T R MILLER

1
INTER-AMERICAN TREATY
OF RECIPROCAL ASSISTANCE

SIGNATORIES AGREE THAT ARMED
ATTACK AGAINST ANY AMERICAN
STATE SHALL BE CONSIDERED
AN ATTACK AGAINST ALL AND
PROMISE TO ASSIST IN MEETING
ATTACK. EXACT STEPS TO BE
STIPULATED BY TWO-THIRDS
VOTE OF ORGAN OF CONSULTATION,
THOUGH INDIVIDUAL STATES MAY
ACT PRIOR TO THAT VOTE.
NO STATE SHALL BE REQUIRED
TO USE ARMED FORCE WITHOUT
ITS CONSENT.

2
NORTH ATLANTIC TREATY

SIGNATORIES AGREE THAT ARMED
ATTACK AGAINST ONE OF THEM
IN EUROPE OR NORTH AMERICA
SHALL BE CONSIDERED AN ATTACK
AGAINST ALL AND PROMISE TO
ASSIST THOSE ATTACKED BY TAKING
FORTHWITH, INDIVIDUALLY OR IN
CONCERT, SUCH ACTION AS EACH
DEEMS NECESSARY, INCLUDING THE
USE OF ARMED FORCE, TO MAINTAIN
THE SECURITY OF THE NORTH
ATLANTIC AREA. ALSO PROMISE TO
DEVELOP BY MUTUAL AID THEIR
INDIVIDUAL AND COLLECTIVE
CAPACITY TO RESIST ARMED
ATTACK.

4
ANZUS TREATY

SIGNATORIES RECOGNIZE THAT
ARMED ATTACK ON ANY ONE OF
THEM IN THE PACIFIC AREA
WOULD IMPERIL THE SECURITY
OF EACH AND DECLARE THEY WILL
ACT TO MEET THE COMMON
DANGER IN ACCORDANCE WITH
THEIR CONSTITUTIONAL PROCESSE.
ALSO PROMISE TO DEVELOP BY
MUTUAL AID THEIR INDIVIDUAL
AND COLLECTIVE CAPACITY TO
RESIST ARMED ATTACK.

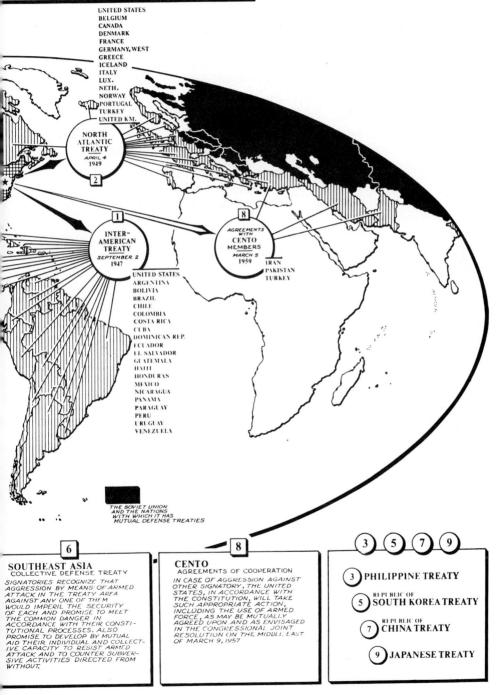

UNITED STATES
BELGIUM
CANADA
DENMARK
FRANCE
GERMANY, WEST
GREECE
ICELAND
ITALY
LUX.
NETH.
NORWAY
PORTUGAL
TURKEY
UNITED KM.

NORTH ATLANTIC TREATY
APRIL 4 1949

2

1
INTER-AMERICAN TREATY
SEPTEMBER 2 1947

UNITED STATES
ARGENTINA
BOLIVIA
BRAZIL
CHILE
COLOMBIA
COSTA RICA
CUBA
DOMINICAN REP.
ECUADOR
EL SALVADOR
GUATEMALA
HAITI
HONDURAS
MEXICO
NICARAGUA
PANAMA
PARAGUAY
PERU
URUGUAY
VENEZUELA

8
AGREEMENTS WITH CENTO MEMBERS
MARCH 5 1959
IRAN
PAKISTAN
TURKEY

THE SOVIET UNION
AND THE NATIONS
WITH WHICH IT HAS
MUTUAL DEFENSE TREATIES

6
SOUTHEAST ASIA
COLLECTIVE DEFENSE TREATY

SIGNATORIES RECOGNIZE THAT
AGGRESSION BY MEANS OF ARMED
ATTACK IN THE TREATY AREA
AGAINST ANY ONE OF THEM
WOULD IMPERIL THE SECURITY
OF EACH AND PROMISE TO MEET
THE COMMON DANGER IN
ACCORDANCE WITH THEIR CONSTI-
TUTIONAL PROCESSES. ALSO
PROMISE TO DEVELOP BY MUTUAL
AID THEIR INDIVIDUAL AND COLLECT-
IVE CAPACITY TO RESIST ARMED
ATTACK AND TO COUNTER SUBVER-
SIVE ACTIVITIES DIRECTED FROM
WITHOUT.

8
CENTO
AGREEMENTS OF COOPERATION

IN CASE OF AGGRESSION AGAINST
OTHER SIGNATORY, THE UNITED
STATES, IN ACCORDANCE WITH
THE CONSTITUTION, WILL TAKE
SUCH APPROPRIATE ACTION,
INCLUDING THE USE OF ARMED
FORCE, AS MAY BE MUTUALLY
AGREED UPON AND AS ENVISAGED
IN THE CONGRESSIONAL JOINT
RESOLUTION ON THE MIDDLE EAST
OF MARCH 9, 1957

3 **5** **7** **9**

3 PHILIPPINE TREATY

5 REPUBLIC OF SOUTH KOREA TREATY

7 REPUBLIC OF CHINA TREATY

9 JAPANESE TREATY

561

by Soviet military forces and then proceeded to get out of hand. The Hungarians lacked a leader of Gomulka's stature and ability, and what had begun as another Titoist bid for national Communist autonomy soon broadened into a sweeping, ill-organized movement to overthrow Communist rule altogether. The Hungarian regime replaced unpopular leaders with moderates who made concession after concession to the rebels—now backed by an almost nationwide general strike—and virtually dismantled the Communist edifice. But, when Hungary threatened to renounce the Warsaw Pact and declare its neutrality, the Soviets responded with a massive invasion. In less than a week, the movement had been crushed and a new pro-Soviet government installed.

The Hungarian uprising coincided with an Anglo-French-Israeli invasion of Egypt in early November 1956. Events leading to the Suez crisis revealed a basic Western disagreement on the colonial question, and the crisis itself transformed this disparity into a split that almost wrecked the Atlantic alliance. The United States not only refused to back its allies in their assault on Egypt but joined the Soviet Union and most other countries in condemning it. Although suspicion and animosity within the Western camp lingered for months, Soviet bellicosity had effectively dramatized the need for unity, and Allied statesmen worked patiently to heal the breach.

Europeans meanwhile grew increasingly restive about their dependence on America's nuclear preponderance. Seeking to escape it, the British developed their own nuclear capability; France followed suit. Although Americans wanted to retain their nuclear monopoly almost as badly as Europeans wanted to break it, the need to mend fences after Suez demanded concessions. The United States agreed in 1957 to a larger measure of collaboration with Great Britain in missile and atomic research and began providing its allies with more nuclear information after Congress amended the Atomic Energy Act in 1958. European NATO contingents received training in the use of American tactical atomic weapons and rockets, and the United States built large stockpiles of nuclear warheads in Europe, to be available to the shield forces in the event of war. In return, Great Britain agreed in 1958 to permit establishment of Thor IRBM squadrons on British soil. Italy and Turkey concluded missile-base agreements with the United States a year later.

Throughout the 1950s, the status of Berlin remained a troublesome—and potentially dangerous—problem. Still under four-power control, the city was divided by a line running irregularly north and south along city streets. On one side was East Berlin, the Soviet sector since 1945 and the capital of East Germany since 1949. Its 1.2 million inhabitants lived drably: a few well-lit modern avenues did not compensate for vast dismal neighborhoods that still carried the scars of war. Across the street lay West Berlin, embracing the three western sectors, a prosperous beehive of 2.2 million energetic inhabitants.

West Berlin both affronted and menaced the Soviet empire. It provided an escape route for the thousands of East Germans who left each year, and its very existence kept discontent alive among those who remained. It contributed substantially to East Germany's economic problems, and the Soviets viewed this situation with understandable nervousness. They had had to quell one East German uprising in 1953. Since then they had experienced major difficulties in Poland and Hungary. Chronic unrest in the German Democratic Republic remained strong.

One further development set the stage for crisis. In 1955, the Russians transferred to East Germany the power to supervise civilian traffic and freight on the surface arteries that linked West Berlin to the Federal Republic. Russian troops continued to inspect military traffic supplying the Allied garrisons, but after 1955 East Germany could harass, delay, or block the flow of civilian goods upon which West Berlin's prosperity depended. The Western powers, which had never recognized the East German regime, warned that they would continue to hold Russia accountable for any disruption of the Berlin traffic or any infringement of their right of access.

Three years passed without major incident. Then Khrushchev announced in November 1958 that four-power occupation of Berlin was out of date and should be terminated. Russia, he said, would shortly hand over its functions in the city to the East German government. If they did not follow suit, the Western allies would henceforth have to deal directly with East Germany. Russia would meet forcible resistance to this new arrangement with force. The Allies promptly reiterated their right to remain until a peace treaty with a reunited Germany had been concluded. They also renewed their promise to protect West Berlin. Khrushchev replied on November 27 that Russia no longer recognized any Western right of access or presence. Continued occupation, he said, was a threat to the security of East Germany, the Soviet Union, and the entire Soviet bloc.

The West met this challenge firmly. The British, French, and American governments refused to recognize Russia's right to act unilaterally in altering the four-power occupation. They also refused to abandon West Berlin and insisted that negotiation was possible only in connection with the entire German question and in the absence of an ultimatum. Although tension eased in 1959 after visits by Deputy Premier Mikoyan to the United States and Prime Minister Macmillan to Moscow, no progress could be made toward a settlement. Negotiations at the Geneva conference of foreign ministers in mid-1959 ended in impasse.

In contrast to the gloomy prospects surrounding the question of Berlin was the early success of the Common Market. Ever since the inception of the six-nation Coal and Steel Community in 1951, statesmen had been laying plans to broaden the area of economic unity. Plans for economic integration went quickly forward, and these six nations—France, West Germany, Italy, Holland, Luxembourg, and Belgium—signed a treaty in Rome in March 1957 creating the

European Economic Community. It called for free movement of labor and capital and gradual abolition of all internal tariff barriers and trade restrictions within the six-nation area. It also envisaged eventual adoption of a uniform external tariff and direction by a network of supranational executive, legislative, judicial, and advisory bodies. The agreement was purposely designed to provide a framework for eventual political union. A companion treaty formed the European Atomic Community, or Euratom, to conduct joint development of atomic power for economic purposes. Both treaties went into force in January 1958.

The first 10 percent reduction in internal tariffs and quota restrictions took place in January 1959, the second a year later. More important, the ability of the supranational governing bodies to prepare long-range programs, resolve complex technical questions, and harmonize conflicting policies gave evidence that this experiment in unity had the power to survive and grow. Economies of member nations flourished spectacularly under the integrated system. A powerful new aggregation, with human and industrial resources on a par with those of the United States and the Soviet Union, was emerging in Europe.

The new arrangement inevitably posed problems for the West as a whole. Plans to link the Common Market with a broader trade area were temporarily stalled when Great Britain, Sweden, Norway, Denmark, Switzerland, Austria, and Portugal formed the European Free Trade Association in 1959—the so-called Outer Seven, as distinguished from the Common Market's Inner Six—in a somewhat looser agreement. Differences in policy between the two groups threatened to bring on a trade war in 1960, as the Common Market effected its second internal tariff reduction and the Outer Seven its first.

The Common Market's economic success and political promise soon showed signs of overcoming most of these troubles. The British government, which had been loath to associate with the Inner Six for fear of endangering its important ties with the Commonwealth nations, reversed a historic policy and made a bid for membership in 1961, but France blocked British admission. In the United States, respect for the Common Market led to adoption in 1962 of one of the most liberal and far-reaching trade bills in American history (see p. 592). And the Soviets, in a not unfamiliar pattern, revealed their respect for this capitalist device by first denouncing it and then copying it. The Soviet bloc's Council for Mutual Economic Assistance, or Comecon, began duplicating Common Market institutions and procedures in wholesale fashion in 1962. This was the sincerest form of flattery and confirmed a general conviction that the European Economic Community marked a historic turning point.

2.   TROUBLES IN THE FAR EAST

Termination of the Korean War in 1953 brought neither peace nor stability to the troubled Orient. Because China's emergence as a superpower under Commu-

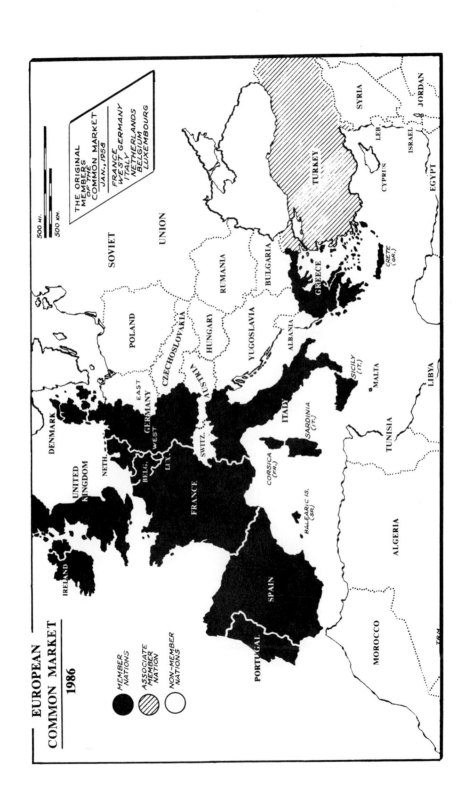

EUROPEAN
COMMON MARKET
1986

MEMBER
NATIONS

ASSOCIATE
MEMBER
NATION

NON-MEMBER
NATIONS

THE ORIGINAL
MEMBERS
OF THE
COMMON MARKET
JAN., 1958

FRANCE
WEST GERMANY
ITALY
NETHERLANDS
BELGIUM
LUXEMBOURG

500 MI.
500 KM.

SOVIET

UNION

DENMARK

EAST
GERMANY

WEST
GERMANY

POLAND

CZECHOSLOVAKIA

AUSTRIA

HUNGARY

RUMANIA

BULGARIA

YUGOSLAVIA

ALBANIA

GREECE

CRETE
(GR.)

TURKEY

SYRIA

LEB.

CYPRUS

ISRAEL

JORDAN

EGYPT

UNITED
KINGDOM

IRELAND

NETH.

BELG.

LUX.

SWITZ.

FRANCE

CORSICA
(FR.)

BALEARIC IS.
(SP.)

SPAIN

PORTUGAL

ITALY

SARDINIA
(IT.)

SICILY
(IT.)

MALTA

TUNISIA

LIBYA

ALGERIA

MOROCCO

nist auspices seemed to pervert long-standing American hopes, Americans tended to view all matters pertaining to China after 1949 with frustration and resentment. The government of Mao Tse-tung, in turn, demonstrated growing anti-Western feelings. It intervened in Korea and assisted Indochinese rebels in their struggle against France. It defied the United Nations, mistreated prisoners of war, and showed a cynical disregard for international law and human rights. It confiscated American property, imprisoned American citizens, conducted a barrage of virulent anti-American propaganda, and accused the United States of aggression and use of germ warfare. It proclaimed its intention to "liberate" Taiwan and the smaller offshore islands held by Chiang Kai-shek's Nationalist government. And, after July 1953, it repeatedly violated the terms of the Korean armistice.

For these reasons, both the Truman and Eisenhower administrations pursued a policy of rigid opposition to the People's Republic of China. Although this course did not lack critics at home or abroad, the prevailing mood in America and the hostility emanating from Beijing left little alternative. The United States continued to withhold recognition and used all its influence to block admission of the People's Republic to the United Nations. It refused to trade with China and tried to persuade its allies to maintain the broad embargo on strategic materials recommended by the UN in May 1951.

The United States adhered to this policy even though many of its allies abandoned it. Great Britain and most other Western states sooner or later accorded recognition and accepted Beijing's sovereignty as an accomplished fact. The majority mustered by the United States against admitting China to the UN dwindled each year in the General Assembly. Great Britain acted unilaterally to ease the embargo on strategic materials in 1957. A year later Japan and most NATO countries agreed upon a reduction in the number of strategic items that could not be sold to the Communist bloc.

The Eisenhower administration firmly supported Chiang Kai-shek's Nationalist government. Although Chiang had been confined since 1949 to Taiwan and smaller islands off the Chinese coast, the United States continued to recognize his regime as the legitimate government of all of China and upheld Chiang's envoy at the UN as the proper occupant of China's permanent seat on the Security Council. American arms and equipment bolstered Nationalist military strength. Although this was an extension of Truman's policy, the Republicans, mindful of their promise to end alleged neglect of the Far East, attempted to go further. They encouraged the belief that a Nationalist reconquest of the mainland was imminent. President Eisenhower announced in February 1953 that the United States Seventh Fleet would no longer be used to "shield" China from a possible Nationalist offensive. Secretary Dulles also brought Taiwan more formally into the Western defensive perimeter by negotiating a mutual defense pact with the Nationalist government in December 1954.

By this time, however, the administration had ceased to look for an alternative to containment in the Far East. Abandoning even the pretense of a possible Nationalist invasion of mainland China, Washington took pains to insure—by official correspondence and by senatorial reservations to the mutual security treaty—that Chiang would undertake no major offensive operations against Peking without American consent. In the treaty, Taiwan and the adjacent Pescadores were specifically named as the Nationalist territory that would be jointly defended against armed attack. Other Nationalist-held islands—notably Quemoy and Matsu, within actual sight and artillery range of the Chinese coast—remained unmentioned.

The renewed importance of a containment policy in the Far East became clear in the Indochinese war in 1954. France, reluctant to grant full independence to the new Indochinese states of Laos, Vietnam, and Cambodia, had been struggling vainly since 1947 to put down local nationalist movements in her Asiatic colonies. The strongest of these movements, the Vietminh, was centered in the coastal state of Vietnam. Increasingly dominated by a well-disciplined Communist element, and assisted by arms and equipment from Peking, the Vietminh employed effective guerrilla tactics and successfully resisted a growing French military effort to crush the uprising.

The Truman administration, perceiving a connection between the struggles in Korea and Indochina, had provided increasing military aid to the French forces. Eisenhower continued this policy, and by 1953 the United States was bearing nearly half the cost of France's Indochinese campaign. Fearful that a truce in Korea would enable China to divert troops to aid the Vietminh, Dulles warned in September that Chinese aggression in southeast Asia would have "grave consequences which might not be confined to Indochina." But Mao Tse-tung did not need to intervene directly. Despite American aid and the commitment of some of France's best troops, an all-out French drive to suppress the rebellion made no progress, and the war dragged on. It became obvious that France could not win without full-scale American participation.

Public opinion in the United States strongly opposed such a step, which promised to mire American soldiers in an even more remote and costly war than the Korean War. For the moment, the possibility of American intervention ended when the French garrison at Dienbienphu surrendered in May 1954. A foreign ministers' conference then convened in Geneva and negotiated an end to this phase of the Indochinese war. The armistice of July 1954 divided Vietnam at the seventeenth parallel between a Communist Democratic Republic in the north, led by President Ho Chi Minh, and a Republic of Vietnam in the south, led by President Ngo Dinh Diem. The Geneva Conference further provided that all-Vietnam elections to unify the country should be held in July 1956. (When that date arrived, the Diem government refused to participate.)

All the other new Indochinese states became fully independent. Laos and

Cambodia were in effect made into neutral states by agreeing not to join regional alliances or to allow foreign bases on their soil. Parties to the Geneva agreement, which included China but not the United States, promised to respect the independence and territorial integrity of the Indochinese states. The settlement was generally unsatisfactory to the American government. Dulles acquiesced in it because he had no choice, but he avoided endorsing it and announced that the United States would resist future Communist attempts to overrun southeast Asia.

Anxious to forestall this possibility, Dulles strove to erect a regional defense system. The result was a treaty, signed in Manila in September 1954 and soon transformed into the Southeast Asia Treaty Organization, or SEATO. It included the United States, Great Britain, France, Australia, New Zealand, the Philippines, Thailand, and Pakistan. Dulles hailed this as the capstone of a Pacific anti-Communist system. But SEATO was full of weaknesses. It possessed no military forces of its own and no centralized command system. More than half of its members were far removed from the actual treaty area, and no two of those within it were geographically contiguous. Strategically, the region posed enormous defensive problems, especially for the United States, upon whom the main burden of defense would fall. The alliance was crippled by the absence of India, Burma, and Indonesia, whose governments preferred neutralism to military alignment with the West.

Not long after the formation of SEATO, Peking began an important test of the extent of American commitment by bombarding Quemoy and Matsu. The bilateral security treaty with Nationalist China in December committed the United States to the defense of Taiwan, but it deliberately omitted specific mention of the offshore islands. Probing still further, Communist forces in January 1955 captured one of the Tachen Islands, the northernmost group of the offshore chain. Concluding that defense of Taiwan did not depend upon the Tachens, Eisenhower ordered the Seventh Fleet to cover the evacuation of the Nationalist troops stationed there. At the same time, he warned Peking that attacks on the other offshore islands might encounter American resistance. To make the country's position clear, he asked Congress for a resolution authorizing him to use armed force to defend not only Taiwan and the nearby Pescadores, already covered by the treaty between the United States and Nationalist China, but also certain unidentified "closely related localities." Congress granted this discretionary authority on January 28 by huge majorities, stipulating that the resolution would remain in effect until the president deemed it no longer necessary.

Intermittent bombardment of Quemoy and Matsu continued for another three months, but Peking did not expand its military action, and Washington carefully dissociated itself from Chiang's warlike flourishes. The crisis tapered off, then subsided completely in April when Chou En-lai offered to negotiate for a

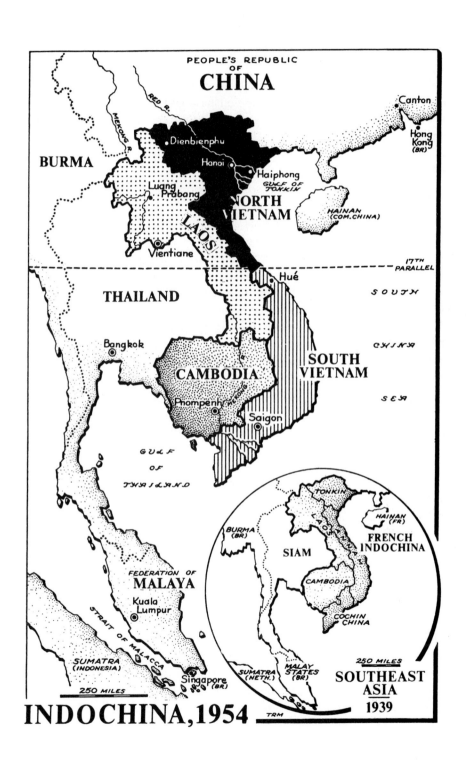

INDOCHINA, 1954

SOUTHEAST
ASIA
1939

relaxation of tensions. The bombardment ceased, and Americans temporarily forgot about Quemoy and Matsu.

More than three years of relative calm followed. Then, in August 1958, China abruptly resumed bombardment of the offshore islands. The American government responded firmly. It would be unwise to assume, Dulles warned, that an invasion of the islands could be a "limited operation." A huge American naval and air striking force assembled in the Formosa Strait, and American warships escorted Nationalist supply convoys from Taiwan to Quemoy. Tension mounted when Khrushchev promised Soviet support to the People's Republic in any clash with the United States and called for an end to American intervention in what he said were China's internal affairs.

The possibility of war over Quemoy and Matsu set off an adverse public reaction in the United States and expressions of alarm from Western Europe, and both sides showed signs of retreat. Dulles announced in late September that the American government had no commitment to defend Quemoy and Matsu. He spoke in favor of reducing Nationalist forces on the islands and added that a dependable cease-fire would make this possible. At the same time, the Chinese seemed almost to welcome the chance to call off what had become a profitless venture. Peking first suspended the bombardment for three weeks in October, then proclaimed the bizarre policy of not shelling Quemoy on even-numbered days while reserving the right to do so on odd ones. It kept up an intermittent and desultory shelling for some months and then abandoned the effort.

Southeast Asia, meanwhile, returned to the spotlight. Forbidden by the Geneva armistice to join regional alliances or to solicit military aid from the East or West, Laos was largely occupied in pacifying the Pathet Lao, its pro-Communist political faction, which received aid from North Vietnam. After years of effort, Prince Souvanna Phouma, the neutralist premier, managed to bring Pathet Lao leaders into a unified national government in July 1958. Yet the political situation in Laos worsened steadily. Neither the Communist bloc nor the United States had approved of Souvanna Phouma's neutralist policy. When he resigned and was replaced by Phoui Sananikone, both sides, in unabashed contravention of the Geneva armistice, maneuvered for advantage in the tiny kingdom. Communist pressure was matched by an expanding American program of military and economic assistance to Sananikone. Thus strengthened, the new premier first excluded all Communist elements from his cabinet, then tried in early 1959 to subdue the Pathet Lao altogether. Fighting spread as guerrillas crossed into Laos from North Vietnam, and the royal government announced in July that the reinforced Pathet Lao was endangering the kingdom.

This internal struggle, temporarily quieted by a UN investigation in late 1959, gradually took on dimensions of an international crisis in 1960. A pro-Western general, Phoumi Nosavan, ousted Premier Sananikone in January and supported a new government which made certain that subsequent elections went against

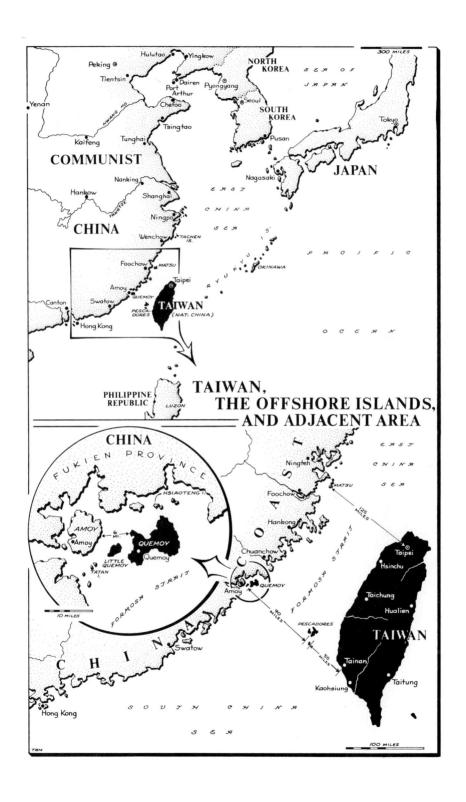

TAIWAN, THE OFFSHORE ISLANDS, AND ADJACENT AREA

the Pathet Lao. Then an enterprising neutralist captain, Kong Le, engineered a coup in August which returned Souvanna Phouma to power. Souvanna argued that only a government of all factions—pro-American, neutralist, and pro-Communist—could restore peace. The Eisenhower administration disagreed, and, when neither diplomacy nor clumsy economic pressure dissuaded Souvanna Phouma from this coalition policy, Washington supported a counterrevolution recently launched by General Nosavan. Nosavan's army, after defeating Kong Le's forces in a battle near the capital, installed a pro-Western government under Prince Boun Oum in December 1960. Souvanna Phouma went into exile in Cambodia, while Kong Le and his followers joined the Pathet Lao.

The tide quickly turned against the new government. Laotian Communists controlled large segments of the kingdom by early 1961 and threatened the capital itself, and they defeated Boun Oum's forces decisively whenever they met. With Boun Oum's collapse imminent, the Eisenhower administration sought the neutralist compromise it had earlier helped to defeat. But Souvanna Phouma, still in exile, blamed the impending disaster on Washington and refused to cooperate, while the resurgent Pathet Lao scented total victory and rejected all compromise proposals. Ngo Dinh Diem's government in neighboring South Vietnam was menaced by guerrilla bands. The row of dominoes to which Eisenhower had likened the fragile governments of southeast Asia six years before seemed about to topple.

3.   THE MIDDLE EAST

The spread of the cold war to the Middle East and sub-Saharan Africa during the 1950s raised new threats to world peace and drew the United States into areas it had hitherto relegated to secondary importance. Responsibility for protecting Western interests in the Middle East had largely been borne by Great Britain and France, but postwar economic and political realities forced these nations to abandon or reduce imperial commitments. The resulting geopolitical power vacuum encouraged Soviet penetration and, in response, expanded American involvement.

After 1950, the Middle East was a region of turbulence and instability. It contained the world's richest known oil deposits and historic land and sea routes connecting three continents. The countries of the area were, except for Israel, ruled by inexperienced, unstable, or reactionary regimes. The Middle East seethed with resentments born of poverty, anticolonial bitterness, extremist agitation, clashing nationalist ambitions, and religious strife.

The mortal conflict between Arab and Jew, bitterest of postwar quarrels, stemmed from the irreconcilable determination of Israel to protect its hard-won independence and of Arab neighbors to destroy the new state. Boundaries between Israel and the encircling ring of hostile Arab nations had been set by an armistice that ended the Arab-Israeli war of 1948–1949. The armistice lines were supervised by a UN truce team and upheld by an Anglo-American-French pledge in 1950. Western diplomacy now faced the well-nigh impossible task of preserving peace and remaining neutral in the Arab-Israeli impasse, while courting Arab favor in erecting a Middle Eastern defensive system.

Secretary Acheson had hoped to forestall Soviet penetration by creating a Middle East Command along NATO lines, but his successor did not consider this project immediately realizable. Instead, Dulles sought Arab friendship by promoting settlement of an Anglo-Egyptian dispute over Britain's huge base at Suez. His efforts were crowned by a treaty in October 1954, whereby England gave up rights to the base and agreed to evacuate all armed forces from the canal zone within twenty months. Egypt agreed in return to keep the base in combat readiness and to permit the reentry of British forces in the event of attack by an outside power against Turkey or any Arab state. Dulles and Eden hoped that Egypt under the new regime headed by Gamal Abdel Nasser would cooperate to reduce Arab-Israeli tensions and build a collective defense system. American offers of economic and military aid to Egypt followed immediately upon conclusion of the Anglo-Egyptian treaty of 1954.

Nasser wanted arms, but mainly for use against Israel and not at the price of the pledges demanded in return for American aid. He professed to see in this program a potential new form of Western imperialism, and he did not share American alarm about the menace of communism. Moreover, Nasser aspired to establish Egyptian primacy in the Arab world. He resented the rival aspirations of pro-Western Iraq and suspected that Iraq's interest in stronger Western ties was designed to bolster its bid for Arab leadership.

A major raid by Israeli units on the Egyptian territory of Gaza in February revealed the relative weakness of Nasser's military forces and naturally increased his desire for better military equipment. At the same time, Dulles's efforts to create a regional defense system culminated in a defensive alliance—the Baghdad Pact—between Turkey and Iraq, soon expanded to include Great Britain, Pakistan, and Iran. This new alliance, which the United States encouraged and aided but did not join, seemed to close the ring of containment around the Communist perimeter. But it also infuriated Nasser, worried the other Arab states, and evoked warnings from the Soviets.

Nasser profited from Soviet resentment and concluded an arms agreement with the Communist bloc in September 1955. Nasser exchanged Egyptian rice and cotton for Czechoslovakian tanks, planes, artillery, and other equipment. Arab nationalists in every country now turned to Nasser for leadership against Israel, and Egypt concluded defensive alliances and military arrangements with Syria and Saudi Arabia in October. Israel, alarmed by this prospective enhancement of Arab military strength, began to lay plans to strike while the advantage still lay in its favor. Armed clashes and raids across the tense armistice lines during 1955 were bloodier than any since 1949.

Nasser then moved more boldly into the center of East-West rivalries in 1956 by seeking foreign loans for a high dam across the Nile at Aswan, eight hundred miles south of Cairo. The project was designed to double Egypt's supply of arable land and stimulate industrial expansion. The British and American governments had already made a trial offer of some $200 million to underwrite initial construction, and the World Bank would advance another $200 million when preliminary work was completed. Nasser rejected the Anglo-American offer in January 1956 on the ground that it threatened Egyptian independence. He also hinted that better terms were available in Moscow.

When Dulles, in June 1956, heard rumors of a $1 billion Russian loan to finance the Aswan Dam, he informed the Egyptian ambassador that the United States had decided not to participate in the project. Events quickly led to the most serious international crisis since Korea. Stung by Dulles's public rebuff, Nasser cast about for a new way to finance his cherished dam. He found it by nationalizing the Suez Canal Company in July. The canal's net annual profits of $30 million would provide money for the dam. Since there would be adequate compensation to shareholders (which the Egyptian government readily promised), there was nothing illegal in Nasser's action. The canal lay in Egyptian territory, and the company that operated it held an Egyptian charter and was subject to Egyptian law. The company's concession, in any case, was due to expire and revert to Egypt in 1968.

What alarmed Western Europe about Nasser's abrupt maneuver was the economic and strategic importance of the Suez Canal. It carried over 100 million tons of cargo a year, three-fifths of which was Middle Eastern oil bound for Western Europe, and its traffic had become a mainstay of European prosperity, NATO security, and world trade. Nasser took pains to announce that, in operating the canal, Egypt would abide by the Constantinople Convention of 1888, which guaranteed all nations free navigation in peace and war.

Great Britain and France took no comfort from these assurances. Treaties and UN protests notwithstanding, Egypt had barred Israeli shipping from the Suez since the birth of Israel. The British doubted that Egypt could operate the canal efficiently. The French had long resented Nasser's open support of rebels in Algeria. Both Great Britain and France regarded Nasser's nationalization of the canal as a blow to their prestige and a threat to their security. Prime Minister Eden cabled Eisenhower on July 27, 1956, that Great Britain was prepared to use force as a last resort if Egypt did not relinquish the canal.

More than two months of intricate and futile negotiations followed. Nasser refused to accept any scheme of outright international control of the canal, and Great Britain and France refused to accept any arrangement that left unfettered control in Nasser's hands. At the same time the Western allies proved unable to coordinate their policy or, in the end, even to communicate with each other. Dulles had initially conceded that Nasser had to be made to "disgorge" the canal and had not ruled out force if other measures failed. But his view soon changed.

The Washington government did not share the Anglo-French sense of urgency or deem vital principles to be at stake, and it insisted upon settlement by negotiation. Eisenhower declared his unwillingness to be a party to aggression, and Dulles insisted that the United States would not "try to shoot its way through the Canal." Thus Great Britain and France went ahead with their plans in full knowledge that they would lack American support. When actual preparation for an attack on Egypt began in mid-October, London and Paris successfully concealed any knowledge of the impending attack from Washington.

Israeli forces launched a sudden invasion of Egypt on October 29, 1956, and their rapid advance across the Sinai peninsula toward the canal gave Great Britain and France a pretext for their own assault. On the excuse that they had the right to insulate the canal from Israeli-Egyptian hostilities, Great Britain and France sent an ultimatum to Cairo and Tel Aviv on October 30. They demanded an end to the fighting, a ten-mile withdrawal of all military forces from the canal, and a temporary right for them to occupy positions along the route in order to safeguard free transit. Then, when Nasser ignored their ultimatum, they executed an aerial bombardment of Cairo and the canal area on October 31. The attack coincided almost exactly with the ill-fated Hungarian revolt.

American leaders, caught completely off guard, were infuriated because they had not been consulted or even notified in advance and were embarrassed by this attack. They recognized that Great Britain, France, and Israel were acting under provocation, but they could not condone an action that betrayed so many commitments. It violated the charters of both the United Nations and the North Atlantic alliance. It flouted an Anglo-American-French pledge of 1950 to oppose any breach in the Arab-Israeli armistice lines and an American promise of 1956 to "support and assist" any country under attack in that region. It went against American policies of keeping the Arab-Israeli and canal controversies separate. The Washington administration took its stand against Great Britain, France, and Israel regretfully but firmly. "There can be no peace without law," Eisenhower declared on October 31. "There can be no law if we work to invoke one code of international conduct for those who oppose us and another for our friends."

Israeli forces occupied most of the Sinai peninsula within a few days. An Anglo-French invasion of the Suez area moved so slowly, however, that Egypt had time to block the canal with sunken ships before enemy troops could occupy the canal zone. Meanwhile, an emergency session of the UN General Assembly passed an American-sponsored cease-fire resolution by a huge majority on November 2. The General Assembly then created an international emergency force to "secure and supervise the cessation of hostilities." Belligerent threats from Moscow added to the growing tension. When the United States rejected Bulganin's proposal for joint Soviet-American military action to end the fighting, the Kremlin avowed its readiness to "crush the aggressors and restore peace in the East through the use of force" and spoke of recruiting "volunteers" to aid the Egyptians. Such threats led Eisenhower to order a global alert of American armed forces on November 6.

The British decided on that day to accept a cease-fire. Israel, having gained most of its military objectives, did the same, and France had no choice but to follow suit. Although arrival of the United Nations Emergency Force (UNEF) enabled the European invaders to withdraw without complete humiliation, their operation had been a fiasco. They had failed to destroy Nasser, whose prestige in Egypt and the Arab world was now higher than before. The Suez Canal not only remained in Egypt's hands but was also closed to traffic until obstructions could be removed. This in turn forced Western Europe in the interim to rely upon American oil and the long route around Africa.

Anglo-French prestige was at an all-time low. The United States won approval among nonaligned nations for its strong opposition to the invasion, but Western influence and prestige had been badly weakened, and the Atlantic alliance was in a shambles. The Soviets reaped substantial benefits by defending Arab nationalism against imperialist aggression. Afro-Asian opinion could overlook Soviet brutality in Hungary because the USSR had shown greater sensitivity to an apparent resurgence of European colonialism. Contrary to European fears, Egypt thereafter proved cooperative in not interfering with canal traffic (save Israel's) and efficient in clearing and operating the busy waterway.

The first response of the United States, in the dazed and tense aftermath of Suez, was the so-called Eisenhower Doctrine. A joint congressional resolution of March 1957 authorized the president to spend up to $200 million for economic and military assistance to Middle Eastern nations that desired it, asserted America's vital interest in preserving the independence and integrity of all countries in the region, and offered American military assistance to any nation that faced "armed aggression from any country controlled by international communism."

As an attempt to deter aggression and clarify American policy in the Middle East, the Eisenhower Doctrine contained certain ambiguities and omissions. It deliberately left the Suez and Arab-Israeli disputes to the United Nations. It did not precisely define the area covered and could not be applied until a nation requested assistance. It did not make any clear distinction between external aggression and internal conflicts. The new doctrine was denounced by the Soviet bloc, described as an imperialist plot by Egypt, hailed by Iraq, Iran, and Turkey, and cautiously approved in Jordan, Lebanon, and Saudi Arabia.

Alarm signals flashed again and again during 1957. Young King Hussein of Jordan, who had recently cut old ties with Great Britain under pressure from anti-Western elements, abruptly ousted his pro-Nasser cabinet in April and appealed to loyal Bedouin tribes to protect his throne. Eisenhower moved to forestall Soviet and Nasserite intervention by pronouncing Jordan's independence "vital" and by ordering the Sixth Fleet to the eastern Mediterranean. This action momentarily stabilized Hussein's throne, but charges of American plot-

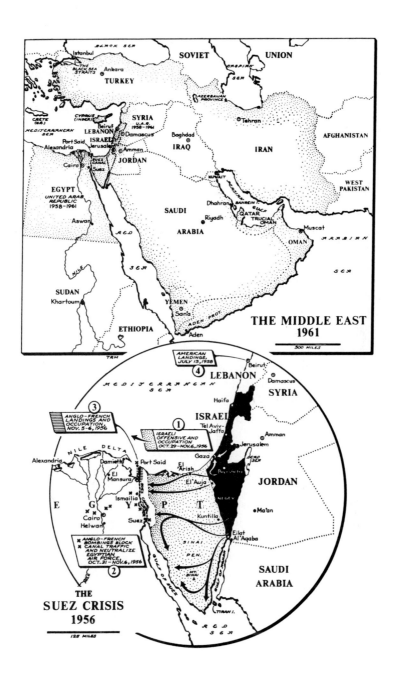

THE MIDDLE EAST
1961

500 MILES

THE
SUEZ CRISIS
1956

125 MILES

ting in Syria culminated in October with a blast from Moscow and a new war scare. Russia accused the United States of inciting a Turkish attack upon Syria and threatened Turkey with rocket attacks. Syria requested a UN investigation, while American and Soviet delegates exchanged accusations, and Egypt sent troops to reinforce Syrian concentrations along the Turkish border. King Saud of Saudi Arabia stepped forward to mediate the Turko-Syrian dispute before UN action was necessary.

A more troublesome challenge was how the United States should respond to the rising tide of Arab nationalism, led by Egypt and pro-Nasser groups everywhere in the Middle East. A Nasserite revolt broke out in Lebanon in May. The Lebanese government accused Egypt and Syria of border violations and interference in its internal affairs and requested an investigation. However, a UN observation group proved unable to seal the frontier, stop the fighting, or substantiate Lebanese charges. When appeals to the Arab League also failed, Lebanon asked for American assistance. Eisenhower hesitated. Then a nationalist group led by General Abdel Karim al-Kassim overthrew the pro-Western regime in Baghdad in July 1958 and signed a mutual defense pact with Nasser. Both Lebanon and Jordan sent out desperate calls for help to the United States and Great Britain.

Eisenhower ordered the Sixth Fleet to deploy off Lebanon for an amphibious landing, and some eight thousand American troops went ashore unopposed in mid-July "to encourage the Lebanese government in defense of Lebanese sovereignty and integrity." Great Britain sent three thousand men to Jordan in response to Hussein's appeal. The operations were executed brilliantly, but diplomatic reactions were ominous. Nasser flew to Moscow, and the Soviet Union responded with warnings and charges of aggression. Fortunately for the United States, there was no actual fighting in Lebanon, and, after a new president acceptable to all factions was elected, all American and British units were withdrawn from Lebanon and Jordan by the end of 1958.

It soon became apparent that Arab nationalists were determined to avoid alignment with either the Western or the Soviet bloc. Actually, genuine neutrality gained ground at the expense of both. Iraq withdrew from the Baghdad Pact in 1959, and the alliance was transformed five months later into the Central Treaty Organization (CENTO), with headquarters in Ankara. Supported but not formally joined by the United States, CENTO lacked a unified command or armed forces of its own, and was more a symbol than a bastion of Western power in the Middle East. Nasser and Arab nationalism remained strong in Egypt and influential in the Middle East, but Nasser became more concerned about internal affairs after the Lebanese crisis. Although Nasser accepted a $100 million loan from Russia in 1958 and began work on the Aswan Dam with help from Russian engineers, he clamped down ruthlessly on Communist activity in Egypt. Despite grave economic troubles, Iraq managed to maintain itself without sliding under the control of either Egypt or Russia. Lebanon became neutral, and Hussein still occupied an uncertain throne in Jordan. However, both countries enjoyed more independence than had seemed possible in 1958.

4.   AFRICA

In Africa, superpower competition was also complicated by a new wave of nationalism. As late as 1955 there were only five independent nations in Africa; twenty-eight more had joined their number by 1962. Only a scattered handful of small dependencies and the two large Portuguese colonies of Angola and Mozambique remained under European rule by this latter date. American diplomatic interest had been limited, by and large, to expressions of good will and friendship toward the emerging African nations.

Only in North Africa, close enough to the main theaters of the cold war to possess strategic value, did the United States show active interest before 1958. The former Italian colony of Libya achieved independence in 1953, French Morocco and Tunisia in 1956. In Tunisia the conservative, pro-Western President Habib Bourguiba was an important counterweight to Nasser. Libya's continued friendship became vital in 1954 when that country leased the huge Wheelus Air Force Base near Tripoli to the United States. Morocco figured even more prominently in American planning because of the airfields and a naval base that the United States built there in 1950–1951. Libya remained well disposed, but Morocco demanded cancellation of American bases on its soil. This demand became so insistent that Washington promised in 1959 to relinquish them by 1963—an agreement made possible by the completion of a new network of American bases in Spain.

Between Tunisia and Morocco lay the French province of Algeria, the oldest and richest possession in France's diminishing empire. American concern here stemmed from the diplomatic and military ramifications of France's prolonged efforts to put down the rebellion of Arab Algerians that broke out in 1954. This war crippled NATO's military strength by draining off nearly all French manpower and resources. It also strained French relations with her allies, diminished Western standing with neutral and ex-colonial nations, and transformed Bourguiba from a pro-Western champion into a neutralist. Washington was torn between loyalty to an ally, on the one hand, and sympathy for the Algerian rebels and concern for anticolonial opinion, on the other hand. Its attempts to offend neither side ended by displeasing both, and it was no more able than Bourguiba, the UN, or any other third party to effect a settlement. France ultimately found a leader, General de Gaulle, who had the courage to terminate the bitter struggle in 1962 by granting independence to Algeria.

Meanwhile, the cold war had sucked sub-Saharan Africa into its vortex. Soviet attacks on Western imperialism and white supremacy in this region began in

1958, as new nations began to emerge from colonial status. Ghana, for example, maintained a policy of nonalignment but espoused a pan-African nationalism that frequently arrayed her against the West. Guinea went much further toward direct alignment with Moscow. The Soviets, unencumbered by liabilities of imperialism in Africa or traditions of white supremacy, enjoyed an advantage over the Western powers in bidding for the friendship of new African nations. The United States again found itself caught between sympathy for African aspirations and the demands of its NATO partners with colonies in the area.

The first real test came when Belgium granted freedom to the Congo in June 1960. Congolese leaders had barely taken the reins of government before mutiny in the native army and looting and violence broke out. Belgium, alarmed for the safety of its nationals still on the scene, reinforced the handful of white troops remaining in the Congo and thereby touched off new violence. Congolese Premier Patrice Lumumba asked the United Nations on July 10 for assistance against "external aggression" and hinted that he would seek help elsewhere if the UN did not provide it.

Chaos quickly engulfed the unhappy Congo. The province of Katanga, from whose rich mineral resources and prosperous mining companies the new republic planned to derive much of its revenue, seceded in July under the leadership of Moise Tshombe. Lumumba, seeking a unified state under a strong central government, tried to put down this secessionist movement and soon won the support of Ghana, Guinea, and the Soviets, who sent technicians and military equipment. Joseph Kasavubu, the Congolese president, grew alarmed at Lumumba's pro-Soviet leanings and dismissed him in September. The Congolese Parliament restored him to power, but the army disbanded Parliament, arrested Lumumba, ousted the Soviet and Czechoslovakian missions, and endeavored to come to terms with Tshombe. The internal struggle became three-cornered when the followers of Lumumba—who was still recognized by the Soviets as premier—organized a new separatist movement. Virtual anarchy prevailed in much of the country.

The United Nations did what it could. The Security Council asked Belgium to withdraw its troops, authorized Secretary-General Dag Hammarskjold to create a multinational peacekeeping force, and recommended that all states refrain from interfering. While the Soviets accused NATO of plotting to restore colonialism in the Congo and affirmed their readiness to combat this move, Moscow and Washington exchanged warnings against introducing troops into the new republic. In assembling the peacekeeping force, Hammarskjold was careful to draw largely upon African and Asian contingents and sought no aid from the major powers. Tshombe's recalcitrance added to the difficulty. He defied the central government and refused to permit UN forces to enter Katanga. This produced another Security Council resolution on August 7. It said that the UN command would have to enter Katanga but must not be employed, as

Lumumba and the Soviets wished, to assist any party in the Congo's civil war.

As it turned out, it proved impossible to obey this last directive. The United Nations force, which eventually totaled twenty thousand men, could not restore peace to the Congo without inadvertently aiding one faction or another. Khrushchev was convinced that the UN had connived against Lumumba in favor of Kasavubu, especially after the General Assembly voted in November to seat Kasavubu's delegates instead of Lumumba's. When Congolese factionalism became more sharply three-cornered after Lumumba's arrest in December 1960, the Soviets supported his cause against both the central government and Katanga and wanted the UN command to do the same. The West backed Kasavubu, and UN troops tried to avoid partisanship in coping with an impossible situation. Involvement led to tragic death for Hammarskjold when his airplane crashed in Northern Rhodesia on September 18, 1961, on a flight to Katanga.

A moderate new premier, Cyrille Adoula, won support from both Western and African governments and achieved a measure of stability for his beleaguered country. He brought Tshombe to terms with the help of UN troops, while Lumumba's Communist-oriented movement gradually faded into impotence after the former premier was kidnapped and murdered in Katanga in 1961 under mysterious circumstances. Even so, the situation remained confused and volatile. The Congo had vividly illustrated both the disruptive effects of East-West rivalry upon local conditions and the internal difficulties that threatened stability and progress in the new African nations.

5. THE COLD WAR AND THE WESTERN HEMISPHERE

Conditions in Latin America after 1945 bred a new era of instability. Poverty, overpopulation, social discontent, reactionary or unstable governments, sensitive nationalism, and hatred of imperialism were facts of life in most countries south of the Rio Grande. Although the status quo was under massive assault, the United States did not awaken to the full implications until Soviet-styled communism established a beachhead in the very center of the hemisphere in 1960.

The United States was partly negligent and partly a victim of circumstances. It could not change the fact that its wealth was a source of envy, its power a source of alarm, its diplomacy in earlier years a source of resentment, and its bases in Panama and Guantánamo, Cuba, a source of irritation south of the border. A wave of revolutions in Latin America during the 1950s swept away many military dictatorships in favor of more or less democratic governments, but the United States lost rather than gained by these upheavals. In the interest of hemispheric security, it had cultivated friendly relations with despotic regimes and thereby antagonized democratic leaders who came to power later. Careful adherence to the doctrine of nonintervention, upon which Latin America insisted, meant that triumphs over dictatorship were achieved without help from Washington. Although it often had no real alternative, the United States was widely criticized for alleged lack of sympathy with democratic movements.

An early test of the Eisenhower administration's Latin American policy came in Central America, where enormous economic problems and stark inequality intersected, sometimes indistinguishably, with superpower competition. In Guatemala, the largest country in Central America, a long-overdue social revolution in 1944 overthrew an oligarchic, repressive regime. But Guatemala was a country with staggering problems. Its economy depended entirely upon the export of coffee and bananas. It was also predominantly a society of large plantations, owned by relatively few families and farmed by a landless peasantry. Before 1952, only 2 percent of Guatemala's people owned 70 percent of its land.

The liberal reformist regime brought to power in the revolution of 1944, confronting these problems, eventually moved to the left. The government, under President Jacobo Arbenz Guzmán, in 1953 instituted an extensive program of land reform, in which large holdings were appropriated and then distributed to the peasantry. Among the largest of the appropriations were 234,000 acres owned by a United States firm, the United Fruit Company.

The Eisenhower administration equated social discontent and nationalism in Guatemala with Soviet-directed subversion. Soon a plan of "covert action" was developed by the CIA to bring down the leftist regime. When news leaked out in May 1954 of the impending arrival of an arms shipment to Guatemala from Czechoslovakia, these plans were set in motion. On June 18, a small force of exiles, trained and equipped by the CIA, invaded from nearby Honduras, while CIA pilots, flying World War II-vintage aircraft, bombed and strafed Guatemala City. After the Guatemalan Army refused to support the government, the leftist regime collapsed, and Arbenz fled into exile. An authoritarian government came to power with the support of the United States.

Meanwhile, similar agitation and discontent in other parts of Latin America continued. Left-wing mobs assaulted Vice-President Nixon in Peru and Venezuela in 1958, dramatizing the depth of anti-American feeling. Economic and social discontent in many countries had clearly passed the point where assurances, palliatives, or stopgap aid would serve. Nixon warned upon his return that there were many non-Communists in the crowds that menaced him in Lima and Caracas. The United States reexamined its economic policies, promoted regional free-trade agreements, and supported an international program to stabilize the price of coffee. Most important, it agreed in 1959 to participate in an Inter-American Development Bank, with a capital of $1 billion, for loans to Latin American countries.

But time was running out. In January 1959, a revolution in Cuba succeeded in overthrowing the harsh dictatorship of Fulgencio Batista. Led by Fidel Castro, the new regime veered with unexpected rapidity toward alignment with the

Soviet bloc. Castro had announced a sweeping land reform program that worried foreign investors, and he had never concealed his antipathy toward the United States for its tolerance of Batista and other Latin American dictators. The Washington administration was therefore expecting some difficulty even after it extended prompt recognition to the new Cuban government. But Washington was not in any way prepared for the intensity of Castro's anti-American policy or the violence of his assault upon the status quo in the Western Hemisphere.

While Castro leaned more and more toward the Communists and became increasingly virulent in his denunciations of the United States, Cuba became a headquarters for intrigue and subversive planning. Communists and radical exiles from other Caribbean republics converged on the island to plot and prepare invasions, accumulate weapons, and conduct training exercises. Reports of imminent armed expeditions led to an inter-American foreign ministers' meeting in August 1959, but Washington's hopes for joint action were reduced to a pair of resolutions condemning totalitarianism and reaffirming democratic principles. Meanwhile, Castro accused the United States of harboring and equipping his enemies, inciting sabotage and counterrevolutionary activity, and permitting air attacks against Cuba. Castro's domestic reform program moved markedly leftward, and Cuban seizures of American property totaled $1 billion by 1960.

American exasperation grew, but the State Department continued its policy of restraint toward Castro. American forbearance weakened when Castro abandoned the hemispheric bloc in the General Assembly and proclaimed a policy of neutralism. Soon afterward, in February 1960, Castro signed an extensive five-year trading agreement with the Soviet Union and hinted at a military alliance with the USSR. Eisenhower's patience snapped when Castro seized a $25 million Texaco refinery in June 1960 for refusing to process Russian crude oil. Eisenhower retaliated by cutting American imports of Cuban sugar. In October 1960, the Washington administration went further and imposed an embargo on all exports to Cuba except food, medicine, and medical supplies. The next month, Eisenhower sent a naval patrol to the Caribbean to prevent rumored Cuban invasions of Nicaragua and Guatemala. In January 1961, Washington formally severed relations with Havana. Meanwhile, Eisenhower ordered the CIA to train and equip Cuban exiles in Guatamela for a military attempt to destroy Castro and his regime.

CHAPTER 26

Toward New Frontiers

In 1960, the Democratic party, led by the young and vigorous John F. Kennedy, recaptured control of the national government. Winning election on a platform that promised activism and renewal from the inertia of the latter years of the Eisenhower administration, Kennedy promised the extension of Democratic policies of past administrations. But most of all, Kennedy offered a new style of presidential leadership boasting youth, energy, and effectiveness. In fact, Kennedy soon confronted grave challenges to his ability to lead. At home, Kennedy defined programs to deal with the increasing complexities of American society and asked for renewed dedication and sacrifice. But he faced serious obstacles to exercising presidential leadership, the most important of which was the deadlock that had gripped Congress in the last years of the Eisenhower administration.

1. THE ELECTION OF 1960

Americans went about the task of choosing a new president in 1960 in an atmosphere of uncertainty, induced largely by vague fears that the nation's position in world affairs had somehow deteriorated. The Democrats, freed by the Twenty-second Amendment from the prospect of running against Eisenhower again, engaged in one of their customary uninhibited contests for the nomination. Four Democratic candidates formally entered the race: Senators Hubert H. Humphrey of Minnesota, John F. Kennedy of Massachusetts, Lyndon B. Johnson of Texas, and Stuart Symington of Missouri. There was also considerable support for Adlai Stevenson, the nominee in 1952 and 1956. Stevenson never became a formal candidate in 1960 but was amenable to a draft.

The forty-two-year-old Kennedy, the first Roman Catholic to contend seriously for the presidency since 1928, emerged as Democratic frontrunner. His triumph over Humphrey in the Wisconsin primary by a six-to-four margin in April was inconclusive, since most of the Kennedy support had come from Catholic districts. But five weeks later, in heavily Protestant West Virginia, Kennedy's efficient and well-financed campaign ended with a decisive triumph over the Minnesotan. Humphrey thereupon withdrew, and Kennedy went on to record impressive primary victories in Nebraska, Maryland, and Oregon. These, together with earlier successes in New Hampshire and Indiana, caused Democratic leaders in the East and Midwest to climb on his bandwagon. Kennedy's well-disciplined organization, working hard for support in other areas, came to the convention in Los Angeles on July 11 confident of at least 600 of the 761 votes necessary for the nomination.

Democrats converged on Los Angeles in a perplexed and sober mood, shaken by recent international events. The party platform proclaimed that an enduring peace could be obtained only by restoring American "military, economic and moral" strength. It charged the Eisenhower administration with having lost America's "position of pre-eminence," and it promised to "recast" national military capacity along more effective lines. Other pledges included better planning for disarmament, reshaping of foreign aid with more emphasis upon economic assistance and international cooperation, promotion of economic growth without inflation, and an end to the Republican "high-interest, tight-money policy" that had allegedly stifled expansion in recent years. The platform also contained the strongest civil rights plank in American history.

The convention then proceeded, after intricate and strenuous maneuvering, to nominate John F. Kennedy on the first ballot. In a move that surprised nearly everyone, Kennedy then requested and obtained Johnson's nomination for the vice-presidency. "The world is changing," Kennedy proclaimed in his acceptance speech on July 15. "We stand today on the edge of a New Frontier . . . a frontier of unknown opportunities and perils—a frontier of unfulfilled hopes and threats. . . . But the New Frontier of which I speak is not a set of promises—it is a set of challenges. It sums up, not what I intend to offer the American people, but what I intend to ask of them."

No such struggle for the nomination took place within the GOP. It had been clear for months that Vice-President Nixon enjoyed overwhelming support from party regulars in all sections of the country. His only serious contender was Governor Nelson A. Rockefeller of New York, a moderate Republican who had won national prominence with an impressive victory over incumbent Averell Harriman in 1958. Rockefeller formed an organization and sought support during 1959. He was popular among independents and party liberals, but he withdrew his candidacy in December upon discovering that Republican regulars and important financial backers were firmly committed to Nixon.

Rockefeller could not win the nomination, but he was nevertheless able to exert decisive influence on the party platform. Disturbed by recent developments and convinced that the administration had permitted American military and economic strength to deteriorate, Rockefeller submitted a sweeping program for reform in these and other areas, including civil rights. It amounted to a repudiation of many of Eisenhower's policies. The governor let it be known that he would accept a draft and threatened an open fight for his program on the convention floor if the platform did not incorporate his views.

Nixon privately agreed with much of Rockefeller's indictment and dreaded a rupture with the moderate wing of the party. Yet he hardly dared endorse so open a repudiation of Eisenhower. Rockefeller flatly rejected a compromise draft platform offered by the Nixon forces. Then the vice-president met the governor secretly at the latter's New York apartment three days before the GOP convention opened in Chicago on July 25 and accepted nearly all of Rockefeller's demands. The "Compact of Fifth Avenue," published in the press on July 23, called for a more imaginative foreign policy, an accelerated defense program, reorganization of the executive branch, stimulation of the economy, strong federal action in behalf of civil rights, a program of medical care for the aged, and aid to education.

News of the compact touched off explosions within the GOP. Senator Barry M. Goldwater of Arizona, leading spokesman of the right wing, denounced it as the "Munich of the Republican Party." From President Eisenhower, then on vacation in Rhode Island, came angry retorts. The platform committee, made up entirely of conservatives, felt betrayed and rebelled openly. The Nixon forces had to use all the political leverage they possessed to placate these dissidents and win partial acceptance of the compact.

The GOP platform was unquestionably more moderate as a result. It praised the Eisenhower record in foreign affairs and national defense but pledged thorough modernization and acceleration of military programs and promised not to let budgetary concerns put a "price ceiling on America's security." The economic plank, while praising the prosperity of the past eight years, admitted the need for a higher growth rate. Warning against "massive new federal spending," the platform promised to stimulate economic expansion through tax reform and other means. The civil rights plank, representing a complete victory for Rockefeller, was almost as strong as that of the Democrats. The convention proceeded to nominate Nixon by acclamation on the first ballot. With equal speed, it nominated Nixon's choice for the vice-presidency, Henry Cabot Lodge, Jr., of Massachusetts, ambassador to the UN.

Personalities and emotions played a more important role than issues in the campaign. The two candidates were in basic agreement on most major questions.

Both were internationalists and moderates, and their programs differed in detail and emphasis but hardly in kind. Kennedy's central theme was the need for positive leadership, public sacrifice, and bold national effort to "get America moving again." Nixon, while denying that the military and economic situation was as grave as his opponent claimed, also affirmed that the United States could not afford to stand still or rest upon past laurels.

The early advantage lay with Nixon, who was free to launch his campaign while Kennedy was tied down in Washington by the barren postconvention session of Congress. Nixon was far better known in the country at large because of his active role in the Eisenhower administration. He emphasized this point over and over, abandoned the narrow partisanship and hard-hitting tactics of his early career, and highlighted the argument that he and Lodge were more qualified for the task of national leadership than the youthful, inexperienced Kennedy. Nixon enjoyed a substantial lead in late-summer opinion polls.

The picture changed drastically, however, on account of an innovation that may have been the most decisive single feature of the campaign—four nationally televised debates between Nixon and Kennedy from September 26 to October 21. Although the candidates were unable to explore issues thoughtfully and few clear distinctions in their positions emerged, Kennedy profited greatly from these encounters. October polls showed him in the lead, and reporters were impressed by the growing size and enthusiasm of his crowds. Democratic confidence and Republican gloom waxed steadily as election time neared. But effective stump speeches by President Eisenhower and a massive Republican television effort during the final week produced a resurgence of Nixon strength and reduced Kennedy's margin to the vanishing point.

Early returns from the East and South on election night, November 8, 1960, indicated a Kennedy landslide. But his lead dwindled steadily as returns from the western states came in. The decision remained in doubt until the next morning. Then returns from Illinois, Texas, and Minnesota gave the presidency to Kennedy by a narrow margin. He received 34.2 million popular and 303 electoral votes; Nixon, 34.1 million popular and 219 electoral votes. Kennedy's popular majority of 120,000 votes was less than one-fifth of 1 percent of the total cast! The large Democratic majorities in Congress were reduced slightly, by a loss of 2 seats in the Senate and 22 in the House, to 64–36 and 263–174.

The election provided much material for analysis. Voting patterns displayed, superficially at least, a sectional hue. The historic Democratic coalition of the East and South gave Kennedy the bulk of his electoral support. He swept the populous Northeast, losing only Maine, New Hampshire, and Vermont. In the South, with the help of Lyndon Johnson, Texas and Louisiana renewed their Democratic allegiance, and five other states returned Democratic majorities. However, Nixon duplicated Eisenhower's triumphs in Virginia, Florida, and Tennessee. In the border region, Kennedy lost Kentucky but won handily in

West Virginia and narrowly in Missouri. Michigan, Illinois, and Minnesota were his only triumphs in the Middle West. And beyond the hundredth meridian Nixon carried every state except Nevada, New Mexico, and Hawaii.

But sectionalism was an inadequate key to American sentiment in this complex campaign. Closer examination revealed that changes in popular voting habits observable during the 1950s—ticket splitting, independent voting, erosion of traditional party loyalties—were more pronounced than ever. Both candidates ran ahead of their tickets in some areas and behind in others. The returns indicated that the disappearance of the Solid South in presidential elections was no temporary phenomenon; the anti-Democratic coalition that had emerged there after 1948 gave Nixon nearly half of the southern popular vote—almost as large a share as Eisenhower had received in 1952 and 1956. Conversely, Kennedy ran quite well in such traditionally Republican areas as northern New England, parts of the Middle West, and the suburbs. He also received heavy support from blacks and other minorities, and demonstrated that a Roman Catholic was no longer automatically barred from winning the nation's highest office.

2. THE NEW FRONTIERSMEN

Kennedy's inaugural address was a clarion call for renewed dedication to traditional American ideals. "Let the word go forth from this time and place, to friend and foe alike," he proclaimed, "that the torch has been passed to a new generation of Americans—born in this century, tempered by war, disciplined by a hard and bitter peace, proud of our ancient heritage." He pledged loyalty to American allies, support to the United Nations, and aid to underdeveloped countries. He also called for a "grand and global alliance" against "the common enemies of man: tyranny, poverty, disease and war itself." As for the cold war, he suggested that "both sides begin anew the quest for peace." He concluded with an eloquent appeal: "In the long history of the world, only a few generations have been granted the role of defending freedom in its hour of maximum danger. . . . The energy, the faith, the devotion which we bring to this endeavor will light our country and all who serve it—and the glow from that fire can truly light the world. And so, my fellow Americans: ask not what your country can do for you—ask what you can do for your country."

As presidential backgrounds go, John Fitzgerald Kennedy's was both unusual and instructive. He was born in Brookline, Massachusetts, on May 29, 1917, the second of nine children. Both his grandfathers were second-generation Irish Catholic immigrants who rose to prominence in Boston's Democratic politics. His father, Joseph P. Kennedy, made a large fortune in banking, stocks, and real estate, later supported Franklin Roosevelt, and served as ambassador to Great Britain during the late 1930s.

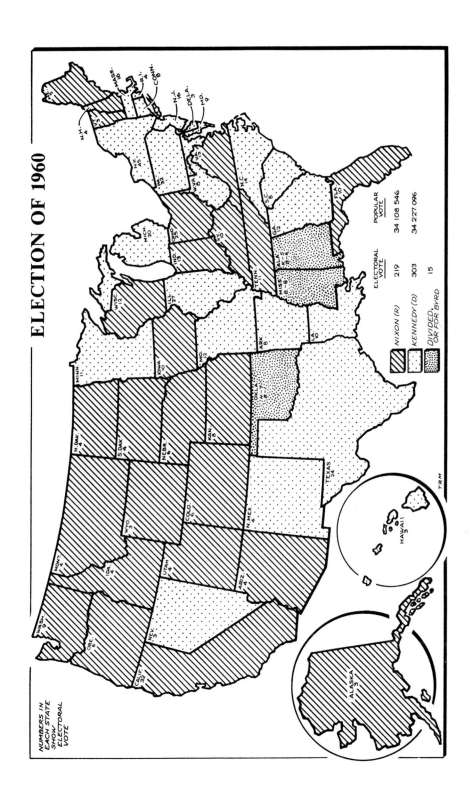

ELECTION OF 1960

NUMBERS IN
EACH STATE
SHOW
ELECTORAL
VOTE

	ELECTORAL VOTE	POPULAR VOTE
NIXON (R)	219	34 108 546
KENNEDY (D)	303	34 227 096
DIVIDED, OR FOR BYRD	15	

WASH. 9
ORE. 6
CALIF. 32
NEV. 3
IDA. 4
MONT. 4
UTAH 4
ARIZ. 4
WYO. 3
COLO. 6
N.MEX. 4
N.DAK. 4
S.DAK. 4
NEBR. 6
KANS. 8
OKLA. 7-8
TEXAS 24
MINN. 11
IOWA 10
MO. 13
ARK. 8
LA. 10
WISC. 12
ILL. 27
IND. 13
OHIO 25
MICH. 20
KY. 10
TENN. 11
MISS. 8-8
ALA. 5-6
GA. 12
FLA. 10
S.C. 8
N.C. 14
W.VA. 8
VA. 12
N.J. 16
DELA. 3
MD. 9
PA. 32
N.Y. 45
MASS. 16
R.I. 4
CONN. 8
N.H. 4
VT.
ME.

HAWAII 3

ALASKA 3

TRM

Graduating cum laude from Harvard in 1940, Kennedy became a junior naval officer during World War II. He won the Navy and Marine Corps Medal for rescuing the surviving crew members of his PT boat after a Japanese destroyer had sunk it off the Solomon Islands in 1943. After the war he entered Democratic politics in Massachusetts and was elected in 1946 to the House of Representatives from the Boston area. After three terms in the lower house he ran for the Senate against the Republican incumbent, Henry Cabot Lodge, Jr., in 1952. It was a formidable undertaking. Eisenhower was headed for a landslide presidential victory, and Lodge, who was serving as the general's campaign manager, had a distinguished name and record. The young Democrat stumped Massachusetts with tireless energy and defeated Lodge by 70,000 votes while Eisenhower carried the state by over 200,000.

Kennedy's congressional career was marked by moderate liberalism, ambition, and remarkable vote-getting ability. He was reelected to the Senate in 1958 by 875,000 votes, the largest majority in Massachusetts history. Almost from the moment of his defeat for the vice-presidential nomination in 1956, Kennedy launched an unrelenting campaign for the presidency that led him to his victory at the Los Angeles convention and culminated in his narrow triumph over Nixon in November 1960.

The youngest man ever elected to the presidency, Kennedy displayed an impressive, if frequently baffling, combination of personal qualities. He had an abundance of poise, charm, self-assurance, and energy, together with a keen sensitivity to the American political process and a leader's fascination for political power. He was well informed, incisive, and articulate, and he respected these qualities in others. Eager to accept responsibility, he inspired fierce devotion and loyalty among his followers. Critics detected a streak of ruthlessness and sometimes worried about his ambition and love of power. Coolly level-headed, he was able at all times to view situations, associates, enemies, and himself with remarkable detachment. This was a practical asset, but some believed that it might also reflect a basic limitation. He was a realist, a believer in the art of the possible. His wife called him "an idealist without illusions." Kennedy's liberalism and interest in human welfare were undoubtedly genuine, but they seemed to represent more of an intellectual than an emotional commitment.

Kennedy's cabinet included a few surprises. Chief among these was the appointment of Dean Rusk, then president of the Rockefeller Foundation, as secretary of state. Rusk was an experienced diplomat, but his name had not been among those mentioned. Adlai Stevenson, mentioned frequently and favored by liberal Democrats for that important office, was named instead as ambassador to the UN. Another surprise, aimed at reassuring "sound money" conservatives, was the appointment of the New York banker C. Douglas Dillon, Eisenhower's undersecretary of state, as secretary of the treasury. Another Republican, Robert S. McNamara, left the presidency of the Ford Motor Company to become secretary of defense.

Most of the other posts went to experienced Democratic politicians. They included the president's brother, Robert F. Kennedy, as attorney general; J. Edward Day of California, postmaster general; former Representative Stewart L. Udall of Arizona, secretary of the interior; former Governor Orville L. Freeman of Minnesota, secretary of agriculture; former Governor Luther H. Hodges of North Carolina, secretary of commerce; and former Governor Abraham Ribicoff of Connecticut, secretary of health, education, and welfare. Arthur J. Goldberg, a prominent labor lawyer, became secretary of labor.

The emphasis in many cabinet appointments, and in most high-level advisory and assistant positions in the executive branch, was upon people with the kind of qualities which Kennedy himself possessed and admired. He wanted to be surrounded by vigorous, activist intellectuals who prided themselves upon their pragmatism and their hardheaded, modern approach to the solution of problems. Confident of their ability to control events, these youthful appointees buzzed energetically about the White House and Capitol Hill during the Kennedy years.

3. KENNEDY AND CONGRESS

As Kennedy had hoped, public imagination was stirred by the new administration's vigor, spirit, and industry. Postinauguration polls indicated that 75 percent of the people "approved" of their new president. But this popularity, he soon discovered, did not automatically mean congressional support for his legislative program. A major obstacle was the coalition of conservative Republicans and southern Democrats that had been blocking or diluting welfare legislation since 1938. Kennedy usually had a reliable working majority in the Senate. But the 263 Democrats in the lower house included some 100 Southerners, at least half of whom voted consistently with the Republicans against progressive measures.

The only parts of Kennedy's program that came through this gauntlet relatively unscathed were those pertaining to defense and foreign policy. Fear of Communist aggression enabled the president to command strong legislative support for nearly all his proposals to strengthen pro-Western governments. Congress readily appropriated $47 billion for defense in 1961 and over $48 billion in 1962. On both occasions it actually exceeded the amount Kennedy had asked for. Congress also approved requests for authority to call reservists into the armed forces for twelve-month periods in 1961–1962 and for a space program designed to put a man on the moon before 1970.

Kennedy encountered more resistance to his far-reaching aid and trade programs, but he obtained much of what he wanted. Congress cut his $5 billion foreign-aid requests in 1961 and 1962 by about 20 percent. It refused to grant long-term borrowing authority, which would have enabled him to avoid the annual battle for new appropriations and develop foreign-aid projects on a long-range basis. But these defeats were more than offset by a number of triumphs. Congress responded to his proposal for a five-year program of aid to underdeveloped countries by creating the Development Loan Fund in 1961 with an appropriation of $1.2 billion in its first year and $1.5 billion annually for the next four years. Kennedy also won approval of his comprehensive program for Latin American aid, the Alliance for Progress. Formally launched at an inter-American conference in Uruguay in August 1961 and signed by all the American republics except Cuba, the Alliance envisaged a massive ten-year program for economic and social development. It promised at least $20 billion in aid, over half to be provided by the United States and the balance by international agencies, European countries, and private capital.

There were other victories. The Senate ratified a treaty in March 1961 making the United States a member of the newly created Organization for Economic Cooperation and Development. The OECD, which also included Canada and eighteen Western European nations in its membership, was designed to improve world trade, promote closer economic ties among members, and evolve a program allocating their future aid contributions to underdeveloped countries. The most dramatic of Kennedy's aid proposals was the Peace Corps, created by executive order in March 1961 to train volunteers for educational and technical service abroad. Thousands of Americans volunteered, and Congress established the Peace Corps on a permanent basis in September 1961.

Kennedy's biggest legislative achievement was passage of the Trade Expansion Act in September 1962. Designed to establish closer ties with the European Common Market through reciprocal concessions, the act permitted him to reduce tariffs by 50 percent, and by as much as 100 percent on articles in which the United States and Common Market countries together accounted for four-fifths of world trade. Another major feature was a system of "trade adjustment assistance" to aid American firms and workers adversely affected by lower tariffs.

In fiscal matters, the new administration proceeded cautiously. Kennedy's economic views were moderate. His plans to stimulate the economy did not envisage massive federal spending or a marked increase in the role of government. Moreover, he was caught in a financial dilemma that jeopardized almost any course of action. On the one hand, the recession that had begun in 1960 was growing worse; business investment and construction had declined, and unemployment was rising. On the other hand, the country faced a near crisis in its international balance of payments. During the last three years of the Eisenhower administration, money spent abroad (for imports, economic and military aid, private investment) had exceeded income *from* abroad (from exports, interest, and services) by a total of $11 billion. The result was an outflow of gold that was increased after the election by the action of European speculators who feared that the new administration would devalue the dollar. Recognizing that this crisis would become more acute if he attacked the recession through large-scale pump-priming measures, Kennedy moved swiftly but circumspectly to ease both problems.

Instead of asking for large appropriations, he countered the recession through a variety of executive actions that did not weaken confidence in the dollar. At the same time, he took action to restore the balance of payments without resorting to the remedies of raising tariffs or reducing foreign aid. Announcement of these measures, together with his financial restraint in domestic policy and his appointment of the conservative Dillon as secretary of the treasury, restored European confidence and ended speculation in gold. The balance-of-payments deficit began to decrease as these policies took effect, and American exports rose sharply. The country began to come out of the recession in 1961.

With the economy expanding again, Kennedy reassured suspicious businessmen that he was not an irresponsible spender. Eager to avoid inflationary action that would nullify returning prosperity, he found it ironic and galling that the first real assault upon a relatively stable price level came from an important segment of the business community. Negotiations between the steel companies and the United Steelworkers over a new wage contract broke down in March 1962. Kennedy and Secretary Goldberg were instrumental in persuading the two sides to renew negotiations, and they were heartened when a noninflationary two-year wage contract was signed on March 31. Kennedy, with assurances from steel executives that the agreement obviated the need for a price rise, praised both labor and management for their "industrial statesmanship" in holding the line against inflation. Ten days later, however, Roger M. Blough, chairman of the board of United States Steel, informed the president that his company was raising its prices by six dollars a ton. Five other major steel companies announced an identical increase on the following day.

Feeling betrayed, Kennedy scathingly denounced the companies in a press conference in April. Quoting figures, he denied any justification for the rise. He was shocked, he said, that "a tiny handful of steel executives, whose pursuit of private power and profit exceeds their sense of public responsibility, can show such utter contempt for the interest of 185,000,000 Americans." The president did more than denounce, and the nation looked on in awe as he mobilized the massive power of the federal government. The FTC launched an inquiry into the possibility of collusive price fixing, while the Treasury Department spoke of a tax investigation. The Department of Justice announced that it would see whether antitrust laws had been violated. The Defense Department hinted that its steel purchases would be made from companies that had not raised their prices.

The offending companies quickly surrendered. Bethlehem Steel announced that it was rescinding its price rise, and the others then followed suit. Kennedy's attempts to cultivate better relations with the business community suffered heavily, but the public on the whole was impressed by his firmness under pressure.

None of this, however, had changed the situation in Congress, where

Kennedy's New Frontier program—designed to bring the country out of recession, stimulate growth, and assist needy groups by economic and social welfare measures—encountered strong opposition from the conservative coalition. Administration Democrats, led by venerable Speaker Sam Rayburn, moved to render the coalition less effective by striking at one of its strongest bastions, the House Rules Committee. This committee included eight Democrats and four Republicans. Its chairman and one other Democrat were southern conservatives who consistently voted with the Republicans to deadlock the committee and bottle up legislation. Rayburn, after a bitter contest, won House acceptance in January 1961 of a resolution to enlarge the Rules Committee from twelve members to fifteen. He appointed two proadministration Democrats and one Republican to the new seats, thereby making possible an eight-to-seven Kennedy majority.

Administration forces then waged a succession of hard-fought battles over each item in the Kennedy program, usually winning or losing by a handful of votes. Honors were about evenly divided during the two sessions of the Eighty-seventh Congress. Conservatives scored a major triumph in the first session by defeating an ambitious school aid bill. It called for a three-year federal grant of $2.3 billion to the states for school construction and teachers' salaries and the allocation of another $3.3 billion over five years for colleges and federal scholarships. The bill passed the Senate easily in May 1961, but Roman Catholic bishops then demanded that parochial schools receive aid on an equal basis with public schools. Kennedy refused to accept this amendment, and the search for a compromise proved futile. Two Catholic Democrats on the Rules Committee joined with conservatives to bury Kennedy's bill, and the House later defeated a weak substitute measure.

The New Frontier recorded a few victories during 1961. One was a new Housing Act which authorized nearly $5 billion for local urban renewal projects over a four-year period. Strenuous administration efforts also mustered a majority in favor of a higher-minimum-wage bill. The new law, which went into effect in September, raised the hourly minimum in two stages over a two-year period from $1 to $1.25 for the 24 million workers already covered, and extended the same coverage to some 3.6 million new workers, primarily in retail and service industries. A third triumph, the Area Redevelopment Act of May 1961, provided nearly $400 million in federal loans and grants for assistance to "distressed areas" of economic stagnation and high unemployment. Kennedy also obtained liberalization of Social Security benefits and new funds for the Federal Water Pollution Control Act, which permitted construction of sewage treatment plants.

The record was different in 1962. Speaker Rayburn, stricken by cancer, died in November 1961, and because his successor was less able to enforce House discipline, the unrepentant southern chairman of the Rules Committee once again kept several bills from coming to a vote. Aside from the Trade Expansion Act, the New Frontier's successes were few and unimportant.

Three key administration measures finally passed, but without the provisions that Kennedy wanted most. One, the Revenue Act of 1962, granted business $1 billion a year in special tax credits to encourage new outlays for machinery and equipment. But it omitted Kennedy's proposals for withholding income taxes on dividends and interest and curtailing expense account deductions. The second, a farm bill designed to impose strict production controls on wheat and feed grains, was defeated in the House in June; a weak substitute measure merely extended the existing voluntary control program for another year. In a third compromise, Congress authorized the president to channel $900 million in public works projects into areas with high unemployment. At the same time, Congress denied Kennedy's request for standby authority to initiate a $2 billion antirecession public works program.

Conservatives defeated several important measures outright during 1962. Chief among these was a bill to provide health insurance for the aged through the Social Security system. This so-called Medicare program, advocated by Kennedy since 1960, was killed in the Senate in July by a vote of fifty-two to forty-eight. Another major loss was a proposed new cabinet Department of Urban Affairs. The House Rules Committee stifled bills that sought to aid unemployed youth, migrant workers, commuter transit, and medical schools. All in all, the legislative record of Kennedy's first two years fell considerably short of fulfilling the New Frontier program.

Nor did the midterm elections promise to improve his prospects. If the past was any guide, the Democrats could expect to lose at least forty seats in the House and six in the Senate. None of these losses was likely to occur in the South. Kennedy wanted to fight for a more amenable Congress, even though (as Franklin Roosevelt and Dwight Eisenhower could testify) presidential intervention frequently backfired. But Kennedy, bent on defeating Republicans because of their opposition to domestic reform, ignored the warnings of his advisers and launched an energetic nationwide campaign on behalf of Democratic candidates. The effects of this bold move will never be fully known, for Kennedy abruptly ended his tour in mid-October in order to deal with the Cuban missile crisis. Although the Democrats went on to score an impressive midterm victory, gaining four seats in the Senate and losing only two in the House, the results could neither be attributed to Kennedy's electioneering nor be interpreted as a mandate for his domestic program. More likely, the victory reflected public approval of his firm stand against the Soviet missile threat.

A time of peace and prosperity appeared at hand as Kennedy faced the new Congress in January 1963. Soviet-American relations had improved; Berlin was quiet; southeast Asia appeared relatively tranquil. The economy was humming. Yet in his annual message Kennedy warned against any temptation to relax and insisted that complacency was unwarranted. Deeply rooted social problems persisted. Material prosperity was only one side of the coin. "The quality of American life," he emphasized, "must keep pace with the quantity of American goods." The United States had to be strengthened by investing in its youth, by safeguarding the health of its citizens, by protecting the basic rights of *all* its people, and by prudent use of its resources. Furthermore, the rate of economic growth had to be sustained and unemployment reduced.

The administration's program, however, fared no better in the first session of the Eighty-eighth Congress than it had in the Eighty-seventh. The lawmakers slashed Kennedy's $4.5 billion foreign aid request by fully 33 percent and pared more than 10 percent from the National Aeronautics and Space Administration's $5.7 billion space program. The fight for a reduction in federal income taxes, which Kennedy had called the "essential" step toward accomplishment of his goals, was symptomatic. The president was determined to sustain an economic growth rate of at least 5 percent. The economy, advisers argued, could be stimulated through either large-scale governmental spending or a tax reduction that would increase consumer purchasing power. Choosing the latter course, Kennedy submitted a detailed proposal to reduce federal tax revenues by $11 billion from individuals and $2.6 billion from corporations. Tightening present schedules would raise an additional $3.4 billion, thus making a net tax reduction of $10.2 billion. The plan immediately came under fire from all sides. Labor demanded further cuts favoring lower-income groups, business claimed discrimination against middle-income groups, and Congress complained that federal revenues could not be cut in the face of a projected $8.3 billion budget deficit. Despite a White House request for prompt action, Congress moved slowly. The Ways and Means Committee did not order the bill reported until September. The House finally passed it, substantially in the form Kennedy had requested, in September 1963, but the Senate adjourned without taking action.

Kennedy's program for improving the quality of American life scored a few successes. Congress approved $150 million in grants to states for construction of nonprofit community health centers for the mentally ill. It also authorized construction grants and student loans for medical and dental schools, an expanded campaign against air pollution, and a one-year extension of the National Defense Education Act. Yet 1963, in terms of congressional response to administration requests, was the least productive of Kennedy's three years in office. Frankly viewing these years as educative and preparative, Kennedy confidently anticipated further legislative triumphs during the 1964 session and the fruition of his program during his second term.

4.   KENNEDY AND CIVIL RIGHTS

The election of Kennedy in 1960 ushered in a new period of heightened expectation—and frustration—among civil rights leaders and black Americans generally. Indeed, black-led organizations began an all-out campaign to end legally enforced segregation soon after the new president's inauguration. The first test came with the "freedom rides" that began in the spring of 1961. Sponsored by several interracial organizations, black and white citizens attacked segregation in interstate travel by chartering buses and riding through the Deep South, deliberately entering segregated restaurants and terminals en route. White resentment quickly boiled over. In Anniston, Alabama, one group of riders was attacked and beaten. A second freedom bus was halted, bombed, set afire, and destroyed by a mob. When the riders tried to proceed from Anniston to Montgomery, the situation deteriorated still further. The governor of Alabama denounced them as "rabble rousers" and made no attempt to curb resentful white citizens. Thus encouraged, they mobbed the riders so ferociously that the Washington government, in the absence of effective action by state or local authorities, had to intervene. Only after Attorney General Robert Kennedy sent several hundred federal marshals to Montgomery to prevent further violence did the governor act. He proclaimed martial law and employed state national guardsmen and police to restore order.

The freedom rides continued. Bruised but unintimidated, most of the original group left Montgomery for Jackson, Mississippi, in a bus under heavy police escort. Many of them were arrested in Jackson for violating a segregation ordinance, but officials were scrupulously careful to prevent further acts of violence. Thereafter, in fact, the riders met with little worse than epithets, angry stares, and occasional mass arrests. State authorities, aware of the unfavorable publicity that Anniston and Montgomery had received in the North and abroad, took steps to avert similar outbreaks.

Results came in late 1961, when the ICC ordered all bus companies to desegregate interstate routes, post signs to that effect on every bus, and cease stopping at restaurants and terminals that maintained segregated facilities. The bus lines complied, and an increasing number of local terminals took down "white" and "colored" signs and grudgingly admitted blacks who sought to enter the white section. Although the freedom rides resulted in partial rather than total victory, they marked a significant erosion in the strength of Jim Crow segregation.

Yet growing numbers of blacks were less impressed by victories won than by dismal evidence of what remained to be done. They were far from free, a century after emancipation. In the South, they still encountered discrimination at nearly every turn. They could not eat in white restaurants or register at white hotels. Few of their children, despite the Brown decision, attended schools with whites. In many southern counties, they still lacked the power to vote and thus seek redress through political action. In the North, millions of blacks lived in urban slums where high unemployment, inadequate opportunities, inferior schools and housing, and disproportionate crime and disease rates were facts of life.

Kennedy's commitment to civil rights was genuine, but his initial performance was, as Martin Luther King, Jr., observed, "essentially cautious and defensive."

The president named a few blacks to positions of high responsibility, including Robert C. Weaver for the sensitive post of federal housing administrator. A new Committee on Equal Employment Opportunity, headed by Vice-President Johnson, persuaded more than fifty of the nation's largest defense contractors to sign "plans for progress" embodying agreements to provide equal opportunity. Firms holding governmental contracts in excess of $10,000 were required to file periodic reports proving compliance with federal antidiscrimination policy. An executive order in November 1962 prohibited racial and religious discrimination in housing built or purchased with federal aid.

Presidential action grew progressively stronger and more forceful in response to events in the Deep South. First came the case of James H. Meredith, a black Mississippian who had instituted a suit charging racial bias after the state university had rejected his two applications to enroll. A variety of legal means to secure his admission all failed in the face of Governor Ross Barnett's defiance of judicial authority. Finally, after Meredith's fourth attempt to register was rebuffed by two hundred state police on September 27, 1962, the United States Circuit Court in New Orleans announced that its powers were exhausted and that further action was up to the executive branch. President Kennedy moved decisively to insure compliance with the court's orders. On September 30 he ordered several hundred federal marshals to accompany Meredith to the university campus at Oxford. Kennedy also sent federal troops to a base at nearby Memphis, Tennessee, and federalized the Mississippi National Guard. That evening a mob of students and bystanders attacked the marshals with rocks and occasional rifle fire, and a fierce riot ensued until dawn of the following day. State police withdrew, and only the prompt arrival of federal troops saved the lightly armed and outnumbered marshals. Two civilians were killed and seventy wounded before order was restored. State resistance thereupon melted away as federal bayonets kept order. Meredith was registered on October 1 and began attending classes under heavy armed guard.

Impressed by a need for stronger action, President Kennedy requested new civil rights legislation in February 1963. He sought to secure greater protection for voting rights, assist areas in the process of desegregating their schools, and extend the Civil Rights Commission. Black leaders demanding "freedom now" were less than satisfied with this moderate program, but the southern catalyst was still at work. Dr. King* began a campaign in April 1963 to end discrimination in shops, restaurants, and employment in Birmingham, a center of deep-southern resistance. The protest, small at first, began with lunch counter sit-ins, picketing, and demonstrations. The mood grew uglier as King met the full force of Birmingham law enforcement authorities, led by Police Commissioner Eugene "Bull" Connor. The climax came on May 3, when Connor used fire hoses and police dogs to break up a protest march. Television forced these events upon the

*About Martin Luther King, Jr., and the civil rights movement, see pp. 647–652.

nation's attention and helped to arouse white middle-class consciences. Civil rights protests spread rapidly; over 750 demonstrations occurred across the nation in the spring and early summer. There were nearly 14,000 arrests in eleven southern states alone.

Kennedy addressed the nation on June 11, 1963, with a call for action. "We face," he declared, "a moral crisis as a country and as a people." Black aspirations could no longer be denied. The United States could not preach freedom abroad and practice discrimination at home. "This is one country," he emphasized. "It has become one country because all of us and all the people who came here had an equal chance to develop their talents." But this had not been true for blacks, and prompt governmental action was imperative. He then submitted a new civil rights bill containing all the features of his February proposal, plus many new ones in the areas of desegregation, equal employment, and equal access to public accommodations. Demonstrations, continuing while Congress considered this proposal, were climaxed by a march on Washington on August 28. Although many feared that the remonstrance would alienate congressmen and might lead to violence, the 250,000 participants conducted themselves with decorum and dignity. The House of Representatives passed a strengthened version of Kennedy's bill. But the Senate Judiciary Committee, headed by James O. Eastland of Mississippi, held the bill so long that little action in the upper house was possible before adjournment. Although a hard fight loomed and a Senate filibuster appeared certain, Kennedy was reasonably confident that Congress would enact civil rights legislation during the next session.

5. TRAGEDY AT DALLAS

In the autumn of 1963, President Kennedy's thoughts turned to next year's election. His first term had been a time of preparation. He confidently expected reelection, a clear mandate, and the fulfillment of his legislative program. He journeyed to Texas in late November, in the company of the vice-president, for the purpose of mending political fences. Texas was badly split between the liberal Democratic forces of Senator Ralph W. Yarborough and a conservative faction led by Governor John B. Connally. Kennedy sought unity for the coming election. He arrived in Dallas, a center of extremist right-wing activities, on the morning of November 22. Ambassador Stevenson, attending the celebration of United Nations Day in the city a few weeks earlier, had been spat upon and hit by a picket sign. But there was no sign of hostility as the presidential motorcade proceeded into downtown Dallas. Friendly, cheering people lined the streets, and Kennedy twice halted the motorcade to greet them.

At 12:30 P.M., local time, just as the motorcade turned on to Elm Street and went past the Texas Book Depository Building, shots rang out. The first hit Kennedy in the back of the neck, exiting through his throat. He stiffened, then lurched slightly forward in his seat. Governor Connally, sitting in front of the president, was also hit. Then Kennedy received a bullet in the back of the head and fell into his wife's lap. The president was sped to Parkland Memorial Hospital, four miles away, but it was too late. He was pronounced dead at 1:00 P.M.

The apparent assassin, soon captured by police, was a twenty-four-year-old malcontent named Lee Harvey Oswald, with a record of emotional disturbance and grievances against society. Another killer murdered Oswald two days later. A special commission headed by Chief Justice Warren later concluded that Oswald's guilt was certain beyond any reasonable doubt and that he had acted as an individual rather than as "part of any conspiracy, domestic or foreign, to assassinate President Kennedy."

No single event in American history, except, perhaps, Lincoln's assassination, had ever caused such trauma. The president's body, taken to the White House, remained there until Sunday, when it was placed in the rotunda of the Capitol on the same catafalque that had held Lincoln's corpse nearly one hundred years before. More than 250,000 people passed by to pay their last respects. Monday, November 25, was clear and cold, and a million people lined the streets of Washington to view the funeral, while millions more watched on television. Eight heads of state, ten prime ministers, and most of the world's royalty added to the pomp and pageantry of the somber occasion. The cortege moved from the Capitol to St. Matthew's Cathedral, where the late president's lifelong friend, Richard Cardinal Cushing, archbishop of Boston, said a funeral mass. The procession then moved down Connecticut Avenue to Constitution Avenue, past the Lincoln Memorial, and over Memorial Bridge to Arlington National Cemetery. There, on a hill overlooking the city of Washington, John F. Kennedy was laid to his final rest.

6.   TO THE MOON AND BEYOND

On May 25, 1961, Kennedy appeared before a joint session of Congress to announce a bold new initiative with major domestic and foreign-policy implications: a crash program to send an American astronaut to the moon by the end of the decade. If the "battle that is now going on around the world between freedom and tyranny" was to be won, Kennedy declared, the United States had to "take a clearly leading role in space achievement, which in many ways holds the key to our future on earth."

Kennedy's call for a moon landing and the enthusiastic response of Congress and public opinion marked the culmination of more than a decade of debate about the objectives, organization, and control of space exploration. Its potential had been limited by two important considerations in the late 1940s and 1950s. First, the early space program was subordinated to the military objective of developing long- and medium-range ballistic missiles. Rivalry within the military resulted, and, despite a commitment by the Eisenhower administration to launch an orbiting satellite, the incipient space program was weakly supported and fell victim to military control over resources and technology. Second, a civilian space program suffered because both Truman and Eisenhower refused strongly to support space exploration because of its great cost and their doubts about its usefulness.

All of this changed, however, with the launching of the Soviet orbiting satellite *Sputnik* on October 4, 1957, which shook Western faith in the technological superiority of the United States and began a new era of cold-war space competition. American technological impotence seemed further confirmed when the navy, on December 6, 1957, failed ignominiously: its Vanguard TV-3 lifted four feet off the launch pad and then exploded before a group of dignitaries and reporters. But in January 1958, a satellite carried by an army Jupiter-C missile, *Explorer 1*, achieved orbit. Facing strong public pressure, Eisenhower and Congress, after the launching of *Explorer*, established a more clearly articulated space policy with the passage of the National Aeronautics and Space Act of 1958. It created a strong civilian agency, the National Aeronautics and Space Administration (NASA), to be responsible for the development of nonmilitary space exploration.

When Kennedy made his call for a unified national effort to conquer space, therefore, a basic structure already existed. As a result of the *Sputnik* scare, the space program became part of Soviet-American competition. We now know that the Soviet space program was part of a bluff, orchestrated by Premier Nikita Khrushchev, which obscured serious weaknesses in Soviet aeronautics and, by the early 1960s, also obscured a decided inferiority in ballistic missiles. But, especially before effective satellite reconnaisance—not established until the early 1960s—the Soviet bluff was less clear. Soviet superiority in space and technology seemed quite possible to Americans. NASA took its first step in the competition with Project Mercury, established in November 1958. Alan B. Shepard, Jr., became the first American in space on May 5, 1961, and John H. Glenn, Jr., the first in actual orbit about a year later. But the Soviet astronauts Yuri A. Gagarin and Gherman S. Titov had already achieved the same feats in April and August 1961.

The race to reach space and to achieve manned orbit stimulated public interest and galvanized congressional support. Hence during the remaining years of the Kennedy administration, NASA, under the leadership of its director, James E. Webb, enjoyed growing largesse from Congress. Responding to Kennedy's call in May 1961 to land an American on the moon, Congress immediately increased NASA's budget by 61 percent. Between 1961 and 1964, NASA's budget grew from under $1 billion to $5.1 billion, while NASA's employees increased in number from 6,000 to 60,000, and civilian space-related employment reached 411,000. This massive deployment of national resources into a crash manned space program soon produced results. Project Mercury's last mission, commanded by the astronaut Gordon Cooper in May 1963, was followed by the more sophisticated Project Gemini, designed to gain the experience and skills necessary for a moon landing. The Gemini program thus involved spacecraft with several crew members; these vehicles could rendezvous with each other, and their crews had the opportunity to emerge from them for "space walks" thousands of miles above the earth.

Project Gemini was followed by Project Apollo in late 1966. Despite a fire which killed the astronauts Virgil Grissom, Edward White, and Roger Chafee and delayed the first launch of an Apollo craft until October 1968, three astronauts successfully orbited the moon aboard *Apollo 8* on Christmas Day 1968. Further dress rehearsals in the spring of 1969 set the stage for *Apollo 11*, which would carry the first astronaut to the moon. After a successful launch on July 16, 1969, Neil Armstrong, Edwin Aldrin, and Michael Collins achieved lunar orbit and, with Armstrong and Aldrin aboard the lunar module *Eagle* and Collins piloting the command module *Columbia*, American astronauts landed on the moon on July 20. *Apollo 11* was then followed by a series of other manned lunar missions, concluding with *Apollo 17* in December 1972.

The successful landing of Americans on the moon—and the victory over the Soviets in the space race it represented—was a remarkable triumph of American technology mobilized by massive and unprecedented governmental direction. Yet live landings on the moon also marked the end of unlimited public and congressional support for NASA and further—and less glamorous—space exploration. Since the early 1960s, an equally important part of NASA's program had been a series of unmanned space probes. Between 1962 and 1973, the Mariner program sent probes to Venus, Mars, and Mercury—with increasingly sophisticated electronic sensors and photographic equipment. Even more spectacular unmanned probes followed with the *Viking* mission to Mars in 1976 and with the *Voyager* probes, which began in 1977 as part of a program of unmanned explorations of Saturn, Jupiter, Uranus, Neptune, and Pluto.

But even after the final Apollo mission, NASA continued its program of manned space exploration. In 1973, it launched *Skylab*, a permanent orbiting space station. Although several missions were conducted on it, a loss of solar panels—and hence of its source of power—doomed *Skylab*. Over the next six years, as it gradually lost power, it began a long descent from orbit. In spite of an all-out NASA effort to save it, *Skylab* crashed to earth in July 1979.

The future of manned space missions lay rather with the Space Transportation Service (STS), or shuttle—a reusable earth-to-space vehicle. Receiving congressional authorization in 1972, NASA made the shuttle the centerpiece of its program and spent about $10 billion over the next decade in development and testing. After a series of mishaps, the first of four shuttles, *Columbia*, was successfully launched on April 12, 1981, and landed two days later. Three further test flights of *Columbia* took place in November 1981, March 1982, and July 1982. They proved the shuttle's ability to carry commercial and military satellites into orbit and to retrieve them for repair. In November 1982, *Columbia* made its maiden full flight and launched two satellites.

It soon appeared that flights of the shuttles *Columbia, Challenger,* and *Discovery* (the fourth, *Atlantis,* was not yet operational) had become an almost routine occurrence. Within three years, NASA had begun an ambitious schedule of shuttle launchings that sought to make them the primary vehicle for orbiting and recovery of defense and civilian satellites. But the worst disaster in the history of the American space program—the explosion of *Challenger* soon after lift-off on January 28, 1986, and the death of its seven crew members—forced a painful reappraisal of both the shuttle program and NASA. After several months of investigation and hearings, a presidential commission, headed by former Secretary of State William P. Rogers, issued its report on June 9, 1986. It concluded that the immediate cause of the explosion was defective design in the shuttle's solid rocket boosters. Even more seriously, the commission cited faulty decision making by NASA—above all, its continued use of the boosters despite knowledge of their structual problems and its decision to launch in conditions of extreme cold—and recommended an overhaul of the space agency and a redefinition of the American space program.

CHAPTER 27

The Great Society

Lyndon Baines Johnson guided the nation during a turbulent period. The expectations of blacks and other minorities had expanded even before Johnson became president. By the time he left office, while an unprecedented amount of federal legislation guaranteed basic political and civil rights, white backlash and divisions among black leaders had seriously drained the strength of the civil rights movement. Along with comprehensive civil rights legislation, Johnson guided through Congress new social and economic welfare measures which significantly extended the New Deal structure. The president had also begun a determined effort to eradicate poverty, malnutrition, and disease at home. Yet Johnson's domestic reforms were, by 1969, overshadowed and weakened, both by public disaffection from them and by deepening American involvement in southeast Asia. Unable to extricate itself from this tragic struggle, rocked also by angry criticism and social turmoil at home, the Johnson administration ended in 1969, leaving American society plagued by violence, dissension, and disarray unequaled since the 1860s.

1. THE JOHNSON PRESIDENCY

Born near Stonewall, Texas, on August 27, 1908, Johnson knew adversity as a youth. He completed his education at Southwest State Teachers College in Texas and taught school for a year, but he was drawn to the world of politics. Both his father and his grandfather had served in the Texas legislature, and he soon developed his own political ambitions. Johnson first came to Washington in 1932 as secretary to Texas Representative Richard M. Kleberg. Four years later, at age twenty-seven, Johnson was appointed head of the National Youth Administration for the state of Texas—a New Deal post which became a springboard for his election to the House of Representatives in 1937. He won the senatorial primary, tantamount to election, in 1948, defeating his opponent by just eighty-seven votes. Only five years later, Senate Democrats, recognizing his political talents, elected him minority leader. When the Democrats regained control of the Senate in 1954, Johnson began his tenure as majority leader and became, by 1960, a leading presidential candidate. After Johnson's bid was swept aside by the Kennedy bandwagon, Kennedy, aware of the strength Johnson would bring to the Democratic ticket, offered him the vice-presidential nomination.

According to one observer, Johnson was "the first uninhibited product of the American frontier" to become president since Andrew Jackson. Direct and earthy, Johnson's speeches frequently sounded like the homilies of a country preacher. Vain, sensitive, and insecure, he desperately needed constant praise and approval and what he termed a national consensus. He was a hard-driving, quick-tempered man, harshly intolerant and abusive of associates who displeased him or critics who opposed him. His most striking personal characteristics were immense energy, drive, and determination—all of which, lacking outside interests, he channeled into politics. Though he was not doctrinaire in political philosophy, he had a deep and passionate concern for the poor, the elderly, and the downtrodden. Government, he believed, existed to serve the people and to do for them what they were unable to do for themselves. Johnson, far more than Kennedy, was thus a direct inheritor of the New Deal tradition and its commitment to social and economic justice.

Not long after he became president, therefore, Johnson made the enactment of Kennedy's New Frontier program a main priority. Congress passed his tax reduction bill in February 1964, enacted a variety of conservation measures, and voted $375 million to promote urban transit systems. When Johnson submitted a "barebones" foreign-aid program calling for the expenditure of $3.5 billion—$1.1 billion less than the previous year's request—Congress reduced it by only $250 million, the lowest percentage cut in the seventeen-year history of the program.

Johnson also continued the fight for civil rights legislation with unrelenting determination. "No memorial oration or eulogy," he stated in his first address to Congress, "could more eloquently honor President Kennedy's memory than the earliest possible passage of the civil rights bill for which he fought so long." Although the bill passed the House in February 1964, a southern filibuster delayed passage in the Senate. But, with only nineteen Southerners participating in the filibuster—and many of them old men like Richard B. Russell of Georgia—the bill's managers maintained unrelenting pressure. They kept two senators loyal to them on the floor at all times, and always had enough supporters on hand to answer quorum calls. Finally, on June 10, fifty-seven days after formal consideration began, the Senate voted cloture on a civil rights debate for the first time in its history. A week later, the bill easily passed by a vote of seventy-six to eighteen.

By late 1964, Johnson could also claim a major legislative triumph of his own. In his first State of the Union message in January 1964, he declared "unconditional war on poverty in America" and proposed a significant expansion of the New Deal welfare state. Congress responded with the Economic Opportunity Act of 1964, which authorized $947.5 million in 1965 to begin a three-year program. It provided, among other things, for a Job Corps to train youths in conservation camps and urban areas and a community action program aimed at job training and improved health care and housing. It also established a domestic peace corps to cooperate with state and local authorities in combating poverty. Finally, the act established the Office of Economic Opportunity to supervise the program. R. Sargent Shriver, Jr., director of the Peace Corps, became head of the new agency.

2.   THE ELECTION OF 1964

By 1964, Johnson was in such a strong position that volunteers for the GOP presidential nomination did not abound. The early favorites were Senator Barry M. Goldwater of Arizona and Governor Nelson Rockefeller of New York, and the contest between the two represented the most serious breach since 1952 between the GOP's right wing and its moderate-centrist element. Goldwater, challenging traditional domestic and foreign policies, advocated voluntary participation in Social Security and suggested that NATO commanders should have the right to order the use of nuclear weapons. Rockefeller, on the other hand, was more moderate in his policy positions but had been badly hurt in public esteem by a recent divorce and remarriage.

Rockefeller and Goldwater faced off in a crucial test in the California primary. Goldwater, who already controlled a large number of delegates to the national convention, won the contest in California and virtually assured his nomination. Although moderate elements of the party, headed by Governor William W. Scranton of Pennsylvania, attempted a last-minute "Stop Goldwater" movement, the GOP National Convention, which opened in San Francisco on July 13, was dominated by Goldwater. The platform committee drafted the most conservative major party platform in modern times. It pledged "limited, frugal and efficient" government at home and "a dynamic strategy aimed at victory" abroad. Nominated on the first ballot, Goldwater showed no inclination to heal wounds. He chose Representative William E. Miller of New York, a former GOP national chairman known for his conservative views, as his running mate. Goldwater's acceptance speech further aggravated Republican infighting and a growing public perception of him as an extremist ideologue. "Any who join us in all sincerity," he said, "we welcome." "Those who do not care for our cause we do not expect to enter our ranks in any case." "Extremism in the defense of liberty," he declared, "is no vice." "And," he added, "let me remind you also that moderation in the pursuit of justice is no virtue."

The conservative wing of the GOP had finally nominated one of its own. Goldwater's political views left little role for federal intervention in domestic affairs such as welfare, education, and civil rights. Federal intervention, Goldwater said, undermined individual initiative, corroding a trait basic to the American character. While Goldwater advocated rolling back big government at home, he favored a reinvigorated anti-Communist foreign policy. There would be no more "capitulation" through fear of nuclear catastrophe.

The Democratic National Convention, which met in Atlantic City in August, duly nominated Johnson. Although some Democrats favored Robert Kennedy for vice-president, Johnson turned instead to Senator Hubert Humphrey of Minnesota, an old friend and a staunch liberal. The convention ratified the president's choice on August 26. To no one's surprise, the Democratic platform endorsed the Great Society.

It was clear from the beginning that Johnson's lead over Goldwater was overwhelming. Goldwater's hopes rested on an anticipated conservative revolt, especially against civil rights and racial disorder. George C. Wallace, governor of Alabama, demonstrated the potential for white backlash throughout the country. In the Democratic primaries, Wallace, a strident segregationist, captured 34 percent of the vote in Wisconsin, 30 percent in Indiana, and 43 percent in Maryland. Republican hopes of profiting from a white backlash rose when riots erupted in black areas of northern cities during the summer. But Goldwater, ignoring the wishes of many supporters, refused to exploit the riots, and civil rights leaders worked effectively to quiet the restive black population. Johnson, shrewdly reading the signs, conducted a restrained campaign; the only thing remaining in doubt was the size of his mandate.

On November 3, 1964, the voters gave Johnson the largest popular vote—43 million—that any presidential candidate had ever received up to that time. His electoral majority was a thumping 486 to 52. Goldwater, trailing far behind with 27 million popular votes, carried only Alabama, Georgia, South Carolina, Louisiana, Mississippi, and Arizona. The sweeping Democratic triumph cut deeply into GOP strength on all levels. The Democrats gained thirty-eight House seats, giving them a 295-to-140 margin in the next Congress, and picked up two seats in the Senate, making their majority 68 to 32. The GOP lost over five hundred seats in state legislatures across the country. Still, a significant result of the election was the reemergence of Republican strength in much of the South. The southern GOP, by adopting a lukewarm if not hostile approach to civil rights and by opposing Great Society programs, now became a strong party which tended to dominate in the region when elections focused on national issues.

3.   THE GREAT SOCIETY

Buoyed by his decisive mandate, Johnson elaborated the goals of the Great Society in his annual message of January 1965. Such a society, he observed, demanded abundance and liberty for all, equality of opportunity, and the improvement of the quality of life. All of this was possible by stimulating the economy, continuing the antipoverty programs, and developing imaginative solutions for the complex problems of modern urban society. It was imperative to control water and air pollution and to preserve the country's natural beauty. A new and expanded program of aid to education was also necessary. In the following months Johnson loosed a flood of specific proposals to implement the Great Society.

Congress responded with an alacrity rarely seen on Capitol Hill. Its first major enactment was the Appalachian Regional Development Act, signed in March 1965. Appalachia, extending from Pennsylvania to northern Alabama and encompassing 182,000 square miles and 17 million people, was a region of poverty, with a per capita income 40 percent lower than the national average and an unemployment rate 50 percent higher. The act provided $1.1 billion for highway construction, health centers, and development of resources. A joint federal-state agency, the Appalachian Regional Commission, would implement the program, while the states would design projects to fit their needs and execute them following approval by the commission.

The administration also strove to alleviate one of the nation's worst problems—urban decay. The Housing and Urban Development Act of 1965, the most sweeping measure of its kind since 1949, expanded the major programs of the Housing and Home Finance Agency, provided assistance for the construction of some 240,000 additional units of low-rent public housing, and authorized $2.9 billion in federal grants for urban renewal over a four-year period. Controversy over payment of direct federal rent supplements to low-income families temporarily stalled this provision, but funds for the purpose were obtained in 1966. Congress, at Johnson's request, also created a cabinet-level Department of Housing and Urban Development to administer the act and related programs. Robert C. Weaver, the first black ever named to the cabinet, became head of the new department in January 1966.

A further milestone was reached in 1965 with passage of the most significant piece of welfare legislation, Medicare, since the New Deal. Truman had proposed a comprehensive plan to assure medical care for the aged in 1945, and during the next twenty years this initiative was blocked by the American Medical Association. But Johnson, having made the program a major issue in his cam-

ELECTION OF 1964

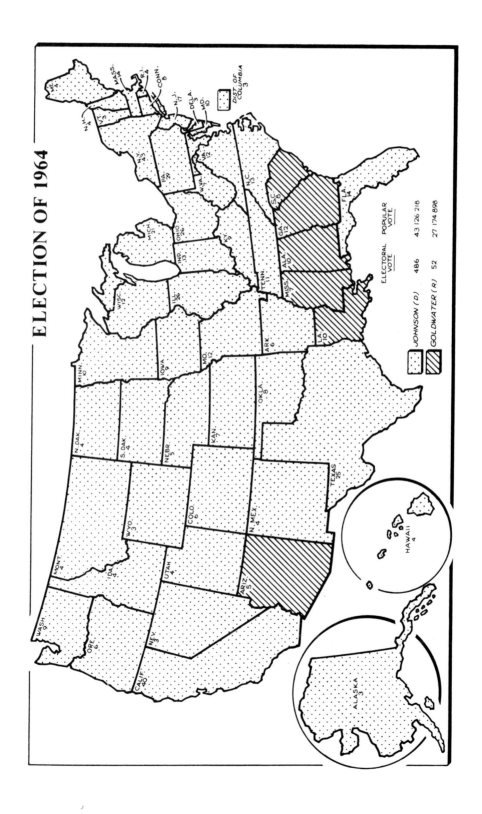

	ELECTORAL VOTE	POPULAR VOTE
JOHNSON (D)	486	43 126 218
GOLDWATER (R)	52	27 174 898

paign, now had both a popular mandate and the necessary votes to enact such a law. Congress approved the Medicare bill by large majorities, and President Johnson signed it on July 30 in Independence, Missouri, with Truman at his side. The act, covering most people sixty-five and older, included a basic health plan that provided up to ninety days of hospital care, one hundred days of nursing-home care, and one hundred home health-care visits. A supplementary plan, available to those who elected to pay a $3 monthly premium, covered 80 percent of the costs for a variety of health services, including doctors' fees, after a standard deduction of $50. General revenues and an increased Social Security tax, rising progressively to 11.3 percent in 1987, financed the program.

Educational legislation, as Johnson repeatedly emphasized, was the most important part of the Great Society since, he said, many Americans were unable to provide their children with full educational opportunities. The Elementary and Secondary Education Act of 1965, passed in April, settled a twenty-year controversy over the use of large-scale federal funds to support primary and secondary education. The $1.3 billion program was designed primarily to aid schools with large numbers of children from low-income families. The act contained a formula for handling the thorny issue of federal aid to parochial schools. Aid would be supplied to children attending both private and public schools, but public agencies would control expenditures. Johnson also won approval of the Higher Education Act of 1965 to expand federal aid on another level. It made scholarships available to more than 140,000 capable but needy college students and authorized a National Teachers Corps to provide qualified personnel for schools in poverty-stricken areas.

After 1965, additional Great Society legislation was inhibited by mounting war costs, inflation, and a less cooperative Congress. Even so, Congress did enact more Great Society programs during the final three years of Johnson's presidency. They included provisions for expanded federal activity in the field of public health in 1966, an amendment to the Social Security Act in 1967 which raised pensions and enlarged coverage for some 24 million people, and an expansion of minimum-wage coverage in 1966. Johnson also won congressional support for further huge infusions of federal aid to education at all levels in 1966, including $3.9 billion over a three-year period for colleges and universities and $6.1 billion for public schools in a two-year extension of the Elementary and Secondary Education Act.

Continued concern for the quality of urban life was reflected in the Demonstration Cities and Metropolitan Area Redevelopment Act of 1966—America's most ambitious effort on behalf of its hard-pressed cities. A housing act in August 1968 called for the construction or rehabilitation of 1.7 million new units of low- and middle-income housing by 1970 and 6 million units by 1978. New concern for consumer protection was reflected in so-called Truth-in-Packaging and Truth-in-Lending acts in 1966 and 1968. Johnson's Great Society also began massive federal involvement in transportation. It granted funds for urban mass transit and the development of fast trains on the metropolitan corridor between Boston and New York and Washington. It created a new cabinet-level Department of Transportation in 1966. And Congress passed a series of highway and traffic safety and automobile emission control laws in 1966–1967.

Federal action on water and air pollution first became significant under Kennedy and expanded markedly during the Johnson administration. Each year brought new legislation and increased appropriations, the cumulative effect of which was to widen the scope of federal responsibility and attack the problem through the formation of regional control agencies and planning commissions. Other laws, notably the Highway Beautification Act of 1965, which the president's wife, Lady Bird Johnson, was instrumental in obtaining, began to attack the man-made blight that lined America's roadways. Concern over an industrial society's steady encroachments upon natural surroundings led to a host of important laws, beginning with the Land and Water Conservation Act and the National Wilderness Preservation Act in 1964. These were followed by statutes setting aside land for parks and recreational use, protecting various endangered species, and safeguarding such threatened national treasures as the Indiana dunes along Lake Michigan, California's giant redwoods, and several wild and scenic rivers.

Aided by prosperity, large congressional majorities, and sympathetic courts, Lyndon Johnson spurred and supervised the enactment of the most ambitious and many-sided program of reform legislation in American history. Yet, by 1968, the Great Society—and the strength of Johnson's presidency—was disintegrating. Congress, expressing voter anxiety about crime, disorder, and inflation, became less favorably disposed toward large welfare expenditures after 1966. The war in Vietnam also diverted funds and attention from the Great Society and its goals.

4. THE BLACK REVOLUTION

Black Americans vastly increased the scope and force of their drive for improved conditions and equal treatment during Lyndon Johnson's presidency. Black progress, although uneven and marred by violence and controversy, was dramatic; not since the 1860s had blacks taken comparable strides toward full citizenship. Federal courts were active agents of change. Empowered by the strong enforcement provisions of the Civil Rights Act of 1964, federal courts required southern school boards to devise plans for desegregation. The results were almost immediate. Only 4 percent of black students in southern states attended integrated public schools in 1957, and no more than 9.2 percent did so in 1964. But this figure increased to 25.8 percent in December 1966, 40 percent in 1968, and 84.3 percent in 1970. Southern white resistance persisted, as hundreds of thousands of white children were sent to private schools to avoid integration. And yet, for the most part, school desegregation after 1964 was accomplished peacefully throughout the South.

The situation in northern cities, which, by 1970, contained nearly half of the nation's blacks, was less encouraging. An exodus to the suburbs by white families, along with retail trade and light industry, narrowed the inner-city tax base and helped to erode the quality of transit, sanitation, and other public facilities. White exodus encouraged residential segregation and brought de facto school segregation. The ghetto poor, meanwhile, were trapped in a vicious circle of inadequate education and training, inadequate job opportunities, inadequate wages, inadequate housing, and all of the debilitating problems of crime and squalor that festered around them. The rapid disintegration of urban areas and growing racial antagonism coincided with a period among urban blacks of rising expectations, resentment, and a growing impatience.

One result was a series of ghetto riots that convulsed urban America during the mid-1960s. A major riot occurred in Harlem in July 1964. It was followed by another riot in the Watts section of Los Angeles during the week of August 11–16, 1965, in which thirty-four persons were killed and over a thousand injured, and which caused some $40 million in damage. During the next three summers, few cities with a substantial black population escaped some sort of racial disorder. Hundreds of communities experienced major riots, the worst of which took place in Newark and Detroit in July 1967. The statistics were dismal and frightening: 26 dead, 1,000 injured, 1,400 arrested, and whole neighborhoods gutted in Newark; over 40 deaths, 350 injuries, 3,800 arrests, 5,000 burned out of their homes, and some 3,000 business establishments sacked and looted in Detroit. Fire bombs and rooftop sniping tore the latter city, and it took some 4,700 federal troops to restore order. Detroit reminded some observers of Berlin in 1945.

Nearly all of these riots were triggered by minor episodes—an arrest, a routine police raid, a shooting, a thrown rock, a street-corner argument—but the upheavals usually expressed black resentment and frustration at symbols of white authority. Studies indicated that the real trouble was rooted in chronic slum conditions, aggravated by resentment of police tactics. By and large, these were not "race riots" between blacks and whites of the sort that many American cities had experienced decades earlier. Most of the action took place within or on the fringes of slum areas. Moreover, most of the destruction was wreaked upon ghetto homes, stores, and businesses (largely white-owned and -operated); and most of the violence occurred between black rioters and the police or national guardsmen.

The traditional mold of racial confrontation was also broken in the rhetoric and tactics of black leaders. Veteran interracial groups like the NAACP, the

Urban League, and the Southern Regional Council emphasized legal and political action to end discrimination, promote opportunity, and bring about a racially integrated society. The leaders of such organizations were increasingly challenged after 1960 by younger, more militant blacks who rejected traditional goals and methods. Between 1960 and 1963, it was these younger blacks who spearheaded nonviolent "direct action" sit-ins and demonstrations across the South through organizations like the Congress of Racial Equality (CORE) and the Student Non-Violent Coordinating Committee (SNCC).

The black militants continued to criticize both the white and the black power structures—even after the major political victories of 1964–1965. Malcolm X, a Black Muslim who broke with Elijah Muhammad to found his own Muslim group, the Organization of Afro-American Unity, in 1964, won wide praise for his advocacy of black dignity and full, uncompromised equality. Stokely Carmichael of Trinidad and New York, educated at Howard University, became chairman of SNCC in 1966 and enunciated a doctrine of "black power" that carried unmistakable overtones of violence. Texas-born Bobby Seale helped to found the Black Panther party for Self Defense in Oakland in 1966 to organize and instill self-respect among ghetto blacks and compel better treatment from police by aggressive confrontations and pressure tactics. The Black Panthers soon dropped "Self Defense" from their title and spoke the language of military preparedness and revolutionary socialism. Eldridge Cleaver, later the Panthers' "minister of information," wrote *Soul on Ice,* a searing, inflammatory look at the race problem. He wrote the book while serving a prison term in California for narcotics possession. H. Rap Brown, an outspoken advocate of black power, urged guerrilla warfare against the white establishment. Playwright and poet LeRoi Jones and essayist and novelist James Baldwin contributed with bitter eloquence to the black protest movement during this period.

By 1968, both the leadership of and public support for the civil rights revolution were seriously undermined. Suspicion and animosity between black militants, black moderates, and white liberals flourished, while white backlash followed the wide media coverage of black power advocates and racial violence. This somber picture was confirmed in March 1968, when the National Advisory Commission on Civil Disorders, appointed by Johnson to investigate the causes of the riots, issued its report. The commission, headed by former Governor Otto Kerner of Illinois, cited poverty and racism in America's inner-city slums as the root causes of racial violence. Unless an all-out effort provided slum dwellers with adequate housing, jobs, training, education, and welfare, the commission concluded starkly, America would continue irrevocably on its way toward "two societies, one black, one white—separate and unequal." A sniper's bullet placed a tragic exclamation point upon the Kerner Commission report. Martin Luther King, Jr., visiting Memphis to aid the city's striking sanitation workers, was assassinated on April 4, 1968, on the balcony of the Lorraine Motel. A new wave of riots erupted in many cities, although police restraint and determined efforts by black leaders and municipal authorities helped to contain these outbreaks.

Despite the failure of what has been called the "Second Reconstruction" to solve fundamental problems of racial injustice, the decade of the 1960s brought real changes for the better. National recognition and acclaim were being won by blacks in unprecedented numbers. Memorable "firsts" included Robert C. Weaver's appointment to the cabinet, Edward Brooke's election to the United States Senate from Massachusetts in 1966 (the first black to sit in the upper chamber since Reconstruction, the first ever from a northern state or by popular vote), and Thurgood Marshall's appointment to the Supreme Court in 1967. Black candidates won mayoral elections in Cleveland, Detroit, Los Angeles, Gary, Newark, Atlanta, New Orleans, Birmingham, Charlotte, and several smaller cities. Charles Evers ran a strong though unsuccessful race for the governorship of Mississippi in 1971; Shirley Chisholm, a black congresswoman from New York, contended seriously for the Democratic presidential nomination in 1972. Psychologist Kenneth Clark and historian John Hope Franklin reached the top of their professions, as did editor LeRone Bennett, reporter Carl Rowan, and writers like Ralph Ellison and James Baldwin. There was also a great galaxy of black superstars in the sports and entertainment worlds, including (to name a few of the very best) slugger Henry Aaron and pitcher Bob Gibson, opera singer Leontyne Price and rock singer Diana Ross, basketball players Bill Russell, Wilt Chamberlain, and Kareem Abdul-Jabbar, running backs Jim Brown, O. J. Simpson, and Gale Sayers, actor Sidney Poitier, and comedians Bill Cosby and Flip Wilson.

For most blacks, however, the battle for full citizenship succeeded in less spectacular fashion. In communities across the United States, change came in small but visible ways. States and cities adopted or strengthened fair employment and open-housing ordinances. Unions, churches, municipalities, business groups, foundations, and community action groups launched campaigns to recruit and hire qualified blacks in white-collar and other skilled positions, to create new job opportunities and training programs for the ghetto's unemployed, to aid and underwrite black businesses and self-help efforts, to improve community recreational facilities, to hire more black policemen and teachers, and so on.

Congress, in the shocked aftermath of King's death, also roused itself. Despite the support of Johnson and much of Congress, the open-housing legislation had failed passage in 1966 and 1967. With all-out presidential support and a determined effort to overcome a Senate filibuster, Congress enacted the Civil Rights Act of 1968. It prohibited discrimination in the sale or rental of most public and private housing and applied to 80 percent of the nation's dwelling units. It banned racial discrimination in the selection of jurors. Finally, the act protected civil rights workers and provided severe penalties for interfering with the exercise of certain specified rights, such as attending school or working.

5. THE SUPREME COURT IN THE 1960s

In a wide variety of areas, the Warren Court continued as a force for activism and for expansion of the powers of the federal government. In a number of decisions, it extended free-speech protection to civil rights workers and sanctioned federal abolition of Jim Crow practices. In *Cox* v. *Louisiana* (1964), the Court reversed the conviction of a civil rights leader under a Louisiana statute prohibiting disturbance of the peace because such laws infringed on the rights of free speech and assembly. The validity of the public accommodations section of the Civil Rights Act of 1964 was sustained in *Heart of Atlanta Motel* v. *United States* (1964). Prohibitions against racial discrimination by hotels providing lodging to transient guests, the Court ruled, constituted a legitimate exercise of federal power over interstate commerce. The same principle was applied to restaurants in *Katzenbach* v. *McClung* (1964). The high bench unanimously dismissed *South Carolina* v. *Katzenbach* in March 1966, thereby upholding the validity of the Civil Rights Act of 1965. In a related matter, the Court struck down the Virginia poll tax in state and local elections, holding, in *Harper* v. *Virginia State Board of Education* (1966), that such a tax violated the Fourteenth Amendment's equal protection clause.

The Civil Rights Act of 1968 was actually upheld even before it went into effect. In 1967 the justices affirmed a decision of the California Supreme Court invalidating a recent amendment to the state constitution that sought to protect property owners' right to sell or lease to whomever they pleased. The effect of this decision was to reinstate a California law of 1963 forbidding discrimination in the sale or lease of houses containing more than four dwelling units. In *Jones* v. *A. H. Mayer Co.* (1968), the Supreme Court went the whole distance and swept aside discrimination in the sale or lease of all public and private housing by applying a century-old civil rights statute. "Racial discrimination which herds men into ghettos and makes their ability to buy property turn on the color of their skin," the Court proclaimed flatly, "is a relic of slavery."

The Warren Court's judicial activism extended even more prominently into the area of civil liberties and the trial rights of accused criminals. A series of decisions literally remade American law enforcement. In *Gideon* v. *Wainwright* (1963), the Court held that a state was obliged to supply defense counsel to indigent defendants even in noncapital prosecutions. The Court expanded the coverage of the Fourteenth and Fifteenth amendments to rule in *Escobedo* v. *Illinois* (1964) that a conviction was invalid when the police had either refused to permit suspects to have counsel during interrogation or had failed to inform them of their right to remain silent. Decisions on June 13, 1966—notably

Miranda v. *Arizona*—established firm guidelines for the treatment of arrested persons. They had to be advised of their right to remain silent or have a lawyer present during interrogation, and counsel had to be provided, even at state expense, if requested by the suspect.

The Court continued to scrutinize—and occasionally to demand revision of—the states' criminal processes. Significantly, the Court applied Bill of Rights protections to the states under the terms of the Fourteenth Amendment. For example, in *Duncan* v. *Louisiana* (1968), the high court held that a misdemeanor case entitled the defendant to a trial by jury under the Fourteenth Amendment's due process clause because the Sixth Amendment would accord him this right in a federal court. Earlier, in a related application of the Bill of Rights, the Court, in *Engel* v. *Vitale* (1962) and *School District of Abington Township* v. *Schempp* (1963), outlawed local or state laws requiring Bible reading and prayers in public schools on the ground that such practices constituted an establishment of religion contrary to the First Amendment.

While the Court decisively affected both civil rights and criminal justice, it had an equally important impact on politics. The result was similar—a wholesale expansion of federal at the expense of state power. In *Baker* v. *Carr* (1962), the Court made legislative apportionment by the states subject to the scrutiny of the federal courts according to the principle of "one man, one vote." The case involved representation in the legislature of Tennessee. The makeup of that body, as in most states, reflected the rural-urban balance of forty or even sixty years earlier. Not wishing to lose their power, rural lawmakers had blocked reapportionment decade after decade, even as their districts lost population and metropolitan areas mushroomed. Urban voters had grown restive under this form of inequality, and when *Baker* v. *Carr* opened the question to judicial review, suits demanding reapportionment were immediately brought in over two dozen states.

The first significant case to be decided involved the legality of Georgia's county unit system, used in primary elections for state offices and United States Senate seats. *Gray* v. *Sanders* (1963) struck down this system as a violation of the Fourteenth Amendment's equal protection clause, in that undue weight had been accorded rural votes. The high-water mark came with *Reynolds* v. *Sims* (1964) and related cases. The Court now held that representation in *both* houses of a state legislature had to be based upon districts having roughly equal population. Casting a wider net, the Supreme Court declared in *Wesberry* v. *Sanders* (1964) that the one-man, one-vote mandate was inherent in Article I of the Constitution as applied to seats in the national House of Representatives. States were instructed to draw the boundaries of their districts so that members of Congress would represent areas of roughly equal population. One man, one vote became the ruling principle across the entire spectrum of American politics when the Court extended it, in *Avery* v. *Midland County* (1968) and other cases, to most local governmental units.

6.   THE ELECTION OF 1968

In November 1967, Senator Eugene McCarthy of Minnesota announced that he opposed Johnson's renomination. McCarthy thus provided a rallying point for sentiment against the Vietnam War. Few took McCarthy's candidacy seriously because they were convinced that Johnson's hold upon the Democratic party was unshakable. But McCarthy's candidacy attracted a host of eager young volunteers, and, in the New Hampshire primary of March 1968, McCarthy scored a surprising upset, polling over 42 percent of the vote and capturing twenty of the state's twenty-four convention delegates. With Johnson now apparently beatable, Senator Robert F. Kennedy of New York, brother of the slain president, announced his own candidacy on March 16. Kennedy, his break with Johnson now complete, was a much more formidable opponent than McCarthy because he could unite party regulars and the new liberal activists.

Johnson, facing eroding public support for his presidency and serious opposition within his own party, in a televised address on March 31, 1968, withdrew from the campaign. He suspended the bombing of North Vietnam indefinitely in the hope of bringing the opposing forces (see p. 708) to the negotiation table—and he announced that he would devote the remaining months of his tenure to an effort to bring the Vietnam War to a satisfactory conclusion. Formal peace talks between the United States and North Vietnam began in Paris in May 1968.

The race now became a three-cornered scramble between McCarthy, Kennedy, and Vice-President Hubert H. Humphrey, who declared his candidacy on April 27 with the tacit support of President Johnson and most "organization" Democrats. Humphrey filed too late to enter the primaries, most of which became battlegrounds between McCarthy and Kennedy. McCarthy's victory over Johnson in Wisconsin on April 2 was inconclusive, since the president had withdrawn from the race two days earlier. Kennedy, his own campaign now fully under way, won decisively in Indiana and Nebraska, but lost in Oregon. Then, following Kennedy's narrow victory over McCarthy in the California primary on June 4, Sirhan Bishara Sirhan fatally wounded the New York senator in his hotel in Los Angeles just before a victory celebration.

The assassination of Robert Kennedy demoralized the antiadministration forces, and Hubert Humphrey came to the convention in Chicago on August 26 with most of the regular party delegations pledged to his support. As expected, the convention nominated Humphrey on the first ballot. A bitter platform battle between proponents of "peace" and "proadministration" Vietnam planks resulted in adoption of the latter. As a result, the Democratic program lauded the president's efforts to end the war, approved the peace negotiations, and proposed an end to the bombing of North Vietnam when such action would not endanger American troops.

The Chicago convention will be remembered not for its platform or its candidates, however, but for the political violence and bitter infighting within the Democratic party it gave rise to. Thousands of youthful antiwar demonstrators converged on Chicago to put pressure on delegates to repudiate the administration's Vietnam policy. In a series of brutal clashes, the Chicago police—in what has been appropriately described as a "police riot"—attacked demonstrators and bystanders alike in a melee of violence and rage. The Chicago riots underscored serious problems for the Democrats. Liberal Democrats were appalled at the repressive savagery of Democratic Mayor Richard J. Daley's police. Other Democrats, in white-collar suburbs and blue-collar wards, either praised or reluctantly supported Mayor Daley's police, seeing in the youthful activists and their heralded lifestyle a threat to cherished values.

In contrast, the Republican primary campaign and convention unified the party behind the candidacy of Richard Nixon, the frontrunner from first to last. He ran largely unopposed in the Republican primaries and won impressive vote totals. He accumulated a mass of delegates and attracted favorable notice for his calm, knowledgeable manner and grasp of local and national issues. The Republican convention, opening in Miami on August 5, gave Nixon an easy first-ballot victory with 692 votes to 277 for Rockefeller, 182 for Ronald Reagan, and 182 scattered elsewhere. The convention also ratified Nixon's rather unexpected choice of Governor Spiro T. Agnew of Maryland as his running mate. The GOP platform, like its Democratic counterpart, was designed to please all and offend none. The Vietnam plank favored peace, but "neither peace at any price nor camouflaged surrender." The party promised a "comprehensive program to restore the preeminence of U.S. military strength" and advocated "more selective use of our economic strength" and multilateral cooperation in foreign affairs. The platform called for federal "encouragement" of job opportunities, fair farm prices, education, health, social security, and control of violence. Metropolitan and rural blight were to be attacked by enlisting "new energies by the private sector and by government at all levels."

Meanwhile, Governor George Wallace of Alabama launched a third-party challenge under the loosely organized, newly formed American Independent party. He preached fear and practiced demagoguery. The bogeys from whom he stridently promised deliverance included blacks, radicals, spenders, planners, bureaucrats, peace demonstrators, hippies, integrationists, do-gooders, big government, high taxes—and "pointy-headed professors," whose fuzzy dogmas were responsible for the country's woes. Wallace favored free enterprise, state rights, property rights, local control over school policy, a greater effort for victory in Vietnam, and, above all, law and order, including the use of troops if necessary. Although no one believed that Wallace could win, experts were predicting that he would poll from 15 to 20 million votes and might well carry enough states to throw the election into the House of Representatives.

Nixon, however, remained a strong favorite until late in the campaign. He

ELECTION OF 1968

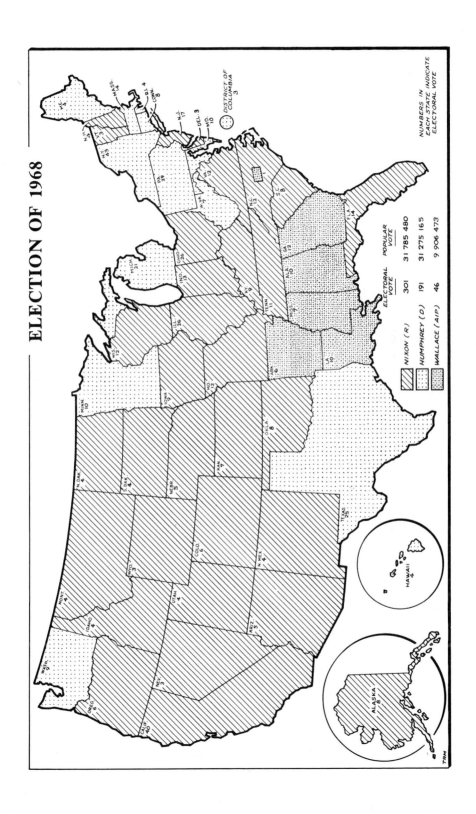

NUMBERS IN
EACH STATE INDICATE
ELECTORAL VOTE

DISTRICT OF
COLUMBIA
3

	ELECTORAL VOTE	POPULAR VOTE
NIXON (R)	301	31 785 480
HUMPHREY (D)	191	31 275 165
WALLACE (AIP)	46	9 906 473

TRM

promised an end to the Vietnam War through an undisclosed "secret plan" and also pledged to end the domestic disorders of rising crime, racial violence, and social disintegration. For most of the campaign, in contrast, the Democrats were paralyzed by internal squabbling, and Humphrey was badly handicapped by his close association with the unpopular Johnson and Johnson's unpopular war. Then, in October, Humphrey's candidacy began to gather momentum. Disaffected liberals drifted back into the ranks as they took clearer stock of the alternatives. Disgruntled union workers and suburbanites, whose frustrations had first inclined them toward Wallace, now began to remember old party loyalties. Humphrey's candidacy received last-minute boosts when McCarthy officially endorsed him on October 29 and when President Johnson, hoping to get the stalled peace talks moving and to help his party, proclaimed a total bombing halt on November 1. Polls showed Nixon's early lead dwindling steadily as election time neared, and on the eve of the election canvassing experts were terming it "too close to call."

A record number of 73 million voters went to the polls on November 5 and, in one of the closest elections in modern times, chose Richard Nixon as their next president. Nixon received 31.8 million popular votes (43.4 percent of the total) as against 31.3 million (42.7 percent) for Humphrey and 9.9 million (13.5 percent) for Wallace. Nixon carried thirty-two states with a total of 301 electoral votes, the smallest number by a winning candidate since Wilson's narrow triumph over Hughes in 1916. Humphrey won thirteen states and the District of Columbia, with a total of 191 electoral votes, while Wallace's 46 votes came from Alabama, Arkansas, Georgia, Louisiana, and Mississippi. The Democrats retained control of Congress by slightly reduced margins: 58 to 42 in the Senate (a net loss of 5 seats) and 243 to 192 in the House (a net loss of 4).

The election of 1968 brought into focus important changes in the pattern of national politics. It made clear the disarray of the Democratic party in national elections. If the New Deal coalition had somehow survived the Eisenhower years, Nixon's victory in 1968 definitely shattered what remained of it. The message delivered by the electorate was dissatisfaction with Democratic policies: impatience with the inability of the United States to win the Vietnamese war, uneasiness about rising crime and violence, and apprehension about the consequences of the civil rights revolution. Although the presidential vote was close, the results did show a large majority—about 57 percent of the electorate—voting against the Democratic candidate. In general, this was a pattern which did not change over the next four elections. With the exception of the election of 1976, Democratic presidential candidates attracted no more than Humphrey's share of the electorate—about 43 percent. Former Democratic bases such as the South, urban ethnic voters, and organized labor all experienced major defections in 1968. Only black voters overwhelmingly supported Humphrey. Only blacks continued to vote Democratic in presidential elections with any constancy.

Nixon could hardly claim a mandate on the basis of so narrow a margin, but Republicans had reason to be confident about the future. They had cut heavily into Democratic strength in all areas. Nixon's popular vote in the eleven former Confederate states exceeded both Wallace's and Humphrey's votes. Favorable response to Nixon's moderate but persistent emphasis upon "forgotten Americans," law and order, and retrenchment and reexamination of domestic welfare programs suggested that the bulk of Wallace's support could be attracted to the GOP in a normal two-party contest.

CHAPTER 28

Challenges to Pax Americana, 1961–1968

While the Kennedy-Johnson years were, at home, a period of vitality, experimentation, and ambitious confidence, they marked a peak of American military power and world economic influence abroad. In almost every area of competition with its global rival, the Soviet Union, the United States in the 1960s appeared to be winning the cold war. With an economy that dominated the western world and outpaced the Soviets and their satellites, with political stability in Europe and Japan, and with a clearly superior nuclear arsenal, American foreign-policy makers of the post-World War II generation could justifiably claim success. But this supremacy began to erode during the Kennedy-Johnson years. Although tensions with the Soviets were reduced significantly, neither Kennedy nor Johnson successfully confronted the tangled confusion of issues and priorities in the relationship between cold-war rivalry and the emergence of third-world nationalism.

1. KENNEDY, JOHNSON, AND THE COLD WAR

The inauguration of John F. Kennedy in January 1961 promised a new departure in American foreign policy. Criticizing what he called the inaction of the Eisenhower years, Kennedy pledged a vigorous reassertion of American power and influence. Rather than offering an end to the cold war, Kennedy warned Americans of a long-lasting struggle which would require sacrifice, risk, and energy. To wage this struggle, both Kennedy and Johnson used the same diplomatic and military tools employed by the Eisenhower administration. They continued to rely heavily on a preponderance of nuclear weaponry to counterbalance the

Soviet superiority of manpower and arms in Western Europe. In the developing nations, they continued to compete for influence and to attempt to contain revolutionary nationalism and wars of "national liberation." Frequently, both Kennedy and Johnson, like Eisenhower, used covert intelligence operations to sustain their public foreign-policy positions.

In other respects, the Kennedy-Johnson years brought a new aggressiveness to the waging of the cold war. Unhappy with the Soviet-American stalemate, both presidents continued to perceive local problems and conflicts in international, cold-war terms. Reversing Eisenhower's policy of reducing military budgets, Kennedy began, and Johnson continued, a sustained buildup in conventional and nuclear forces. Just as important, the Kennedy-Johnson foreign policy involved an aggressive posture of counterinsurgency in local conflicts and, in several minor and major instances, began a policy of employing American combat troops.

This new assertiveness partly reflected both Kennedy's and Johnson's public commitment to take the initiative in Soviet-American competition and their penchant for personal presidential control over foreign policy. In fairness, however, American aggressiveness abroad was also a response to real challenges from the Soviets. Although Khrushchev warmly welcomed Kennedy's inauguration, he also soon made it clear that he would test the mettle of the new and inexperienced president. Exuding confidence about the ultimate triumph of communism over capitalism as a world economic and political system, Khrushchev declared in January 1961 that there was "no longer any force in the world capable of barring the road to socialism." While he rejected nuclear war and embraced "peaceful coexistence" as a principle of Soviet policy, Khrushchev maintained that an intense, worldwide struggle with the United States would continue through diplomacy and support for revolutionary "wars of national liberation" in Asia, Africa, and Latin America.

Soviet assertiveness became clear in June 1961 during Kennedy's first meeting with Khrushchev in Vienna. It was not a summit meeting but a private encounter, permitting the two leaders to exchange views and take each other's measure. Hoping to overawe the younger man, Khrushchev adopted a truculent and at times bellicose posture on Berlin. Without setting a deadline, he renewed demands for an "immediate" peace treaty with Germany and the concomitant end to the four-power occupation of Berlin. Khrushchev made it plain that he would sign such a treaty with East Germany (whether the Western allies participated or not) and thus force them to negotiate their rights in Berlin directly with a government they refused to recognize. Months of tension over Berlin followed. The NATO allies flatly rejected any solution that did not guarantee Western presence, Western access, and unhampered freedom for the citizens of West Berlin. "We do not want to fight, but we have fought before," Kennedy declared in late July 1961. "We cannot and will not permit the Communists to drive us out of Berlin, either gradually or by force."

The situation grew steadily more ominous when East Germany, determined to end the flood of refugees to the West, closed the boundary between the eastern and western sectors in August while Soviet troops surrounded the city. The Soviets ignored the protests of the Western allies, and East German authorities physically sealed off the entire Berlin border by a wall of concrete blocks and barbed wire—the Berlin Wall—running across the city. To reassure anxious West Berliners, Kennedy provided three symbols to show that America stood by them. He sent Vice-President Johnson on a visit to the city to renew American pledges of support. He appointed General Lucius D. Clay, symbol of Western firmness during the Berlin blockade of 1948–1949, as his personal representative there. And, in a dramatic move, Kennedy reinforced the American garrison by dispatching a battle group of fifteen hundred troops down the hundred-mile Autobahn from West Germany to Berlin. Diplomatic exchanges failed to break the impasse, but tensions eased when Premier Khrushchev announced in October that he would no longer insist upon a settlement before the end of the year. Soviet harassment of air corridors was halted in March 1962. Then, in May, General Clay, expressing the belief that Berlin was no longer in immediate peril, returned to the United States.

Although the crisis over Berlin ended without definite resolution, it had clear consequences. In the spring and summer of 1961, Kennedy announced a military buildup through increases in the defense budget, increases that went well beyond the spending levels of the Eisenhower administration. In order to prepare the country for possible military responses to the Soviet challenge, Kennedy also called up reserve and National Guard units, expanded the civil defense program, and initiated new weapons systems and the modernization of existing military equipment. Signaling the administration's commitment to an invigorated military, Kennedy also made clear that the United States would respond forthrightly to any future challenges.

2.   REVOLUTIONARY NATIONALISM
IN LATIN AMERICA

One such challenge to Pax Americana was in clear evidence well before the Berlin crisis: the emergence of revolutionary nationalism in the Western Hemisphere—a product of purely local political and economic conditions and Soviet-American cold-war competition. As we have seen, President Eisenhower severed diplomatic relations with Cuba in January 1961. Kennedy, who had criticized Nixon during the campaign of 1960 for inaction and weakness on Cuba, promised a tough policy. Already personally antagonistic toward Castro, Kennedy raised no objection to the plans (about which he was briefed during the presidential campaign) begun during the Eisenhower administration for a CIA-directed covert operation against Castro.

Earlier, in 1959, the Eisenhower administration had supported a small group of anti-Castro guerrillas operating inside Cuba. But, a year later, when Castro began to communize the Cuban economy and a stream of refugees fled to southern Florida, the administration decided instead to support an invasion by an anti-Castro exile army, based in a secret camp in Guatemala. The CIA was convinced that a well-timed assault by these refugees would set off a massive general uprising of disaffected Cubans and topple Castro. Blueprints for such an invasion, prepared before Eisenhower left office, awaited only Kennedy's approval before being put into action. Kennedy, despite some misgivings, in April ordered the assault to take place—against the advice of several White House staff members and Senator J. William Fulbright, chairman of the Foreign Relations Committee.

The operation was doomed from the start. As sponsor of the Cuban exile army, the CIA helped to elevate less competent, but pro-American, former supporters of Batista rather than anti-Batista exiles. Because of its identification with the unpopular former dictator, the uprising probably had little chance of attracting mass support. Internal divisions also seriously weakened morale. Perhaps even more important, in order to win Kennedy's agreement, the CIA had to insure that the operation took place without any American military involvement.

Kennedy thus became responsible for one of the most ill-conceived, dismally planned, carelessly managed, and ineptly executed episodes in American history. Cuban airfields were attacked on the morning of April 15, 1961, by B-26 fighter bombers, which the United States claimed were flown by defecting Cuban air force pilots, but which were later revealed to have taken off from a refugee base in Central America. The actual landing took place before dawn on April 17 in the Bahía de Cochinos—the Bay of Pigs—on the southern coast of Cuba. An estimated fifteen hundred Cuban refugees took part in the landing. In the absence of air or naval artillery cover, the invaders were pinned down and overwhelmed within three days by Castro's forces. Contact with the underground was not made, and the anticipated anti-Castro uprising did not occur.

At home, Congress, the press, and the American people rallied to Kennedy's support. Public opinion polls taken just after the Bay of Pigs disaster showed approval of the president at 83 percent, while only 5 percent disapproved. Yet the fiasco had disastrous repercussions. The United States suffered widespread international condemnation and loss of prestige in Latin America. Khrushchev combined threats of possible Soviet intervention in defense of Cuba with pious lectures to Kennedy on good conduct and the importance of observing international law. Other Latin American governments, disturbed by the reemergence of interventionism, refused to cooperate with Washington's attempts to generate inter-American action against Cuba. Castro, strengthened rather than weakened by the episode, proceeded to make Cuba an even greater storm center in hemispheric affairs. He reaffirmed his ties with Russia, claimed that only Soviet offers of armed assistance had deterred further American assaults, formally proclaimed Cuba a socialist country, and quickened the pace of socialization.

The Bay of Pigs brought at least two other policy consequences. First, the administration was now committed not only to an anti-Castro posture but also to pursuing other measures to overthrow him. If anything, the administration increased pressure by beginning another CIA program, Operation Mongoose, which involved intelligence gathering and a secret war against Castro's regime. Led by a White House special group headed by Attorney General Robert Kennedy, Mongoose eventually had a budget of $50 million a year, employed four hundred American and two thousand Cuban agents, and operated a small, independent navy and air force. Among the more bizarre plans proposed by Mongoose was chemical warfare against Cuban farm workers, which would disable them for several days and thus paralyze the sugar harvest. Without the direct support or official knowledge of Mongoose—but nonetheless under the sponsorship of the CIA—at least eight attempts were made to assassinate Fidel Castro by the end of 1965.

A second policy consequence of the Bay of Pigs disaster was an ambitious program, the Alianza para el Progreso, or Alliance for Progress, designed to forestall the further development of revolutionary nationalism in Latin America by stimulating rapid economic growth. Based upon the assumption that a Cuban-styled revolution was only possible because of underlying economic causes, the Alliance for Progress would be for Latin America what the Marshall Plan had been for post-World War II Western Europe. In a striking departure from Eisenhower's Latin American policy and from the emphases in both the Bay of Pigs invasion and Operation Mongoose, the Alliance for Progress sought modernization as a tool to encourage internal political reform and a democratic center-left alternative to both revolutionary nationalism and right-wing dictatorship.

Kennedy formally proposed the Alliance in March 1961. Describing it as a "vast cooperative effort, unparalleled in magnitude and nobility of purpose," Kennedy offered massive American aid for improved housing, land reform, health, and education. The international crisis over the Bay of Pigs then gave the Alliance added momentum. It was formally organized in August 1961 at a conference in Punta del Este, Uruguay. The twenty Latin American nations participating in the program agreed, in principle at least, to democratic political reforms, to housing improvements and a plan of "comprehensive" agrarian land redistribution, to the end of illiteracy and ill health, and to the reformation of tax laws and fiscal policies which favored the rich. Each participating country was also required to formulate a national program of economic development and modernization. In return, the United States, in the Charter of Punta del Este, promised to provide at least $20 billion in development aid over the next decade. This aid would, theoretically, increase Latin American economic growth to an annual rate of 2.5 percent.

The Alliance for Progress resulted in an outpouring of Latin American affection for Kennedy which was comparable to the pro-American sentiment during Franklin Roosevelt's administration and the Good Neighbor policy. Over the next decade, however, the program's results were mixed. Two years after Kennedy's assassination, the Alliance was in deep trouble. In Latin America in 1963, for example, per capita GNP decreased by 0.4 percent; during the next five years, it increased by only 1.8 percent. The countries with the greatest natural resources and industrial and agricultural potential—Brazil and Argentina—recorded disappointing, even dismal, economic performances during the 1960s. Although official American lending under the Alliance for Progress increased from $981 million in 1963 to $1.7 billion in 1968, the expected surge of outside private investment—upon which the success of the program depended—never materialized. One reason that it did not was the continuing problem of political instability, and it was in this respect that the Alliance most clearly failed. The Alliance did not usher in a democratic constitutionalist alternative to revolutionary nationalism. On the contrary, it coincided with the overthrow of elected democratic governments in Brazil and Argentina in 1964 and in Peru four years later.

In the balance between economic and military tools of foreign policy, Kennedy and Johnson both came to rely more on the latter than on the former. Both presidents became committed to an aggressive anti-Cuban hemispheric policy designed to isolate Cuba and to prevent the contagion of revolutionary nationalism from spreading. Especially under the Johnson administration, increased American military aid, training for Latin American military personnel and police in counterinsurgency and crowd control, and hemispheric foreign policy itself all became instruments in the effort to contain the spread of Cuban influence.

A test of the willingness to use force to prevent the expansion of Cuban-Soviet influence—and to violate Good Neighbor pledges of nonintervention—occurred in the Dominican Republic, where the Kennedy administration, seeking to make the country a showpiece of the Alliance for Progress, supplied economic aid and encouraged the election of the liberal-left politician Juan Bosch in December 1962. When Bosch was unable to alleviate chronic social and economic problems, the Dominican military ousted him in September 1963, and Kennedy responded by withholding recognition from the new regime and by suspending economic aid. President Johnson restored diplomatic relations in December but maintained an attitude of cautious reserve as sabotage, strikes, and underground resistance led to armed rebellion by the army in April 1965. With little confidence in the army's promise to hold free elections, Bosch's supporters demanded that he resume the presidency. Violence broke out in the city of Santo Domingo when the army refused to meet these demands; the army attacked the city, while the defiant rebels elected a provisional president.

Johnson feared that pro-Castro groups had infiltrated the rebel forces and ordered an invasion by American marines on April 28, 1965. Over twenty thousand American troops soon followed. The United States tried to generate support for the intervention by requesting the creation of an Inter-American Peace Force, which the OAS, with some reluctance, approved on May 6. Units from Paraguay, Nicaragua, Honduras, and Brazil later joined American forces in the Dominican Republic. In September, the American occupiers installed a provisional president, Héctor García-Godoy, who laid the basis for free elections. Held in June 1966, the elections resulted in a surprising victory by Joaquin Balaguer, a moderate, over the favored Juan Bosch, who had returned from exile. A measure of peace and stability returned to the Dominican Republic, and Johnson withdrew American troops in September.

Although forestalling further turbulence in the Dominican Republic, American intervention involved the first overt use of military force by the United States in Latin America since the inauguration of the Good Neighbor policy. The extent of Cuban involvement in the Dominican crisis remains unknown. What is clear is that policy makers in the Kennedy and Johnson administrations took Castro's rhetoric about hemispheric revolution seriously and were determined to prevent leftist upheaval by any and all measures—including, as a last resort, military force.

3. THE CUBAN MISSILE CRISIS

American attempts to contain Latin American revolutionary nationalism, in combination with heightened aggressiveness and adventurism by both the Soviets and the United States during the early Kennedy administration, brought an end to the stasis in superpower relations under the Eisenhower administration. Soviet-American tensions over Berlin and Cuba culminated in late 1962 in the Cuban missile crisis, the first genuine approach to worldwide nuclear holocaust. The roots of the confrontation lay in the militarization of Cuba during 1961 and 1962, following the failure of the Bay of Pigs invasion. By early 1962, Cuba had become a Soviet satellite and military base. When large numbers of Soviet technicians and arms began to arrive in Cuba during the summer of 1962, Kennedy received explicit assurances from Soviet Foreign Minister Andrei Gromyko in a White House meeting on October 18 that such arms were exclusively defensive in character. But four days earlier, Kennedy had learned from aerial reconnaissance that medium-range ballistic missiles were already present in Cuba and that the construction of launching pads was nearing completion.

The reasons why the Soviets pursued this high-risk policy are, to this day, obscure. Since medium-range American Jupiter missiles were then stationed in Turkey, Khrushchev might have been attempting to force their removal. Soviet missiles in Cuba probably did not pose any significant new danger to American security, since the United States was already well within range of either Soviet

ICBMs or submarine-launched missiles. As he maintained during the crisis and in his memoirs, Khrushchev was under considerable pressure to demonstrate Soviet reliability to what had become a major client state. Placing nuclear weapons there would provide security for Cuba against any future American invasion and demonstrate a symbolic international credibility. Nonetheless, Khrushchev's decision carried considerable risk—of nuclear holocaust, but also, given the logistical problems of defending Cuba, of international humiliation.

For Kennedy, the presence of Soviet missiles in Cuba clearly required some sort of strong response. Having already lost face at the Bay of Pigs and under pressure from the Republican opposition, Kennedy and his party were facing off-year congressional elections in only a few weeks. Kennedy's main advisers disagreed about the best policy. Some of them, such as General Maxwell Taylor and former Secretary of State Dean Acheson, recommended an air strike or invasion. Others, such as Robert Kennedy and Secretary McNamara, counseled deferring an invasion and favored a blockade to prevent the introduction of Soviet warheads. By October 22, in a nationally televised address, Kennedy announced his decision. "Unmistakable evidence" existed that Soviet missiles were "now in preparation" on Cuban soil. Announcing establishment of a "strict quarantine of all offensive military equipment under shipment to Cuba," Kennedy asserted that the United States would demand "prompt dismantling and withdrawal" of all offensive bases at an emergency meeting of the Security Council and would maintain the quarantine—actually a selective blockade—until the bases had been removed.

It was the most direct and ominous confrontation in the history of Soviet-American relations, and the world hovered on the brink of war. The Soviets, caught off balance, replied hesitantly and with restraint. The American people, the Western allies, and the OAS rallied overwhelmingly behind President Kennedy, and Russia backed away from the challenge. American planes reported on October 24 that Soviet vessels carrying jet aircraft and other "contraband" had altered course away from Cuba. Two Cuba-bound Soviet ships bearing no offensive equipment submitted to American inspection and were permitted to proceed. Khrushchev first offered to remove Russian bases in Cuba in exchange for America's evacuation of its obsolete bases in Turkey. When Kennedy refused, the Soviet premier agreed to the substance of the president's demands on October 28. The USSR would remove all offensive weapons and submit to international inspection if the United States would pledge not to invade Cuba. Kennedy agreed to these terms and suspended the blockade. Dismantling and removal of the bases took place promptly.

While Kennedy enjoyed considerable domestic political and international credit for his resoluteness under pressure, Khrushchev and the Soviets suffered a serious blow to their prestige. Within two years, in October 1964, the Politburo deposed the Soviet premier, replacing him with the joint leadership of Leonid I. Brezhnev and Aleksei N. Kosygin. The aftermath of the Cuban missile crisis also moved both superpowers toward arms control negotiations and an easing of cold-war tensions. Of particular importance was a breakthrough in test ban negotiations. During the Berlin crisis in 1961, the Soviets announced resumption of atmospheric nuclear testing, and the Americans responded by promising the same. By early 1963, however, the Soviets, in private talks, indicated greater willingness to negotiate.

Taking the initiative in a speech at American University in June 1963, Kennedy called for a reexamination of American attitudes toward the Soviet Union and the cold war. He emphasized that negotiation of a test ban treaty was the first step along the road to peace and dispatched Undersecretary of State Averell Harriman, one of the nation's ablest and most experienced negotiators, to Moscow in July. Harriman found the Russians both willing and eager to conclude a treaty. The question of underground testing, which would require on-site inspections, was put aside in favor of an agreement banning atmospheric explosions. The treaty, initialed on July 25, provided that there should be no atmospheric or underwater testing and banned other tests that would spread radioactive debris outside the territorial limits of the testing state. Both nations pledged to refrain from "causing, encouraging, or in any way participating in" tests anywhere else. Either party could withdraw from the agreement upon three months' notice if its supreme interests were in jeopardy. Eventually, more than one hundred nations signed the treaty, but the two powers close to a nuclear capacity—France and China—refused.

The test ban treaty was favorably received in the United States, notwithstanding claims that the agreement endangered American security. The Senate approved it by a vote of eighty to nineteen in September 1963. Other signs of lessening tensions followed. President Kennedy proposed a joint Soviet-American expedition to the moon and authorized the sale, through private channels, of American wheat to the Soviet Union. Progress was not disrupted by Nikita Khrushchev's fall from power in October 1964. His successors—Kosygin, who became premier, and Brezhnev, who replaced Khrushchev as party chairman— were sober, cautious leaders who sought an end to Khrushchev's adventurism and a new stability in Soviet-American relations. A noticeable thaw set in between the superpowers, including cultural exchange agreements, a treaty establishing consulates in both countries, and the inauguration of direct air service between New York and Moscow.

In 1967, both nations agreed to a treaty banning the use or deployment of nuclear weapons in outer space. A five-year attempt to reach accord in the matter of preventing the spread of nuclear weapons culminated in a nonproliferation treaty, initialed by the United States, the USSR, Great Britain, and fifty-eight nonnuclear countries in July 1968. Even the invasion and occupation of Czechoslovakia by Russian troops a month later, which ruthlessly crushed a liberalization policy pursued by Czech party leader Alexander Dubĉek, did not seriously impair Soviet-American relations. Sympathy for Czechoslovakia and condemnation of the Russian move were voiced in all quarters—not only in the United States and other Western nations but in most Communist countries and even among Russian intellectuals. And yet the United States Senate, after delaying consideration of the nuclear nonproliferation treaty for a number of months, voted to approve its ratification in March 1969. Before President Johnson left office the two countries had also agreed to hold talks on the crucial subject of limiting the arms race.

Meanwhile, the so-called Communist monolith, however real it might have been, was clearly and irrevocably shattered. Suspicion and antagonism between the Soviet Union and China expanded into outright hostility during the late 1960s. Sino-Soviet relations deteriorated to the point not only of shrill recriminations but also of troop buildups and border clashes. Meanwhile, their fierce rivalry for leadership of world communism divided or confused Communist party organizations everywhere. Smaller Communist countries deviated or dissented from the overlordship of either Russia or China with increasing frequency and boldness. All of these developments encouraged a belief in the United States and elsewhere that the era of the cold war was essentially over.

4.   KENNEDY AND THE INDOCHINESE WAR

One of the most important decisions in American history—the decision to involve the United States in the Indochinese war—took shape during the Kennedy and Johnson administrations. American intervention had begun under Truman but was substantially expanded—through military aid to the fledging nation of South Vietnam and through involvement in Vietnamese politics—during the Eisenhower administration. For a variety of reasons, the most important of them being the deterioration of the South Vietnamese ability and willingness to wage a civil war against a growing Communist insurgency, Kennedy began, and Johnson increased, a commitment to employ American military forces in Indochina.

In early 1961, Kennedy was confronted with a crisis, not in Vietnam but in Laos, where three rival governments—pro-Communist, anti-Communist, and neutralist—contended for primacy. When it became apparent that only large-scale American intervention could save the right-wing government, Kennedy instead affirmed the goal of a "neutral and independent Laos" and pressed for a diplomatic solution. The Soviets agreed in April 1961 to discuss the problem at an international conference and to join other powers in requesting a cease-fire. All three Laotian factions and representatives of thirteen nations assembled in Geneva in May and, over the next fourteen months, hammered out an international agreement to safeguard Laotian neutrality and independence. In July 1962, the conference approved two neutrality pacts. They pledged respect for Laotian neutrality, territorial integrity, and independence and specified procedures for the withdrawal of foreign troops and the future guarantee of Laotian neutrality.

Meanwhile, the situation in South Vietnam had deteriorated steadily. Despite massive American aid—about $300 million a year after 1954—the pro-Western government of Ngo Dinh Diem faced crippling problems. Diem had been encouraged by Secretary Dulles to form an anti-Communist regime in South Vietnam. He refused to hold nationwide elections in 1956 (as specified by the Geneva armistice of 1954) and consolidated his position by ruthlessly suppressing any opposition, Communist and non-Communist alike. Apparently against the wishes of Ho Chi Minh and the North Vietnamese Communists, opponents of Diem—eventually known as the Vietcong—formed the National Liberation Front (NLF) in March 1960, and they began a widespread guerrilla war in the South. By the end of 1960, there were perhaps fifteen thousand Vietcong, and Ho had made a clear decision to support the southern rebellion. In the countryside and the cities, opposition to Diem's repression and to the concentration of power in his family further eroded the stability of the fragile South Vietnamese state.

The Kennedy administration harbored few illusions about Diem, but it faced a shrinking set of options. Some advisers, such as Vice-President Johnson, who visited Vietnam in May 1961, recommended an expanded American military commitment; others, like Undersecretary of State Chester Bowles, favored neutralizing all of Indochina. After General Maxwell Taylor and National Security Adviser Walter Rostow visited Vietnam in October 1961, they recommended active American intervention in the burgeoning civil war. Kennedy, determined not to retreat from an American security commitment, ordered an infusion of American arms in December 1961.

By early 1962, over four thousand American military personnel were on the scene, instructing and at times assisting South Vietnamese troops in more efficient supply and combat operations. American military forces in Vietnam gradually swelled to over sixteen thousand during the next eighteen months, and sixty American soldiers were killed in action in 1963. American troops and arms spearheaded a new, aggressive counterinsurgency plan—the strategic-hamlet program, begun in April 1962. Designed by Taylor and modeled on the successful British war against Malayan guerrillas, the program provided for the relocation of peasants into fortified pro-Diem villages. Each of the hamlets would become a secure center of an intense educational, medical, and economic program to win popular support. By mid-1963, some 7 million South Vietnamese were relocated in seven thousand hamlets.

Although his regime was temporarily bolstered by the American military intervention, Diem's main problem—his inability to build or to sustain a viable nation-state—remained unsolved. His fundamental political weakness, the tenuousness of his regime, and the extent of domestic opposition were revealed in

a series of Buddhist protests against Diem beginning in June 1963. The protests—which included self-immolation by Buddhist monks—soon exploded into
an anti-Western, anti-American protest. Diem, who had never responded to
American pleas that he initiate needed reforms and broaden the base of his
government, declared martial law and attacked the Buddhist pagodas. Washington finally gave up on him and virtually conceded the bankruptcy of its previous
policy. In November, a military coup, tolerated if not inspired by the Kennedy
administration, finally overthrew the regime and resulted in the assassination of
Diem.

5. JOHNSON AND THE DECISION TO ESCALATE

Diem's overthrow and murder solved none of South Vietnam's problems while
it aggravated a growing political chaos and disintegration. Politically and militar-
ily, the South Vietnamese government verged on collapse by the summer of
1964. The South Vietnamese Army—the Army of the Republic of Vietnam
(ARVN)—suffered steady losses against Vietcong guerrillas and the stream of
North Vietnamese troops infiltrating the South. Weakened by corruption and
low morale, the ARVN was virtually incapable of waging war in 1964. An equal
degree of disintegration affected the political structure. Within sixteen months
of Diem's murder, no fewer than nine new South Vietnamese governments came
and went.

By mid-1964, Johnson was faced with a major decision. Cutting his losses,
withdrawing from Vietnam, and allowing a Communist victory was unthinkable
for Johnson, a man of great personal pride who was acutely aware of the
domestic consequences of another "loss" to the Communists. The choice was
rather whether to hope for political stabilization and a revitalization of the
ARVN's capacity to fight or to escalate the American military role in the war.
During 1964, Johnson gradually chose the latter alternative by undertaking a
variety of measures short of total military involvement. General Taylor replaced
Henry Cabot Lodge as ambassador to South Vietnam in June 1964, while
General William C. Westmoreland took command of the American military
mission in Saigon. Expanding its role in the war, the American government
strengthened its forces in southeast Asia and launched a program of covert
military operations against North Vietnam: U-2 observation flights, South Vietnamese commando raids and American naval intelligence operations along the
North Vietnamese coastline, and selective bombing by American aircraft over
Laos. Contingency plans for full-scale American bombing of North Vietnam
were also prepared, and administration officials spoke in early 1964 of seeking
a congressional endorsement for American military involvement in Indochina.

Johnson and his advisers meanwhile had concluded that growing North
Vietnamese military intervention was the main reason behind the deteriorating

situation in South Vietnam. To Johnson, the solution was also military: a steadily increasing combination of threats and military actions that increased the cost of the war to the North. In turn, escalating the war would mean large-scale participation of American combat troops and heavy retaliatory bombing by American aircraft. Such a dramatic expansion of the war required, however, some sort of congressional approval. In August 1964, American destroyers conducting intelligence operations in the Gulf of Tonkin were allegedly attacked by North Vietnamese patrol boats—apparently on the assumption that the American craft had taken part in recent commando raids. Planes from the carrier *Ticonderoga* promptly took off on a retaliatory strike that destroyed some two dozen North Vietnamese patrol boats and various support facilities. A deployment of American planes and bases looking toward the projected full-scale bombing campaign was ordered.

Anxious to obtain congressional approval both of what it had done and of what it might feel compelled to do, the administration backed a joint resolution pledging full support for American action in Vietnam "to promote the maintenance of international peace and security in Southeast Asia." The House approved this, the Gulf of Tonkin Resolution, by a vote of 416 to 0 on August 7. In the Senate, when Wayne Morse of Oregon spoke in opposition, J. William Fulbright of Arkansas, chairman of the Foreign Relations Committee and later an outspoken critic of administration policy, responded by claiming that North Vietnam was guilty of aggression. The United States, Fulbright added, had no choice but to fight back and make it clear to the Communists "that their aggressive and expansionist ambitions, wherever advanced, will meet precisely that degree of American opposition which is necessary to frustrate them." The Senate speedily approved the resolution by a vote of eighty-eight to two.

Although now given broad authority to intensify American participation, Johnson resisted pressures to begin bombing the North during the autumn of 1964. Within a month of a Vietcong attack on an American base near Saigon in November 1964, however, he approved a plan for retaliatory air strikes followed by graduated air warfare against North Vietnam. As part of the plan, Johnson's advisers also recommended introducing ground combat forces. A sustained bombing offensive against the North, known as Operation Rolling Thunder, began in February 1965, after Vietcong attacks on American installations and billets at Pleiku and Quinhon in which some thirty Americans lost their lives. A contingent of 3,500 marines went ashore to protect the huge Da Nang air base in March, bringing the total of United States forces to 27,000. Johnson took a more decisive step in April when he ordered these marines to take part in offensive combat. Troop buildups began in earnest, and American forces in Vietnam reached 74,000 by June and 190,000 by the end of 1965.

American ground troops soon took the offensive against an elusive foe in a series of "sweep," or "search and destroy," operations. For the time being, at least, the infusion of men and arms averted the collapse of South Vietnam. Yet, despite enormous military superiority and an aggressive pacification program in rural Vietnam, the Americanization of the war did not bring defeat for the NLF and North Vietnamese.

In April 1966, when American troop strength approached 250,000, B-52 bombers began large-scale raids on North Vietnam, extending their strikes to include oil installations in the Hanoi-Haiphong area in June. A steady stream of reinforcements brought American strength in South Vietnam to nearly 400,000 by the end of 1966 and to 500,000 a year later. Costs and casualties mounted in their turn, yet a kind of deadlock, rather than victory, appeared to be all that this massive effort was able to achieve.

The deadlock, in turn, took on an air of permanence. The American effort undoubtedly prevented a total Communist triumph in Vietnam, but neither incessant bombing attacks nor heavy casualties among its ground forces appeared to diminish Hanoi's capacity or will to continue the struggle. The South Vietnamese government achieved a measure of stability after June 1965 under a military regime headed by Air Vice-Marshal Nguyen Cao Ky as premier and Nguyen Van Thieu as chief of state. This government later acquired a certain legitimacy when relatively peaceful elections in September 1967 led to the choice of Thieu as president and Ky as vice-president. Nonetheless, Saigon had not solved most of its major problems—opposition from Buddhists and others, harsh repression, low morale, and corruption and favoritism. Unable to reform itself, the South Vietnamese government made little progress in winning support among the peasantry.

In late 1967, several attempts had been made by the United States and by third-party nations to negotiate a limitation to the war or end it altogether. Johnson made several offers to halt, partially or completely, the bombing of North Vietnam, to engage in direct negotiations, and to use American aid to reconstruct the Vietnamese economy. But both the North Vietnamese and the United States had rigid and incompatible war aims and negotiating positions: the North Vietnamese wanted the formation of a government dominated by the NLF and the eventual reunification of Vietnam; the United States insisted on the establishment of a secure, independent, non-Communist South Vietnam.

The failure of diplomacy was the result of the conviction of both sides that they could win on the battlefield. Johnson, buttressed by reports from his generals that more troops and increased bombing would eventually end the Communists' ability to fight, sought a middle course. He rejected the demands of so-called hawks that he further escalate the bombing, mine Haiphong harbor, use atomic weapons, or otherwise generally increase military pressure on North Vietnam and the Vietcong. He also resisted pressure from the growing ranks of "doves," who variously advocated an end to the bombing, an unconditional cease-fire and immediate negotiations, or a unilateral withdrawal of American forces.

A decisive break in the psychological, if not the military, deadlock occurred

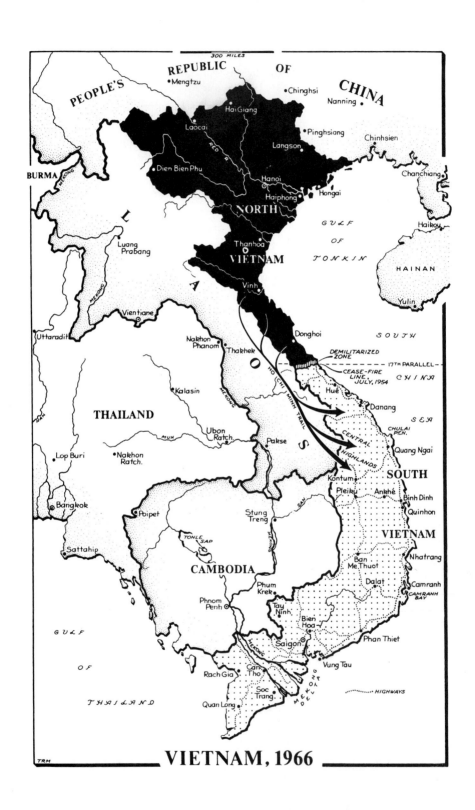

VIETNAM, 1966

in early 1968 when the Communists launched their so-called Tet (lunar New Year) offensive. Catching both American and South Vietnamese authorities completely off guard, North Vietnamese and Vietcong units attacked all of the major South Vietnamese towns and cities, including Saigon. Some of the bitterest fighting of the war took place before the onslaught was contained. The Tet offensive inflicted great material damage, hurt the rural pacification program by forcing Saigon to divert funds and manpower to the shattered cities, shook the Saigon government, and proved that Communist forces could strike almost at will in the very heart of southern urban centers. Yet from the military and political point of view, the offensive fell short of its major objectives. Communist efforts to topple the Saigon government, retain control of the areas under attack, improve their strategic position, or touch off an uprising of disaffected southerners all ended in failure. The Communists, particularly the NLF, suffered heavy casualties, which weakened the impact of follow-up offensives in May and August.

Nevertheless, Tet was an unquestioned psychological victory for the North Vietnamese. Its greatest impact and most decisive influence was upon the American people. They had been led to believe by the news media that the Tet offensive had been a great victory for the Vietcong. Now they saw no end to the war. The ferocity of the Tet offensive belied recent optimistic reports of General Westmoreland, who had proclaimed as recently as November 1967 that he had "never been more encouraged in my four years in Vietnam." No part of South Vietnam was secure; Saigon could not defend itself adequately; search-and-destroy campaigns had not weakened the enemy's capacity to strike hard blows. By mid-1968 there were some 530,000 American military personnel on the scene. The conflict had become the longest war in American history and one of the bloodiest: over 35,000 Americans had died in combat, another 75,000 had been injured, and hundreds more were confined in North Vietnamese prison camps. The financial cost approached $100 billion. The cost to the people of Vietnam—in deaths, injuries, suffering, dislocation, devastation of homes, villages, towns, and the very land itself—had been incalculable.

The conviction that victory in southeast Asia was neither worth such a cost nor even attainable gained wide currency in the United States. Antiwar sentiment, which had been gathering force for three years, spread on college campuses and among intellectuals. It grew much stronger in Congress, where Senators Fulbright (long since regretful of his support for the Tonkin Resolution), Mike Mansfield of Montana, Eugene McCarthy of Minnesota, and George McGovern of South Dakota had been outspoken critics for some time. Antiwar demonstrations became more vociferous and angry and attracted more support from the general public. Disillusionment, bitterness, and distrust of the credibility and motives of the United States government reached ominous proportions. No more divisive or agonizing issue had ever confronted the American people, and the Johnson administration moved into its final months with the nation's collective morale at an all-time low.

6.   THE SIX-DAY WAR

In another crucial region, the postwar order also experienced a new era of instability. Since the 1950s, the same social, economic, and political factors in the Middle East that had undermined Anglo-French colonialism—poverty, overpopulation, and Arab nationalism—also helped to erode American power.

Poverty, political instability, and unrest plagued most of the Arab states. Egyptian President Nasser's aggressive efforts to foster pan-Arab unity under his leadership by harnessing and abetting the forces of revolutionary nationalism merely added to the antagonisms that underlay Middle Eastern politics. His ambitions, fanned by Soviet technological, economic, and military aid, were resisted by conservative rulers such as King Faisal of Saudi Arabia and pro-Western leaders like Tunisia's Habib Bourguiba. Soviet interest and influence in the region waxed steadily. Further complications stemmed from the tangled network of economic and political interests bound up with oil, pipelines, and strategic trade routes.

The underlying problem of the Middle East, however, remained Arab hostility to the state of Israel. Since Israel's creation in 1948, no Arab nation had recognized or maintained diplomatic relations with Israel, and, in effect, a state of war existed. A UN Emergency Force, created after the war of 1956 as a peacekeeping body, patrolled the Israeli-Egyptian border, but the danger of another war remained constant. A potential for violence persisted in the periodic shelling and raids into Israeli territory by Palestinian guerrillas and terrorists, launched from neighboring Arab states with or without the knowledge of the governments involved. Such episodes invariably provoked drastic reprisals from Israel and kept the region in turmoil.

Arab-Israeli tensions grew steadily in the spring of 1967, when Palestinian raids from Syria's Golan Heights, just across the Israeli border near the Sea of Galilee, touched off a retaliatory air attack on April 7 that destroyed several Syrian planes and penetrated within sight of Damascus. Renewed raids against Israel prompted a severe warning from Tel Aviv in early May. Syria, claiming an Israeli military buildup along its borders, invoked the defense pact it had concluded in November 1966 with Egypt, and both Arab countries began to mobilize. Nasser now moved recklessly to the fore. During the week of May 1 he requested the UN to withdraw its forces from the Israeli-Egyptian border, sent his own troops into the buffer region thus vacated (including strategic Sharm El Sheikh, commanding entry to the Gulf of Aqaba), and proclaimed a blockade of Israel's Red Sea port of Elath.

Israel could only regard all this as a blow at its vital interests—virtually an

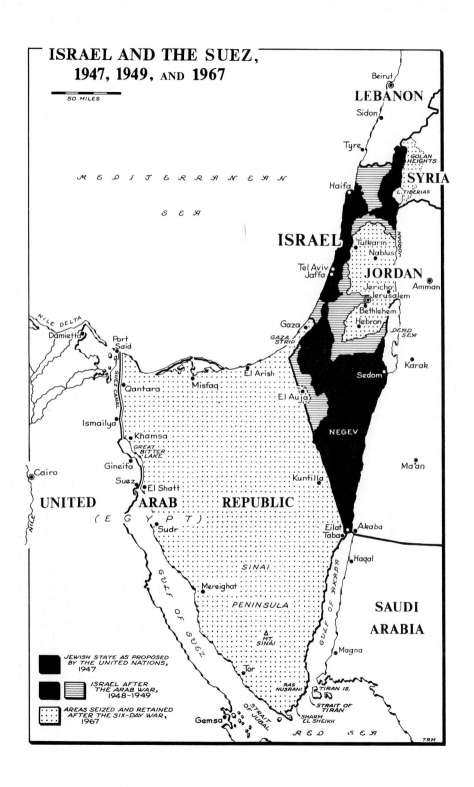

ISRAEL AND THE SUEZ,
1947, 1949, AND 1967

50 MILES

Beirut
LEBANON
Sidon

MEDITERRANEAN

Tyre

GOLAN
HEIGHTS
SYRIA

L. TIBERIAS

Haifa

SEA

ISRAEL
Tulkarm
Nablus

JORDAN

Tel Aviv
Jaffa

Jericho
Jerusalem
Bethlehem
Hebron

Amman

DEAD
SEA

Gaza
GAZA
STRIP

Karak

Sedom

NILE DELTA

Damietta
Port
Said

El Arish

Qantara
Misfaq

El Auja

NEGEV

Ismailya

Ma'an

Khamsa

GREAT
BITTER
LAKE

Cairo

Gineifa

Kuntilla

Suez
El Shatt

UNITED   ARAB   REPUBLIC

(E G Y P T)

Eilat
Taba

Akaba

Sudr

Haqal

SINAI

SAUDI

Mereighat

PENINSULA

ARABIA

MT.
SINAI

Magna

Tor

RAS
NUSRANI

TIRAN IS.

STRAIT
OF TIRAN

SHARM
EL SHEIKH

Gemsa

RED   SEA

TRM

JEWISH STATE AS PROPOSED
BY THE UNITED NATIONS,
1947

ISRAEL AFTER
THE ARAB WAR,
1948-1949

AREAS SEIZED AND RETAINED
AFTER THE SIX-DAY WAR,
1967

act of war. When two weeks of futile international diplomacy failed to persuade Egypt to lift its blockade, Israel prepared to settle the issue. Nasser, whose posture became more bellicose each day, concluded an agreement with King Hussein of Jordan on May 30 that placed Jordanian armed forces under "united" Arab command. This action further convinced the Tel Aviv government that an all-out Arab attack was imminent.

Accordingly, Israel launched a sudden offensive on the morning of June 5. Flying low to avoid radar detection, Israeli aircraft attacked enemy air bases and destroyed Egypt's air force. Armored columns, enjoying complete air protection, fanned out swiftly across the Sinai peninsula, routed the Egyptian Army, and captured or destroyed hundreds of Egypt's Soviet-made tanks and other armored vehicles. When Jordan loyally entered the war on Egypt's side, Israel struck similarly devastating blows at this enemy. Other units kept Syria at bay.

By the time that both sides agreed to a UN cease-fire on June 10—six days after the offensive began—Israel had achieved one of the most brilliant and stunning military successes in modern history. Its forces occupied the entire Sinai peninsula and camped along the east bank of the Suez Canal. They held all Jordanian territory west of the Jordan River and were entrenched inside Syria on the Golan Heights. Nasser's military capacity had been wiped out, his prestige shattered.

The Six-Day War had convincingly demonstrated Israel's prowess and resolve, but little seemed to have changed. Israel ignored Soviet and Arab protests and retained possession of the captured territories—determined to use them to protect its security, either as buffer zones or bargaining chips in return for Arab recognition and related guarantees. Military success had reopened the Gulf of Aqaba and blocked the Suez Canal, thus depriving Egypt of a major source of revenue. But Nasser proved amazingly resilient. Egyptians supported him despite the debacle, and new infusions of Soviet aid brought Egypt's military strength back to its prewar level within a few months. UN diplomacy made no progress in bringing the Arab-Israeli dispute appreciably closer to solution. President Johnson and Soviet Premier Kosygin conferred briefly in Glassboro, New Jersey, in late June 1967 to try to find a settlement of the Middle Eastern question, but no significant progress resulted from this meeting. Terrorist activities and violations of the cease-fire persisted.

The Soviet Union intensified its involvement in the area by refurbishing Egypt's armed forces, supporting Arab demands that a return of all captured territory precede negotiations with Israel, and enlarging its naval forces in the Mediterranean until they rivaled the strength of the United States Sixth Fleet. It seemed apparent that Russia would not permit another Arab humiliation at Israel's hands; and it was equally apparent that the United States would not let the Zionist state suffer defeat and destruction.

CHAPTER 29

Affluence and Anxiety

For many Americans, the 1940s and 1950s were quiet decades in which families, suburbs, and the new institution of television provided an idyllic and tranquil setting. Yet appearances were deceiving, for this superficial social calm disguised an underlying turbulence that became more apparent in the 1960s and early 1970s. To many, the contradictions of American life became glaringly obvious. The United States was a nation of affluence, the richest nation on earth by 1960, yet it was unable properly to feed, educate, or keep healthy a significant portion of its population. As late as the mid-1960s, despite its worldwide protestations of democracy, Americans maintained a system of apartheid and institutionalized racial oppression in much of the country. The moment of its greatest triumph was also a time of its greatest challenge for the American system. On a number of fronts, accepted norms were questioned and, in some instances, tossed aside. Young Americans embraced new forms of music, loudly rejected the new domesticity of the 1950s, and advocated a liberalized sexuality. To their parents, their youthful rebellion often seemed baffling and confusing, and the clash between the parents and children of the baby boom generation was unprecedented in American history in its intensity.

1. THE TRANSFORMATION OF THE FAMILY

In many respects the greatest challenge facing American society in the postwar era came from within—in the changes in the American family of the 1960s and early 1970s. The self-assured domesticity that pervaded popular culture through-out the two decades after World War II constituted only a thin veneer beneath which lay another reality: the American family had undergone a significant alteration of its character and composition that would become fully clear only after 1960.

Americans in the 1960s were still in the midst of the baby boom, yet that phenomenon was coming to a close. The birthrate, which had been 19.4 per thousand in 1940, reached a twentieth-century peak of 25.0 per thousand in the year 1957. Thereafter it declined over the next two decades to 23.7 in 1960 and 18.2 in 1970. Family size, which had been growing throughout the 1950s, began a similar drop during the next decade. The percentage of families that had three or more children rose to a postwar high of 22.3 percent in 1964. Yet it subse-quently declined to 6.2 percent by 1975.

The end of the baby boom in the mid-1960s had significant implications. Baby boom children entered a world of unprecedented wealth. To a degree quite unlike the experience of their parents or grandparents, they lacked for few things and were provided for lavishly. The first generation to grow up with television, they lived in a world of different images and cultural symbols. With an expanded system of education, they were likely, much more so than their parents, to experience peer-group socialization in schools; they were more likely to attend high school; and they were more likely to have the chance to go to college. But they also grew up with clashing expectations: a traditional message of economic justice and social democracy in contrast to the pervasive cultural message of consumerism, along with an emphasis on the traditional family and an often rigid adherence to its norms combined with new choices generated by rapid social change.

Children of the cold war, the baby boomers began to test the limits of domesticity and the family hierarchy. As we shall see, they asserted themselves in various ways, all testing the constraints of family. In particular, baby boomers tested the authority of their parents, which had been taken for granted for generations and which had been reasserted in a different language in the 1940s and 1950s. Middle-class white children and adolescents began to develop a distinct youth culture in the 1950s and 1960s that reflected their spending power and expressed their rebellion against the traditional family.

The authority of the family was challenged in another way in the 1960s: with the increasing incidence of marriage breakup. The cold-war family, as it appeared in movie, television, and advertising images in the 1950s, was stable and orderly, with clear and defined gender roles. To a certain extent, this reflected social reality. Among married women in 1962, 96 percent indicated that they were either extremely happy or fairly happy; an equally large percentage of women reaffirmed their desire to fulfill traditional roles as wives and mothers.

Yet the position of women within families defied these attitudes. The most visible evidence of change appeared in the erosion of the traditional structure of marriage. Compared with the first half of the twentieth century, divorce became commonplace. By the late 1970s about half of all marriages were ending unsuccessfully. While the marriage rate leveled off in the postwar period, between 1940 and 1980 the divorce rate increased by 260 percent. This increase became particularly acute after 1970: during the decade that followed, the divorce rate rose from 3.5 per thousand to 5.2 per thousand, an increase of 149 percent.

These trends reflected several new conditions. One was the liberalization of divorce laws, which made marriage breakup, during and after the 1960s, much easier than it had ever been. In most states by 1970, mutual consent or even the initiative of one party sufficed to bring about the end to a marriage; in most states before then, divorces could result only from much stricter criteria. Divorce was now available to spouses caught in unhappy marriages, and the fact that millions of Americans took advantage of this possibility suggests that cold-war matrimony defied its superficial appearance.

Divorce also reflected a greater degree, at least among white middle-class families, of independence among working wives. The mass departure of American wives during and immediately after World War II from the home to the workplace accelerated during the 1960s and 1970s. In 1960, close to a third of all married women worked in paid labor; by 1970, that proportion had increased to about two-fifths. In the early 1980s, a majority of all married women worked outside the home. Meanwhile, working women penetrated previously all-male occupations during the 1970s, particularly highly paid and high-status professions. The proportion of women among all architects during this decade rose from 4 to 8 percent; of women college and university teachers, from 29 to 36 percent; of women lawyers, from 5 to 14 percent; and of women physicians, from 10 to 13 percent. During the 1970s, the overall proportion of women in executive or managerial positions rose from 19 to 31 percent.

New opportunities for working women also shaped the African-American experience. For much of the nineteenth and early twentieth centuries, the most significant difference between white and black women had been that, while black wives worked, white wives did not. After 1960, that difference vanished, and, by 1980, equal numbers—roughly half of both black and white married women—were employed outside the home. Particularly during the 1960s, black women found expanded opportunities in occupations that heretofore had been closed to them. Thus during that decade the proportion of black women working in the clerical and sales force grew from 3 to 11 percent in the South and from 17 to 33 percent in the North. In the beginning of the decade, black women's median income was almost 80 percent that of white women; at the end of the decade, this proportion had risen to about 95 percent.

By no means did this mean real independence or equality for working women; far from it, since the greater share of married women entering the work force in this era continued to be employed in female-dominated and underpaid occupations such as teaching, nursing, and secretarial work. Balanced against the increase in the economic power of married women was the persistence, then, of forces limiting that power. Because they were largely employed in underpaid jobs and because they often worked part-time, women earned substantially less than men. Through the five decades after World War II, the median income of women compared with that of men deteriorated despite the increase in the numbers of working women. While the median income of white women in 1945 was 63 percent that of white men, by 1982 this proportion had actually declined to about 41 percent.

In sum, traditional domesticity was eroding among black and white families at a rapid rate during the 1960s. Among black families, an even higher rate of disintegration occurred for different reasons. The percentage of working black wives tended to correspond with greater family stability—to a greater degree than was true among white families. In the late 1970s, about three-fifths of all black married women living with their husbands were employed outside the home, as compared with 48 percent of white wives. Yet black women continued to work at the lowest-paid jobs; almost a third of all working black women were employed as domestics as late as 1980.

Among the many differences between whites and blacks were the greater strains experienced by black families. Family breakup was strongly associated with continuing poverty. By 1980, some rather disturbing facts existed about the black family, particularly in urban ghettos. In that year, one-third of all black households—as compared with only about a tenth of white households—were poor, and more than two-thirds of them were headed by women. Of all black children, about half grew up without a father at home. Of black babies, more than half would be born out of wedlock, and most of them to teenage mothers. Among blacks, the most disturbing ramification of family breakup were its connections with a continuing cycle of despair and poverty.

The roots of the transformation of the black family lay in the 1950s but came to full fruition thereafter. The proportion of female-headed households among blacks grew steadily after World War II. In 1950, 17.6 percent of all black families were female-headed; by 1970, this proportion had increased to 28.3 percent; by a decade later, to 40.2 percent. These female-headed households were likely to be centers of further poverty. A minority, about two-fifths in 1980, held jobs; most tended to be young and undereducated and therefore with little hope for the future. When they did work, their income remained low. In 1981, female-headed households earned about a third of what two-parent black families earned in income.

The erosion of the black family was the result of external strains and stresses. Black migrants to cities, especially black males, soon faced high rates of unemployment; throughout the 1960s and 1970s, black male unemployment remained about twice that of whites. When black men did work, their income levels tended to be significantly lower than those of their white male counterparts. Combined with a growing mortality rate for black men that continued to climb in the three decades after the 1960s, these conditions substantially reduced the numbers of potential husbands and breadwinners and played a major role in the high rates of poor single-parent black households.

The cold-war family in which the male breadwinner coexisted happily with a homemaker wife and docile children may well have been a myth; even if it was not, its sanctity suffered devastating damage in the 1960s and 1970s. Whatever its sources and effects, the transformation of the American family was a central event in the contradictory events of those decades.

2. ORIGINS OF THE CIVIL RIGHTS REVOLUTION

Perhaps the greatest challenge to the postwar status quo came from the millions of African-Americans who lived oppressed in a system of segregation enforced by both custom and law. For most of the twentieth century, southern blacks remained excluded politically; without political power, they suffered discrimination not only in public places of accommodation but also in jobs and housing.

The relegation of black people to a second-class Jim Crow status represented the central contradiction of postwar American life. In a cold-war society that sought to combat international communism by representing itself as free and democratic, the oppression of black people made these claims ring hollow. Yet cold-war America offered ripe conditions for challenging racial segregation, for American culture was experiencing, to an unprecedented degree, nationalizing influences: not only were white middle-class Americans directly exposed to the inequities of Jim Crow through national media such as television, but, through these very same media, southern blacks were made aware of the degree of injustice that they suffered.

It is a central irony of the Jim Crow system that the seeds for its demise lay within that system. White segregationists had long held that black progress lay in separation, which, they contended, fostered responsible leadership. The development of black leadership during the first half of the twentieth century was a clear by-product of segregation. From within black urban communities grew a black middle class, which sustained black-owned business that catered to an all-black clientele. Black undertakers, dentists, doctors, lawyers, and small businessmen all thrived in an environment that denied black people effective access to white professionals and businessmen. All-black colleges and universities that came into existence because of segregation also emerged as centers of leadership. Many of these institutions, such as Morehouse College in Atlanta or Fisk University in Nashville, grew out of abolitionist efforts to educate freedmen after the Civil War. Others, such as North Carolina College for Negroes in Durham, first came into existence as halfhearted attempts by state governments to provide access to public higher education, but later they developed as centers of a black educational renaissance. Whatever their origins, black colleges experienced a period of intellectual creativity during the middle of the twentieth century; they became centers of critical inquiry that challenged the justice of the Jim Crow system itself.

Black leaders mounted that challenge. The war had provided great hope among African-Americans for change, as did other developments in the postwar era, including Harry S Truman's decision to integrate the armed forces and the Democratic party's decisive commitment in 1948 to favor federal protection of civil rights. But nothing gave black people higher expectations than the monumental Brown decision. Decided in May 1954 by a unanimous vote, the case overturned segregation in education but, by overthrowing the Plessy case's "separate but equal" rule, which had allowed segregation if it were nominally equal, Brown called into question the entire legal basis of legally required segregation.

The Brown decision seemed to undermine the very assumptions of postwar American society. To many southern whites, Court-mandated integration would upset the foundations of society and unleash social chaos. Especially in the Deep South, some whites responded violently to the black aspirations for freedom. Perhaps no instance of violence better exemplified the tensions that existed in the aftermath of Brown than the Emmett Till case. Till was a fourteen-year-old boy who was visiting relatives in Money, Mississippi, in 1959. Born and raised in Chicago, Till had little respect for southern racial taboos; in addressing a white woman one day in a local store, he apparently was disrespectful. When the woman's husband, Roy Bryant, heard of the incident, he and another man, J. W. Milam, abducted Till and murdered him.

Till's body was discovered the next day in the Tallahatchie River, and Bryant and Milam were tried by a local court. Quickly and rather typically they were found innocent by an all-white jury. Although subsequent attempts to obtain a conviction failed, the Emmett Till case displayed the gulf in perceptions that divided whites and blacks. For whites, it revealed the sudden assertiveness of southern blacks; even if they denounced the crime, many southern whites would probably cite the challenge to racial etiquette as its chief cause. For blacks, in contrast, it showed the basic inequity of the Jim Crow system that tolerated murder of blacks by whites and permitted random violence, especially in the Deep South. White paternalism, which offered justice despite segregation, was exposed as a complete sham. Black people, especially young black people the same age as and older than Till, had lost confidence in southern whites to lead the region toward a different future.

By the early 1960s, despite its immediate promise, the Brown decision had brought little real change. Most of the South's public schools remained segregated and unequal; facilities and public services were allocated unequally. The strategy of traditional black leadership meanwhile underwent challenge. That strategy, at both the local and the national levels, had been primarily gradualist. In towns and cities where segregation had permitted the emergence of a black middle class, the black elite served as the main communication link between white and black communities; yet the black elite's chief interest was often the preservation of cautious and incremental progress that would not disrupt lines of communication to white leadership. At the national level, organizations such as the NAACP sought change primarily through the legal and political process, and they were willing to wait decades for that change to occur.

Many blacks, however, were unwilling to wait. In the Deep South, challenges emerged from within the black community, which was growing impatient and restive at the slow pace of change. In the late 1940s, in Montgomery, Alabama, a black professor at the segregated Alabama State College organized the Women's Political Council (WPC). It eventually became the most important voice for black militancy in that city. By the mid-1950s, after a few political successes, the WPC challenged the segregated local bus system, which required black people to relinquish their seats to whites and sit in the rear of the bus. On December 1, 1955, Rosa Parks, a Montgomery seamstress, tired from a long day's work, refused to give up her seat. As a result, Parks was arrested.

This incident might have seemed random, but, like many other aspects of the civil rights movement, it was the product of careful planning. Parks, a high school graduate, had earlier attended the Highlander School, in Monteagle, Tennessee, which pioneered interracial contacts and became a spawning ground for further activism. Two weeks at Highlander plus membership in the NAACP and the WPC were enough to steel Parks's courage to challenge bus segregation. It was also enough to ignite a mass movement. In response to Parks's arrest, local leaders began a black boycott of the city's buses. Attempting to broaden their base further, boycott leaders persuaded a young minister recently arrived in the city, the Reverend Martin Luther King, Jr., to lead the movement.

On the surface, King seemed a poor choice. Son of one of the most powerful black ministers in Atlanta, King had spent most of his life as a privileged member of the black elite of Atlanta. Yet he soon rose to the occasion. His oratorical skills and his unique sense of timing transformed the Montgomery movement and stiffened the determination of local blacks to maintain the boycott, despite extraordinary pressure and considerable hardship, for almost a year. Then, on November 13, 1956, the Supreme Court, in *Gayle et al.* v. *Browder* ruled that the segregation of the Montgomery bus system was unconstitutional. On December 21, after 381 days of boycott, King boarded a Montgomery bus and sat in its front row.

Although the Court decision rather than the boycott successfully desegregated the buses, blacks derived important lessons from the Montgomery movement. If they had possessed any doubts before, southern blacks were now utterly convinced that little help would come from liberally minded whites, who remained immobilized in responding to rapidly changing events. In the boycott and other measures like it, blacks learned that power lay in numbers and in collective, united action and that organization into a mass movement could affect segregation, perhaps even play a role in breaking it down. And, as in the case of the Montgomery bus boycott, the new activists sought some form of federal intervention, whether through the courts or through the executive.

In the aftermath of the Montgomery success, King and other black ministers in February 1957 created the Southern Christian Leadership Conference (SCLC), which sought to extend the Montgomery model regionwide. At the same time, black mobilization occurred at another level—among college-age blacks who had grown up in the baby boom generation and were increasingly unable to stomach racial injustice. These younger blacks would spearhead a new approach designed to upend Jim Crow immediately through even more ambitious tactics.

3.   FROM GREENSBORO TO SELMA

When four students from the all-black North Carolina A&T State College staged a sit-in at a Woolworth's department store in downtown Greensboro, North Carolina, on February 1, 1960, they demonstrated the degree of impatience many young blacks felt about the slow pace of change. There was nothing new in the sit-in technique: sit-ins had occurred before Greensboro. The Congress of Racial Equality (CORE) had staged a sit-in at Chicago almost twenty years before; in 1958 and 1959, students had successfully desegregated lunch counters in Tulsa and Miami. Closer to Greensboro, Durham blacks had conducted a sit-in three years earlier in a local all-white ice cream parlor. But while the Durham sit-in and others elsewhere had gained little attention from other blacks and from the news media, the Greensboro sit-in set off a nationwide movement.

The A&T students chose Woolworth's for carefully considered reasons. Woolworth's was a national chain that was susceptible to media pressure. As in many chain stores, blacks could purchase personal items such as toothpaste and soap but could not sit down to eat at the lunch counter. Having purchased a few items from the store, the black students sat down politely at the lunch counter and requested service. Refused, they then sat and awaited an outcome; when no outcome resulted, even after a visit from a policeman, they left after staying about forty-five minutes. The next day, however, they were joined by other students; within a few days the numbers of protesters were in the thousands.

The sit-in movement, which was led and directed by students at all-black colleges, quickly evolved into a well-coordinated regional and national movement. Sit-ins occurred across the South during the spring of 1960; fifteen southern cities were experiencing them by the end of February. By April fifty-four cities in nine southern states had witnessed sit-ins. These demonstrations offered a direct challenge to the Jim Crow system. Unlike the participants in the NAACP's long legal campaign or the Montgomery bus boycott, the demonstrators wholeheartedly adopted Mahatma Gandhi's doctrine of nonviolent civil disobedience, in which they willingly risked arrest in order to test the legality and to dramatize the immorality of Jim Crow. The sit-in movement of the spring of 1960 yielded significant accomplishments. The Greensboro Woolworth's had been desegregated by July, while lunch counters in twenty-eight other cities were opened to blacks. Nonetheless, the Jim Crow system had survived this assault, and black student activists were determined to overthrow segregation once and for all. In April 1960, about two hundred veterans of the sit-in movement gathered in a conference sponsored by the SCLC organizer Ella Baker, who urged the students to expand their campaign beyond the lunch counters. At the urging of Baker and King, students formed the Student Nonviolent Coordinating Committee (SNCC) in Atlanta about a month later and elected Marion Barry, then a young leader from Nashville and later mayor of Washington, as its first chairman.

Civil rights activists then moved into high gear. About a year after the sit-in movement, CORE inaugurated a campaign to desegregate interstate bus travel by sponsoring, across the South, "freedom rides" to force the integration of bus terminals. In May 1961, two groups of interracial travelers boarded buses and headed south from Washington. Their journey was uneventful through Virginia and North Carolina. Then, in Rock Hill, South Carolina, freedom rider John Lewis was turned back when whites refused to permit him to enter the all-white waiting room. After their safe arrival in Atlanta on May 13, the freedom riders faced the most difficult part of their journey in Alabama and Mississippi. One group of freedom riders was assaulted by a white mob outside Anniston, Alabama, which fire-bombed the bus and attacked the civil rights activists with clubs and blackjacks. In Birmingham, another group was viciously attacked by local Klansmen operating with the connivance of local police. Then, in Montgomery, despite the addition of both new SNCC volunteers and federal protection, a mob again attacked. In response, the Kennedy administration dispatched four hundred marshals to Montgomery, and they protected the freedom riders on the last leg of their journey through Mississippi.

By dramatizing images of racial hate, CORE and SNCC organizers achieved their immediate goal. Then, in late 1961, the Interstate Commerce Commission (ICC) banned segregated carriers and terminal facilities. Yet activists realized that only direct action and civil disobedience, and the national display of white racism, would bring down segregation. Organizers were fully aware, moreover, that direct action alone was insufficient; their ultimate objective was massive federal intervention and coercion.

The most ambitious attempt to date to overthrow segregation occurred in Albany, Georgia. Responding to the appeals of local leaders in the autumn of

1961, King helped to organize a grass-roots movement. The Albany local government, rigidly segregationist, had ignored the ICC ruling outlawing segregation in terminals and had arrested students who attempted to integrate them. By the time King arrived, SNCC organizers had already assembled what became known as the Albany movement. It sought to challenge local segregationists' ability to persevere despite massive black pressure. Yet the movement stalled at Albany. Local police chief Laurie Pritchett developed an effective response to the movement's civil disobedience tactics. Arranging with jails around the county to house thousands of arrested demonstrators, he insisted that prisoners be treated fairly and without brutality and remained conscious that the movement's most effective weapon against segregation was adverse publicity in the national media. Pritchett instructed his arresting officers in courses in nonviolence, mimicking the demonstrators' methods. After persisting into the summer of 1963, the Albany movement finally gave up.

It was in this context of intense self-doubt that King and supporters sought greater successes in Birmingham, Alabama. There King faced an openly racist opponent in Police Commissioner Eugene "Bull" Connor, who, unlike Pritchett, would reject nonviolence. King planned a series of marches seeking the desegregation of public accommodations and of city parks, to begin in April 1963. In contrast to Albany, the results at Birmingham were electrifying. Although King was arrested and jailed and although the full force of the Birmingham police was turned on the demonstrators with police dogs and fire hoses, national public opinion turned decisively against the segregationists. Local business leaders conducted negotiations with King's forces that amounted to a virtually total surrender, and local merchants agreed to the end of visible signs of segregation.

The Birmingham marches had even more important effects, however. The spectacle of Connor's police violence, displayed before a national audience, forced President Kennedy to intervene by pressuring local southern officials to accelerate the pace of integration. At the same time, Kennedy, in June 1963, making a national address that pushed civil rights to the center of the domestic-policy agenda, called for a greatly strengthened federal civil rights bill. The Birmingham triumph buoyed the hopes of blacks everywhere, and in the spring and summer of 1963, the tactics of grass-roots organizing and mass demonstrations were replicated throughout the South. By late 1963, much of the region was in rebellion against segregation.

King's movement culminated in the March on Washington, which occurred in August 1963. King and supporters sought to revive the march that had originally been scheduled for the summer of 1941 by A. Philip Randolph but had been canceled in exchange for Franklin Roosevelt's pledge of nondiscrimination in federal wartime hiring and his issuance of Executive Order 8802 in June 1941. Gathering in front of the Lincoln Memorial on August 28, 1963, the marchers, who numbered as many as 200,000, listened to speakers urge Congress to enact strong civil rights legislation. The most stirring speech, however, was that of King himself, who delivered probably the best-known address of his life, the fifteen-minute "I Have a Dream" speech.

After the assassination of John Kennedy and the inauguration of Lyndon Johnson, the new president made civil rights legislation his top priority. Shepherded through Congress by this master of legislative processes, the Civil Rights Act was signed by Johnson on July 2, 1964. It was one of the most important laws that Congress ever enacted. In one stroke of legislation, segregation of public accommodations, theaters, and parks—of any public facilities—was declared illegal, and through these provisions the most visible indicators of Jim Crow were swept away. But the Civil Rights Act did much more. It established an Equal Employment Opportunity Commission (EEOC), whose primary purpose was to insure fair hiring and to recommend sanctions in cases in which it found discrimination. It required more vigorous action on school desegregation and mandated the withholding of federal funds from those state agencies that were found to continue to discriminate. And, in a last-minute addition, the law required that such antidiscriminatory features of the act also applied to cases of gender discrimination.

The movement then turned to the issue of voting rights. Even after the enactment of the Civil Rights Act and even with the full force of the federal government behind them, African-Americans faced terrific obstacles to real political power. In the cities of the upper South, blacks had possessed the effective right to vote since the 1930s; the real repression and violence were centered in rural areas, especially in the Deep South. It was in these rural areas that the movement thus directed its main thrust in 1964 and 1965. Working together through the Voter Education Project (VEP), which was conceived at the urging of the Kennedy administration and financed by several philanthropies, all the major civil rights organizations combined to conduct efforts in 1962 to expand voter registration.

Perhaps the most ambitious and daring of all these efforts was that of SNCC, which attempted voter registration in Alabama and Mississippi. Predictably, its efforts evoked a violent response on the part of whites. After a frustrating beginning, SNCC conducted a renewed registration drive in the summer of 1964. Eventually known as "Freedom Summer" and "Mississippi Summer," it involved hundreds of white college students who streamed into Mississippi to participate; civil rights leaders hoped to attract greater national attention and perhaps even a strong national response if violence also threatened young whites. It soon did: in June 1964, three civil rights workers, two of them whites, were reported missing near Philadelphia, Mississippi, and after an extensive search their bodies were discovered six weeks later. The net result of Freedom Summer was to dramatize further the plight of southern rural blacks—during the summer there were thirty homes and buildings burned and six murders.

Further action followed when King and the SCLC intervened in the burgeon-ing voting rights movement. They chose Selma, Alabama, a center of white obstructionism on voting rights just as Birmingham had been a center on the issue of public accommodations. In January 1965, King organized marches to the Dallas County Courthouse in Selma that provoked thousands of arrests. He then convened a march from Selma to Montgomery, the state capital, on March 7, 1965. When state troopers and Selma police attacked and pursued the marchers on Edmund Pettis Bridge, national outrage was the result. Joined by hundreds of white clergymen, SCLC leaders marched again on March 21, but, more important, Johnson, a week earlier, had addressed Congress to urge enactment of a new Voting Rights Act.

The Voting Rights Act was enacted by Congress and signed by Johnson on August 6, 1965. Just as the Civil Rights Act of 1964 had revolutionized public accommodations and education, the Voting Rights Act dramatically altered the nature of southern politics. The act did away with those various mechanisms, such as the literacy test, that white Southerners had employed since the 1890s to disfranchise black voters. Applying to those states, all of them southern, that had a history of significant voter discrimination, the law required that federal registrars and observers be posted across the South to supervise elections. The results were almost immediate: a surge in black registration and voting across the South.

4. AMERICAN HIGHER EDUCATION UNDER SIEGE

With the rebellion of its young, the cold-war family was under attack from another quarter in the 1960s. Just as women began to challenge the constrictions of the new domesticity established a decade earlier, so too young Americans, most of them born at the beginning of the baby boom generation, defied many of these conventions. The center of this rebellion in many respects was the American college and university. Experiencing a surge in enrollments, in public and private support, and in the numbers of faculty and staff employed, American higher education was in flush times of unlimited budgets and expansion. Yet it was during these flush times that American students would challenge the struc-ture and authority of higher education and, in a sense, the structure and authority of their parents.

In the 1950s, students had periodically challenged college and university authority through such events as "panty raids," but those challenges had focused mostly on parietal rules governing the hours and social life of undergraduates. Never had students banded together to upset the entire nature of university authority, at least until the eruption of the free-speech movement in Berkeley, California, in 1964. In September of that year, a University of California adminis-trator ordered students to remove tables that displayed political literature from the main gate of the university. In response, students defied the ban until a member of their group, Jack Weinberg, was arrested on October 1. When police attempted to jail Weinberg, who later was immortalized with the declaration "You can't trust anyone over thirty," students encircled the police car and refused its passage. After a long siege, the administration agreed to release Weinberg.

Then, about a month later, student leaders of the Weinberg affair were charged with acts of violence; one of their leaders, Mario Savio, was accused of having bitten a policeman. Students responded militantly, demanding that these charges be withdrawn. The university administration, led by President Clark Kerr, then refused, and students occupied the administration building, Sproul Hall. The administration responded by arresting hundreds of students, and a student strike ensued. The final upshot was that the faculty sided with the students and concurred with what had become known as the free-speech movement, the right of all students to express diverse political opinions.

The Berkeley uprising reflected restive conditions on American campuses. In order to accommodate surging enrollments, colleges and universities had developed large administrative bureaucracies; public universities in many states such as California had developed multicampus structures that evolved in response to the enrollment explosion. On campuses such as Berkeley, large classes prevailed and student alienation was common. All the while, however, university administration ruled student life with an iron hand and regulated it on the assumption of *in loco parentis,* the ancient principle of college life that transferred parental authority to collegiate authorities.

The time was thus ripe in many ways for a wholesale challenge to this authority, and the Berkeley free-speech movement was only the first round. As in Berkeley, students derived their model of organization and activism from the civil rights movement, which stressed grass-roots organizing and had pioneered methods of defiance toward entrenched, powerful authority. Many of the leaders of the free-speech movement had participated in civil rights organizing; Mario Savio, for example, had just returned from the Freedom Summer, which was designed to increase black voter registration in Mississippi during the summer of 1964.

What gave the student movement added urgency was the Vietnam War, a cause that aroused normally indifferent students and swelled the ranks of student activists. As early as 1965 and 1966, student activists began to organize campus "teach-ins," which sought to educate the campus community about the expanding American role in the Vietnam War. Student groups began to grow and spread across the country thereafter. Perhaps the most important of these groups was the Students for a Democratic Society (SDS). SDS activists rejected the central assumptions shared by both social democrats and liberals: the rectitude of the cold war and of the welfare state. The United States, they contended, shared in the responsibility for the coming of the cold war, while the nation's leadership had institutionalized oppression and suppressed what SDS organizers called "economic democracy." Loosely organized in decentralized campus chapters around the country, the SDS viewed large social organizations, whether they were multinational corporations or university bureaucracies, with deep suspicion.

For most of the early 1960s, the SDS challenge to the social order fell on deaf ears. Beginning in 1961, white student radicals joined in a loose coalition with black student radicals and their most important organization, SNCC. By then, many SDS activists were energized by participation in the black uprising against segregation. But the real turning point came after Lyndon Johnson's escalation of the American involvement in the Vietnam War. In 1965, SDS leaders harnessed antiwar sentiment by inaugurating a national antidraft campaign; in response, SDS membership swelled, and local chapters conducted public burnings of draft cards, obstruction of military recruiters, and counseling for draft evasion. With the SDS leading the way, other campus organizers spawned student movements across the country during 1967 and 1968. Most of these were fueled by opposition to the war and the draft; but behind most of the uprisings was a context of almost dictatorial control by university administrators and increased assertiveness by student protesters, who began to view the war only as a symptom of a larger condition. A new peak of student activism was reached in the year 1968, when there were some 221 student demonstrations at 101 colleges and universities in which about forty thousand students participated.

Perhaps the most important of these uprisings occurred at Columbia University in the spring of 1968. A strong SDS chapter existed on that campus, as in many others, because of the depth of student resentment of the draft and opposition to the war. But the issue that eventually erupted in crisis was Columbia's determination to build a new athletics facility by razing houses in a nearby black community. SDS had already been conducting an antiwar campaign that sought to force off campus the Institute for Defense Analysis, an interuniversity, mostly Ivy League group that conducted military-related research. Student activists, with the gymnasium issue, now succeeded in widening their base and making an elaborated critique of university structure and governance.

On April 24, 1968, black and white students at Columbia occupied two administration buildings, rummaging through administration files and sacking offices. After negotiations for their departure failed, Columbia President Grayson Kirk ordered in the police. Bedlam ensued, and about 700 students were arrested and another 150 injured. The rest of the university community, in response, rallied around the cause of the students, and Columbia remained closed for the remainder of the spring. As a result of the furor, the university dropped its plans for a new gymnasium and loosened its campus regulations. Meanwhile, Kirk resigned his post as president.

The climax of campus activism occurred in 1970, when American colleges experienced a wave of uprisings after the American incursion into Cambodia. These revolts exploded after four college youths were killed and several others wounded by gunfire from national guardsmen during an outbreak at Kent State University in Ohio on May 4. Further inflamed by news of the killing of two black youths by police gunfire during a melee at Jackson State College in Mississippi ten days later, students closed down many of the nation's colleges and universities. Some 750 institutions, of every size and description from coast to coast, experienced upheaval in the tense weeks that followed, and at least 130 schools canceled classes for the balance of the spring term.

5. THE NEW LEFT

Although probably most of the participants in these campus uprisings were inspired by opposition to the Vietnam War, what emerged out of them was a wide-ranging critique of American society. In the 1950s, a number of intellectuals, such as Herbert Marcuse and C. Wright Mills, had criticized the anti-Communist consensus. Radicalism was not over, they claimed: a "New Left"—a term that was coined by Mills—opposed bureaucratic organizations of the military, big business, and universities.

New Left ideology supplied a radical language emerging out of the campus turmoil of the 1960s. The most important New Left organization was SDS, which grew out of the Student League for Industrial Democracy (SLID). Tracing their roots to the Socialist party of America, SLID leaders had created SDS at Ann Arbor, Michigan, in 1960. In December 1961, SDS began almost a decade of activism when its leaders composed the Port Huron Statement, which became a program of action for the SDS. The Port Huron Statement culminated several years of activism in which students or former students from the University of Michigan, such as Al Haber, Sharon Jeffrey, and Tom Hayden, developed the SDS into an organization independent of SLID, with an agenda that largely rejected its social democratic program. The Port Huron Statement offered a classic synopsis of the emerging New Left analysis of cold-war America. The statement, drafted primarily by Hayden, marked a break between Old and New Left. SDS leaders called for an end to American interventionism abroad and the inauguration of what they called genuine "participatory democracy" at home. Committing the SDS to the creation of a New Left, the Port Huron Statement sought to transform universities into centers of social action.

SDS and other New Left organizations drew much of their inspiration from the civil rights movement. By the early 1960s, New Left activists had been exposed to activism and to social problems through participation in the civil rights struggle. Many of them had witnessed the violence of Freedom Summer and had been deeply affected by the face of white racism. New Left students sought to apply the lessons of the movement to a wider field: the sources of racism, they came to believe, lay in an unjust society that had inequitably distributed its resources and had stifled democracy.

In the early 1960s, SDS attempted its Economic Research and Action Project (ERAP), which paralleled, by organizing workers in the North, the movement's voter registration drive in the South. ERAP would become, SDS organizers hoped, a grass-roots basis for both what they called "economic democracy" and, eventually, a coming social revolution. Yet ERAP soon proved to be a failure. Few workers were attracted to a middle-class student organization in the middle of good economic times. In the meantime, moreover, the pressing issue of the Vietnam War attracted the attention of the New Left.

In October 1967, the antiwar movement organized a Stop the Draft Week that attracted demonstrations and draft-card burnings across the country. This was followed by larger demonstrations attracting an even wider following that culminated in the convergence of activists on the Democratic convention of 1968 in Chicago. The Youth International party, the "Yippies," led by cultural radicals Jerry Rubin and Abbie Hoffman, organized a festival of life to protest the convention. The National Mobilization to End the War meanwhile staged street demonstrations. In what experts later described as a "police riot," Chicago police attacked the demonstrators and bloodied their ranks, indiscriminately clubbing journalists and activists. In 1969, the moratorium movement sought to end the war, and in 1970 came the widespread campus revolt in response to the American invasion of Cambodia in April.

The campus uprisings of spring 1970 were a high-water mark for New Left radicalism. Several reasons account for the failure of student radicalism. Because the Old Left, which had offered the only real hope of a political base, had been effectively dispersed and dispirited during the anticommunism purges of the 1950s, the New Left lacked any support from or communication with labor organizations and social democrats. Aside from the unpredictable student population, the New Left lacked popular appeal, and many of its tactics provoked and even offended working-class and middle-class opinion. The New Left also suffered from serious internal divisions. From its inception, the SDS and organizations like it were faction-ridden: some of its leaders were social democrats, others were Maoist, and others Marxist-Leninist. Still others, rejecting any political philosophy or any authority, were nihilists. By 1969, these differences had resulted in the splintering of the SDS into competing organizations. In its national meeting in June 1969, a faction, eventually known as the Weathermen, seceded and formed an underground revolutionary organization; at this point, the SDS ceased to function as an effective group.

Part of the New Left's ineffectiveness also lay in its confused message. Its critique of cold-war American society was partially accurate but also diffused and unclearly focused. It was a political movement, yet it rejected political solutions. And it was very much part of the emerging counterculture. The convergence of the counterculture and the New Left was best exemplified by the Youth International party, which expressed a rejection of politics as usual but did so by flouting middle-class standards of probity. Formed in late 1967 by political activists Jerry Rubin and Abbie Hoffman, the Yippies sought a cultural revolution which would defy sexual and behavioral conventions.

Scholars of the New Left now know that its demise was also fostered by subversion sponsored by the FBI. Beginning in the Johnson administration, FBI Director J. Edgar Hoover inaugurated a program in which FBI agents penetrated most of the existing New Left and civil rights organizations. In most instances, they sought to gather intelligence about these organizations and, at least nominally, to determine the extent of their loyalty to foreign agents. On some occasions, acting as agent provocateurs, they themselves committed criminal activities. Yet the FBI also, through the use of undercover agents, spurred on the internal divisions and differences and helped to speed the disintegration of these groups.

6. THE REEMERGENCE OF FEMINISM

Another challenge to the status quo came from women, especially white middle-class women, who pressed forward a revival of the feminist agenda of the early twentieth century. Feminists directly attacked the domesticity of the post-World War II era. They criticized the notion that all women should become wives and mothers and relinquish work outside the home. They challenged the vestiges of a male-dominated society that barred women from male-only public places and from male-only occupations. And they pushed hard for greater equality in the workplace, specifically in the payment of equal wages for equal work.

A pioneer feminist and author, Betty Friedan, has often been described as the founder of the modern women's movement. In what started as a sociological and psychological inquiry into the fate of the Smith College graduating class of 1942, Friedan, in *The Feminine Mystique* (1963), disputed the conclusion that women were happier in domestic life. She maintained that the domesticity of the post-World War II era, which Friedan described as a "mystique," imprisoned women and forced them to believe that only the home offered the source of happiness and fulfillment. Domestic life was, she wrote, a "comfortable concentration camp" that degraded women and reduced them to an eventual loss of independence and autonomy. Although the book had less relevance to working-class or African-American women, thousands of middle-class white women devoured the contents of *The Feminine Mystique*, which quickly hit the best-seller lists.

The publication of Friedan's manifesto coincided with a new political awareness on the part of women and a new spate of national legislation. In 1963, Congress enacted the Equal Pay Act. Prior to the passage of this act, employers openly practiced gender discrimination in the area of pay. The law now required employers to pay for equal work equally, and it enabled women to file wage grievances and expect redress through federal intervention. Of even greater importance in spurring on gender equality in the workplace was Title VII of the Civil Rights Act of 1964. It had been added to the bill in Congress by Howard W. Smith of Virginia, who sought to weaken its prospects of passage. Out of the welter of complicated maneuvering, however, Congress outlawed gender discrimination and made it coequal with racial discrimination. The passage of Title VII was the most important event in the history of feminism since the ratification of the Nineteenth Amendment. It banned gender discrimination in employment, hiring, and promotion, and also education, but, more important, it placed the full weight of the federal government behind antidiscrimination efforts.

This critical legislation was enacted in the absence of an organized grass-roots feminist movement. Much of the impetus for it had come from the appointment by John Kennedy of Esther Peterson as assistant secretary of labor and director of the Women's Bureau. A longtime women's activist, Peterson was able to persuade Kennedy to endorse the Equal Pay Act of 1963 and, even more important, to form a presidential commission to investigate the condition of American women. Entitled the President's Commission on the Status of Women (PCSW), it was established by presidential order in December 1961, with Eleanor Roosevelt as its chair. Issuing its report in 1963, the PCSW made a number of recommendations seeking to eliminate gender discrimination while maintaining a domestic role for women. Meanwhile, the example of the PSCW spawned the creation of state and local commissions examining the status of women.

The convergence of these factors—new federal legislation and the publication of *The Feminist Mystique*—coincided with the civil rights movement, with which women had been involved since its inception. Women had spearheaded the Montgomery bus boycott; in the Deep South, they risked their lives in the Freedom Summer. The movement raised questions about the meaning of equality and for many women established a model for a new feminist revival. Just as racism permeated American society, many women believed, "sexism," a term new to the 1960s, also affected it. Indeed, women activists, discovering that sexism was as prevalent in the movement as anywhere else, eventually concluded that the agenda of gender equality needed separate attention and nurturing.

The emergence of a feminist movement that was patterned on the civil rights movement came in the creation of the National Organization for Women (NOW) in October 1966. The founding members, who numbered about thirty, came from diverse backgrounds. They included the black woman legal scholar and activist Pauli Murray; Marguerite Rawalt, a member of the National Woman's party and an advocate of an equal rights amendment (ERA); and Caroline Davis, a labor organizer from the United Auto Workers. It also included

Friedan, who had been instrumental in creating the organization and became its first president. NOW developed an ambitious agenda. It called for the effective enforcement of Title VII of the Civil Rights Act and the inclusion of gender as part of any federal antidiscrimination policy. On the heels of the passage of the Civil Rights Act, Lyndon Johnson had issued an executive order in 1965 that required that all recipients of federal funds end discrimination on the basis of race, creed, and national origin. Under pressure from NOW and other feminist organizations, he added gender to this list in 1967. In effect, affirmative action programs henceforth included women and blacks as the two major target groups in the area of employment, and these policies would have a major impact in eliminating barriers to women, especially in higher-paying professional occupations.

By the late 1960s, feminists were concentrating on several issues. Pressing ahead on the issue of pay equity, they promoted equality in the workplace. A number of them favored reform of mostly state legislation that had criminalized abortions, and with the Supreme Court's landmark *Roe* v. *Wade* case in 1973, these laws were swept away. For NOW leaders by the late 1960s, moreover, "empowerment" became a catchword, and that meant the acquisition of political power through the creation of a women's vote and the solidification of women as a pressure group. By 1968, Friedan was advocating a NOW strategy in which women would cross party lines and vote for candidates sympathetic to women's issues.

Political power for women was, however, beyond the purview of NOW, which saw itself primarily as a lobbying organization. In July 1971, three hundred feminist leaders, including Friedan, Elly Peterson, vice-chair of the Republican National Committee, Bella Abzug and Shirley Chisholm, both members of Congress, and Gloria Steinem, founder-publisher of *Ms.* magazine, a feminist publication, convened in Washington and formed the National Women's Political Caucus (NWPC). The new organization, which was bipartisan in nature, sought to increase the role of women and to spur their election to political offices around the country. But it also sought better representation within both major parties and the promotion of a broad range of women's issues that included an equal rights amendment, abortion, and child care. Within several years, the NWPC had spread across the country, included some five hundred chapters, and had a mailing list of over thirty thousand.

Despite these successes, problems accompanied the emergence of the new feminist movement. The new organizations continually sought to widen their base, but the fact remained that their appeal was limited among both working-class and African-American women. For whatever reason, whether it be cultural, class, and racial barriers that separated feminist leaders from the masses they needed to attract, feminism never attracted a truly wide following. It also suffered from significant internal divisions. Major divisions persisted on strategy:

many women's groups in the early and mid-1960s continued to oppose the ERA, although many of them rallied behind it in the 1970s.

There were, in addition, deep divisions between moderate and radical camps of the feminist movement. All feminists believed in equality, but their definitions of it varied considerably. Conservative feminists, for example, broke away from NOW in 1968 to form a new organization, the Women's Equity Action League (WEAL). It sought to avoid direct political involvement and favored neutrality on issues such as abortion and birth control in favor of more narrowly defined subjects such as jobs, education, and taxation. In contrast, moderate feminists believed that gender equality could be accomplished through the model of the civil rights movement: affirmative action programs which would persuade, cajole, or coerce employers into hiring more women in higher-paying jobs in the workplace. Moderate feminists believed in the elimination of all sex-typed advertising and all other gender barriers, just as the moderate wing of the civil rights movement favored the removal of Jim Crow signs and equal access for all black Americans. Like other liberal reformers before them, the moderates had a high degree of confidence in the power of law and rational discourse to alter folkways.

Other feminists adopted a different approach. In the radicalized milieu of the late 1960s, many of them saw an intersection of gender and class; they believed that the oppression of women was related to the oppression of all people. These socialist feminists sought reform through socialist solutions. Still others believed in complete gender equality, but, for various reasons, they came to believe that it was impossible to achieve it by operating within a male-dominated society. Accordingly, they favored gender separatism; like black nationalists within the civil rights movement, they had become convinced that empowerment lay in separation and the establishment of a separateness. They attempted to construct women-controlled enterprises; their sexuality was often lesbian as the best means of declaring independence from men.

Although eventually frustrated on the ERA, feminists could claim significant progress by the end of the 1970s. Barriers to women in hiring and employment had fallen; women entered the professions in large numbers during the decade. Further legislation by Congress during the 1970s expanded federal control over affirmative action. It was not uncommon for a variety of appropriation bills to include antidiscrimination clauses. In 1972, Congress amended the Equal Pay Act of 1963 to include upper-level professional positions in business and government. In the same year, the Equal Employment Opportunity Act gave federal agencies stronger powers to enforce gender equality. And, in a crucial law also enacted in 1972, Congress passed the Educational Amendments Act; Title IX of that act prohibited sexual discrimination in education. It had a particularly important effect in women's sports, which, beginning in the 1970s, experienced an infusion of resources and funds.

7. POPULAR MUSIC AND THE YOUTH REVOLUTION

The domesticity of the 1950s received another stinging blow in a distinctive culture of youth that emerged in that decade and came into its own during the next decade. As the baby boom reached adolescence, this large age cohort began to express a revolt against the conventions of its parents. In the 1950s and 1960s, the baby boomers embraced a new, more liberal sexuality. On campuses, they challenged the strict conventions and regulations that had governed student conduct for centuries and began to test the codes of dress and behavior. They rejected the new "multiuniversity" that had emerged to house the expanding higher-education enrollments in the postwar era, in particular the depersonalized environment that came with it. They embraced new music styles such as rhythm and blues (R&B) and rock and roll, and they became avid consumers of this sector of the entertainment industry.

Out of the black migrants to southern and northern cities of the 1930s and 1940s came a new cultural market for high-energy dance music known as rhythm and blues. Although R&B attracted a primarily black audience, the advent of rock and roll marked a fusion of southern white "hillbilly" music with these African-American forms. One of the most successful and earliest practitioners of this new style was Elvis Presley, originally of Tupelo, Mississippi; he was followed by other southern white performers, such as Jerry Lee Lewis, Carl Perkins, and Buddy Holly. By the mid-1950s, they were joined by black performers Chuck Berry, Little Richard, and Fats Domino, whose slightly modified R&B style appealed to white audiences.

The forces behind the music explosion lay in both economic and cultural changes in postwar American society. The delivery system for the developing recording industry was radio, which in the 1950s fueled the rock-and-roll explosion. By the end of the decade, television played a major role as well. In 1957, Dick Clark inaugurated his highly successful *American Bandstand*, which displayed visual images of the new performers to even greater audiences. But clearly rock and roll was part of the cultural changes sweeping through the baby boom generation. R&B and rock and roll were musical styles that embodied the urge to rebel and defy convention: they were, at least for their time, openly sexual, and they parodied the domesticity of the 1950s family.

The musical rebellion of the 1950s, with the emergence of the Beats, was joined by rebellion at another level. Emerging out of metropolitan cultural centers such as New York and San Francisco, the Beats strongly rejected postwar American cultural norms. They embraced bohemianism and self-discovery. They appeared in public forums denouncing public morality with one hand and brandishing a brandy flask with another. They actively sought fulfillment through physical pleasure, whether through drinking, experimentation with drugs, or sexual promiscuity. A leader of the Beats was the poet Allen Ginsberg, whose verse epitomized the entire Beat generation. Jack Kerouac's *On the Road* described the new lifestyle of the Beats and became a kind of bible for that generation. By the early 1960s, Beat ideas had spread to well-defined cultural pockets across the nation. In coffeehouses, student gathering spots, and jazz clubs, the language of liberation from conventions was having an extensive cultural impact.

The emergence of rock and roll and of the Beats during the 1950s set the stage for other changes in the early and mid-1960s. To many Americans, the defiant styles of Jerry Lee Lewis and Elvis Presley were deeply disturbing, as were what was, to them, the incomprehensible nihilism of Ginsberg and Kerouac. More assuring were crooners such as Frankie Avalon, Paul Anka, Bobbie Vinson, and Fabian, who muted the original driving message of early rock and roll. By 1963, however, the apparent calm was destroyed. Bobbie Zimmerman, who became Bob Dylan, offered a new message and medium: rebellion that drew on the folk music traditions of protest and social critique of Woody Guthrie and Pete Seeger. Dylan's ballads became ballads for a leftist commentary that criticized racism and the cold war and embraced a new insurgency. Dylan's "The Times They Are A-Changin' " became a ballad for an entire generation.

The musical style of Dylan and other folk music balladeers who followed him, such as Joan Baez, was matched by a biting cultural critique offered by a new wave of rock and rollers. From Britain came new bands that had developed their style from R&B and rock and roll but were also forming a distinctive sound. The Beatles were by far the most successful of the British rock and rollers, and their arrival in the United States in 1964 set off a storm of enthusiasm for their music. They were joined by a new "British invasion" by the mid-1960s that included the Rolling Stones, the Kinks, and the Who. In their first introduction, the music of these British bands was complacent and reassuring; the Beatles' early harmonies performed before American audiences offered variations on Fabian's croonings. In contrast, the Rolling Stones offered a more disturbing message of conflict and discontent; their song "I Can't Get No Satisfaction" embodied this message.

In the mid-1960s, rock and roll, although a highly commercialized, multibillion-dollar industry, was expressing a message of youth revolt. In some cases, the lyrics of rock musicians directly paralleled the message of the New Left: the Beatles, the Rolling Stones, and a California group, the Jefferson Airplane, included a theme of revolution. In some cases there were even direct connections between music and the New Left; Bob Dylan, for example, once sat in on an SDS meeting and offered to participate in an ERAP project, while other musicians lent some support. Yet, for the most part, the revolution rock musicians had in mind was more a cultural than a political revolution, and its roots lay more with Jack Kerouac than they did with C. Wright Mills. The cultural revolution that rock music came to exemplify appeared first in cities such as San Francisco, New York, and London. There and on the campuses, the counterculture offered a message of rejection of traditional middle-class respectability. It also rejected war, but less in a political than in a cultural sense. "Coming together" and "love" were the catchwords; in the era of the Vietnam War, "Make love, not war" became a commonplace. That message ultimately was to reject conventionality by withdrawing from it; marijuana became the drug of choice for scores of Americans on campuses and elsewhere, while hallucinogens such as mescaline and LSD became more widely available. The counterculture that emerged in the 1960s thus carried a mixed message. On the one hand, it embraced the language of the New Left, sharing with it a rejection of middle-class conventionality and joining in a vague call for "revolution." But Timothy Leary's call for Americans to "Tune in, turn on, and drop out" also implied a quiescence about worldly affairs and an urge to withdraw from an outer world of turmoil to an inner world of calm.

PART SIX

Troubles and Transformations, 1968–1992

CHAPTER 30

The Constitution Imperiled

The early years of the Nixon presidency seemed to signify the beginning of a new era in American politics. The GOP, extending earlier inroads made by Eisenhower and the Republicans, recorded a triumph in 1968 which was more decisive than the small margin of difference between Nixon and Humphrey might suggest. Most persons who voted for George Wallace were, for the future, probable Republican rather than Democratic voters—a bad omen for subsequent Democratic presidential candidates. Moreover, especially in national contests for the presidency and the Senate, Republicans found new strength in an anxious "silent majority" of disaffected blue-collar workers, southern whites, middle- and lower-middle-class urban dwellers, and traditional Republican voters in the Middle and Far West.

In his first term, Nixon moved to solidify this new coalition. At least in his rhetoric, he appealed to strong desires among Americans for patriotism, stability, and law and order. At the same time, he identified his Democratic opponents as responsible for the tumultuous changes of the 1960s. He criticized the extension of the welfare state under Johnson and proposed to restrict the growth of the federal government. Finally, he promised limitations on the civil rights revolution by opposing school desegregation efforts that involved massive "forced" busing. Ultimately, however, a wide gap existed between the rhetoric and the reality of the Nixon presidency. Promising stability, Nixon brought further unrest and disorder through the impact of his political personality. He promised limits to big government and brought a steady expansion in welfare and regulatory federal intervention. He promised law and order and displayed a calculated disrespect for law and constitutional probity unequaled in American history.

1.   THE NIXONIAN PERSONA

The Nixon years brought a confused combination of hope and despair, idealism and cynicism at least partly because of the elusive and perplexing personality of Richard Milhous Nixon. Born on a farm in Yorba Linda, California, on January 9, 1913, Nixon was a self-made man. He grew up in nearby Whittier, where he worked long hours in his parents' grocery store and, from an early age, exhibited a driving ambition. He was graduated from Whittier College and Duke University Law School and practiced law in the Whittier area until World War II, when he entered military service as a naval supply officer. Ambition led him into politics; in 1946, he ran for Congress as a Republican in California's twelfth district and defeated Democratic incumbent Jerry Voorhis.

Soon Nixon was a figure with a national reputation as an ambitious, vigilant anti-Communist. As a young congressman serving on the House Un-American Activities Committee, Nixon earned this reputation in his aggressive performance as the chief inquisitor in the Alger Hiss case. Nixon ruthlessly exploited the Communist issue. Having depicted Voorhis, a liberal Democrat, as pro-Communist, Nixon ran for the Senate in 1950 by painting his Democratic opponent, Helen Gahagan Douglas, as at least sympathetic with subversives. His reputation as an able, hard-line anti-Communist in 1952 persuaded GOP strategists that he would make a good running mate for General Eisenhower. Nixon's subsequent career displayed not only political ability and ambition but also stubborn persistence. After eight years as Eisenhower's vice-president there came the narrow loss to John F. Kennedy in the presidential election of 1960—and then apparent oblivion two years later with his decisive defeat in the California gubernatorial election. But the tireless Nixon transferred his base to New York and rebuilt his political standing to the point where he could seek and capture the GOP nomination in 1968. His ensuing victory over Humphrey marked one of the most spectacular political comebacks on record.

Nixon's inauguration in January 1969 thus was a moment of triumph for this driven man. His rise was a triumph also of a pure political opportunist—of a man who had mastered politics and, in particular, the political language of television. As a policy maker, the new president would show little attachment to any fixed principles and would instead pragmatically employ a variety of solutions in domestic policy. But, for Nixon, the long road to power had created a political personality mired in contradictions. Genuinely believing in hard work, thrift, and individualism, Nixon also had an obsessive need for approval and a paranoid suspicion of his enemies. He was a secretive, private, and lonely man, aloof and remote from all except a small inner circle of family and close associates. Easily hurt, and prone to lash back in anger and reveal too much of himself, he had practiced the discipline of self-control until it became a mask that sometimes quavered but rarely slipped. Wariness and defensiveness seemed to inform his every public gesture, every smile, every glance. No previous president had guarded or shielded himself so closely.

Nixon's cabinet included both moderates and conservatives, with an accent upon experienced men from a variety of business, academic, legal, and public service backgrounds. For secretary of state, Nixon chose his longtime adviser William P. Rogers, while the new secretary of defense was the veteran GOP congressman Melvin R. Laird of Wisconsin. David M. Kennedy, a prominent Chicago banker and believer in monetary restraint, was named secretary of the treasury. The president's erstwhile law partner, John N. Mitchell, a conservative, became attorney general. Even more important—given Nixon's obsessive need for privacy and secrecy—was the inner circle at the White House: Henry A. Kissinger, special adviser on foreign policy; John Ehrlichman, special adviser on domestic affairs; and H. R. Haldeman, White House chief of staff.

2.   DOMESTIC POLICY, 1969–1972

Given Nixon's concern with foreign affairs and the control of Congress by the opposition party, it is not surprising that domestic legislative accomplishments were modest during Nixon's first term. Rather than curtailing the social welfare programs of the Great Society, Nixon's administration supervised a moderate extension of them. Social Security benefits were increased and liberalized by enactments in 1969, 1971, and 1972. Production of federally subsidized housing for low- and middle-income families proceeded at a brisk pace.

Similar moderation on domestic policy was also evident in the area of environmental protection. By the late 1960s and early 1970s, an environmental movement had emerged. In 1962, Rachel Carson's *Silent Spring* documented the damage which the pesticide DDT had inflicted on the environment. In states and localities, Americans had begun to demand greater regulation over pollution and the deterioration of the environment. This grass-roots movement culminated with the organization, on April 22, 1970, of the first annual Earth Day. In this context, Nixon's record became moderately proenvironmental. In 1969, his administration issued an order banning the use of DDT. In the same year, Nixon signed the National Environmental Policy Act. Subsequently both the Environmental Protection Agency (EPA) and the Occupational Safety and Health Administration (OSHA) were established.

Nixon experienced less success in other areas of domestic policy. Two of his most innovative proposals—the family assistance plan and revenue sharing—became embroiled in partisan and ideological conflict in Congress. The family assistance plan was designed to provide a minimum income for all families with dependent children ($1,600 for a family of four). Soon, however, the proposal was caught in a cross fire between conservatives, who objected to the proposed increase in total welfare costs, and liberals, who maintained that the minimum income figures were unrealistically low. When a "workfare" provision was added to the scheme, the family assistance plan further alienated potential supporters. Although the House passed a family assistance bill in 1970, the Senate blocked it for the next two years. Just before adjournment in December 1971, however, Congress suddenly passed the workfare provision. It required all welfare recipients under the Aid to Families with Dependent Children program, except for a few exempt categories, to register for work or training beginning in July 1972.

Nixon's other major domestic-policy initiative—revenue sharing—encountered similar difficulties in Congress. The administration's plan called for distribution of some federal revenues to states calculated on a combined basis of population and taxable resources and for subdividing this amount between a state and its localities. Despite objections in Congress which delayed its passage for three years, revenue sharing became law in October 1972. It provided for the sharing of $30.2 billion in federal revenue over a five-year period, with $5.3 billion to be distributed in 1972 on a basis of two-thirds to local governments and one-third to the states. Although the plan was widely hailed as "reversing the flow of power" and inaugurating a new era of "refreshed and renewed" government at all levels, mayors and other spokesmen for urban areas and inner cities were soon complaining that the new system, coinciding as it did with drastic cutbacks or freezes in various federal programs, threatened to leave them worse off than before.

Both Congress and the president oscillated near the political center in other areas of domestic policy. The tendency was toward a moderate and generally flexible conservatism, with the president inclining a bit more strongly in this direction than Congress. His inclination was most apparent in the field of civil rights. The administration did move boldly in the area of job opportunity by experimenting with the so-called Philadelphia Plan, which was designed to increase the ratio of blacks and other minorities in the building trades by assigning quotas to firms engaged in federally financed construction projects. In other areas of civil rights policy, however, Nixon began a slowdown: in the kind of candidates he nominated for the Supreme Court, in several attempts to delay school desegregation in the Deep South, and, above all, in his opposition to the busing of schoolchildren to achieve integration. In January 1971, Nixon publicly opposed what he described as federal efforts to "force integration of the suburbs." In March 1972, demanding that Congress enact a temporary halt to further court-ordered busing until mid-1973, he requested that Congress, not the courts, control the practice. Although Congress delayed further implementation of court-ordered busing until the end of 1973, Nixon's plan to end judicial control was frustrated, and busing remained the most important tool of school desegregation.

Nixon's antibusing efforts enraged his liberal opponents but endeared him to a large portion of southern and northern Americans alarmed by the drastic changes they feared in their schools. In similar fashion, Nixon exploited the issue of law and order. With strong support from the White House, Congress, in 1970, enacted the District of Columbia Criminal Justice Act as a model piece of anticrime legislation. Meanwhile, the Nixon administration also increased efforts against organized crime through the use of wiretaps and other electronic surveillance equipment.

Sensing the attractiveness of law and order as a political issue, Nixon and Republicans used it in an attempt to capture control of Congress in the off-year elections of 1970. The Republicans portrayed Democratic liberals as softheaded and permissive and launched an all-out partisan attack (spearheaded by Vice-President Agnew), with occasional forays by President Nixon. Both campaigned by denouncing biased news media, rioting, "spoiled" college youth, pornography, radicals, crime, drugs, Democrats, and various other social evils. "Will Americans be led by a president elected by a majority of the American people?" Agnew thundered in September. "Or will we be intimidated and blackmailed into following the path dictated by a disruptive radical and militant minority—the pampered prodigies of the radical liberals of the United States Senate?" All in all, it was an appeal to a great "silent majority" fed up with the ills of the past decade.

At least as measured by the elections of 1970, the silent majority never quite found its tongue. Only once in the twentieth century—in 1934—has the president's party *not* suffered losses in off-year congressional elections. Republicans were also hurt by popular impatience with the Vietnam War and by the intemperateness of Agnew's assaults, and the net result of the election of 1970 was a virtual standoff. The GOP gained two seats in the Senate, and the Democrats increased their majority in the House by nine. Democrats scored even more impressive victories in state elections. They captured thirteen contested governorships from the GOP while losing only two and making substantial gains in many legislatures. The election was hardly a conservative mandate.

Partly because of Nixon's sharply partisan attack in the elections of 1970, the president and Congress were deadlocked during the remainder of the first Nixon administration. Congressional opposition was strongest on issues involving the power of the presidency. Democrats and Republicans united to oppose the confirmation of two Supreme Court nominees in 1969 and 1970. Nixon struck back after 1971 by thwarting congressional attempts to reform campaign spending and by casting two major vetoes in 1971—of a $5.7 billion public works and regional development bill and of a $2.1 billion comprehensive child care bill for preschool children. When Nixon vetoed both measures for ideological and budgetary reasons, his doing so marked the end of the cooperative relationship between the early Nixon administration and Congress.

Other issues pitted the president against Congress. Strong support was emerging, because of what was regarded as excessive executive control over foreign policy, for a reassertion of congressional control over the war-making power. There was marked recalcitrance, for the first time since the 1930s, to approve swollen defense budgets. Presidential claims of executive privilege, periodically invoked as a means of excusing members of the executive branch from testifying before congressional committees, became a source of friction. This was accompanied by a steadily growing resentment of the president's inaccessibility and remoteness and the studied arrogance and uncooperative attitude of many of his chief advisers on the White House staff.

Congress also began to realize that its control over the federal budget, and specifically over the way in which authorized sums were actually allocated and spent, was fast disappearing. On a few occasions the president calmly proceeded to impound funds already appropriated by Congress when he disagreed with the purposes for which they had been authorized. Budgetary control became a major issue in the fall of 1972, when Congress angrily rejected an administration proposal which limited federal spending in fiscal 1973 to $250 billion and empowered the president to eliminate appropriations for any program, as he saw fit, in order to stay within the $250 billion limit. Nixon retaliated by vetoing a $24.7 billion, three-year program designed to clean America's polluted waterways. When the incensed lawmakers sweepingly overrode this veto, the president struck back in the name of fiscal responsibility by pocket-vetoing eleven public works and social welfare bills that exceeded the amounts he had requested.

3. THE NIXON COURT

Two developments in 1968 seemed to suggest that the Supreme Court would soon enter a distinctly new phase. The first was Chief Justice Earl Warren's announcement that he intended to retire at the end of the 1967–1968 term. The second important development was Nixon's intention, clearly stated during the campaign of 1968, to end the activism of the Warren Court by appointing conservative "strict constructionist" justices.

More than any president since Franklin D. Roosevelt, Nixon had an opportunity to determine the Court's future. Warren had announced his retirement early enough for Johnson to nominate as chief justice Associate Justice Abe Fortas, an old friend and brilliant attorney appointed to the Supreme Court in 1965. But conservative Republicans and southern Democrats blocked his appointment. Nixon, given this opportunity to choose a chief justice, selected Warren E. Burger, a Minnesotan who had served as assistant attorney general under Eisenhower and later as judge of the Court of Appeals for the District of Columbia. Respected in legal circles, Burger had a reputation as a strict constructionist prepared to interpret the Constitution with rigor and caution. Quickly confirmed by the Senate in January 1969, the new chief justice presided at the opening of the 1969–1970 term.

Nixon soon had an opportunity to appoint another justice when, in 1969, the disclosure that Fortas had accepted an annual fee of $20,000 from a private foundation (whose head was under prosecution in federal court) forced him to resign. Nixon, determined to appoint another strict constructionist, also hoped to appoint a Southerner to the bench as a way to strengthen his support in the South. But when he nominated Clement Haynsworth, a federal circuit court judge from South Carolina, opposition arose because of Haynsworth's conservative opinions in labor and civil rights decisions. Haynsworth's nomination took a turn for the worse when the Judiciary Committee learned that Haynsworth, an active stock investor, had financial ties with litigants in cases over which he had presided. Notwithstanding administration pressure, the Senate rejected the Haynsworth nomination in November 1969 by a vote of fifty-five to forty-five.

Nixon, stung by the Senate's refusal to approve Haynsworth and still determined to appoint a conservative Southerner, nominated G. Harrold Carswell, a Florida circuit judge. Soon objections to the Carswell nomination arose because of his racial views and because of his general reputation for mediocrity. By a vote of fifty-one to forty-five, in April 1970 the Senate again rejected a Nixon nominee—the first time a twentieth-century president had been twice rebuffed on Supreme Court appointments. Nixon then nominated a more capable strict constructionist, Circuit Court Judge Harry A. Blackmun of Minnesota, whom the Senate confirmed unanimously in May.

In 1971, the retirement of two more justices, John M. Harlan and Hugo Black, gave Nixon another opportunity to strengthen the conservative presence on the Court. Nixon's choices—Lewis F. Powell, Jr., of Virginia, a respected corporation lawyer and former president of the American Bar Association, and Assistant Attorney General William H. Rehnquist of Arizona—were quickly confirmed. With Powell and Rehnquist joining Blackmun and Burger as moderate conservatives, the Nixon Court moved away from judicial activism. Yet the Nixon Court, rather than ending activism, only slowed and moderated it. Almost all of the tribunal's major opinions not only reaffirmed the Warren Court's precedents but in some areas also extended and broadened them.

In the field of civil rights, for example, the Court under Burger guarded minority rights and reinforced school desegregation. Contravening the Nixon administration's attempts to delay desegregation, the Court, in *Alexander* v. *Holmes County Board of Education* (1969), unanimously ordered an end to all school segregation "at once." In *Swann* v. *Charlotte-Mecklenburg Board of Education* (1971) and four related cases, the Court approved massive busing to achieve desegregation.

While continuing the Warren Court's activism, the Burger Court was moderate, even cautious and conservative, in two areas of civil rights. In school desegregation cases, civil rights lawyers argued—and found a receptive audience in the lower courts—the need to merge school districts as a way, along with busing, to achieve racial balance. Soon, the Supreme Court sent an important message. In *School Board of Richmond* v. *State Board of Education* (1973), the Court upheld an appellate court ruling that had blocked the proposed merger of Richmond school districts. Even more decisively, in *Rodriguez* v. *San Antonio Independent School District* (1973), the Court ruled that, in local taxation and appropriations for schools, disparities between rich and poor districts did not violate the equal protection clause of the Fourteenth Amendment.

The high bench displayed similar restraint in moderating Warren Court decisions in the area of women's rights. In three important cases—*Phillips* v. *Martin Marietta* (1971), *Reed* v. *Reed* (1971), and *Drewrys Ltd.* v. *Bartmess* (1972)—the Court began to affirm the extension of equality under the law to women under Title VII of the Civil Rights Act of 1964, as well as to other disadvantaged groups. In what became its most controversial decision, the Court under Burger ruled, in *Roe* v. *Wade* (1973), that a state could not constitutionally prevent a woman from having an abortion during the first six months of pregnancy. At the same time, however, the Court refused to go beyond moderate protection of the legal and economic status of women. In January 1973, it refused to rule whether sex discrimination, per se, was unconstitutional, and it therefore refused to extend to women the full protection of law—until and unless an equal rights amendment was passed.

The Supreme Court's shift from activism to restraint was more evident in the complex field of criminal law and procedure. Earl Warren, in his last year as chief justice, combined with a majority of the Court to extend Bill of Rights restrictions to the states in *Benton* v. *Maryland* (1969) and *Chimel* v. *California* (1969). Altogether, during Warren's final term, the Court decided against the prosecution in eighteen out of twenty-six appeals involving criminal law and procedure.

The new Court, clearly departing from this tradition of activism, ruled for the prosecution in eighteen out of twenty-nine criminal law decisions during the 1969–1970 term. In a series of decisions, the Burger Court restricted the rights of alleged criminals and attempted to expand the powers of law enforcement agencies. In *Williams* v. *Florida* (1970), it held that a six-person rather than a twelve-person jury would meet the requirements of the Sixth Amendment in noncapital cases. In *Johnson* v. *Louisiana* (1972), it upheld state laws abandoning the requirement of a unanimous jury vote in criminal convictions. And in *Milton* v. *Wainwright* (1972), it held that a confession obtained by unconstitutional means would not invalidate a conviction if there was enough legitimate evidence of guilt to sustain the original verdict.

While attempting to implement greater moderation for criminal procedure cases, the Burger Court carefully protected, and even expanded, the Court's protection of civil liberties. In the landmark case of *Furman* v. *Georgia* (1972), it said that inconsistently imposed death penalty statutes—which tended to fall more frequently upon the poor and minorities—were an unconstitutional violation of the Eighth Amendment's prohibition of cruel and unusual punishment.

(At the same time, the Court made clear that *Furman* was a procedural ruling which did not outlaw an equitably administered death penalty.) In two other important decisions, moreover, the Court imposed restrictions on the government's ability to spy on Americans and its ability to control information. In *United States* v. *U.S. District Court, Eastern Michigan* (1972), an opinion written by Powell held that wiretapping was not constitutional without authorization by a court order. And, in *New York Times* v. *United States* (1971), the Court held that that newspaper's publication of the Pentagon Papers—a highly classified governmental study of the Vietnam War—could not be restrained by the government.

4.   GROWING ECONOMIC PROBLEMS

The atmosphere of conflict and uncertainty which characterized Nixon's relations with Congress, his posture toward the press, and his conduct of the Vietnam War (see pp. 707–711) was accentuated by the sudden emergence by 1972 of a host of troubling economic problems. By then the quarter-century era of economic growth and prosperity after World War II had come to an end, and at least two new factors brought instability and uncertainty to the performance of the American economy. One was the end of cheap energy and the beginning of almost a decade, after 1973, of steady price increases paid by oil-consuming nations to oil-producing nations. The other was the growing prosperity of Western Europe and Japan and the increased ability of their industries to compete with those of the United States even in the American market itself.

Rising energy prices, the higher cost of food and raw materials, and a rate of productivity growth which slowed to a crawl caused a persistent problem of the 1970s: a steady rise in the Consumer Price Index. The Vietnam War, and the heightened demand for goods and services it caused, overstimulated the economy and generated slow but steady increases in prices after 1966. By the early part of Nixon's first administration, inflation had become a matter of great public concern. The 7.7 percent growth in the GNP in 1969 was accounted for entirely by price increases rather than gains in real output. During that year, the average worker's real spendable earnings actually declined. Inflation continued unchecked during 1970 and much of 1971 at a rate of 4 to 5 percent a year. Meanwhile, in a baffling development, unemployment rose from 3.5 percent in December 1969 to 6.2 percent a year later—the highest level in nearly a decade—and the United States faced the onset of severe recession simultaneously with continued inflation.

The administration first responded by reducing spending and curbing the money supply to slow the pace of economic activity. But, primarily because of the monetary constriction, interest rates shot up to the highest point in a century, depressing the housing and automobile industries. In further antiinflationary moves in 1969 and 1970, the government raised certain taxes and effected large cutbacks in defense spending and missile and space projects. When these policies seemed by 1971 to have caused a recession, Nixon responded by pronouncing himself a Keynesian and deliberately permitting an unbalanced federal budget in the hope of stimulating economic recovery. Although the result was budget deficits of $23 billion in 1971 and 1972, the economy did not recover until late 1972, and both 5 percent inflation and 6 percent unemployment persisted through the spring and summer of 1971.

In the summer of 1971, Nixon, in a dramatic reversal, began an economic policy which startled his conservative supporters. In August, he announced a broad new program of economic stabilization. To begin with, the administration imposed a three-month freeze on prices, wages, rents, and dividends. Phase Two, initiated in November 1971, imposed a system of controls to be administered by a price commission and a pay board and set maximum guidelines of 5.5 percent for most wage increases and 2.5 percent for price and rent increases. When Nixon ended Phase Two in January 1973 and replaced mandatory with voluntary wage and price controls, the results of his anti-inflation program were far from clear. However, by the autumn of 1972, a booming economy had brought recovery in major manufacturing industries and lowered the unemployment rate from 6 percent to 5.5 percent.

An international monetary crisis in the summer of 1971 paralleled the growing prominence of economic problems at home. Although the United States enjoyed an uninterrupted annual trade surplus between 1893 and the 1960s, a number of factors after 1945 assumed increasing importance. Despite the annual trade surplus, payments for imports, foreign aid, military expenditures abroad, amounts paid to foreign shipping, tourist spending, private overseas investments, and earnings on foreign investments in the United States often matched and sometimes exceeded the total annual income from exports, American shipping earnings, foreign travelers and investments in the United States, and returns on American investments abroad. Deficits in this overall balance of payments produced a momentary loss of confidence in the American dollar and a drain of gold reserves from a postwar high of $25 billion to a low of $10.5 billion in 1971.

But the trade deficit was the product of another, more important factor: the eroding position of the American economy relative to the expanding economies of Western Europe and Japan. Underwritten by postwar American aid, the Western allies, particularly the defeated enemies West Germany and Japan, were beginning to compete successfully with American steel, automobiles, and consumer goods. As productive efficiency in these nations grew, American goods became subject to increasing competitive pressure in the world market. At first the pinch could be felt in items of low unit costs—such as shoes, clothing, and textiles—for which labor differentials were a major factor. Then, more painfully, foreign goods began elbowing American goods off the shelf—both in the international and the domestic market—in steel, photographic equipment, television sets and other electronics items, aircraft, and automobiles. The American product, frequently matched or surpassed in quality by the foreign output, was placed at a further disadvantage by the effects of inflation. In early 1971, a trade deficit was recorded for the first time in nearly eighty years. Soon, the trade deficit sparked a conversion crisis, in which domestic and foreign investors stampeded during the summer of 1971 to convert dollars into other currencies and, in the process, further hastened the dollar's decline.

Nixon responded on August 15 by ending convertibility into gold and imposing a 10 percent import surcharge. Representatives from Western industrialized nations then met at the Smithsonian Institution in Washington and produced an interim agreement. It provided for the devaluation of the dollar by 8 percent and an upward revaluation of other currencies. Under the agreement, the dollar remained unconvertible into gold, while currencies were allowed to fluctuate against each other in value. In exchange for reform of the international currency system, the United States dropped the 10 percent import surcharge.

Yet the Smithsonian agreement soon proved to have been only a holding action. During the first year of operation with a devalued dollar, American trade and payments balances showed a persistent, nagging deficit. Because international confidence in the American economy was lacking, pressure on the dollar continued until a second devaluation of about 10 percent in February 1973.

5. THE ELECTION OF 1972

Despite conflicts with Congress, a troubled economy, and domestic discontent with the Vietnam War, Nixon and the GOP occupied an advantageous position as the presidential election of 1972 approached. Especially in an election whose main issues were of national concern—economic policy and international affairs—the coalition put together by Eisenhower in 1952 and 1956 of Westerners, southern whites, and a sprinkling of blue-collar ethnics, had reemerged in 1968. By establishing the GOP as a party of stability abroad and orderly growth at home, moreover, Nixon was politically secure in 1972.

Meanwhile, the Democratic party remained seriously divided, ridden with factionalism and scarred by the experiences of 1968, its various blocs and interests disagreeing, sometimes bitterly, over issues such as busing, law and order, and welfare. The battle for the party's nomination reflected these internal conflicts. The early favorite was Senator Edmund Muskie of Maine, who soon gathered the largest number of endorsements by state and national party leaders. Hubert Humphrey, standard-bearer in 1968, still commanded support among party regulars, organized labor, and blacks. In active pursuit of these frontrunners were Senator Henry F. Jackson of Washington, a firm advocate of a stronger defense program, and Senator George McGovern of South Dakota, chiefly known for his long record of outspoken opposition to the Vietnam War. The unknown factor was the impact of sweeping reforms in the party's nominating procedure that democratized delegate selection by opening access to activist grass-roots organizations and also by decreasing the power of party regulars.

The contest for the nomination was, from the beginning, an all-out fight. When Muskie faded in early primaries, McGovern soon became the frontrunner. Despite a last-ditch effort by Humphrey, the Democratic convention which met at Miami Beach in July was dominated by McGovern forces. Chosen under the new party rules, it contained unprecedentedly high ratios of women (40 percent), blacks (25 percent), people under thirty (21 percent), and relatively inexperienced grass-roots enthusiasts. McGovern's triumphant nomination, a stunning political upset, was due to several causes. Unlike any other of the candidates, he had strong support among the party's liberal activists—support galvanized by his advocacy of the rights of minorities, expanded social welfare legislation, tax reform, and immediate withdrawal from Vietnam. McGovern's victory also resulted from a superior organization that was well adapted to the new party rules. Energy, dedication, teamwork, and shrewdness enabled the McGovern forces to find grass-roots support, organize it, get out the vote, and capture delegates right from under the noses of startled veterans.

After refusals by Senator Edward M. Kennedy, Senator Abraham Ribicoff of Connecticut, and Governor Reubin Askew of Florida, McGovern chose Senator Thomas F. Eagleton, a Roman Catholic from Missouri, as his running mate. The convention endorsed a platform which promised reduced military spending, immediate withdrawal from Vietnam, and restricted presidential war-making powers. As for domestic policies, it endorsed full employment, tax reform, and vigorous law enforcement, and it supported busing as "another tool" of school desegregation.

In comparison, the selection of a Republican candidate was relatively easy, and in late August the GOP, whose national convention also met at Miami Beach, enthusiastically renominated Nixon and Agnew. The party also had no trouble in making clear how it differed from the Democrats. Accepting the nomination, Nixon claimed that the differing philosophies of the opposing candidates constituted "one of the clearest choices of the campaign." The platform spelled it out: the choice, it said, was "between moderate goals . . . and far-out goals of the far left." The Republican platform supported arms limitation, a volunteer army, full employment, and tax reform. It opposed de jure segregation but rejected busing to achieve school integration. It advocated equitable financing, law enforcement with equal justice, fair prices for farmers, drug control, preservation of natural resources, and equal rights for women. In foreign policy, the platform spoke of "a full generation of peace" based upon "a strategy of national strength" combined with "a new sense of international partnership." It called for a Vietnamese settlement that would guarantee self-determination for the peoples of southeast Asia and insisted that United States forces should not be completely withdrawn until all American prisoners were returned.

It soon became clear that Nixon's advantages, combined with McGovern's liabilities, made the results of the election a foregone conclusion. In spite of McGovern's apparently decisive popular mandate in the primary campaign, his nomination left serious discords between the party's moderate-centrist and liberal-left wings. Veteran party leaders, including Chicago's Mayor Richard A. Daley, still smarted over the treatment they had received at the hands of the McGovern organization before and during the convention, where they were outmaneuvered, unseated, and rebuffed. Organized labor was dissatisfied with McGovern at two levels: members of the high command were upset by his indifferent labor record and certain aspects of his program, while many ordinary workers regarded him as too far removed from their concerns.

But McGovern's greatest liability was the charge of radicalism. Although he made an unlikely radical (he was the son of a Methodist minister and a distinguished war veteran), his association with liberal activism and his identification with liberal issues—distinct advantages in the primary campaign—were distinct liabilities in the general election. Thus, his hastily put-together proposal for a guaranteed income, his support for busing to achieve school desegregation, his support of amnesty for Vietnam War deserters and those who had resisted or evaded the draft, and his desire to liberalize the laws against marijuana and abortion all stamped him as a "radical" in the public's mind.

Hampered by this image, the McGovern campaign also suffered from bad luck. McGovern had hoped to electrify the nation with his acceptance speech at the July convention, but party wrangling delayed it until the wee hours of the morning—well after the prime-time television audience had gone to bed. Even more serious was the public furor over McGovern's handling of the disclosure that his running mate, Senator Eagleton, had been hospitalized on three occasions for nervous exhaustion and fatigue and had undergone brief psychiatric treatment for depression. The McGovern staff had not discovered these facts about Eagleton before the nomination, and Eagleton had neglected to tell them himself. Thrown off balance by the discovery, McGovern wavered—first declaring that he was "one thousand percent" behind his running mate and then abruptly deciding to drop him. He replaced the Missourian with R. Sargent Shriver, brother-in-law of the Kennedys and former director of the Peace Corps and the Office of Economic Opportunity.

But the damage had been done. McGovern was caught in a cross fire of criticism. He was accused of carelessness and poor staff work, for not having learned of Eagleton's background before selecting him; for indecisiveness, in having first backed and then dropped his running mate; and for unfairness and disloyalty. It was, in short, one of those predicaments for which no right solution existed. The affair took the McGovern strategists a month to settle, precious time which they had planned to spend organizing their campaign, and McGovern's hard-working forces never recaptured the drive or confidence that had swept them to victory in Miami Beach.

Given all the political advantages that Nixon enjoyed in 1972, however, probably nothing McGovern might have done could have carried him to victory. Nixon was in an all but impregnable position. He was supervising a decreased American combat role in Vietnam, claiming an impressive number of foreign-policy triumphs, and was in office while both inflation and unemployment were declining. He adeptly sensed and then expressed the public mood. He represented stability at home and opposition to the lawlessness and the disorder of the cultural revolt.

McGovern was swimming against a powerful tide, and he made almost no headway. Among the minority who agreed with him, he did well. He spoke with earnest conviction and raised ample funds through hundreds of thousands of small contributions. He had found one potentially vulnerable spot in his opponent's formidable armor and pressed it hard. He charged that the Nixon administration was the "most corrupt in history." As proof, McGovern pointed to allegations that a $400,000 offer by the International Telephone & Telegraph Company to defray GOP convention costs was connected with an antitrust decision by the Justice Department in 1971 approving ITT's acquisition of the Hartford Fire Insurance Company.

Increasingly, McGovern hammered home the message of corruption in the Nixon administration by pointing to a break-in at the Democratic National Committee headquarters in the Watergate hotel-office complex in Washington on June 17, 1972. Seven men, including two former White House aides and a member of the Committee for the Reelection of the President (CREEP), were apprehended and indicted—and later tried, convicted, and sentenced—on charges of conspiring to obtain information illegally, breaking and entering, planting wiretaps and other electronic bugging devices, and stealing and photographing documents. It appeared that individuals connected with the Republican campaign, and perhaps with the White House itself, had been engaged in acts of espionage and sabotage against the Democratic party.

White House officials dismissed these events as a "caper" and a "third-rate burglary attempt." Although McGovern tried to make corruption an issue— during the waning days of the campaign, with increasing freneticism—most voters had already made up their minds. More impressed by returning prosperity and imminent peace, they dismissed Watergate as a species of typical political infighting.

Content with a few personal and television appearances and the strength of his record, Nixon campaigned very little. All indications pointed to a Nixon landslide, and the electorate behaved according to prediction. On November 7, 1972, Nixon and Agnew received over 47 million votes (61 percent of the total) and carried forty-nine states with an electoral total of 520. McGovern and Shriver polled about 29.2 million popular votes and won only the 17 electoral votes of Massachusetts and the District of Columbia. Nixon's margin ranked with the victories of Johnson in 1964, Roosevelt in 1936, and Harding in 1920 as among the greatest on record.

Nixon's victory in 1972 further extended the majority he had gained four years earlier. With George Wallace out of the race after an unsuccessful but crippling assassination attempt, nearly all of the Wallace supporters cast their ballots for Nixon. The same voters who supported Nixon in 1968—a silent majority of middle- and lower-middle-class white voters, blue-collar workers, ethnic minorities, Southerners, and Midwesterners—endorsed him in even greater numbers. Although closely watched by political pundits, the youth vote—eighteen-year-olds were enfranchised by constitutional amendment in 1972—had no measurable impact. Among minorities, only blacks, Hispanics, and, by much reduced margins, Jews appear to have supported the Democratic ticket.

In spite of the Nixon landslide, the Republicans made few gains in Congress. The Democrats easily retained control of both houses, picking up 2 seats in the Senate to make their new margin 57 to 43, and losing 12 in the House to reduce their majority to 242 to 192. Republicans gained 8 new southern congressmen, including 4 from the Deep South—and yet the South also sent 2 black members to Congress (both Democrats, from Texas and Georgia) for the first time in the twentieth century. The new House of Representatives would include record totals of 16 blacks and 14 women. The Democrats also won 11 of 18 gubernatorial races, increasing their total number of governorships from 30 to 31.

6.   ROOTS OF THE WATERGATE CRISIS

Returned by a decisive mandate from the American people, Nixon prepared to extend his domestic and foreign-policy accomplishments. Abandoning his acquiescence in Great Society measures, he soon made clear that his second term would attempt a sharp departure in domestic policy. His budget message in early 1973 announced the reduction or complete elimination of over one hundred federal programs in the fields of public welfare, the drive against poverty, and education. Among the programs to be phased out were the Economic Development Act, a Great Society measure designed to stimulate growth in depressed rural and urban areas, and the Office of Economic Opportunity, the coordinating agency for the network of antipoverty programs. A recent moratorium on new public housing and housing-subsidy schemes was extended. Programs for employment training, school and public library construction, regional medical care, aid to state education departments, and a planned extension of the Head Start program were a few of the other items marked for cutbacks or elimination.

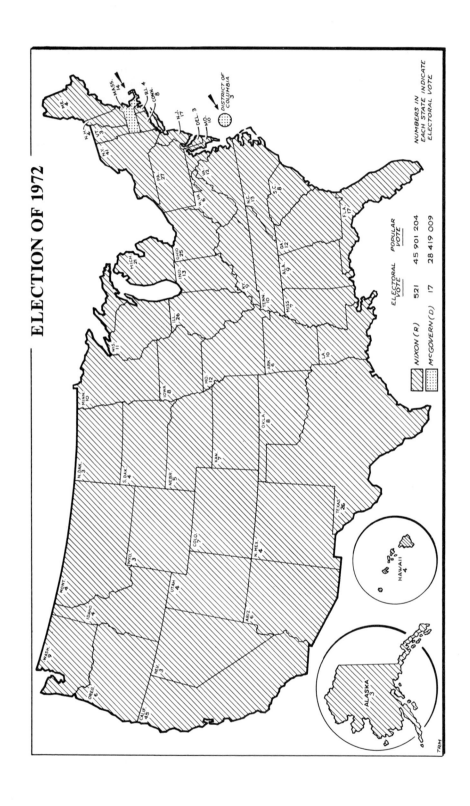

ELECTION OF 1972

NUMBERS IN
EACH STATE INDICATE
ELECTORAL VOTE

	ELECTORAL VOTE	POPULAR VOTE
NIXON (R)	521	45 901 204
McGOVERN (D)	17	28 419 009

DISTRICT OF COLUMBIA 3

ME. 4
MASS. 14
R.I. 4
CONN. 8
N.H. 4
VT. 3
N.Y. 41
N.J. 17
DEL. 3
MD. 10
PA. 27
W.VA. 6
VA. 12
N.C. 13
S.C. 8
FLA. 17
GA. 12
ALA. 9
MISS. 7
TENN. 10
KY. 9
MICH. 21
IND. 13
OHIO 25
ILL. 26
WIS. 11
IOWA 8
MO. 12
ARK. 6
LA. 10
OKLA. 8
KAN. 7
MINN. 10
N.DAK. 3
S.DAK. 4
NEBR. 5
TEXAS 26
COLO. 7
WYO. 3
N.MEX. 4
MONT. 4
IDAHO 4
UTAH 4
ARIZ. 6
WASH. 9
OREG. 6
NEV. 3
CALIF. 45

HAWAII 4

ALASKA 3

TRM

Although the need for fiscal responsibility and the danger of higher taxes and more inflation were among the reasons for this new retrenchment policy, Nixon made it clear that its rationale was, at bottom, ideological. His budget proposals, he said, would create "a leaner federal bureaucracy, increased reliance on state and local governments to carry on what are primarily state and local responsibilities, and greater freedom for the American people to make for themselves fundamental choices about what is best for them."

Yet, within a month of Nixon's inauguration on January 20, 1973, these ambitious plans had been shattered by a crisis over the corrupt use of power, the limits of presidential authority, and the ability of the American constitutional system to right itself. The crisis sprang from the involvement of key White House officials in the burglary of the Democratic National Committee headquarters on June 17, 1972. The precise motives of the Watergate affair remain obscure; nor is it clear to what extent Nixon himself was involved in its planning and execution. What is clear is that the burglary was part of a broad plan, conceived of and directed by CREEP, to monitor Democratic strategy and affect the campaign of 1972. The chief target of the break-in was the chairman of the Democratic National Committee, Lawrence F. O'Brien, whose political skills and connections were supposed to make his telephone conversations and office files worth tapping and burglarizing. In addition, CREEP had been conducting a "dirty tricks" campaign since the summer of 1971. It hired people to write and distribute slanderous letters impugning Democratic candidates, concoct misleading telegrams and newspaper advertisements that would create an impression of popular support for the president, and disrupt and discredit opposition gatherings. The scandal also involved the misuse of millions of dollars of GOP campaign funds, much of which had been raised in violation of the Federal Election Campaign Act of 1972. Large donations, including $250,000 to finance the actual break-in, had been "laundered" through Mexican banks in an effort to make them untraceable and then placed in unaudited funds that were used to support political sabotage, espionage, and so on.

Actually, these activities were only part of a larger pattern of White House behavior that began in 1969. In that year, the Nixon administration employed a small group of investigators, paid out of campaign funds, to gather information about the personal habits and finances of political opponents. From 1969 to 1971, in the name of "national security," the White House had ordered the placing of taps on the telephones of several reporters and governmental employees suspected of leaking information or, as often as not, simply of being "anti-Nixon"—all in clear violation of existing laws on wiretapping. White House aides compiled an "enemies list" and sought to harass the people on it by instructing the Internal Revenue Service to audit their tax returns. The threat of FCC action was similarly used against "unfriendly" newspapers, notably the *Washington Post*. In 1970, Nixon himself had approved an intelligence-gathering plan—the Huston Plan—that called for the use of illegal mail surveillance, wiretapping, and burglary against dissident groups by federal intelligence agencies. When FBI Director J. Edgar Hoover torpedoed the scheme, the White House organized its own special investigating group known as the "plumbers," which the White House formed in 1971 in order to find and plug security "leaks" like that involving Daniel Ellsberg and the Pentagon Papers (see p. 675). In September 1971, the plumbers—much the same crew that would later be caught at Watergate—broke into the office of Daniel Ellsberg's psychiatrist in Beverly Hills, California, in search of evidence that could be used against the defendant in his trial for theft and espionage.

The plumbers involved themselves in a variety of legal and illegal activities. In May 1972, they orchestrated the heckling and roughing up of demonstrators at a Capitol antiwar rally. A few months earlier, the *Washington Post* published an ITT memorandum documenting a connection between the corporation's $400,000 contribution toward GOP convention costs and its efforts to win approval of its merger plans. The White House then ordered a plumber to fly to Denver to persuade the ITT lobbyist Dita Beard to deny her authorship of the memorandum and denounce it as a hoax.

The plumbers' activities were part of a larger pattern of the corruption of power which lay at the center of the Nixon presidency. That the White House resorted to this variety of illegal or unethical means to protect itself suggested at least two important characteristics of the Nixon regime. The first was an isolation from, and intense suspicion toward, the public, Congress, and the print and electronic media. The second was an aggressiveness about asserting a view of the presidency which placed that office at the center of governmental power and elevated it above any constitutionally established limits. In and of itself, the June 17, 1972, burglary was only a minor part of a much larger White House plumbers political operation. But soon it came to symbolize the abuse of power—a "cancer," as White House Counsel John Dean would later describe it, which was eating away at the Nixon presidency.

7.   THE COVER-UP

Of much greater significance than the Watergate break-in itself was the White House's reaction to its exposure. From the last days of June 1972 to early 1973, Nixon and his chief lieutenants conducted deliberate efforts to impede and obstruct the prosecution of the criminals. Three days after the Watergate burglary—on June 20, 1972—White House Chief of Staff H. R. Haldeman, in a meeting with Nixon, revealed the extent of White House involvement and proposed a plan to prevent the courts or the public from finding out the whole truth. Launched with Nixon's full support, the cover-up lasted through and beyond the election—indeed, for as long as the participants could manage it.

And the cover-up led step by step into a deepening morass of illegality that threatened the constitutional system itself.

The White House succeeded at first in containing the break-in as a political issue, for the seven Watergate defendants—supported by the White House by $400,000 in "hush money" and the promise of presidential pardons—remained silent about any ties to the Nixon administration. But the beginning of their trials in January 1973 initiated a series of events which broke the defendants' silence and revealed the extent of the Watergate cover-up. When the defendants pleaded guilty, the presiding judge, John J. Sirica, announced that he was "not satisfied" with the results and that he would impose harsh sentences of up to forty years unless the burglars cooperated. Under Sirica's stern pressure, one of the defendants, James W. McCord, Jr., began to disclose the extent of White House involvement. In response, the Senate unanimously voted on February 7, 1973, to establish a Select Committee on Presidential Campaign Activities, eventually known as the Watergate Committee, with the veteran North Carolina Democrat and respected constitutional lawyer Samuel J. Ervin, Jr., as chairman.

The cover-up dam was almost at once swept away by a flood of new disclosures. By the end of April, a procession of White House intimates had been forced to resign: Herbert Kalmbach, Nixon's private attorney and veteran fund raiser; John W. Dean III, counsel to the president; Attorney General Richard G. Kleindienst; the director of the SEC and the recently named head of the FBI; and, above all, Nixon's top aides John D. Ehrlichman and H. R. Haldeman.

Nixon, publicly affirming his determination to get at the whole truth, appointed Secretary of Defense Elliot Richardson, a Boston patrician of unassailable integrity, as the new attorney general. Events followed swiftly. In May 1973, the Senate demanded, and Richardson was instructed to appoint, a special Watergate prosecutor with broad powers of investigation and subpoena. Richardson selected Archibald Cox, professor of law at Harvard and a blue-blooded Yankee like himself. While Cox assembled a staff and started to gather evidence, the nationally televised public hearings of the Senate Watergate Committee, which began on May 17, brought more and more testimony into open view. These hearings made public a sordid tale of the corruption of political power, including the cover-up with its promises of clemency and future aid as well as perjured testimony, a parade of misleading affirmations and denials, constant evasions and distortions of the truth, and a good deal of unadorned lying. The hearings made clear the White House's misuse of the Justice Department, the FBI, and the CIA. Most damaging of all, the hearings demonstrated that these activities belonged to a pattern of repeated, calculated, and systematic criminal wrongdoing of massive proportions unparalleled in the history of the presidency.

Almost inevitably, the main unanswered question in the Watergate crisis became the extent of Nixon's direct involvement in the cover-up. In June 1973, in a dramatic appearance before the Senate Watergate Committee, Nixon's former counsel, John W. Dean, directly charged that the president had knowingly conspired in the cover-up. But it was Dean's word against that of the president of the United States. And if Dean's testimony was often persuasive, it was not accompanied by proof, and the case against Nixon rested upon unsubstantiated testimony.

All this changed on July 16, 1973, when Alexander Butterfield, a former presidential aide, testified before the Watergate Committee that Nixon had ordered a taping system installed in his White House offices in early 1971 to record conversations and telephone calls. The next day, Senator Ervin formally requested that Nixon give the committee access to five of the tapes and other relevant presidential documents. Nixon flatly refused, and the committee voted unanimously on July 23 to issue subpoenas for the tapes and other materials. Meanwhile, on the same day, Special Prosecutor Cox issued a subpoena for nine of the tapes. When the White House rejected these subpoenas, the case went to district federal court and Judge John J. Sirica. Nixon's lawyers maintained that the constitutional doctrine of separation of powers provided for sweeping powers of "executive privilege" which made the president virtually immune from congressional subpoenas or court orders.

When Sirica rejected Nixon's argument in late August 1973—and when the federal court of appeals upheld the decision in October—the stage was set for a showdown between Cox and Nixon. Realizing that full compliance with the subpoena meant disaster, Nixon, facing a court deadline of October 19 to turn over the tapes, frantically searched for alternatives. One option that Nixon had long been contemplating was to exercise his authority over the special prosecutor by firing Cox.

Thus, when Attorney General Richardson was summoned to the White House in mid-October, Chief of Staff Alexander M. Haig, Jr., informed him that Nixon intended to prepare his own "summary" of the tapes for Judge Sirica and then dispose of Cox's subpoena by having Richardson, as Cox's superior, fire the special prosecutor. But Richardson, who had promised the Senate during his confirmation hearings that he would give Cox complete freedom, said that he would resign if ordered to fire Cox. Although Haig attempted a compromise by arranging for verification of the tape transcripts by Senator John C. Stennis of Mississippi, Cox continued to insist on his right to the actual tapes.

In response, Nixon ordered Richardson to fire Cox, and the "Saturday Night Massacre" ensued. When Richardson resigned rather than comply with Nixon's command, the same order went to Deputy Attorney General William D. Ruckelshaus. But Ruckelshaus agreed with his former superior about Cox; so he, too, elected to resign rather than carry out the order. It remained for the third-ranking official, Solicitor General Robert Bork, to perform the actual act. He did so only to prevent the decimation of the Justice Department by mass resignations.

8.   IMPEACHMENT AND RESIGNATION

The outcry was so strong against the firing of Cox and the resignations of Richardson and Ruckelshaus that Nixon was forced to appoint another special prosecutor, the Texas lawyer Leon Jaworski. Jaworski, granted full powers of investigation, convened a grand jury which indicted seven presidential aides involved in the cover-up and named Nixon as an "unindicted co-conspirator" in March 1974. But the chief result of the Saturday Night Massacre was that it further undermined Nixon's standing in public opinion and prompted the beginning of impeachment proceedings. Congressional Democrats, anxious to avoid haste and partisanship, decided to turn the issue over to the House Judiciary Committee with instructions to begin an "inquiry" as to whether impeachment proceedings might be in order. At the outset, this thirty-eight-person committee—twenty-one Democrats and seventeen Republicans—moved with what struck partisans on both sides as maddening slowness. Under the skillful leadership of Chairman Peter Rodino, a New Jersey Democrat, and Chief Counsel John Doar, the Judiciary Committee laid a careful groundwork. Its first task was to decide what constituted an impeachable offense, which the committee defined as "substantial"—although not necessarily criminal—presidential misconduct. Next, in a vote of the House of Representatives in early February, the Judiciary Committee was empowered to subpoena anything and anyone, including the president. Now in full motion, Doar's staff began to compile evidence and organize it meticulously.

By late February, the committee, in a major step, requested some forty additional tapes from the White House. After being pressed further with subpoenas from the Judiciary Committee and from Jaworski, Nixon responded by releasing edited transcripts of the tapes. It was a calculated risk and a bold stroke characteristic of Nixon. But it was soon apparent that the move had backfired. The transcripts released on April 30, 1974, revealed a picture of shoddy, petty, backroom wheeling and dealing in the highest office in the land. Calls came for impeachment or resignation, even from those who had been the president's staunchest defenders.

While release of the transcripts further damaged Nixon's public standing, it did not satisfy either Jaworski or the House Judiciary Committee, and, while the special prosecutor pressed his case in the courts, Rodino and Doar went ahead with the impeachment process. The president's defenses gave way completely during the final week in July, when both the Supreme Court and the Judiciary Committee reached decisions that destroyed his last hopes of remaining in office. In *United States of America* v. *Richard Nixon,* the Court upheld Judge Sirica's order to the president unanimously, eight to none. Burger conceded that executive privilege had a legitimate constitutional basis; however, the evidence being sought did not enjoy such protection. Moreover, the chief justice added, executive privilege could not "prevail over the fundamental demands of due process of law in the fair administration of criminal justice." Burger ordered the president to give the tapes to Sirica "forthwith."

Also in late July, the Judiciary Committee began its formal public debate before a nationwide television audience. By July 30, after thirty-five hours of debate, the committee had voted to send three articles of impeachment to the House of Representatives. Passed by bipartisan votes, the articles of impeachment charged the president with obstruction of justice, abuse of power, and refusal to heed the committee's subpoenas. What the president's defenders did not yet know was that their other hope of defeating impeachment—the absence of the "smoking gun" that would prove a specific criminal act—had been dashed by the Supreme Court on July 24. One of the tapes that the Court had ordered Nixon to turn over contained a conversation between Nixon and Haldeman on June 23, 1972, in which the president had explicitly instructed his assistant to have the CIA fabricate a "national security" operation and keep the FBI away from Watergate. Here was incontrovertible proof that the president had ordered the cover-up, six days after the break-in, and had sought to subvert one governmental agency in order to prevent another one from investigating a crime. It would be difficult to conceive of a presidential directive that offered more specific evidence of obstruction of justice and abuse of power.

Nixon was in San Clemente when the Court handed down its momentous decision. His immediate reaction was a resentful outburst against the three justices he had appointed—Burger, Blackmun, and Powell. However, there was no way out in the face of a unanimous Court decision. Thus the president—knowing, as no one else yet knew, that compliance would almost certainly insure impeachment and conviction—reluctantly permitted his attorney, James St. Clair, to announce that the White House would hand over the tapes as ordered. Then Nixon asked one of his aides to review the fatal June 23 tape to see if it was as bad as he feared it was. Within the next few days, while the Judiciary Committee wound up its debate and passed its resolutions, Haig and St. Clair also learned about the incriminating conversation. Both of them were stunned. They had labored beyond the call of duty in Nixon's defense. They had believed in his innocence, yet Nixon had been actively involved in the cover-up from the start. And he had lied about it—to his advisers, to the public, to Congress, even to his family—for over two years.

While Nixon himself wavered and agonized, unwilling to surrender, Haig quietly set about to convince him that resignation was the only solution. In early August, Haig conveyed the news of the "smoking gun" tape to Vice-President Ford,* cabinet members, Nixon loyalists on the Judiciary Committee, Republican

*About Agnew's resignation and Ford's appointment as vice-president, see pp. 712–713.

leaders in the House and Senate, and the White House staff. Nearly everyone felt betrayed. Nixon's remaining support, outside of a tiny corporal's guard of fanatics, simply vanished.

Meanwhile, the president was still undecided. He agreed that an accurate transcript of the damning conversation should be made public; in fact, he published it on August 5. But he accompanied it with an explanatory statement that suggested that he was not giving up. The conversation of June 23, he admitted, was "at variance" with certain of his previous statements. He had also neglected to inform his counsel or anyone else about it. He regretted this "act of omission" and conceded the likelihood of impeachment. However, he urged the Senate to look at events "in perspective" and proclaimed his confidence "that the record, in its entirety," did not justify "the extreme step of impeachment and removal of a President."

The appeal, of course, was useless. The mind of the Senate—and the country—was already made up. Haig, determined to avoid actually recommending that the president resign, now deftly arranged to have the hopelessness of the situation brought home to Nixon from a source he could not ignore. Senator Goldwater, indignant beyond measure at this last, conclusive evidence of Nixon's culpability, was already seeking to convey a demand for resignation to the White House from a group of senior Republican senators. Haig and Goldwater conferred, and, on the afternoon of August 7, the senator from Arizona, accompanied by the Republican minority leaders, Senator Hugh Scott of Pennsylvania and Congressman John Rhodes of Arizona, had a final meeting with the president. Without urging resignation—Haig had cautioned them against this, fearing that it might make Nixon dig in and fight—the three Republican leaders quietly went over the prospects. Rhodes estimated that Nixon had no more than ten supporters left in the House; Goldwater and Scott agreed that there were no more than ten or fifteen supporters left in the Senate.

In short, impeachment and removal were inevitable. Now even Nixon could see the futility of further resistance. He decided to resign. The careful Haig already had a writer at work drafting a speech of resignation. Vice-President Ford met with the president for a thorough briefing session on Thursday, August 8.

It was all over, now, except for the formalities. The resignation speech, delivered from the White House to a huge national television audience at 9:00 P.M. on August 8, was quietly eloquent, the delivery calm and controlled. Nixon admitted that he had made some mistakes in judgment and expressed regret for any harm he might have done to others. But those mistakes, he insisted, had been made in what he believed at the time "to be in the best interests of the nation." Much of the speech he devoted to reviewing his accomplishments and voicing his hopes for the future of America. At no time did he admit wrongdoing or guilt. He was essentially announcing a political defeat, saying that he had decided to resign because his "political base" in Congress had shrunk so much that he could no longer lead effectively. He was resigning, as he had always tried to govern, "in the interest of America."

On the following morning, again before a national audience, Nixon bade his staff good-bye. He visibly controlled his emotions, and the ceremony was restrained and informal. The high drama and tension had already passed. Richard Nixon, his battle ended, now simply took his leave. He strolled with his wife and the Fords in friendly fashion across the White House lawn to the helicopter that would take him to his plane. In accordance with specified procedure, Nixon had written to the secretary of state, formally announcing his resignation in a single sentence. It became effective at noon on August 9, with his plane high over middle America on its way to the Pacific coast.

The national disillusionment and sense of tragedy that had grown along with the revelations of the dimensions of the scandal during the last eighteen months of Nixon's presidency were all too real, but the final days were quietly reassuring. The American constitutional system had worked, slowly but implacably. The transition occurred without a tremor. Gerald Ford took the oath of office on schedule at noon and announced, while the nation breathed a collective sigh of relief: "Our long national nightmare is over."

CHAPTER 31

The Kissinger Years

Richard Nixon was a president who had long been fascinated by foreign affairs and was determined to reshape the role of the United States in international relations. Although he left office in disgrace over the Watergate crisis and although his policy record at home was ambiguous at best, historians will surely be generous to Nixon when they consider his foreign policy. With the help of Henry A. Kissinger—who quickly became his primary foreign-policy adviser and, by 1974, a kind of prime minister—Nixon redefined the parameters of American foreign policy for the first time since the postwar era began. Dramatic changes resulted—the first opening toward Communist China, the easing of superpower tensions known as "détente," and the strengthening of the Western alliance.

The Kissinger years were also years of failure. Nixon and Kissinger came to office facing a world of international crises in which American power and authority had steadily lessened. The challenges to American global preponderance which preceded them under Kennedy and Johnson, far from disappearing, multiplied after 1969. In Latin America, revolutionary nationalism posed a major challenge in 1970 when Salvador Allende, an avowed Marxist, was elected president of Chile. In what remained a major foreign-policy preoccupation—Vietnam—Nixon and Kissinger attempted to terminate United States military involvement in a way that would preserve America's prestige abroad and political unity at home. But in the end, they failed dismally.

1. NIXON, KISSINGER, AND THE SHAPING OF AMERICAN FOREIGN POLICY

As president, Nixon's liking for bold strokes and his affinity for secrecy and isolation found international relations highly congenial. For twenty years, Nixon had sought the presidency as a culmination of his political career, and he ardently desired to leave a permanent impact on the position of the United States in the world.

Kissinger, Nixon's collaborator in shaping a new American foreign policy, could not have come from a more unlike background than Nixon's. Born in the Bavarian town of Fürth on May 27, 1923, Kissinger, as a German Jew, had suffered from Nazi discrimination but was able to emigrate to the United States in 1938 and eventually settled in New York. The experience was one which Kissinger did not forget. America, he later wrote in his memoirs, "acquired a wondrous quality"; it became "an incredible place where tolerance was natural and personal freedom unchallenged." Later on, he was "enormously gratified" to have the chance "to repay my debt to a society whose blemishes I recognized but also saw in a different perspective."

Drafted into the American Army in 1943, Kissinger returned to Germany with the Allied occupation force at the end of World War II. Demobilized in 1947, the young veteran won a scholarship to attend Harvard University. In 1950, he earned the B.A. summa cum laude and, in 1954, the Ph.D. Kissinger soon established a brilliant record as an expert on postwar international relations. After serving as director of the prestigious Council on Foreign Relations, Kissinger achieved wide influence through several of his books, especially *Nuclear Weapons and Foreign Policy* (1957) and *The Necessity for Choice: Prospects of American Foreign Policy* (1961). Subsequently, he served as a consultant under the Kennedy and Johnson administrations and as the chief foreign-policy adviser to Nelson A. Rockefeller. Despite the fact that Kissinger had met Nixon only once before 1968, the president-elect appointed him to be his national security adviser because of his connection with Rockefeller and because Kissinger was part of the eastern "liberal" diplomatic establishment.

Although they soon developed a productive working relationship, Nixon and Kissinger never were completely comfortable with each other. The president was attracted to Kissinger precisely because the latter was part of an academic world which had scorned Nixon since the Hiss case. For his part, Kissinger was fascinated by Nixon and attracted by the opportunity for power, although he was repelled by Nixon's deviousness and paranoia. Their personalities clashed, but the ideas of Nixon and Kissinger converged as to the proper objectives, organization, and implementation of presidential foreign policy. From the outset, Nixon made it clear that he intended to lead foreign policy by circumventing the normal channels of diplomacy and policy making that involved the State and Defense departments. Doubting the loyalty of the Foreign Service since the McCarthy era, Nixon was also impatient with the slow processes required by normal diplomatic channels. Nixon was thus determined to centralize decision making inside the White House and to ignore the State Department if possible.

Accordingly, he appointed his close friend, former Attorney General William P. Rogers, as secretary of state. Kissinger concurred in Nixon's impatience with normal diplomacy and in his contempt for the governmental bureaucracy. Kissinger was also determined to centralize his control over the flow of information and decisions that passed across Nixon's desk. No sooner had Nixon's inauguration taken place than Kissinger, with the president's strong approval, began to redesign decision making in such a way as to exclude Rogers and the State Department from real power. As a consequence, all of the important decisions on foreign affairs reached by Nixon occurred outside of normal channels and were implemented by Kissinger through his own, personally controlled network.

This style of diplomacy satisfied Nixon's penchant for isolation and secrecy and Kissinger's for centralized power. It also became the main vehicle for implementing foreign-policy objectives. Convinced that the 1960s had begun an era of diminished American world hegemony, both Nixon and Kissinger believed that this was partly due to a growing pluralism in international relations. But both men also agreed that the root cause of world instability, along with the relative deterioration of American power, was the steady increase of Soviet influence, unchecked by any mechanism—or "new equilibrium," according to Kissinger—to accommodate Soviet-American competition and thus maintain global stability. To both Nixon and Kissinger, the fundamental force behind late-twentieth-century international relations remained superpower competition. Therefore, both believed that a new balance of strategic interests and the realities of power should replace traditional moral principles in American foreign policy to allow for continuity and stability in international relations.

These foreign-policy assumptions brought at least two important consequences for the Nixon-Kissinger foreign policy. First, a determined and partly successful effort began, for the first time since World War II, to reach an understanding with the Soviets and to defuse cold-war tensions which could conceivably lead to war. Second, Nixon and Kissinger reaffirmed the "bipolarity"—that is, the priority of Soviet-American competition in world affairs—of American foreign policy and extended it, even more systematically than had their predecessors, to conflicts which appeared to be primarily local. Soviet-American cooperation, rather than ending superpower competition, would simply lay out new ground rules for such competition and help to reduce the risks of nuclear holocaust. Bipolarity led to the important concept of "linkage"—that superpower relations embraced a wide range of activities, each of which was affected by the other, and that the United States could thwart the Soviet Union by selectively applying a range of penalties and incentives.

These new emphases added up to a fundamental reformulation of postwar American foreign policy. In their rapprochement with the Soviet Union, Nixon and Kissinger placed new emphasis on negotiation and arms limitation. As part of their overarching global perspective, they also emphasized the value of a new, trilateral relationship between the United States, the Soviet Union, and China. Even more dramatically, these new emphases reversed many of the most important principles guiding liberal foreign policy since World War I. Kissinger and Nixon asserted the importance of national interest as the most important part of foreign-policy making, thus discarding the historically American primary emphasis on the moral value of diplomacy. They also replaced liberal internationalism—which stressed collective security and international organizations—with adherence to the theory of a new, invigorated global balance of power that assumed stable and orderly relations between the Soviet Union and the United States. On the other hand, the Nixon-Kissinger years marked a reversal of another long-standing American principle in their clear recognition of the limitations of American power to influence world affairs. Both Nixon and Kissinger delegated considerably more power under the "Nixon Doctrine" to regional American allies. Among American statesmen for the first time since 1945, they also recognized and acquiesced in the establishment of rough nuclear parity by the Soviet Union.

2. ORIGINS OF SOVIET-AMERICAN DÉTENTE

At the center of the Nixon-Kissinger world system was therefore a new relationship with the Soviet Union. Their policy embraced two basic objectives. First, they believed that the United States should be prepared to counter Soviet expansionism and adventurism, but, because of the new realities of world affairs over which American power had less influence, American military preponderance was not sufficient. Instead, while the United States would retreat from its role as the world's policeman, it would further its own interests and counter those of the Soviets by supporting regional "proxies"—states or movements whose aims were compatible with American policy. Second, when this system of counterweights to Soviet expansionism was in place—and only then—Nixon and Kissinger would seek a new, stabilized framework for superpower competition with the USSR.

Side by side with the administration's rapprochement with the Soviets was therefore the assumption that negotiation could only take place from a position of strength or at least of parity. In 1969, there was strong domestic support for broad reductions in military spending and for continued attempts to begin strategic arms limitation talks (SALT). However, Nixon and Kissinger before 1971 opposed both on the grounds that "linkage" meant that agreement on arms limitation and access to American trade and technology depended upon Soviet cooperation in ending the Vietnam War. At the same time, they contended that progress in arms limitation would not occur unless the United States negotiated from a position of strength. As a result, the administration in 1969 endorsed a significant increase in two new weapons systems: the ABM and the MIRV. Mainly as a defense against the new Soviet SS-9 ICBM missile, the Defense Department proposed to build and deploy an antiballistic missile (ABM). It also began to test a new offensive weapon, the multiple independently targeted reentry vehicle (MIRV), a multiple warhead that could be fired from the parent missile in midflight at several targets in a kind of controlled buckshot effect. Introduction of the MIRV effectively reduced the importance of Soviet ABMs.

In the Senate, a growing number of opponents, most of them liberal Democrats, fought hard against the ABM during the summer of 1969. The Senate opposition made a strong case for discarding the ABM program because of its high cost and because MIRV technology—which the Soviets were also developing—had rendered the ABMs obsolete. In contrast, the administration made Senate support for the ABM an all-out test of defense policy and defended it as a vital bargaining chip in any future negotiations with the Soviets. In the end, the Senate passed the ABM system—by a single vote—in August 1969.

Even as he supported a buildup of new weapons systems, Nixon pursued a policy of moderate but steady reductions in conventional strength, including cancellation of or cutbacks in a variety of installations and projects. He was reinforced in this approach by changing attitudes in Congress, and particularly in the Senate, where growing numbers of lawmakers were no longer willing to rubber-stamp all proposals from the Pentagon for new appropriations and hardware. Military retrenchment went hand in hand with a frank downward revision of America's global commitments. At Guam in mid-1969, the president proclaimed a new policy, known as the Nixon Doctrine, in which the nation's role was redefined in more modest terms as that of helpful partner rather than military protector. Looking first at Asia, Nixon provided assurances that the United States would continue to honor its treaty and mutual defense obligations. But its goal, he added, would henceforth be to help Asian countries, through economic and technological aid, to assume a larger share of the responsibility for their own development and security. As a substitute for American ground troops, the Nixon Doctrine proposed to build up regional powers which would act as American proxies: in Asia, South Vietnam, South Korea, and the Philippines; in the Middle East, Israel, Iran, and, after 1974, Egypt.

Nixon later extended his advocacy of American partnership and greater self-reliance on the part of other nations to Latin America in a redefinition of the Alliance for Progress. He also made it plain to European leaders that he regarded the era of American hegemony as over, and he talked about applying the new partnership principle to NATO.

It was in the context of these changes that Nixon and Kissinger, in 1971, undertook to reshape Soviet-American relations. During the Johnson administration, the Soviets—even while they began a sustained and eventually successful effort to overcome American nuclear superiority—also sent clear signals that they welcomed the further easing of cold-war tensions. After delays in beginning the negotiations, three rounds of talks during 1971 produced an agreement that the two powers would seek to reduce the risk of nuclear war by concentrating upon limiting the number of ABMs and strategic offensive weapons. A host of other agreements followed—a total of twenty by 1972—that fostered international cooperation, trade, cultural exchanges, and even a joint space mission in 1975. Still other agreements provided for the modernization and strengthening of the hot-line communications link between Moscow and Washington.

But the most important Soviet-American accords in 1972 were two agreements to limit nuclear arms. The first, a full-fledged treaty, limited the number of ABM sites in either country to two, one near its national capital and the other at least eight hundred miles distant. No ABM site could contain more than one hundred launchers and interceptor missiles, and both countries pledged not to develop, test, or deploy further ABM systems on land, sea, or in space. Rather than providing for international or on-site inspections, long a stumbling block in disarmament negotiations between the United States and the Soviet Union, the ABM treaty permitted each side to monitor the other by "nonintrusive" means, which meant photoreconnaissance satellites. The treaty represented a recognition by both countries that a policy of mutual deterrence afforded the surest key to peace under present circumstances, and that only by prohibiting either side from working toward an effective nationwide ABM system could such mutuality be preserved.

The second accord was not a treaty but an interim agreement that put a five-year freeze on the number of strategic offensive missiles in both arsenals, including ICBMs, submarine-launched ballistic missiles (SLBMs), and modern ballistic-missile submarines. Modernization of launchers and submarines on a one-to-one replacement basis was permitted, and no limits were placed on the number of nuclear warheads or upon such programs as America's current MIRV development. As with the ABM treaty, the interim agreement relied upon mutual monitoring via satellites rather than on-site inspections. The agreement gave the Soviet Union a distinct edge in the number of missiles and submarines but recognized an American lead of 2.5 to 1 in the number of warheads. The United States Senate approved the ABM treaty promptly by a vote of eighty-eight to two but expressed concern over the Soviet missile lead sanctioned by the interim agreement (which, not being a treaty, did not require formal Senate approval). Nixon requested that Congress pass a joint resolution endorsing the agreement, so as to strengthen his hand in negotiating a full-fledged treaty after the next round of SALT talks. In complying, Congress attached an amendment sponsored by Senator Henry Jackson of Washington which urged that in future negotiations the United States should insist upon missile equality with the Soviet Union.

The ABM treaty and interim agreement were clearly no more than first steps. Certain features tending to intensify the arms race—production of nuclear warheads, improvement of guidance systems, and qualitative advances—were not only permissible but likely to continue, since each side would feel a competitive pressure to improve its strategic bargaining position in future talks. But the SALT accords of 1972 represented a genuine breakthrough in the long and generally unproductive record of East-West arms limitation negotiations. The freeze on strategic weapons did not guarantee that there would be no war, as Nixon said when he signed the interim agreement on September 30, 1972, but he called it "the beginning of a process that is enormously important, that will limit now, and we hope, later reduce the burden of arms."

Other agreements followed in the wake of Soviet-American détente. In April 1972, Great Britain, the United States, and the Soviet Union signed a convention prohibiting the production and stockpiling of bacteriological weapons. The biological weapons convention, later signed by eighty-six other nations, was the first accord of the postwar era to provide for the actual destruction of existing weapons. Conferences between NATO and Warsaw Pact nations regarding mutual reductions in armed forces were scheduled to take place in 1973. With such agreements in effect or pending and a new phase of SALT negotiations under way at Geneva, Nixon could justly point with pride to his record in the field of arms control.

There were parallel accomplishments in other important areas of Soviet-American relations. The Big Four foreign ministers were able, after thirty-three sessions over a seventeen-month period in 1970–1971, to reach formal accord on the thorny subject of Berlin, a periodic source of tension since 1945. The Quadripartite Berlin Agreement of 1971, while pledging that "there shall be no use of force in the area and that disputes shall be settled by peaceful means," provided for "simplified and unhindered" transit to and from West Germany. It also carefully defined the city's political status, the four-power presence, and regulations for visits between East and West Berlin. The Berlin accord was followed by a series of agreements between East and West Germany. After signing pacts that provided for improving the flow of traffic to and from Berlin, easing travel and visit restrictions, and granting amnesty to many political prisoners, the two German states concluded a major treaty in November 1972. The document defined and established relations between the two countries to the satisfaction of both, including pledges of peaceful coexistence and mutual recognition of sovereignty and independence. This long-awaited normalization of German relations was followed in turn by the ratification of treaties of friendship and nonaggression between West Germany and Poland and between West Germany and the Soviet Union.

Among the results of the rapprochement between the United States and the Soviet Union were Nixon's visit to Moscow in May 1972 and the conclusion of several agreements. Cordial talks between the president and the Russian leaders (which included signing of the two SALT accords on May 26) culminated in a cluster of pacts covering a variety of issues. Most important, Nixon's visit paved the way for a comprehensive Soviet-American trade agreement, signed in October. The agreement provided, among other things, for reciprocal credits, reduction of tariff levels on a most-favored-nation basis, availability of Soviet business facilities to American businessmen, and establishment of an American commercial office in Moscow and a Russian trade representative in Washington. It was estimated that the pact would result in a tripling of trade levels between the two countries, from $500 million in 1969–1971 to $1.5 billion in 1973–1975. These figures, moreover, did not include a $1 billion contract for Soviet purchases of American grain over a three-year period, authorized in July 1972. The two countries also signed a maritime treaty in October and agreed to liquidate an old lend-lease debt that dated back to World War II.

3. THE OPENING TO CHINA

Along with Soviet-American détente, the single most important foreign-policy accomplishment of the Nixon-Kissinger years was the beginning of good relations with the People's Republic of China (PRC). During the twenty years after the Korean War, Chinese-American relations remained embittered, as American presidents from Truman to Johnson succeeded in isolating China (the world's largest nation) by refusing to recognize the Communist regime, preventing the PRC's admission to the UN, and pressuring American allies to cut off economic ties. This policy was based upon the assumption that Communist China, working in conjunction with the global ambitions of Soviet Russia, was a dangerous power which threatened American interests in Asia, and that the proper response was diplomatic and military containment. It was this assumption, at least in part, that led American foreign-policy makers to regard local conflicts in Korea and Asia as part of a global Communist design.

By 1969, however, these assumptions no longer corresponded to new international realities—the most important of which was the Sino-Soviet split. Tensions between China and the Soviet Union, which were rooted both in historical enmities and in an ideological rivalry in the Communist world, were apparent as early as 1959, when the Soviets ended economic aid and withdrew their technical advisers. In the summer of 1969, the Sino-Soviet conflict took on new dimensions and new risks when armed clashes between Soviet and Chinese troops erupted along the border between the two countries.

Facing a major Soviet military threat, China began to emerge from its two-decades-long isolation, cultivate friendships abroad, and strengthen its international position. Peking made overtures to Communist, Western, and third-world nations alike, and several countries, led by Canada and Italy in late 1970, responded by recognizing Peking as the sole legal government of China and establishing diplomatic relations. For the first time, the United Nations General Assembly in November 1970 cast a majority vote (although short of the necessary two-thirds) for the admission of the PRC to the United Nations.

Nixon spoke several times, before and after his election, of his interest in opening a direct dialogue with Peking and in seeking to review and improve the relationship between the two countries. China's only response to these overtures was an agreement to resume the Warsaw talks it had broken off in 1968; intermittent conversations between the Chinese and American ambassadors to Poland had constituted the sole channel of direct communication between the two powers. The Warsaw talks duly reopened in February 1970, but American efforts to focus on relatively safe subjects like an exchange of visitors and expanded trade were met by a Chinese desire to discuss political problems, and particularly Taiwan. This last issue, along with Indochina and Korea, was the main Sino-American disagreement. Peking had never ceased to claim Taiwan as an integral part of China and hoped someday to "liberate" and absorb the island. This of course would mean an end of the Nationalist regime to which the United States remained tied by mutual security obligations and a strong sense of commitment. The Warsaw talks consequently got nowhere, and Peking discontinued them in May 1970 in protest against American military action in Cambodia.

At the same time, in other areas the interests of the two nations converged. Above all, both wanted security against Soviet expansionism, and improved relations between Peking and Washington might induce a more cooperative spirit in Moscow toward both countries. Based on these and other mutual interests, Washington made a number of overtures to Peking in early 1971, chiefly by relaxing trade and travel restrictions. The response emerged in calm and polite fashion during the spring and summer. It began with an indirect, good-natured gesture: an invitation in April 1971 to an American table tennis team to visit China and play a match with a Chinese team—the first official invitation to an American delegation since 1949. Soon after this outbreak of Ping-Pong diplomacy, the Nixon administration responded in April 1971 by ending the twenty-one-year American embargo and other trade restrictions with China. Détente emerged more tangibly from a series of private interviews between Premier Chou En-lai and a succession of American visitors, including

James Reston of the *New York Times*. Chou reaffirmed China's Taiwan policy but deftly outlined a possible agenda for more official conversations.

The breakthrough came with a secret visit to Peking by Henry Kissinger in early July 1971. The world first learned of Kissinger's trip when Nixon addressed the nation on July 15 to announce that his adviser had conferred with the Chinese leaders and had arranged for a presidential visit to China in early 1972. There would be no preconditions, Nixon added; the purpose of his visit would be to seek "normalization" of relations between the two countries. Kissinger returned to China in October to arrange the details for Nixon's forthcoming visit.

The trip took place as planned during the last week in February 1972. It was the first meeting between American and Chinese heads of state since Roosevelt conferred with Chiang Kai-shek in Cairo in 1943, and the first time that any American president had set foot in China or engaged in top-level negotiations with a country which the United States did not officially recognize. Nixon met with Mao Tse-tung on February 21, the day of his arrival in Peking. The entire American party were guests at a huge banquet that evening, at which American and Chinese officials (including Nixon and Premier Chou En-lai) mingled and drank to one another's health.

After several conferences, Nixon and Chou issued a joint communiqué on February 27 that summed up divergent but not irreconcilable views in certain key areas. Peking called itself the sole government of China and defined Taiwan's "liberation" as an internal Chinese concern. The United States agreed that Taiwan was part of China, affirmed its desire for a peaceful settlement, and spoke of reducing its armed forces near China "as the tension in the area diminishes." The Chinese placed priority upon the unification of Korea; the United States again called for relaxing tensions there. China expressed concern over the revival of "Japanese militarism," while the United States emphasized the value that it placed upon friendly relations with Tokyo. Peking's expression of sympathy for the peoples of Indochina was countered by American emphasis upon self-determination for both Vietnams and an eventual withdrawal of American forces. Having expressed itself on the issues where differences were most acute, the communiqué went on to discuss areas of agreement and proposed wider contacts in the fields of science, culture, sports, technology, journalism, and trade development. The presidential party began its homeward trip on February 28.

The spirit of the joint communiqué was soon given practical form. A delegation of Chinese doctors visited the United States in October 1972, and arrangements were made for several American editors to visit China. The Chinese government bought ten Boeing 707 transports from the United States in September and followed this with the purchase of $50 million worth of American grain. In early 1973, the two countries agreed to exchange diplomatic missions. Both Nixon and Chou, as befitted veteran negotiators, were well aware that their meeting and the events flowing from it represented a mere beginning in what would perforce be a long search for full accord and normal relations. Yet the cordiality and good will in evidence on both sides during the presidential visit were obviously genuine, and few doubted that a historic turning point had been reached and passed.

These months of dramatic improvement in Sino-American relations also witnessed a veritable spate of diplomatic action elsewhere, as other nations tacked and yawed to adjust their courses to the changing direction of the political wind. The Soviet readiness to negotiate treaties with the United States and West Germany in 1971–1972 was not unrelated to this change. In the United Nations (where the United States had finally made known its willingness to support the PRC's entry after years of blocking such a move), the enthusiastic delegates went far beyond the American goal of letting Peking join while Taiwan remained. In an emotional session in October 1971, the General Assembly rejected American resolutions looking toward "two-China" membership. Instead, by a vote of seventy-six to thirty-five, it exuberantly admitted Peking and ousted Taiwan altogether. The Nationalist Chinese seat on the Security Council, as well as its membership in the United Nations, was thus taken over by the mainland regime twenty-two years after the displacement in China itself. Great Britain established full diplomatic relations with Peking in March 1972. It also acknowledged that Taiwan was a part of China and withdrew its consular offices from Taiwan. Japanese elections in 1972 ended the long premiership of Eisaku Sato, who had stubbornly upheld Japan's friendship with Taiwan. His successor, Kakuei Tanaka, visited Peking in September and arranged for an important accord between the two countries: Japan officially recognized Peking (and its claims to Taiwan), while China, in return, dropped its demand for indemnities stemming from Japanese damages during World War II.

4. THE NIXON-KISSINGER SYSTEM AND LATIN AMERICA

By the end of Nixon's first term, Nixon and Kissinger had made significant strides toward creating what they thought would be a new era in American foreign relations. They had accepted the limits to American military power in imposing stability upon the world, and they had sought instead the creation of a working relationship with the USSR by building a network of mutually binding interests and a framework within which peaceful competition could take place. Having struck an accommodation with the Soviets by 1972, Nixon and Kissinger had also achieved a remarkable breakthrough by ending two decades of Sino-American hostility and by establishing a new, triangular relationship between China, the Soviet Union, and the United States.

Both Nixon and Kissinger believed that, with this superpower accommodation, local conflicts and threats to the stability of the international order could be limited and contained. The sources of such instability were obvious to most observers of the international scene in 1969—those areas in the Middle East, Latin America, and Indochina which had to varying degrees confounded American policy makers since 1950. The objectives of the Nixon-Kissinger policy, moreover, remained the same as those of their predecessors: to curtail Soviet opportunities for greater influence.

In Latin America, Nixon and Kissinger continued to warn of Soviet expansionism and to practice the containment of revolutionary nationalism. Cuba remained a chief source of irritation. In September 1970, American reconnaissance aircraft discovered an enlarged Soviet presence at the naval base of Cienfuegos (on the southern coast of Cuba), which amounted to a full-fledged Western Hemispheric facility for Soviet submarines. Kissinger responded by informing the Soviet ambassador to the United States that the United States would regard any "offensive" Soviet military facility in Cuba as being in violation of the Cuban missile understanding of 1962. In mid-October 1970, the Soviets reassured Washington that they had not built a military base in Cuba. A week later, Foreign Minister Gromyko assured Nixon that the understanding of 1962 would be in the future "upheld." Reconnaissance soon confirmed that construction at Cienfuegos had been halted.

Although Soviet-American détente brought tangible benefits regarding Cuba, it could do little elsewhere to contain problems and disorder of a mainly internal domestic origin. One demonstration of the inability of Soviet-American détente to reduce the appeal of revolutionary nationalism came in Chile, where a Marxian Socialist, Salvador Allende Gossens, won a plurality of the vote in the presidential election in the autumn of 1970.

Allende's election occasioned a general panic in the Nixon administration, which had been preoccupied with apparently more pressing problems in Vietnam and in Soviet-American relations. Nixon and Kissinger believed that Allende's victory might eventually bring the establishment of a Marxist-Leninist dictatorship, which would align this strategically located country with the Cuban-Soviet bloc. They were deeply disturbed at the prospects for American influence in South America. As Kissinger later wrote, Allende's election did not just concern issues like nationalization and expropriation—these had been irritants in Latin American relations for over fifty years. Rather, the main threat of Allende, according to Kissinger, was his "stated goal" of bringing about a totalitarian dictatorship and undermining American interests in the Western Hemisphere. "No responsible President," concluded Kissinger, "could look at Allende's accession to power with anything but disquiet."

The Nixon administration thus began a policy of intervention in Chilean affairs whose ultimate purpose was to destabilize the Allende administration and bring about its downfall. Actually, American covert intervention in Chilean politics was not new to the Nixon administration. In the presidential election of 1964, which Allende narrowly lost, the CIA had secretly funneled some $3 million to his Christian Democratic opponents. In 1971, the 40 Committee—an interagency White House group which supervised all CIA covert activities—attempted to prevent Allende's accession to the presidency. Once he became president, the committee provided financial support to opposition political parties and newspapers. By 1973, about $6.5 million in secret American funds had been spent in Chile.

But Allende's chief problems were his inability to prevent a dangerous polarization in Chilean politics during 1972 and 1973. Allende lacked a clear mandate—almost 64 percent of the electorate had voted *against* him in 1970. He proposed amendments to the constitution which would have consolidated greater power in the presidency, restructured the bicameral legislature into a unicameral "popular assembly," and reduced the influence and independence of the Supreme Court. At the same time, Allende attempted to stifle political and media opposition. But the most significant obstacles in the path of Allende's consolidation of power were the growing international isolation and spiraling problems of the Chilean economy. Governmental inefficiency and greatly reduced productivity, which followed Allende's policy of nationalization and expropriation, brought massive inflation—163 percent in 1972 and 258 percent in 1973.

Allende faced an economic crisis and a domestic political stalemate in which his opponents controlled the Chilean legislature. He responded with measures that further radicalized the situation. In January 1973, he imposed a new system to distribute and ration foodstuffs. In March, he promulgated an executive order reorganizing public and church-controlled elementary and secondary education. A wave of strikes by copper workers and truck drivers followed in the spring and summer of 1973, and Chile was on the verge of civil war.

In this context of increasing political and social chaos, the Chilean military intervened on September 11, 1973, and staged a coup, or *golpe*, which ousted Allende and imposed a military dictatorship. The extent of American involvement in the coup is still the subject of considerable debate. In his memoirs, Kissinger maintains that American intervention was confined to the funneling of money, through the CIA, to opposition political parties and newspapers. The destabilization and overthrow of Allende, he contends, was the product of internal Chilean revulsion against his heavy-handed attempts to consolidate political and economic control. "The United States was hardly the crucial determinant of events. It was Allende who brought the economic and political system . . . close to breakdown" and prompted the coup. Critics of American policy in Chile, including a Senate Select Committee which investigated CIA involvement in the coup, have concluded that the United States at least helped to "destabilize" the Allende regime and at most encouraged the coup.

Whatever the extent of American involvement, the leaders of the *golpe*, who believed that the overthrow of Allende would save Chile from chaos and that their actions had at least the tacit approval of the United States, unleashed a total war against all left-wing elements. Tens of thousands of Chileans were arrested or abducted and then permanently "disappeared." The Chilean democracy, long one of the strongest in Latin America, was thus destroyed in the name of halting the internal subversion of revolutionary nationalism. The coup in Chile had important implications that affected United States–Latin American relations. The Chilean *golpe* was part of a hemispheric trend toward right-wing, repressive military regimes. Thus, Uruguay (another country with strong democratic traditions) in 1973 and Argentina in 1976 both experienced social and political chaos and urban terrorism which provoked military coups. In both countries, these *golpes* unleashed "dirty wars" against not just terrorists but a wide variety of left-wing dissidents as well. For American policy, the Chilean coup was a final blow to attempts begun under the Alliance for Progress to foster nonrevolutionary democratic alternatives to Cuban-styled revolutions. At least indirectly, they were the fruition of a decade-long American counterinsurgency program which trained Latin American military personnel to suppress revolution and terrorism. Increasingly, American policy looked less toward moderate and constitutional political solutions to Latin American instability and, under the guiding assumption that East-West relations were crucial, more toward military solutions.

5. CRISIS IN THE MIDDLE EAST

On another front, the Middle East, the Nixon-Kissinger international system experienced serious testing. Israel's decisive triumph in the Six-Day War in 1967 and its conquest and continued occupation of the former Arab territories of the West Bank, the Sinai, and the Golan Heights only further aggravated Arab-Israeli tensions. During the six years after the Six-Day War, the prospects for peace grew bleak. Israel's conquests further strengthened Arab radicals and brought to power the new anti-Western regime of Colonel Muammar al-Qaddafi in Libya in 1969. In Jordan, a virtual civil war between the Palestinian fedayeen and the moderate Arab government of King Hussein brought bloody conflict, with Hussein emerging as the victor in September 1970. Beginning in 1969, moreover, an undeclared war raged between Israel and the "frontline" Arab states of Egypt, Syria, and Jordan. In early 1969, President Nasser of Egypt began what he called a "war of attrition" against the Israelis, who responded with devastating bombing raids against Cairo. The threat of full-scale war remained ever present. An American initiative and several months of negotiations with Israel, Jordan, and Egypt finally brought a genuine cease-fire in 1970, but it was little better than an armed truce.

For the next three years, Middle Eastern negotiations remained deadlocked.

Nasser's death in September 1970 apparently brought few changes, for his successor, Anwar el-Sadat, was at first unable to build up Arab unity or attract the Israeli respect needed to begin serious negotiations. Beginning in 1972, however, Sadat began to reshape the deadlocked Middle Eastern situation. In a surprise move in July 1972, he reversed Nasser's Russian alliance by expelling all Soviet technicians and military personnel from Egypt. During the next year and a half, moreover, he began plans for a coordinated attack on Israel by both Egypt and Syria. The main purpose of Sadat's attack was not to win a military victory but to shock the Arab world and the Israelis out of the stalemate of 1967–1973. As was later learned, Egypt had no serious plans even to conquer the Sinai.

On the morning of October 6, 1973, Egyptian and Syrian forces launched an all-out attack during the Jewish rites of Atonement, Yom Kippur. The Arabs fought much more effectively than in earlier contests and recorded several initial gains on both the Golan Heights (Syrian) and Suez (Egyptian) fronts. Determined Israeli counterattacks, launched first against Syria and then against Egypt, were terribly costly in men and equipment and could not have been sustained except for a massive American airlift of military equipment. The Soviets were equally busy replenishing the Arab armies, which were also supported by 18,000 Iraqis and units from Morocco and Saudi Arabia. Jordan sent troops to fight alongside the Syrians on the Golan Heights but did not open a third front.

Within a week, the Israelis had pushed the Syrian invaders back across the 1967 boundaries and were rolling their tanks toward Damascus. A few days later, although they had lost some 400 square miles of the Sinai desert to the Egyptians, the Israelis were able to establish a bridgehead on the west side of the Suez Canal and enlarge it with a sizable force. Material losses on both sides were heavy. Meanwhile, the UN, supported by both superpowers, promoted a cease-fire. A Security Council resolution, embodying a formula agreed upon in Moscow by Brezhnev and Kissinger, was approved on October 22 and tentatively accepted by the three main warring states. In the absence of a policing mechanism, however, Israel decided to strengthen its bargaining position and quickly fanned troops and armor out from the Suez bridgehead. Then the Israelis advanced toward Cairo and trapped an Egyptian army on the west bank of the canal. On the Syrian front, Israeli units pressed closer to Damascus.

Facing all-out defeat, Sadat on October 24, 1973, invited the United States and the USSR to send a joint task force to police the cease-fire. When Moscow accepted and Washington refused, a Soviet-American confrontation ensued. The Kremlin threatened a unilateral airlift of Soviet troops, and the United States responded by placing its forces on worldwide alert. Whether or not this was, as Nixon later called it, "the most difficult crisis we've had since the Cuban confrontation of 1962," the confrontation was soon over. The Security Council, supported by both the Soviets and the United States, passed a resolution calling for a seven-thousand-man peacekeeping force that would not include troops from any of the major powers. Kissinger then traveled to the Middle East and negotiated a six-point Israeli-Egyptian cease-fire, which both sides signed on November 11. The cease-fire provided for an armistice line, a peacekeeping force, an exchange of prisoners, a corridor for sending nonmilitary supplies to the besieged Egyptian Third Army, and an end to the Arab blockade of the Red Sea. The cease-fire also mandated negotiations for an overall settlement.

Thus began an intense period of Arab-Israeli diplomacy in which American mediation—and, in particular, "shuttle diplomacy" by Henry Kissinger—played a prominent role. Largely at Kissinger's initiative, Israel and Egypt agreed to disengagement talks in Geneva. With Kissinger's help, they concluded an agreement in January 1974 that called for an Israeli withdrawal to a line a few miles east of the canal, a buffer zone along this line, patrolled by UN troops, and a thinning out of Egyptian and Israeli forces for some miles on either side of the zone. This made possible the clearing of the canal, which had been closed since 1967. Kissinger, in May 1974, also engineered a disengagement between Israel and Syria. Israel withdrew from territory captured in 1973 but relinquished only a portion of the strategically important Golan Heights.

While a smaller UN force patrolled this cease-fire line, Kissinger's diplomacy began to bear fruit. Egypt, Syria, and Algeria restored diplomatic relations with the United States. In June 1974, Nixon made a visit to the Middle East, where he conferred with heads of state in Syria, Egypt, Israel, and Jordan. The Geneva peace talks, which looked toward an overall settlement, made little progress, chiefly because no one could agree upon the role to be played by the Palestinians. But American influence grew considerably in the aftermath of the Yom Kippur War. Arab nations previously hostile to the United States now welcomed its mediation. Egypt, before 1972 a staunch Soviet ally, by 1974 had completed a policy reversal under Sadat in which it eventually became the largest Arab recipient of American economic and military aid. Arab enthusiasm for the United States was marked by Nixon's triumphant visit to the Middle East in June 1974. In spite of mounting crises at home, Nixon was greeted by millions of Arabs in Egypt, Saudi Arabia, and Syria.

By no means did these new turns in American diplomacy end the root causes of Middle Eastern instability. Continuing as secretary of state under President Gerald Ford, Kissinger worked his way through a succession of setbacks and finally achieved an important new Sinai agreement between Israel and Egypt in September 1975. The UN force was to be retained, and an elaborate "early warning system" was to be set up on either side of the line to guard against surprise attacks. The United States also agreed upon aid programs to both countries, while Egypt and Israel pledged not to use force or the threat of blockade to resolve their differences. The Sinai accord was a genuine achievement. Moreover, throughout the strenuous diplomacy that followed the Yom Kippur War, President Sadat had greatly enhanced his reputation both among his own people and abroad, as a patient, courageous, flexible leader of integrity and good will.

6. THE WIDENING OF THE INDOCHINESE WAR

The greatest single challenge to the Nixon-Kissinger international system—and to any American leader since World War II—was how to end American involvement in Vietnam. Nixon and Kissinger inherited a war which was not of their own making but was rather the product of American intervention over several decades—an intervention that had culminated in Johnson's decision to engage large numbers of American combat troops in the war. Nixon won election in 1968 at least partly because of popular impatience with the American military's inability to defeat the Vietcong and North Vietnamese. And Nixon acted upon what he believed was a popular mandate to disengage American troops from this long and costly war.

Domestic dissatisfaction with the Indochinese war, which had figured largely in Johnson's decision not to run for reelection in 1968, was a dark cloud over Nixon's future. During the autumn of 1969, a nationwide moratorium on behalf of peace evoked mass participation in hundreds of cities and campuses and drew over 250,000 peaceful antiwar demonstrators to Washington in mid-November. Then new shocks and revelations began, and the antiwar mood grew louder and uglier. News of the invasion of Cambodia in the spring of 1970 touched off a wave of protest in many quarters and a virtual scream of anguish from the nation's colleges and universities. This was the springtime of strikes, arson, disruption, shutdown, and violence on American campuses. A few instances of bombing and arson—a bank here, a business office there—took place off campus as well.

Public dissatisfaction with the war also affected Nixon's relations with Congress. The Senate, having gone on record in December 1969 against military involvement in Laos or Cambodia, responded sharply to the invasion of the latter country. It repealed the Gulf of Tonkin Resolution of 1964, which had given President Johnson blank-check support for any action that he might take to counter aggression in southeast Asia. The Senate also passed a military sales bill amendment, sponsored by Democrat Frank Church of Idaho and Republican John Sherman Cooper of Kentucky, which sought to deny funds for American military action in Cambodia; the House later defeated this measure. Senators Mark Hatfield of Oregon and George McGovern of South Dakota introduced an amendment (which their colleagues finally rejected in September by a vote of fifty-five to thirty-nine) which required withdrawal of all American troops from Vietnam by December 1971. The Senate again discussed and rejected this amendment in June 1971 by a vote of fifty-five to forty-two, but bipartisan opposition to administration policy was growing.

At the same time, both Nixon and Kissinger were determined to leave

Vietnam only after avoiding a humiliating defeat for American interests in Asia. They also believed that events in Indochina were at least partly tied to super-power relations—that the North Vietnamese were susceptible to influence from their Soviet and Chinese sponsors. Based on these assumptions, American policy toward Vietnam under Nixon had several main themes. First, Nixon continued to hope for a negotiated settlement which would bring "peace with honor"—at a minimum, American withdrawal, but not defeat, and the secure establishment of a non-Communist government in South Vietnam. Nixon thus gave whole-hearted support to both the phased withdrawal of American troops as well as to the Paris negotiations begun under Johnson in 1968 and, later, to a series of secret high-level negotiations between Kissinger and the North Vietnamese. Second, Nixon and Kissinger both believed that Soviet-American détente and the opening with China would result in concessions by North Vietnamese leaders, particularly their willingness to accept something less than total victory. Third, and perhaps most important, as a way to increase pressure upon the North Vietnamese to negotiate, Nixon and Kissinger began a studied escalation of the war by increasing American bombing and by extending the war to other parts of Indochina.

The war during the Nixon years thus had three concurrent, interrelated dimensions: a military front, centered in Vietnam but spilling over into Laos and Cambodia; a diplomatic front, centered in Paris but rippling into other capitals as negotiators and emissaries hastened here and there; and a political-psychological front that throbbed irregularly across the length and breadth of the United States. The military phase was simply an extended version of what had gone on during the Johnson years, with one major difference. Under Nixon, the level of American troop strength was on the wane rather than on the rise. The American effort had two principal components. One was the process, called Vietnamization, of assigning a greater share of the military action to the South Vietnamese as their units were deemed ready and as United States ground forces were withdrawn. Second, Nixon made heavy use of American air power, tactical and strategic, in direct support of ground operations and in attacks upon North Vietnamese supply routes, bases, depots, and production centers.

Nixon also expanded the theater of war against his Vietnamese adversaries to prevent them from mounting major ground offensives. Portions of eastern Cambodia had long served as "sanctuaries" for the North Vietnamese and Vietcong, who had evacuated Cambodian civilians and operated as this region's de facto government. As a way to impair the Communist military potential, Nixon in mid-March 1969 ordered the secret bombing by B-52 bombers of sanctuaries in Cambodia. When Prince Norodom Sihanouk was overthrown in a coup in April 1970, and when the North Vietnamese responded by penetrating deep into Cambodian territory, Nixon responded with a bold invasion of Cambodia. The joint United States–South Vietnamese offensive was intended to locate and destroy North Vietnamese headquarters, sanctuaries, and supply caches in Cambodian territory used by the enemy to support offensive operations around Saigon. Some supplies were located and duly destroyed, but the enemy command headquarters eluded discovery. Terming the operation a success, Nixon withdrew the American forces at the end of June.

Meanwhile, by early 1971 Vietnamization of the war had proceeded so smoothly that ARVN commanders and their American advisers believed that a major South Vietnamese–run offensive was possible. After massing troops in its northernmost provinces, South Vietnam launched a heavy attack into Laos in February in an effort to cut the jungle trails by which Hanoi supplied its forces in the South. The operation was in part a costly setback, with some South Vietnamese units breaking in panic and others suffering heavy casualties in the face of determined North Vietnamese counterattacks. It was also partly successful, in that the military situation directly below the seventeenth parallel became more secure, and the withdrawal of American forces was facilitated.

The last major military operation involving American forces began in March 1972, when Hanoi launched its heaviest offensive since the Tet offensive of four years before. The Communists struck simultaneously in several areas and both inflicted and sustained serious losses. They captured considerable territory and routed several South Vietnamese units. But southern resistance later stiffened and regained some of the lost territory. The United States, whose military role by this time was confined to air strikes and support operations, retaliated in April by stepping up the bombing raids—hitherto in process of deescalation—on North Vietnamese installations, supply centers, and rail links to China. In an even more audacious move, the president ordered the mining of Haiphong and other northern harbors in May in an effort to cut off the flow of Soviet military supplies and equipment that sustained the northern war effort.

None of these operations had interfered with Nixon's sustained program of reducing the American military commitment while trying to negotiate a satisfactory peace. The withdrawal of American ground forces proceeded steadily, from a peak of 543,000 in April 1969 to 430,000 a year later, and to 280,000 in the spring of 1971. The president continued to announce withdrawals and reduced the total to 139,000 by November 1971 and to 70,000 by May 1972. The American ground combat role terminated that summer, with a residue of fewer than 60,000 advisers, technicians, and helicopter pilots remaining. These support forces had been reduced to 27,000 by December.

Meanwhile, progress at the Paris peace talks was slow and tortuous. After the formal talks began in May 1968, discussions were confined to bickering over the shape of the conference table and the related question of whether two, three, or four separate delegations—American, North Vietnamese, South Vietnamese, and the National Liberation Front (Vietcong)—should be present and recognized. Indeed, a principal reason for the prevailing deadlock that plagued the

Paris negotiations from 1968 to 1972 was the intractable antagonism between the Thieu government in Saigon and the NLF, neither of whom, for a time, could even admit the other's claims to valid existence.

Another issue contributing to the deadlock at Paris was a fundamental disagreement over the exact timing of and relationship between a cease-fire, troop withdrawals by both sides, an end to American bombing, and a comprehensive peace agreement. While the North Vietnamese insisted upon a total withdrawal of American forces as a precondition for further negotiation, the United States insisted upon certain conditions of its own—including the release by Hanoi of several hundred American prisoners of war—before removing its capacity to apply military pressure. The talks dragged on and were frequently stalled and occasionally broken off.

The logjam broke only through the inauguration of secret talks between Kissinger and the principal North Vietnamese diplomats, Xuan Thuy and Le Duc Tho. These secret meetings became more frequent during 1972, and from them the basis for an acceptable agreement slowly emerged. Rumors of an impending settlement flew faster during early autumn, heightened by a Hanoi radio announcement in October 1972 which claimed that the United States had agreed to sign a nine-point settlement by the end of the month. Kissinger, at a press conference, denied the deadline but told reporters that an agreement was indeed imminent. It could be reached, he thought, after one more round of private talks lasting three or four days. "Peace," the presidential adviser solemnly announced, "is at hand."

But, when Kissinger returned to Paris in November, the talks broke down because of both North and South Vietnamese intransigence. In mid-December, in response, Nixon ordered the renewal of massive B-52 bombing and mining attacks on North Vietnam "until such time as a settlement is arrived at." At the end of the month, after the loss of fifteen B-52s and ninety-three airmen killed or captured, the administration halted the bombing above the twentieth parallel. Kissinger and Tho went back to work in January and conferred in Paris for thirty-five hours over a six-day period. Reports of progress led the president to order an end to all bombing and mining of North Vietnam. Agreement was announced on January 23, 1973, and the accord was formally signed in Paris on January 27. A cease-fire went into effect in Vietnam on the same day.

In brief, the Paris accord called for the removal and deactivation by the United States of the mines it had sown along the Vietnamese coast, the withdrawal of all remaining American troops within sixty days, and the dismantling of United States military bases in Indochina. All foreign troops, including Vietnamese Communist forces, were to be withdrawn from Laos and Cambodia. American prisoners of war, together with other military and civilian prisoners on both sides, were to be released at phased intervals over the next sixty days, and the Vietcong and Saigon were to negotiate the status of various Vietnamese "political prisoners." Two truce teams—an international group composed of Canadian, Hungarian, Polish, and Indonesian observers and another who represented each of the four participant factions (the United States, North Vietnam, South Vietnam, and the NLF)—would supervise the cease-fire. An international conference that included Russia and China was to be convened to "guarantee peace in Indochina." Finally, a council composed of representatives of the Saigon government, the NLF, and the South Vietnamese neutralist factions was to organize and conduct a national election for a new South Vietnamese government, with the present Saigon regime remaining in power until this was done.

The Paris accord permitted the United States to withdraw its last troops, recover its prisoners of war, and end its involvement. But it did not end the Indochinese war. North and South Vietnam continued to grapple and maneuver for advantage in violation of the cease-fire. Although the regime of President Nguyen Van Thieu did what it could to consolidate its power in South Vietnam, time was running out for the American client state. Its hold upon the people had always been tenuous because of corruption, favoritism, an angry dismissal of legitimate opposition as Communist-inspired, and a refusal to undertake meaningful reforms. Its military capacities had improved after years of fighting, but it relied too much upon American equipment, training, and support. That support was now gone, and Congress greatly reduced the flow of aid and equipment after the cease-fire. The military situation was in a seeming stalemate in 1974, but South Vietnam's economic and political situation weakened steadily.

Hopes that stalemate and economic exhaustion might lead the two sides closer to accommodation were dashed in 1975 when disaster overtook the Thieu regime. North Vietnam mounted a new offensive in January. Thieu first announced a "strategic withdrawal" from the northern and then the central regions of South Vietnam, but the retreat suddenly became a wholesale rout. South Vietnamese army units abandoned some $5 billion worth of American equipment, ceased their resistance, and joined the masses of refugees that clogged every road in a headlong flight from the advancing enemy. Thieu stepped down on April 21, and a dissident general surrendered Saigon to Communist forces on April 30. In the same month, the Khmer Rouge triumphed over Lon Nol's Western-backed regime in Cambodia, and a Communist faction peaceably supplanted the neutralist government of Laos.

The long war that had devastated Vietnam and had taken an estimated 1.3 million Vietnamese lives was finally over, but the quality of peace was uncertain. Although no "bloodbath" took place, Hanoi reunified the country with a heavy hand and subjected hundreds of thousands of southerners to prolonged detention in "reeducation" camps. Moreover, the Hanoi government displayed aggressive tendencies in its hour of triumph. It kept troops in Laos and Cambodia and sought hegemony over all of Indochina.

CHAPTER 32

The Crisis of the 1970s

The six years that followed the downfall of Richard Nixon in 1974 were both turbulent and uncertain. Public revulsion over the Watergate crisis and Nixon's misconduct was expressed against Republican candidates in 1974 and 1976. Yet the political reaction to Watergate became as much antipartisan as partisan, and successful candidates in the decade after Watergate ran against Washington, against concentrated governmental power, and against the political establishment, Democratic as well as Republican.

These were not happy years, either for the American people or for American political leaders. It was a period during which presidents enjoyed neither sustained popular support nor the cooperation of Congress, and executive leadership was weaker than it had been since Herbert Hoover. Throughout the 1970s, despite overwhelming Democratic dominance in Congress, partisan control over policy making declined as the influence of well-organized, usually single-issue interest groups grew. The domestic economic and international challenges continued to erode Americans' faith in their government and in the ability of policy makers to lead it.

1. THE FORD INTERLUDE

The inauguration of Gerald Rudolph Ford, Jr., on August 9, 1974, was greeted with relief. Nixon's resignation was widely hailed as a vindication of the ability of the American constitutional system to right itself. Gerald Ford had become vice-president in December 1973 and president in August 1974 primarily because he was a GOP loyalist. In August 1973, Spiro Agnew was charged with receiving bribes from Baltimore contractors before and after he was vice-president, and, in a plea-bargained settlement, he resigned his office on October 10, 1973. Nixon chose Ford as the first unelected vice-president in American history because Ford was a GOP loyalist who commanded strong congressional support.

Born in Omaha, Nebraska, on July 14, 1913, Ford grew up in Grand Rapids, Michigan. In 1935, he graduated from the University of Michigan, where he was a star football player. Ford worked his way through Yale Law School and received his law degree in 1941. He returned to Grand Rapids to enter private practice and enlisted in the navy after Pearl Harbor. In 1948, he was elected to the House of Representatives as a Republican from Michigan's fifth district, and he went on to win thirteen consecutive terms. As a congressman, Ford, if not particularly brilliant, was distinguished by hard work, party loyalty, and service on several important committees. Steadily advancing in the GOP leadership, he was elected House minority leader in 1965.

Ford represented what was in 1974 the mainstream of the Republican party—internationalism, strong support for Nixon's Vietnam policy and détente, and moderate conservativism on domestic issues. Not surprisingly, the Ford presidency was a caretaker administration, dominated by Nixon's main advisers and policies. A stalemate in domestic politics resulted from two problems. One was the continuing deadlock between a Republican president and a Democratic Congress, which stemmed partly from philosophical differences and partly from the rebellious, angry mood that Nixon and Watergate had engendered on Capitol Hill. The second problem was a troubled economy for which no satisfactory or readily agreed-upon solutions existed.

The harmony and good feeling which accompanied Ford's inauguration ended abruptly on September 8, 1974, when Ford announced that he was granting Richard Nixon a "full, free and absolute pardon" for any crimes that the former president "committed or may have committed" during his term of office. The White House also announced an agreement giving Nixon custody of his presidential papers—including the notorious tapes, which were to be destroyed after his death. This news came a bare month after Nixon's resignation, sparked a national uproar, and cost Ford considerable support and good will. Despite Ford's insistence that there had been no advance bargain or deal between himself and Nixon about the pardon, Ford's administration was tainted by its association with Watergate. Although the uproar eventually subsided, Ford never regained the bipartisan support that he had enjoyed before the pardon.

Congress soon seized the initiative. A new campaign finance bill, signed by Ford in October 1974, established contribution limits of $1,000 for individuals and $5,000 for organizations in campaigns and provided public financing of presidential elections. Yet election reform, while eliminating some abuses, provided room for abuse—particularly for much heavier spending in congressional campaigns in the late 1970s and for the rise of independent, single-issue political action committees (PACs). Because it made candidates more dependent than before on small contributions, the law encouraged the development of a computer-based technology of direct-mail solicitation of contributors. Although some candidates mastered the new science of political campaigns, the main beneficiaries were single-issue interest groups. In subsequent elections, PACs—with the blessing of the Supreme Court—were able to circumvent the spending limitations of the legislation of 1974.

In two areas—impoundment of congressional funds and war powers—Congress and the courts also asserted greater power over the president. Several lower-court decisions in 1973 and 1974 ruled against specific presidential acts that withheld funds, but no one regarded the issue as settled until a ruling could be had from the Supreme Court. In *Train* v. *New York* (1975), that tribunal held that Nixon had lacked the authority to impound $9 billion appropriated by Congress for sewage treatment plants, and it thus ended the impoundment issue. Under Nixon, Congress asserted greater control over war making with the passage, over a presidential veto, of the War Powers Act in November 1973. The measure required the president, within forty-eight hours of any commitment of American forces to hostile action overseas, to report all the circumstances and details of such action to Congress and to cease the operation within sixty days unless Congress specifically approved it.

But the most telling repudiation of presidential leadership came in the congressional off-year elections of 1974. Although Ford campaigned hard for his party, the Democrats scored impressive victories on all levels. They gained 43 new seats in the House and 4 in the Senate and enlarged their majorities to 291–144 and 61–38 respectively. Democrats even elected a senator from Vermont, for the first time in the state's history. They made a net gain of four governorships, including California and New York, and added to their strength in many state legislatures. Voter turnout was low (38 percent), even for a midterm canvass, which suggested disillusionment with government and elected officials. Widespread independent voting and ticket splitting reinforced a long-standing trend away from party regularity. The new Congress was more liberal than the old one: several conservatives in both parties retired or went down to defeat, while moderates and liberals won handsomely. It was also the youngest Congress to be elected since World War II. The voters had spoken, but their message remained unclear. Although many of the new congressmen elected in 1974 were liberal Democrats, the public mood had not swung leftward. More than anything, voters wanted to exorcise Watergate by voting against Republican incumbents.

2. FORD AND THE ECONOMIC CRISIS

Ford's political problems were compounded by a worsening economy. After holding fairly steady during 1972, prices rose sharply thereafter. Inflation became so bad during the spring of 1973 that Nixon ordered a sixty-day freeze of consumer prices in June, followed by a system of "phased" or modified controls that tied price increases to cost increases and retained a flexible 5.5 percent guideline for wage increases.

When Congress allowed this system to expire in 1974, it was clear that inflation had not abated. If anything, it had been exacerbated by wage and price controls. A major factor in stimulating inflation was the increase in petroleum prices charged by OPEC nations. By January 1974, within a space of less than three months, the price of oil had quadrupled. This brought a huge shift of hundreds of billions of dollars to oil-producing nations and fueled inflation around the world. Actual shortages were brief and temporary—Arab nations had lifted their embargo by the spring of 1974, and supplies were back to normal—but more damaging was the increase in price. Other prices rose with oil prices. Virtually every economic calculation had to be recast.

In the United States, the "oil shock" of 1973–1974 had a profound impact. Its first effect was to accelerate inflation into a double-digit range. Then, in late 1974, the worst recession of the postwar era began. Key industries, such as automobiles, steel, and construction, experienced lean times. Unemployment reached 9.2 percent in May 1975, the highest rate since the Great Depression; the level was even higher among industrial workers, minorities, and young people. Although there were signs of recovery by the end of 1975, the economy was still wobbly from the effects of the rise in oil prices.

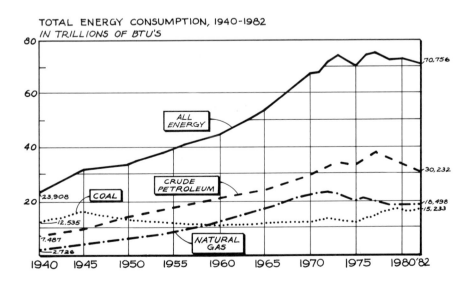

TOTAL ENERGY CONSUMPTION, 1940–1982
IN TRILLIONS OF BTU'S

These economic problems contributed to public disaffection with government—an attitude reinforced by the paralysis of the presidency under Nixon and Ford after 1973. In spite of the gravity of the oil price increases, neither president nor Congress shaped a coherent response. In November 1973, Nixon proposed what he called Project Independence, which would make the United States self-sufficient in energy by 1980. He called for an increase in domestic oil production by tapping the Alaskan field and drilling for offshore deposits. He also called for an increase in the output of natural gas, a greatly increased use of coal and nuclear power, the conversion of coal to synthetic oil and natural gas, the extraction of oil from shale, and the development of nonexpendable sources like solar and geothermal energy and the wind and tides.

Despite the urgency that surrounded Project Independence, paralysis rather than action characterized the response of government to the oil shock of 1973–1974. By mid-1974, as the crisis apparently ended and as Americans grew accustomed to higher prices, the need for a comprehensive energy policy seemed less urgent. Along with public apathy, another cause of the logjam was the opposition of some of the country's most powerful interest groups—environmentalists, antinuclear groups, and domestic oil producers—who, for different reasons, opposed federal intervention in energy policy.

Nixon vetoed an energy act in March 1974 because Congress added a windfall profits tax on the domestic oil industry. Ford was also soon at odds with a congressional majority. Ford's energy program, which he advocated in vain throughout 1975, stressed voluntary conservation. It also called for stiff levies on foreign oil to reduce imports, deregulation of domestic oil and natural gas prices, production of oil from the naval reserve lands, and an easing of environmental restrictions to encourage greater use of coal. Congress saw all of this as spurring inflation and aiding business at the expense of consumers and refused to enact any of it. Democrats advocated financing energy development by an increase in the federal gasoline tax and an excess profits tax on the oil companies. They also urged continuation of price controls and enactment of tax incentives to encourage the manufacture and use of fuel-efficient automobiles. But they could not combine enough support behind these proposals to override a veto, so the result was stalemate.

Congress and the president finally agreed on a compromise bill that Ford signed in December 1975. The key provisions of this, the Energy Policy and Conservation Act, authorized the Federal Energy Administration to order utility companies to switch from oil or natural gas to coal and increased the president's authority over the supply, allocation, and production of energy. The act also gave the president standby authority to impose gas-rationing and conservation measures and created a billion-barrel strategic petroleum reserve. It set mandatory fuel economy standards for post-1977 automobiles, looking toward a 26-MPG average by 1985. Finally, the act extended oil price controls into 1979 and rolled back the average market price of domestic oil by about one dollar per barrel.

Economic policy was also paralyzed by the political problems of the Nixon-Ford years. The simultaneous emergence of inflation and unemployment aggravated the power struggle between the Republican president and the Democratic Congress. Especially under Ford, the major emphasis of public policy was on reducing inflation even if the effort caused an increase in unemployment. Ford eschewed the experimentation with wage and price controls of the Nixon era and favored fiscal conservatism. He called for voluntary wage and price restraint and a restrictive monetary policy as the way to bring down prices. In contrast, the Democratic Congress, chiefly concerned with the problem of unemployment, passed a number of bills to alleviate unemployment through public works projects and temporary tax cuts. The result was a sharp divergence between president and Congress, a legislative stalemate, and Ford's use of the veto, which he employed some fifty times during his presidency.

3. THE ELECTION OF 1976

In 1976, the GOP suffered from a lethal combination of political problems. The association between the Republicans, Nixon, and the Watergate trauma remained fresh, and, on account of his pardon of Nixon, Ford was implicated as well. As the incumbent administration, the Ford presidency was held responsible for what seemed to be a deteriorating international position and a declining, perhaps even decaying, economy. Although the loss of public confidence in elected officials eventually affected Democrats as much as Republicans and although economic problems were the fault of no single administration, the fact remained that Gerald Ford and the Republicans received most of the blame.

Given the public mood of despair over conventional politics, it is not surprising that the campaign for the Democratic nomination was dominated by the emergence of a political unknown, Jimmy Carter, who ran his campaign as a political outsider opposed to the Washington establishment. Carter was little known beyond his native Georgia, where he had been governor from 1971 to 1975. He had laid his plans well in advance. Announcing his candidacy in December 1974, he won the Iowa caucus in early 1976 and then finished first in a field of nine candidates in the New Hampshire primary. This victory established Carter's credentials. Then his surprising victory in March over George Wallace in the Florida primary gave him a momentum that he never really lost. A tireless and effective campaigner, Carter stressed general themes rather than specific issues—above all, the need for a leader untainted by Washington who could restore morality and integrity to government. Despite losses in western primaries, Carter came to the Democratic National Convention in New York in July 1976 assured of the nomination.

The convention, compared with the previous two Democratic conventions, proceeded smoothly. With credentials, rules, representation, and platform all settled in advance, Carter won easily on the first ballot and chose the popular liberal senator from Minnesota, Walter F. Mondale, as his running mate. Unity was the Democratic watchword. In his acceptance speech, Carter called for a "time of healing" to replace the recent "time of torment" and promised efficient government and new efforts to end racial and sex discrimination. Carter voiced a populist theme and denounced "a political and economic elite who have shaped decisions and never had to account for mistakes." He praised the American character and the strength of American ideals and predicted that Americans would soon be "on the move again, united . . . entering our third century with pride and confidence." Democrats left New York in a cheerful mood.

In contrast, the battle for the Republican nomination was bitter and divisive. For the first time since 1964, the intraparty struggle between moderate centrists and right wingers threatened to divide the party. Ford, who had decided in 1975 to seek the presidency in his own right, was challenged by the former governor of California and hero of the party's conservative activists, Ronald W. Reagan. Ford won the early primary contests by projecting the image of a moderate leader who was healing America's wounds, presiding over economic recovery, and keeping the nation at peace. After Ford defeated Reagan decisively in the first three Republican primaries in early 1976, his supporters urged the Californian to withdraw in the interest of party unity.

But Reagan refused to give up and scored an upset victory over Ford in North Carolina in March. Then Reagan surged back into contention with a string of triumphs in the sun-belt states. Ford fell behind in the delegate count in May but stayed close with a big home-state triumph and strong performances in two border states. He regained a slight lead by persuading uncommitted supporters in New York and Pennsylvania to declare for him. He then rounded out the primaries in June with victories in New Jersey and Ohio, while Reagan took California by a landslide. Overall primary results had left the two candidates so close that everything depended on who could capture a majority of the uncommitted delegates.

The issue remained in doubt when the GOP convention assembled in Kansas City in mid-August. Ford gained a small lead in delegates, but Reagan countered with the surprise announcement that he had chosen Senator Richard S. Schweiker of Pennsylvania, a liberal, as his running mate—a strategy that alienated several uncommitted conservative delegates. Ford, able to hold his ranks intact, won the nomination on the first ballot and then chose Senator Robert A. Dole of Kansas as his running mate. In his acceptance speech, Ford praised the state of the nation as "sound," "secure," and "on the march to full economic recovery and a better quality of life for all Americans." He pledged continuing fights against inflation and unemployment, called for reduced taxes, and spoke of his record as "one of performance, not promises."

Partly because of the contrast between Democratic harmony and Republican infighting, Carter enjoyed a huge lead in the public opinion polls at the outset of the campaign. But, by September, that lead had dwindled significantly; by October, the race had become a dead heat. Of crucial importance, therefore, were a series of three debates between the presidential candidates and one between the vice-presidential candidates in late September and October. Although most observers credited Ford as "winning" the first debate, Carter bested the president in the second and third encounters and gained important momentum several weeks before the election. Nearly 82 million Americans went to the polls on November 2, 1976, and it was not until the next morning that Carter could be declared a winner. He received 40.8 million popular votes (51 percent) to Ford's 39.2 million (48 percent). Carter carried the District of Columbia and twenty-three states to Ford's twenty-seven, and Carter's electoral margin of 297 to 241 was the smallest since 1916.

Carter's triumph was based essentially upon the same East-South axis that had been a mainstay of Democratic success in John Kennedy's time, in Franklin Roosevelt's, and, indeed, in Thomas Jefferson's. Carter carried New York, Pennsylvania, and all but one state in the Old South. These, together with victories in Massachusetts and Rhode Island, accounted for more than two-thirds of his total. Carter also ran well in the border states, capturing Delaware, Maryland, the District of Columbia, West Virginia, Kentucky, and Missouri. He won three midwestern states (Ohio, Wisconsin, Minnesota) and lost everywhere in the West except Hawaii.

Carter had proved, as Kennedy in 1960 had proved for Catholics, that a person from the Deep South was no longer unable to seek and obtain the nation's highest office. In an ironic twist, southern black voters, newly enfranchised since the 1960s, voted overwhelmingly Democratic and gave Carter his margin of victory in most, if not all, of the ex-Confederate states—and indeed in the election as a whole. Urban, labor, Jewish, liberal, and other traditionally Democratic voters also supported Carter, and he ran well among midwestern and eastern farmers, who liked his rural origins.

The results of the election of 1976 also maintained Democratic control of Congress, by margins of 292–143 in the House and 62–38 in the Senate. Yet, far from being a decisive endorsement of the Democratic party, the election of 1976 betrayed a public mood which was suspicious of both parties and hostile to Washington insiders. Carter's election did not alter the main reality of national politics since 1952—that the GOP, all things being equal, would normally win presidential elections. Carter's election simply reflected public dissatisfaction over Watergate and over the recession of the mid-1970s. Moreover, Carter,

ELECTION OF 1976

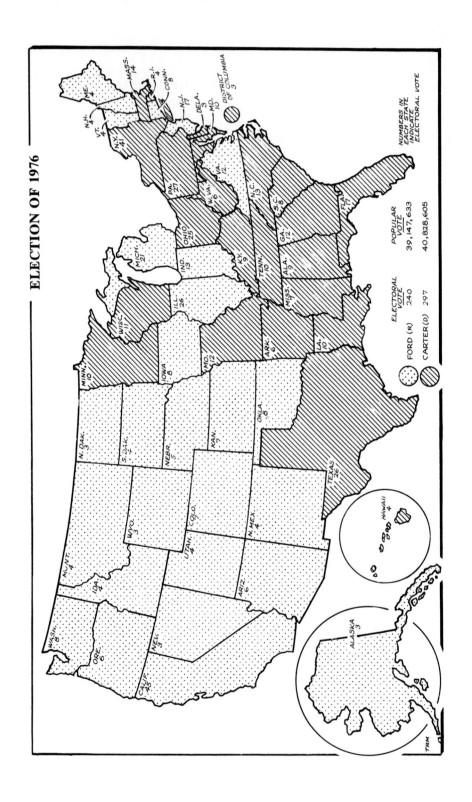

NUMBERS IN EACH STATE INDICATE ELECTORAL VOTE

	ELECTORAL VOTE	POPULAR VOTE
FORD (R)	240	39,147,633
CARTER (D)	297	40,828,605

MAINE 4
N.H. 4
VT. 4
MASS. 14
R.I. 4
CONN. 8
N.Y. 41
N.J. 17
DELA. 3
MD. 10
DISTRICT OF COLUMBIA 3
PA. 27
W. VA. 6
VA. 12
N.C. 13
S.C. 8
GA. 12
FLA. 17
MICH. 21
OHIO 25
IND. 13
KY. 9
TENN. 10
ALA. 9
MISS. 7
WISC. 11
ILL. 26
IOWA 8
MO. 12
ARK. 6
LA. 10
MINN. 10
N. DAK. 3
S. DAK. 4
NEBR. 5
KAN. 7
OKLA. 8
TEXAS 26
WYO. 3
COLO. 7
UTAH 4
N. MEX. 4
MONT. 4
IDA. 4
ARIZ. 6
WASH. 8
ORE. 6
NEV. 3
CALIF. 45
HAWAII 4
ALASKA 3

TRM

elected as an outsider, would now have to maintain public confidence while he worked with a Congress suspicious of his intentions and accustomed to opposing presidential leadership.

4.   THE CARTER PRESIDENCY

James Earl Carter, Jr., was born on a farm near the village of Plains in southwestern Georgia on October 1, 1924. He graduated from high school during wartime, spent a year in the navy ROTC program at Georgia Tech, and then received an appointment to the United States Naval Academy. He was graduated from Annapolis in 1946 in the upper tenth of his class and served in the navy for seven years. He rose to the rank of lieutenant and worked in Admiral Hyman Rickover's nuclear submarine program. He did a year of graduate work in nuclear physics at Union College and looked forward to a naval career, but he decided to leave the service and return to the family farm upon his father's death in 1953. He entered Georgia Democratic politics and served two terms in the state senate. He then ran unsuccessfully for his party's gubernatorial nomination in 1966.

Elected governor of Georgia four years later, Carter enjoyed a reputation as one of a new breed of southern politicians. Earlier an opponent of desegregation, as governor he took a forthright stand against racial discrimination. Hanging portraits of Martin Luther King, Jr., and other black leaders in the Georgia state capitol, he also increased black appointments to state offices. Although his record as governor was creditable, it was not outstanding. His principal achievements included governmental reorganization, improved budget procedures and state services, prison reform, and some modest welfare legislation.

Carter's presidency was shaped by a combination of personality and experience. A deeply religious "born again" Christian, Carter vaguely promised a moral reinvigoration of American domestic and foreign policies and a departure from the policies of Nixon and Ford. As a Georgian with no national experience and no important Democratic allies in Congress, Carter, undeniably an outsider, promised a general reform of excessive and irresponsible government. With even less experience in foreign affairs, he represented a repudiation of American interventionism abroad and a return to the primacy of morality in international affairs. While Carter had strong convictions about the importance of ideals in policy making, he was also obsessed with the complex and often highly technical details of its implementation. Indeed, he was a pragmatic realist who frequently saw decisions less in terms of ideology or political consequences than as a matter of problem solving.

Carter's inaugural address set an ambitious agenda for his presidency. It proclaimed "a new beginning, a new dedication within our government, a new spirit within us all." He urged caution and restraint in attacking problems and thanked his predecessor "for all he has done to heal our land." Carter also promised to humanize the imperial presidency. As a start, he and his family walked down Pennsylvania Avenue to the White House on Inauguration Day. He discouraged the traditional fanfare of playing "Hail to the Chief" and stopped the limousine service for White House aides. He answered questions on a two-hour radio call-in show and met with local citizens at televised "town meetings" in Massachusetts and Mississippi.

Carter's major appointments combined a manager's search for competence, a politician's search for balance, and a newcomer's desire to surround himself with a few trusted friends. Most of the new cabinet members were veterans of the Kennedy and Johnson administrations. Cyrus R. Vance, his secretary of state, was a New York attorney who had been a diplomat and deputy defense secretary under Lyndon Johnson. W. Michael Blumenthal, chosen as secretary of the treasury, was formerly head of the Bendix Corporation and a Kennedy tariff negotiator. Harold Brown, Johnson's secretary of the air force and later president of the California Institute of Technology, became secretary of defense. Joseph A. Califano, Jr., another Johnson official, assumed control of the mammoth apparatus at the Department of Health, Education and Welfare (HEW). There were, at the same time, new faces. Griffin B. Bell, a friend and fellow Georgian whose legal career had led to a federal judgeship, became attorney general. Juanita M. Kreps, professor of economics and vice-president of Duke University, was chosen as secretary of commerce. As secretary of housing and urban development, Carter appointed Patricia R. Harris, a distinguished black woman with varied experience as a diplomat, corporate board member, and professor of law.

Rather than appointing a chief of staff, Carter dispersed power among key White House staff members—Jody Powell, the press secretary; Hamilton Jordan, chief political adviser; and Stuart Eisenstat, domestic policy adviser. Although Carter attempted to humanize the presidency by preventing any concentration of power in the executive office, the White House staff inevitably played an important role. Included in any major decisions was a circle of advisers composed of the "Georgia Mafia" of Powell and Jordan; presidential opinion poll specialist Patrick Caddell; former Columbia University professor of foreign affairs and, under Carter, national security adviser, Zbigniew Brzezinski; former aide to Martin Luther King, Jr., black congressman from Georgia, and Carter's UN ambassador, Andrew Young, Jr.; and Rosalynn Carter, who played a greater role in presidential politics than any First Lady since Eleanor Roosevelt.

In January 1977, public expectations were greatly elevated about prospective changes in American domestic and foreign policies. The new president promised a clean break from the secrecy and political corruption of the Nixon years, and he offered a presidency which in style and substance would operate under stricter limits and fewer pretensions. Yet he also promised action on a range of issues long of interest to Democratic constituencies. These were tax reform, reinvigoration of environmental protection, stronger civil rights protection for minorities and women and renewed efforts to end discrimination in housing and employment, and the establishment of a comprehensive system of national health insurance. Carter had equally high expectations for dramatic changes in American foreign policy. In broad terms, he sought to reverse the guiding principles of the Nixon-Kissinger policies, in particular what he considered its excessive preoccupation with Soviet-American competition and its emphasis on realism and international power rather than morality as the standard of American conduct.

Carter began his term with strong public support for these objectives but met serious political obstacles that eventually undermined his presidency. Leading a contentious and demanding coalition of Democratic interest groups—each of which wanted immediate and unqualified results—required great political skill, and Carter's problem-solving, analytical approach often ran against the realities of power. In deciding issues which he considered of vital national interest but which were also politically sensitive, Carter typically ignored political considerations. Carter advanced an ambitious agenda but was unable either to simplify complex issues into emotionally compelling themes or to communicate the goals and accomplishments of his presidency to the American people.

5.   ENERGY POLICY UNDER CARTER

Carter's political problems were at least partly caused by an array of issues which were as challenging as any postwar president had faced. On the first day of his administration, Carter's staff began to draft a national energy plan, and, in a "fireside chat" on April 18, 1977, Carter proposed a comprehensive energy policy which would require national sacrifice and cooperation—the "moral equivalent of war." Carter presented his plan to a joint session of Congress two days later. It called for an ambitious conservation program designed to reduce the growth rate in overall energy use, reduce gasoline consumption by 10 percent, and cut oil imports virtually in half by 1985. It recommended more nuclear power plants and a two-thirds increase in coal production. But the major emphasis was upon conservation—specifically, reduced consumption of oil and natural gas. The core of this conservation plan was a complex system of taxes, tax incentives, and tax rebates and credits. A heavier tax on gasoline would raise its price and encourage fuel efficiency, while taxes on gas-guzzling cars and rebates for buyers of fuel-efficient cars would help to accomplish the same objective. Meanwhile, through deregulation, domestic crude oil and newly discovered natural gas would reach a higher open-market price.

This energy program was the single most important piece of legislation of the early Carter administration, and its fate displayed the fundamental problems that hampered close relations between the president, Congress, and the public. Although the House of Representatives quickly passed the energy bill in August 1977 with no important changes, the Senate dismembered the proposal and passed so different a measure that it took the conference committee nearly a year to produce a workable compromise.

Carter's energy policy stalled mainly because, at one and the same time, it satisfied no single energy interest group and alienated most of them. The centerpiece of his proposals—energy deregulation and higher taxes—encountered a cross fire of opposition. While intrastate sales of natural gas were unregulated, interstate sales since 1938 had been subject to severe and rigid price controls. The price of oil produced in the United States had been controlled since 1970. In the case of both natural gas and oil, the results of regulation not only kept prices down but also frequently resulted in serious shortages, disruptions in supply, and disincentives for new well exploration and development. A three-cornered battle over the issue of deregulation took place in Congress. Democratic liberals wanted to retain price controls; Carter and his backers wanted higher prices as a deterrent to consumption and would achieve this by a wellhead tax; oil-state senators wanted higher prices for the producer as an incentive to increased output and would achieve this by deregulation. The result was a compromise that included annual phased increases bringing natural gas prices up to the open-market level by 1985, when controls would cease altogether.

An exhausted Congress finally reached agreement in October 1978 and passed the National Energy Act. It represented something less than a victory for Carter. The wellhead tax on crude oil—which Carter had described as his program's "cornerstone"—was gone, as were the gasoline tax and the rebate for buyers of gas-saving automobiles. The tax on gas-guzzling cars was reduced, as were the rebates and credits designed to promote the use of coal in power plants and to encourage better insulation and the use of solar energy in homes. The president's request for a wellhead tax on natural gas had been replaced by deregulation.

Spurred on by the Iranian Revolution and the ensuing oil "shock" of 1979, Carter proposed further legislation to encourage energy conservation and production. In early April 1979, Carter proposed a conservation program which included decontrol of oil prices to encourage production and a windfall profits tax on decontrolled oil to pay for energy assistance for low-income families, public transportation, and the development of alternative synthetic fuels. Carter met a tepid response to these proposals and then attempted to build a broad consensus for them—and revive his presidency—by conferring for about ten days in early July with experts, scholars, labor leaders, and politicians at the presidential retreat at Camp David.

Then, on July 15, 1979, Carter emerged from his talks to deliver an address—perhaps the most important of his presidency—to an estimated audience of 100 million people. He described a "crisis of confidence" that was gripping the American people; confessed his own mistakes; and said that he had not provided enough leadership. He pledged to do better, called for the people's help and cooperation, and assured them that he would lead the fight and would act. Carter then unveiled the details of a new energy plan. He set a goal of cutting oil imports to half their current level by 1990 and announced a freeze on imports in 1979 and 1980 at a level not to exceed 8.5 million barrels a day. But his major proposals were designed to increase energy production by building more nuclear power plants under stricter safeguards, encouraging the use of solar energy, and, above all, by decontrolling oil prices in combination with a windfall profits tax. In addition, another major component of Carter's new policy was increased synthetic fuel production, stimulated by a new Energy Security Corporation financed by the proposed windfall profits tax.

In contrast to the fate of Carter's energy plan of 1977, these initiatives were enacted largely intact by Congress in the spring of 1980. Congress created a Synthetic Fuels Corporation and enacted the centerpiece of Carter's proposal—decontrol of oil prices combined with the windfall profits tax. Carter proposed a phased decontrol, together with a tax of 50 percent on the portion of the price above $13 per barrel, which was then the controlled price. In spite of vigorous

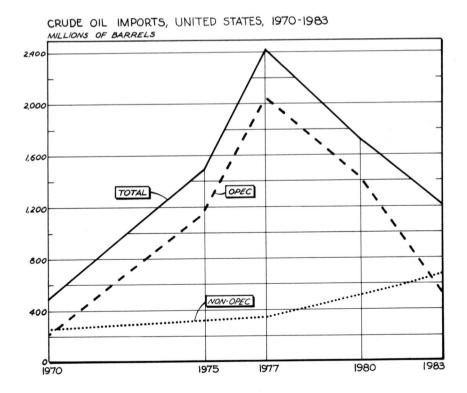

CRUDE OIL IMPORTS, UNITED STATES, 1970-1983
MILLIONS OF BARRELS

opposition from the oil industry, Congress enacted decontrol and a tax which included a variable rate of 30 to 70 percent on oil produced by existing wells. The tax, according to the act, would only last until 1993, or until a total of $227 billion was collected.

Carter later claimed that the passage of his energy program in 1980 constituted a major success of his presidency. In 1977, the United States imported 48 percent of its oil; by 1980, this percentage had declined to 40 percent. In 1978, Americans consumed about 19 million barrels of oil per day; in 1980, they consumed about 17 million barrels. These results "speak for themselves," wrote Carter, and Americans were now "better equipped" to deal with potential shortages. Nonetheless, as Carter freely conceded, his accomplishments in the field of energy came at a high price. His early struggles in 1977–1978 preoccupied his administration and won him few friends and little respect in Congress, the public, or the media. Even more damaging was the impact of the oil shock of 1979, which seemed to demonstrate the paralysis and impotency of the Carter presidency.

By 1979, meanwhile, Carter's political strength was also being undermined by inflation. It steadily increased, from 7 percent in 1977 to 9.6 percent in 1978 to 12.4 percent in 1980. The causes of this phenomenon are complex. An inflationary cycle had begun under Johnson and Nixon, fueled by the stimulative effects of the Vietnam War. Excessive regulation in certain industries restricted price competition, while the success of unionization increased labor costs. But the two long-term causes of inflation were rising energy costs and declining productivity.

Reducing inflation became the major objective of Carter's economic policy only gradually. In 1977, Carter proposed and Congress enacted a stimulative package of $6 billion for local public works; $7.9 billion in public service jobs; a three-year, $34 billion tax cut; increased farm supports; and a phased increase of the minimum wage from $2.30 to $3.35 per hour by 1981. By 1978, however, stimulation was the last thing that the American economy needed, and Carter began an anti-inflation policy. In the spring of 1978, he announced a 5.5 percent limit upon governmental pay increases and froze the salaries of top-level White House staff members and federal officials. Then, in October 1978, he began a new anti-inflationary program which established voluntary guidelines aimed at limiting wage increases to 7 percent and keeping price increases to between 6 and 6.5 percent.

The ineffectiveness of Carter's anti-inflation policies was made clear after the impact of the oil price increases of 1979, which further exacerbated the problem of inflation during 1979 and 1980. By the summer of 1979, Carter was forced to act decisively. He did so by replacing the chairman of the Federal Reserve Board, William Miller, with a monetary conservative, Paul Volcker. Through a policy of restraining the growth in the nation's money supply and encouraging interest rates to rise to historically high levels, Volcker began a determined effort to reduce inflation. But tight monetary restraint had caused a recession by the spring of 1980 in industries such as automobiles and construction that were sensitive to interest rates.

6. CARTER AND SUPERPOWER FOREIGN POLICY

During the campaign of 1976 and early in his administration, Carter made it clear that his foreign policy would differ from that of Nixon, Ford, and Kissinger. Carter's new departure abroad had three principal components. First, in contrast to the *Realpolitik* of his predecessors, Carter proposed to reintroduce a moral component into American foreign policy as a way to rally domestic and international support. This moral component, he believed, lay in an emphasis on human rights, applied equally to the Soviet Union and to nations as diverse as South Korea, Iran, Argentina, and South Africa. Second, Carter proposed to deemphasize Soviet-American competition. Third, partly as a product of the first two components of his foreign policy, Carter placed greater emphasis on expanding American influence in the developing world. Although none of these objectives can be said to have been fully achieved by the end of the Carter presidency in 1980, American foreign policy did change significantly during the Carter administration.

In spite of Carter's claim to the contrary, his foreign policy was an extension of some of the policies of his immediate predecessors, Nixon and Ford. In relations with the superpowers—China and the Soviet Union—Carter attempted to preserve the general structure established during the first Nixon administration. The success of détente was based on the success of arms control, begun in 1972 with the signing of the first SALT accords (see pp. 694–695). Under the Ford administration, further strides in arms limitation and détente were made in a Soviet-American agreement at Vladivostok in November 1974. Under the terms of this agreement, the United States and the Soviet Union agreed to a limit of 2,400 launchers and 1,320 MIRVed missiles; of these the Soviets were allowed 308 modern heavy missiles, the United States, none.

Soon after his inauguration, Carter proposed deep cuts in the superpowers' nuclear arsenal. In a comprehensive scheme submitted by Secretary of State Cyrus Vance in Moscow in March 1977, Carter proposed that both superpowers agree to reduce launchers to an 1,800–2,000 limit and MIRVed ICBMs to an 1,100–1,200 limit, while the Soviets would be restricted to 150 heavy missiles. The Soviets claimed that Carter was seeking unilateral advantages, harshly rejected the American proposal, and sent Vance packing. During the next two years, long and grueling negotiations toward a second SALT treaty followed. Not until June 1979, in a summit meeting in Vienna between Carter and Brezhnev, were all the details of the accord worked out and SALT II signed.

The treaty set a limit of 2,400 long-range missiles and bombers for each side at the time of signing, to be reduced to 2,250 by 1981. It restricted the total number of nuclear warheads to 10,000 per country, whereof 1,320 might be MIRVs, and placed a limit of 10 upon the number of warheads that a single ICBM could carry. The American cruise missile was included in the limitation, while the Soviet Backfire bomber was not. However, Brezhnev did pledge to limit production of these medium-range aircraft to the then present rate of thirty a year. The two leaders also agreed that SALT III talks would concentrate upon reducing nuclear stockpiles.

The Vienna summit and the signing of SALT II coincided, however, with a decline in support among the American public for détente and a growing suspicion of Soviet intentions. A sizable portion of the Republican party— primarily its right wing, led by Senator Jesse Helms of North Carolina and Governor Ronald Reagan of California—had always considered détente and the improvement in Soviet-American relations as inimical to American interests. They claimed that SALT II legitimized Soviet nuclear superiority and encouraged Soviet adventurism around the globe.

Undeniably, Soviet aggressiveness in exploiting what it perceived was post-Vietnam American weakness contributed to the decline of détente. The Soviets, beginning in the mid-1970s, inaugurated an active policy of intervention in African affairs. In 1975, a Soviet-backed group took power in Angola, formerly a Portuguese colony, after the infusion of Russian arms and thousands of Cuban troops. Then, in 1977, the USSR made a bold move to gain influence in the strategic Horn of Africa region. A revolution in Ethiopia against Emperor Hailie Selassie eventually brought a Communist dictatorship and a pro-Soviet alignment. In 1977 and 1978, the Soviets and their Cuban proxies intervened in a border war between Ethiopia and Somalia and helped the Ethiopians attempt to suppress the secession of Eritrea.

These actions added to the perceptions of American opinion makers and the public that détente was not restraining Soviet expansionism. Two other developments during the late 1970s accounted for a further deterioration in Soviet-American relations. The first was the decision of Kremlin leaders to deploy hundreds of medium-range nuclear SS-20 missiles which would be aimed at the NATO countries of Western Europe. Because this decision appeared to alter the balance of power in Europe, NATO, in December 1979, responded with a decision to deploy cruise missiles and advanced Pershing II medium-range missiles in Europe. Still more damaging was the Russian invasion of Afghanistan in December 1979. After a coup in 1978 had toppled a neutralist government and installed a pro-Soviet regime there, the deterioration of popular support and a spreading rebellion forced the Soviets' hand. The Russians, confronted with the real possibility of an Islamic anti-Soviet government on their border, occupied Afghanistan with an army of over 100,000 men. Subduing the Afghans was not easy, and the Soviets were soon bogged down in a costly and brutal guerrilla war.

In direct proportion to the decline of détente was a substantial improvement in Sino-American relations. After the opening toward China in 1971, the visit of Nixon to Peking, and the signing of a joint Chinese-American communiqué (see pp. 699–700), liaison offices established low-level relations between the United States and the PRC. Yet further improved relations, as Carter discovered after taking office, were obstructed by American recognition of Taiwan. In discussions held during 1977, the Chinese made clear three conditions for better relations: the end of the United States–Taiwan defense treaty, the severance of diplomatic relations with Taiwan, and the withdrawal of American military forces from Taiwan. Although Carter was willing to accept these conditions, he insisted upon his own conditions: the right to sell "defensive" weapons to Taiwan, the preservation of Taiwan-American trade, and the maintenance of "unofficial" relations with Taiwan.

After almost a year of negotiations, the national security adviser, Zbigniew Brzezinski, visited Peking in May 1978 and began to lay the groundwork for a general Chinese-American settlement. Secret talks followed during the summer and autumn which eventually brought an agreement in mid-December 1978. The United States would break relations with Taiwan and recognize the People's Republic of China as the sole legitimate government of China on January 1, 1979. In exchange, the Chinese agreed to the maintenance of the United States–Taiwan defense treaty for one year; sanctioned the continued sale of American "defensive" equipment to Taiwan; and acquiesced in an American statement that the Taiwan issue would be settled "peacefully and with patience." The new era of harmonious Chinese-American relations culminated with the visit to the United States of the Chinese premier, Deng Xiaoping, in January 1979.

7. CARTER THE PEACEMAKER

Carter's foreign policy differed in its emphasis on human rights, open diplomacy, accommodation, and principle from the *Realpolitik* that characterized Nixon-Kissinger diplomacy. Carter dramatized his new approach by signing an Inter-American Convention on Human Rights and then asked the Senate to approve the UN Human Rights Covenants of 1966. He further urged that the UN human rights machinery be strengthened by withholding assistance from nations that did not meet the UN's standards in this area.

At the same time, Carter opposed restrictive import quotas (preferring to help American producers through marketing agreements or governmental aid) and took the lead in supporting a freer world trading system at a Western summit conference in London in May 1977. The United States contributed heavily to the International Development Association, increased its support for UN development programs, and joined in the creation of a new international fund for agricultural development.

Carter's patience and skill in negotiation won for him two truly notable triumphs in foreign policy—the Panama Canal treaties and the Camp David accords. Success in the Panama negotiations came in two stages. The United States and Panama concluded thirteen years of talks by agreeing upon a pair of treaties in September 1977. One provided for American operation and defense of the canal until the year 2000, an increase in Panama's share of canal revenues, a slow decrease in the number of American employees in the Canal Zone, the immediate abolition of the zone itself, and a return to Panama of all territory unconnected with the actual operation of the canal. The second document—a neutrality treaty—designated the canal as an international waterway, permanently neutral in war and peace, and open to peaceful passage by ships of all nations. American and Panamanian warships would have priority of passage in times of war and emergency. Although Panama would maintain defense sites and military installations after 2000, the United States would retain a permanent right to act along with Panama to defend the canal's neutral status. Panamanians approved the treaties by a two-to-one margin in a plebiscite in October 1977.

The canal negotiations touched off a loud controversy in the United States, and it took a considerable amount of skill, maneuvering, and persuasive logic by Senate supporters and administration leaders to get the treaties approved. Opposition was vocal and strong. Conservatives denounced the agreements; bitter American residents in the Canal Zone demonstrated angrily against them. To allay legitimate fears, the Senate attached reservations which strengthened the priority of American warships in times of war or emergency and provided for America's right to use force to reopen or secure safe operation of the canal. When Panama objected to this latter point, the Senate modified it by stipulating that the right of the United States to take unilateral action did not extend to intervening in or impugning Panama's independence. The Panamanian head of state, Brigadier General Omar Torrijos, soon reported that his country found the amendments and reservations acceptable.

The Senate approved one treaty on March 16 and the other on April 18, 1978, by identical votes of sixty-eight to thirty-two—only one more than the necessary two-thirds. President Carter and General Torrijos met in Panama City in June and exchanged the instruments of ratification. But the opponents of the treaty did not give up, and, during 1978 and 1979, they concentrated on blocking congressional legislation which was needed to implement the treaties. These maneuvers included attempts in the House of Representatives to prohibit any changes in American military forces in Panama; to cut off economic and military aid to Panama; to raise canal tolls to prohibitive levels; and to require Panama to pay for operating the canal. After a fierce lobbying effort by the White House, Congress enacted implementation legislation on September 27,

1979, only three days before the treaties became effective. Although in negotiating and persuading the Senate to approve the Panama Canal treaties, Carter had succeeded where Johnson, Nixon, and Ford had failed, Carter had done so at considerable political cost. The ratification battle expended precious political capital, and it exposed Carter to subsequent charges that his policy of accommodation was actually a policy of weakness and vacillation.

The second great Carter achievement in foreign policy—the Camp David accords—was a monumental breakthrough in relations between Egypt and Israel. The first sign of a break in the impasse between these two countries came in November 1977. When Egyptian President Sadat announced his willingness to visit Israel, the new Israeli premier, Menachem Begin, responded with an invitation. Immediately accepting, Sadat addressed the Israeli Parliament in Jerusalem and spoke soberly of the need to break down the "psychological wall . . . that constitutes 70 percent of the problem between Arab and Jew." Then Sadat proclaimed that Egyptians wanted to live with Israelis in a "just and lasting peace." Moreover, he said that the existence of Israel was "an established fact."

Negotiations, under American sponsorship, proceeded slowly during 1978, and, by early summer, had ceased altogether. To break the stalemate, Carter invited Sadat and Begin to Camp David for a summit conference in September— and kept them there for two weeks in an intense round of negotiations. On September 17, an exhausted but triumphant president announced that two accords had been reached—a Framework for Peace in the Middle East and a Framework for the Conclusion of a Peace Treaty between Egypt and Israel. Israel and Egypt agreed to negotiate a treaty within three months. Sadat acquiesced in a separate peace with Israel rather than insisting upon inclusion of other Arab states and the Palestinians. Begin agreed to return the Sinai to Egypt. The Framework for Peace spoke in deliberately vague terms of "self-governing authorities" in the West Bank and the Gaza Strip, "freely elected" by the inhabitants—an indirect reference to the explosive Palestinian question. The status of the West Bank and Gaza was to be settled by negotiations among Israeli, Egyptian, Jordanian, and local authorities over a five-year period.

Agreement to negotiate a treaty was one thing; successful negotiation itself was another. The euphoric glow of the Camp David meeting soon subsided. Follow-up talks raised touchy questions of detail and implementation which the broadly phrased frameworks had been able to skirt, and the two nations could not come to terms within the three-month deadline. Indeed, by early 1979 it looked as if the negotiations would fail altogether. Sadat began to demand that the peace treaty be linked to an agreement about the exact status of the Palestinians. Israel resented this request for linkage because it had not been part of the Camp David accords. In turn, Begin angered Egypt by building new Israeli settlements in the West Bank. The rest of the Arab world, including the Palestine Liberation Organization (PLO), the largest of several refugee groups, kept up a drumfire of criticism against the whole idea of any peace treaty with Israel.

Carter now renewed the earnest personal diplomacy that had worked so well at Camp David. After strenuous new discussions, capped by a presidential visit to Tel Aviv and Cairo in March for marathon sessions, the pieces suddenly fell into place. A weary, smiling president arrived home with the surprise announcement that Israel and Egypt had agreed upon terms.

With Carter presiding, Sadat and Begin signed the peace treaty in Washington on March 26, 1979. Israel pledged to withdraw its military forces and remove its civilian settlements from the Sinai over a three-year period, with two-thirds of the territory to be relinquished within nine months of ratification. At that point, Egypt and Israel were to establish normal friendly relations and exchange ambassadors. UN forces were to be deployed in border areas to monitor the agreement. The United States, which had pledged some $5 billion in military and economic aid to both countries as part of the bargain, was to assist in security arrangements by conducting surveillance flights. Egypt was to end its economic boycott of Israel, whose ships and cargoes were granted free right of passage through the Suez Canal. Israel could purchase oil from the Sinai fields that it was about to return to Egypt. The two countries also agreed to begin to negotiate the question of Palestinian autonomy within a month after ratification. Formal approval of the treaty took place almost immediately in both capitals. The first Sinai evacuation began the day after the treaty was signed; the second phase took place on schedule in the early summer.

Thus peace returned to a large part of the Middle East. More important, war against Israel by other Arab states was now futile, if not inconceivable.

8.   THE HOSTAGE CRISIS

The most serious test of Carter's policy of accommodation occurred in his response to new turbulence in Iran. In 1951, the government of Mohammed Mossadegh had nationalized the Anglo-Iranian Oil Company. In 1953, the CIA cooperated with local Iranians, particularly the army, to overthrow Mossadegh. The oil controversy was settled, and Shah Mohammed Reza Pahlavi increasingly assumed dictatorial control in Iran. By Carter's inauguration, Iran under the shah had been America's strongest ally in the Middle East for over twenty-five years. Like six American presidents before him, Carter welcomed the shah in a visit in late 1977, and Carter described Iran as "an island of stability in one of the most troubled areas in the world." Yet Carter also urged the shah to loosen police-state restrictions, broaden participation in the government, and begin a more liberal human rights policy. The shah responded positively, but his attempts to liberalize his absolutist regime came too little and too late. When he began awkward attempts to liberalize in 1978, he only aroused a fury of popular opposition, particularly from the Moslem mullahs (holy men). Riots broke out in major Iranian cities in the summer of 1978, and the shah declared martial law in September.

The crisis in Iran now moved steadily toward revolution. Demonstrations against the shah were contained only by the killing of hundreds of demonstrators. Then the shah attempted to quiet opposition by granting amnesty to opposition leaders. His greatest mistake was to permit the return from exile in France of Ayatollah Ruhollah Khomeini, the charismatic leader of the Islamic fundamentalists. With the return of Ayatollah Khomeini to the Iranian capital of Teheran on February 1, 1979, an Islamic republic was proclaimed, and the shah and his family fled into exile in Egypt. During the rest of 1979, a power struggle ensued between Western-oriented supporters of the shah and the Islamic fundamentalists, who were bitterly anti-American and anti-Western.

With the fall of the shah, Carter pursued a risky policy in Iran—he attempted to establish friendly relations with the Khomeini regime. During the spring and summer of 1979, Carter's policy appeared to be working. Relations were good or improving with the government headed by Mehdi Bazargan, a Western-oriented Iranian who had the support of Khomeini. However, the Islamic fundamentalists continued to exploit the anti-American issue to discredit the Bazargan government, and Ayatollah Khomeini's hatred of the United States—at least as expressed in his public statements—grew daily more venomous.

The fragile condition of United States–Iranian relations and the dynamics of internal Iranian politics became apparent when Carter, pressured by the shah's American supporters and advised that the shah needed medical care inside the United States, decided to allow the shah to come to the United States for treatment. The arrival of the shah at a hospital in New York from Mexico, then his place of exile, in late October 1979 set off a series of antishah and anti-American demonstrations in Teheran. Then, on November 4, 1979, about three thousand Islamic militant "students" invaded and occupied the American Embassy and held about sixty of the embassy staff hostage. Assurances came to Washington from the Bazargan government, but the militants who had seized the embassy held its occupants as hostages for the delivery by the United States of the shah to Teheran. More important, the militants had Khomeini's complete support.

In response, Carter considered a military rescue but then rejected it. Instead, he cut off all American imports of Iranian oil and froze all Iranian assets in American banks or in their branches overseas. Abroad, Carter succeeded in isolating the Khomeini regime among Western European nations and Japan. At home, he succeeded in the winter of 1979–1980 in rallying American opinion, at least temporarily, around a policy of patience and negotiation. But public patience began to wear thin in the early spring of 1980, especially after the collapse of several nearly successful attempts to negotiate a settlement which would bring the hostages home. These attempts were futile for the crucial reason that no central authority existed in Iran with which the American government could negotiate. Indeed, as the crisis dragged on, it became apparent that the American hostages were the most effective weapons which the Islamic fundamentalists possessed to purge Iran of Western, especially American, influence. As important was the fact that, at every juncture, Ayatollah Khomeini undermined the ability of the Iranian president, Abolhassan Bani-Sadr and his foreign minister, Sadegh Ghotbsadeh, to settle the crisis.

In early April 1980, after the failure of Bani-Sadr to obtain the approval of either the ruling Revolutionary Council or Khomeini for the release of the hostages, Carter gave up hope of any quick resolution of the crisis. He imposed additional economic sanctions (which embargoed the shipment of all goods to Iran except food and medicine) and broke relations with Iran. By mid-April, Carter began to reconsider a military rescue and ordered military leaders to devise a plan. American military officials were convinced that the long occupation of the Teheran embassy had made the Iranian captors lax and carefree in their security—apparently a perfect situation for a surprise rescue operation. The rescue plan called for eight navy helicopters, based on aircraft carriers in the Gulf of Oman, to rendezvous with six C-130 transport planes carrying an American commando team six hundred miles inside Iran to a remote landing strip known as Desert One. After the rendezvous, the commando team would fly aboard the helicopters to a base outside of Teheran, rush the embassy compound, and then, with the freed hostages, escape from Iran to Saudi Arabia in two of the C-130s.

Having received reports suggesting that the hostages might be held for another six months, Carter gave the order for the rescue mission to proceed. The operation, launched on April 24, 1980, met with one disaster after another. En route to Desert One, two of the eight helicopters malfunctioned. One of them was left on the aircraft carrier, the other in the Iranian desert. Then, during the rendezvous at Desert One, another helicopter developed mechanical difficulties. Because the mission could not be carried out without a minimum of six helicopters, Carter gave the order to abort the mission. Worse luck occurred. While taking off, one of the helicopters crashed into the nose of a C-130 because of bad visibility and eight members of the rescue team were killed.

The failure of the mission had disastrous repercussions for Carter at home. Up to this time, he had been able to avoid major public criticism and to maintain a degree of public patience. After the rescue disaster, which he announced at once, Carter increasingly suffered political damage, first in the primary fight with Senator Edward Kennedy and then in the general election campaign with Ronald Reagan. At the same time, the failed mission also foreclosed any future rescue attempts, for their captors now dispersed the hostages to different locations in Iran. It now seemed likely that the hostage crisis would not be resolved until after the presidential election.

Over the summer and fall of 1980, virtually no progress was made toward a settlement. Slowly, several considerations persuaded the Iranian Islamic hard-liners that they had derived maximum benefit from the crisis. The first was the death of the shah on July 27, 1980. This eliminated what had been the major—and, for the United States, the unacceptable—Iranian demand that the shah be delivered to Iran for trial and certain execution. Then, on September 22, 1980, neighboring Iraq invaded Iran in order to settle a long-standing territorial dispute with Iran. The beginning of the Iran-Iraq war meant that the diplomatic and economic isolation of Iran—and its lack of access to Western arms and supplies—was now important. For Iran, fighting the war against Iraq effectively depended upon ending the hostage crisis. Finally, the internal power struggle between Western-oriented moderates and Islamic fundamentalists was over by the fall of 1980. The hostage crisis had so undermined the moderates that the Islamic fundamentalists were now dominant throughout Iran. The American hostages were no longer useful to the fundamentalists as pawns in the internal Iranian struggle.

As early as September, there was evidence that Iran wanted to solve the crisis. It demanded, throughout the fall of 1980, that, in exchange for the return of the hostages, the United States should agree to return the frozen assets, transfer the shah's personal fortune back to Iran, and promise never to interfere in internal Iranian affairs. Just two days before the American presidential election, the Majles, the Iranian Parliament, approved these conditions and authorized President Bani-Sadr and Prime Minister Mohammed Ali Rajai to negotiate with the United States. But on election day, November 4, 1980—the first anniversary of the Teheran embassy takeover—it was obvious that a long period of negotiating would occur before the hostages' release. Not until December did Iranian and American officials, working through Algerian intermediaries, begin to narrow remaining differences, particularly over the return of the frozen Iranian assets. After difficult and tense interchanges, the two sides agreed on January 17—the Sunday before Ronald Reagan's inauguration—to a complex settlement. Of the almost $12 billion in Iranian assets in the United States, two-thirds were to be immediately unfrozen and deposited in an escrow account in London under Algerian control; the remaining third would be first subject to American claims through American courts. This massive transfer of funds occurred during the next two days. Then, only after the inauguration of Ronald Reagan, at 12:33 P.M. on January 20, 1981, did the Iranians release the fifty-two hostages from their captivity of 444 days.

CHAPTER 33

The Reagan Revolution

Ronald Reagan's election to the presidency in 1980 marked the most decisive turning point in American national politics since the New Deal. Reagan was the hero of the Republican right wing, which, denied power since about 1930, was united by opposition to the New Deal's welfare policies and to the post-1960 growth of federal power in civil rights, education, and criminal justice. The right wing was also united by its opposition to the further secularization of American life, the erosion in the status of the traditional American family, and by hostility toward any compromise with Soviet totalitarianism. Republican conservatives grew stronger primarily because they forged successful alliances with single-issue splinter groups, such as Protestant fundamentalists—awakened from a political hibernation which dated back to the late 1920s—and antiabortion groups. Moreover, by the mid-1970s, the conservative argument in favor of reducing taxes and governmental activities began to have a wider, populist appeal to a broad range of Americans suspicious of the intentions and abilities of Washington politicians.

1. THE REVOLUTION BEGINS: THE ELECTION OF 1980

It was clear to most political observers in the autumn of 1979 that the Carter presidency was in grave trouble. According to public opinion polls, Carter, during the summer of 1979, was the most unpopular president in modern history. He faced a major intraparty challenge, and it appeared likely that he would become the first incumbent president in the twentieth century to be denied renomination by his own party. A procession of party leaders, who sensed political disaster, encouraged Senator Edward M. Kennedy of Massachusetts to challenge Carter and unite the party. Throughout the summer and autumn of 1979, polls showed Kennedy leading the president among Democratic voters by a margin of two to one. Kennedy's nomination seemed assured, and in September he unofficially announced his intention to run.

But translating popularity into votes, as Kennedy discovered, proved difficult to accomplish. Much of that popularity reflected a nostalgia for the Kennedy legacy, and, when the inheritor of that legacy became a presidential candidate, he experienced the full brunt of public scrutiny of his abilities, leadership, and character under stress. The early months of the Kennedy campaign witnessed an uninterrupted series of failures and growing public misgivings about his candidacy. In early November 1979, in a nationally televised interview, Kennedy appeared indecisive and inarticulate, unsure about why he was running for president, and unwilling to address questions about his numerous personal problems. Added to Kennedy's inability to get his flagging candidacy off the ground was another problem: a resurgence of popular backing for Carter, largely because of the foreign-policy crises in Iran and Afghanistan.

Kennedy's weaknesses became obvious in early tests in February and March 1980. In the Iowa caucuses, the first major test, Carter defeated Kennedy by 59 percent to 31 percent. While Carter remained in a self-imposed isolation and refused to campaign until the hostages were released, the Massachusetts senator suffered a defeat in the New Hampshire primary and a string of losses in the South. When Carter also won an important primary victory in Illinois in late March, it appeared that Kennedy would surely withdraw. Kennedy lagged far behind in opinion polls, but he defeated Carter in the New York primary in early April by sixteen points and revived his candidacy. During April and May, Kennedy now capitalized on public disaffection with Carter and impatience about the hostages and won important primaries or caucuses in Pennsylvania, Michigan, and California.

Although Carter had three hundred more delegates than were necessary to win the nomination, Kennedy stubbornly refused to withdraw between the last primary in early June and the Democratic convention in mid-August. Carter's political problems thereafter only grew worse with further bad news in the summer of 1980: rising inflation and unemployment, the continuing hostage stalemate, and the revelation that Billy Carter, the president's brother, had accepted a $220,000 "loan" from the Libyan government. Some Democrats in Congress worried about a Republican sweep in November. Kennedy supporters, hoping to capitalize on an anti-Carter stampede, proposed an "open" convention, in which delegates could support any candidate. When the Democratic convention opened in New York in August, a bitter Carter-Kennedy split was inevitable. Although the Carter forces won the open-convention rules fight easily, Kennedy delivered what sounded like an acceptance speech. It was so effective that it salvaged his reputation and rallied the support of the convention behind a platform plank—opposed by Carter—which called for a $12 billion public works program that would employ 800,000 workers. The Carter forces left the convention dispirited, and the party entered the campaign deeply divided.

The Republican campaign, in contrast, quickly demonstrated the political prowess and strong voter appeal of Ronald Reagan. Reagan, losing to challenger George Bush in the Iowa caucuses, regained his balance and decisively won enough victories in subsequent primaries to have secured the nomination by April 1980. The Republican convention, which met in Detroit, emphasized unity and moderation. In spite of a platform which was largely written by conservative activists (it contained vigorous denunciations of détente, abortion, and the Supreme Court's school prayer decisions), Reagan presented himself as a moderate candidate squarely in the centrist tradition of American politics. As part of his move to the political center, he chose as his vice-presidential candidate his principal opponent, George Bush, previously a Texas congressman, director of the CIA, and head of the Republican National Committee.

When the general election campaign formally opened on Labor Day, the polls showed Reagan in a commanding lead. Attempting to narrow the margin, Carter launched a series of increasingly strident attacks which sought to reduce Reagan's support among moderates. In a speech at the Ebenezer Baptist Church in Atlanta, Carter accused Reagan of injecting "hatred" and "racism" into the campaign. Carter later charged that the election was a choice between "war and peace." But this strategy backfired and thereby overshadowed a bumbling start and well-publicized misstatements by Reagan in September. More damage to the Carter campaign ensued after the League of Women Voters insisted that the independent candidate John B. Anderson of Illinois be included in any televised presidential debate—a condition which Reagan immediately accepted. Carter, fearing the inroads that Anderson's candidacy would make into Democratic strength, refused.

In October, public doubts about the Reagan candidacy grew, while support for Anderson partly dissipated, and Carter steadily began to gain ground. His own polls showed him behind by only two percentage points in mid-October. Then Carter proposed and Reagan agreed to a one-on-one debate in Cleveland on October 28. In the debate, Carter appeared stiff, if fully informed in his answers; Reagan seemed at ease, amiable, and completely unthreatening. The debate apparently solidified and expanded support for Reagan among independents and Democratic voters on the eve of the election. On election day, November 4—the first anniversary of the takeover of the American embassy in Teheran—Reagan won a decisive victory, capturing 43.5 million votes and 51 percent to 34.9 million and 41 percent for Carter and 5.6 million and 7 percent for Anderson. Even more impressive was Reagan's electoral vote: 489 electoral votes, compared with only 49 for Carter, who won only Minnesota, Rhode Island, Georgia, West Virginia, Hawaii, Maryland, and the District of Columbia.

Although contemporary observers exaggerated the significance of Reagan's victory as a landslide, it was nonetheless impressive. Many traditionally Democratic labor, ethnic, Jewish, and southern voters all defected to the Republicans; the only group that remained overwhelmingly loyal were blacks. As important were the results of the congressional elections, which returned thirty-three more Republicans to the House of Representatives and gave the GOP control of the Senate for the first time since 1954. Reagan's victory obviously constituted a mandate for change and a strong rejection of Carter's presidency. It reflected public suspicion of excessive governmental involvement in the economy as the cause of inflation and unemployment. More important, the election also expressed public frustration because of Carter's inability to free the hostages in Iran.

2. RONALD REAGAN AND AMERICAN POLITICS

Ronald Wilson Reagan's election in 1980 marked the high point of a remarkable career. He was born on February 6, 1911, in Tampico, Illinois, the son of Nelle Wilson and John Edward "Jack" Reagan. Reagan owed much to each of his parents. Nelle was warm-hearted and boundless in her generosity, while Jack was an expansive and witty storyteller. But Jack was also an alcoholic who was never able to support his family beyond bare subsistence. When their son was two years old, the Reagans moved to Chicago, where Jack worked as a clerk in a department store. The family moved to a succession of small towns in Illinois, and, in 1920, finally settled in Dixon, the place that Reagan always considered his home. Reagan was graduated from Dixon High School and entered Eureka College, twenty-one miles east of Peoria, Illinois, where he gained campus prominence as a football player and actor. Graduating in 1932, he became a radio announcer in Davenport and Des Moines, Iowa. Soon "Dutch" Reagan was famous throughout the Middle West as a sportscaster of the Chicago Cubs' baseball games.

In 1937, Reagan began a long career in motion pictures. Among some fifty feature-length films in which he acted were *Brother Rat* (1938), *Dark Victory* (1939), *Knute Rockne—All American* (1940), and *King's Row* (1941). By the mid-1940s, however, Reagan's acting career was in decline, and he steadily became more involved in labor politics. He served as president of the Screen Actors' Guild in the late 1940s and led a fight to preserve the integrity of the actors' union and to root out Communist influence. Reagan remained a loyal New Deal Democrat, and his hero was Franklin D. Roosevelt. Reagan also

ELECTION OF 1980

NUMBERS IN
EACH STATE
INDICATE
ELECTORAL VOTES

	ELECTORAL VOTE	POPULAR VOTE
REAGAN (R)	489	43,904,153
CARTER (D)	49	35,483,883
ANDERSON (I)	0	5,719,222

MASS. 14
R.I. 4
CONN. 8
N.J. 17
DELA. 3
MD. 10
DISTRICT OF COLUMBIA 3
ME. 4
N.H. 4
VT. 3
N.Y.
PA. 27
W. VA. 6
VA. 12
N.C. 13
S.C. 8
GA. 12
FLA. 17
MICH. 21
IND. 13
OHIO 25
KY. 9
TENN. 10
ALA. 9
MISS. 7
WISC. 11
ILL. 26
IOWA 8
MO. 12
ARK. 6
LA. 10
MINN. 10
N. DAK. 3
S. DAK. 4
NEBR. 5
KAN. 7
OKLA. 8
TEXAS 26
WYO. 3
COLO.
N. MEX. 4
MONT. 4
IDA. 4
UTAH 4
ARIZ. 6
WASH. 9
ORE. 6
NEV. 3
CALIF. 45
HAWAII 4
ALASKA 3

actively campaigned for Harry S Truman and liberal Democratic candidates in the election of 1948.

Thereafter, however, Reagan underwent a conversion experience from a New Deal liberal to a New Right conservative. A number of factors contributed to this change. Reagan's experience in fighting Communists and his defense of the film industry before HUAC and other congressional investigations made him a staunch anti-Communist, much as he had earlier been a staunch anti-Fascist. After his first marriage—to the actress Jane Wyman—ended unhappily, he married another actress, Nancy Davis, a woman of political skill and conservative political opinions. With the decline of his acting career, Reagan found a new vocation in television as host of the popular *General Electric Theater* and as chief touring spokesman for General Electric products. In the late 1950s, by impromptu speeches at dinners across the country, Reagan gained a reputation as a conservative critic of the welfare state and governmental regulation.

By the early 1960s, Reagan had developed a successful combination of political skills. An accomplished speaker and master of the radio and television media, he had cultivated a dedicated following of conservative activists drawn to his message of limiting the power of government and opposing world communism. In the waning days of the presidential campaign of 1964, when it was clear that Johnson would win a landslide victory over Goldwater, Reagan suddenly emerged as a political figure of nationwide appeal. In a nationally televised address entitled "A Time for Choosing," he stressed the themes of individual independence and freedom from governmental intrusion. Borrowing language from his hero, Franklin D. Roosevelt, Reagan told Americans that they had a "rendezvous with destiny." "We can preserve for our children this the last best hope of man on earth or we can sentence them to take the first step into a thousand years of darkness."

"The Speech," as this address became known, made Reagan a viable candidate for political office, and, in 1966, he challenged long-standing incumbent Edmund G. "Pat" Brown for the governorship of California. Reagan capitalized on discontent with the Johnson presidency and disaffection over Brown's administration. But Reagan also showed unique, almost instinctive, abilities to communicate his message to a broad spectrum of voters. Shedding the image of an ideologue, Reagan moved to the center and won the election with almost 58 percent of the vote. In two terms as governor of California—from 1966 to 1974—Reagan also began to plan to run for the presidency. After a brief and unsuccessful bid for the Republican nomination in 1968, he mounted a major effort in 1976 and only narrowly lost the nomination to the incumbent, President Ford (see pp. 717–718).

The new Reagan administration, elected with what conservatives said was a decisive mandate for change, took shape in late 1980 and early 1981. Although Reagan's cabinet included individuals who had served in past Republican administrations, new faces outnumbered the old ones. The cabinet members principally in charge of economic policy were Secretary of Commerce Malcolm Baldrige and Secretary of the Treasury Donald T. Regan, both successful businessmen. As secretary of state, Reagan chose Alexander M. Haig, formerly an assistant to Kissinger, White House chief of staff during the last year of Nixon's presidency, and former commander of NATO forces in Europe. Reagan appointed Caspar W. Weinberger, former California finance director and, under Nixon, budget director, to lead the Department of Defense. The new attorney general was William French Smith, Reagan's personal attorney. As heads of two new cabinet positions which Reagan had promised to eliminate—education and energy—Reagan appointed Utah educator Terrel H. Bell and the former governor of South Carolina, James B. Edwards. In his most controversial appointment, Reagan named as secretary of the interior James G. Watt, a western conservative and head of an antienvironmentalist lobbying group.

As was true for all presidents since Franklin Roosevelt, the most important appointments were those which provided the most direct access to the chief executive himself. Reagan's principal aides—both of whom had served him since his California governorship—were Edwin Meese III, who became counselor to the president and served as his chief domestic policy adviser, and Michael K. Deaver, who became deputy chief of staff. The third member of this White House "trio" was James A. Baker III, a former adviser of Gerald Ford and George Bush who became Reagan's chief of staff and quickly established himself as the most powerful member of the White House staff. Other important advisers included Jeanne Kirkpatrick, a conservative Democratic critic of Jimmy Carter's human rights policy in Latin America, who was appointed ambassador to the United Nations; William P. Clark, a California lawyer who had been chief of staff while Reagan was governor and now became deputy secretary of state in 1981, national security adviser in 1982, and secretary of the interior in 1983; and Richard V. Allen, a longtime foreign-policy aide to Reagan, who was appointed national security adviser.

3.   THE REAGAN REVOLUTION IN ACTION

In January 1981, Americans faced serious economic problems: during the previous year the inflation rate had been 13 percent; the prime rate of interest, 20 percent; and unemployment, 7.4 percent. Reagan had maintained that these problems were predictable consequences of intrusive governmental intervention, which stifled individual initiative and creative entrepreneurial drive. Reagan, inaugurated as president on January 20, 1981, announced plans to reverse almost five decades of federal policy. He cited economic problems of "great proportions" and declared: "Government is not the solution to our problem; it is the problem." He then pledged to begin a campaign to limit the size and scope of government and to protect the "freedom and dignity of the individual" from "unnecessary and excessive growth of government."

What his admirers would call the "Reagan Revolution" began soon thereafter. In a televised address on February 5, the new president repeated the themes of his inaugural speech. The problems of inflation, unemployment, and stagnant productivity were the consequences of a generation of unnecessary regulation and extravagant spending by big government. Reagan announced plans to forbid federal agencies to replace personnel who retired or resigned and also said that he would appoint a task force, headed by Vice-President Bush, to abolish unnecessary governmental regulations. In an even more important part of the address, Reagan announced what would become the most important legislative proposal of his first administration—reduction of social spending and substantial cuts in the income tax.

Two weeks later, in his State of the Union address, Reagan spelled out this program. He promised reductions in the growth of spending and in taxes, the promotion of a "consistent" monetary policy by the Federal Reserve Board, and the reform or abolition of unnecessary or inefficient regulations. He presented to Congress the first full-fledged attempt since the New Deal to alter the role of government in society and requested that Congress enact $41.4 billion in cuts in social spending, while he assured it that the "truly needy" would be protected in a "social safety net." Reagan pledged the protection of Social Security and Medicare—whose expenditures totaled $216 billion and primarily benefited middle-class Americans—and proposed broad reductions in antipoverty expenditures and cultural programs such as the National Endowment for the Arts and the National Endowment for the Humanities. Most important, he asked Congress to pass a three-year, across-the-board, 30 percent reduction in federal income taxes; a reduction in the maximum marginal tax rate from 75 to 50 percent; substantial reductions in taxes on unearned income; and increases in depreciation schedules for business.

The effect of Reagan's two speeches, which were masterfully delivered, was that his economic program experienced little congressional or public opposition. After Reagan survived an assassination attempt in March 1981, his popularity reached new highs—and stayed there for most of the spring and summer of 1981. On May 7, after attracting the support of forty-seven southern and western Democrats in the House of Representatives, Reagan won a decisive victory for his budget bill. The next week, after the bill passed unscathed in the Senate by a vote of seventy-eight to twenty, Reagan signed it. When the White House proposed another $5.2 billion in cuts in June, Congress dutifully enacted the proposal. The second part of Reagan's program—a 30 percent tax reduction—encountered more opposition, but the substance of Reagan's proposal survived. In late July, Congress, by votes of 238 to 195 in the House of Representatives and 89 to 11 in the Senate, passed a three-year 25 percent

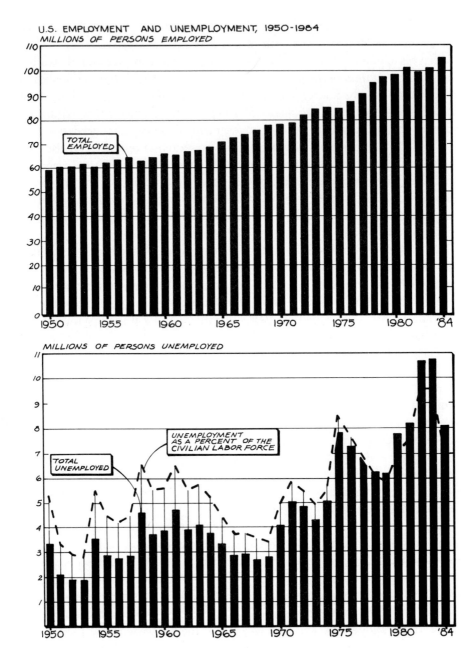

U.S. EMPLOYMENT AND UNEMPLOYMENT, 1950-1984
MILLIONS OF PERSONS EMPLOYED

TOTAL
EMPLOYED

MILLIONS OF PERSONS UNEMPLOYED

UNEMPLOYMENT
AS A PERCENT OF THE
CIVILIAN LABOR FORCE

TOTAL
UNEMPLOYED

reduction in income taxes. The first year's reduction of 5 percent, which was delayed until October 1, would be followed by cuts of 10 percent during the next two years.

Advocates of Reagan's new economic policy maintained that the combination of reduced federal spending and lower taxes would make possible an American economic renaissance. Critics, on the other hand (who quoted George Bush's words during the primary campaign of 1980 to the effect that Reagan's program was "voodoo economics"), claimed that the combination of budget cuts and tax reductions disproportionately hurt the poor while primarily benefiting the rich. Whatever its effects, the fiscal and political consequences of these policies were obscured by the most serious recession since the 1930s, set off by the Federal Reserve Board's effort, begun in 1979, to restrain inflation by restricting monetary growth. The American economy was in deep recession during 1981 and 1982. Industries such as automobiles and construction, which were traditionally most sensitive to high interest rates (above 14 percent during 1982), experienced a collapse in consumer demand. At the same time, intensified foreign competition, partly brought on by the emergence of industrializing economies in Asia and Latin America and partly by the inflated value of the American dollar, hurt basic industries such as automobiles, steel, mining, and textiles. At the worst part of the recession, almost 12 percent of the American work force was unemployed, and between 1980 and 1982 Americans experienced a decline of 3.5 percent in their real income. As the party in power during the most severe recession since 1937, the GOP suffered serious losses in the congressional off-year elections of 1982. The Republicans retained control of the Senate but lost twenty-six seats and effective control of the House of Representatives.

Another important consequence of Reagan's fiscal experiment was the appearance, after 1982, of massive deficits in the federal budget. Not since the Eisenhower administration had any president been able to balance the budget with any regularity. The last balanced budget had been in 1969, and it occurred, almost by accident, during the first year of Nixon's presidency. When Reagan took office in 1981, he faced a budget deficit of $56 billion. In his economic program of 1981, Reagan argued that the consequences of reduced social spending and taxes and steep increases in military spending would be counterbalanced by strong economic growth that would bring offsetting federal revenues. In reality, it was clear that Reagan's program had made a catastrophe out of the problem of budget deficits. In 1981–1982, the deficit was $111 billion; during the subsequent three years, deficits grew to about $200 billion a year. In August 1982, Congress enacted a three-year reduction of $30 billion in Medicaid, Medicare, food stamps, and federal pension benefits. At the same time, with Reagan's support, it passed a three-year $98.3 billion tax increase which raised taxes on cigarettes and telephone service, reduced income tax deductions for medical expenses, and tightened reporting procedures for interest and dividend income.

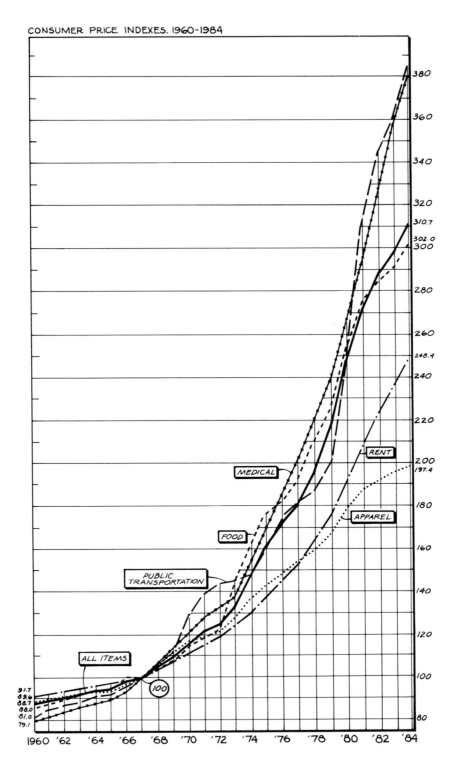

CONSUMER PRICE INDEXES, 1960-1984

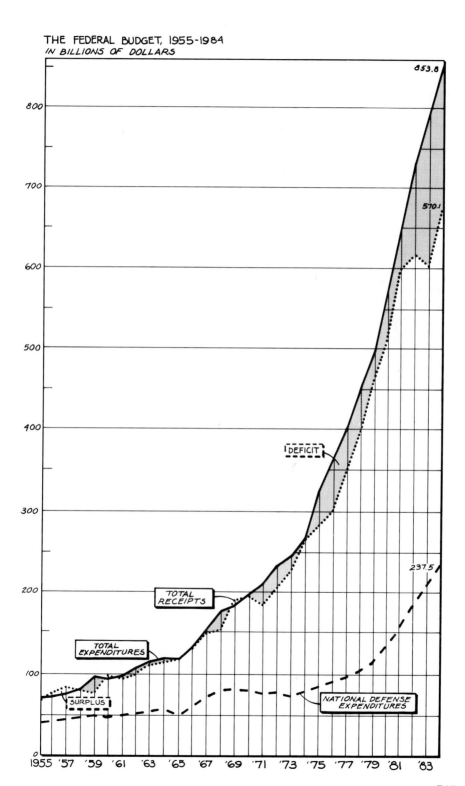

THE FEDERAL BUDGET, 1955-1984
IN BILLIONS OF DOLLARS

853.8

570.1

DEFICIT

237.5

TOTAL
RECEIPTS

TOTAL
EXPENDITURES

NATIONAL DEFENSE
EXPENDITURES

SURPLUS

1955 '57 '59 '61 '63 '65 '67 '69 '71 '73 '75 '77 '79 '81 '83

4.   A NEW SOCIAL POLICY

The Reagan Revolution had important effects in a variety of other areas aside from economic policy. To begin with, the administration began a determined effort to cut back or end a number of social programs. It did so for two reasons. One was a need to reduce the rising budget deficit. Administration budget cutters, especially the budget director, David Stockman, permitted few domestic programs to escape their scrutiny. Another factor was ideological: a strong belief among Reagan and his advisers that the elimination of federal intervention was a necessary precondition for an "opportunity society" and a social, cultural, and economic rebirth.

An important example of this new approach was the administration's environmental policy. Reagan and Secretary of the Interior Watt strongly favored the accelerated development of American natural resources. They believed that the array of federal environmental laws passed during the 1970s—the Clean Air acts of 1970 and 1977, the Clean Water Acts of 1972 and 1977, and the Superfund Toxic-Waste Cleanup Act of 1980—unnecessarily impeded economic growth. While proposing a wholesale revision of these laws, the Reagan administration acted to loosen federal control over natural resource development. In 1981, Watt proposed to open up millions of acres of oil lands to private development. Some of these lands were in or near wilderness and national park areas or in environmentally sensitive coastal and offshore regions. Watt also proposed further reductions in the public domain by prohibiting any additions to national parks and by offering some 35 million acres of federal lands for sale to the public.

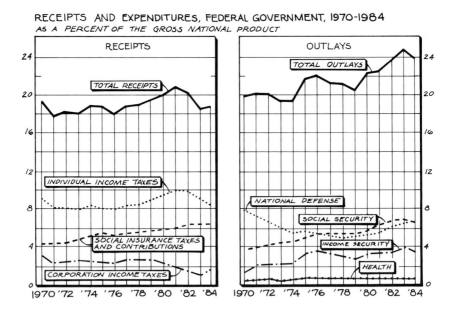

RECEIPTS AND EXPENDITURES, FEDERAL GOVERNMENT, 1970-1984
AS A PERCENT OF THE GROSS NATIONAL PRODUCT

More particularly, Watt moved to weaken the regulatory power of the Environmental Protection Agency (EPA). As head of the EPA, Watt chose Anne Gorsuch (later Burford), who, without any experience in environmental policy, worked hard to reduce staff, gut programs, and dilute the EPA's regulatory powers. In these activities, the Reagan administration could claim considerable success. Between 1981 and 1984, the EPA's staff was reduced by 29 percent, while funds for EPA programs declined by 44 percent.

It soon became clear that Reagan's environmental policy and his appointment of Watt were notably less popular than his economic policy. Watt's proposals to dismantle federal environmental protections were greeted by vigorous opposition; he and the administration were soon opposed by every major environmental group in the nation. In 1982, public opinion polls showed that 67 percent of those questioned opposed the weakening of environmental protection, even if it did impede economic growth. Watt lacked public support and experienced increasing problems with Congress. It rejected his attempt to curtail national park expansion in 1981 and a year later refused to give him authority to lease wilderness lands for mineral development. Similarly, proposals to revise antipollution legislation languished in Congress.

By the end of the first Reagan administration, Watt's and the administration's indifference and even hostility to environmental protection were clear political liabilities. Irregularities in the administration of the multibillion-dollar Superfund for the cleanup of toxic wastes led to the trial and conviction of its administrator, Rita Lavelle, and forced the resignation of Burford and twenty other top EPA officials in early 1983. Attempting to mollify public opinion, Reagan then appointed a former Nixon administration official, William Ruckelshaus, as EPA chief. In 1982, some forty congressmen and most of the nation's environmental groups demanded Watt's resignation. After Watt was quoted in 1983 as having made derogatory remarks about handicapped persons, he found himself forced to resign on October 9, 1983. He was replaced by the national security adviser, William P. Clark.

In another area of late-twentieth-century federal intervention—civil rights— the Reagan administration also attempted to introduce significant changes. Reagan had earlier expressed his hostility to affirmative action programs, which attempted to increase minority representation in employment, housing, or politics. Once in office, the Reagan administration made clear its intention to reverse federal civil rights policies in effect since the Eisenhower presidency. The Reagan administration contended that policies designed to increase black employment, reduce discrimination in housing, and expand black political participation had produced as many harmful as beneficial effects. "Reverse discrimination," the administration charged, was itself unfair discrimination and reduced overall efficiency through the hiring of unqualified applicants. Administration officials proposed several major changes. While planning the strict limitation of coercive intervention, they encouraged voluntary compliance with nondiscriminatory employment and housing practices. Perhaps even more important, the administration proposed, first, that *proof* of intent to discriminate had to be established before federal intervention occurred and, second, that quotas, numerical goals, and timetables be rejected as means to compensate for past discrimination.

This narrow interpretation of federal civil rights responsibilities was soon put into practice. As part of its attempt to reduce federal expenditures, the administration between 1981 and 1983 reduced the budgets of the two major antidiscriminatory agencies—the Equal Employment Opportunity Commission (EEOC) and the Office of Federal Contract Compliance Programs (OFCCP)—adjusted for inflation, by 10 and 24 percent, respectively. During the same period, the Civil Rights Division of the Justice Department experienced a budget reduction of 13 percent. In key areas of education, housing, and employment, enforcement of antidiscrimination declined precipitately. The number of employment-related complaints filed by the OFCCP against governmental contractors declined from fifty-three in 1980 to five in 1982 and to eighteen in 1983. The EEOC filed 60 percent fewer cases in 1983 than it had three years earlier.

Even more dramatic changes occurred in education. The Civil Rights Division of the Justice Department, departing from the practice of the previous four administrations, rejected any coercive means of achieving school desegregation and supported only the removal of "official impediments" to racial balance. As a result, by 1983 it had filed only one school desegregation case. In two important cases which eventually reached the Supreme Court, Reagan's Justice Department filed briefs opposing traditional means of desegregation. In January 1982, in a case brought by Bob Jones University of Greenville, South Carolina, and the Goldsboro, North Carolina, Christian Schools against the Treasury Department, the administration supported abolition of the two-decades-old policy of refusing tax-exempt status to nonprofit institutions which discriminated against blacks. The Supreme Court, by a vote of eight to one, ruled in 1983 that the Treasury Department's policy was legal. A year later, however, in another decision, the Court held that withdrawal or denial of federal funds could be used as an antidiscriminatory weapon only in those particular educational *programs*, as opposed to institutions, in which discrimination was practiced.

As was the case in its environmental policy, the Reagan administration's new approach toward civil rights encountered strong opposition. In 1981, when the Voting Rights Act came before Congress for renewal, the administration was lukewarm toward the measure and opposed amendments to strengthen it. Only after considerable public and congressional pressure did Reagan endorse passage of the bill and sign it in 1982. During the spring of 1982, meanwhile, the administration evoked strong opposition when it attempted to discharge certain members of the United States Civil Rights Commission and replace them with supporters of administration policies. Congress responded with legislation, passed in November 1982, which extended the authority of the commission but provided that four of its eight members would be appointed by Congress. Even so, the administration's social policy was more successful in the area of civil rights than in any other.

In other areas, Reagan's ability to translate rhetoric into legislation and policy was less clear. The president, elected in 1980 with the support of Protestant fundamentalist and New Right groups, was strongly committed to reversing the liberalization of restrictions on abortions and to permitting some form of organized prayer in public schools. Both of these issues were produced, in a sense, by Supreme Court decisions that had banned governmental intervention in individual decisions, so it was not without considerable irony that Reagan's position on these so-called social issues meant greater, not less, governmental interference. However, advocates of restricting abortion and mandating school prayer made scant progress in changing federal policies. Attempts to introduce constitutional amendments to permit "voluntary" school prayer in public schools and to ban abortions were frustrated by threats of liberal filibusters in the Senate. More important still was the fact that the administration provided virtually no support for either cause.

Whether judged ultimately successful or not, the experiment in social policy begun by the Reagan administration marked a historic reversal of federal policies. For the first time since the New Deal, antipoverty programs were substantially reduced, on the assumption that excessive "dependency" of the poor on federal welfare actually encouraged poverty rather than reducing it. Similarly, new policies on the environment and on civil rights attempted and largely succeeded in reducing federal intervention in the marketplace.

5. SUPERPOWER RELATIONS AND THE REAGAN PRESIDENCY

Ronald Reagan brought clearly defined foreign-policy objectives to the White House. Because his administration was guided by an ideological predisposition about the need to combat the global power and influence of the Soviet Union, it should come as little surprise that a significant deterioration in Soviet-American relations ensued. Deeply suspicious of the Soviet Union, Reagan believed that SALT I and SALT II and other treaties simply legitimized Soviet nuclear superiority. Although the administration tacitly agreed to abide by the unratified SALT II treaty—which Carter had withdrawn from consideration by the Senate after the Soviet invasion of Afghanistan—it began the largest peacetime military buildup in American history.

A new anti-Soviet rhetoric accompanied the military buildup. Typical of the administration's tone was the speech that Reagan delivered before the British

Parliament during his first visit to Europe, on June 8, 1982. He denounced Soviet expansionism and attempted to rally Western opinion around a "crusade for freedom." Later, in what became a frequently quoted statement, Reagan, speaking before the National Association of Evangelicals on March 8, 1983, described the Soviet Union as an "evil empire." "While they preach the supremacy of the state, declare its omnipotence over individual man, and predict its eventual domination of all peoples of the earth," he declared, "they are the focus of evil in the modern world." Reagan's rhetoric was matched by polemics from Moscow. In a visit to Bonn, West Germany, Soviet Foreign Minister Gromyko denounced the members of the Reagan administration as "compulsive gamblers and adventurists who declare that they are ready to plunge mankind into a nuclear catastrophe."

The battle of words was based not only upon ideological differences but also upon real strategic differences. Soviet-American relations had already worsened during the late Carter years as a result of Soviet adventurism in Africa and the invasion of Afghanistan. Then political instability in Poland, which was produced by the emergence of the anti-Communist and anti-Soviet labor union Solidarity, in the summer of 1980, provoked a severe crackdown in December 1981. In response, the Reagan administration instituted a series of harsh economic sanctions against the Polish regime and its Soviet sponsor, including an unsuccessful attempt to persuade Western European nations not to participate in the construction of a multibillion-dollar Siberian-European natural gas pipeline.

Perhaps the main source of Soviet-American tension, however, was NATO's decision in December 1979 to modernize its intermediate-range nuclear forces (INF) in response to a buildup of hundreds of mobile and highly accurate Soviet SS-20 missiles. The NATO countries of Great Britain, West Germany, Italy, Belgium, and the Netherlands agreed to a "two-track" policy of planning for deployment of new INF missiles while making greater efforts at negotiation. Almost immediately, the Soviets responded with a high-pressure campaign designed to sway European public opinion, block deployment, and effectively drive a wedge between the United States and its NATO allies. In part in response to this campaign, but probably more directly in response to the aggressive rhetoric of the Reagan administration, public opposition to installation grew in Europe during 1981 and 1982 and culminated in large demonstrations in Great Britain, the Netherlands, and West Germany.

There were also Soviet-American negotiations to reduce INF missiles in November 1981, but they were soon stalled by Soviet insistence that the independent British and French nuclear forces be counted as part of NATO's armament. By late 1983, with these negotiations stalemated, the United States began deployment of its new cruise missiles and Pershing II missiles in Great Britain, Italy, and West Germany. The Soviets had warned that installation of these weapons would end the INF negotiations and worsen East-West relations.

On November 23, 1983, a day after the West German Bundestag reaffirmed its support for deployment, Soviet negotiators walked out of the INF talks. Yuri Andropov, who had succeeded to power after Brezhnev died in late 1982, announced that the Soviets would deploy additional SS-20s and that medium-range missiles would be positioned aboard submarines off the American coast.

Along with the basic divergence on "Euromissiles" came the bitter recrimination that followed the shooting down by a Soviet war plane, on September 1, 1983, of an unarmed airliner—Korean Air Lines flight number 007—after it flew into a sensitive area of Soviet airspace. The disaster cost 269 lives. Reagan subsequently announced sanctions against the USSR, including restrictions on travel by Soviet citizens and the suspension of negotiations to establish new consulates. Despite a noticeable moderation in the anti-Soviet rhetoric of the Reagan administration during early 1984, the atmosphere of superpower relations remained poisoned. In May, the Soviets announced a boycott—supposedly because of inadequate security for Soviet athletes—of the 1984 summer Olympic games in Los Angeles.

Superpower relations had, in this way, reached what many experts were characterizing as the nadir since 1945. George F. Kennan, historian and former ambassador to the Soviet Union, described relations as "dreadful and dangerous" and as having the "unfailing characteristics of a march toward war." By late 1983, trade between the two countries had almost ground to a halt; the immigration of Soviet Jews, which had numbered in the tens of thousands annually in the late 1970s, had virtually ended; efforts for arms control had collapsed. And the extensive scientific and cultural exchanges begun under Nixon had also slowed to a halt. Some improvement in relations appeared possible when Reagan met with Gromyko in September 1984—the first such high-level Soviet-American meeting since the beginning of the Reagan presidency—and when arms control talks resumed in Geneva in January 1985. The coming to power of Mikhail Gorbachev after the death of the Soviet leader Konstantin Chernenko, Andropov's successor, in late 1984 brought to these negotiations rather more posturing by both sides than any real progress.

It appeared that Sino-American relations would also deteriorate after Reagan's inauguration. Reagan, long a supporter of Taiwan and an inveterate opponent of the People's Republic of China, had criticized the normalization of relations during the campaign of 1980. The Chinese thus remained cool to the new administration and were particularly irritated by its expressed willingness to continue the sale of arms to Taiwan. Not until August 1982, when the two countries agreed to a joint communiqué, was the impasse broken. Under its terms, the Reagan administration disavowed a long-term policy of arms sales to Taiwan and promised that any sales would not exceed, "either in qualitative or in quantitative terms," existing levels. For its part, China promised to pursue a policy of peaceful reunification with Taiwan.

Relations between the United States and China continued to improve. George

Shultz, who replaced Alexander Haig as secretary of state in June 1982, visited Peking in early February 1983 and reestablished the high-level military contacts between Chinese and American officials which had begun under Carter but had been suspended after Reagan became president. Despite persisting differences over Taiwan and trade issues, further visits by American officials during the spring and autumn of 1983 brought a general improvement in relations. In late May 1983, Secretary of Commerce Baldrige assured the Chinese that restrictions on the export of sophisticated technology with military applications would be relaxed. In June 1983, administration officials announced that China would be given the more favorable trade status of "friendly non-allied" nation. Then, in late September 1983, Secretary of Defense Weinberger visited Peking, where he conducted talks with his Chinese counterpart, General Zhang Aiping. As a result of this meeting, Weinberger announced a further relaxation of restrictions on the sale of "defensive" military technology (including antitank weaponry and antiaircraft systems). Weinberger further said that military exchanges would begin between the two countries in 1984 and that American warships would be permitted to call on Chinese ports for the first time since 1949.

Sino-American relations reached a high point of cordiality in early 1984, when the Chinese and American leaders exchanged state visits. In January, the Chinese premier, Zhao Ziyang, visited the United States, where he was received warmly by the Reagan administration. Then, in late April and early May, Reagan visited China, his first trip to a Communist country and the first visit by an American president since the normalization of relations in 1979. In an address at the Great Hall of the People on April 27, Reagan declared that he had come to China "to build on what binds us." He also signed four agreements two days later for nuclear cooperation (providing for the sale of American nuclear power technology), scientific and technical cooperation, cultural exchanges, and reciprocal tax benefits.

6.   REAGAN AND THE MIDDLE EAST

Sorely testing the foreign-policy abilities of the Reagan White House were the complex problems of the Middle East. During the first year of the Reagan presidency, Secretary Haig attempted to persuade conservative Arab states that it was in their vital interest to form an anti-Soviet "strategic consensus." He said that the pro-Western regimes of Saudi Arabia, Egypt, and Jordan had more to gain by opposing Soviet objectives than they did in perpetuating a pointless conflict against Israel. As an incentive to join in unofficial cooperation with Israel, the United States promised to extend the benefits of sophisticated American military technology. As a token of such future benefits, the administration— despite strong opposition from Israel's congressional supporters—sold Saudi Arabia three airborne warning and command systems (AWACS) in 1981.

It was almost immediately apparent, however, that the Israelis and Arabs agreed that the Middle East's main threat was not the Soviet Union but each other. When its intelligence services became convinced that Iraq was on the verge of producing nuclear weapons, Israel launched a preemptive bombing raid on Baghdad and destroyed its antagonist's main nuclear research and production center there. Even more apparent Arab-Israeli differences persisted over the Palestinian issue and the related question of which foreign power would dominate Lebanon. In the early 1970s, after its expulsion from Egypt and Jordan, the Palestine Liberation Organization (PLO) made Lebanon and its capital, Beirut, its diplomatic and military base. When civil war broke out between the politically dominant but numerically inferior Christians and the majority Sunni and Shiite Moslems in 1975, the PLO allied itself with the Moslems and succeeded in altering Lebanon's balance of power.

Syria intervened in the Lebanese civil war in 1976, but this intervention solved none of the problems that underlay the conflict in the first place. If anything, sectarian violence grew worse, restrained only by the presence of 35,000 Syrian troops. Yet, because Syrian and PLO dominance over Lebanon seriously threatened Israeli security, the Israelis, in response to terrorist attacks in northern Israel, launched a full-scale invasion in 1978 and briefly occupied the southern third of Lebanon. For the next four years, the Israelis continued to bomb Palestinian positions with impunity. Then, growing tensions led to an all-out Israeli invasion of Lebanon in June 1982. It was designed to uproot and destroy PLO strength and to end Syrian dominance of Lebanon.

The Israelis soon destroyed the Syrian Air Force and occupied Lebanon as far north as the outskirts of Beirut and as far east as the strategic Bekaa Valley. The Israeli invasion disrupted the internal unity and greatly diminished the fighting abilities of the PLO and demoralized the Palestinian movement, but it also induced direct American intervention and new instability in the Middle East. Sensing an opportunity to arrange a general settlement, the Washington administration in August 1982 agreed to send American marines to sponsor the evacuation of the remaining PLO fighters in West Beirut. Subsequently, it also provided strong support to a Lebanese government dominated by Christians and friendly to Israel, and helped in May 1983 to negotiate an Israel-Lebanon peace treaty which provided for Israeli evacuation. In late September 1982, the administration had proposed an overall Middle Eastern settlement. Under this arrangement, Israel would grant autonomy to West Bank Palestinians federated with Jordan in exchange for Arab recognition and security guarantees to Israel.

Soon, however, events made a shambles of the administration's policy. Both Israel and the Arab states in question emphatically rejected the American peace proposals. Meanwhile, in the power vacuum created by the defeat and partial withdrawal of the Syrians, Christian-Moslem conflict created new turbulence in Lebanon. Having committed himself to the pro-Western regime of President

Amin Gemayael, Reagan decided in the summer of 1983 to send a detachment of marines to guard the Beirut airport and dispatched, as a show of force, a naval flotilla. American marines, who were joined by a large detachment of French paratroopers, aroused intense anti-Western feeling and provoked terrorism. In 1983 and 1984, suicide terrorists attacked the American Embassy in Beirut. An even more serious incident occurred on October 23, 1983, when Islamic terrorists simultaneously drove trucks loaded with explosives into the American and French compounds, killing some 300 soldiers, about 260 of whom were Americans.

The waning strength of the Gemayael government in late 1983 and early 1984 had its counterpart in the inability of the American military presence to influence events to any good purpose. After Syrian antiaircraft batteries opened fire on American naval reconnaissance flights in early December 1983, Reagan responded by ordering air strikes on Syrian positions in central Lebanon. When the Syrians continued to harass naval reconnaissance, the battleship *New Jersey* opened fire in mid-December with over eighty 16-inch shells. Reagan declared before Congress that the "international credibility" of the United States depended upon its steadfast support of its commitment to Lebanon. But it was obvious by early 1984 that the American position was untenable and, with little fanfare, Reagan ordered the withdrawal of the marines on February 7, 1984.

7. REAGAN AND LATIN AMERICAN REVOLUTIONS

The foreign region which soon drew the greatest attention of the Reagan administration was Central America. The unpopular Nicaraguan regime of Anastasio Somoza Debayle was overthrown in July 1979 by a coalition of left-wing Sandinista guerrillas, businessmen, and the urban middle class. During the last year of the Carter administration, and especially with Reagan's inauguration, Nicaraguan-American relations steadily deteriorated. Although Carter attempted to maintain American influence through economic aid, the Reagan administration, deeply suspicious of the Sandinistas and convinced that they were proxies for the expansion of Soviet and Cuban influence in Central America, terminated all aid in the spring of 1981 and grew increasingly hostile.

By 1982, the Reagan administration was openly supporting the anti-Sandinista military organization known as the Contras—the Nicaraguan Democratic Force (FDN), formed in August 1981 and composed primarily of exiled members of Somoza's National Guard. Operating from bases in neighboring Honduras, the FDN received training and funds from the CIA. In September 1982, a second, smaller Contra group, the Democratic Revolutionary Alliance (ARDE), composed primarily of disillusioned former supporters of the Sandinistas, was founded and began to operate in southern Nicaragua from bases in Costa Rica.

These groups succeeded in harassing, but not in seriously undermining, the revolutionary government. By 1985, they had conducted a campaign of terrorism, blown up oil installations, and mined Nicaragua's harbors, but they had evoked no real popular support or won any important military victories. American support for the Contras met increasing skepticism and even opposition from the Congress of the United States. When, in April 1984, it was disclosed that CIA frogmen had played a key role in the mining of Nicaraguan harbors, the Senate passed a resolution that stated that "no funds heretofore appropriated . . . shall be obligated or expended for the purpose of planning, executing or supporting the mining of the ports or territorial waters of Nicaragua."

By 1984, congressional fears of entanglement in Nicaraguan affairs led to an increasing assertion of control on Capitol Hill over Central American policy. Despite several efforts by Reagan to rally the American people behind his policy, public opinion polls showed a determined resistance to any further military intervention. Bolstered by public doubts about, and a lack of support for, Reagan's policy, the House in July 1983 defeated an administration proposal of $50 million in aid for the Contras. After pressure from Senate Republicans and the White House, the House agreed to a scaled-down version which provided $24 million in aid but stipulated that the CIA had to return six months later for any additional funds. But, in an amendment added by Representative Edward Boland of Massachusetts, Congress banned any American actions designed to overthrow the Nicaraguan government. Several developments further eroded congressional support for the administration's Nicaraguan policy. In late 1983 and 1984, CIA-sponsored terrorism alienated congressional opinion, as did the admission by the CIA in April 1984 that the Contras lacked the military strength or popular support they needed if they were to succeed. To most observers, it had become obvious that the original purpose of "covert" aid—the interdiction of the flow of arms from Nicaragua to insurgents in El Salvador—had been replaced by the objective of harassing, destabilizing, or even overthrowing the Sandinista regime.

When the administration attempted to obtain further congressional aid for the Contras, it encountered strong opposition. In late May 1984, the House of Representatives refused to finance covert aid; when the administration renewed its request in October, it was again rebuffed. Moreover, in what became known as Boland II, Congress banned any agency involved in "intelligence activity" from engaging in covert action in Nicaragua. Then, in May 1985, the House refused to extend even the paltry sum of $14 million in "humanitarian" aid for the Contras. As relations between the Sandinista government and the United States deteriorated even further, the Reagan administration exerted even greater pressure. Despite the holding of apparently free elections in Nicaragua in the autumn of 1984, the Reagan administration refused to characterize the regime as anything but totalitarian. Then, in early May 1985, after the House had cut off all aid to the Contras, Sandinista leader Daniel Ortega visited Moscow and

Eastern Europe. In response, Reagan imposed a total embargo on Nicaraguan-American trade, and the House of Representatives agreed to the extension of a modicum of humanitarian aid to the Contras.

The Reagan administration's fears about the contagion of Marxist-Leniinst revolution appeared to be borne out in El Salvador, a tiny and impoverished Central American nation. Its repressive political system, even worse than Nicaragua's under Somoza, only aggravated overpopulation, maldistribution of wealth, and underdevelopment, thus making it ripe for revolution. After decades of control by right-wing military regimes, a military coup brought a reformist junta to power in 1979 which promised wide-ranging political reforms and a program of land redistribution. Within a year, however, the junta—despite the support of the Carter administration—was caught in a polarization between the left and the right: a bitter civil war ensued between the government and a rebel group eventually known as the Farabundo Martí National Liberation Front. By 1982, 34,000 Salvadorans had died in the conflict.

The early response of the Reagan administration was to emphasize El Salvador as the area of vital American interest and to internationalize its civil war. Soon after Reagan's inauguration in 1981, the State Department, at the urging of Secretary Haig, published a white paper which charged extensive Soviet and Cuban intervention in El Salvador and proposed a major military and economic effort to thwart Communist expansion in Central America. A presidential commission, headed by Henry Kissinger, came to the same conclusions when it issued its report in January 1984. The report maintained that Central America was a region which "critically" concerned American security interests and stated that the origins of the crisis lay in conditions which were "both indigenous and foreign." Accordingly, it recommended what had become the main features of Reagan's Salvadoran policy: the infusion of large amounts of economic and military aid. In particular, the Kissinger Commission proposed that the annual level of American aid should increase from $200 million in 1984 to $400 million in 1990.

Along with its emphasis upon aid, however, the Kissinger Commission also recommended what had become—mainly because of public and congressional pressure—a cardinal tenet of Reagan's Central American policy: incentives for the development of stable, democratic political systems. Beginning in 1981, Congress provided Salvadoran aid on the condition that the State Department annually certify that progress in human rights had been made. Under American pressure, El Salvador made considerable strides toward the development of a democratic political system: the election in March 1982 of a constituent assembly, the writing and adoption of a constitution in December 1983, the election of the moderate reformer José Napoleón Duarte as president in May 1984, and further legislative elections in 1984.

Frequently, the objective of encouraging democratic development ran head-on into the Salvadoran oligarchy's control over the military—and, through it, the political system. Consequently, before 1983, progress came slowly in effecting land reform or ending the human rights violations of military "death squads" which abducted, tortured, and murdered with virtual impunity. According to one study by the Roman Catholic Church's legal aid office, about 4,800 Salvadorans were killed in military operations and about 5,300 were killed in assassinations by regular military or paramilitary units during 1983. Since 1982, there had been a pattern of violence against civilians which was "persistent, grave, and massive."

Nonetheless, a determined effort by the Reagan administration, beginning in late 1983, to end these gross human rights abuses eventually brought results. About the same time, the Salvadoran military reorganized its senior command structure and began to emphasize professionalism and combat prowess. After Duarte's Christian Democrats captured control of the Salvadoran legislature in March 1985, the armed forces refused to allow a violent right-wing backlash by the oligarchy. On the military front, the Salvadoran government by 1985 had managed to prevent a guerrilla victory. Under a program of aid and training— much of it done in American bases in neighboring Honduras—the United States succeeded in building counterinsurgent Salvadoran army units that took the offensive and actively engaged rebel units after 1983. Urged on by the United States, Duarte began negotiations with rebel groups in September 1984 and continued them intermittently, although with little success, through 1985.

Closely linked to Reagan's Central American policy was a renewed attention to the Caribbean Basin. In 1981, the president proposed the Caribbean Basin Initiative (CBI), which would provide extensive American economic aid to Caribbean and Central American nations. As Reagan put it in an address, the CBI sought to "bring the power of private enterprise—America's most potent weapon—to help Latin America and the Caribbean." Although the House approved the bill in December 1982, it was delayed in the Senate and not approved by both houses of Congress until August 1983. The act provided a long-term program of aid and development support for non-Communist nations which cooperated with American antidrug programs, had concluded an extradition treaty with the United States, and met American conditions about their nationalization and expropriation policies.

Perhaps the most serious test of Reagan's Caribbean policy occurred in the tiny island republic of Grenada, where a revolution in 1979 had brought to power Maurice Bishop and the Marxist New Jewel Movement. When Bishop declared a People's Revolutionary Government (PRG) and established closer ties with Cuba and the Soviet Union, Grenada's relations with the United States grew very tense. Bishop's government, excluded from the CBI, suffered severe economic problems and Bishop attempted to improve relations by visiting the United States during May 1983. But his attempt at diplomacy—rebuffed by the Reagan administration—further worsened his standing among hard-line New

Jewel Movement supporters. He was overthrown and murdered in October and replaced by a Revolutionary Military Council.

Reagan was now worried about the safety of more than six hundred American medical students studying in Grenada. He also saw a chance to strike a decisive blow against Soviet-Cuban influence in the Western Hemisphere. Rumors of an American invasion spread as an American naval task force, led by the aircraft carrier *Independence,* was sent to the Caribbean on October 21. Four days later, an American invading force of over two thousand paratroopers, navy commandos, and marines landed on the island. They were supported diplomatically by the Organization of East Caribbean States (OECS). The invaders met stiff resistance from the fifteen-hundred-man Grenadan Army, which was expecting an invasion and was well fortified, and about the same number of Cuban construction workers. After two days of fighting, the Americans overcame resistance, but at the cost of 42 American, 160 Grenadan, and 71 Cuban lives. Within weeks, the American invaders began to turn over control of the Grenadan government and the administration of justice to an OECS and Caribbean peacekeeping force and, eventually, to the new Grenadan government.

There was strong domestic support in the United States for this show of force, and Reagan derived almost immediate political benefit from it. But less clear were the consequences of the invasion. Reagan partly justified it because he claimed that there was extensive Soviet-Cuban influence in Grenada. A year earlier, he had displayed aerial photographs of efforts to lengthen the airstrip in Grenada's Point Salines and claimed that it was designed to accommodate large Soviet-supplied Cuban aircraft and to militarize the island (the Grenadans claimed that the airport expansion would stimulate tourism). Reagan told Congress that Grenada was becoming a "Soviet-Cuban colony being readied for use as a major military bastion to export terror." Despite these claims, the American occupiers could find no clear evidence of an extensive effort to establish a major military base in Grenada; once in control of the island, they themselves helped to complete the airport. Even more damaging, moreover, was the international condemnation that greeted the invasion. Fidel Castro characterized the American invasion as "an enormous political error." It also attracted widespread condemnation from Latin Americans, who regarded it as an example of resurgent Yankee interventionism. Even the NATO allies—and especially Great Britain, formerly Grenada's colonial master—privately criticized the American invasion and questioned its objectives and accomplishments. Further evidence of the international isolation of the United States came in a UN General Assembly resolution, proposed by Nicaragua and Zimbabwe and passed by a vote of 108 to 9, which condemned the invasion and called for the immediate withdrawal of all foreign troops.

8.   THE ELECTION OF 1984

By the spring and summer of 1984, it was becoming increasingly obvious that Ronald Reagan occupied an impregnable political position. At home, the nation was experiencing a vigorous recovery from the recession of 1981–1982 as personal income rose at the highest yearly rate since World War II. Reagan had fulfilled his major campaign pledges of 1980 to reduce federal taxation, assault the federal bureaucracy, and lower inflation (which declined from over 12 percent in 1980 to 3.8 percent in 1983). At the same time, Reagan had suffered no major foreign-policy disaster, and the nation was enjoying a period of renewed self-confidence and optimism.

Because Reagan's invincibility was less apparent during 1983, the campaign for the Democratic nomination attracted a number of candidates, most of whom were organizing and soliciting support and endorsements fully two years before November 1984. Representing the party's activist liberal wing were Senator Alan Cranston of California; the former senator and presidential nominee in 1972, George McGovern; and the Reverend Jesse Jackson of Illinois, whose appeal was made almost entirely in the name of increased black political power. Another candidate was Senator Gary Hart of Colorado, a leader of "neoliberal" Democrats; he (and they) favored continuing the party's commitment to social justice but also advocated a new emphasis upon economic growth and a strong defense. But the frontrunners soon became Senator John Glenn of Ohio and the former senator and vice-president, Walter Mondale of Minnesota.

Mondale at first appeared to be unbeatable: he built the best and most extensive organization and won the endorsement of the AFL-CIO, feminists, and teachers' unions. When, in the Iowa caucuses, Mondale won a big victory, the momentum behind his nomination seemed irresistible. But Mondale also had clear weaknesses: an excessively strong identification with unions and minority groups, the traditional welfare-state liberalism of the Democratic party, and, most of all, the legacy of the unpopular Carter administration he had served in. Beginning with the New Hampshire primary in March and then with a string of New England primaries, the Mondale bandwagon lost speed and was overtaken by the accelerating campaign vehicle of Hart, whose appeals to youth, change, and a vaguely articulated set of "new ideas" became a force to be reckoned with.

By April 1984, it was clear that the campaign had narrowed down to a Mondale-Hart contest, with Jackson attracting a large percentage of black voters. The campaign in the South was crucial. Just when it appeared that Mondale was facing elimination, he scored victories in the Georgia and Alabama primaries. With the momentum shifted in his favor, Mondale went on to important victories in Illinois, Pennsylvania, and New York. Despite a strong resurgence of support for Hart, who decisively won primaries in California and New Jersey,

the Mondale forces went to the Democratic National Convention in San Francisco in July with an ample majority of the delegates committed to their candidate. Hart's managers attempted to persuade Mondale delegates to switch to
their candidate on the basis of public opinion polls, which showed strong voter
dissatisfaction with Mondale. But the convention nominated the Minnesotan
with little bickering and chose Representative Geraldine Ferraro of New York as
the first woman vice-presidential candidate of a major party in American history.

Actually, it mattered little, because Reagan and the Republican party were
enjoying a period of unrivaled popularity. Unopposed for renomination, Reagan
benefited from an unprecedented degree of public support when the GOP
convention opened in Dallas in August. The convention renominated Reagan
and Bush and endorsed a platform expressing conservative positions on abortion, the equal rights amendment, and school prayer. Little that Mondale did
during the months that followed made any significant impact on Reagan's large
lead in the polls. In a bold gamble, Mondale had attempted to make rising
budget deficits an issue by offering a deficit reduction plan based upon tax
increases. But this strategy failed, for Reagan successfully contrasted Mondale's
tax-increasing proposals with his own tax-cutting policies. In another gamble,
Mondale had hoped that choosing Ferraro might attract the votes of women and
those of Italian-American and Catholic voters. But the disclosure of financial
irregularities on the part of Ferraro and her husband, John Zaccaro, made her
candidacy more of a liability than an asset.

With Reagan's election seemingly assured, the campaign's only dramatic
moments came in October, when, in a televised debate in Louisville, Reagan
appeared faltering and inarticulate. For the next few weeks, Reagan's age and
competence briefly became an issue and accounted for a slight increase in
Mondale support. But after a second debate in Kansas City, in which Reagan was
able to hold his own, public doubts were dispelled. The general election on
November 6, 1984, resulted in a decisive Reagan victory. He won 53.4 million
votes, or 58 percent of the total, as compared to 36.9 million and 41 percent for
Mondale. Reagan won forty-nine states (he only lost—narrowly—in Mondale's
home state of Minnesota) and garnered 525 electoral votes. Thus he bested
Franklin Roosevelt's record of 523 electoral votes in 1936.

Postelection polls showed that Reagan had the support of virtually every
sector of American society. Attracting about a quarter of the Democratic vote,
he also won a majority of the vote of independents and strong majorities in the
South and Middle West. With a majority of Catholic voters behind him, he also
attracted the solid support of white Protestants, especially born-again Christians.
Reagan's support tended to increase according to wealth, although every class—
with the exception of the poorest—endorsed his reelection. In contrast, Mondale attracted a narrower constituency and had little appeal to middle-class
voters. His base among minorities remained strong, for he won strong majorities

ELECTION OF 1984

NUMBERS IN
EACH STATE
INDICATE
ELECTORAL VOTES

	ELECTORAL VOTE	POPULAR VOTE
REAGAN (R)	525	59,428,357
MONDALE (D)	13	36,930,923

N.H. 4
ME. 4
VT. 3
MASS. 13
R.I. 4
CONN. 8
N.Y. 36
N.J. 16
DELA. 3
MD. 10
DISTRICT OF COLUMBIA 3
PA. 27
W.VA. 6
VA. 12
N.C. 13
S.C. 8
FLA. 21
MICH. 20
OHIO 23
IND. 12
KY. 9
TENN. 11
ALA. 9
GA. 12
MISS. 7
ILL. 24
WISC. 11
MINN. 10
IOWA 8
MO. 11
ARK. 6
LA. 10
N. DAK. 3
S. DAK. 3
NEBR. 5
KAN. 7
OKLA. 8
TEXAS 29
MONT. 4
IDA. 4
WYO. 3
UTAH 5
COLO. 8
N. MEX. 5
ARIZ. 7
WASH. 10
ORE. 7
NEV. 3
CALIF. 47
HAWAII 4
ALASKA 3

of the black and Hispanic vote; he attracted thinner majorities among low-income and union voters. But exit polls showed that the Ferraro candidacy had had small effect: Mondale attracted only a minority of both women and Italian-American voters.

Despite the magnitude of the presidential election landslide, except in the South the "coattails" effect of Reagan's victory was small. Preelection polls revealed that Americans liked and admired Reagan but disagreed with many of his policies. Americans, perhaps reflecting this ambivalence, returned a Congress in 1984 which would almost certainly check any vigorous assertion of Reagan's policies. The Republicans maintained control of the Senate, albeit by a smaller majority of 53 to 47; the Democratic majority in the House was only slightly reduced, by 15 seats, to 253 to 182. Reagan's reelection thus testified to voters' confidence in his ability to communicate and to lead. However, there were obviously many doubts about the wisdom of further expansion of the Reagan Revolution.

Reagan's second inaugural address was a restatement of his presidency's accomplishments and a program for future changes. He had assumed office four years before at "a time of economic stress." Through reduced tax rates, lower inflation, and greater employment, he said, "we are creating a nation once again vibrant, robust, and alive." In order to foster this "opportunity society," Reagan promised further efforts to reduce the role of government in American life. Pledging a government of "social compassion," he announced the objective of reducing dependency and raising "the dignity of those who are infirm or disadvantaged." Promising deficit reduction, primarily through budget cuts, he also proposed the general objective of tax simplification. In foreign policy, Reagan, while endorsing the "ancient prayer for peace on earth," pledged resolute steadfastness against the Soviets as "those who scorn our vision of human dignity and freedom." As an important element in negotiations with the USSR from a position of strength, he stressed the need for a crash research program on space-based antiballistic weapons, the Strategic Defense Initiative (SDI)—popularly known as the "Star Wars" program—which would, he said, render nuclear weapons "obsolete" and so make possible a real end to the arms race.

CHAPTER 34

Reagan, Bush, and a New World Order

The landslide victory of Ronald Reagan in 1984 not only solidified his political mandate but seemed to verify the new course that he was steering. The Reagan White House could claim significant accomplishments. At home, Reagan had reoriented the political agenda by launching an attack on the New Deal and post-New Deal welfare bureaucracy. In a host of areas, from airlines to the environment, Reagan pushed for a reduction of governmental involvement so as to unleash the economic potential of the United States. Probably his most important accomplishment was the enactment in 1981 of a major, 25 percent reduction in the federal income tax—the largest such reduction since 1945—and the slashing of marginal rates for higher incomes. Yet Reagan's second term and the term of his successor, George Bush, would bring new uncertainties and challenges to the partisans of the Reagan Revolution. At home, the domestic political agenda stalled on the shoals of a Democratically controlled Congress and a rising tide of budget deficits. Like other presidents, Reagan in his second term and Bush in his term turned to foreign affairs, where they would possess significantly greater freedom of action but where they would also encounter much greater risks.

1. DOMESTIC POLICY IN THE SECOND TERM

Soon after Reagan's inaugural, the White House committed its energies to the passage of what it heralded as the most significant reform in the federal income tax code since 1945. Weeks after the election, Treasury Secretary Donald Regan presented Reagan with a tax reform proposal. Soon after Reagan's State of the Union message in January 1985, the president ordered the formation of a team of experts at the Treasury Department to prepare a new tax plan. Meeting for 310 days, the Treasury group, headed by Regan, kept its deliberations a closely guarded secret. The final form of the administration proposal closely resembled the proposals of two Democrats, Senator Bill Bradley of New Jersey and Representative Richard Gephardt of Missouri, who had been advocating changes in the tax code since 1982.

The result, in a different form from that advanced by either the Bradley-Gephardt or the administration version, was the Tax Reform Act of 1986, which Reagan signed on October 22, 1986. The Tax Reform Act of 1986 brought the most sweeping changes to the tax code since World War II and could justifiably be described as the second Reagan administration's most significant domestic-policy accomplishment. The law reduced the existing number of marginal income tax rates from fourteen to two by 1988. Lowering the maximum marginal tax rate paid by upper-income Americans to 33 percent, it eliminated a number of deductions, including that for consumer interest, while it shifted much of the tax burden toward corporations. The capital gains tax was increased from a previous-level maximum of 20 percent to 28 percent.

The successful effort to enact tax reform, coming after a fierce political battle involving an assortment of special-interest groups, marked a high point in Reagan's influence over Congress during his second term. Yet it was at least partially overshadowed by the budget deficits and the inability of Congress and the president to come to terms with how to deal with them. Although Congress enacted a major tax increase in 1982 and although Walter Mondale attempted to make the budget deficits an issue in 1984, they remained the most troubling political issue of the 1980s. The election of 1984 seemed to confirm the political wisdom of Reagan's pledge not to increase taxes to reduce the deficit, yet neither a Republican White House nor a Democratic Congress was able to arrive at a workable formula that could reduce spending. In December 1985, Congress and the Reagan White House agreed on a new mechanism of fiscal restraint: a formula of phased, targeted reductions in the deficits which would be enforced, if need be, by across-the-board cuts in spending. The Balanced Budget and Emergency Deficit Act of 1985—otherwise known as the Gramm-Rudman Act—incorporated these features and was signed into law on December 12, 1985. By the end of 1986, Reagan had reached a domestic political stalemate lasting the remainder of his presidency. The congressional elections of 1986 sealed Reagan's political future. As the result of those elections, the Democrats succeeded in regaining control of the Senate, which they had lost in 1980, and in increasing their majority in the House. As a result, the 100th Congress would contain 55 Democrats and 45 Republicans in the Senate and 258 Democrats and 173 Republicans in the House. Yet the elections meant no decisive political mandate for the Democrats. Turnout was low—at 37 percent, it was the lowest since 1942—and the probable reason for Republican defeat lay in the fact that twenty-two of the thirty-four contested Senate seats were Republican.

Although generally unsuccessful in relations with Congress, Reagan and his successor, George Bush, had their greatest impact on domestic policy on the Supreme Court. In February 1981, only weeks after the beginning of his presidency, Reagan received the news that Justice Potter Stewart would leave at the end of the Court's term. Although he personally favored more conservative justices, Reagan had made the appointment of the first woman to the Court a campaign promise in 1980. Accordingly, in July 1981 Reagan named Sandra Day O'Connor, an Arizona appeals court judge and former state senator, and she was soon confirmed by the Senate with little opposition.

Five years later, the retirement of Chief Justice Warren Burger provided an even greater opportunity for Reagan to bequeath a lasting legacy. Burger's departure meant the end of a long era in Supreme Court history; it also meant the advent, perhaps, of a completely new character of Court rulings. By appointing Associate Justice William Rehnquist, who had been appointed to the Court by Richard Nixon in 1971, Reagan left little doubt that he was seeking to shift the court rightward. Although opposition to Rehnquist's nomination focused on his views on civil rights and civil liberties, he won confirmation by a comfortable margin of sixty-five to thirty-three in September 1986. To replace Rehnquist, Reagan appointed Antonin Scalia, a federal judge for the District of Columbia since 1982, and the Senate confirmed him unanimously on the same day that it confirmed Rehnquist. Scalia joined Rehnquist as a vigorous advocate of judicial restraint and "strict construction" and would become the most articulate voice for a new conservative majority on the Court.

Reagan had a further opportunity to solidify conservative domination of the Court in June 1987, when Lewis Powell retired. Perhaps overconfident because Scalia, a conservative ideologue, had won such strong approval, the Reagan White House underestimated the opposition when it put forward the nomination of Robert Bork as Reagan's third appointee to the bench in the summer of 1987. Bork had strong credentials and had long been high on Reagan's list of potential appointees. Serving as solicitor general under Nixon, Bork had advocated rolling back the judicial activism of the Warren and Burger Courts. For example, Bork had long attacked the famous *Griswold* v. *Connecticut* (1965) case, which had struck down a Connecticut law making contraceptives illegal on the basis of an "unenumerated" but constitutional right to privacy. Rejecting the "right to privacy," Bork also openly opposed the *Roe* v. *Wade* decision. Since 1982, he had served as a judge on the United States Court of Appeals for the District of Columbia—serving with Scalia—and his decisions there had evoked the opposition of civil rights groups.

As it turned out, however, the Reagan administration miscalculated. Scalia had achieved easy confirmation not so much because of his conservatism as because of his support among Italian-Americans; many senators were unwilling to vote against an Italian-American Supreme Court justice. When Bork's nomination came before a Democratically controlled Senate, that party's leadership had coalesced around the use of Bork's nomination as an opportunity to humiliate the White House. Bork supporters were unprepared for what followed, as civil rights, prochoice, and other liberal groups organized a grass-roots campaign to defeat the nomination. His opponents, led by Senators Edward Kennedy and Joseph Biden of the Judiciary Committee, focused on Bork's written and spoken opinions. The national grass-roots campaign was led by an umbrella organization, the Leadership Conference on Civil Rights, which succeeded in portraying Bork as an opponent of civil rights and of the right to abortion. What ultimately undid the Bork nomination, however, was the testimony of Bork himself before the Senate Judiciary Committee in September 1987. Bork seemed aloof and unfeeling, and public opinion polls showed that, by the end of his testimony, Americans had decided against him. On October 23, 1987, Bork's nomination went down to defeat in the Senate by a margin of fifty-eight to forty-two.

The defeat of the Bork nomination was followed by a comedy of errors, as the Reagan White House nominated Douglas H. Ginsburg, a former Harvard law professor who had also served on the United States Court of Appeals with Bork and Scalia and had earlier been an assistant attorney general in the Reagan administration. Ginsburg had the backing of conservative Republicans, who regarded him as one of their own. Yet his nomination seemed endangered when it became known that his wife had performed abortions and that he had been involved in a potential conflict of interest while in the Justice Department. But what eventually doomed the nomination were reports that Ginsburg had used marijuana while he was a student and a law professor at Harvard. Ginsburg, as a result, withdrew.

After the demise of the Bork and Ginsburg nominations, the Reagan administration nominated Anthony Kennedy, who had been appointed to the federal bench by Ford. Nominated on November 11, 1987, Kennedy won unanimous confirmation on February 3, 1988, in the Senate, where Democrats judged him to be the most moderate justice that they were likely to get. As it turned out, however, although he was something of a civil libertarian, Kennedy otherwise was as conservative as either Bork or Ginsburg likely would have been. In subsequent decisions on the court, Kennedy would play a prominent role in weakening the defense of abortion rights.

By the time Reagan left office in 1989, it had become clear that he was widely viewed as a lame-duck president, especially as regarded domestic issues. His ineffectiveness was the result of several factors. One was the constitutional requirement that he not succeed himself. Toward the end of his presidency, Reagan loudly complained that the constitutional restriction against presidents succeeding themselves—which had been pushed through by Republicans who were frustrated by the four-term presidency of FDR—had limited his influence with Congress. But there were other problems as well. Achieving control over Congress in 1986, the Democrats sabotaged his legislative proposals. His standing with public opinion sagged during the middle of this second term, mainly because of the Iran-Contra affair, discussed below. Perhaps just as important was the turbulence in the White House staff. Reagan's team during his first term—Michael Deaver, Richard Darman, and, most important, Chief of Staff James Baker—departed early in the second term and were replaced by less politically skilled managers. In particular, under the command of Chief of Staff Donald Regan, who had exchanged his post as treasury secretary with Baker, the relations of the White House with the press and Congress and its effectiveness plummeted.

2. A SECRET OPENING TO IRAN

The weakening of Reagan's political strength during the last two years of his presidency lay less with domestic than with foreign affairs. After the unsuccessful intervention in Lebanon and American withdrawal, political and legal authority in that country collapsed, and Lebanon became a center of random violence and terrorism. In 1984, Shiite fundamentalists seized three American hostages and in the next year abducted four more. Although Reagan's public position since taking office in 1981 had been a refusal to negotiate with terrorists, the imprisonment of Americans in the Middle East spurred on an effort by Reagan's foreign-policy staff, especially National Security Adviser Robert C. McFarlane (who had been present during the earlier American debacle in Lebanon) and his successor, John M. Poindexter, to seek negotiations to free the Americans.

McFarlane's ability to develop a policy that eventually was conducted despite the opposition of Reagan's secretaries of defense and state testified to the chaotic condition of presidential leadership during the second term. McFarlane was a career marine officer who had been a military assistant to Henry Kissinger and then served as a deputy to National Security Adviser William Clark beginning in 1982. Under both Clark and his predecessor, Richard V. Allen, the National Security Council (NSC) was in considerable turmoil, and with the confusion in the White House, McFarlane gained direct influence with Reagan. Although McFarlane was a skilled bureaucratic operator, he preferred to work the behind the scenes; one critic charged that he had won White House influence "under cover of dullness." Close to the Israelis, he was convinced that Soviet influence in Iran needed to be deflected and that this strategic interest coincided with the humanitarian need to free the hostages.

McFarlane believed that the best approach to the Shiite terrorists was through Iran, their primary sponsor. But to do so would be to contradict the long-standing American policy of isolating Iran that had been followed since the seizure of the American hostages in Teheran in 1979. Indeed, beginning in December 1983, both Secretary of Defense Weinberger and Secretary of State George Shultz had agreed on what was known as Operation Staunch, an effort to prevent the flow of arms to Iran during its eight-year war with Iraq. In January 1984, moreover, Shultz had designated Iran officially as a sponsor of international terrorism and, on that basis, had imposed export controls on that nation.

Nonetheless, despite official policy to the contrary, McFarlane sought an opening with Iran. But because diplomatic relations had remained broken since the beginning of the Iranian hostage crisis in 1979, McFarlane could work only through an Iranian arms dealer, Manucher Ghorbanifar, who assured him that an opening was possible that would free the hostages. After this tenuous beginning, Reagan secretly approved, on August 2, 1985, the shipment of 100 American TOW antitank missiles to Iran. According to a presidential "finding" (required by law in the event of a covert operation), Israel would serve as the intermediary in the transaction, and the United States would replenish Israeli arms shipped to Iran. A month later, despite the release of no hostages, another arms shipment followed, also approved by Reagan, this one composed of 408 TOWs. Rather than resulting in freedom for all of the hostages, the shipment obtained the release of only a single American, Benjamin Weir, on September 15, 1985.

It should have been apparent at this point that Iran was an unreliable negotiator for the Lebanese Shiites and that its vague promises of freedom for the hostages were meaningless. It should have also been obvious that the overture to Iran and the arms-for-hostages exchanges were undermining existing American policies toward terrorism and toward Iran. Even at this late date, American negotiators McFarlane and his associates could have gracefully ended the talks, conducted via middlemen such as Ghorbanifar, with minimal political and diplomatic damage. Israel itself by the fall of 1985 had ended its involvement in the arms-for-hostages scheme. But the Americans, determined to obtain a hostage breakthrough and operating outside the usual channels of foreign-policy leadership, persisted. McFarlane, lacking Israeli support, developed his own delivery system that was operated by former Air Force General Richard Secord and his associate Albert Hakim, who worked with McFarlane's deputy, Marine Colonel Oliver L. North, but did so as private, for-profit entrepreneurs.

By late 1985 Secord was able to deliver eighteen Hawk antiaircraft missiles to the Iranians, who continued to raise the price for freeing the hostages. In the meantime, lacking legal authorization for these shipments, McFarlane and Poindexter, who succeeded him in late 1985, also faced the opposition of both Weinberger and Shultz. Poindexter secured three additional presidential findings in late 1985 and early 1986 that sanctioned further shipments of arms to the Iranians in order to free the hostages. Meanwhile, McFarlane's deputy, North, was assuming an increasingly prominent role in managing the arms-for-hostages exchanges and in maintaining the Secord-Hakim network.

Yet the arms-for-hostages deal eventually went off track. McFarlane and North found Ghorbanifar, a former member of the Shah's secret police turned arms dealer, an untrustworthy intermediary who relayed a constantly changing set of terms from the Iranians. Although negotiations continued and even involved a secret mission by McFarlane to Teheran in late May 1986, Reagan administration officials found it impossible, despite the shipment of 1,500 missiles, spare parts, and intelligence about Iraqi positions to Iran, to secure an unqualified commitment that all of the hostages would be released. That mission failed in a bizarre four-day, Kafkaesque visit that led nowhere. Indeed, after Secord and North had made an additional delivery of 1,000 TOWs in February 1986, no hostages gained their freedom. Lawrence Jenco was freed in July, but three new hostages were abducted in the fall of 1986. David Jacobsen was freed on November 2, following another delivery of 500 TOWs, but three more Americans had been seized by January 1987.

3.   THE IRAN-CONTRA AFFAIR

At the same time that the Reagan administration was conducting a secret overture to Iran, it had already embarked on a clandestine effort to resupply the Contras despite the congressional cutoff of funds and the restrictions of the Boland amendments of 1983 and 1984 that specifically prohibited intelligence from involvement in Nicaragua. When it seemed likely that Congress would end covert aid to the Contras in early 1984, Reagan had ordered McFarlane to circumvent congressional restrictions by finding alternative sources of money; such noncongressional funds, as Reagan instructed McFarlane, should sustain the Contras "body and soul." McFarlane, working with North, first approached nations that were friendly to the United States but had no direct interest in Central America—countries, in other words, that might seek to expand their influence with the White House through generous contributions to the Contras. In May 1984, the Saudis—who had no national interest in Nicaragua—pledged $1 million a month as a way to curry American favor. By 1985, their commitment had been increased to $2 million a month. Meanwhile, the sultan of Brunei contributed another $10 million. North, who had become McFarlane's primary fund-raiser, solicited contributions from wealthy American donors; contributors often earned a meeting with Reagan himself.

The efforts to achieve a strategic opening to Iran, to free the hostages, and to circumvent congressional restrictions over Contra support ran in parallel tracks during 1984 and 1985. Both were under the direct supervision of the National Security Council and ignored the usual foreign-policy apparatus and bureaucracies at the Department of State and the Department of Defense.

Moreover, even while Reagan was seeking to negotiate with terrorists, publicly he delivered a different message. On April 14, 1986, after a terrorist attack on American servicemen in West Berlin, Reagan ordered United States Air Force and Navy bombers to attack Libya, which he identified as a state sponsor of terrorism. Delivering more than ninety 2,000-pound bombs on the Libyan cities of Tripoli and Benghazi, American bombers scored a direct hit on the barracks of Libyan leader Muammar al-Qaddafi, killing his adopted daughter and wounding two of his sons. The attack was enormously popular with American public opinion, which had long been frustrated by the inability to strike back at terrorism.

Despite its public antiterrorist posture, the secret policies of the Reagan administration were taking a different path. Both of the secret policies, toward Iran and Nicaragua, involved significant risks. Both required the pursuit of a policy that had been publicly repudiated, the subversion of usual constitutional processes, and the establishment of a secret and ultimately unaccountable foreign-policy apparatus. The joining of these two enterprises in early 1986 set the stage for a major disaster. From the start, the enterprises were both connected: the trio of McFarlane, Poindexter, and North controlled both, and they depended on the advice and consent of CIA Director William Casey and the participation of private contractors such as Secord.

By the spring of 1986, the secret Iranian and Contra policies had become directly intertwined. By this point, North, with the concurrence of Secord and Hakim, had been overcharging the Iranians for the arms transferred by Secord's "enterprise." North and the enterprise were charging the Iranians more than four times the arms' market value. In what North later characterized as a "neat idea," the secret effort had now become joined: arms shipments and their "residuals" (or profits) to Iran would not only seek the release of American hostages but also would pay off Ghorbanifar and the Secord-Hakim operation and help to finance the Contra resupply operation. In May 1986, North described the diversion to McFarlane, who had left as national security adviser in December 1985 and was involved as a secret negotiator. The circle of White House advisers involved in this illegal and probably unconstitutional activity included North, his associate Robert Owen (who was not on the White House payroll), and Poindexter, who had known of the diversion since February 1986. Although direct evidence has not survived, it seems likely that the diversion scheme enjoyed the support of CIA Director Casey and some of his deputies. At the same time, a number of White House officials were informed of the secret opening to Iran by the summer of 1986.

It is clear, however, that the diversion scheme was run primarily out of North's office and lacked the participation of the foreign-policy bureaucracy. The Iranian overture continued, with few results. In August, North and other negotiators agreed to the shipment of 500 additional TOW missiles and American radar to Iran in exchange for the release of a single hostage; this was to be followed by a similar shipment to free another hostage. While North described this as a breakthrough to his superiors, two additional Americans were seized in Lebanon in September 1986, along with another American in the next month. Meanwhile, on October 5, 1986, a Contra resupply plane was shot down over Nicaragua. An American crew member, Eugene Hasenfus, parachuted from the plane and was captured by Nicaraguan forces; two other Americans perished. Soon questions arose about the extent of official American involvement. The White House's secret enterprises further unraveled when, on November 3, a Lebanese newspaper reported that McFarlane had earlier conducted a secret mission to Teheran; a day later, Ali Akbar Hashemi Rafsanjani, the Iranian premier, admitted the same thing.

The controversy remained contained through the congressional elections of 1986. Yet in the first week of November 1986, the affair exploded in Reagan's face. Poindexter, North, and McFarlane prepared a chronology of events for public distribution that contained deliberate falsifications. A speech by Reagan to the nation claimed that the effort had resulted from an attempt to strike a new relationship with Iran. In false information supplied by Poindexter, Reagan declared that the arms were "defensive" and could "easily fit into a single cargo plane." About a week later, on November 19, Reagan conducted a disastrous press conference in which he repeated even more falsehoods. By late November 1986, the entire Iran-Contra enterprise had begun to unravel. Casey, Poindexter, and North all testified to Congress and lied about their involvement. Poindexter, on his return from testifying, proceeded to destroy documents; he was joined in his efforts by North throughout the weekend of November 21–23.

Attorney General Edwin Meese had been ordered by Reagan to conduct an investigation on November 21. Alerted to the Meese investigation by Poindexter, North worked hard that weekend in a "shredding party" that destroyed thousands of documents; all but one of the memoranda that North wrote documenting the diversion were thus lost. So many documents were destroyed that at one point North's shredding machine jammed. At the same time, North attempted to alter other documents that were preserved on the White House's computer system. Meese meanwhile declined the support of the FBI and did not move to seal the NSC's records. Despite having uncovered evidence of the existence of the Contra diversion on Saturday, November 22, Meese moved slowly, only informing Reagan on Monday.

When news of the diversion became public on Tuesday, November 25, a political bombshell hit Washington. The disclosure was followed by the firing of North, the resignation of Poindexter, and the appointment by Reagan of a special review board headed by former Senator John G. Tower of Texas. Reagan also directed Meese to direct a federal court to appoint an independent counsel to take over the investigation; on December 19, former Judge Lawrence Walsh was appointed. The recent congressional elections had returned Democratic control of the Senate, and there was increasing likelihood that a congressional investigation would result. After considerable discussion, the House and Senate formed select committees to investigate, and they began joint hearings on May 5, 1987. Meeting in the summer of 1987, the joint committee held nationally televised hearings, including testimony from all of the administration figures. Some of them, including Poindexter and North, testified only under grants of limited immunity—which would, as it turned out, later cripple Walsh's criminal prosecutions—but by July 1987 the country had heard enough. The committee never was able to address the extent of Reagan's knowledge and involvement in the illegalities of the affair—which had been the primary charge of the committee—nor did it attempt to probe aggressively in directions that might have embarrassed a still-popular president. Then, in the summer of 1987, public opinion appeared to turn decisively against the congressional investigators. In a strange turn of events, "Olliemania" raged through the summer, as Oliver North became a sort of folk hero. At the same time, Walsh's independent counsel's office conducted prosecutions against the main perpetrators of the diversion; they resulted in the convictions of Secord, Poindexter, and North. Although North's conviction was subsequently overturned because his protected testimony to Congress had "tainted" his prosecution, Walsh was able to continue the investigations into 1992. By the end of 1991, Elliott Abrams, a former assistant secretary of state, had pleaded guilty to a charge of lying before Congress, while Alan Fiers, a CIA official, pled guilty to a charge of participation in the diversion. For Reagan, the chief result of the Iran-Contra affair was the weakening of his presidency for the remainder of his term. After a prolonged battle within the White House, Chief of Staff Donald Regan resigned in February 1987; he was replaced by former Senate Majority Leader Howard Baker.

4.   THE ELECTION OF 1988 AND THE REAGAN LEGACY

Early in the second Reagan administration, it became clear that George Bush would inherit the Reagan legacy. He had been intently preparing himself for that role for eight years, as a loyal team player, vice-president, and heir apparent. Those eight years had blurred the sharp divisions of the primary campaign of 1980—in which Bush had criticized Reagan's "voodoo economics"—and partially obscured the political compromise of the Detroit Republican National Convention in 1980, in which the two rivals had joined forces in a common cause. A loyal vice-president and a principal player in the administration, Bush enjoyed the strong support of the president, who chafed at the constitutional restrictions against a three-term presidency but saw the election of Bush as a vindication of his presidency.

Nonetheless, Bush confronted a major political challenge in winning the presidency. Martin Van Buren had been the last sitting vice-president to achieve election as president, more than 150 years earlier, in 1836. With a moderate Republican record, Bush needed the support of the now-dominant conservative wing of the party, which had never fully accepted him as a genuine part of the Reagan Revolution and remained suspicious of his intentions. Stiff opposition to Bush arose within his own party. New York Congressman Jack Kemp and former Delaware Governor Pierre du Pont IV both sought to assume the Reagan mantle from conservative Republican voters. They were challenged by television evangelist Pat Robertson, founder of the Christian Broadcasting Network. Alexander Haig, the former Nixon official and secretary of state, had joined the contest by 1987. But Bush's most serious challenger was Senate Majority Leader Robert Dole, Republican vice-presidential candidate in 1976.

Early on, Bush's primary problem was his lack of an identity independent from Reagan; a widespread public perception prevailed that he was weak and somewhat elitist. Formally entering the race on October 12, 1987, Bush endorsed the Reagan record and described the American economy as the "strongest in history." But he also asserted a different political identity from the Reagan presidency. He described the present prosperity as "incomplete" and "not an end but a beginning" and promised greater "moral leadership" in the areas of economic justice, race relations, and the environment.

The Democrats, meanwhile, sensing an opportunity, presented a wide field of candidates. Gary Hart, the early frontrunner, withdrew from the race in May 1987 following disclosures of sexual improprieties. Six candidates had entered the race by the summer of 1987: Joseph Biden, senator from Delaware; Bruce Babbitt, former governor of Arizona; Michael Dukakis, governor of Massachusetts; Richard Gephardt of Missouri; Albert Gore, senator from Tennessee; and Paul Simon, senator from Illinois. After it became known that Biden had plagiarized a speech by the British Labor leader Neil Kinnock, he withdrew in September. In October, Jesse Jackson joined the race, promising that he would bring "justice to our land, mitigate misery in the world and bring peace to our earth." In December, Gary Hart rejoined the race.

The early primaries and caucuses soon winnowed this field. In Iowa, Bush suffered a shocking defeat when Dole and Robertson finished ahead of him, while Gephardt, emphasizing a theme of economic nationalism, finished first among Democrats. The sagging Bush campaign revived in New Hampshire, however, when aggressive TV commercials against Dole resulted in a decisive Bush victory. The vice-president then won caucuses and primaries in Maine, Vermont, and South Carolina. On "Super Tuesday," March 8, 1988, seventeen Republican and twenty-one Democratic primaries and caucuses were held. Among Republicans, Bush swept the field and established a commanding and unbeatable lead over all other candidates. For the Democrats the results were not so clear-cut. Dukakis and Jackson emerged as frontrunners, with Gore trailing behind, but none of these candidates yet possessed enough delegates to claim the nomination. The Dukakis campaign appeared stalled after the Illinois primary, which Simon captured on March 15, and the Michigan caucus, which Jackson won. The decisive battle occurred in the northeastern states. On April 19, in the New York primary, Dukakis won decisively after a bitter campaign; a week later he received 67 percent of the vote in Pennsylvania. Then, in primaries held on June 7 in California, Montana, New Jersey, and New Mexico, Dukakis won enough delegates to claim the nomination.

The Democratic convention, meeting in Atlanta in July, nominated Dukakis on the first ballot. But, armed with a large bloc of delegates, Jackson sought to influence the shaping of the party platform and the nomination of a vice-presidential candidate. On July 11, Jackson announced that he would accept the vice-presidential nomination if it were offered; when Lloyd Bentsen, senator from Texas, was chosen the following day, Dukakis aides sought to soothe an angered Jackson. Despite strains between the Dukakis and Jackson camps, the convention went smoothly and secured Jackson's firm support for the Dukakis-Bentsen ticket. Indeed, Dukakis left the Atlanta convention boosted by public opinion polls that showed him, in late July, with a commanding, seventeen-point lead over Bush.

In their New Orleans convention, the Republicans met and nominated Bush in mid-August. Bush stunned the convention by nominating J. Danforth "Dan" Quayle, senator from Indiana, as his vice-presidential nominee. The selection of Quayle, who had been elected to the Senate in 1980, was another step in Bush's declaration of independence from Reagan, but a controversy brewed over Quayle's presidential qualifications and his apparent avoidance of the draft by joining a National Guard unit in 1969 during the Vietnam War. In his acceptance speech, however, Bush set the tone of the coming campaign. Promising to lead a "kinder, gentler" America, Bush went on the attack. Citing Dukakis' veto of a Massachusetts law requiring schoolchildren to recite the pledge of allegiance, Bush led the convention in reciting the pledge. He also attacked Dukakis for what he said were "liberal" values: Dukakis, he claimed, was weak on national defense, weak on crime, opposed to the death penalty, and in favor of higher taxes. Bush then pledged to the convention that if Congress sought higher taxes, he would tell them: "Read my lips, no new taxes."

By late August, the now-familiar pattern of Republican supremacy in presidential elections had reasserted itself. Bush had reversed his position in the polls and held a commanding lead. Continuing his attack on Dukakis, Bush criticized his patriotism, ridiculed his environmental record, and claimed—in a controversial television ad that raised the specter of black criminals—that his support for a prison furlough system had resulted in greater crime. Despite two presidential debates, Dukakis could not effectively respond to these attacks and regain the momentum. In a desperate whirlwind of campaigning in the last three weeks before the election, Dukakis reaffirmed his support of the liberalism of Franklin D. Roosevelt and John F. Kennedy. With the lowest turnout since 1924, with 49.1 percent of the electorate voting, Bush recorded a resounding victory, capturing 426 out of 538 electoral votes.

On January 20, 1989, Bush was sworn in as the forty-first president of the United States, before a crowd of 150,000 people before the Capitol. In his inaugural address, Bush paid tribute to Reagan; he had earned "a lasting place in our hearts in our history" and had accomplished "wonderful things . . . for America." Bush then turned to what he conceived as the mission of his adminis-tration: promoting the growth of democracy worldwide until "the day of the dictator is over" by stimulating economic as well as political freedoms. But he also distanced himself from the Reagan administration by stressing the concepts of duty and public-spiritedness rather than absolute individualism.

George Herbert Walker Bush was born into a family of wealth and considera-ble prestige. His father, Prescott Bush, was a United States senator from Con-necticut. Educated at elite prep schools, George Bush enlisted as a young navy pilot in World War II, in which he served with distinction. After the war, he was graduated from Yale University and moved to Texas, where he established a successful oil-drilling business. In the 1950s, he was drawn into the challenge of establishing a viable Republican party in Texas, and he eventually won election to Congress from Houston. After an unsuccessful run for the Senate in 1970, Bush joined the Nixon administration, first as chairman of the Republican Na-tional Committee, then as head of the American delegation in China; during Ford's administration, he also served as director of the CIA. In 1980, he was defeated by Reagan in a bid for the presidency but, by becoming a loyal vice-president, he inherited the Reagan legacy.

In many respects, the Bush administration extended that legacy. This was the first instance since 1929 in which the successor to an incumbent came from the same political party, and it was inevitable that Reagan holdovers were part of the Bush administration. On November 10, 1988, Reagan requested the resigna-tion of the entire cabinet so that it could be reconstituted according to Bush's choosing during the next two months before the inauguration. The Bush cabinet included familiar names: Richard Thornburgh as attorney general and Nicholas Brady as treasury secretary had both been appointed and confirmed before the election and continued in the new administration. James Baker became secretary of state after having served as White House chief of staff and secretary of the treasury. Newcomers included James Watkins, in energy; Louis Sullivan, in health and human services; Jack Kemp, in housing and urban development; and Lauro Cavazos, in education.

Given his experience, however, it was likely that Bush would also seek to transform the Reagan legacy. While Reagan had had virtually no experience in foreign affairs and operated effectively but instinctively in domestic politics,

Bush's experience drew him to world affairs. Elected with a Congress that remained under Democratic control, he realized the difficulty of setting the domestic agenda. On key matters such as the budget, moreover, Bush at times seemed pragmatic, at other times almost indifferent. In contrast, in foreign affairs Bush held well-defined ideas. Given his experience in China, he was committed to maintaining the diplomatic and economic cooperation with that country that had existed since the 1970s. He was deeply suspicious of the Soviet Union, yet he encircled himself with pragmatists, such as Secretary of State Baker, a long-time and trusted associate, Secretary of Defense Richard Cheney, and National Security Adviser Brent Scowcroft.

5.   DOMESTIC POLITICS AND
THE BUSH PRESIDENCY

The preoccupation of George Bush with foreign policy became evident early in his first term, as in domestic politics he fought to a standstill with the Democratic Congress. His nominee as secretary of defense, John G. Tower, had had a long career as Texas senator and chairman of the Armed Services Committee; he had also been a longtime Bush loyalist. But Tower was also a hard-drinking woman-izer, and when his nomination went before the Senate, Democrats, sensing political victory, sought to block it. Despite intense pressure from the Bush White House, the Senate refused to confirm the Tower nomination and dealt Bush a severe blow early in his presidency.

Bush's record on civil rights also revealed a combination of confusion and ineffectiveness. Although he had made an appeal for black support during the campaign, his use of the crime issue fused with racial innuendo had polarized the electorate; 90 percent of the black electorate voted Democratic. When Congress enacted the 1990 Civil Rights Act, which sought to reverse the Supreme Court's ruling in the Grove City case, Bush vetoed it, denouncing it as a "quota bill." Moreover, Bush sought to make the quota issue significant in the 1990 congressional elections; in at least one instance, in the North Carolina senatorial election between Jesse Helms and Harvey Gantt, that issue played a significant role. For much of 1991, when congressional supporters sought to enact a slightly altered version of that bill, Bush expressed strong opposition. Only under pressure from congressional Republicans did he agree to support a compromise civil rights bill on October 25, 1991.

But the most important domestic-policy issue of Bush's presidency was the question of the budget; it was also the issue that displayed the most obvious weaknesses of his style and approach. In the summer of 1990, the Office of Management and Budget projected larger deficits than were permitted under the Gramm-Rudman deficit law, which had been enacted in December 1985 and provided for deficit targets and, if necessary, across-the-board budget reductions.

While the Gramm-Rudman target was $64 billion for 1991 (and a balanced budget in 1993), the OMB was predicting a $169 billion deficit.

There followed, during the summer and fall of 1990, intense negotiations between Congress and the White House that sought to narrow the deficit. While Congress was reluctant to cut expenditures, Bush, bound by his "read my lips" campaign pledge of 1988, refused to raise taxes. In late June, however, Bush suddenly abandoned this pledge and agreed that a budget package would have to include not only cuts but also tax increases. Yet House Republicans, facing the election of 1990, revolted and refused to support Bush, and the Democrats hesitated to associate themselves with tax increases without bipartisan support. In August, after a month's impasse, Bush mounted a highly partisan attack on the Democratic Congress for foot-dragging.

Not until late September did a budget agreement emerge that satisfied the Democratic leadership and the president. In a key development, Bush agreed to abandon his demand that the capital gains tax be reduced. Coming only twelve hours before automatic Gramm-Rudman cuts would have come into effect, the agreement provided for a $500 billion reduction in the deficit over a five-year period. It called for a tax increase of $134 billion during the first year, primarily through taxes on luxury items, alcohol, and gasoline. But the agreement, when it came before Congress, was caught in a cross fire between revolting conservative Republicans and liberal Democrats who objected to the spending cuts, and it was defeated on October 5, 1990, in the House by a 362 to 179 vote.

Intense talks followed while Congress enacted a temporary funding measure to avert the Gramm-Rudman ax. Yet these talks stalled over House proposals to raise the maximum income tax rate from 28 to 33 percent and to establish a 10 percent surtax on incomes above $100,000. The result was that Congress remained in session through the month of October—its longest session since World War II—despite the fact all of the House and a third of the Senate faced reelection. Not until October 27 did Congress enact a budget package that ended the crisis.

It was not a distinguished performance by either Congress or the president. Coming on the eve of elections, it contributed to a prevailing public mood of dissatisfaction with the Washington leadership. Nonetheless, that dissatisfaction did not translate into changes in the status quo. Indeed, an even greater proportion of incumbents in the House remained in office; the anti-incumbent mood, it seemed, applied only to other people's congressmen. While Democrats gained nine seats in the House, they gained an additional member in the Senate. With firm Democratic control of Congress continuing, it was clear that Bush's domestic agenda faced further frustration.

The only area of domestic policy on which the Bush presidency had a decisive effect was the Supreme Court. In the Reagan years, the Court had been in transition, with the appointment of three new justices: Sandra Day O'Connor, the first woman to serve, Anthony Kennedy, and Antonin Scalia. Their addition turned the Court's decisions in a conservative direction, but the most conservative justices, Rehnquist and Scalia, were held in check by swing justices such as O'Connor, who voted with the liberal faction on some issues. The retirement of two of the Court's most liberal justices, William J. Brennan, who retired in the summer of 1990, and Thurgood Marshall, who retired a year later, provided Bush with an unusual opportunity to solidify conservative dominance of the Court. Bush, determined to avoid the political problems of the Bork nomination in 1987, sought a conservative justice whose public views on issues such as abortion were scanty. In David H. Souter, a New Hampshire state judge with no known views on the abortion issue, Bush found a candidate who fitted that bill, and following his nomination on July 23, 1990, Souter was confirmed by the Senate in October by a vote of ninety to nine.

Bush encountered more trouble when he nominated Clarence Thomas to succeed Marshall to the bench. Thomas, a black conservative Republican who had served as an assistant secretary of education and as chairman of the Equal Employment Opportunity Commission under Reagan, appeared to have ideal credentials. The White House could maintain that a black justice would remain on the Supreme Court. Yet because he was strongly conservative, his addition would appear to guarantee a decisive conservative majority on key decisions regarding issues such as affirmative action and abortion. Although encountering strong opposition as liberal interests rallied, the Thomas nomination seemed assured by late September 1991. The Senate Judiciary hearings resulted in a split seven-to-seven vote along party lines, and the full Senate seemed poised to confirm him. Then, on October 6, 1991, came charges that Thomas had sexually harassed a lawyer, Anita Hill, who served under him at the Department of Education and at EEOC, and in a dramatic, nationally televised series of hearings, Hill and Thomas presented their cases. On October 15, the full Senate voted and confirmed Thomas by the margin of fifty-two to forty-eight.

The addition of Souter and Thomas during the Bush presidency assured a decidedly new character to the Supreme Court. In a controversial term in 1991—between the Souter and Thomas nominations—the Court issued sweeping decisions that sharply limited the rights of criminals to counsel, widened the rules of police search and use of evidence, and permitted the imprisonment and holding of suspects for longer periods of time. In two other crucial cases that seemed to indicate the Court's attitude toward abortion, the justices permitted a highly restrictive law enacted in Missouri to stand in a decision in 1990, while a year later it upheld new federal rules, issued by the Reagan-Bush administrations, that prohibited physicians in birth control clinics to give any advice about abortion.

6. THE "NEW WORLD ORDER"

In contrast to domestic policy, where Bush had to work with a Democratic majority in Congress, the president found much greater freedom of action in foreign affairs. He was also blessed with the most favorable conditions confronting an American president abroad in a generation. The first two years of the Bush presidency affirmed the arrival of a new day in foreign affairs. By 1991, the Soviet empire had crumbled in Eastern Europe, while the Soviet system was crumbling from within. As the Soviets restricted or cut off aid to their allies and satellites across the globe, and as a democratic tide seemed to be sweeping through Asia, Africa, and Latin America, the cold war came to an end. These developments supplied Bush and his foreign-policy team with unusual opportunities to promulgate what Bush would later describe as a "new world order."

The new world order was based on the end of Soviet-American hostility. This new relationship began with the coming to power of Mikhail Gorbachev on March 11, 1985. Gorbachev was cut of a new Soviet cloth. In April 1985, he announced a moratorium in the deployment of SS-20 missiles; he later pledged to reduce the number of missiles fixed on European targets. Then, in November 1985, Gorbachev met for the first time with Reagan at a summit held in Geneva, and there he offered to reduce Soviet nuclear weapons in exchange for Reagan's pledge to confine SDI development to the laboratory. This was followed by an aggressive effort by Gorbachev to achieve an arms control breakthrough. In January 1986, he offered a plan that would reduce Soviet and American nuclear arsenals by half in a period of five to eight years and would eliminate all nuclear arsenals by the year 2000. These proposals were enlarged at another Reagan-Gorbachev summit at Reykjavik, Iceland, in October 1986, when the Soviet leader offered the elimination of all nuclear weapons in a decade and the limitation of SDI to the laboratory. Despite what seemed to be the possibility of a breakthrough, Reagan's refusal to consider SDI as a bargaining chip doomed the Reykjavik negotiations.

Arms control negotiations nonetheless continued in the aftermath of Reykjavik. In February 1987, Gorbachev separated the INF treaty from other agreements, and quick progress in negotiations resulted. On September 18, Secretary of State Shultz and Soviet Foreign Minister Eduard Shevardnadze announced agreement on an INF treaty that eliminated intermediate nuclear weapons from Europe and provided for an unprecedented system of verification. In early December 1987, Gorbachev arrived in Washington for a third superpower summit in which the INF treaty was signed. The two leaders solidified a close relationship when Reagan was invited to come to Moscow the following summer. Signed on December 8, the INF treaty was the first in world history in which nuclear weapons would actually be eliminated, although it reduced nuclear arsenals by only 4 percent. The treaty provided for the destruction of 859 American missiles and 1,836 Soviet missiles over a three-year period. After conservative Republican opposition during Senate debate, the INF treaty was ratified on May 27, 1988, by a vote of ninety-three to five.

By the end of Reagan's presidency, the Gorbachev policies of *glasnost*, or opening to the West, and *perestroika*, or restructuring at home, had brought real benefits to the United States. Although subsequent negotiations on the reduction of strategic arms stalled, the Soviets adopted a less aggressive posture in regional conflicts. On February 8, 1988, Gorbachev announced that the Soviets would withdraw over 100,000 troops from Afghanistan, ending an eight-year occupation that had devastated that country and involved the Soviets in an intractable quagmire. In April, after talks with the United States, the Soviets agreed to withdraw their forces by February 1989.

Although Bush inherited these hopeful developments when he was inaugurated president in January 1989, the early months of his presidency were marked by cautiousness toward the Soviets and fears that Gorbachev might soon be replaced by a hard-line successor. Events soon overcame American reluctance, however, and confirmed a fundamental change in the Soviet-American relationship. The most important of these events was the crumbling of the Soviet empire. By 1989, the Soviet Union and its satellites were suffering severe economic problems—low productivity, an eroding standard of living, and acute shortages of food and other commodities. The information revolution in telecommunications and computers, in which the West possessed a decided advantage, further undermined the credibility of the Soviet system, while Gorbachev's opening to the West informed the peoples of the Soviet empire of the gross disparities between theirs and Western societies. Meanwhile, the loosening of the Soviet system and the gradual attempt by Gorbachev to institute a peaceful transition to a representative system aggravated national ambitions among the peoples of the Soviet empire. The liberalization of Stalinist controls had raised the hopes of divergent nationalities such as the Baltic states, Georgia, and Azerbaijan. In Eastern Europe, moreover, restiveness against Soviet control manifested itself. In Poland, an anti-Soviet coalition headed by Solidarity movement leader Lech Walesa was swept to power in 1989, while a non-Communist government took power in Hungary. In East Germany and Czechoslovakia, in late 1989 popular uprisings overthrew pro-Soviet regimes and replaced them with democratically elected governments. By the end of that year, the Berlin Wall had been torn down; in September 1990 East Germany and West Germany were reunited into one country. By 1991, Communist regimes had been replaced in Romania, Bulgaria, and even Albania.

These developments tested the Bush administration's resolve, yet they were developments that occurred without its participation. The United States played a more active role on August 18, 1991, when Gorbachev was deposed in a hastily assembled coup by hard-line Communists that sought to reverse the liberalization policies of *perestroika*, restore central control over the declining economy, and discipline the unruly nationalities within Soviet Union. With active American encouragement, however, democratic forces, led by Russian Federation President Boris Yeltsin, resisted the coup leadership and succeeded in restoring a much-weakened Gorbachev to power. The end of the coup marked the completion of the end of Soviet power. The Baltic states successfully seceded from the Soviet Union, and it was obvious by late 1991 that that empire was disintegrating.

The end of the Soviet threat and what amounted to a Western victory in the forty-five-year-old cold war promised a new era of peaceful development. Yet it also occasioned new challenges for the Bush presidency. Inheriting the Reagan administration's policy, Bush found a turbulent Central American situation upon his inauguration in 1989. In El Salvador, the expenditure of over $200 million in American aid over almost a decade had failed to suppress an insurgency there. In Nicaragua, meanwhile, the Contras were a failed military and political force, and the new Bush foreign-policy team of Baker and Scowcroft sought a quick end to the Central American quagmire of the Contras. In early 1989, the United States announced a plan that provided for the end of the Contra military threat and the holding of free elections in Nicaragua. When those elections were held, they resulted in the election of an anti-Sandinista candidate, Violeta Barrios de Chamorro, to that nation's presidency.

In Panama, Bush faced a more intractable problem. In July 1981, after the plane crash death of Panama's leader Omar Torrijos under suspicious circumstances, Colonel Manuel Antonio Noriega, then chief of the Panamanian military's intelligence, took command. Declaring himself general, Noriega assumed dictatorial control and made his country a center of criminal enterprise. While under CIA sponsorship, Noriega in the early 1980s had transferred arms to the Contras. He meanwhile had established a rewarding partnership with Colombian drug lords that laundered, or made legitimate, billions of dollars in illegal cocaine profits. According to some accounts, Noriega received as much as $2.5 billion for his efforts.

As these activities became known during the early months of Bush's presidency, pressure grew to isolate the Noriega regime. A nearly complete financial and trade embargo failed to dislodge the dictator, and after two coup attempts had failed, Noriega grew increasingly defiant. After a disputed election that was won by Noriega's opponents but stolen by the regime, the United States pressed for his removal. In response, the Panama National Assembly on December 20, 1989, made Noriega head of state, granting him wide powers; he then announced a state of war with the United States. On December 16, Panamanian-American relations grew tense after the killing of an American marine and violent threats against the thousands of American citizens in Panama.

On December 20, citing the threat against the 35,000 Americans in Panama, Bush acted decisively, ordering 13,000 troops in the Canal Zone and dispatching 9,500 more from American bases to launch an invasion. Within a day, American forces, despite minor resistance, had secured control of the country and had installed Guillermo Endara Gaillimany, victor of the stolen election, as Panama's head of state. By Christmas Eve, it became known that Noriega had sought and received refuge in the Papal Embassy in Panama City, and on January 3 he surrendered and was immediately extradited to the United States to face drug and money-laundering charges. In 1991, he faced a criminal trial in a Miami courtroom.

7. THE PERSIAN GULF WAR

The new world order received its gravest challenge in the summer of 1990, when President Saddam Hussein of Iraq invaded and conquered Kuwait on August 2. Despite an early promise to withdraw, the Iraqis were in Kuwait to stay. Less than a week after they invaded, on August 6, Iraq formally annexed Kuwait, while by the end of the month, Saddam had negotiated a treaty with Iran that formally ended its long and bloody war with Iraq at the price of substantial Iraqi concessions. Those concessions bought Iranian neutrality but signified a major investment in the Kuwaiti adventure.

The invasion and conquest of Kuwait marked a shift in Saddam's territorial ambitions away from the east, in Iran, toward the south and the Persian Gulf. In the course of his war with Iran, he had secured a formidable military force composed of thousands of tanks, chemical weapons which he had used against Iranians and against rebellious Kurds inside Iraq, Soviet Scud missiles, and a growing nuclear weapons development program. The attack was led by three divisions of Saddam's elite armored and mechanized assault force, the Republican Guards. Despite a quick conquest, the Iraqi forces failed to capture the Kuwaiti government; led by the emir, it escaped into neighboring Saudi Arabia and formed a government in exile. Almost immediately, the exiled Kuwaiti government called for worldwide assistance and, at the same time, transferred its massive cash assets to overseas banks. The Saudis, meanwhile, became convinced that Saddam intended to push his forces southward to dismember their country and the gulf states. In response, within days they requested that American forces be stationed to deter such an attack.

The Iraqi invasion had come after growing tensions. In mid-July, Saddam had demanded that Kuwait agree to production cuts to stem the collapse of world oil prices. Although Kuwait, at a meeting on July 10–11 at Jeddah, Saudi Arabia, promised to reduce its output by 300,000 barrels a day, the Iraqis claimed only a week later that Kuwait was violating the agreement. Moreover, Iraq demanded that Kuwait cancel the multibillion-dollar debt it owed the Kuwaitis from the

Iran-Iraq war. It also charged that Kuwait had stolen vast amounts of oil from the disputed Rumalia oil field, the southern portion of which lay on the Iraq-Kuwait border.

For Saddam, the invasion of Kuwait was a risky adventure, but it fulfilled long-standing Iraqi objectives. Historically, the Iraqis had coveted the oil-rich emirate and had claimed that Kuwait, as a national entity, was only a product of British colonialism. The Iraqis had also long sought access to the Persian Gulf, which the annexation of Kuwait would have provided them. Whatever their motivation, the Iraqi invasion took the world by surprise. Fellow Arab nations had, only hours before the invasion, received assurances of no military action, and on August 3 fourteen Arab League nations condemned the invasion and demanded an immediate withdrawal.

Meanwhile, Bush orchestrated a coordinated world response. Despite an Iraqi appeal to Arab support in the name of the Palestinian cause, no Arab nation joined him, while sympathetic nations such as Jordan and Yemen could only remain neutral. In a startling move, James Baker and Soviet Foreign Minister Eduard Shevardnadze issued a joint declaration on August 3 that condemned the invasion, demanded an Iraqi withdrawal, and called for a global arms embargo of Iraq. Four days later, on August 7, Defense Secretary Cheney, after meetings with the Saudis, announced that a massive American ground force would be dispatched to Saudi Arabia, along with jet fighters and a naval flotilla; by early September there were some 100,000 Americans in the region. The American arms buildup, code-named Operation Desert Shield, effectively dissuaded Saddam from invading Saudi Arabia. At the same time, the arms embargo by late August was expanded, as an American-led international blockade sealed off the flow of goods into Iraq. By the end of the Persian Gulf War, some 7,000 ships had been intercepted by the international blockade, while 30 to 40 ships were being inspected daily.

Over the next months, Bush pressed for coordinated action by the United Nations in a series of resolutions establishing a total embargo on imports into Iraq, the most important of which was UN Security Council Resolution 678. Passed on November 29, 1990, it authorized "all necessary means," including that of force, to obtain Iraq's withdrawal from Kuwait by a deadline of January 15, 1991. The first UN resolution to authorize the use of force since the Korean War, it indicated the extent of world unity in the post-cold-war era. The passage of UN Resolution 678 was followed by intensive efforts to resolve the crisis. The Iraqis made some gestures, including the announcement on November 18 that 20,000 Westerners held by Iraq would be freed, while at the end of the month Bush, announcing that he was going the "extra mile for peace," proposed direct talks. Yet, by December, events seemed to move inexorably toward confrontation. Frustrated at minimal progress, Bush on November 9 had announced a major escalation of American forces. Meanwhile, the planned Iraqi-American talks foundered at the end of the year after a disagreement on when they should begin. Intense diplomatic activity occurred during the first half of January. The French sought, unsuccessfully, to mediate; the last-minute efforts of UN Secretary-General Javier Pérez de Cuéllar were no more fruitful. A meeting between Baker and Iraqi Foreign Minister Tariq Aziz yielded no change in the Iraqi position. With the passing of the January 15 deadline, the outbreak of war seemed imminent.

In early January 1991, Bush sought congressional approval for the use of force. Congressional critics claimed that Bush was exceeding his war-making powers under the Constitution; they demanded that Congress be given a chance to debate the use of force. Democrats, while generally in favor of using economic sanctions as the primary means of pressure, were reluctant to criticize a president directly during a time of international crisis. After a nationally televised debate, Congress voted a resolution authorizing force on January 12, 1991. Some eighty-six Democrats joined Republicans in supporting the administration in the House, while the resolution narrowly passed with only ten Democratic votes in the Senate.

With both international and domestic support, Bush approved a military operation, named Operation Desert Storm, the weekend before the January 15 deadline. Beginning on January 16, the allied coalition, represented by forces from twenty-nine countries, mounted an unrelenting air campaign. Coalition fighters on the first day established uncontested air supremacy, destroying Iraq's radar, bombing its airfields, and driving its aircraft from the skies. They next struck at the Iraqi command structure and destroyed communications, missile sites, power plants, and nuclear and chemical weapons production facilities. By the end of January, the allies had mounted over 30,000 sorties, or air attack missions; by late February that figure had increased to nearly 100,000.

Iraq responded by launching ground-to-ground Scud missiles against Saudi Arabia and Israel. Despite fears that these missiles might contain chemical weapons, and despite some casualties that came with them, they served primarily as weapons of terror. Cut off from contact with Iraqi commanders in Baghdad, terrorized by day and night American attacks, including carpet bombing from high-altitude B-52s, the occupying Iraqi Army grew increasingly dispirited. The Iraqi regime, although publicly defiant, was no doubt impressed by the extensive destruction that had been inflicted on its country. Mediation by Iranians and the Soviets seemed to bring some Iraqi movement, yet the Iraqis persisted in refusing to leave Kuwait. By February 22, Iraq had agreed to a withdrawal, but Bush insisted that such a withdrawal occur immediately and unconditionally.

Following the expiration of an ultimatum that accompanied Bush's message, Allied ground forces launched an all-out invasion on February 24. On Iraq's western flank, the United States XVIII Corps, in combination with French forces, launched an airborne invasion of western Iraq that secured bases and cut off the Iraqi Republican Guard's retreat to the north. At the same time, American and British armored divisions drove directly north into western Iraq to engage the Republican Guard divisions, which were positioned in southern Iraq. A successful frontal assault, after an amphibious assault on Kuwait's beaches had been feigned, was launched into southern Kuwait by American marines and by Arab forces.

The war quickly proved to be a mismatch. By the third day, February 26, coalition forces had liberated Kuwait City, and most of the Iraqi forces were routed. By then, the Iraqis had lost untold numbers of soldiers, perhaps as many as 100,000 in the entire war, along with most of their armor. The vaunted Republican Guard, which had acquired a reputation as an elite fighting force during the Iran-Iraq war, was decimated through coalition air supremacy and superior coalition technology and logistics. In a nationwide televised address, Bush declared a cease fire on February 27, and a formal cease fire had been negotiated by March 3. Within a month, Iraq had accepted all of the United Nations' resolutions as the basis for future settlement.

Yet the war did not, by any means, solve the problems of the Persian Gulf. Disparities between the rich and poor nations of the Arab world persisted; intra-Arab conflict, particularly between the gulf states and the Palestinians, North Africans, and Yemenis, who to varying degrees supported Saddam, grew more acute. The end of the war left Kuwait in shambles; the return of Kuwaiti control was accompanied by widespread questioning of the legitimacy of the regime. Iraq was reduced through the unprecedented coalition bombing to a preindustrial condition. Saddam remained in power, and uprisings by Shiite Iraqis in southeastern Iraq and by Kurds to the northeast were ruthlessly suppressed. The Kurdish revolt, which like the Shiite uprising looked to the Americans for support, resulted in the flight of over 2 million refugees and, eventually, in the intervention of American military forces to protect them from further Iraqi retribution.

CHAPTER 35

Toward a New Century

In the last quarter of the twentieth century, Americans entered an era of uncertain and contradictory historical trends. Since the mid-1970s, they had witnessed the triumph of technology both at home and abroad, the continued abundance of great wealth, and the most sustained economic boom in American history. The early 1970s saw the victory of the United States in the race to the moon and the inauguration and application of undreamed-of new technologies. With the continued attraction of the United States to the rest of the world, the American dream for many continued with the migration of hundreds of thousands of people and the onset of new immigrant waves to American shores. Yet these were also years of national self-doubt. Balanced against economic boom and the triumph of technology were the erosion of the American position in the world economy and the deterioration of the United States manufacturing base in the face of intense European and Far Eastern competition. The family continued to experience a transformation, but it too showed signs of decline through an even higher divorce rate, an increasing incidence of unwed mothers, and a continuing cycle of intergenerational poverty.

1. FROM STAGFLATION TO ECONOMIC BOOM

Beginning in the mid-1970s, inflation began to become a major affliction of the American economy. It had several sources. The first was the Vietnam War, which, at the peak of the buildup, Lyndon Johnson had decided could be financed without a major tax increase or major domestic spending cuts—financed, that is, through budget deficits. The second cause was rooted in structural characteristics of the American economy. Between World War II and the beginning of the 1970s, Americans realized regular increases in wages and income that were accomplished through equally steady rises in productivity. Increased productivity was the result of new technology, and when those technological advances were exhausted, productivity slowed while wage increases or the expectation thereof continued, thus spurring on inflation.

Probably the most important spur to inflation, however, was the end of the long era of cheap petroleum. Since 1945, American economic expansion had been fueled on cheap oil, first available from domestic producers and then, by the late 1960s, from new and seemingly unlimited sources in the Middle East. The onset of the 1973 Yom Kippur War between Israel and its Arab enemies changed this equation, however, when the Arabs, led by Saudi Arabia, embargoed exports to the United States to punish it for its support of Israel. As a result, oil prices skyrocketed from under $5 a barrel to over $12 a barrel. Subsequently collective action by the Organization of Petroleum Exporting Countries (OPEC) maintained that price, and, with the onset of the Iranian Revolution in 1978–1979, prices rose to over $40 a barrel.

These "oil shocks" had the effect of further spurring inflation and, more important, of encouraging an inflationary psychology in which producers and services of all sorts regularly imposed cost-of-living increases and passed the cost along to the consumer. The statistics on inflation since 1945 bear this pattern out. Inflation had been a short-term problem in the years immediately after World War II, particularly during 1946–1947, and during the last part of the Korean War. Yet between 1953 and the mid-1960s it remained low, averaging an increase of only about 1.2 percent per year. Then, beginning with the Vietnam era, along with the inflationary pressures of the oil shortages of the 1970s, the longest and most sustained price increases in American history occurred. In the worst years, 1974 and 1980, the Consumer Price Index (CPI) rose by 11 percent and 13.5 percent, respectively.

The advent of inflation had a devastating effect, both real and perceived, on Americans in the 1970s. Inflationary psychology led to a cycle in which workers sought wage increases to beat inflation but thereby contributed to increases in the price level. Some groups, particularly those that held low-interest debt, profited by inflation, but other groups, particularly those who lived on fixed incomes or whose salaries did not keep pace with the rapidly increasing price level, saw their real income decline appreciably. Overall, the advent of inflation was an indicator of a relative decline in American wealth: in constant dollars, personal income between 1970 and 1983 rose by only 22 percent—the slowest decennial increase since 1940.

Just as suddenly as it had appeared, however, inflation subsided during the early 1980s. After 1981, inflation declined to its lowest level since the 1960s.

While exceeding an increase of 10 percent in 1981, the CPI declined to a 3.3 percent increase in 1983 and 4.2 percent a year later. The end of hyperinflation was the result of several factors. A contributing force was the decreasing price of oil, food, and most raw materials. A further collapse of oil prices in 1986 further dampened inflation for most of the rest of the decade despite a booming economy. Also important was a determined effort on the part of the Federal Reserve System to restrain growth in the money supply and hence to curb inflation; this policy began to bear fruit after a severe recession in 1981–1982— the worst since the Great Depression—brought powerful anti-inflationary pressures to bear.

After 1983, the American economy began an economic expansion that lasted for the rest of the decade; the eight-year recovery would be the longest in American history. Its roots lay in new federal fiscal policies of the 1980s and in the ascendancy within the Reagan administration of so-called supply-side economists. Since the New Deal, they believed, the federal government had aimed its fiscal policies toward the manipulation of consumer purchasing. The result was, according to supply-side economists, inflation, sluggish growth, and reduced productivity. Rather than on the consumer, or demand, side, supply-side economists argued that federal fiscal policies should focus on supply, primarily by reducing the restraining influence of taxes. A general reduction of income taxes would unleash the American economy to new and higher levels of production and wealth and, in the process, resolve the budget deficits that they might otherwise create.

The Reagan administration's tax cut of 1981—which amounted to a 25 percent reduction over three years—provided a real stimulative effect on the American economy, as did the federal budget deficits of the decade. The national debt, which was $908.5 billion in 1980 had nearly tripled, to almost $2.7 trillion, by the time Reagan left office. This greatly increased deficit spending served to fuel the economic expansion of the 1980s, and by the middle of the decade employment and income were increasing at a steady pace. Particularly affected were service industries such as banking, financial services, and real estate, some portions of the computer industry, and defense-related manufacturing.

The budget deficits of the 1980s were brought on by the combination of tax cuts and an unprecedented increase in military spending. Much of the costs of this buildup went toward modernizing and updating conventional weaponry. New funds were infused into naval forces; soon into his administration, Reagan endorsed the concept of a 600-ship navy capable of projecting American power around the globe. The army received a new tank, the M-1, which became operational in the latter part of the decade, along with a new Bradley armored personnel carrier (APF). The air force also greatly benefited from the buildup. Not only did it develop the expensive F-117A fighters, which employed radar-evading "stealth" technology and became operational at the end of the decade, the air force also developed new long-range bombers, including the B-1B and the stealth B-2, both of which were designed as alternatives to the aging fleets of B-52 bombers, as an essential element in America's nuclear deterrent. Yet these weapon systems were constructed at great cost, chiefly because of their dependence on high technology.

A similar infusion of money and high technology occurred elsewhere as a result of the military buildup. In several instances, high-tech military hardware was first developed during the Carter years but then expanded and deployed during the Reagan era. Cruise missiles could be launched by submarine, by surface naval vessel, or by air. Carrying either conventional or nuclear warheads, these new aircraft were subsonic but could successfully evade radar by flying low and could strike targets with near-pinpoint accuracy. The expensive and controversial MX missile system, a subject of bitter debate during the late 1970s, was designed to deter a perceived Soviet threat of missile superiority, and it became a centerpiece of the Reagan administration's new missile force.

Meanwhile, Reagan defense officials belittled the long-standing nuclear doctrine of mutual assured destruction, which had sought to prevent nuclear war by maintaining rough superpower parity in nuclear weaponry. Instead, they endorsed nuclear superiority through the military buildup on the one hand and, on the other, the construction of an effective antimissile defense system. Despite the fact that the United States was a signatory, with the Soviet Union, of the Antiballistic Missile Treaty of 1972, which permitted only a limited antimissile system on both sides, Reagan, in March 1983, endorsed a full-scale effort to develop what he called a Strategic Defense Initiative (SDI). It would be a multibillion-dollar effort, using high-powered lasers and computers, to shoot down incoming Soviet missiles in outer space and thereby, according to Reagan, end the terrible possibility of nuclear war. Yet the challenge of SDI was daunting. Not only were its costs staggering—estimates ran as high as several hundred billion dollars—but many scientists doubted if a feasible and effective antimissile defense could ever be deployed.

Spurred on by the tax cut of 1981 and the military buildup of the first half of the decade, the American economy lifted out of the worst post-World War II recession in 1983 and entered a period of prolonged expansion. Leading the way were service industries—real estate, banking, insurance—while manufacturing began to recover by the end of the decade. Unemployment declined steadily, and by 1989, it was only 5.3 percent. The 1980s were a decade in which wealth and conspicuous consumption returned to fashion. On Wall Street, prices on the New York Stock Exchange began a steady climb after 1983; the Dow-Jones average rose from below the 1,000 level to new and unheard-of heights: first, the 2,000 level and, then, in 1991, the 3,000 level. Riding the crest of this new wave of opportunity was a new class of entrepreneurs and investors such as Michael Milken, who pioneered the use of low-rated "junk" bond offerings as a tool of raising the necessary capital to buy out or take over American firms. Financiers such as Milken, once in charge of these companies, amortized or leveraged their debt, sold off parts of these companies, and restructured them to further reduce costs. The corporate "raiders" who engineered takeovers or leveraged buyouts (LBOs), however, realized huge profits. Milken thus earned more than $550 million in 1987; by the age of forty he had become a billionaire.

The 1980s consequently saw a spurt of merger activity, as hundreds of companies experienced major reorganization. During the Reagan years, the value of mergers and buyouts involved firms whose value totaled more than $82 billion. The merger wave was particularly concentrated between 1984 and 1987, when twenty-one buyouts occurred, whose value was greater than $1 billion each. The biggest of these buyouts occurred in the fall of 1988, with the acquisition of RJR Nabisco by the Wall Street firm of Kohlberg Kravis Roberts & Company for the record price of nearly $25 billion.

In the first half of 1987, euphoria and visions of quick money were on the minds of most stock market investors. By late August the New York Stock Exchange had set another record high, the fifty-fifth of the year. By Labor Day, the Dow-Jones average stood at over 2,700, and many were predicting even greater gains as capital poured into Wall Street from around the world. Then the bubble burst. On Friday, October 16, 1987, the New York Stock Exchange experienced a dramatic drop, while the news over the weekend got no better. By early Monday morning, October 19, financial markets in Tokyo had experienced panic selling and virtual collapse, and markets throughout Asia were reeling from the shock waves.

The opening of the stock exchange in New York was greeted by a wave of panic selling; in Chicago, commodity markets went into a tailspin. The extensive use of computerized trading, in which large blocks of stock were automatically sold when the price declined to a certain price, compounded the crisis. During the first thirty minutes of the morning of October 19, more than 71 percent of the stock sales came from computer-generated block trading. Soon, the price decline in the New York Stock Exchange became an avalanche. By the time the market closed, the Dow-Jones average had declined more than 500 points; stock prices had dropped almost 23 percent; and almost 605 million shares of stock had been traded, double the previous record.

It was clearly the gravest financial crisis since the great crash of 1929. Financiers later recalled that, during the middle of what became known as Black Monday, it seemed as if there were no buyers for any stock and that the stock market was in a downward free fall. In this moment of great peril, the Federal Reserve intervened decisively. In a dramatic statement, Fed chairman Alan Greenspan announced that credit restrictions, which had earlier been imposed to restrain inflationary pressures, were being relaxed. The Federal Reserve proclaimed its willingness to serve a "source of liquidity" during the crisis. In response, buying resumed and total disaster was averted, and during the rest of the week the infusion of additional bank capital brought a partial restoration of market confidence; by Tuesday and Wednesday, the Dow had regained its equipoise.

Yet the crash of 1987 had an important effect on economic performance and attitudes. Although the economy continued to expand during the next two years, it grew at a significantly slower rate; gone was the unbridled optimism of the mid-1980s. The psychological impact of the crash coincided with a downturn, during the last years of the decade, of the key automobile industry. In areas of the nation that had experienced a real-estate boom, moreover, a sharp downturn had occurred by the middle of 1990. Then, in the summer of 1991, a recession began that spelled the end to the long period of economic expansion, and unemployment rose from 5.3 percent in 1989 to 6.7 percent by the end of 1991.

Other bad economic news of the late 1980s came in the unfolding of another financial crisis. A decade earlier, in the late 1970s, savings and loan banks (S&Ls) had experienced severe problems, as depositors withdrew their money in favor of money-market accounts which paid higher interest rates than the regulated S&Ls were permitted to offer. Meanwhile, caught in a squeeze in the high-interest environment, the S&Ls held lower-rated home mortgage loans. In 1980, Congress responded by allowing S&Ls to offer higher interest-bearing accounts; at the same time, it also lowered requirements for capital reserves and raised the maximum amount of federal insurance per depositor from $40,000 to $100,000.

Subsequent legislation was passed with the blessing of both the Reagan administration and Democratic congressmen who were the beneficiaries of S&L campaign contributions. In 1982, Congress permitted S&Ls to expand loans from home mortgages to a variety of other investments. Meanwhile, the Federal Home Loan Bank (FHLB), in charge of overseeing the S&Ls, permitted the banks to conceal loan losses and even insolvency. In April 1982, the FHLB abolished a rule that had required the S&Ls to have at least four hundred stockholders; this encouraged a single unsupervised operator to take over a bank.

The result was fraud and mismanagement in the S&L industry on a massive, unprecedented scale. By 1989, government regulators were reporting that hundreds of the S&Ls were on the verge of bankruptcy and that the federal deposit insurance corporation, the Federal Savings and Loan Insurance Corporation (FSLIC), was insolvent. By late 1990, over 600 S&Ls had failed; less than half of the rest of the 2,500 institutions were judged to be in good financial health. Furthermore, it was estimated that the total cost of a taxpayer bailout might eventually reach $500 billion over a thirty-year period.

2.   THE TRIUMPH OF TECHNOLOGY

A key part of the new economy of boom and bust in the 1970s and 1980s was the shifting basis of wealth and production. For the century between 1870 and

1970, the United States had been primarily a manufacturing economy, and it had become a world leader in basic industries such as steel, automobiles, and textiles. By the late 1970s, however, American world supremacy in these areas had eroded. The United States was facing intense competition from abroad, and European and especially Japanese goods were flooding American markets and often overwhelming the competition.

At the same time, the United States continued to lead in the introduction of new technologies and the development of new high-tech industries. A dynamic sector of the post-1945 economy had long been the electrical appliance and electronics industries. New appliances—air conditioners, electric blankets, dehumidifiers, automatic washing machines and clothes dryers, home freezers, dishwashers, waste disposal units, power lawn mowers, and many others—came on the market after 1945 in an unending stream, and American producers led the way for the global market. As foreign competitors also began production of these goods for American markets in the 1980s, American manufacturers turned to the development of new goods. Electronics experienced rapid growth, especially in the 1960s and 1970s, and by 1982 it was employing 1.2 million workers and generating $148 billion in income. Television, a prime mover in electronics, became one of the fastest-growing industries of the postwar era. Production increased from 7,000 sets in 1947 to 6 million in 1952 and to 19.7 million in 1983. Also leading the way in electronics was the growth of stereo and audio parts production. In 1983, a total of 81.3 million audio parts were manufactured and sold by American producers.

But foreign manufacturers in the electronics industry provided stiff competition. The pattern here was similar to that of other industries experiencing foreign competition. Foreign producers, especially the Japanese, were able successfully to imitate American-pioneered technology and then enter the American market with cheaper-produced goods. As in other industries, that competition overwhelmed American producers and drove many of them from the scene.

Closely connected with the growth of the electronics industry were changes in computer processing and information technology. A mere 200 computers were in use in the United States in 1954; 100,000 were in use by 1970. After 1960, the spread of computer technology had an extensive impact on the American economy. As the capabilities of computers increased, the tasks that lent themselves to computerization multiplied. In manufacturing, computers were employed in the making of consumer goods such as food and clothing, the fabrication and assembly of heavy industrial equipment, and the processing of chemical products. They were used in cost accounting, market research, production scheduling, test grading, hospital diagnosis, legal research, criminal identification, and engineering design. Even trains, highways, and air traffic were capable of direction and control by electronic systems.

Computer technology was even further extended into the American economy during the 1970s and 1980s. Computer-controlled robots became common in manufacturing. The use of computer-directed robots in the United States rose rapidly during the 1980s, roughly doubling from 3,849 in 1980 to 7,232 in 1983. Very important were the invention and mass marketing of the personal computer (PC), a microcomputer designed to suit the needs of individuals and small businesses. PCs, whose popularity expanded greatly during the early 1980s, were pioneered by Apple, which by the middle and latter part of the decade had developed a highly popular model known as the MacIntosh. The industry leader for much of the decade, however, was the International Business Machines Corporation (IBM). It developed an early entry in the PC market that soon became dominant.

Nonetheless, as it matured during the 1980s, the computer industry followed a familiar pattern: pioneered by Americans, it was soon besieged by foreign competition. Strong competition first developed in the manufacturing of computer chips, the key element in the manufacturing of PCs. By the middle of the decade, Japanese competitors were able to produce chips at significantly lower cost than Americans and were dominating the world market. Meanwhile, although IBM had set the industry standard for the PC, foreign competitors were able to produce PC "clones" that could perform the same computing functions at a substantially lower price.

A high-tech industry in which American producers retained supremacy, aerospace, also grew in importance after the mid-1970s. Earlier, in 1958, the most significant breakthrough had been the successful adaptation of the jet engine to commercial aircraft, and aerospace manufacturers grew rapidly thereafter. By 1968, sales surpassed $30 billion; by 1983, they had increased to almost $75.8 billion.

3. THE SEXUAL REVOLUTION

There was, perhaps, no greater measure of the altered lifestyles of Americans in the 1970s and 1980s than the sexual revolution. Like most social changes, although it appeared to have an almost immediate impact, the sexual revolution marked the culmination of long-standing trends. Well before the 1970s, Americans were already practicing sexual habits quite different from those of their parents. The key distinction was that by the 1970s these practices were becoming an open and often-discussed part of American culture.

By the 1960s, the legal and customary restrictions that had prohibited the public display or discussion of sexuality were breaking down. The clash between the new and more liberal patterns of sexuality among Americans and the American position in public policy and law had become focused in the 1960s on the issue of pornography. Before that decade, the Comstock law of 1873 and its narrowly defined notion of obscenity had prevailed. Yet a host of cases challenged it and the extensive legal controls over the public display of sexuality. In 1957, in the landmark Roth decision, the Supreme Court affirmed the conviction of a bookstore owner but ruled that sexuality was obscene only when it appealed to the "prurient interest." Other cases followed, culminating with the *Fanny Hill* case in 1966, in which the court held that publications were obscene only if they were found to be *"utterly* without redeeming social value."

The result of the *Fanny Hill* case was to sweep away previous restrictions on the publication and display of overtly sexual material. A rapid growth in the hard-core pornographic industry followed in the 1970s. Lacking legal restrictions, that industry, which had long flourished outside the law, now became public, indeed ever present, in most American cities. Although an antipornographic backlash resulted, subsequent restrictions that came from the Burger Court only imposed the restriction of "community standards," which allowed for limited local regulation of pornography. Of much greater significance, however, was the impact of the end of legal restrictions on public sexuality. In the wake of the Court's *Fanny Hill* decision, Hollywood now felt increasingly free from public censure, and it responded with a much greater display of sexuality and sex-related issues. The removal of limitations on popular literature meanwhile meant that what might have been considered obscene now became commonplace in popular fiction. By the 1980s, even television was including a much franker role for sexuality.

After about 1970, sexuality noisily entered the public sphere, and what some observers were calling a "sexual revolution" was beginning to have an extensive impact on American life. Sexual practices meanwhile underwent another major change with the advent of new, more easily used, and more reliable methods of birth control. In 1960, the FDA approved "the pill," a new, orally ingested contraceptive that was highly effective, easy to use, and did not interrupt sexual activity. The pill achieved rapid popularity. Whereas most couples in the 1940s and 1950s had employed a diaphragm, by 1970, 58 percent of married couples used the pill, an intrauterine device (IUD), or sterilization. By the mid-1970s, the proportion of couples using the pill had increased to 75 percent. Also important in limiting unwanted pregnancies was the availability of abortions. The Supreme Court's decision in *Roe* v. *Wade* (1973) invalidated most restrictions on abortion that states and localities had imposed. As a result, abortion, especially in the first trimester of pregnancy, became universally available. Between 1975 and 1985, the number of legal abortions increased from about 1 million to almost 1.6 million annually. The rate of abortions among black women by the mid-1980s was almost three times that among white women. Overall, moreover, for every ten live births in 1985 there were slightly more than four abortions.

Along with the expansion of nonreproductive sexuality came a growth of sexuality outside marriage. Publications such as *Playboy* celebrated the end of sexual restrictions and promoted sexual activity outside marriage. Other publications such as *Cosmopolitan* urged its readership, mostly women, to reject the conventionality of marriage; the unmarried working woman should seek out sexual adventure and shun marriage. *Cosmopolitan* editor Helen Gurley Brown, in her early-1960s bestseller, *Sex and the Single Girl,* urged young women to explore sexuality outside marriage. *Playboy* and *Cosmopolitan* existed because they were satisfying a growing cultural market. Even at the peak of the post-war domesticity, there had always been Americans disaffected with it: in bohemian centers in New York and San Francisco, young Americans openly rejected sexual conventionality. Yet, by the 1960s, what had been bohemian and outside the mainstream gained wider acceptance, as the population of young, unattached, and sexually active men and women grew significantly. In urban America, appeals to singles dominated the media and popular culture; gathering places catering exclusively to singles known as "singles bars" sprang up everywhere. They were matched by dating services and a host of singles groups. By the 1970s, this singles culture had contributed significantly to a new ethos of sexual permissiveness. Other cultural media also spurred the sexual revolution outside marriage. The youth rebellion and the counterculture of the 1960s promoted liberation from constraints, including those of marriage, and urged a new cultural radicalism that paralleled the political radicalism of the decade. The counterculture challenged the nuclear family and defied the conventions that required that sexual intercourse be confined to marriage or—more commonly in the mid-twentieth century—be associated primarily with the late stages of courtship.

By the 1980s, the sexual revolution had about run its course. Although it had succeeded in overturning tradition and taboos, that decade saw the emergence of critics who came from diverse backgrounds. A revitalized conservative movement claimed that the erosion of traditional sexuality was the main culprit in the decline of marriage. The conservative movement's energies were focused particularly on homosexuals, and it fought pitched battles to restrict the equalization of rights for homosexuals in jobs, churches, and employment. On the left, feminists at the same time criticized the sexual revolution as providing, at least in some of its manifestations, a vehicle for the exploitation of women, who became sexual objects through the commercialization of sex.

Other factors figured more importantly in limiting the sexual revolution. Persons born during the baby boom of the 1940s, 1950s, and 1960s had pioneered a transformation in attitudes toward sexuality. Indeed, public opinion polling revealed a sharp contrast in attitudes on sexuality between baby boomers and their parents' generation. In the 1950s, less than 25 percent of Americans approved of premarital sex; by the late 1970s, less than 25 percent disapproved. While about 75 percent of Americans in the late 1970s over the age of sixty-five disapproved of cohabitation, about 75 percent of Americans under thirty approved of it. By the 1980s, the baby boom generation was aging, with many of its members reaching their forties. As they aged, a growing proportion of baby boomers developed more stable immediate family relationships. By the mid-1980s, marriage rates had increased, although not to their rates of the 1950s and 1960s, while childbearing and childbirth became increasingly popular. Men and women who had deferred childbirth and parenting into their thirties or even forties turned, by the mid-1980s, with increasing fervor to the production of babies. The result was a marked increase in the fertility rate by the end of the decade. Perhaps even more significant, by the late 1980s and early 1990s, was the increasing prominence of parenting and babies in the popular media. The appearance of films such as *Three Men and a Baby* and *Baby Boom*, both appearing in 1989, told the stories of how participants in the all-singles culture were converted to the joys of parenting. Similarly, in popular television shows such as *Cheers* and *Murphy Brown*, the lead characters, who had been singles in their forties, faced the so-called biological clock and sought, in episodes appearing in 1991, to become parents.

But the most chilling impact on the sexual revolution came from the advent of the acquired immune deficiency syndrome (AIDS), which grew to near-epidemic proportions in the 1980s. In the early years of the decade, doctors began to detect a new disease, concentrated primarily among homosexual men, that devastated the body's immune system and, in virtually all cases, resulted in death from some form of opportunistic infection. While the HIV virus that carried AIDS was first identified by French and American researchers in 1983, public health officials and physicians saw increasing numbers of AIDS patients through the 1980s: from 225 Americans in 1981 to over 100,000 afflicted with the disease a decade later. AIDS had a decided impact on the sexual revolution. Unlike other diseases, AIDS could be transmitted only by bodily fluids; casual contact did not spread the disease. The disease was at first confined to three groups: homosexual men transmitting the disease by sexual contact, intravenous drug users who shared needles and the HIV virus, and hemophiliac patients who could receive the virus by means of transfusions. By the end of the 1980s, other significant but also much smaller groups of people were at risk: health professionals directly exposed to the virus, patients of infected health professionals, and women whose partners were bisexual males.

The AIDS outbreak carried a mixed message. Like most epidemics in American history, it evoked panic and fear among many Americans, who sought to shun the infected. Many Americans labeled the AIDS outbreak the "gay plague"; many of them even saw the disease as some sort of divine retribution for the moral transgressions of homosexuals. Some victims of AIDS infection, especially gay men, suffered ostracism; many even lost their jobs. AIDS was closely tied to the casual sexuality that had characterized the 1970s and thereafter. With neither a cure nor even a vaccine in sight, public health workers focused their efforts on the modification of the sexual habits of gay males; by the end of the decade, public opinion polls showed an appreciably lower rate of homosexuals with multiple partners. In the same period, moreover, increasing numbers of gay men practiced what became known as "safe sex," primarily by using condoms.

Yet the implications of AIDS extended beyond the homosexual community, despite the fact that the epidemic wreaked a terrible human cost among gays. Interestingly, media coverage of AIDS victims focused particularly on two victims who were heterosexual, Ryan White, a boy who had contracted the disease by transfusion, and Kimberly Bergalis, who was infected by an AIDS-carrying dentist. Clearly, the fears of Americans outside the gay community were out of proportion to the threat; nine out of ten AIDS victims were gay males. Yet infection increased among promiscuous heterosexuals, and the risk of AIDS infection among this group was high. More broadly, among heterosexuals—especially drug users—AIDS called into question the risk-free illusion of multipartner sexuality and marked a distinct period in the history of American sexuality.

4.   SOCIAL STRESS AND SOCIAL CHANGE

The sexual revolution of the 1970s and 1980s reflected a welter of wrenching social changes. Attitudes toward personal behavior, not only sexuality but also religious attitudes, became in many respects more tolerant. Mainline Protestant denominations, the Roman Catholic Church, and Eastern Orthodoxy drew closer as Christians muted their differences and joined in statements against nuclear war, poverty, and discrimination. To an unprecedented degree, all three Christian faiths were demonstrating a sense of mutual tolerance, understanding, and accommodation unmatched since the split between Rome and Byzantium. The growth of ecumenism and toleration among Christians and a similar liberalization of attitudes between Christians and Jews were revealed in changes in opinions. The proportion of Americans who held a highly favorable opinion of Jews increased from 33 percent to 40 percent between 1975 and 1981. Similarly, during the same period, the percentage of Catholics with a highly favorable opinion of Protestants increased from 48 percent to 56 percent, while the percentage of Protestants with a highly favorable opinion of Catholics rose from 34 percent to 40 percent.

With new notions of sexuality came the further transformation of the family and the role of women within it. Within the institution of marriage, a steep drop in fertility occurred, particularly during the 1970s. The post-1945 peak in the birthrate was reached in 1957, when there were 25.3 births per 1,000 population. Thereafter, it declined steadily, and by 1970 it was about 73 percent of the 1957 rate. Five years later, the birthrate reached a post-1945 low, at only slightly more than half of the 1957 rate. Although the birthrate rose in the late 1970s and 1980s, the increase was slight and remained well below baby boom fertility rates. In 1988, for example, the birthrate was 63 percent that of the year 1957.

Meanwhile, in the post-1970 decades especially, the divorce rate exploded. In

1950, there were 2.6 divorces per 1,000 people in the United States. Thereafter, the rate expanded significantly, to 3.5 per 1,000 in 1970 and 5.2 per 1,000 in 1980; by 1988, the rate had leveled off, to just under 5 per 1,000. Yet it was clear that divorce had become a commonplace in American society. In the mid-1980s, one estimate had it that three-fifths of all married women in their thirties would be divorced by the next century. This incidence of divorce reflected wholesale changes in attitudes toward marriage and, of course, the liberalization of laws regarding marriage and divorce.

Further evidence of the changing nature of the family came in the numbers of unmarried Americans. In 1960, about 17 percent of Americans were unmarried; by 1983, that proportion had increased to 25 percent. The growth in the number of unmarried and divorced persons was particularly marked among young Americans. In 1960, about 17 percent of Americans in the 25–44 age group lived alone; in 1983, about 29 percent lived alone. In addition, the number of couples who were unmarried rose dramatically, as did the number of single parents. Between 1970 and 1984, the number of unmarried couples almost quadrupled, while the number of families not maintained by a married couple about doubled.

Another important development in gender relations that became fully apparent during the 1970s and 1980s was the acceleration of the earlier trends of the entrance of married women into the work force. The decade of the 1970s witnessed a surge of women into the labor force; of all new workers during the decade, 60 percent were women. Nearly two-thirds of all women of working age were employed by the mid-1980s, and the greatest increases in working women during the 1970s and 1980s were those in their childbearing years. As Americans entered the 1990s, men and women were entering the work force at roughly the same ages and in roughly the same proportions. The most important change affecting working women in the 1970s and 1980s, as these data suggest, was in younger married white women with children. By the 1990s, the differences between the employment of white and black married women were minimal, as they were employed at the same proportion. Seven out of ten mothers having children between the ages of six and seventeen worked in 1984; the proportion in 1950 had been one out of ten. Six out of ten women with children aged under six also worked in 1984; this was double the proportion of 1970.

Despite the plenty of the 1980s, poverty, for both black and white Americans, became a more pervasive problem. About 24 million Americans, or one-eighth of the population, were officially defined as living below the poverty level in 1969. Thereafter, economic growth and the expansion of opportunity reduced this percentage, and federal and state antipoverty programs also had an impact. The percentage of persons living at or below the poverty level decreased from 13.7 in 1969 to 12.4 in 1979. The war on poverty, it seemed, was having something of an impact.

In this case, however, appearances were deceiving, and during the 1980s millions of Americans were dragged perilously closer to poverty. First came the recession of 1981–1982, which resulted in an unemployment rate of 12 percent, the highest since the Great Depression. Coinciding with the impact of recession was the decline, for much of the 1980s, of the American manufacturing base and the loss of jobs in key industries such as steel, automobiles, and textiles. Many of these jobs, which often tended to be unionized and high-paying, were not recouped; new jobs added in the expansion of the 1980s were mostly low-paying nonunion service sector jobs. Between 1979 and 1985, more than 1.7 million jobs were lost in manufacturing.

The automobile industry, for example, had long been an important generator of jobs, and, at its peak in the late 1970s, the American automobile industry employed about 900,000 workers and was responsible for $37 billion in value added by manufacture. The story of the automobile industry was, however, also the story of the intensive pressures and changes of the late 1970s and 1980s. Insulated from international competition for most of the postwar era, American carmakers in the 1960s began to suffer from inroads by European and Japanese producers of lower-priced and better-quality automobiles. Combined with the oil crisis of 1979, which created a greater demand for fuel-efficient cars, and the recession of 1981–1982, American automobile manufacturers faced the greatest competitive challenge in the history of the industry. In 1981, relief came when the Japanese government agreed to restrict the numbers of cars Japan exported to the United States. American manufacturers, shaken from their complacency, began a program of plant modernization and worker layoffs which made their industry more competitive. But between 1977 and 1983, some 260,000 auto workers lost their jobs, and, despite recovery after 1983, most of them were never rehired.

Coinciding with recession and economic decline in some sectors of the American economy were changes in federal policies. Key antipoverty programs were slashed during the Reagan years; housing subsidies and programs for the poor were cut in the first two years of the Reagan presidency. With rising real-estate prices in many markets of the country, this often meant that low- or middle-income families simply could not afford to rent an adequate home, let alone buy one. By the mid-1980s, an unknown number of Americans—by some estimates as many as 3 million—were homeless.

The net result of all of these factors was, beginning in the early 1980s, the reemergence of poverty as a significant social phenomenon of American life. The number of Americans living below the poverty line rose significantly to 14.8 percent in 1982 and to 15.2 percent in the next year. Although the economic boom of the 1980s improved the lot of many Americans, poverty remained a nagging problem. From a peak of 35 million i 1983, the number of poor, as defined by the Bureau of the Census, declined to around 31 million in 1989. At the same time, the percentage of poor had also declined to 12.8 percent in 1989. Yet poverty remained a persistent problem. The recession of the early 1990s

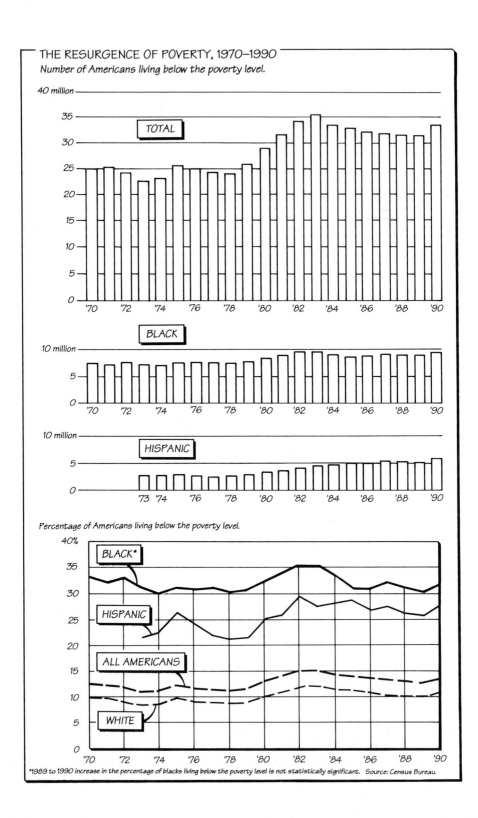

THE RESURGENCE OF POVERTY, 1970–1990
Number of Americans living below the poverty level.

TOTAL

BLACK

HISPANIC

Percentage of Americans living below the poverty level.

BLACK*

HISPANIC

ALL AMERICANS

WHITE

*1989 to 1990 increase in the percentage of blacks living below the poverty level is not statistically significant. Source: Census Bureau.

only worsened the plight of the poor, while it expanded their ranks. In 1990, 2.1 million more Americans lived in poverty than did in 1989; a total of about 33 million lived in poverty, or 13.5 percent of the population, with the most important increases coming among whites of European ancestry and Hispanics.

Another major source of social change and social stress was the advent of a new wave of immigration beginning in the 1970s and culminating in the 1980s. The latter decade was particularly crucial: during the 1980s, the racial character of the United States changed more than it had during any other decade in American history. In 1990, almost one out of every four Americans was of either African, Asian, Hispanic, or Native American ancestry; a decade earlier, the same proportion had been one in five. This demographic transformation reflected a transformation in the sources of immigrants. Whereas before 1970 most immigrants had come from Europe, thereafter a swelling wave originated from Latin America, the Philippines, China, South Korea, southeast Asia, and India. By the 1980s, more than four out of every five immigrants to the United States had non-European backgrounds.

Among certain groups with non-European backgrounds, the increases of the 1980s were rapid. The numbers of Asians thus grew by 108 percent, and those of Hispanics by 53 percent. In certain states these increases were especially dramatic. In California—which recorded the largest overall increases in population in the 1970s and 1980s—the proportion of residents of European ancestry declined from about two-thirds in 1980 to 57 percent in 1990. By the latter year, nearly 13 million people out of the state's population of almost 30 million claimed non-European ancestry. Moreover, California had become a magnet for much of the new immigration of the post-1970 period: in 1990, it possessed nearly 35 percent of the Hispanic population and 39 percent of the Asian population resident in the United States.

Social change and social stress were no better exemplified than in the growth in drug use that characterized the 1970s and 1980s. Beginning in the 1960s, recreational and experimental use of drugs such as marijuana and hallucinogens such as mescaline, peyote, and LSD was common in the counterculture and among many college-age young. Other, more addictive drugs such as heroin grew in popularity, especially among the urban poor. An illegal and highly profitable importing and distribution system arose. By the late 1960s, four-fifths of the heroin imported into the United States came from Turkey. Under pressure from the Nixon administration, that country agreed to ban the cultivation of opium poppies (which are processed into heroin) and inaugurated an effective program of suppression. Heroin then came from other sources. By the mid-1970s, it was estimated that 87 percent of the heroin consumed in the American market originated in Mexico. When a suppression program restricted the source there, new centers of heroin arose in the Far East.

Despite these developments, heroin consumption remained isolated from the mainstream of drug culture. The drug of choice for many was "pot," or marijuana. A large illicit network of supply and distribution soon arose. In the 1960s, most marijuana was smuggled from Mexico, but after a vigorous eradication program began there in the 1960s and early 1970s, other sources such as Jamaica, Colombia, and Thailand filled the market. By the late 1970s, Colombia was emerging as the dominant supplier for the large American market—estimated to be about 9,000 tons annually—and by then it was supplying three-quarters of the marijuana consumed in the United States. Colombian suppliers, even while they operated only at the wholesale level, were earning profits as high as $1 billion annually. In their country, it had become a major industry that employed 50,000 peasants who grew the crop and an equal number of other Colombians who had some role in the trade.

By the 1980s, the popularity of marijuana and the hallucinogens declined as the baby boom generation aged. Meanwhile, however, cocaine, which had been a minor drug in the 1960s and 1970s, suddenly expanded in popularity. The Colombian suppliers of marijuana shifted to cocaine, and they soon dominated the production centers in the Andes mountains of Colombia, Bolivia, and Peru. By the 1980s, cocaine was flooding into the United States via an elaborate network of smugglers and distributors. At the same time, the drug became fashionable among middle-class Americans, while many others made the shift within the drug culture. In the twenty years after 1970, cocaine came to dominate the drug scene. In 1970, federal agents seized 305 pounds of cocaine. By 1985, the total had increased to over 50,000 pounds.

In the mid-1980s, cocaine importation and consumption had become an epidemic that was spilling into most reaches of American society. Young professionals were discovered secretly or openly to be addicts. As public exposure in the decade increased, Americans became increasingly aware of the dangers of this highly addictive drug, and cocaine specifically and drugs in general became an important political issue. At both state and federal levels, state legislatures and Congress significantly stiffened the penalties for drug offenders. In the Comprehensive Crime Control Act of 1984, Congress raised maximum terms for cocaine "dealers" and authorized the confiscation of property "used or intended to be used" in the commission of a drug violation. In combination with the stiffening of state and local penalties, the partial result was a rapid rise in the nation's prison population in the 1980s. Between 1985 and 1988 alone, the prison population grew from just over 480,000 to over 600,000. Employers also began systematic drug testing, despite criticisms that this constituted an excessive violation of privacy.

5.   THE NEW RIGHT

Americans faced these social, economic, and cultural changes with considerable uncertainty. A single generation had witnessed a complete economic transformation; yet the awakening of the American economic dynamo was matched by problems of inflation and unemployment and what seemed, to many Americans, to be signs of real economic decline. Americans continued to exalt the family, yet they watched as the family structure underwent terrific stress and strain. These sociocultural and socioeconomic stresses were wrapped up in what many Americans perceived to be the decline of a once-great nation.

Nothing reflected uncertainty among Americans about sexuality and social change more than the abortion controversy. Through the 1960s, most state laws had held that physicians or others performing abortions were subject to felony convictions and prison terms, and despite a state-level liberalization campaign that resulted in some "abortion on demand" states, abortion remained generally illegal until the Supreme Court's *Roe* v. *Wade* in 1973. The Roe decision marked the culmination of more than a decade's effort on the part of prochoice activists seeking to liberalize abortion law.

Yet the Roe decision also sparked a strong antiabortion movement, and for the next two decades, the abortion issue became controversial and divisive. The antiabortion movement attracted a diverse constituency that included evangelical Christians, conservatives committed to a "profamily" social agenda, and Roman Catholics. In response to the Roe decision, the National Conference of Catholic Bishops in 1973 established a National Committee for a Human Life Amendment to press for the adoption of a constitutional amendment that would overturn the Supreme Court's decision. Within two years, moreover, the Catholic hierarchy had issued detailed plans for use by local groups in organizing themselves into antiabortion pressure groups.

Still more effective were secular organizations. Among the most prominent was the National Right to Life Committee, which emerged in the 1970s as a coalition of antiabortion organizations. By the mid-1970s, the right-to-life movement had become a highly effective single-issue movement that was having a potent political effect. Its impact was felt at the state level, where well-organized activists attempted various restrictions on abortions. Because these state laws often faced reversal in federal courts, antiabortion activists looked to the federal government for redress. In 1976, right-to-life activists succeeded in placing an antiabortion plank in the platform of the Republican National Convention. In subsequent elections involving senators and congressmen, activists targeted prochoice congressmen and, in 1978 and 1980, claimed that they had succeeded in defeating leading figures who included Dick Clark, senator from Iowa; Birch Bayh, senator from Indiana; George McGovern, senator from South Dakota; and Frank Church, senator from Idaho. In 1977, activists were able to flood Congress with telegrams, phone messages, and petitions seeking to end all federal funding for abortions; for several months, Congress became logjammed over the issue. Although the activists failed to obtain complete abolition, in an amendment offered to the appropriations bill of 1977 by Representative Henry Hyde of

Illinois, Congress ended federal financial support for all abortions except in cases where the life of the mother was endangered or where rape or incest had occurred. A year later, the Supreme Court upheld this prohibition. Meanwhile, states followed suit; by 1979, only nine states still financed abortions.

By the 1980s, antiabortion campaigners enjoyed a peak period of political influence. In that decade, they championed the election of both Ronald Reagan and George Bush, both of whom campaigned as opposed to "abortion on demand." Although Reagan and Bush both appointed federal justices opposed to abortion—and although, in the early 1990s, the Supreme Court seemed poised to overturn or severely limit the Roe decision—antiabortion activists were experiencing increasing frustration. That failure was linked to the unwillingness of Congress to enact any further restrictions, the limited support (despite their rhetoric) of Republican presidents, and, most important, the solidification of public opinion in the late 1980s against the antiabortion activists. Throughout the 1970s and 1980s, according to public opinion surveys, those Americans opposed to abortion remained a minority; most favored abortion on demand. While right-to-life activists were mobilized, prochoice public opinion remained dormant until the late 1980s, when Supreme Court decisions permitting some state restrictions on abortion occasioned widespread public alarm. In Virginia in 1989, for example, the Democratic candidate for governor, Douglas Wilder, became the first elected black governor in American history by running on as a prochoice candidate.

Out of the frustration of right-to-life activists came more desperate measures. In 1988, some of their movement maintained that because of the legal and political stalemate more drastic measures were required. In that year, a former salesman, Randall Terry, organized a new movement, Operation Rescue, that employed the civil disobedience tactics of the civil rights movement in abortion clinics around the country. Antiabortion campaigners encircled clinics and sought to prevent, in a peaceful fashion, the entrance of patients; like civil rights crusaders, they openly welcomed arrest as a way to dramatize their cause. Operation Rescue attracted attention when it began operations in Atlanta during the Democratic convention in that city in the summer of 1988. Over the next three years, it mounted similar "rescues" elsewhere. Perhaps the most dramatic of these occurred in the summer of 1991 in Wichita, Kansas, where thousands of demonstrators were arrested.

The social changes of the post-1945 era in family, race, residence, and culture brought the traditions of American life into sharp focus. To many, social change meant social breakdown. The altered role of women within the family and the new conceptions of sexuality, among other new conditions of late-twentieth-century life, suggested the erosion of the basic fundamentals of American life. It was in reaction to what many Americans conceived of as a collapsing society that a new, reinvigorated conservatism emerged. The New Right embraced a diverse coalition that included longtime opponents of the welfare state, antiabortion activists, anti-Communists, and advocates of a nationalist foreign policy. But the most active and best-mobilized element in the coalition was the so-called Christian Right, evangelical Protestants who, beginning in the late 1970s, favored a new moral agenda that stressed antifeminism and a return to a more "traditional" sexuality.

Revivalists such as the Moral Majority's Jerry Falwell and the Christian Broadcasting Corporation's Pat Robertson were committed to a revitalized but also strongly conservative brand of Protestant Christianity. Throughout the postwar era, revivalists had advocated a return to the traditional cultural authority of the church and the moral authority of the Bible, while they denounced the erosion of father-dominated family cohesion. They were conservative opponents of Communists abroad and the welfare state at home. They opposed birth control, abortions, and the new sexuality, just as they were alarmed by feminism and the assertiveness of women within the family. Most of all, they favored restoring the prominence of religion in public life by restricting the teaching of evolution and reinstituting prayer, or at least "moments of silence" for meditation, in public schools.

The Christian Right's political involvement in sexual politics dated to the 1950s and 1960s, when its efforts focused on antipornography campaigns and efforts to restrict the teaching of sex education in the schools. When the Supreme Court effectively stymied these efforts and then forbade mandatory school prayer, the Christian Right emerged in the 1970s with a clearly developed program. Its members maintained that institutions, above all schools, had been invaded by a tidal wave of secularism—what they called "secular humanism"—resulting in the elimination of public morality and the triumph of feminists, homosexuals, and humanists. Although public opinion polls recorded a decline in Protestant fundamentalism overall from 65 percent in 1963 to 37 percent in 1981, conservative evangelicals began to wield increasingly effective political power. After Dade County, Florida, enacted a gay rights ordinance, Anita Bryant, a former Miss America and New Right activist, led a successful repeal campaign. With backing from other moral conservatives in the Miami area, Bryant's supporters won repeal by a two-to-one majority. The victory of the antigay coalition in Miami was duplicated elsewhere, as Christian Right and moral conservatives overturned gay rights laws in St. Paul, Wichita, and Eugene, Oregon, within a year.

The antigay movement overlapped an antifeminist campaign that was dedicated to the defeat of the equal rights amendment (ERA). Introduced in Congress at the instigation of Alice Paul and the National Woman's party (NWP) in 1923, the proposed amendment ("Men and women shall have equal rights throughout the United States and every place subject to its jurisdiction") gained little support in Congress and fell victim to infighting among women's groups. Both the

League of Women Voters and the National Consumers' League opposed the amendment, for example, on the ground that it would strip women of the benefits of the "protective legislation" enacted during the progressive era.

At Paul's urging, the ERA was introduced at every session of Congress between 1923 and 1971. The Senate approved it in 1950 and 1953 after adding a proviso that the ERA would not deprive women of the benefits of protective legislation, but it failed approval in the House. With the passage of the Civil Rights Act in 1964, however, the issue of gender equality was redefined. Title VII of the act forbade discrimination on account of race *or* sex, and the Equal Employment Opportunity Commission began to enforce antigender discrimination. On the heels of Nixon's Citizens Advisory Council on the Status of Women, which strongly urged adoption of the ERA, the House of Representatives voted approval by a vote of 350 to 15 in August 1970. The fight was much longer and harder in the Senate because of opposition from the AFL-CIO, the National Council of Catholic Women, and Senator Sam Ervin of North Carolina. But, in March 1972, the Senate overcame this opposition and approved the amendment by a margin of eighty-four to eight. The ERA, as passed, said that equal rights under the law should not be abridged on account of sex by the United States or any state, that Congress should enforce the amendment, that it would go into effect two years following ratification, and that it had to achieve ratification within five years.

The ERA soon became a lightning rod for opposition to the feminist movement. Hours after Congress had passed the ERA, Hawaii became the first ratifying state, and eighteen other states soon followed. By the end of 1973 a total of thirty-one state legislatures had ratified the amendment, three short of the necessary margin. These dazzling successes made ERA supporters confident that national ratification would come quickly and with little opposition. To make matters worse for them, as it turned out, pro-ERA groups competed with each other for leadership of the ratification drive, and not until 1977 did NOW emerge as the leader and launch a coordinated national drive. By 1982, NOW had emerged reinvigorated, as its membership swelled from 55,000 in 1977 to over 200,000 by 1982, while, in the latter year, it received $1 million to finance its ratification campaigns.

Yet it was at this point of near triumph that ERA supporters encountered powerful and increasingly well-organized opposition. The anti-ERA coalition was composed of fundamentalist Christians, the Mormon Church, and the right-wing John Birch Society. The National Conference of Catholic Bishops refused to endorse the amendment because it associated ERA with support for abortion. But perhaps the best-known opponent of ERA and the leading antifeminist was Phyllis Schlafly, a conservative Republican activist from Illinois. A leading member of what congealed as the New Right, Schlafly had, since the 1950s, opposed big government and endorsed limits to its power.

Schlafly was spectacularly successful when she made her case against ERA. She had organized Stop ERA in October 1972, soon had a national organization, and spoke tirelessly. The amendment, she and other opponents charged, would further erode the traditional family. Not all opponents of ERA, it should be noted, were as far right as Schlafly: both the Daughters of the American Revolution and the National Council of Catholic Women opposed the amendment. They, along with other women, saw the ERA as a symbol for disturbing new trends. They feared that the ERA would reverse sex roles and would result in such horrors as women in combat and sex-blind public restrooms. It would threaten the obligation of men to be breadwinners and providers for the family and thereby further undermine the position of the average woman. Mobilized by the message of Schlafly and others, anti-ERA activists descended on the remaining state capitols and pressed beleaguered legislators to defeat the measure. Like feminist activists, they became adept at the methods of modern pressure-group politics in the use of sophisticated, targeted direct-mail fundraising and the mobilization of massive letter-writing campaigns to wavering legislators.

By the mid-1970s, supporters of the ERA realized that they faced an uphill struggle. Feminists had poured resources into congressional passage without creating and sustaining an effective state-level machinery to achieve ratification. Meanwhile, strong opposition had congealed and was focused on those remaining states that were still about to consider the amendment. Even more troubling news came in 1975, when both New Jersey and New York rejected the ERA in statewide referenda. NOW responded to the slow pace of ratification in 1977 by announcing a boycott of all states that refused ratification; eventually some 350 organizations joined the boycott. Meanwhile, supporters of the ERA were able in 1978 to secure a congressional extension, until 1982, of the time necessary to obtain ratification, and NOW and its allies put all their energies and resources into a last-ditch drive. They failed. Not a single additional state legislature voted in favor of ratification, and time ran out for the ERA. In retrospect, it seems probable that the pro-ERA leaders were simply outmaneuvered, unable and unwilling to reply in kind to a smear campaign. Ironically, as had been the case with the abortion issue, public opinion polls showed that the majority of Americans supported the ERA. To be sure, there was some erosion of this support from its peak in 1974, when 74 percent of Americans endorsed ratification. But even as late as 1982, one respected poll revealed that 61.5 percent of respondents favored the amendment, 23.4 opposed it, and 15.1 percent said "don't know." Public support for defeat of the ERA, meanwhile, never exceeded 31 percent. Defeat of the ERA was perhaps the strongest evidence of what a well-organized, well-financed special-interest group could accomplish in a politically fragmented society.

The coalescence of the New Right marked the coming of age of a formidable political force. Opponents of the ERA also extended their campaign into a generalized antifeminist effort. Between 1977 and 1980, as a result, nine states abolished their commissions on the status of women, while in other states these commissions were filled with opponents of the ERA, antiabortion activists, and others. The organization of groups such as the National Conservative Political Action Committee, the Conservative Caucus, and, for conservative evangelicals, the Moral Majority, became well-heeled and sophisticated pressure groups. These groups played a major role in the election of Ronald Reagan in 1980 and 1984 and had a major impact on the electoral politics of the 1980s.

6.   AFRICAN-AMERICANS IN THE 1970s AND 1980s

For African-American families, the trends that had become apparent in the 1960s and early 1970s were more fully elaborated. On the one hand, economic expansion and federal antipoverty programs in the 1960s had substantially expanded the black middle class. Along with other minorities, blacks markedly improved their status during the 1960s. The proportion of nonwhites officially classified as below the poverty level fell from 56.2 percent in 1959 to 31.1 percent a decade later. Blacks earned a median family income which was 54 percent of that of whites in 1950; twenty years later this proportion stood at 58 percent. A primary reason for these increases in black income was the expansion of the black middle class. In 1948, only 9 percent of nonwhite workers had white-collar jobs. In contrast, in 1970, nearly 28 percent of nonwhite workers were in white-collar categories, including 9 percent in the professions and over 15 percent in clerical and sales work. Middle-class blacks tended to have stable family relationships, to live in suburbs, and to have internalized most of the expectations of middle-class Americans.

The demographic pattern among African-Americans—in which they departed from the South for northern cities—was reversed after 1970. The Great Migration, which saw the departure of millions of southern blacks in the decades after 1915, finally slowed to a trickle by the late 1960s, partly because of worsening conditions in northern ghettos and partly because of the end of legally required segregation in the South. By the mid-1970s, the pattern was reversed: northern blacks were beginning to migrate southward. In the period 1975–1979, 193,000 more blacks migrated southward than migrated northward. In 1980–1985, that figure was 89,000; in 1985–1989, it was 355,000. By 1988, for the first time since the early twentieth century, the proportion of blacks who lived in the South actually grew, to 56 percent of the total African-American population in the United States.

Matched against these developments was the fact that the bulk of African-Americans saw their condition deteriorate during the 1970s and 1980s, and for this majority, family disintegration produced by grinding poverty was the rule.

Black Migration to the South, 1975–1989

Numbers of non-Hispanic blacks who moved between regions (thousands).

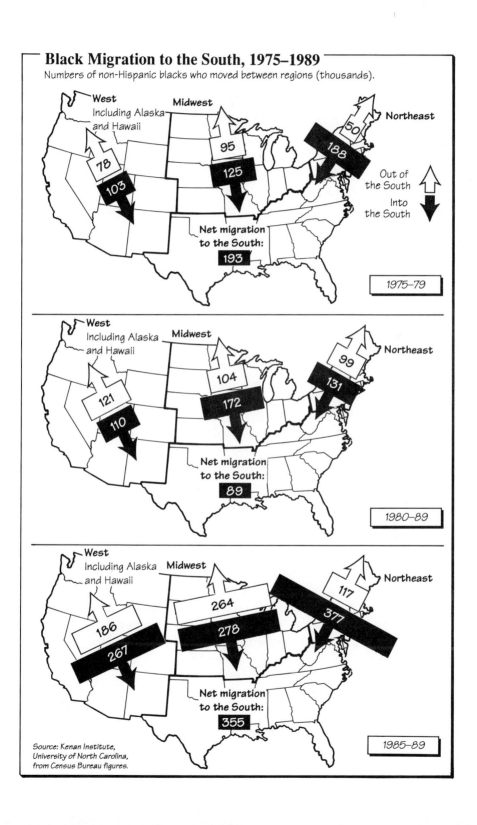

West Including Alaska and Hawaii

Midwest

Northeast

78
103

95
125

50
188

Out of the South

Into the South

Net migration to the South:
193

1975–79

West Including Alaska and Hawaii

Midwest

Northeast

121
110

104
172

99
131

Net migration to the South:
89

1980–89

West Including Alaska and Hawaii

Midwest

Northeast

186
267

264
278

117
377

Net migration to the South:
355

1985–89

Source: Kenan Institute, University of North Carolina, from Census Bureau figures.

Overall, the economic status of African-Americans declined during the 1970s and 1980s. In 1970, median black family income was 58 percent of median white family income; in 1975, it was 57 percent; and, in 1983, it stood at 56 percent. The numbers of poor blacks remained stubbornly high during the 1970s and 1980s. In 1959, a majority of all blacks—55 percent—lived at or below the poverty line; by 1979, that figure had declined to 31 percent. Yet thereafter it inched upward, from 33 percent in 1980 to 34 percent in 1984, and then declined slightly to 32 percent in 1988. The pattern was similar for Hispanics. Separate statistics on Hispanic median family income became available only in 1972, when it was recorded that 23 percent of all Hispanics lived at or below the poverty level. This proportion—partly reflecting growing Hispanic immigration—increased to 27 percent in 1975, 26 percent in 1980, and 27 percent in 1988.

Many African-Americans and other Americans believed that the deterioration of their economic status was tied to a hostile political environment. Ronald Reagan believed that his mandate in 1980 impelled him to reduce the role of government in yet another area: federal protection of the civil rights of African-Americans in voting, housing, employment, and education. Reagan had long been suspicious of federal civil rights policies. In 1965, he had opposed the passage of the Voting Rights Act; as late as 1980, he described it as "humiliating to the South." In 1970, he made welfare fraud the centerpiece of his gubernatorial reelection campaign in California; in his 1976 campaign for the Republican presidential nomination he frequently told the story of a "welfare queen" who bilked the system. The implication, which was patently untrue, was that most recipients of welfare, especially black recipients, were somehow guilty of fraud. And in the 1980 campaign, Reagan opened his successful run for the presidency with a speech at Philadelphia, Mississippi, scene of the murder of three civil rights workers in 1964 and symbol to many persons of white resistance and racial conflict.

Once Reagan was elected president, his appointees favored reversing a two decades' old consensus about federal civil rights policy. His appointee as assistant attorney general for civil rights, William Bradford Reynolds, led an effort to challenge the legality of affirmative action programs in housing, employment, and education. As part of its effort to reduce federal intervention in the workplace, the Reagan administration supervised the slashing of staff and funds of important agencies, including the Equal Employment Opportunity Commission, the Office of Federal Contract Programs, and the Civil Rights Division of the Justice Department (which Reynolds headed).

In education, the Reagan administration also made it clear that the previous practice of using coercive measures to enforce school desegregation would be abandoned. In 1982, the Justice Department filed briefs in two cases involving a private Christian academy in Goldsboro, North Carolina, and the fundamentalist Bob Jones University, in which the plaintiffs challenged the long-standing policy of denying tax-exempt status to institutions that discriminated on the basis of race. Although the Supreme Court eventually endorsed this as a legitimate use of federal power, the Reagan administration sent a powerful message nationwide. Moreover, in the crucial *Grove City College* v. *Bell* case decided a year later, the Court at least partially assumed the administration's position by limiting the application of antidiscrimination laws to those programs engaged in discrimination rather than to the entire institution. And when Congress enacted legislation restoring the previous construction of the law in March 1988, Reagan vetoed it. An almost identical measure enacted by Congress in 1990 was vetoed by George Bush; a subsequent law faced a veto in the following year.

Symbolism on the issue of civil rights also became an essential part of the Reagan record. When the Voting Rights Act came up for renewal in 1982, the administration only reluctantly, after strong public pressure, agreed to support and sign the act. In the spring of 1982, an uproar ensued when Reagan replaced, or attempted to replace, members of the United States Civil Rights Commission and substitute appointees who agreed with administration policies. Congress, responding to the controversy, enacted new legislation that required that half of the commission's members be congressional appointees. A still more important issue came on the question of a national holiday commemorating the birthday of Martin Luther King, Jr. Reagan had long opposed creating a King holiday, and when Congress enacted one, he signed the act only after publicly questioning the validity of King's claims to national honor.

*   *   *

As Americans entered the 1990s, they confronted an uncertain future, full of new challenges. George Bush, appropriately, was almost certainly the last president to serve in that office who was a veteran of World War II; with his departure in the 1990s so also will depart the postwar generation of leaders. In the recession of the early 1990s, Americans expressed a deep pessimism about the future. Looking forward to the end of the twentieth century, many Americans saw a future clouded by economic stagnation, a vacuum of political leadership, and a social structure that was buffeted by poverty, rising crime, and renewed racial and cultural conflict. The old structure of politics, established in mid-century during the New Deal and World War II, was giving way to a new system of leadership, while new forces were remaking the social, economic, and cultural landscape.

Suggested Additional Reading

1. AMERICAN POLITICS SINCE WORLD WAR II

A. General Studies

Among the best general studies of the postwar era are Herbert Agar, *The Price of Power: America since 1945* (1957); Eric F. Goldman, *The Crucial Decade and After, 1945–1960* (1961); Everett Ladd, Jr., and Charles D. Hadley, *Transformations of the American Party System: Party Coalitions from the New Deal to the 1970s* (1975); Herbert S. Parmet, *The Democrats: The Years after FDR* (1976); David W. Reinhard, *The Republican Right since 1945* (1983); Robert D. Marcus and David Burner, eds., *America since 1945* (1972), which includes both historical essays and documents; William E. Leuchtenburg, *In the Shadow of FDR: From Harry Truman to Ronald Reagan* (1983); Alonzo L. Hamby, *Liberalism and Its Challengers: F.D.R. to Reagan* (1985); and Paul A. Carter, *Another Part of the Fifties* (1983). A valuable documentary collection dealing with all important phases of national policy during the period is National Archives and Records Service, *Public Papers of the Presidents of the United States*; volumes covering all presidents since 1945 have been published annually. The fourth volume of Arthur M. Schlesinger, Jr., Fred L. Israel, and William P. Hassen, eds., *History of American Presidential Elections* (4 vols., 1971), covers the elections from 1940 through 1968 and includes interpretative essays, documents, and statistics for each canvass. Radical and reactionary political viewpoints in the postwar era are placed in historical context by Christopher Lasch, *The Agony of the American Left* (1969), and Seymour M. Lipset and Earl Raab, *The Politics of Unreason: Right-Wing Extremism in America, 1790–1977* (1978). The best general survey of recent southern history is Charles P. Roland, *The Improbable Era: The South since World War II* (1975), which can be supplemented by James C. Cobb, *The Selling of the South: The Southern Crusade for Industrial Development, 1936–1980* (1982). Otis L. Graham, Jr., *Toward a Planned Society: From Roosevelt to Nixon* (1976), is the best study of that subject.

B.   The Home Front during World War II

For general studies of the home front during World War II, see Allan M. Winkler, *Home Front U.S.A.* (1986); Richard Polenberg, *War and Society: The United States, 1941–1945* (1972); John M. Blum, *V Was for Victory: Politics and American Culture during World War II* (1976); and Geoffrey Perrett, *Days of Sadness, Years of Triumph: The American People, 1939–1945* (1973). Jack Goodman, ed., *While You Were Gone: A Report on Wartime Life in the United States* (1946), contains some useful essays. Alan S. Milward, *War, Economy, and Society, 1939–1945* (1977), surveys the impact of the war on the American economy in a worldwide setting. Francis E. Merrill, *Social Problems on the Home Front* (1948), is excellent on social tensions and changes.

Donald M. Nelson, *Arsenal of Democracy* (1946), is an "official" history of industrial mobilization, while Eliot Janeway, *The Struggle for Survival* (1951), is extremely critical of the administration. Nelson Lichtenstein, *Labor's War at Home: The CIO in World War II* (1982), treats organized labor's response. Frederick C. Lane et al., *Ships for Victory* (1951), is excellent for the shipbuilding program; E. R. Stettinius, Jr., *Lend-Lease, Weapon of Victory* (1944), is good on the export of war materials; James P. Baxter III, *Scientists against Time* (1946), is a superb account of American scientific achievement during wartime; and Leslie R. Groves, *Now It Can Be Told* (1962), is the story of the Manhattan Project, written by its director. Walter Wilcox, *The Farmer in the Second World War* (1947), is excellent, while Randolph E. Paul, *Taxation for Prosperity* (1947), recounts wartime tax struggles with commendable objectivity. Herman M. Sowers, *Presidential Agency OWMR* (1950), is especially good on plans for reconversion of the wartime economy. Davis R. B. Ross, *Preparing for Ulysses: Politics and Veterans during World War II* (1969), is also a good study. Dorothy S. Thomas et al., *The Spoilage* (1946), Roger Daniels, *Concentration Camps, U.S.A., Japanese Americans and World War II* (1972), Peter H. Irons, *Justice at War* (1983), and John W. Dower, *War without Mercy: Race and Power in the Pacific War* (1986), are scholarly studies of the wartime mistreatment of Japanese-Americans.

C.   The Truman Era, 1945–1952

The historical literature about the Truman years has grown significantly in recent decades. Richard S. Kirkendall, ed., *The Truman Period as a Research Field* (1967), has been supplemented by the same author's *The Truman Period as a Research Field: A Reappraisal* (1974). The best general accounts are Cabell Phillips, *The Truman Presidency: The History of a Triumphant Succession* (1966); Alonzo L. Hamby, *Beyond the New Deal: Harry S Truman and American Liberalism* (1973); Robert J. Donovan, *Conflict and Crisis: The Presidency of Harry S. Truman, 1945–1948* (1977) and *Tumultuous Years: The Presidency of Harry S. Truman, 1949–1953* (1982); Bert Cochran, *Harry Truman and the Crisis Presidency* (1973); and Donald R. McCoy, *The Presidency of Harry S Truman* (1984). For an interesting, if not always persuasive, radical critique of New Deal and Fair Deal reform, see the relevant essays in Barton J. Bernstein, ed., *Towards a New Past: Dissenting Essays in American History* (1968).

On Truman, David McCullough, *Truman* (1992); Harry S Truman, *Memoirs by Harry S Truman* (2 vols., 1955–1956), and Merle Miller, *Plain Speaking: An Oral Biography of*

Harry S Truman (1974), are invaluable. William Hillman, ed., *Mr. President* (1952), includes brief excerpts from Truman's diaries and letters. See also Morris B. Schnapper, ed., *The Truman Program* (1949), a collection of Truman's speeches on Fair Deal policies; Robert H. Ferrell, ed., *Dear Bess: The Letters from Harry to Bess Truman, 1910–1951* (1983); and Ferrell, ed., *Off the Record: The Private Papers of Harry S. Truman* (1980). Jonathan Daniels, *The Man of Independence* (1951), is a good biography that carries the story as far as 1949. Margaret Truman, *Harry S Truman* (1973), is a fascinating personal reminiscence by a president's daughter, which includes excerpts from Truman's letters. Donald R. McCoy and Richard T. Ruetten, *Quest and Response: Minority Rights and the Truman Administration* (1973), is an excellent overall study of the administration's policies in this realm. A revealing insider memoir is Clark Clifford, *Counsel to the President* (1991).

American politics during this turbulent era has been the subject of several important studies. Samuel Lubell, *The Future of American Politics* (1965), is a penetrating analysis of shifting political alignments. See also Louis L. Gerson, *The Hyphenate in Recent American Politics and Diplomacy* (1964), and Jack Redding, *Inside the Democratic Party* (1958). The background of the changing political outlook in the South is superbly treated in V. O. Key, Jr., *Southern Politics in State and Nation* (1949). The story is carried forward in George B. Tindall, *The Disruption of the Solid South* (1972). Other general surveys of postwar southern politics include Jack Bass and Walter DeVries, *The Transformation of Southern Politics: Social Change and Political Consequence since 1945* (1976); Numan V. Bartley and Hugh D. Graham, *Southern Politics and the Second Reconstruction* (1975); and Steven F. Lawson, *Black Ballots: Voting Rights in the South, 1944–1969* (1976) and *In Pursuit of Power: Southern Blacks and Electoral Politics, 1965–1982* (1985). Among more specialized studies, see J. Harvie Wilkinson III, *Harry Byrd and the Changing Face of Virginia Politics, 1945–1966* (1968); Andrew Buni, *The Negro in Virginia Politics, 1902–1965* (1967); and Numan V. Bartley, *From Thurmond to Wallace: Political Tendencies in Georgia, 1948–1968* (1970).

For the campaign of 1948, see Irwin Ross, *The Loneliest Campaign: The Truman Victory of 1948* (1968), and Jules Abels, *Out of the Jaws of Victory* (1959). Arthur M. Schlesinger, Jr., *The Vital Center* (1949), is a liberal Democrat's thoughtful contemporary analysis of Fair Deal liberalism and contrasting political pressures from right and left. For developments on the left, the best accounts are Karl M. Schmidt, *Henry A. Wallace, Quixotic Crusader* (1960), and Norman D. Markowitz, *The Rise and Fall of the People's Century: Henry A. Wallace and American Liberalism, 1941–1948* (1973). See also Edward L. and Frederick H. Schapsmeier, *Prophet in Politics: Henry A. Wallace and the War Years, 1940–1965* (1971). Two excellent studies by Christopher Lasch provide historical contexts for postwar left-wing politics: *The Agony of the American Left* (1969), and *The New Radicalism in America, 1889–1963: The Intellectual as a Social Type* (1965).

Other important issues of the Truman era are treated in Allen J. Matusow, *Farm Policies and Politics in the Truman Years* (1967); Richard O. Davies, *Housing Reform During the Truman Administration* (1966); and Arthur F. McClure, *The Truman Administration and the Problems of Postwar Labor, 1945–1948* (1969). Walter Millis and E. S. Duffield, eds., *The Forrestal Diaries* (1951), is especially revealing on military and naval policies.

For economic issues in the postwar era, the best single volume is George A. Steiner, *Government's Role in Economic Life* (1953). Lester V. Chandler, *Inflation in the United States,*

1940–1948 (1950), is comprehensive and clearly written. On the Employment Act of 1946, see Edward S. Flash, Jr., *Economic Advice and Presidential Leadership: The Council of Economic Advisers* (1965). But see also Stephen K. Bailey, *Congress Makes a Law* (1957); Edwin G. Nourse, *The 1950s Come First* (1951) and *Economics in the Public Service* (1953); and Seymour E. Harris, *Economic Planning* (1949). For the mobilization following the outbreak of the Korean War, see L. V. Chandler, ed., *Economic Mobilization and Stabilization* (1951), and Steiner, *Government's Role in Economic Life,* just cited.

Charles W. Tobey, *The Return to Morality* (1952); Paul H. Douglas, *Ethics in Government* (1952); Blair Bolles, *How to Get Rich in Washington* (1952); H. Hubert Wilson, *Congress: Corruption and Compromise* (1951); Karl Schriftgiesser, *The Lobbyists* (1951); and Andrew J. Dunar, *The Truman Scandals and the Politics of Morality* (1984), describe the causes and consequences of corruption during the Truman era.

D.   McCarthyism and the Domestic Cold War

The rise of the Republican right is treated in James T. Patterson, *Mr. Republican: A Biography of Robert A. Taft* (1972), and the earlier book by William S. White, *The Taft Story* (1954). Arthur S. Vandenberg, Jr., ed., *The Private Papers of Senator Vandenberg* (1952), deals mainly with foreign affairs but also reveals the tensions that divided the Republican party. Several competent studies have pointed up the close connection between foreign-policy issues and domestic politics during the Truman years. Among the best are H. Bradford Westerfield, *Foreign Policy and Party Politics: Pearl Harbor to Korea* (1955); Ronald J. Caridi, *The Korean War and American Politics: The Republican Party as a Case Study* (1968); John W. Spanier, *The Truman-MacArthur Controversy and the Korean War* (1965); and Athan G. Theoharis, *The Yalta Myths: An Issue in U.S. Politics, 1945–1955* (1970). Alan D. Harper, *The Politics of Loyalty: The White House and the Communist Issue, 1946–1952* (1969), argues that the Truman administration was the victim of an irresistible climate of anti-Communist opinion. In sharp contrast is Richard M. Freeland, *The Truman Doctrine and the Origins of McCarthyism: Foreign Policy, Domestic Politics, and Internal Security, 1946–1948* (1972), which maintains that postwar anticommunism grew directly out of Truman's purposeful strategy of rousing public opinion in support of the Marshall Plan and other cold-war policies. Also critical of Truman's policies toward left-wing opposition is Michael R. Belknap, *Cold War Political Justice: The Smith Act, the Communist Party, and American Civil Liberties* (1977).

The most virulent aspect of postwar anti-Communist sentiment, McCarthyism, has been the subject of much analysis and conflicting interpretations. Goldman, *The Crucial Decade and After,* includes a penetrating sketch and judgment of the Wisconsin demagogue. Richard H. Rovere, *Senator Joe McCarthy* (1959), is hostile but judicious. The best case for the senator is made by William F. Buckley, Jr., and L. B. Bozell, *McCarthy and His Enemies: The Record and Its Meaning* (1954). But the definitive biography is David M. Oshinsky, *A Conspiracy So Immense: The World of Joe McCarthy* (1983). The prevailing "intellectual" view during the 1950s—that McCarthyism was a kind of mass populist movement fed by antiestablishment "status envy"—has been provocatively challenged by two recent authors who see McCarthyism as a direct extension and outgrowth of GOP partisanship and conventional right-wing sentiment: Robert Griffith, *The Politics of*

Fear: Joseph R. McCarthy and the Senate (1970), and Michael P. Rogin, *The Intellectuals and McCarthy: The Radical Specter* (1967). On the other hand, Seymour M. Lipset and Earl Raab, *Politics of Unreason: Right-Wing Extremism in America, 1790–1977* (1978), suggests that McCarthyism was not a right-wing extremist movement but simply a "tendency of the times" and "more hysteria than a political movement." For other studies of McCarthyism and the cold war at home, see David M. Oshinsky, *Senator Joseph McCarthy and the American Labor Movement* (1976); E. J. Kahn, Jr., *The China Hands: America's Foreign Service Officers and What Befell Them* (1975); Richard M. Fried, *Men Against McCarthy* (1976) and *Nightmare in Red: The McCarthy Era in Perspective* (1990); David Caute, *The Great Fear: The Anti-Communist Purge under Truman and Eisenhower* (1978); Edwin R. Bayley, *Joe McCarthy and the Press* (1981); Thomas C. Reeves, *The Life and Times of Joe McCarthy: A Biography* (1982); Stanley I. Kutler, *The American Inquisition: Justice and Injustice in the Cold War* (1982); Kenneth O'Reilly, *Hoover and the Un-Americans: The FBI, HUAC, and the Red Menace* (1983); Ellen W. Schrecker, *No Ivory Tower: McCarthyism and the Universities* (1986); and Athan G. Theoharis, ed., *Beyond the Hiss Case: The FBI, Congress, and the Cold War* (1982).

Closely related to these works is a substantial literature on communism and civil liberties. David A. Shannon, *The Decline of American Communism* (1959), is the best general work, but see also John P. Diggins, *The American Left in the Twentieth Century* (1973); Joseph R. Starobin, *American Communism in Crisis, 1943–1957* (1972); Wilson Record, *The Negro and the Communist Party* (1951); and three volumes in the superb Communism in American life series: Ralph L. Roy, *Communism and the Churches* (1960); Robert W. Iverson, *The Communists and the Schools* (1959); and Daniel Aaron, *Writers on the Left* (1961). While Allen Weinstein, *Perjury: The Hiss-Chambers Case* (1978), is definitive on the controversy surrounding Alger Hiss, Alistair Cooke, *A Generation on Trial* (1950), is a balanced analysis of the Hiss trials and their consequences, and Robert E. Cushman, *Civil Liberties in the United States* (1956), is a dispassionate survey. R. K. Carr, *The House Committee on Un-American Activities, 1945–1950* (1952); Clair Wilcox, ed., *Civil Liberties under Attack* (1951); and John W. Caughey, *In Clear and Present Danger* (1958), condemn the excessive fear of internal communism. A highly polemical but stimulating indictment of anti-Communist attitudes in the twentieth century is Michael Parenti, *The Anti-Communist Impulse* (1969).

E.   The Eisenhower Years

In addition to the relevant *Public Papers* volumes, important documents are available in Robert L. Branyan and Lawrence H. Larsen, eds., *The Eisenhower Administration, 1953–1961: A Documentary History* (2 vols., 1971), and Alfred D. Chandler, Jr., et al., *The Papers of Dwight D. Eisenhower* (1970–). The president's own view is capably set forth in Dwight D. Eisenhower, *The White House Years: Mandate for Change* (1963), and *The White House Years: Waging Peace, 1956–1961* (1965). The best histories of the period are Herbert Parmet, *Eisenhower and the American Crusades* (1972), and Charles C. Alexander, *Holding the Line: The Eisenhower Era, 1952–1961* (1975). Many of the political studies of the Truman period cited above also bear upon the Eisenhower years. An excellent analysis of the shifting political attitudes that underlay the election of 1952 is Samuel

Lubell, *The Revolt of the Moderates* (1956). Emmet John Hughes, *The Ordeal of Power: A Political Memoir of the Eisenhower Years* (1963), is candid and critical. Three contemporary studies contain useful information about the first term: Merlo I. Pusey, *Eisenhower the President* (1956); Robert J. Donovan, *Eisenhower: The Inside Story* (1956); and Richard H. Rovere, *Affairs of State: The Eisenhower Years* (1956). Richard M. Nixon, *Six Crises* (1962), is an interesting performance.

The most recent studies of Eisenhower have portrayed him as an activist president in firm control of domestic and foreign policy. See Douglas Kinnard, *President Eisenhower and Strategy Management: A Study in Defense Policies* (1977); Stephen E. Ambrose, *Eisenhower: Solider, General of the Army, President-Elect, 1890–1952* (1983) and *Eisenhower: The President* (1984); Fred I. Greenstein, *The Hidden-Hand Presidency: Eisenhower as Leader* (1982); and William Bragg Ewald, Jr., *Eisenhower the President* (1981).

Other relevant studies include Aaron Wildavsky, *Dixon-Yates: A Study in Power Politics* (1962); William J. Miller, *Henry Cabot Lodge* (1967); Joseph B. Gorman, *Kefauver: A Political Biography* (1971); Patterson, *Mr. Republican*, already cited; John Barlow Martin, *Adlai Stevenson of Illinois* (1976) and *Adlai Stevenson and the World* (1977); and Richard G. Hewlett and Jack M. Holl, *Atoms for Peace and War, 1953–1961: Eisenhower and the Atomic Energy Commission* (1989).

F.   The Presidency under Kennedy and Johnson

For general studies, consult Jim Heath, *Decade of Disillusionment: The Kennedy-Johnson Years* (1975); Harris Wofford, *Of Kennedys and Kings: Making Sense of the Sixties* (1980); David Burner and Thomas R. West, *The Torch Is Passed: The Kennedy Brothers and American Liberalism* (1984); and Allen J. Matusow, *The Unraveling of America: A History of Liberalism in the 1960s* (1984).

On Kennedy, good introductions are Donald C. Lord, *John F. Kennedy: The Politics of Confrontation and Conciliation* (1977); Henry Fairlie, *The Kennedy Promise: The Politics of Expectation* (1973); James T. Crown, *The Kennedy Literature: A Bibliographical Essay on John F. Kennedy* (1968); and Thomas C. Reeves, *A Question of Character: A Life of John F. Kennedy* (1991). The only attempt at a definitive biography is Herbert Parmet, *Jack: The Struggle of John F. Kennedy* (1980) and *JFK: The Presidency of John F. Kennedy* (1983). Parmet's volumes may be supplemented by Ralph G. Martin, *A Hero for Our Time: An Intimate Story of the Kennedy Years* (1983); Benjamin Bradlee, *Conversations with Kennedy* (1975); and Montague Kern, Patricia W. Levering, and Ralph B. Levering, *The Kennedy Crises: The Press, the Presidency, and Foreign Policy* (1983). Two recent reassessments are Garry Wills, *The Kennedy Imprisonment: A Meditation on Power* (1982), and Peter Collier and David Horowitz, *The Kennedys: An American Drama* (1984).

Interesting evaluations of Kennedy's leadership are contained in Carl M. Brauer, *John F. Kennedy and the Second Reconstruction* (1977); Aida deP. Donald, ed., *John F. Kennedy and the New Frontier* (1967); and Irving Dernstein, *Promises Kept: John F. Kennedy's New Frontier* (1991). Two excellent, detailed, and highly favorable accounts by men who worked closely with Kennedy are Arthur M. Schlesinger, Jr., *A Thousand Days: John F. Kennedy in the White House* (1965), and Theodore C. Sorenson, *Kennedy* (1965). Also valuable on the Kennedy years is Richard N. Goodwin, *Remembering America: A Voice from the Sixties* (1988). A significant legislative study is Richard Harris, *The Real Voice*

(1964), dealing with the background of the drug industry bill. Jim F. Heath, *John F. Kennedy and the Business Community* (1969), is a penetrating and judicious study. An important area of domestic policy is well covered in Vernon W. Ruttan et al., *Agricultural Policy in an Affluent Society* (1969), and somewhat more broadly in Robert J. Morgan, *Governing Soil Conservation: Thirty Years of the New Decentralization* (1966), and R. Burnell Held and Marion Clawson, *Soil Conservation in Perspective* (1965).

Tom Wicker, *JFK & LBJ: The Influence of Personality upon Politics* (1969), is an incisive comparison of the two Democratic presidents. A personal memoir by Kennedy's White House secretary, Evelyn Lincoln, *Kennedy and Johnson* (1968), includes some perceptive observations. Michael Davie, *LBJ: A Foreign Observer's Viewpoint* (1966), and Rowland Evans and Robert Novak, *Lyndon B. Johnson: The Exercise of Power* (1966), contain useful insights. Doris Kearns, *Lyndon Johnson and the American Dream* (1976), is as close as possible to an authorized biography. See also Eric F. Goldman, *The Tragedy of Lyndon Johnson: A Historian's Personal Interpretation* (1969). These may be supplemented by the interesting first-person observations contained in Lyndon B. Johnson, *The Vantage Point: Perspectives of the Presidency, 1963–1969* (1971); Lady Bird Johnson, *A White House Diary* (1970); and Jack Valenti, *A Very Human President* (1975).

For other studies of Johnson, see Robert A. Caro, *The Years of Lyndon Johnson: The Path to Power* (1982) and *Means of Ascent* (1990); Vaughn Davis Bornet, *The Presidency of Lyndon Johnson* (1983); Robert A. Divine, ed., *Exploring the Johnson Years* (1981); Ronnie Dugger, *The Politician: The Life and Times of Lyndon Johnson: The Drive for Power, from the Frontier to Master of the Senate* (1982); Merle Miller, *Lyndon: An Oral Biography* (1980); George Reedy, *Lyndon Johnson: A Memoir* (1982); and Robert Dallek, *Lone Star Rising: Lyndon Johnson and His Times, 1908–1960* (1991), the first of a multi-volume biography.

G.   Nixon and Constitutional Crisis

The best studies of the Nixon presidency are Jonathan Schell, *The Time of Illusion* (1976), and Arthur M. Schlesinger, Jr., *The Imperial Presidency* (1973). Garry Wills, *Nixon Agonistes: The Crisis of the Self-Made Man* (1970), reviews the life and career of Richard Nixon through the election of 1968 and into the early months of his presidency. Robert E. Osgood et al., *Retreat from Empire? The First Nixon Administration* (1973), carries the story forward to 1972. Bruce Mazlish, *In Search of Nixon: A Psychohistorical Inquiry* (1972), is an attempt at a psychobiography, as is Fawn M. Brodie, *Richard Nixon: The Shaping of His Character* (1981). Recent biographies include Stephen E. Ambrose, *Nixon: The Education of a Politician, 1913–1962* (1987), and *The Triumph of a Politician, 1962–1972* (1989); Tom Wicker, *One of Us: Richard Nixon and the American Dream* (1991); Herbert Parmet, *Richard Nixon and His America* (1990); and Roger Morris, *Richard Milhous Nixon: The Rise of an American Politician* (1990). The rise of H. R. Haldeman and John Ehrlichman to positions of great power within the administration is the subject of Dan Rather and Gary Paul Gates, *The Palace Guard* (1974). Also essential to understanding the Nixon presidency are Richard M. Nixon, *RN: The Memoirs of Richard Nixon* (1978), and Henry Kissinger's memoir, *The White House Years* (1979) and *Years of Upheaval* (1982).

Domestic politics are discussed in Daniel P. Moynihan, *The Politics of a Guaranteed*

Income: The Nixon Administration and the Family Plan (1973); Vincent Burke and Vee Burke, *Nixon's Good Deed: Welfare Reform* (1974); James Reichley, *Conservatives in an Age of Change: The Nixon and Ford Administrations* (1981); Joseph C. Spear, *Presidents and the Press: The Nixon Legacy* (1984); and Herbert G. Klein, *Making It Perfectly Clear* (1980).

Accounts of the Watergate affair are rich and lively. Theodore H. White, *Breach of Faith: The Fall of Richard Nixon* (1975); Barry Sussman, *The Great Coverup: Nixon and the Scandal of Watergate* (1974); and J. Anthony Lukas, *Nightmare: The Underside of the Nixon Years* (1976), are excellent general surveys. Carl Bernstein and Bob Woodward, *All the President's Men* (1974), describes the initial investigation by two reporters from the *Washington Post*. Jimmy Breslin, *How the Good Guys Finally Won: Notes from an Impeachment Summer* (1975); Frank Mankiewicz, *U.S. v. Richard Nixon: The Final Crisis* (1975); and John R. Labovitz, *Presidential Impeachment* (1978), offer thoughtful reflections on Nixon's judicial troubles. Other valuable surveys are the 1974 volumes put together by the *New York Times* and the *Washington Post*, called *The End of a Presidency* (1974) and *The Fall of a President* (1974), respectively. For the most recent assessment, see Stanley I. Kutler, *The Wars of Watergate: The Last Crisis of Richard Nixon* (1990).

For a superb account of the scandal from a judicial perspective, see John J. Sirica, *To Set the Record Straight: The Break-In, the Tapes, the Conspirators, the Pardon* (1979). James Doyle, *Not Above the Law: The Battles of Watergate Prosecutors Cox and Jaworski, a Behind-the-Scenes Account* (1977), is a description of the Watergate crisis by the press spokesman. Leon Jaworski, *The Right and the Power* (1976), gives an account of his own particular role. Howard Bell, *"We Have a Duty": The Supreme Court and the Watergate Tapes Litigation* (1990), is useful. Fred D. Thompson, *At That Point in Time: The Inside Story of the Senate Watergate Committee* (1975), tells the story of the Senate investigation, as does Samuel Dash, *Chief Counsel: Inside the Ervin Committee—the Untold Story of Watergate* (1976). Philip B. Kurland, *Watergate and the Constitution* (1978), discusses the judicial implications of the scandal. For a vivid description of Nixon's last weeks in office, see Bob Woodward and Carl Bernstein, *The Final Days* (1976).

H.   Post-Watergate Politics

The literature on the brief Ford presidency is sparse. Gerald Ford, in *A Time to Heal: An Autobiography* (1979), reflects upon his truncated presidential term. The campaign of 1976 is explored in Jules Witcover, *Marathon: The Pursuit of the Presidency, 1972–1976* (1977), and Elizabeth Drew, *American Journal: The Events of 1976* (1977). An interesting discussion of the evolution of the Democratic party during the 1970s is provided in Byron E. Shafer, *Quiet Revolution: The Struggle for the Democratic Party and the Shaping of Post-Reform Politics* (1983). Jimmy Carter is the subject of several studies. Early assessments, generally negative, are James T. Wooten, *Dasher: The Roots and the Rising of Jimmy Carter* (1978); William Lee Miller, *Yankee from Georgia: The Emergence of Jimmy Carter* (1978); Gary M. Fink, *Prelude to the Presidency: The Political Character and Legislative Style of Governor Jimmy Carter* (1980); Betty Glad, *Jimmy Carter: In Search of The Great White House* (1980); Haynes B. Johnson, *In the Absence of Power: Governing America* (1980); Clark Mollenhoff, *The President Who Failed: Carter Out of Control* (1980); and Laurence F. Lynn, *The President as Policymaker: Jimmy Carter and Welfare Reform* (1981).

More sympathetic treatments of Carter's presidency include M. Glenn Abernathy et al., eds., *The Carter Years: The President and Policy Making* (1984); Jack Germond and Jules Witcover, *Blue Smoke and Mirrors: How Reagan Won and Why Carter Lost the Election of 1980* (1981); George D. Moffett III, *The Limits of Victory: The Ratification of the Panama Canal Treaties* (1983); and Gaddis Smith, *Morality, Reason, and Power: American Diplomacy in the Carter Years* (1985). Also see Charles O. Jones, *The Trusteeship Presidency: Jimmy Carter and the United States Congress* (1988). The memoirs of officials in the Carter administration are another important source. They include Jimmy Carter, *Keeping Faith: Memoirs of a President* (1982) and *The Blood of Abraham* (1985); Rosalynn Carter, *First Lady from Plains* (1984); Joseph E. Califano, *Governing America: An Insider's Report from the White House and Cabinet* (1981); Hamilton Jordan, *Crisis: The Last Year of the Carter Presidency* (1982); Zbigniew K. Brzezinski, *Power and Principle: Memoirs of the National Security Advisor, 1977–1981* (1983); and Jody Powell, *The Other Side of the Story* (1984).

The history of the Reagan and Bush presidencies remains to be written. Haynes Johnson, *Sleepwalking through History: America in the Reagan Years*, surveys the 1980s. Garry Wills, *Reagan's America: Innocents at Home*, is a brilliant analysis of Reagan's political personality. A revealing account is available in Jack Germond and Jules Witcover, *Whose Broad Stripes and Bright Stars? The Trivial Pursuit of the Presidency, 1988* (1990). Two memoirs of cabinet officials who left before the end of Reagan's first term are Alexander M. Haig, *Caveat: Realism, Reagan, and Foreign Policy* (1984), and James Watt and Doug Mead, *The Courage of a Conservative* (1985). Another account which studies the struggle for power inside the White House is Laurence I. Barrett, *Gambling with History: Ronald Reagan in the White House* (1983). Other memoir accounts include David A. Stockman, *The Triumph of Politics: How the Reagan Revolution Failed* (1986); Michael Deaver, *Behind the Scenes* (1987); Larry Speakes, *Speaking Out: The Reagan Presidency from Inside the White House* (1988); Donald T. Regan, *For the Record: From Wall Street to Washington* (1988); Martin Anderson, *Revolution* (1988); Maureen Reagan, *First Father, First Daughter* (1989); Caspar W. Weinberger, *Fighting for Peace: Seven Critical Years in the Pentagon* (1990); and Nancy Reagan, *My Turn* (1990) and Edwin Meese III, *With Reagan: The Inside Story* (1992). The best single biography is Lou Cannon, *Reagan* (1982) and *President Reagan: The Role of a Lifetime* (1991). Other assessments are available in Robert Dallek, *Ronald Reagan: The Politics of Symbolism* (1984); Rowland Evans and Robert Novak, *The Reagan Revolution* (1981); and Richard Reeves, *The Reagan Detour* (1985). A valuable study of the domestic policies of the first Reagan administration is John L. Palmer and Isabel V. Sawhill, eds., *The Reagan Record: An Assessment of America's Changing Domestic Priorities* (1984).

On Reagan's foreign policy, see Theodore Draper, *Present History: On Nuclear War, Detente, and Other Controversies* (1983); Coral Bell, *The Reagan Paradox: American Foreign Policy in the 1980s* (1989); Fred Halliday, *From Kabul to Managua: Soviet-American Relations in the 1980s* (1989); and Don Oberdorfer, *The Turn: From Cold War to a New Era, the United States and the Soviet Union, 1983–1990* (1991). Further studies of the Reagan presidency include Wayne Greenhaw, *Elephants in the Cottonfields: Ronald Reagan and the New Republican South* (1982); Joan Claybrook, *Retreat from Safety: Reagan's Attack on America's Health* (1984); Strobe Talbott, *The Russians and Reagan* (1984) and *Deadly Gambits* (1984); and George C. Eads and Michael Fix, eds., *The Reagan Regulatory*

Strategy: An Assessment (1984). On new political configurations and the question of a Republican realignment, see Gillian Peele, *Revival and Reaction: The Right in Contemporary America* (1984); Thomas Ferguson and Joel Rogers, *Right Turn: The 1984 Election and the Future of American Politics* (1986); and Elizabeth Drew, *Campaign Journal: The Political Events of 1983–1984* (1985).

There are several outstanding biographies or autobiographies of important political leaders of the 1960s, 1970s, and 1980s: Arthur M. Schlesinger, Jr., *Robert Kennedy and His Times* (1978); Hubert H. Humphrey, *The Education of a Public Man* (1976); Edward C. Schapsmeier and Frederick H. Schapsmeier, *Dirksen of Illinois: Senatorial Statesman* (1985); George S. McGovern, *Grassroots: The Autobiography of George McGovern* (1977); James MacGregor Burns, *Edward Kennedy and the Camelot Legacy* (1976); Max Lerner, *Ted and the Kennedy Legend* (1980); Theo Lippman, Jr., *Senator Ted Kennedy: The Career Behind the Image* (1976); Eugene Brown, *J. William Fulbright: Advice and Consent* (1985); and Marshall Frady, *Wallace* (1968), on Governor George C. Wallace of Alabama.

I.   The Supreme Court since 1940

Among the best studies of the Supreme Court and the Constitution are William F. Swindler, *Court and Constitution in the Twentieth Century* (2 vols., 1969–1970); Alpheus T. Mason, *The Supreme Court from Taft to Burger* (1979); Paul L. Murphy, *The Constitution in Crisis Times, 1918–1969* (1972); and Robert G. McCloskey, *The Modern Supreme Court* (1972), which includes material on the Stone (1940–1946), Vinson (1946–1953), and Warren (1954–1969) Courts. See also Kathryn Griffith, *Judge Learned Hand and the Role of the Federal Judiciary* (1973); C. H. Pritchett, *Civil Liberties and the Vinson Court* (1954); Mary Frances Berry, *Stability, Security, and Continuity: Mr. Justice Burton and Decision-Making in the Supreme Court, 1945–1957* (1978); Arthur J. Goldberg, *Equal Justice: The Warren Era of the Supreme Court* (1972); and Archibald Cox, *The Warren Court: Constitutional Decision as an Instrument of Reform* (1968). Walter F. Murphy, *Congress and the Court* (1962), is an important analysis of congressional opposition in the late 1950s. More specialized studies include Richard C. Cortner, *The Apportionment Cases* (1970); Charles A. Miller, *The Supreme Court and the Uses of History* (1969); Richard Claude, *The Supreme Court and the Electoral Process* (1970); Raoul Berger, *Government by Judiciary: The Transformation of the Fourteenth Amendment* (1977). A recent Court controversy is the subject of Robert Shogan, *A Question of Judgment: The Fortas Case and the Struggle for the Supreme Court* (1972). For an account of the inner workings of the Court by an investigative reporter, see Bob Woodward, *The Brethren: Inside the Supreme Court* (1979).

2.   AMERICAN FOREIGN POLICY SINCE 1940

A.   Origins of World War II

The body of literature on the background of American participation in World War II is immense. The two outstanding works on the subject are William L. Langer and S. E. Gleason, *The Challenge to Isolation, 1937–1940* (1952) and *The Undeclared War, 1940–1941* (1953). Other general works are Robert Dallek, *Franklin D. Roosevelt and American Foreign Policy, 1932–1945* (1979); James MacGregor Burns, *Roosevelt: The Soldier of*

Freedom (1970); Robert A. Divine, *The Reluctant Belligerent: American Entry into World War II* (1965); T. R. Fehrenbach, *F.D.R.'s Undeclared War, 1939 to 1941* (1967); and James V. Compton, *The Swastika and the Eagle: Hitler, the United States, and the Origins of World War II* (1967). Robert E. Sherwood, *Roosevelt and Hopkins* (1948); and Winston S. Churchill, *The Gathering Storm* (1948) and *Their Finest Hour* (1949), are invaluable sources. See also Charles A. Beard, *American Foreign Policy in the Making, 1932–1940* (1946), and *President Roosevelt and the Coming of the War, 1941* (1948), critical studies worthy of serious consideration. Particular works relating to the United States and Europe from 1938 to 1941 are Alton Frye, *Germany and the American Hemisphere, 1933–1941* (1967); John M. Haight, *American Aid to France, 1938–1941* (1970); Philip Goodhart, *Fifty Ships That Saved the World* (1965); Warren F. Kimball, *The Most Unsordid Act: Lend-Lease, 1930–1941* (1969); Theodore A. Wilson, *The First Summit: Roosevelt and Churchill at Placentia Bay, 1941* (1969); and David Reynolds, *The Creation of the Anglo-American Alliance: A Study in Competitive Cooperation* (1982).

Relations with Japan during the 1930s to 1941 are traced by A. Whitney Griswold, *The Far Eastern Policy of the United States* (1938); Dorothy Borg, *The United States and the Far Eastern Crisis of 1933–1938* (1964); Waldo H. Heinrichs, Jr., *American Ambassador: Joseph C. Grew and the Development of the United States Diplomatic Tradition* (1966); and Joseph C. Grew, *Turbulent Era, a Diplomatic Record of Forty Years, 1904–1945* (2 vols., 1952). The Langer and Gleason volumes contain the best account of events leading to the rupture in Japanese-American relations, but see also Manny T. Koginos, *The Panay Incident: Prelude to War* (1967); John Toland, *The Rising Sun: The Decline and Fall of the Japanese Empire, 1936–1945* (1970); Herbert Feis, *The Road to Pearl Harbor* (1950); Paul W. Schroeder, *The Axis Alliance and Japanese-American Relations, 1941* (1958); Robert J. C. Butow, *Tojo and the Coming of the War* (1961); Roberta Wohlstetter, *Pearl Harbor: Warning and Decision* (1962); and Gordon W. Prange, *At Dawn We Slept: The Untold Story of Pearl Harbor* (1981). Insightful essays on various aspects of Japanese and American foreign policies are contained in Dorothy Borg and Shumpei Okamoto, eds., *Pearl Harbor as History* (1973).

For the debate over American intervention, we now have adequate studies for both the internationalists and the isolationists: Walter Johnson, *The Battle against Isolation* (1944); Mark L. Chadwin, *The Hawks of World War II* (1968); Donald J. Friedman, *The Road from Isolation: The Campaign of the American Committee for Non-Participation in Japanese Aggression, 1938–1941* (1968); Wayne S. Cole, *America First, the Battle against Intervention, 1940–1941* (1953); and Manfred Jonas, *Isolationism in America, 1935–1941* (1966).

B.   The Diplomacy and Conduct of World War II

The best and most revealing source on the Anglo-American wartime relationship is Warren F. Kimball, ed., *Churchill and Roosevelt: The Complete Correspondence* (3 vols., 1984). Dallek, *Franklin D. Roosevelt and American Foreign Policy;* Burns, *Roosevelt: Soldier of Freedom;* and Herbert Feis, *Churchill, Roosevelt, and Stalin* (1957), are the best one-volume accounts, but see also Churchill's magisterial *The Grand Alliance* (1950), *The Hinge of Fate* (1950), *Closing the Ring* (1951), and *Triumph and Tragedy* (1953); Warren

Kimball *The Juggler: Franklin Roosevelt as Wartime Statesman* (1991); John S. D. Eisenhower, *Allies: Pearl Harbor to D-Day* (1982); Sherwood, *Roosevelt and Hopkins;* and W. Averell Harriman and Elie Abel, *Special Envoy to Churchill and Stalin, 1941–1946* (1975). Akira Iriye, *Power and Culture: The Japanese-American War, 1941–1945* (1981), is a reconsideration of that subject. Other general studies are Robert A. Divine, *Roosevelt and World War II* (1969); Gaddis Smith, *American Diplomacy during the Second World War* (1965); Christopher Thorne, *Allies of a Kind: The United States, Britain, and the War against Japan* (1978); and William Roger Louis, *Imperialism at Bay: The United States and the Decolonization of the British Empire, 1941–1945* (1978), a monumental study. For more specialized works, see Mark A. Stoler, *The Politics of the Second Front: American Military Planning and Diplomacy in Coalition Warfare, 1941–1943* (1977); Herbert Feis, *The China Triangle* (1953); Paul A. Varg, *The Closing of the Door: Sino-American Relations, 1936–1946* (1973); E. J. Kahn, Jr., *The China Hands: America's Foreign Service Officers and What Befell Them* (1975); Keith Eubank, *Summit at Teheran: The Untold Story* (1985); John L. Snell, ed., *The Meaning of Yalta* (1956); Stephen E. Ambrose, *Eisenhower and Berlin: The Decision to Halt at the Elbe* (1967); Robert A. Divine, *Second Chance: The Triumph of Internationalism in America during World War II* (1967); Herbert Feis, *Between War and Peace: The Potsdam Conference* (1960), *Japan Subdued* (1961), and *From Trust to Terror: The Onset of the Cold War, 1945–1950* (1971); Frank D. McCann, Jr., *The Brazilian-American Alliance, 1937–1945* (1973); Robert J. C. Butow, *Japan's Decision to Surrender* (1954); and William L. Neumann, *After Victory: Churchill, Roosevelt, Stalin, and the Making of the Peace* (1969). Gabriel Kolko, *The Politics of War: The World and United States Foreign Policy, 1943–1945* (1969), challenges, not always successfully, and rarely without bias in favor of the Soviet Union, many traditional assumptions about relations between the Western allies and the Soviet Union and about Soviet policies.

The sad story of the Roosevelt administration's failure to do much to help European Jews in danger of extermination is related in David S. Wyman, *Paper Walls: America and the Refugee Crisis, 1938–1941* (1968) and *The Abandonment of the Jews: Americans and the Holocaust, 1941–1945* (1984); Henry L. Feingold, *The Politics of Rescue: The Roosevelt Administration and the Holocaust, 1938–1945* (1970); Arthur D. Morse, *While Six Million Died* (1968); and Saul S. Friedman, *No Haven for the Oppressed: United States Policy toward Jewish Refugees, 1938–1945* (1973).

Churchill, *The Grand Alliance, The Hinge of Fate, Closing the Ring,* and *Triumph and Tragedy,* include brilliant summaries of all major military operations. The best single-volume history is Martha Byrd Hoyle, *A World in Flames: The History of World War II* (1970). But see also Chester Wilmot, *The Struggle for Europe* (1952); Charles B. MacDonald, *The Mighty Endeavor: American Armed Forces in the European Theater in World War II* (1969); Ronald Schaffer, *Wings of Judgment: American Bombing in World War II* (1985); and Gary R. Hess, *The United States at War, 1941–1945* (1985). The Department of the Army's Office of Military History has published numerous volumes in its large and generally excellent series, *U.S. Army in World War II.* Samuel E. Morison, *History of the United States Naval Operations in World War II* (15 vols., 1947–1962), is definitive; but see Gordon Prange, *Miracle at Midway* (1982), and Walter Lord, *Incredible Victory* (1967), on the Battle of Midway; see also Ronald H. Spector, *Eagle against the Sun: The American War with Japan* (1984). Kent Roberts Greenfield, ed., *Command Decisions*

(1959), contains a number of brilliant analyses of crucial military events and also reveals how considerations of military strategy affected diplomacy. Greenfield, *American Strategy in World War II: A Reconsideration* (1963), is another provocative assessment. For British perspectives on Anglo-American strategic planning and operations, see Michael Howard, *The Mediterranean Strategy in the Second World War* (1966), and John Keegan, *Six Armies in Normandy* (1982).

For American military and naval leaders, see Alfred D. Chandler, Jr., Stephen E. Ambrose, and Louis Galambos, eds., *The Papers of Dwight D. Eisenhower: The War Years* (9 vols., 1970, 1978); Stephen E. Ambrose, *The Supreme Commander: The War Years of General Dwight D. Eisenhower* (1970) and *Eisenhower: Soldier, General of the Army, President-Elect, 1890–1952* (1983); Dwight D. Eisenhower, *Crusade in Europe* (1948); Forrest C. Pogue, *George C. Marshall* (3 vols., 1962–1973); William Raymond Manchester, *American Caesar, Douglas MacArthur, 1880–1964* (1978); Gavin Long, *MacArthur as Military Commander* (1969); D. Clayton James, *The Years of MacArthur*, vol. I (1970); Douglas MacArthur, *Reminiscences* (1964); H. Essame, *Patton: A Study in Command* (1976); E. B. Potter, *Nimitz* (1976); Henry H. Arnold, *Global Mission* (1949); Omar N. Bradley, *A Soldier's Story* (1951); Ernest J. King and W. M. Whitehill, *Fleet Admiral King* (1952); and William D. Leahy, *I Was There* (1950). Richard F. Haynes, *The Awesome Power: Harry S. Truman as Commander in Chief* (1973), is a significant study of the military power inherent in the office of the presidency.

C.   The Cold War

During the past two decades, considerable scholarly attention has been focused on the origins of the cold war. Much of it, written by New Left revisionist historians, has criticized American diplomacy and placed the burden of responsibility for the coming of the cold war on the United States. See D. F. Fleming, *The Cold War and Its Origins, 1917–1960* (2 vols., 1961), the pioneering study; Gar Alperovitz, *Atomic Diplomacy: Hiroshima and Potsdam* (1966), which argues that the United States consciously used the atomic bomb as a diplomatic weapon in its negotiations with the Soviet Union in 1945, as does, more judiciously, Martin J. Sherwin, *A World Destroyed: The Atomic Bomb and the Grand Alliance* (1975). Also critical of U.S. policies are Diane S. Clemens, *Yalta* (1970); Bruce Kuklick, *American Policy and the Division of Germany: The Clash with Russia over Reparations* (1972); Lloyd C. Gardner, *Architects of Illusion: Men and Ideas in American Foreign Policy, 1941–1949* (1970); Barton J. Bernstein, ed., *Politics and Problems of the Truman Administration* (1970); David Horowitz, *From Yalta to Vietnam* (1967); D. Horowitz, ed., *Containment and Revolution* (1967); and Walter La Feber, *America, Russia, and the Cold War, 1945–1966* (1967). The most extensive case for revisionism has been made by Gabriel Kolko in three studies: *The Politics of War: The World and United States Foreign Policy, 1943–1945* (1968); *The Roots of American Foreign Policy: An Analysis of Power and Purpose* (1969), an examination of American relations with the third world; and (with Joyce Kolko), *The Limits of Power: The World and United States Foreign Policy, 1945–1954* (1972).

Revisionist historiography has been directly or indirectly responsible for the writing of several penetrating studies that seek either to refute its contentions or reexamine the documents in light of its claims. Revisionist findings are attacked harshly in Robert J. Maddox, *The New Left and the Origins of the Cold War* (1973), and Robert W. Tucker, *The Radical Left and American Foreign Policy* (1971). Lloyd C. Gardner, Arthur M. Schlesinger, Jr., and Hans J. Morgenthau, *The Origins of the Cold War* (1970), presents three forceful conflicting essays in which the basic revisionist and nonrevisionist interpretations may be compared and contrasted. Martin F. Herz, *The Beginnings of the Cold War* (1966), and Paul Seabury, *The Rise and Fall of the Cold War* (1967), reflect but partially transcend revisionist influence. Robert Hunter, *Security in Europe* (1969), argues that conflict was more a consequence of lack of understanding or agreed-upon guidelines than of real clash of interest. William L. Neumann, *After Victory: Churchill, Roosevelt, Stalin and the Making of the Peace* (1969), suggests that wartime realities and exigencies were instrumental in determining the nature of the peace; while Louis J. Halle, *The Cold War in History* (1967), sees a high probability, if not the inevitability, of conflict between two emerging superpowers with incompatible aims and assumptions.

Balanced, realistic correctives to the revisionist views are presented by Adam Ulam, *Expansion and Coexistence: The History of Soviet Foreign Policy, 1917–1967* (1968), and George S. Herring, Jr., *Aid to Russia, 1941–1946: Strategy, Diplomacy, and the Origins of the Cold War* (1973). Herbert Feis, *Contest over Japan* (1967), counters revisionist claims by stressing an unbroken American desire to create a democratized and independent postwar Japan rather than a bastion against Communist expansion in Asia. See also the same author's *From Trust to Terror*, cited earlier. The best recent assessment of Soviet responsibility for the cold war is Vojtech Mastny, *Russia's Road to the Cold War* (1979). Raymond Aron, *The Imperial Republic: The United States and the World, 1945–1973* (1974), is an eloquent defense of American foreign policy during the period.

The best and most judicious studies of the entire problem are Melvin P. Leffler, *A Preponderance of Power: National Security, the Truman Administration, and the Cold War* (1991); John Gaddis, *The United States and the Origins of the Cold War, 1941–1947* (1972), *Russia, the Soviet Union, and the United States: An Interpretive History* (1978), and *Strategies of Containment: A Critical Appraisal of Postwar American National Security Policy* (1982); Thomas G. Patterson, *Soviet-American Confrontation: Postwar Reconstruction and the Origins of the Cold War* (1974) and *America's Half-Century: United States Foreign Policy in the Cold War* (1984). Daniel Yergin, *Shattered Peace: The Origins of the Cold War and the National Security State* (1977) and Randall B. Woods and Howard Jones, *Dawning of the Cold War* (1991). Other studies include Michael Schaller, *The American Occupation of Japan: The Origins of the Cold War in Asia* (1985); Gregg F. Herken, *The Winning Weapon: The Atomic Bomb in the Cold War, 1945–1949* (1981); Bruce R. Kuniholm, *The Origins of the Cold War in the Near East* (1980); Michael M. Boll, *Cold War in the Balkans: American Foreign Policy and the Emergence of Communist Bulgaria, 1943–1947* (1984); Bradley F. Smith, *The Shadow Warriors: O.S.S. and the Origins of the C.I.A.* (1983); James F. Trent, *Mission on the Rhine: Reeducation and Denazification in American-Occupied Germany* (1982); Robert L. Messer, *The End of an Alliance: James F. Byrnes, Roosevelt, Truman, and the Origins of the Cold War* (1982); Lawrence Wittner, *American Intervention in Greece, 1943–1949* (1982); Howard Jones, *"A New Kind of War": America's Global Strategy and the Truman Doctrine in Greece* (1989); and William H. McNeill, *Greece: American Aid in Action, 1947–1956* (1957). On Latin America, see Morris H. Morley, *Imperial State and Revolution: The United States and Cuba, 1952–1986* (1987).

D. The Diplomacy of the Truman Era

Richard L. Walker and George Curry, *E. R. Stettinius, Jr.—James F. Byrnes* (1965); Robert H. Ferrell, *George C. Marshall* (1966); and Gaddis Smith, *Dean Acheson* (1972), study Truman's secretaries of state. Of crucial importance is Dean Acheson, *Present at the Creation: My Years in the State Department* (1969), memoirs covering the period 1941–1953. See also McGeorge Bundy, ed., *The Pattern of Responsibility* (1952), a collection of Acheson's major speeches. Arnold Wolfers, *Alliance Policy in the Cold War* (1959), and George Liska, *The New Statecraft: Foreign Aid in American Policy* (1960), are invaluable for aspects of Truman's diplomacy. Also useful is Walter Isaacson and Evan Thomas, *The Wise Men: Six Friends and the World They Made: Acheson, Bohlen, Harriman, Kennan, Lovett, McCloy* (1988).

For the United Nations and American international economic policies in the immediate postwar period, see Leland M. Goodrich, *The United Nations* (1959); Abraham H. Feller, *United Nations and World Community* (1952); Raymond F. Mikesell, *United States Economic Policy and International Relations* (1952); Brian Tew, *International Monetary Cooperation, 1945–1952* (1952); Clair Wilcox, *A Charter for World Trade* (1949); and Alfred E. Eckes, Jr., *A Search for Solvency: Bretton Woods and the International Monetary System, 1941–1971* (1975).

Hajo Holborn, *American Military Government* (1947); Eugene Davidson, *The Death and Life of Germany: An Account of the American Occupation* (1959); and Trent, *Mission on the Rhine*, are useful for American occupation policies in Germany. See Robert H. Jackson, *The Case against the Nazi War Criminals* (1946) and *The Nuremberg Case* (1947), for a justification of the proceedings. For a study of American opinion on the subject, see William J. Bosch, *Judgment on Nuremberg: American Attitudes toward the Major German War-Crime Trials* (1970). For a highly critical view of the postwar trials in Japan, see Robert Minear, *Victors Justice: The Tokyo War Crimes Trial* (1971). See also Frederick S. Dunn, *Peace-Making and the Settlement with Japan* (1963); Hugh Borton et al., *The Far East, 1942–1946* (1955); Kazuo Kawai, *Japan's American Interlude* (1960); and Michael Schaller, *The American Occupation of Japan: The Origins of the Cold War in Asia* (1985).

The causes of the disruption of the Grand Alliance have been told many times. One of the best early studies is William H. McNeill, *America, Britain, and Russia: Their Co-operation and Conflict, 1941–1946* (1953). Other good accounts are contained in Churchill, *Triumph and Tragedy;* Sherwood, *Roosevelt and Hopkins;* Wilmot, *The Struggle for Europe;* and Messer, *The End of an Alliance,* all cited earlier; two excellent studies by Herbert Feis: *Churchill, Roosevelt, and Stalin* (1957), and *Between War and Peace;* and James L. Gormly, *The Collapse of the Grand Alliance, 1945–1948* (1987). Snell, *The Meaning of Yalta,* is the best introduction to that controversial conference. For related developments in the Far East, see Herbert Feis, *The China Triangle* (1953), and *Japan Subdued* (1961), together with Butow, *Japan's Decision to Surrender.* James F. Byrnes, *Speaking Frankly* (1947), relates his futile struggle for postwar cooperation with the Soviets. There are a few glimpses of Truman's private views in Hillman, ed., *Mr. President,* and Margaret Truman, *Harry S Truman,* and detailed discussions of the growing tensions in Mills and Duffield, eds., *The Forrestal Diaries,* and Vandenberg, ed., *Private Papers of Senator Vandenberg,* all cited previously. Truman's *Memoirs* are indispensable. George F. Kennan, *American Diplomacy, 1900–1950* (1951), contains an incisive chapter on the Truman Doctrine and Kennan's own influential "Mr. X" article on containment. Also see Walter L. Hixson, *George F. Kennan: Cold War Iconoclast* (1989); David Allan Mayers, *George Kennan and the Dilemmas of U.S. Foreign Policy* (1988); and Kennan, *Sketches from a Life* (1989). Penetrating comments on Soviet interests and attitudes are set forth in Kennan, *Memoirs* (2 vols., 1968–1972), and Charles E. Bohlen, *Witness to History* (1973). For the first Berlin crisis, see Lucius D. Clay, *Decision in Germany* (1950); W. Phillips Davison, *The Berlin Blockade* (1958); and Avi Shlaim, *The United States and the Berlin Blockade, 1948–1949: A Study in Crisis Decision-Making* (1983).

Other studies include Joseph M. Jones, *The Fifteen Weeks* (1955), which analyzes the change in opinion during the development of the Greek-Turkish aid program and the Marshall Plan; Harry B. Price, *The Marshall Plan and Its Meaning* (1955); and Theodore H. White, *Fire in the Ashes* (1953), a moving record of American success in Western Europe. Halford L. Hoskins, *The Atlantic Pact* (1949), and Drew Middleton, *Defense of Western Europe* (1952), recount the movement toward Atlantic unity and mutual defense.

Questions of nuclear weapons, the arms race, and disarmament are capably treated in Herken, *The Winning Weapon*, already cited; Herken, *Counsels of War* (1985), on postwar strategic thinking; Chalmers M. Roberts, *The Nuclear Years: The Arms Race and Arms Control, 1945–1970* (1970); Fred M. Kaplan, *The Wizards of Armageddon* (1983); UN Secretariat, *The United Nations and Disarmament, 1945–1965* (1967); and Richard G. Hewlett and Francis Duncan, *A History of the United States Atomic Energy Commission, Vol. I: The New World, 1939–1946* (1972) and *Vol. II: Atomic Shield, 1947–1957* (1972). Excellent sources for this and related subjects are David E. Lilienthal, *The Journals of David E. Lilienthal: The Atomic Energy Years, 1945–1960* (1965), and Harland B. Moulton, *From Superiority to Parity: The United States and the Strategic Arms Race, 1961–1971* (1973). See also Joseph I. Lieberman, *The Scorpion and the Tarantula: The Struggle to Control Atomic Weapons, 1945–1949* (1970). An interesting pioneer study of a basic related question is Eugene B. Skolnikoff, *Science, Technology, and American Foreign Policy* (1967).

American policies in the Middle East after 1945 are discussed by McNeill, *Greece: American Aid in Action*, cited earlier, Lawrence Wittner, *American Intervention in Greece, 1943–1949* (1982); Ephraim A. Speiser, *The United States and the Near East* (1947); L. V. Thomas and R. N. Frye, *The United States and Turkey and Iran* (1951); James G. McDonald, *My Mission in Israel, 1948–1951* (1951); and Bruce Kuniholm, *The Origins of the Cold War in the Near East* (1980).

The debate over the failure of American policy in China has stimulated the printing of most of the basic documents and the writing of some first-rate scholarly studies. U.S. Department of State, *United States Relations with China* (1949), is the "white paper" that presents the official version and documents. Feis, *The China Triangle*, cited above, covers the story through the end of the Marshall mission, while Tang Tsou's excellent *America's Failure in China, 1941–1950* (1963), carries the story forward to the outbreak of the Korean War. These works can be supplemented by Ernest R. May, *The Truman Administration and China, 1945–1949* (1975), and William Stueck, *The Wedemeyer Mission: America Politics and Foreign Policy during the Cold War* (1984). Foster Rhea Dulles, *American Policy toward Communist China, 1949–1969* (1972), is the best general survey of Chinese-American relations during this period.

An account critical of American intervention in Korea is Rosemary Foot, *The Wrong War: American Policy and the Dimensions of the Korean Conflict, 1950–1953* (1985). The best general work on the Korean War is David Rees, *Korea: The Limited War* (1964), but see especially Spanier's *Truman-MacArthur Controversy*, cited above, for the recall of General MacArthur. The general's side of the story is presented in MacArthur, *Reminiscences*, and Manchester, *American Caesar, Douglas MacArthur*. Mark W. Clark, *From the Danube to the Yalu* (1954), recounts events of the last months of the war and the armistice negotiations. An interesting personal assessment by another important participant is Matthew B. Ridgway, *The Korean War* (1967). J. Lawton Collins, *War in Peacetime: The History and Lessons of Korea* (1969), adds little to what was already known. Robert F. Fetrell, *The United States Air Force in Korea, 1950–1959* (1983), is the only systematic study of this subject. Glenn D. Paige, *The Korean Decision* (1968), is a detailed account of the American decision in June 1950 to intervene, while Bruce Cumings, *The Origins of the Korean War: Liberation and the Emergence of Separate Regimes* (1981), traces its roots. Allen S. Whiting, *China Crosses the Yalu* (1960), treats the question of Chinese intervention, while Robert E. Osgood, *Limited War* (1957), considers important strategic discussions and decisions.

E.   Diplomacy under Eisenhower

Walt W. Rostow, *The Diffusion of Power, 1957–1972* (1972), is an interpretive study by an important witness to the making of American foreign policy. An interesting study is Justus D. Doenecke, *Not to the Swift: The Old Isolationists in the Cold War Era* (1979). The basic sources for the Eisenhower years are Eisenhower, *Mandate for Change* and *Waging Peace*, cited above. Townshend Hoopes, *The Devil and John Foster Dulles* (1973); Roscoe Drummond and G. Coblentz, *Duel at the Brink: John Foster Dulles' Command of American Power* (1960); Mark G. Toulouse, *The Transformation of John Foster Dulles: From Prophet of Realism to Priest of Nationalism* (1986); and Richard H. Immerman, ed., *John Foster Dulles and the Diplomacy of the Cold War: A Reappraisal* (1990) are appraisals of Eisenhower's secretary of state, while Andrew H. T. Berding, *Dulles on Diplomacy* (1965), recounts conversations with the secretary. These may be supplemented by Louis L. Gerson, *John Foster Dulles* (1967), a biography that is longer on summary than on evaluation or analysis. Robert R. Randle, *Geneva 1954: The Settlement of the Indochinese War* (1969), praises Dulles's astuteness. Eisenhower's other secretary of state is the subject of G. Bernard Noble, *Christian A. Herter* (1970).

Recent historians have stressed Eisenhower's involvement in foreign policy. See Richard A. Melanson and David Mayers, *Reevaluating Eisenhower: American Foreign Policy in the 1950s* (1987); Stephen E. Ambrose, *Eisenhower: The President* (1984), and Fred I. Greenstein, *The Hidden-Hand President, Eisenhower as Leader* (1982); William Bragg Ewald, Jr., *Eisenhower the President* (1981); and Douglas Kinnard, *President Eisenhower and Strategy Management: A Study in Defense Policies* (1977). For more specialized works, see Keith Eubank, *The Summit Conferences, 1919–1960* (1966); Donald Neff, *Warriors at Suez: Eisenhower Takes America into the Middle East* (1981); Burton I. Kaufman, *Trade and Aid: Eisenhower's Foreign Economic Policy, 1953–1961* (1982); and Stephen G. Rabe, *Eisenhower and Latin America: The Foreign Policy of Anticommunism* (1988). On the evolution of the CIA and its activities under Eisenhower, see Stephen E. Ambrose and Richard H. Immerman, *Ike's Spies: Eisenhower and the Espionage Establishment* (1981); Richard H. Immerman, *The CIA in Guatemala: The Foreign Policy of Intervention* (1982); Stephen C. Schlesinger and Stephen Kinzer, *Bitter Fruit: The Untold Story of the American Coup in*

Guatemala (1982); and Kermit Roosevelt, *Countercoup: The Struggle for Control of Iran* (1979).

F.   Kennedy, Johnson, and Pax Americana

Schlesinger, *A Thousand Days*, and Sorenson, *Kennedy*, both cited above, contain good "inside" accounts of New Frontier diplomacy. A specific episode is the subject of Robert F. Kennedy's fascinating *Thirteen Days: A Memoir of the Cuban Missile Crisis* (1971). For accounts of the president's behavior during this and other foreign policy crises, see Peter Wyden, *Bay of Pigs: The Untold Story* (1979); Herbert Dinerstein, *The Making of a Missile Crisis: October 1982* (1976); Desmond Balls, *Politics and Force Levels: The Strategic Missile Program of the Kennedy Administration* (1980); Richard D. Mahoney, *JFK: Ordeal in Africa* (1983); and Michael R. Beschloss, *The Crisis Years: Kennedy and Khrushchev, 1960–1963* (1991). Also useful are the biographical accounts by Parmet, Wills, and Heath. For two highly critical evaluations of Kennedy's foreign policy as a whole, see Richard J. Walton, *Cold War and Counterrevolution: The Foreign Policy of John F. Kennedy* (1972), and Louise FitzSimons, *The Kennedy Doctrine* (1972). On Johnson, see Divine, ed., *Exploring the Johnson Years*, already cited, along with general accounts by Heath, Burnet, Kearns, and Reedy.

Various issues and areas of cold-war diplomacy under Kennedy and Johnson are treated in Jack M. Schick, *The Berlin Crisis, 1958–1962* (1971); Henry A. Kissinger, *The Troubled Partnership: A Reappraisal of the Atlantic Alliance* (1965); John Newhouse, *De Gaulle and the Anglo-Saxons* (1970); Carl H. Amme, Jr., *NATO without France: A Strategic Appraisal* (1967); the essay by Lawrence Kaplan in John Braeman, Robert H. Bremner, and David Brody, eds., *Twentieth-Century American Foreign Policy* (1971), which reviews NATO's first two decades; Robert S. Walters, *American and Soviet Aid: A Comparative Analysis* (1970); R. H. Dekmejian, *Egypt under Nasser: A Study in Political Dynamics* (1971); Stephen R. Wissman, *American Foreign Policy in the Congo, 1960–1964* (1974); and Timothy P. Maga, *John F. Kennedy and the New Pacific Community, 1961–63* (1990). For Latin America, see William D. Rogers, *The Twilight Struggle: The Alliance for Progress and the Politics of Development in Latin America* (1967); R. Harrison Wagner, *United States Policy toward Latin America: A Study in Domestic and International Politics* (1970); Lynn Darrell Bender, *The Politics of Hostility: Castro's Revolution and United States Policy* (1975); Trumbull Higgins, *The Perfect Failure: Kennedy, Eisenhower, and the C.I.A. at the Bay of Pigs* (1987); Jerome Slater, *Intervention and Negotiation: The United States and the Dominican Revolution* (1970); and Abraham F. Lowenthal, *The Dominican Intervention* (1972). On the arms race, see Roberts, *The Nuclear Years*, UN Secretariat, *The United Nations and Disarmament*, and Balls, *Politics and Force Levels*, all previously cited, and Harland B. Moulton, *From Superiority to Parity: The United States and the Strategic Arms Race, 1961–1971* (1972).

G.   Nixon, Kissinger, and a New World Order

An interesting collection of essays on Nixonian diplomacy is Lloyd C. Gardner, ed., *The Great Nixon Turnaround: America's New Foreign Policy in the Post-Liberal Era* (1973). The best single history is the two-volume memoir by Henry Kissinger, *The White House Years* (1979) and *Years of Upheaval* (1982). Although, like most memoirs, Kissinger's are self-serving, they express a sophisticated understanding of modern history and an eloquent defense of Nixon-Kissinger policies which is richly documented. Other general studies are John G. Stoessinger, *Henry Kissinger: The Anguish of Power* (1976); David Landau, *Kissinger: The Uses of Power* (1972); Stephen R. Graubard, *Kissinger: Portrait of a Mind* (1973); Coral Bell, *The Diplomacy of Détente: The Kissinger Era* (1977); Seyom Brown, *The Crises of Power: An Interpretation of United States Foreign Policy during the Kissinger Years* (1979); Peter W. Dickson, *Kissinger and the Meaning of History* (1978); Marvin Kalb and Bernard Kalb, *Kissinger* (1974); Harvey Starr, *Henry Kissinger: Perceptions of International Politics* (1984); and Robert D. Schulzinger, *Henry Kissinger: Doctor of Diplomacy* (1989). Two specialized studies are Bruce Mazlish, *Kissinger: The European Mind in American Policy* (1976), and Ishaq I. Ghanayem, *The Kissinger Legacy: American–Middle East Policy* (1984).

Kissinger has attracted his share of critics. They include Roger Morris, *Uncertain Greatness: Henry Kissinger and American Foreign Policy* (1977); Tad Szulc, *The Illusion of Peace: Foreign Policy in the Nixon Years* (1978); and, above all, Seymour M. Hersh, *The Price of Power: Kissinger in the Nixon White House* (1983).

H.   The United States and the Indochinese War

The basic sources on foreign affairs, previously cited, discuss the developments leading to America's involvement in Vietnam. Many of the recent studies of the cold war also include material on the conflict in southeast Asia. The best single account of American involvement in all of its dimensions is George C. Herring, *America's Longest War: The United States and Vietnam, 1950–1975* (1979). Other accounts include Bernard Fall, *Two Viet Nams: A Political and Military Analysis* (1967), *Vietnam Witness, 1953–1966* (1968), and *Last Reflections on a War* (1972); David Halberstam, *The Best and the Brightest* (1972), undocumented, rambling, and brimful of devastating insights; Don Oberdorfer, *Tet* (1971); Frances Fitzgerald, *Fire in the Lake: The Vietnamese and the Americans in Vietnam* (1972); Daniel C. Hallin, *The "Uncensored War": The Media and Vietnam* (1986); David L. Dilco, *George Ball, Vietnam, and the Rethinking of Containment* (1991); John Hellman, *American Myth and the Legacy of Vietnam* (1985); and Lloyd C. Gardner, *Approaching Vietnam: From World War I through Dienbienphu, 1941–1954* (1988). William Shawcross, *Sideshow: Kissinger, Nixon, and the Destruction of Cambodia* (1979), is devastating. Leslie L. Gelb and R. K. Betts, *The Irony of Vietnam: The System Worked* (1979), is a balanced study of American decision making during the war. For the military aspects, see Bruce Palmer, Jr., *The 25-Year War: America's Military Role in Vietnam* (1984). One of the best accounts of the Vietnam tragedy is Neil Sheehan, *A Bright Shining Lie: John Paul Vann and America in Vietnam* (1988).

Valuable excerpts from Daniel Ellsberg's celebrated revelation are contained in *The Pentagon Papers as Published by the New York Times* (1971), and the much longer Senator Gravel edition, *The Pentagon Papers: The Defense Department History of the United States Decision-Making on Vietnam* (4 vols., 1971). See also Townsend Hoopes, *The Limits of Intervention: An Inside Account of How the Johnson Policy of Escalation in Vietnam Was*

Reversed (1969), which should be supplemented by Clifford, *Counsel to the President*; John Galloway, *The Gulf of Tonkin Resolution* (1970); Henry F. Graff, *The Tuesday Cabinet: Deliberation and Decision on Peace and War under Lyndon B. Johnson* (1970); Larry Berman, *Planning a Tragedy: The Americanization of the War in Vietnam* (1982) and *Lyndon Johnson's War: The Road to Stalemate in Vietnam* (1989); Robert J. Donovan, *Nemesis: Truman and Johnson in the Coils of War in Asia* (1984); Kathleen Turner, *Lyndon Johnson's Dual War: Vietnam and the Press* (1985); and Brian Vandemark, *Into the Quagmire: Lyndon Johnson and Escalation of the Vietnam War* (1991). Merlo Pusey, *The Way We Go to War* (1969), studies the Vietnamese war as the latest example of a long-standing tendency for the executive to encroach upon congressional war-making powers. Herbert Y. Schandler, *The Unmaking of a President: Lyndon Johnson and Vietnam* (1977), is superb. William C. Westmoreland, *A Soldier Reports* (1977), is a firsthand account of the American military involvement. See also Townsend Hoopes and Maxwell D. Taylor, *Swords and Plowshares* (1972); Ronald H. Spector, *Advice and Support: The Early Years, 1941–1960* (1983). Guenter Lewy, *America in Vietnam* (1978), is comprehensive on the moral and legal issues of American involvement. A study which criticizes American motives but is uncritical of those of the Vietnamese Communists is Gabriel Kolko, *Anatomy of a War: Vietnam, the United States, and the Modern Historical Experience* (1985).

3.   SOCIAL AND ECONOMIC CHANGE SINCE 1940

A.   Demographic Changes and Economic Development

The handiest reference for general economic and social data is the *Statistical Abstract of the United States*, published annually. The best sources for demographic changes are the summary volumes of the Census. For two case studies of postwar demographic change, see Jean Gottmann, *Megalopolis: The Urbanized Northeastern Seaboard of the United States* (1961), and David Lavender, *California: Land of New Beginnings* (1972). On the growth of suburbs, see Kenneth T. Jackson, *Crabgrass Frontier: The Suburbanization of the United States* (1985).

For discussions of American economic development in the postwar period, see W. Elliot Brownlee, *Dynamics of Ascent: A History of the American Economy* (1979); Harold G. Vatter, *The U.S. Economy in the 1950s: An Economic History* (1963); Ralph E. Freeman, ed., *Postwar Economic Trends in the United States* (1960); and David C. Smith, *A History of Papermaking in the United States, 1691–1969* (1971). Milton Friedman and Anna J. Schwartz, *A Monetary History of the United States, 1867–1960* (1963), is a monumental study. It should be supplemented by Margaret G. Myers, *A Financial History of the United States* (1970), and Herman E. Krooss and Martin R. Blyn, *A History of Financial Intermediaries* (1971), an important study of the various financial institutions that now control over half the nation's wealth. For the regulation of one of the nation's most important industries, see Arie and Olive Hoogenboom, *A History of the ICC* (1976). Robert Sobel, *Amex: A History of the American Stock Exchange, 1921–1971* (1972), is a definitive study of this basic economic institution. John W. Kendrick, *Postwar Productivity Trends in the United States, 1948–1969* (1973), is invaluable. For changing patterns of income distribution in the twentieth century, see Simon Kuznets, *Shares of Upper Income Groups in Income and Savings* (1953), and Robert J. Lampman, *The Share of Top Wealth-Holders in National Wealth, 1922–1956* (1962). Simon Kuznets, *Capital in the American Economy* (1961), and

Raymond W. Goldsmith, *The National Wealth of the United States* (1962), are more general studies.

The most valuable analytic overview of recent economic development is Thomas C. Cochran, *American Business in the Twentieth Century* (1972). Other thoughtful interpretive insights are provided by John K. Galbraith, *American Capitalism* (1952), *The New Industrial State* (1967), *The Affluent Society* (1969), and *Economics and the Public Purpose* (1973); and by Adolf A. Berle, Jr., in *The Twentieth-Century Capitalist Revolution* (1954) and *Power without Property: A New Development in American Political Economy* (1959). Robert L. Heilbroner, *The Limits of American Capitalism* (1965), is an outstanding brief assessment of trends in American economic development. John W. Oliver, *History of American Technology* (1956); Leonard S. Silk, *The Research Revolution* (1960); and Elting E. Morison, *From Know-How to Nowhere: The Development of American Technology* (1974), are good surveys of the technological revolution.

On concentration in American industry, see Willard F. Mueller, *A Primer on Monopoly and Competition* (1970); Ralph L. Nelson, *Merger Movements in American Industry, 1895–1956* (1959); and the more specialized studies by the Federal Trade Commission, *The Merger Movement* (1948), *Interlocking Directorates* (1951), and *The Concentration of Productive Facilities* (1949). See also Wassily W. Leontief, *Studies in the Structure of the American Economy* (1953). A more recent analysis is Robert Sobel, *The Age of Giant Corporations: A Microeconomic History of American Business, 1914–1970* (1972).

B.   American Labor

Foster Rhea Dulles and Melvyn Dubofsky, *Labor in America: A History* (1992); Philip Taft, *Organized Labor in American History* (1964); and Henry Pelling, *American Labor* (1960), have chapters on the postwar labor movement; see also Joel I. Seidman, *American Labor from Defense to Reconversion* (1953). John Hutchinson, *The Imperfect Union: A History of Corruption in American Trade Unions* (1970); Walter Sheridan, *The Fall and Rise of Jimmy Hoffa* (1972); and Robert F. Kennedy, *The Enemy Within* (1960), analyze labor racketeering; while C. Wright Mills, *The New Men of Power* (1948), and Eli Ginzberg, *The Labor Leader* (1948), are sociological studies of the rise of a new labor leadership since the Wagner Act. For postwar labor policies, state and federal, see Charles C. Killingsworth, *State Labor Relations Acts* (1948); Harry A. Millis and E. C. Brown, *From the Wagner Act to Taft-Hartley* (1950); Emily C. Brown, *National Labor Policy* (1950); and John L. Blackman, Jr., *Presidential Seizure in Labor Disputes* (1967). McClure's *Truman Administration and the Problems of Postwar Labor*, already cited, is also pertinent. Robert L. Tyler, *Walter Reuther* (1973), and John Barnard, *Walter Reuther and the Rise of the Auto Workers* (1983), treat the most important American labor leader since John L. Lewis.

4.   SOCIAL AND INTELLECTUAL TRENDS SINCE 1940

A.   Social Trends

Most of the important social development in the postwar era are examined in William O'Neill, ed., *American Society since 1945*, and William Manchester, *The Glory and the Dream: A Narrative History of America, 1932–1972* (1973). Daniel J. Boorstin, *The Ameri-*

cans: The Democratic Experience (1973), is a fascinating discussion of many recent social changes. William O'Neill, *Coming Apart: An Informal History of America in the 1960s* (1971), is uneven, opinionated, but nonetheless full of insights. For different views on the same subject, see Todd Gitlin, *The Sixties: Years of Hope, Days of Rage* (1987), and Jim Miller, *"Democracy Is in the Streets": From Port Huron to the Siege of Chicago* (1987). Joseph F. Kett, *Rites of Passage: Adolescence in America 1970 to the Present* (1977), is excellent on its subject. Several studies on the history of childhood are now available: N. Ray Hiner and Joseph M. Hawes, eds., *Growing Up in America: Children in Historical Perspective* (1985); Viviana A. Zelizer, *Pricing the Priceless Child: The Changing Social Value of Children* (1985); Fred M. Hechinger and Grace Hechinger, *Growing Up in America* (1975); and Daniel P. Moynihan, *Family and Nation* (1986).

Francis E. Merrill, *Social Problems on the Home Front* (1948), is an excellent analysis of social tensions and changes during World War II. The postwar American character is perceptively analyzed in David Riesman, *The Lonely Crowd: A Study of the Changing American Character* (1950); William S. Whyte, *The Organization Man* (1956); and Christopher Lasch, *The Culture of Narcissism* (1978). Irwin Unger, *The Movement: A History of the American New Left, 1959–1972* (1974), is a reflective study. For a more favorable view, see Edward J. Bacciocco, Jr., *The New Left in America: Reform to Revolution, 1956–1970* (1974). For urban and suburban influences, see Sam B. Warner, Jr., *The Urban Wilderness: A History of the American City* (1972); Zane L. Miller, *The Urbanization of Modern America* (1973); Gottmann, *Megalopolis,* already cited; Robert C. Wood, *Suburbia: Its People and Their Politics* (1959); and Jackson, *Crabgrass Frontier,* cited earlier.

On the transformation of the post-1945 South, see Pete Daniel, *Standing at the Crossroads: Southern Life since 1900* (1986) and *Breaking the Land: The Transformation of Cotton, Tobacco, and Rice Cultures since 1880* (1985); Jack Temple Kirby, *Rural Worlds Lost: The American South, 1920–1960* (1987); Bruce J. Schulman, *From Cotton Belt to Sunbelt: Federal Policy, Economic Development, and the Transformation of the South, 1938–1945* (1991); and David Goldfield, *Promised Land: The South Since 1945* (1987).

For studies on women in the war and postwar eras, see Karen Anderson, *Wartime Women: Sex Roles, Family Relations, and the Status of Women* (1981); D'Ann Campbell, *Women at War with America: Private Lives in a Patriotic Period* (1984); Maureen Honey, *Creating Rosie the Riveter: Class, Gender, and Propaganda During World War II* (1984); and Judy Barrett Litoff and David C. Smith, *Since You Went Away: World War II Letters from American Women on the Home Front* (1991). More general in scope are Alice Kessler-Harris, *Out to Work: A History of Wage-Earning Women* (1982); Susan E. Kennedy, *If All We Did Was to Weep at Home: A History of Working-Class Women in America* (1979); Carl N. Degler, *At Odds: Women and the Family from the Revolution to the Present* (1980); Peter G. Filene, *Him/Her/Self: Sex Roles in Modern America* (1975); William H. Chafe, *Women and Equality: Changing Patterns in American Culture* (1977). Other fine general studies are Linda K. Kerber and Jane DeHart Mathews, eds., *Women's America: Refocusing the Past,* 2d ed. (1986); Glenda Riley, *Inventing the American Woman,* vol. 2 (1986); and Anne Firor Scott, *Making the Invisible Woman Visible* (1984). The best book on the ERA is Joan Hoff-Wilson, ed., *Rites of Passage: The Past and Future of the ERA* (1986).

B.   The Media

The effect of the media on American politics and the public has recently aroused much interest. A marvelous study of the power of major news media is David Halberstam, *The Powers That Be* (1979). On federal regulation of broadcasting, see James C. Baughman, *Television's Guardians: The FCC and the Politics of Programming, 1958–1967* (1985). For ways in which the media manipulate public opinion, see Edward Jay Epstein, *News from Nowhere: Television and the News* (1973). For an in-depth study of one instance, see Peter Braestrup, *Big Story: How the American Press and Television Reported and Interpreted the Crisis of Tet 1968 in Vietnam and Washington* (2 vols., 1977). Hunter S. Thompson, *Fear and Loathing on the Campaign Trail '72* (1973), and Timothy Crouse, *The Boys on the Bus* (1972), provide colorful accounts of political reporting. On the relationship between television and sports, see Benjamin G. Rader, *In Its Own Image: How Television Has Transformed Sports* (1984).

C.   American Thought

Merle Curti, *The Growth of American Thought* (1964); Ralph Gabriel, *The Course of American Democratic Thought* (1958); and Henry S. Commager, *The American Mind* (1950), discuss important developments in the twentieth century. Morton White, *Social Thought in America* (1949), is indispensable if specialized. There are no adequate works covering the postwar period as a whole, although the two previously cited studies by Lasch, *Agony of the America Left* and *The New Radicalism in America*, examine one important strand of postwar thought. For its opposite number, see Daniel Bell, ed., *The New American Right* (1955). Other studies of postwar intellectuals include William L. O'Neill, *The Great Schism: Stalinism and the American Intellectuals* (1982); Mary Sperling McAuliffe, *Crisis on the Left: Cold War Politics and American Liberals, 1947–1954* (1978); Richard H. Pells, *The Liberal Mind in the Conservative Age: American Intellectuals in the 1940s and 1950s* (1986); and Paul S. Boyer, *By the Bomb's Early Light: American Thought and Culture at the Dawn of the Atomic Age* (1985).

D.   Education

The best general accounts of recent educational developments at all levels are Ernest L. Boyer, *High School: A Report on Secondary Education in America* (1983) and *College: The Undergraduate Experience in America* (1988); Charles E. Silberman, *Crisis in the Classroom: The Remaking of American Education* (1970); Diane Ravitch, *The Troubled Crusade: American Education, 1945–1980* (1983); and David B. Tyack, *The One Best System: A History of American Urban Education* (1974). See also Edgar W. Knight, *Education in the United States* (1951). Lawrence A. Cremin, *The Transformation of the School: Progressivism in American Education, 1876–1957* (1961), is excellent social history. See also the parallel but more specialized book by Patricia A. Graham, *Progressive Education: From Anarchy to Academe; A History of the Progressive Education Association, 1919–1955* (1967). Lawrence A. Cremin, *The Genius of American Education* (1965), is a thoughtful, brief analysis. The following studies highlight the immediate postwar crisis: Benjamin Fine, *Our Children Are Cheated: The Crisis in American Education* (1947); James B. Conant, *The American High School Today*

(1959) and *The Education of American Teachers* (1963); Arthur E. Bestor, Jr., *Educational Wastelands* (1953) and *The Restoration of Learning* (1955); and Albert Lynd, *Quackery in the Public Schools* (1953). One of the gravest problems is examined in James B. Conant, *Slums and Suburbs: A Commentary on Schools in Metropolitan Areas* (1961). See also the pertinent items listed under "Race Relations" below. The turbulence of the college campus in the 1960s is treated in Nathan Glazer, *Remembering the Answers: Essays on the American Student Revolt* (1970), and more specifically in James A. Michener, *Kent State* (1971). The opening of educational opportunities by the ending of Jewish quotas and affirmative action on behalf of minority groups is related in Marcia G. Synnott, *The Half-Opened Door: Discrimination and Admissions at Harvard, Yale, and Princeton, 1900–1970* (1979). An important study of educational policy making by the federal government is Hugh Davis Graham, *The Uncertain Triumph: Federal Education Policy in the Kennedy and Johnson Years* (1984).

E. Religious Institutions and Thought

Sydney E. Ahlstrom, *A Religious History of the American People* (1972), and James W. Smith and A. Leland Jamison, eds., *Religion in American Life* (4 vols., 1961), are the best introductions. Another recent survey is Winthrop S. Hudson, *Religion in America* (1973). Clifton E. Olmstead, *History of Religion in the United States* (1960), includes material on the 1940s and 1950s. R. Laurence Moore, *Religious Outsiders and the Making of Americans* (1986), discusses the rise of white and black folk Protestantism in the twentieth century. More detailed, for the immediate postwar years, is Herbert W. Schneider, *Religion in Twentieth-Century America* (1952). About the theologian who had the greatest impact upon American intellectuals in the postwar years, see Richard Fox, *Reinhold Niebuhr: A Biography* (1985). Social and religious history are provocatively blended in Will Herberg, *Protestant-Catholic-Jew: An Essay in Religious Sociology* (1960). Excellent general surveys include John T. Ellis, *American Catholicism* (1969); David J. O'Brien, *The Renewal of American Catholicism* (1972); Andrew M. Greeley, *The American Catholic* (1977); Nathan Glazer, *American Judaism* (1972); Joseph L. Blau, *Judaism in America* (1976); Naomi W. Cohen, *American Jews and the Zionist Idea* (1975); Winthrop S. Hudson, *American Protestantism* (1961); Kenneth K. Bailey, *Southern White Protestantism in the Twentieth Century* (1964); and Martin E. Marty, *Righteous Empire: The Protestant Experience in America* (1970), a stimulating and highly critical account that covers the past two hundred years. Martin E. Marty, *The New Shape of American Religion* (1959), and Arthur R. Eckhardt, *The Surge of Piety in America* (1958), raise some important questions about the so-called return to religion during the 1950s. William G. McLoughlin, Jr., *Modern Revivalism: Charles Grandison Finney to Billy Graham* (1959), places modern revivalism in historical perspective. W. G. McLoughlin, Jr., *Billy Graham: Revivalist in a Secular Age* (1960), and Marshall Frady, *Billy Graham: A Parable of American Righteousness* (1979), are excellent for the most influential Protestant religious leader since World War II. For one of the most recent movements in American religion, see David Edwin Harrell, Jr., *All Things Are Possible: The Healing and Charismatic Revivals in Modern America* (1975). On the new political activism of the religious right, see Leo P. Ribuffo, *The Old Christian Right: The Protestant Far Right from the Great Depression to the Cold War* (1983).

F.   American Literature

The basic general history of American literature is Robert E. Spiller et al., *Literary History of the United States* (3 vols., 1963), which contains discussions of virtually every American writer worthy of mention, lengthy essays on the major writers, and a good general bibliography. See also Leon Howard, *Literature and the American Tradition* (1960); Willard Thorp, *American Writing in the Twentieth Century* (1960); and Frederick J. Hoffman, *The Modern Novel in America, 1900–1950* (1951). Walter B. Rideout, *The Radical Novel in the United States, 1900–1954* (1956), is useful for the literature of protest. The best study of postwar fiction is Alfred Kazin, *Bright Book of Life: American Novelists and Story Tellers from Hemingway to Mailer* (1973). Biographical data and excerpts from critical appraisals of modern writers, including poets and dramatists, are contained in the semiannual series *Contemporary Authors;* see especially Barbara Harte and Caroline Riley, eds., *Two Hundred Contemporary Authors* (1969), derived from that series.

G.   Race Relations

The literature on this complex subject is voluminous. General histories of the black experience abound, but the best is John Hope Franklin, *From Slavery to Freedom: A History of Negro Americans,* 6th ed. (1987). Indispensable background is provided by Gunnar Myrdal, *An America Dilemma* (2 vols., 1944), a massive, penetrating study of all phases of race relations. Arnold M. Rose, *The Negro in America* (1948), is an abridgment of Myrdal's volumes. See also August Meier and Elliott M. Rudwick, *From Plantation to Ghetto: An Interpretative History of American Negroes* (1976) and *Along the Color Line: Explorations in the Black Experience* (1976); Lawrence W. Levine, *Black Culture and Black Consciousness: Afro-American Folk Thought from Slavery to Freedom* (1977); and Harvard Sitkoff, *The Struggle for Black Equality, 1954–1980* (1981). An eloquent statement is John Hope Franklin, *Racial Equality in America* (1976).

On the Great Migration, see Robert Coles, *The South Goes North* (1971), and Nicholas Lemann, *The Promised Land: The Great Black Migration and How It Changed America* (1991). For developments in the 1940s and 1950s, see Arnold M. Rose, *The Negro in Postwar America* (1950); Bucklin Moon, *The High Cost of Prejudice* (1947); Walter B. Weare, *Black Business in the New South: A Social History of the North Carolina Mutual Life Insurance Company* (1973); Frank S. Loescher, *The Protestant Church and the Negro* (1948); Dwight W. Culver, *Negro Segregation in the Methodist Church* (1953); J. Saunders Redding, *On Being Negro in America* (1951); Carl T. Rowan, *South of Freedom* (1952); E. Franklin Frazier, *Black Bourgeoisie* (1957) and *The Negro Church in America* (1973); Jack Greenberg, *Race Relations and the American Law* (1959); Margaret Price, *The Negro and the Ballot in the South* (1959); C. E. Lincoln, *The Black Muslims in America* (1973); E. U. Essien-Udom, *Black Nationalism* (1962); Robert Burke, *Eisenhower and Civil Rights* (1984); and two previously cited works: Berman, *Politics of Civil Rights in the Truman Administration,* and Dalfiume, *Desegregation of the U.S. Armed Forces.* See also Daniel O. Price, *Changing Characteristics of the Negro Population* (1969), a 1960 Census monograph. A study of residential segregation in one urban community is Arnold R. Hirsch, *Making the Second Ghetto: Race and Housing in Chicago, 1940–1960* (1983).

The thoughts and actions of black activists are examined in Jervis Anderson, *A. Philip*

Randolph (1973); David L. Lewis, *King: A Critical Biography* (1978); Peter Goldman, *The Death and Life of Malcolm X* (1973); George Brietman, ed., *Malcolm X Speaks* (1965); S. P. Fullinwider, *The Mind and Mood of Black America: Twentieth Century Thought* (1969); Doug McAdam, *Political Process and the Development of Black Insurgency, 1930–1970* (1985); August Meier and Elliott Rudwick, *CORE: A Study in the Civil Rights Movement, 1942–1968* (1973); and Clayborne Carson, *In Struggle: SNCC and the Black Awakening of the 1960s* (1981). See also David J. Garrow, *Bearing the Loss: Martin Luther King, Jr., and the Southern Christian Leadership Conference* (1986); Adam Fairclough, *To Redeem the Soul of America: The Southern Christian Leadership Conference and Martin Luther King, Jr.* (1987); and, most especially, Taylor Branch, *Parting the Waters: America in the King Years* (1989). For studies of single communities, see William H. Chafe, *Civilities and Civil Rights: The Struggle for Black Freedom in Greensboro, North Carolina* (1980), and David R. Colburn, *Racial Change and Community Crisis: St. Augustine, Florida, 1870–1980* (1985), and J. Anthony Lukas, *Common Ground: A Turbulent Decade in the Lives of Three American Families* (1986). White responses, including backlash, are analyzed in William Brink and Louis Harris, *Black and White: A Study of U.S. Racial Attitudes Today* (1967), and Louise K. Howe, ed., *The White Majority: Between Poverty and Affluence* (1970).

Good introductions to the Brown decision and desegregation are available in David R. Guldfield, *Black, White, and Southern: Race Relations and Southern Culture, 1940 to the Present* (1989); Richard Kluger, *Simple Justice: The History of Brown v. Board of Education and Black America's Struggle for Equality* (1976); Henry A. Bullock, *A History of Negro Education in the South: From 1619 to the Present* (1967); Bernard H. Nelson, *The Fourteenth Amendment and the Negro Since 1920* (1946); C. H. Pritchett, *The Roosevelt Court* (1948) and *Civil Liberties and the Vinson Court*, cited above; Robert J. Harris, *The Quest for Equality* (1960); Harry S. Ashmore, *The Negro and the Schools* (1954); and Benjamin Muse, *Ten Years of Prelude: The Story of Integration Since the Supreme Court's 1954 Decision* (1964). A synthesis is Raymond Wolters, *The Burden of Brown: Thirty Years of School Desegregation* (1984). The impact of desegregation on two communities is explored in Richard A. Pride and J. David Woodard, *The Burden of Busing: The Politics of Desegregation in Nashville, Tennessee* (1985), and David R. Colburn, *Racial Change and Community Crisis: St. Augustine, Florida, 1877–1980* (1985). For various aspects of the controversy following the Brown decision in 1954, see John B. Martin, *The Deep South Says "Never"* (1957); Benjamin Muse, *Virginia's Massive Resistance* (1961); Harry S. Ashmore, *The Other Side of Jordan* (1960); J. W. Peltason, *Fifty-eight Lonely Men* (1961), on southern federal district judges and desegregation; James W. Silver, *Mississippi: The Closed Society* (1964); Russell H. Barrett, *Integration at Ole Miss* (1965); I. A. Newby, *Challenge to the Court: Social Scientists and the Defense of Segregation, 1955–1966* (1967); Earl Black, *Southern Governors and Civil Rights: Racial Segregation as a Campaign Issue in the Second Reconstruction* (1976); Numan V. Bartley, *The Rise of Massive Resistance: Race and Politics in the South during the 1950s* (1969); Neil R. McMillen, *The Citizens Council: Organized Resistance to the Second Reconstruction, 1954–1964* (1971); and Gary Orfield, *The Reconstruction of Southern Education: The Schools and the 1964 Civil Rights Act* (1969). Segregation and desegregation in transportation are treated in Catherine A. Barnes, *Journey from Jim Crow: The Desegregation of Southern Transit* (1983).

The new self-awareness on the part of American Indians are well set forth in Vine

Deloria, Jr., *Custer Died for Your Sins: An Indian Manifesto* (1969), and Alvin M. Josephy, *Red Power: The American Indians' Fight for Freedom* (1972). New studies of Mexicans in the United States are now available. The best of them are Matt S. Meier and Feliciano Rivera, *The Chicanos: A History of Mexican Americans* (1972); Peter N. Kirstein, *Anglo over Bracero: A History of the Mexican Worker in the United States from Roosevelt to Nixon* (1977); and Peter Matthiessen, *Sal Si Puedes: Cesar Chavez and the New American Revolution* (1973).

H.   Gender and Sexuality

On women, since 1945, see the following works: Sara Evans, *Personal Politics: The Roots of Women's Liberation in Civil Rights Movement and the New Left* (1979); Eugenia Kaledin, *Mothers and More: American Women in the 1950s* (1984); Cynthia Harrison, *On Account of Sex: The Politics of Women's Issues, 1945–1968* (1988); Elaine Tyler May, *Homeward Bound: American Families in the Cold War* (1988); William H. Chafe, *The Paradox of Change: American Women in the Twentieth Century* (1991); and Beth L. Bailey, *From Front Porch to Back Seat: Courtship in Twentieth-Century America* (1988).

On the issue of the ERA, see Jane J. Mansbridge, *Why We Lost the ERA* (1986); Mary Frances Berry, *Why ERA Failed: Politics, Women's Rights, and the Amending Process of the Constitution* (1986); and Donald G. Mathews and Jane Sherron De Hart, *Sex, Gender, and the Politics of ERA: A State and the Nation* (1990). On the abortion controversy, see Kristin Luker, *Abortion and the Politics of Motherhood* (1984); Marian Faux, *Roe v. Wade: The Untold Story of the Landmark Supreme Court Decision That Made Abortion Legal* (1988); Faye D. Ginsburg, *Contested Lives: The Abortion Debate in an American Community* (1989); and Suzanne Staggenborg, *The Pro-Choice Movement: Organization and Activism in the Abortion Conflict* (1991).

For the best account of sexuality, see John D'Emilio and Estelle Freedman, *Intimate Matters: A History of Sexuality in America* (1988), but also see Barbara Ehrenreich, Elizabeth Hess, and Gloria Jacobs, *Re-Making Love: The Feminization of Sex* (1986). The best general account of homosexuality in America since World War II can be found in John D'Emilio, *Sexual Politics, Sexual Communities: The Making of a Homosexual Minority in the United States, 1940–1970* (1983), but also see Allan Berube, *Coming Out under Fire: The History of Gay Men and Women in World War II* (1990).

Index

Aaron, Henry, 614
Abdul-Jabbar, Kareem, 614
Abortion rights, 659–660, 674, 751, 768, 780, 796, 805–806
Abrams, Elliott, 774
Abzug, Bella, 659
Acheson, Dean, 479, 485, 492, 493, 573, 629
Acquired immune deficiency syndrome (AIDS), 798–799
Admiralty Islands: and Allied offensive, 418
Adoula, Cyrille, 581
Advertising industry, 518
Aerospace industry, 795
Afghanistan: Soviet invasion of, 728–729; Soviet withdrawal from, 782
Africa: nationalism in, 558–559, 579–581
African-Americans: during World War II, 396, 397, 399–400, 403–404; and migration to the North, 403, 513; and election of 1944, 428; and election of 1948, 454, 456; and Democratic party, 456, 463, 538, 678, 681, 719, 739, 764, 778; and Truman, 457–458, 552–553; and election of 1952, 461; and black women in the postwar period, 520–522, 643–644; and southern agriculture and industry, 523–524; and literature, 528; and Eisenhower, 549; and Warren Court, 549–551; organize civil rights challenge, 552–555, 645–648; and civil rights during

African-Americans (*Cont.*):
1960s, 596–599, 611–615, 648–652; and election of 1968, 620; and transformation of family (1960s and 1970s), 643–645; and student protests, 654–655; and popular music, 661; and Burger Court, 673–674; and Carter, 721; during 1980s, 749–751, 803, 810–813; and abortion rate, 796
Afrika Korps, 411
Agnew, Spiro T., 618, 671, 678, 680; resignation of, 713
Agricultural Act: of 1949, 457, 545; of 1954, 545; of 1956, 545; of 1958, 545
Agricultural Adjustment Administration (AAA), 523, 524
Agricultural Trade Development and Assistance Act (1954), 546–547
Agriculture: during World War II, 392–393, 397; during postwar period, 452, 457, 509; and election of 1948, 456; and transformation of rural South, 522–524; federal policy toward in 1950s, 544–546; federal policy toward in 1960s, 595
Aid to Families with Dependent Children, 670
Air Force: increase in expenditures for, 495
Airborne warning and command systems (AWACS), 754
Alabama: and school desegregation, 555
Albania: non-Communist government in, 782